PASSING
THE
TORCH

PASSING THE TORCH

LESSONS LEARNED • WISDOM SHARED

Conversations with Louisville Leaders
About Life, Leadership and Service

BUTLER BOOKS • GREATER LOUISVILLE INC.
LOUISVILLE, KENTUCKY

gli Greater Louisville Inc.

The Metro Chamber of Commerce

Passing the Torch

Publisher	Butler Books, Louisville in partnership with Greater Louisville Inc. and the Leadership Louisville Center
Editors	William S. Butler Carol K. Butler Tracee B. Troutt Lisa M. Mills Carmen A. Hickerson Dr. Robert L. Taylor Heather Holladay Gates Sharon A. Receveur
Profile Writer	Joe Ward
Project Advisers	Dr. Robert L. Taylor Christine D. Johnson
Jacket Designer	Stacey Wade, NIMBUS, Inc.

ACKNOWLEDGMENTS

Producing and publishing *Passing the Torch* took more than a year, but it was well worth our efforts. Now, for the first time, Louisville has a collection of oral histories from 54 of Louisville's most influential living leaders. The wisdom and advice they share in their interviews will delight people who have known and admired them over the years and, we hope, inspire future generations of leaders.

Conducting, transcribing and editing the leaders' interviews was an immense effort, but many people who believed in the project stepped forward to help. Greater Louisville Inc. and Butler Books would like to thank the following individuals and organizations who played key roles in the publication of *Passing the Torch*:

• First, the 54 community leaders who are profiled in this book, who took time from their very busy schedules to be interviewed by Leadership Louisville alumni, and to edit and finalize their pieces for publication;

• President Christine Johnson and Heather Holladay Gates at the Leadership Louisville Center, who became our partners in the publication of *Passing the Torch*. Their mission every day, and for over 20 years, has been to train tomorrow's community leaders. They saw these interviews as invaluable mentoring opportunities and recruited a team of 34 Leadership Louisville alumni to interview the leaders who are profiled in this book. They also helped train and prepare the interview team, and provided them with the equipment they needed to be able to conduct and record their interviews;

• Our outstanding interview team – the 34 Leadership Louisville alumni listed on page 24 – who voluntarily took time from their busy careers to conduct and transcribe their interviews with the leaders who were assigned to them;

• Veteran journalist Joe Ward, who researched and wrote profile pieces on the 54 leaders featured in this book;

• Dr. Robert L. Taylor, professor of management and dean emeritus at the University of Louisville's College of Business and Public Administration — a mentor himself to many of the leaders in this book and to scores of "leaders-in-training" over the 21 years he has lived and taught in Louisville. Bob served as an invaluable project adviser and editor, and helped train and prepare our interview team members;

• Ed Manassah and Sharon Bidwell at *The Courier-Journal*; Tom Monahan and his staff at *Business First*; and Dan Crutcher and his staff at *Louisville Magazine*, who combed through their archives to help us create background files on the 54 leaders, which we shared with their interviewers;

• The law firm of Ogden, Newell & Welch, title sponsor of GLI's Business at Breakfast Series, the genesis for the *Passing the Torch* book project. The firm also made a generous donation to the book project to help us purchase professional transcribing equipment;

• Jim Hall, of Veranda Communications Inc., who donated professional tape recording equipment for our interviewers to use to create these oral histories;

• Charlie Green, of the Magnetic Tape Recorder & Stereo Center, who helped us secure equipment to transcribe the leaders' interviews, and helped train the interview team members on using the recording and transcribing equipment;

• Rick Redding, who helped coach our volunteer interview team.

To all of the above people and organizations, and to the support staff in our own offices, we want to say thank you. It "takes a village" to produce a book of this magnitude and historic importance to our community, and we are grateful to all those who believed in this project and helped us make it a reality.

GREATER LOUISVILLE INC.   BUTLER BOOKS

CONTENTS

STEVE HIGDON

President and CEO
Greater Louisville Inc.

INTRODUCTION

We at Greater Louisville Inc. have been fortunate to know and to have access to some of the brightest thinkers and greatest leaders in our community's recent history. With help from generous sponsors like the law firm of Ogden Newell & Welch, which underwrites our *Business at Breakfast* series, we have heard successful and brilliant people discuss a wide variety of issues. However, we have often regretted that only the few hundred people attending a particular *Business at Breakfast* event were being exposed to the wisdom of these leaders.

As the Chamber of Commerce celebrates its 55th anniversary in 2005, we wanted to find a way to share these important lessons with a wider audience. We looked for a vehicle that would capture the great ideas and experiences these leaders have to offer, because they are great lessons – not just for our generation, but for generations to come.

This book is a result of that effort.

Passing the Torch captures the thoughts, feelings and experiences of some of Louisville's greatest thinkers and visionaries of the past five decades. We interviewed 54 of Louisville's most influential leaders and documented their oral histories – what they did back in the '50s, '60s and '70s, and why they did it. Their experiences and insights help us understand how we as a community got to where we are today so that we can better plan where we're going and how we want to get there.

When I think about leadership, two qualities stand out in my mind – vision and courage. Vision is about seeing the possibilities and reaching beyond our grasp to achieve them. Courage is about taking risks and doing what our convictions say are the right things to do that will ultimately benefit the community as a whole.

Few of us are born with those leadership qualities, but we can learn much from those who do have them. During my tenure at GLI, I've had the benefit of learning from many different types of leaders and of hearing their perspectives on how to run a company, how to improve a community, and how to bring about positive change. Those leaders have greatly influenced the way we do things at GLI.

The nature of leadership has changed tremendously over the past half-century. Fifty years ago, a small group of influential individuals could unilaterally make decisions for the entire community. In today's diverse communities, leaders must build consensus. They gain respect because of what they do and say every day and because of the way they treat people. Real leaders don't demand respect; they earn it.

Leaders inspire people. They can get the masses behind them and can move things in one direction with their compelling vision and their ability to get people to buy into the dream. They have a day-in, day-out ability to lead by example, to be passionate about what they believe in, to be consistent and to be fair. Great business leaders can also be great community leaders, if they are willing to share their time and talent and if they have a genuine passion to improve what is around them.

In the past, community leadership typically came from the large corporations headquartered here. But with the mergers and consolidations of the last 20 years, many of our largest employers are no longer headquartered here. That's why we need a much greater grassroots effort from people who don't necessarily run the Fortune 500 companies – people who were born and raised here, who have kids here and who want to see Louisville get better.

You don't have to be a multimillionaire or run a huge company to become a leader in our community. Anybody can become a community leader. We need to recruit community leaders of all shapes, sizes, colors and sexes.

Our community has changed immeasurably and has accomplished so much over the last 55 years, but a number of challenges remain. Three recently launched initiatives in particular will continue to require a major commitment of leadership, vision, risk-taking and capital if they are to succeed.

1. The vision to change Louisville from being a nice average city into an economic hotspot. So much has resulted from our community leaders' publicly stating where we want our community to be in 2010. Merging our governments was a major step toward achieving that vision, but it was also a major risk. Not many people thought we could do it, but we did it. It required not only a ton of vision, but a ton of boldness.

2. The "Every 1 Reads" program. This program was created by the business community and GLI, but it has challenged our entire community – our school district, our government partners, all citizens – to raise the reading level of every child in the community, regardless of their demographic, sociographic or economic background. It is a huge challenge and a huge risk, but it's the right thing to do. We will know the results of the program in about three years.

3. Downtown revitalization. It took great vision and leadership, but our community is much better off today because we have Waterfront Park, Louisville Slugger Field and Fourth Street Live! So many things are happening downtown. People are living downtown. It's a big vision, but it is one that we have only just begun, and we are making things better every day.

A community is no different from a business — it must grow or it will stagnate. For Louisville to become the absolute best it can be, we must build on what is really great and unique about our city — its neighborhoods, cleanliness, friendliness, low cost of living, park system, easy commutes. We need to take the very best of Louisville and make it even better.

Over the next 55 years, I want Louisville to become the very best it can be. I would like every citizen to have an improved quality of life. I want to see a place where our kids can graduate from college, whether here or elsewhere, and find challenging careers right in their hometown.

I want Louisville to be a city that can offer people the right jobs, the right quality of life — a place that thrives, and is a great place for everyone to live, regardless of income, race, gender, religious preference or ethnicity.

We need leaders who represent all segments of the community to work together strategically toward a common vision. Whether we live in Hurstbourne, Park DuValle or Southern Indiana, every single one of us has the same thing at stake, and that's the quality of life in this community. My hope is that we will start today — all of us — to find common links with people with whom we have not historically had common links, so that we can become one community — not multiple communities within one city limits.

Passing the Torch is full of real-life examples of how people have made significant accomplishments in this community. It's easy to get caught up in the day-to-day rut and to act tactically on what we have to get done that day. We don't leave ourselves time to think about tomorrow or next year, much less ten years from now. We need to spend more time dreaming and envisioning a better world, a better place.

I hope this book inspires you to act, to do things differently and to make a difference. I hope you will be inspired to take risks you otherwise might not take, but to do due diligence — to make sure the risks you take are thought-through and smart. I hope you will be inspired to visualize and to think, "Here's where we are today, here's where we want to be in ten years, and here's how we can get there."

DAVID G. WILKINS

**2005 Past Chair, Board of Directors
Greater Louisville Inc.**

**Chairman & CEO
Doe Anderson, Inc.**

HOW GLI CHOSE LEADERS TO FEATURE IN THE BOOK

Louisville has been blessed with many tremendous leaders over the years, so narrowing down the list to feature in this book was a huge task. Over 200 people were nominated, which unfortunately was far more than we could fit into the book. We decided to screen the nominees against a set of tough criteria: How many years have they been in Louisville? Were they a pioneer? Were they a true leader? Did they make some really important things happen? How much involvement did they have in the community – not just in one area, but did they lend their talents to a number of different areas? Have they given back to the community? Have they made a difference with those contributions? Are they people who have stood up and taken leadership roles as opposed to people who said "Yes, I believe in that and I'll follow you?" We looked at all these things. Obviously, the selection committee had a difficult task.

We ended up selecting 54 people. It goes without saying that there are many very worthy people who were not selected to be featured in this volume, but who certainly could have made the list. Some of the decision-making, as you might expect, was subjective because some things are more important to you than they are to me. But we think that everybody who is in this book is deserving, and we think it is clear that a second book may be in the offing because we still have many people who ought to be recognized for their leadership and contributions to this community and who ought to be interviewed from a historical perspective.

Louisville has come a long way, and there have been huge changes in the community under the generation of leaders profiled in this book. As individuals, and as groups of individuals, they have had the ability to think big – to think beyond what was going on at any given time, to believe that anything was possible and that there was nothing we couldn't accomplish in the city of Louisville if we all decided we wanted to get it done.

13

This "can do" attitude is pervasive not only among the people in this book, but among leaders in general. Leaders are people who believe that change is the way to make things happen, instead of sticking with the status quo. Once things begin to move, people begin to believe that progress is possible and they will follow along. But it takes someone first to stand up, take a risk, and say "Let's make this happen." That's what the people in this book have done. They have devoted a tremendous amount of time and energy, as well as personal and corporate resources, to a variety of different projects that have been accomplished over the years to make our city a better place to live.

Leaders have to have the vision to see ways to make things better and then have the courage to stand up in the face of "naysayers." Many people are averse to change, as it makes them uncomfortable. It takes a lot of courage to stand up and say something is wrong and needs to be changed. When you change things you change and affect people's lives, hopefully for the better in the long-term, and hopefully for the better of the majority of people. Some people are averse to change, however, because they are going to have less of a say in what's going on or less of an ability to dominate things themselves. Great leaders have the ability to get us beyond such petty concerns. I heard someone once say, "Kiss change on the lips." Change is a good thing for growth. It's a good thing for excitement. It's a good thing for energy. It's a good thing for making positive things happen. Having an attitude that change is a positive thing has to be mixed with the courage to stand up in order for something to actually happen.

Louisville learned from its merger campaign a few years ago not to give up. If you have an idea that makes sense, push forward – continue to strive to make it happen. We also learned not to worry about being politically correct. You're going to step on some toes periodically if you voice your opinion, but you have to be more concerned with doing what is right than about doing what is politically correct.

One of the traits for all of the people who are in this book is that they have been able to build consensus. When you have a community as diverse as Louisville Metro, that consensus must cut across widely different lines if positive things are to be achieved. The leaders in this book were able to sell people on their ideas, their vision and the passion they have had for those visions. If they didn't have the ability to sell and they couldn't articulate the vision clearly, then building consensus would have been a very difficult thing for them to do.

The leaders in this book have characteristics that set them apart. They have not only been good business people in general, but they have been business people who decided that part of being a good business person is being a good citizen as well. They have made it a big part of their agenda to give their time and energy and, in some cases, millions of dollars back to the city so the rest of us could benefit as well. They never gave up. They kept pushing. If one channel was closed when they tried to get something done, they would find other ways to do things and to sell their ideas. They would find other ways to build a coalition of minds. None of the people featured in this book knew how to take "no" for an answer, and that's important.

In some cases, it was their business savvy that helped them achieve great things, but in other cases it was their ability to organize; their ability to apply the right resources, the right amount of energy, or the right amount of financial support in the right place at the right time. It was, in some cases, their ability to raise money to get projects seeded and started. All of those skills aren't necessarily found in one person but they are found in groups of people. Someone's idea spurs another idea which makes it stronger. That gets somebody else thinking about it and pretty soon the group has purpose and the ability to move forward.

"Ego management" is important, too. All of the people in this book were driven because they wanted to be driven, and for many, that attitude was based on a healthy ego. But when you get a lot of smart people in a room, you have to be willing to defer every once in a while and let somebody else get up on their feet and take charge. These people not only had the ability to be leaders, but they also had the ability to be very strong followers and strong supporters when the situation called for it. That's part of the sense of team that is at the core of building consensus.

It was a team that made merger happen – a team from across the community – and there were huge egos involved. At some points, those egos were front and center, and at other points in time, people were willing to pull them back. If you have 20 good leaders in a group and, at the right point in time, 19 of them have the ability to be good followers, then you're going to have an awesome organization.

The people who were nominated to be included in this book were about driving big ideas and big visions. They are the tireless leaders who decided to make something happen. We need more people who, like them, want to improve our quality of life and make Louisville a better place to live and raise our families. I hope that the next generation of leaders in our community understands how competitive the environment is for luring business to our city, for creating jobs, for keeping our smart people here, and for luring smart people from outside. It's going to require a continuing focus and lots of hard work to keep good things happening. Yes, we have created jobs and we have had social change, but there's more to do. The bottom line is that the people in this book have made Louisville a better place to live because of their efforts, and that's what the next generation has to continue to push for.

E.C. "EDDY" ROBERTS

**2005 Chairman, Board of Directors
Greater Louisville Inc.**

State President–Kentucky–BellSouth

PASSING THE TORCH OF LEADERSHIP: THE INTERVIEWS

Many of us in this community are getting ready to pass the torch of leadership on to the next generation. It is important we do all we can to help develop those coming behind us into the leaders of tomorrow.

The leaders of tomorrow no doubt will have to be able to adapt to an increasingly faster pace and tremendous change. Yet there are consistent qualities that distinguish good leaders at any time. They have vision. They set the example for their organizations. And they connect with their community.

Good leaders are visionaries – people with new ideas, new thoughts. They are progressive thinkers who push us to reach, to stretch our thinking, to stretch what we are are trying to accomplish. Their leadership causes us to become more competitive and more aggressive, to want our city to be the best that it can be.

Good leaders lead by example. They start leading in their own businesses or organizations, then branch out to encourage people in the community to take on an initiative, to be aggressive, to grow. The impact of their leadership can often be felt beyond the city of Louisville as well, which encourages further, more far-reaching growth and investment in Louisville.

Most leaders come into their position with a drive that's part of their makeup. Leadership can be contagious, however. Someone initially just willing to watch or help may see good things happening, be inspired by a good leader and step forward.

Leadership can also be learned. Opportunities often come to you because someone sees something in you. You get exposed to someone who has already been where you want to be – someone you respect, someone in whose footsteps you would like to follow. That helps you to be ready when a new opportunity comes along.

Truly great leaders are connected to the community where they live and work. Louisville has a wonderful quality of life, but people who live here want their granchildren to grow up with an even greater quality of life. They love our city, and want to see it prosper. They also want future leaders to succeed.

Great leaders are everywhere in our community, and in all segments of our community – business, social, the arts. They come from all races, all income levels, all ages, all types of jobs and careers. The real magic in Louisville happens when someone or some project pulls leaders in our community together for a common cause. When that happens, there is tremendous excitement and great things happen.

This book is meant to inspire existing leaders throughout the community, as well as those who are aspiring to leadership positions. The diverse and impressive list of leaders featured in this book share their thoughts, visions and experiences for anyone aspiring to leadership. It is interesting to learn about their experiences, what caused them to think a certain way, how they developed their vision of where they wanted to take Louisville.

This book will give our next generation of leaders valuable insight and help anyone who is trying to figure out where they would like to see Louisville go and how they can help take it there.

We have some outstanding young people in Louisville who are going to do great things. I am looking forward to watching where they take us. We need to encourage these new leaders to step forward and say "I have an idea. I have a vision. Work with me on this." Then we need to get people who have already been through the wars to step forward to work with them on their new ideas. That's how we will train our community's new leaders.

Younger leaders will increasingly take on more more responsibility, larger roles. We just need to give them opportunities, let them grow, help them along the way, then let them go.

THE INTERVIEW PROCESS

Greater Louisville Inc. was proud to partner with Leadership Louisville in the publication of this book, because both of our organizations understand how important it is to our community's continuity and long-term future that one generation of leaders train and mentor those coming behind them.

As one generation prepares to "pass the torch" to the next, oral histories like the ones contained in this book become valuable tools for leaders-in-training.

All of the leaders profiled in this book were interviewed by alumni of Leadership Louisville. The volunteer interviewers did a terrific job, and reported back to us that their sessions with these leaders were invaluable mentoring experiences.

THE INTERVIEW QUESTIONS

Each leader interviewed was asked to answer the same set of questions:

- When and why did you decide you wanted to become a leader in our community?

- Who were your mentors and what did you learn from them?

- How would you describe your leadership style? How would others describe it?

- Describe your most significant accomplishment or success and what you learned about leadership from that experience.

- Describe your biggest failure or disappointment and what you learned from that experience.

- What, in your opinion, are the characteristics of a good follower and what do you, as a leader, expect from followers today?

- What would you do differently now, if you could do it all over again?

- What advice would you give to young people aspiring to leadership?

- Who or what do you think has contributed most to the growth, development and improved quality of life in Louisville over the last 50 years? What role, if any, did you play in this?

- What do you think are the biggest challenges facing our city in the future and what advice would you give its next generation of leaders?

- What are the most valuable lessons you have learned in your own life and career that you would like to share with the next generaton of leaders in Louisville?

We have removed the questions from the leaders' first-person interviews to make them easier to read, but we thought it important for readers to understand the context of the interviews, and the questions each leader addressed.

E.C. "Eddy" Roberts

Greater Louisville Inc. is proud of the role it has played in creating this exciting collection of oral histories of some of Louisville's most influential living leaders. Through their stories and personal recollections, future generations of citizens in Louisville will be able to trace the growth and development of their community during the second half of the 20th century, and to understand the important roles that these leaders played in that progress.

Robert L. Taylor

Project Adviser, Interview Team Trainer

**Professor of Management
and Dean Emeritus**

**College of Business
and Public Administration
University of Louisville**

Words of Advice for Tomorrow's Leaders

The stories in this volume reflect our past and our present. Younger readers can now study some of the leaders who shaped our community. They have a wonderful opportunity to consider the challenges of leadership success, and to prepare to take charge.

But first, we must recognize that there are differences between leaders, managers, and those who are "at the top." Simply because one is awarded the role of president, head, or chief executive says nothing about whether that individual is a leader. There are differences.

Headship is the descriptor for people to whom a title is given but who are unwilling or unable to perform in the role assigned. Management is the appropriate term to use when an individual is good at planning, organizing, and controlling people, money, material, information and time in the pursuit of organizational goals and objectives. Leadership is that special impact that a person has on others, where an influence process emerges to energize people to achieve a common goal. Effective leadership is found in the most successful organizations, where everyone experiences the excitement of a shared future.

As you experience the leadership lessons contained in this volume, think about whether a particular individual reflects great management, effective leadership, or both. Most importantly, ask yourself what that individual's interview communicates to you about your own potential for leadership.

As we look to the future, how shall we define leadership? You might want to consider the following list, as qualities and characteristics of an effective leader:

Vision – The ability to define a future state of affairs not clearly understood by the followers;

Communication – Telling the story of that future while listening carefully to the wants and needs of followers so that they can eventually own the vision;

Commitment — Waking up each day with the energy to pursue the vision despite obstacles, conflicts and failures;

Loyalty — Working with others in a way that makes them loyal to the vision and the organization, not to the leader;

Timing — Understanding when it is time to follow and when it is time to lead (and the ability to choose wisely);

Risk — Willingness to take the risks necessary to achieve the vision, and ability to ignore criticisms and challenges;

Trust — Understanding that leaders and followers must reciprocate with transparent communications to trust each other in the pursuit of shared goals.

Ultimately your own definition of leadership will drive what you do, and our hope is that you will choose to lead.

Our community offers many opportunities for leadership. Whether people are local or from out-of-town, the Louisville region welcomes those who want to be involved and make a difference. Those who decide to volunteer and to get involved early will find themselves on non-profit boards, community task forces and other groups where time, talent, and intellect are needed.

The key is not to be shy. Ask, and you will discover that groups and organizations are ready to embrace you. Network with friends and others you meet. Learn about the community and identify those places where you want to make a contribution. You will ultimately connect with the places you choose, and your leadership journey will start. Once you demonstrate your capacity and willingness to lead, the invitations to serve will come — in organizations, politics, and even business.

Understand that there are no courses, programs, seminars, or workshops that can transform you into a leader. We can learn management tools and techniques, but because leadership is an influence process dependent upon the personalities of leader and followers, a simple approach does not exist.

Rather, the best preparation for leadership is self-knowledge. Do everything you can to learn about your own strengths and shortcomings. Study the stories that follow and think about what you can learn from those who preceded you. Explore the education and training that helps you learn who you are. From these experiences will come self-confidence — a belief that you can lead others. Then develop your network by volunteering for civic and social projects to test your leadership.

Give time to boards of community organizations. Ultimately, your self-confidence will result in leadership experience that will allow you to make critical leadership choices in your career, as well as your personal life.

Good luck!

CHRISTINE D. JOHNSON

Project Adviser

President
Leadership Louisville Center

LEADERSHIP LOUISVILLE'S PARTNERSHIP WITH GLI
IN THE PUBLICATION OF *PASSING THE TORCH*

How appropriate it is to have the Leadership Louisville Center play such an important role in the creation of *Passing the Torch*. Not only have the leaders profiled in this book left their mark on Louisville, they have also shaped our organization – as founders, alumni and speakers who have generously shared their stories with our participants over the past 27 years.

More than 30 of our Leadership Louisville graduates conducted the personal interviews that formed the foundation for this living history of our community. Sitting face-to-face with Louisville's icons proved to be a transformational leadership experience in itself. For what this book points out is that a community's success is ultimately the story of its leaders, the relationships they nurture, the risks they take, the visions they pursue and the passions they share for the values they hold dear.

I'm reminded of the unforgettable comments the late Wilson Wyatt used to make at our annual Leadership Louisville programs about "power and influence." I was particularly fascinated by the unique impact he had on each new class eager to learn the "how-to" of great leadership from a living legend.

One of Mr. Wyatt's favorite stories was his insider account of serving as President Kennedy's special envoy to negotiate an oil agreement with Indonesia. His eyes still sparkled more than 30 years later, as he recalled the memory of the unexpected summons to the White House. He admitted his own doubts about whether he was truly up to the task. But if President Kennedy thought he was the man for the job, then he was.

While the class participants waited in anticipation of hearing some profound secret on how to successfully wield power and influence, Mr. Wyatt instead shared a simple lesson about the importance of building trust and personal relationships. The job of international negotiator, as he saw it, wasn't much different from walking the city precincts as mayor. The task was the same: bringing people together and working to let them see that their common interests far outweighed their differences.

Passing The Torch makes certain that the stories of Louisville's leaders in the pivotal last half of the 20th century won't be lost. They will be here to inspire the next generation of leaders who are already eager to step up to the challenge.

THE LEADERSHIP LOUISVILLE INTERVIEW TEAM

The following Leadership Louisville program graduates accepted the challenge of interviewing the 54 community leaders who are featured in *Passing the Torch*:

Carolee Allen	David Klein
Christy Ames	Susan Lehmann
Lynn Ashton	Jessica Loving
Stephanie Bateman	Cissy Maloney
Mark Brashers	Lynnie Meyer
Dan Burgess	Daugherty Murphy
Joni Knight Burke	Eileen Pickett
Tricia Burke	Mary Lea Quick
Carole Christian	Joan Riehm
Diane Cornwell	Sandy Ringer
Terri Giltner	Kerry Walsh Skelly
Cece Hagan	Daryl Snyder
Maria Gerwing Hampton	Gordon Strauss, M.D.
Tim Hellige	Lynn Wangerin
Carmen Hickerson	Michael D. Ward
Linda McGinity Jackson	Carla Whaley
A. Dale Josey	Tom Williams

THE INTERVIEW QUESTIONS

Each of the leaders profiled on the following pages was asked to answer the same set of questions:

- When and why did you decide you wanted to become a leader in our community?

- Who were your mentors and what did you learn from them?

- How would you describe your leadership style? How would others describe it?

- Describe your most significant accomplishment or success and what you learned about leadership from that experience.

- Describe your biggest failure or disappointment and what you learned from that experience.

- What, in your opinion, are the characteristics of a good follower and what do you, as a leader, expect from followers today?

- What would you do differently now, if you could do it all over again?

- What advice would you give to young people aspiring to leadership?

- Who or what do you think has contributed most to the growth, development and improved quality of life in Louisville over the last 50 years? What role, if any, did you play in this?

- What do you think are the biggest challenges facing our city in the future and what advice would you give its next generation of leaders?

- What are the most valuable lessons you have learned in your own life and career that you would like to share with the next generaton of leaders in Louisville?

PASSING THE TORCH

The Interviews

Jerry E. Abramson

Mayor
City of Louisville Metro

Former Three-Term Mayor
City of Louisville

Former Third Ward Alderman
City of Louisville

THE LATE ROY ABRAMSON liked to tell a story about his son, Jerry, who helped out in the family's grocery store at Preston and Jacob Streets near downtown Louisville. Jerry's father was frustrated because city garbage collectors would regularly take away the corner trash can along with the trash. "Don't worry, Dad," his son would say. "Someday I'll be mayor and I'll get your trash can bolted down for you."

Jerry Abramson did grow up to become mayor of Louisville and has served so many years in office that residents affectionately refer to him as "Mayor for Life."

He first ran for mayor in 1985 and won handily. When a new state law permitted mayors to succeed themselves, he ran a second time, then a third — the maximum allowed in Kentucky. After 13 years as mayor, he left office in 1999 with one of the highest public approval ratings of any elected official in the Commonwealth.

After Louisville and Jefferson County voters approved merging city and county governments a few years later, it was no surprise that they chose Abramson by a margin of three to one to serve as the first mayor of the new city of Louisville Metro, which overnight became the 16th largest city in the United States.

Abramson has deep roots in Louisville. He graduated from Seneca High School in 1964, then Indiana University in 1968. After IU, he headed to law school at Georgetown University in Washington, D.C. He was drafted into the Army after his first year of law school, then returned to Georgetown where he became editor of the law journal. Before graduating with honors in 1973, he considered New York and Washington law firms. But he decided to come home to a place where he felt he "could personally make a difference." Louisville's Greenebaum Doll McDonald quickly hired him as a junior attorney.

In 1975, Abramson won the Third Ward seat on Louisville's Board of Aldermen. He served two terms and chaired the Board's finance committee for four years.

When John Y. Brown Jr. was elected governor of Kentucky in 1980, he asked Abramson to serve as his general counsel. After two years, Abramson returned to Louisville to practice law and to prepare to run for mayor.

As mayor, Abramson's achievements have changed the landscape of Louisville. He oversaw a period of economic growth and downtown revitalization. And he created award-winning local government programs: CityCall (now MetroCall); Mayor's Night In and Mayor's Night Out (now Community Conversations); and the Brightside city beautification program.

He bucked significant opposition to advocate a bold expansion of Louisville's airport that required relocating thousands of families. That $700 million expansion paved the way for the billion-dollar UPS international air cargo hub that has brought in thousands of new jobs. He also helped recruit the headquarters for the world's largest fast food company, YUM! Brands (KFC, Pizza Hut, Taco Bell and others), and the Presbyterian Church (USA).

Abramson spearheaded efforts to reclaim the city's historic riverfront and replace piles of sand and scrap metal with projects like the Louisville Slugger Field ballpark and the 70 acres of lawn, trees, fountains and playgrounds known as Waterfront Park. Neighborhood revitalization projects have won national awards. New museums and attractions like the Muhammad Ali Center, the Frazier Historical Arms Museum and Fourth Street Live! have fueled further economic development and sweeping changes downtown.

At the same time, the merger of city and county governments has been a huge milestone for the community. Abramson was at the forefront of a bipartisan group of elected officials and community leaders that led the successful merger campaign.

Two years into the new merged government, Abramson had streamlined departments and agencies, trimmed the workforce by ten percent and improved services — without raising taxes. Public protection has been a top priority — including establishing MetroSafe, a new emergency communications system for all the community's first responders.

Abramson's achievements as mayor also earned him national recognition — including serving as president of the U.S. Conference of Mayors in 1993-94, and being named one of *Governing* magazine's Public Officials of the Year in 2003 for his work as "Merger Maestro."

Humana founder and civic leader David Jones says Abramson is "probably the best mayor in the country."

Abramson and his wife, Madeline, have a teenage son, Sidney.

MY LEADERSHIP GOALS took shape while I was in college. I was energized by my experiences with United States Senator Robert Kennedy during his presidential campaign. I was a student at Indiana University at the time, serving as chairman of Students for Robert Kennedy in Indiana.

Indiana was the first state primary that he entered, so it became my job to introduce the senator as we traveled to state colleges and universities. What a tremendous experience it was to get to know him personally – and to see his idealism and commitment to bringing people together: rich and poor, urban and rural, black and white.

I knew then that I wanted to make a difference in public life. I didn't know whether it would be in my hometown of Louisville, in Congress or in the U.S. Senate. After graduating from college, I went to Georgetown University Law School in Washington, D.C. – where I appreciated the front-row perspective it gave me on our federal government.

As a law student, I volunteered with Indiana Senator Birch Bayh's campaign and George McGovern's campaign for president. I continued to think: Should I stay in Washington and work as a staffer on the Hill? Or should I go back home and try to be a leader in a place where I could personally make a positive difference?

I came home. I felt I could make the greatest contribution here, and I began getting involved in civic activities that provided opportunities for leadership: Big Brothers/Big Sisters, the Louisville Orchestra, the March of Dimes, Forward Louisville.

When I was elected mayor in 1985, it was the fulfillment of a promise I had made as a child – and a pledge I had made to myself after spending time with Robert Kennedy.

It was also clear, immediately, that Louisville's progress was hampered by Kentucky's one-term limit for large-city mayors. It seemed to me that it took at least one year to learn the ropes, then you would serve as mayor for two years and by the fourth year, you were widely viewed a lame duck. That discouraged long-term planning and big-picture thinking.

In 1986, thanks to support in Louisville, Northern Kentucky and Lexington, Kentucky voters approved extending large-city mayor term limits to three terms, laying the groundwork for more visionary planning in all our cities.

When I look back at the people who shaped my interests and ambitions, it's clear that my parents were my first mentors. My father owned a three-aisle grocery. He went to work at six in the morning, came home at six at night, and worked six days a week, so I certainly learned a work ethic. My mother helped out at the grocery and was a homemaker.

My debate coach at Seneca High School – Mr. Stickler – gave me confidence in articulating ideas. Other mentors included Ron Snyder, adviser to high school clubs at the Jewish Community Center, where I spent a lot of time as a teenager; and the director of the Student Union at Indiana University.

But it was Senator Robert Kennedy who made the most impact on my thinking as a young adult. I was with him in an African-American neighborhood in Indianapolis the night Martin Luther King was killed – and I will always remember his words empowering individuals to stand up and make a difference: "That which unites us must be stronger than that which divides us."

At Georgetown, Professor Sherman Cohen helped me sort through job decisions – offers from prestigious law firms in Washington and New York, as well as Louisville.

As a Louisville attorney, my first mentors were Larry Leatherman and former Kentucky Attorney General Bob Matthews. Larry told me first to become a good lawyer and to learn my trade, then to do other public service. Bob told me it was important to watch for opportunities in public service because good people are always needed.

I have had a number of mentors since I've been in elected office – too many to list here – Bob Allison, Charles Weisberg, Bill Lomicka, Mason Rudd, and Wilson Wyatt, among others.

As a leader, my strength is having ideas, crystallizing them into a vision and being able to articulate that vision in a positive way so that people feel trust and enthusiasm – and are inspired to follow.

The best ideas come from dialogue with a team of advisers with different perspectives. When I am weighing complex issues like expanding the airport, public ownership of LG&E or an air-toxics reduction program, I like to have people around who argue with me, who bring different points of view and have varied experience. I mull over their advice and ask questions. Then I come back a second time, have another discussion and perhaps a third.

When quick decisions need to be made, of course, I shorten the process considerably. But I always rely on dialogue with people I trust.

It's also important that those whose judgment I trust don't read about decisions in the paper the next day, when they haven't had an opportunity to share their thoughts.

If I had to pick my most significant accomplishment so far, the top of the list would be our airport's expansion. While many progressive cities bought up property around their airports on a systematic basis so they would be ready to expand, Louisville's airport never did that.

So the question I faced back in the late 1980s was: Do we take a bold step and cause upheaval for 4,000 people, 180 businesses and 11 churches? Or do we just sit back and say, "We are what we are, and we're never going to be much more?"

We pressed forward, of course, and worked hard to relocate the folks whose land we needed. From that decision, I learned that you need to think out 20 years and to be prepared for what your community will need on that 20-year horizon.

What ultimately came out of the airport expansion was better air service and UPS' expansion with a billion-dollar package-sorting hub. Today UPS is the largest employer in Louisville – and the entire state of Kentucky.

To accomplish really great things, you have to be willing to take risks and, sometimes, to undergo a lot of grief and trouble for them.

Here is another example:

Some people looked at Louisville's waterfront years ago and saw piles of scrap and steel and sand and salt and said, "It's a working waterfront." Others said, "We have a vision. This could be our city's front door."

It took us ten years of litigation and heartache and headache to be able to get the scrap yard property we needed to begin the project. The result was the opportunity to build Waterfront Park and Louisville Slugger Field – investments that are serving as catalysts today for more than $100 million of private investment in housing, hotels, shops and offices.

The real success of leadership is when you can soldier through very difficult times and come out at the end with everyone looking back and saying: "You know, he was right."

On the other hand, my biggest disappointment was the garbage-to-steam plant that we proposed in my second term in office. My administration put together a well-engineered proposal: An experienced operator would oversee a plant that would create steam from garbage, sell the power and extend the community's options for garbage disposal beyond a single, privately-owned landfill.

But I could never get the Board of Aldermen to take ownership of the complicated proposal. What I learned from that experience is this: When you're going to try to get public support on a very complicated issue, you have to take time to explain it, and to work patiently with everyone who has a stake in it.

Timing, of course, is always important. The proposal might have won more support if there were a crisis – no more landfill space. But we were told that the landfill would serve our community's needs for 20 more years. And since then, that landfill has been expanded, so there is plenty of space. Life goes on. Timing is everything.

Creating a strong team is critical to effective leadership. I've always tried to attract people who love the community – first and foremost – not just because they want to work with me.

If I ever tried to take the community in a completely wrong direction, I hope they would do a lot of arguing and soul-searching – then they would all quit, because their first loyalty is love for their hometown.

As a leader, I believe it's my responsibility to delegate to my team – and to let them know that I trust their intuitive thinking and their judgment. I want to foster leadership skills all down the line and throughout government. Any organization going through change – like our new government – needs that.

Where is the next generation of leaders? I am asked that question frequently. It troubles me that many young folks these days want to become instant leaders. Few want to start at the bottom and work their way up.

I tell them that I learned something from every organization I worked with over the years. My organizational skills were honed by planning events and functions for non-profits and civic organizations. You learn how to work with folks who are helpful, how to handle people who are recalcitrant and how to make sure that the end product is as good as it can possibly be. You also learn how to create a good team.

I advise young people today to get involved now in whatever interests them because leadership is getting along with people, and letting people see that when you give your word, you deliver on your word. A leader is not just a name on the side of a letterhead. It's the person who says, "I'll do it."

Looking back half a century, so much has happened to improve our quality of life, and so much of it is the product of terrific teamwork by our local government and business leaders.

You can see benefits of this teamwork everyday – when you appreciate Waterfront Park, Brightside flower plantings and the expansion and improvement of other parkland throughout our community.

You can appreciate it in the education realm – where we now have one united public school system, a vital community college system and University of Louisville's embrace of a strong urban mission, research and the creation of centers of excellence.

You can witness teamwork in our community's economic-development growth – from life sciences to health care to logistics. And you can appreciate it in the renaissance of our downtown and cultural assets.

We're one of very few cities our size with a professional orchestra, ballet, opera, repertory theater and children's theater – not to mention our zoo, science center and other attractions.

Two additional examples:

Millions of dollars have been generated for our parks through the Olmsted Parks Conservancy. It was modeled on a similar group supporting New York City's Central Park. Our Conservancy developed a master plan for improving Louisville's major parks and parkways designed by landscape architect Frederick Law Olmsted – and I pledged to match private dollars with public funds.

Long before our city-county government merger, the Louisville-Jefferson County Compact was a significant step toward greater cooperation in local government. This agreement, negotiated when I became mayor and Harvey Sloane was Jefferson County judge-executive, set forth ways the city and county could work together for what was best for all our residents: sharing occupational tax revenue, creating a single economic development office, and freezing the annexation wars.

Merger was, of course, a major change for this community – supported by a bipartisan team of elected officials and local business. Another effective public-private partnership, Louisville-style.

As we look ahead, our city is facing some big challenges in the future. One of the most important challenges is balancing growth with quality-of-life issues. We must ensure that the center of our new 386-square-mile city continues to be vibrant; that housing stock is preserved and enhanced; that office space and entertainment venues are strengthened; and that our educational institutions are supported. The continued upgrade of our public school system is critical to building a strong workforce, raising educational attainment all the way up to the Ph.D. level and, ultimately, creating opportunity.

Our city is clearly a regional city now – so we have to consider the best ways for the region to grow and prosper. Some 80 percent of the jobs in the seven-county region are in this city, and 70 percent of the people in the region live in this city. Clearly issues like healthy air, economic development and transportation reach across the river and over county lines.

We must figure out how to have growth in our suburban areas that is responsive to residents. Density is good for the delivery of public services because as our geographic dimensions expand, it costs taxpayers a lot of money to provide new services like roads. And density is good for a city's vitality and "chemistry" – bringing together the rich diversity of individuals who make up a city's population.

That is another challenge: We must work to create a community where people have an interconnected concern for one another.

If our community is going to be a patchwork quilt made vibrant by diverse individuals and neighborhoods, then we all have a stake in our community's fabric being strong. I applaud residents who get outside their comfort zones and engage with other areas and individuals who share common concerns — whether it's affordable housing or crime, education or poverty.

It's boring to talk about infrastructure, but we still have a lot of needs — from small bridges to roads, from sewers to water. We have areas in this community where the water lines are 100 years old. We have sewers still made of wood. We have an enormous number of farm-to-market roads, where two school buses can't safely pass. It's going to take an infusion of significant capital and it's going to take leadership from the political and civic side to educate the community in terms of the needs, costs and options.

The most important lesson that I have learned is this: You can't do things by yourself. You will achieve the best results when you work in partnership — and work at building a consensus.

The days are over when one person stands up and says, "Follow me. Trust me. I have all the answers."

One good example occurred when the Park DuValle redevelopment project was coming online in the late 1980s — a plan to replace old public housing with a mixed-income neighborhood.

A large citizen advisory board of Park DuValle residents was formed, and held numerous evening and weekend meetings to plan how they could use millions of dollars in potential federal funds to rebuild their neighborhood.

It took longer to give that board a strong voice. But the result was a process that gave them a stake in the outcome: a decision that Park DuValle needed to be redeveloped, that a Community Development Bank needed to be created, and that a transportation facility should be built to get people from where they live to where the jobs are.

In today's era of consensus-building, it's important to put your listening ears on — as I tell my 13-year-old son — and to pay attention to what people are saying who are affected by whatever you are proposing as a leader. Then involve them in the ultimate decisions. With all those stakeholders, your odds of being successful as a leader will be far better.

I really like this quote from Margaret Mead, the anthropologist and author:

"Never doubt that a group of thoughtful, committed citizens can change the world. Indeed it is the only thing that ever has."

DAVID L. ARMSTRONG

Of Counsel
Greenebaum Doll & McDonald
PLLC

Former Mayor
City of Louisville

Former County Judge-Executive
Jefferson County

WHEN DAVE ARMSTRONG was finishing up his term as the last mayor of the old city of Louisville in 2002, then-University of Louisville president John Shumaker asked him to come to UofL to teach urban issues and leadership as an Executive-in-Residence. Shumaker wanted to give students exposure to someone of "proven ability to meet the leadership challenges of public office, and the skills necessary to build consensus among diverse constituencies," he said.

Armstrong had an impressive résumé. After graduating from UofL's law school in 1969, he had served as a juvenile court judge, a prosecutor at local and state levels, Kentucky's attorney general, Jefferson County judge-executive for two terms, and mayor of the City of Louisville.

Throughout his career, *The Courier-Journal* said in an editorial, Armstrong "delivered progress wherever he went."

He was appointed to his first two jobs — police court prosecutor and juvenile court judge — in 1970. That experience led to a 1973 run for county attorney, which he lost to Bruce Miller. But he bounced back to unseat incumbent commonwealth's attorney Edwin Schroering in 1975. He served as commonwealth's attorney for eight years, during which time President Jimmy Carter recognized him as one of ten outstanding prosecutors in America, and the National District Attorneys Association elected him president.

Armstrong jumped to statewide office with a victorious run for Kentucky attorney general in 1983. What might have been a train ride to the governor's chair was derailed in 1988, however, when he came up against Brereton Jones's vastly superior war chest in a campaign for the office of lieutenant governor of Kentucky.

After a brief stint in Louisville's Wyatt, Tarrant & Combs law firm, Armstrong turned to local politics instead. He won two terms as Jefferson County judge-executive — one that spanned five years — before crossing the street to serve as Louisville's mayor.

As commonwealth's attorney, as attorney general, and even as county judge-executive, Armstrong championed advocacy for victims of crime. One of his landmark achievements was the creation of V.I.N.E. (Victims' Information Notification Everyday), a system for notifying victims when perpetrators of crimes against them are released from jail. The program has now been implemented across the country.

As Kentucky's attorney general, he led efforts for adoption of a "Crime Victim's Bill of Rights," and a "lemon law" that protected buyers of new cars. He also looked after the interests of the elderly and utility ratepayers, earning a reputation as a principled man with a strong social compass.

As Jefferson County's judge-executive, Armstrong built a new jail and justice center and pushed for expansion of the Jefferson County Forest. Another signature achievement was his restoration of Riverside, The Farnsley-Moremen Landing — a museum and cultural center in southwest Jefferson County, an area that had long complained of neglect by a downtown government.

When he became mayor of Louisville, Armstrong moved quickly and dramatically on the theme of building a strong urban core for all of Jefferson County. He championed downtown housing, fostered technology jobs along the ten blocks of "eMain USA," and launched an effort to make the old Galleria into a vibrant, new "Fourth Street Live!" The idea, he said — as a sort of mantra repeated whenever he got a chance — was to encourage people to "live, work and play" downtown.

And he meant that for everybody. Armstrong put Louisville on the country's skateboarding and extreme cycling map with his cutting-edge Louisville Extreme Park. He pushed for expansion of the city's medical research center and supported private projects like the Muhammad Ali Center and the Frazier Historical Arms Museum. He has received innumerable awards for accomplishments and years of service to the city, the latest being Greater Louisville Inc.'s Silver Fleur-de-Lis Award in 2005.

Armstrong worked very hard for merger of Louisville and Jefferson County, which he considered essential to preservation of the city's core. Many expect Armstrong's mark on Louisville Metro to be detectable for a long time. Among the endeavors that gave him his broadest impact, *The Courier-Journal* said, was "his persistent effort to raise the community's level of aspiration."

I WAS BORN IN HOPE, ARKANSAS – yes, Bill Clinton's home town is also my home town. My parents, Lyman G. Armstrong Sr. and Elizabeth Evans Armstrong had three sons – Lyman, Dave and Tom, in that order.

Our home was a regular stop for politicians when they campaigned in our region. My grandfather – my mother's father – was Thompson Leroy Evans, whom I admired greatly. He was an alderman in Hope. He was also the station master at the railroad depot and he, along with another member, sponsored an ordinance to remove the "white only" signs at the station. He lost his re-election bid because of it. He kept the job as station master, though, because he had a good reputation as a former railroad detective.

My grandfather is mentioned in a special section of the train station museum. He did a number of important things, like opening the depot to African-Americans and allowing African-Americans to farm part of his property. He made a big impression on me when I was young, teaching me that good character was more important than material gain. My father also was an important mentor to me, teaching me to give back to the community.

I first became involved in civic activities as a student at Murray State University. I was given an opportunity to campaign for a new constitution for the Commonwealth of Kentucky. I got to meet people like Ed Prichard, a very good lawyer in Frankfort, who became a reformer for education and a reformer for the structure of state government.

Former Governor Ned Breathitt and other luminaries were involved in the campaign for a new constitution as well. I began to attend meetings with them and, whenever they got together to discuss the campaign, they also discussed strategies for improving western Kentucky. I found it appealing to try to find ways to change things for the better in that part of the state.

I majored in English and Political Science at Murray State and was active in a lot of projects on campus. I can't remember all of the issues that arose on campus while I was there, but I can remember that one issue arose about married students' housing being taken away on campus and, since I was married, I became involved in that issue. The more I got involved on campus, the more I was able to meet and get a good look at the type of people who were interested in politics and who became leaders on campus and in the community. I also got to know a lawyer from Owensboro named Wells Lovitt, who had long been involved in Democratic politics in Kentucky. He became a life-long political supporter.

I wanted to be closer to my family in Madison, Indiana, so I decided to come to Louisville to attend law school at the University of Louisville. I got a scholarship to law school but also worked in the law library while I was a student there.

David L. Armstrong

I knew no one in Louisville but I ended up meeting many of my life-long friends during that time. I met then-State Senator Wendell Ford one day when he visited campus. He asked me, as one of the first people he ran into, where he could find more people. It was noontime, so I took him over to the student union. He gave me his name and phone number when he left campus. I followed up with him, and he became a political ally from then on.

In the 1971 Democratic primary for governor, I supported Ford when most other political leaders in Louisville were for former governor and federal court judge Bert Combs.

I passed the bar in 1969 in both Kentucky and Indiana and opened a practice in Louisville. I was appointed an assistant police court prosecutor and also gained the International Electrical Workers Union as a client. This led to the opportunity of going to federal court to argue that the IUE members, while on strike, were entitled to receive food stamps. Kentucky government argued against it, but we won. This allowed the strike to continue.

Running for county attorney in the 1973 Democratic primary appealed to me because it seemed to be an office that would allow me to continue to practice law while also being a community leader. I lost the election that year but was able, in 1975, to take on and defeat the Republican commonwealth's attorney, Ed Schroering. I ran on a platform that we would reduce plea bargains by taking more cases to trial.

As commonwealth's attorney, I hired the first African-American and also the first female prosecutors. One problem we had to overcome, however, was the fact that only three courts handled criminal cases at the circuit court level. I was the first commonwealth's attorney to ask to appear before all the circuit court judges to ask that all the circuit court divisions be able to hear criminal cases. It took awhile but, within a couple of years, we merged the 16 circuit courts into a general term that could hear all criminal cases.

I also worked very hard to obtain the first grants from the Law Enforcement Assistance Administration of the U. S. Justice Department. It gave me the opportunity to work with many national leaders on crime issues. The money allowed me to computerize the courts, to hire more prosecutors and victim's rights advocates, and to bring other new innovations to our community. Using the federal grant monies, we were also able to set up sting operations – a new crime fighting tool at that time.

I was very proud of what my office was able to accomplish when I was commonwealth's attorney, and I ended up being recognized by President Jimmy Carter as one of the top ten prosecutors in America.

When I became attorney general of Kentucky, I led reforms that brought stronger laws to combat drunk driving, child sexual abuse and prosecution of corrupt state and local officials.

We created a new victim's advocacy unit in our office and, with the state legislature's help, we enacted a Victim's Bill of Rights and the first used car "lemon law" to protect consumers.

I think people would describe my leadership style as persistent and straightforward. I've always told people what needed to be done and what I wanted to accomplish and, once we did it, what we had accomplished. I have a deliberate style of leadership. I took that same kind of leadership national, in 1981, as president of the National District Attorneys Association.

I think Louisville has been served well by a number of outstanding community leaders over the years who have worked hard to keep Louisville's progress going forward. In my opinion, all leaders stand on the shoulders of prior leaders to accomplish objectives, but they seldom give them credit.

Growth and improvement in Louisville's quality of life have been brought about with the help of a number of companies in my time – Ford and UPS, for sure. Ford Motor Company used $2 million we provided them when I was county judge to train workers, and they kept and expanded their truck plant here. This is work that could have been done anywhere, but we made an investment in our workforce and in Ford that showed Ford that we were willing to partner with them on important community initiatives. We also worked with them on their emissions problems. They saw we valued them as a corporate citizen, and that paved the way for them to tell us when they needed help with their Fern Valley Road plant on more emissions problems.

David Jones, Wendell Cherry and Humana stepped up again and again as well when they were called upon to provide leadership. Law firm leaders like Larry Leatherman were always there for us when needed. Wallace Wilkinson, when he was Kentucky's governor, worked closely with us to make important things happen, like the property trade that made the UofL stadium possible.

Louisville's air quality and its connection to medical problems like heart disease and the general quality of life in our community are very important issues in our community. We need to find ways to deal with these challenges in new ways. As county judge, I worked with UPS to help them obtain money to buy new planes and to upgrade older plane engines to meet air quality standards.

I am proud that I've had an opportunity to play several key leadership roles in the community. When I was county judge, during Kentucky Governor Brereton Jones's administration, we needed to acquire additional land near the Riverport. Part of the land in question was occupied by a trailer park.

We knew that the property would be a huge boon to the county. If we had been able to acquire the land, it would have become the site for a large employer that instead went to Kansas City. Had it come here, it would have been something as big as GE's Appliance Park. They wanted a $3 million-a-year commitment in tax abatements and some pollution regulation help. The state said it couldn't offer that much, but the truth is, it just wasn't on the state's radar screen. That plant now employs over 4,500 people and almost has grown a separate city around it, with suppliers and other job-producing activities.

As county judge, I also had a vision that we could change the fortunes of a number of neighborhoods and other areas within Jefferson County – areas like Southwest Jefferson County, Fairdale, Newburg, Highview and others. The other county commissioners and I accomplished a lot, I believe.

We strengthened the county's finances, tackled jail overcrowding by building an additional facility and constructing a state-of-the-art justice center.

We streamlined the delivery of social services by creating one-stop community centers called Neighborhood Places to handle the health and social service needs of citizens in those areas.

We expanded the Jefferson Forest and even bought a riverboat – which we named the "Spirit of Jefferson" – for Farnsley-Moremen Landing.

We built parks, libraries and – perhaps most importantly – we created a new blueprint for developing our entire community called "Cornerstone 2020."

We developed three industrial parks and filled them with plants and headquarters. One became the seventh-best in America, with 24-hour day care, a worker training center, new TARC routes and affordable "fair" housing.

We created the VINE program, so that victims of violent crimes could be notified before a prisoner was released from jail.

We also worked hard for another bridge in eastern Jefferson County which, after all these years, looks like it's finally going to be a "go."

When I campaigned to be elected mayor of the City of Louisville in 1998, I discovered there was great interest among young and older citizens alike to move back downtown if we could provide them jobs, good housing options, and exciting entertainment venues. The demand for those things became a mantra for me as mayor. I created a slogan and a campaign for the City of Louisville to become a "place to live, work and play." For many people, that slogan became a rallying call to "come to the city." After three years, $2.3 billion of new monies were planned or invested in Louisville's downtown. During my term, Louisville also received two "Most Livable Cities" awards, I am proud to say.

I was pleased to have led those efforts, and gratified to have had so much help from many citizens in Louisville.

In 1999 and 2000, as mayor of Louisville, I participated on the local government task force and my office drafted the merger legislation that was ultimately passed, with some changes, by Kentucky's legislature. A task force was formed, after voters approved merger, that was headed by me and then-County Judge-Executive Rebecca Jackson. Our challenge was to prepare for one new government, thus avoiding potential problems that were anticipated for the new metro mayor and metro council members.

If you study the evolution of leadership, you know that people used to believe that leaders were ordained to be leaders or born into leadership. That's how kings and queens and others gained power. Common people could not become leaders. People now understand that leadership is not a birthright, it can be acquired.

I would urge young people who aspire to assume leadership roles in our community to take more risks and not to settle for small objectives. There are two kinds of leaders — those who take a series of small steps to reach their goals, and others who want to leap forward. The risks are higher when you leap forward, but you do not get as high a payoff with smaller steps. Remember, leadership is not a place, but rather a process.

Challenge people who tell you your ideas won't work. You need to go out and make them work. When I came in as mayor, I decided I wanted to truly revitalize the city and make downtown a nice neighborhood to live in. I look back today and it's all coming together.

People who have spoken to my classes at UofL, including some developers who were about ready to leave and go elsewhere and to leave the city abandoned, now say they saw my vision and built downtown. With Fourth Street Live!, Louisville Slugger Field, Waterfront Park and other projects downtown, people now want to live downtown. They are not looking for big homes in the suburbs anymore. They are contributing property taxes to our city.

People from all walks of life are now looking for places to live downtown so they can be closer to their work. And people our children's age are also now looking for places to live downtown because it has become a vibrant center for nightlife, the arts and entertainment.

I am proud of the role I was able to play in creating ways for our citizens to "live, work, and play" downtown, and I look forward to watching how our city is going to continue to develop in the years to come.

Minx M. Auerbach

Former Executive Assistant to County Judge-Executive Mitch McConnell

Former Director of Consumer Affairs, City of Louisville

Former Chair, Louisville-Jefferson County Planning Commission

FOR DECADES, NO NEWCOMER to Louisville went very long without hearing about Minx Auerbach — a woman who started volunteering a little when she first moved to Louisville in the mid-1950s and saw her activity snowball into several careers and a long record of public service.

Auerbach headed the city of Louisville's first office of consumer affairs for Mayor Harvey Sloane, served as Jefferson County Judge-Executive Mitch McConnell's executive assistant, then chaired both the Louisville and Jefferson County Planning Commission and the University of Louisville Board of Trustees.

She was one of the founders of Louisville's Community Coordinated Child Care (4-C) organization, which advocates for quality child care services and funding for children and families in Jefferson County. She also led efforts to expand and upgrade programs at the Louisville Science Center that have boosted its number of visitors from 70,000 to 500,000 a year, and have extended its outreach to all 120 Kentucky counties and to 18 counties in southern Indiana.

At 83, Auerbach is still on the board of the Tumbleweed restaurant chain and of the River Fields environmental watchdog organization. Her résumé of community service and accomplishments is long and impressive.

Minx Mansbach Auerbach was born in Ashland, Kentucky, one of six children born to prominent, activist parents. She and her three sisters shared three goals, she told *Business First* several years ago — to get a good education, to get out of Ashland, and to marry doctors.

Auerbach met her first two goals by going to Ohio State University for two years, then to the University of Miami in Florida for two more. She took care of the third by picking out a husband — Sy Auerbach — at Miami, and helping him get through medical school. He is a prominent orthopedic surgeon in Louisville and is himself a civic activist. They have three adult children – one daughter and two sons.

In the mid-1950s, Auerbach found herself in Louisville with three small children and an itch to volunteer. She quickly dispatched a project assigned to her by the Louisville section of the National Council of Jewish Women and soon found herself chair of the women's division of the United Jewish Appeal. She also served as local, then regional president of the NCJW, and ultimately served on that organization's national board.

While she was working with 4-C in the early 1970s, she was asked by then-Governor Louie Nunn to chair the Kentucky Commission on Children and Youth.

Harvey Sloane soon became aware of her leadership abilities and civic activities and, when he became mayor in 1974, he tapped her to run his new office of consumer affairs, a job that brought her national attention and praise.

When Sloane left office, Auerbach accepted an invitation from then-County Judge-Executive Mitch McConnell – a Republican who called her his "favorite liberal" – to balance out his administration as his executive assistant. In that position, she created a formal system for selecting programs and organizations worthy of county funding and chaired a variety of community projects, including revival of a then-waning Louisville Community Foundation, and planting trees throughout the city through the Comprehensive Employment and Training Act (CETA), a federally-funded jobs program for disadvantaged youth.

Auerbach was appointed to the Louisville-Jefferson County Planning Commission in 1984. She served on the Commission until 1997 and, from 1986 to 1997, served as its first woman chair.

Auerbach served on the UofL Board of Trustees from 1991 to 1998 and was its first woman chair from 1996 to 1998. She was instrumental in creating the Commission on the Status of Women at the university, and in effecting a significant increase in the number of women professors and administrators now serving in key positions. To commemorate her efforts on behalf of women and women's issues at UofL, Auerbach's husband established an endowment in her honor that now funds an annual Minx Auerbach Lecture in Women's and Gender Studies during Women's History Month each spring.

Auerbach says she is proudest of her work with the Science Center and 4-C. "Hundreds of teachers come to learn about science, and thousands of children are weekly visitors now to the Louisville Science Center. That is a real success story," she says with pride.

I NEVER REALLY CONSIDERED becoming a leader in the community. My leadership just evolved gradually.

My husband Sy and I moved to Louisville from Ashland in 1948 so he could attend medical school. We had one child and knew no one here. I had come from a family who was involved in community life, so when I was asked to participate, it was natural for me to do so.

My first involvement was with the Louisville section of the National Council of Jewish Women. I was asked to make some phone calls for them and when I finished them quickly and efficiently, I continued to get calls to work. I eventually became chair of the Louisville section, then went on the board of the regional division, became regional chair, then went on the national board. Because the work of the Council interfaced with many of the things that were happening in the community, I got to know a wide variety of people in the community and was asked to sit on other boards.

Some of the issues the Council was involved in at that time were mental health, open housing and child care. Though my leadership in those areas evolved gradually, I would like to think that my efforts back then have resulted in enduring positive results.

Take child care, for example. I served on a child care committee of what was then called the Community Chest, now Metro United Way. The federal government decided to award grants to 12 communities to coordinate child care. The $15,000 grant came to the Community Chest and was funneled to the child care committee of which I was chair. I knew that other states were taking advantage of programs for children that Kentucky was missing out on, simply because they had not written grants or established programs. I went to Governor Louie Nunn's assistant at that time to encourage the state to submit a grant that would assist the program we were starting in Louisville called Community Coordinated Child Care, known as 4-C. We used the federal grant we received to leverage other money and actually ended up with $40,000 which enabled us to set up a board, hire staff and establish a lasting program.

Of the 12 communities that received money from the grant, Louisville is the only community that still has a coordinated child care program 30 years later. Our ability to raise money in Louisville, however, helped state government create programs around the state with federal money.

Two important things happened to me as a result of those efforts. Governor Nunn put me on the board of the Kentucky Commission on Children and Youth and a few months later made me chair; and Mitch McConnell, who was chairing the Jefferson County campaign for the Republican nominee for governor that year, asked me to write an issue paper for him on child care, which I very happily did. That was my introduction to Mitch.

I was doing a great deal of volunteer work when Harvey Sloane was elected mayor of Louisville. Harvey asked me to set up a department of consumer affairs for the city. I realized I could probably do it very easily, since that was essentially what I was doing as a volunteer. To make sure I was qualified, I went to New York to meet with Bess Myerson, who was director of consumer affairs in New York. She supposedly had the best office in the country. After that meeting, I believed I could do the job, so I came back to Louisville and accepted the job that Harvey offered me.

I had a wonderful time in that job. Harvey was an inexperienced mayor and had his hands full, so he let me do what I wanted to do. For example, there was an old unused firehouse on Hill Street with some vacant land attached to it. I decided to help the neighbors use the land for a community garden. Then I went to the Ball Corporation in Indiana and persuaded them to put equipment in the firehouse so people could can the produce they raised for ten cents a jar. It was a huge success.

I used students from UofL as interns to search for data. We put out a pamphlet which reported bank's interest rates and other information that was not available at that time, though it is so commonplace today.

We created a book on doctors that reported which doctors took Medicaid and Medicare patients and included what their charges were. Not all the doctors responded to our inquiries, but the majority did. I could not have done all this with the small staff I had, but the interns supplied invaluable leg work.

An interesting thing happened to me when I was serving as Harvey's director of consumer affairs. I received an anonymous call from a mortgage company in Indiana. The man on the telephone said that he was calling to tell me that an elderly lady in Louisville was about to lose her home. He said she could not keep up the payments because she only had income from social security. Her husband had died three years before, but part of the mortgage payment was an insurance policy that paid off the loan at his death. He gave me the name of his mortgage company and said the following week they were going to repossess the woman's house. He gave me the address of the woman. I sent a staff person to see if she had any documents pertaining to the mortgage, which she did, and they very clearly stated that she was entitled to the house at her husband's death. Well, I had absolutely no authority to do anything in Indiana, so I called the manager of the mortgage company and said "Look, I have this story and I will give you 24 hours to give that woman her deed and repay her the $3,000 she has paid you over the past three years, plus interest. If you don't do it, I am going to the press with this story." The man did what I asked. Then I told the press anyway, because I figured this was not the only woman he was trying to cheat.

I loved that job because it was wonderful to be able to help people in a positive way and to improve the community along the way.

We started the first farmers markets in Louisville. Now they are all over the place. I created Food Day, a one-day food fest on the Belvedere that promoted healthy eating, and we got the food purveyors to supply the food. The local ordinance we now have dealing with solicitations was put into effect when we saw the need.

At that time, Louisville had two newspapers and three television stations, all with consumer reporters. They came to me for stories because they had nowhere else to go. I quickly learned the power of the press and let them report all the good things we were doing.

As a result of all this public work, I became well known. In fact, I received a call from an AP reporter who said she had asked ten national consumer affairs organizations to name the best local consumer affairs director in the country, and my name was the only one on all ten lists. She came to Louisville and did a lengthy interview which was published in dozens of papers all over the country except Louisville ironically, because they did not think it was news.

At that time, of course, mayors couldn't succeed themselves. Bill Stansbury was elected mayor and I didn't think I wanted to work for him. I was mulling over what to do next when I got a call from Mitch McConnell, who had just been elected Jefferson County judge-executive, the only Republican to be elected in Kentucky that year. My, haven't things changed? He said he was looking for a high-profile Democrat to serve in his administration. I knew Mitch was going to run an honest administration, so I decided to take the job.

At that time, the county was doling out a lot of money to General Hospital, the Board of Health and a number of other social service agencies. I served as the county's liaison to all agencies that received county money. I took that job seriously and sat on all those boards with two hats, one as a liaison and the other as a dedicated member of that board. The previous county judge had handed out money to whatever organization came to ask for it. It was millions of dollars. Mitch decided he wanted that organized and asked me to handle it.

I created a community committee to review requests for funding from all groups requesting money. They had to apply in writing on forms that we created and had to report how the money was being spent. From then on, money was designated for these groups in the annual budget.

When I was raising money for 4-C, I learned about a Community Foundation in Louisville that had been established many years before but was now inactive. It had $1 million – the same $1 million it had 20 years earlier.

The foundation was being run by an elderly banker. When I looked into its charter, I learned that the board members of the foundation were appointed by the county judge.

One of my jobs for Mitch was to find capable people to sit on the many boards to which he made appointments. I had a friend in Boston who sat on the board of the Boston Community Foundation, so I knew how valuable a really good foundation could be to a community.

Maxine Brown moved to Louisville from Indianapolis and was urging me to help create a good community foundation. So I went to leaders like Wilson Wyatt and Baylor Landrum and offered that Mitch would appoint a good board under their leadership if they would they help. Wilson Wyatt was particularly interested. Though he did not sit on the board, he was very helpful in creating what is now the well-known Louisville Community Foundation. I sat on the board for a number of years. Not many people know the role I played in that.

Also at that time, the federal government was pouring money into communities to help disadvantaged youth through the Comprehensive Employment and Training Act (CETA) program. The money came to the county but was rerouted to the CETA board. Since the young people worked in the summertime, it was hard finding useful things for them to do. So we went to Trees, Inc., which Henry Heuser, Jr. chaired, and said "If you provide trees for the streets, we will guarantee you that they will be watered every week during the summer for two years." That way, we knew the trees would live. So if you go down Market Street today or to Butchertown and see all the trees alive and well, know that they were planted and kept alive by youth who worked for the CETA program back then.

I enjoyed working for Mitch. I learned a great deal about politics from him. But after about five or six years with him, I decided it was time to move on. He asked me to sit on the Louisville and Jefferson County Planning Commission. Since that would keep me in public service as a volunteer, I decided to do it. I was on the Commission for 13 years and chaired it for eight.

One of my biggest disappointments was that after all the time I served on the Planning Commission, I could not get the "powers that be" to implement impact fees. Every time a developer moves out to a farm to create yet another subdivision, the taxpayers pick up the tab for the schools, the roads, the water, the sewers, and all that infrastructure is expensive. Many communities require developers to pay impact fees to create the infrastructure. If you mentioned the words impact fees in our community, however, it would send developers up a tree, and the elected officials did not want to deal with it.

I thought there was a chance to create some smart growth when the plan for Cornerstone 2020 was proposed. Lots of money and years of time was put into that planning document, which was to be a guideline for future growth. Larry Leatherman was the representative from the Chamber of Commerce to the Cornerstone planning committee. Larry understood exactly what needed to be done and how to do it and I was so encouraged that we would eventually do what needed to be done – not to slow growth, but to have smart growth. Larry died, however, and his role on the committee was taken over by people who seemed more interested in helping developers than in doing what was best for the community's growth. I have always regretted that I did not have the ability to make impact fees and a plan for smart growth happen.

As chair of the Planning Commission, one of the most difficult things I had to do was chair the joint meeting of the Urban Renewal Board and the Planning Commission to clear the way for the airport expansion. Unfortunately, in order to do this, Urban Renewal had to declare the Highland Park community as "blighted" and the Planning Commission had to rezone it for industrial use.

The public meeting was held at the fairgrounds because the crowd was so large. It started at 7:00 p.m. Joe Corradino was the engineer who planned the details of the expansion and, as was customary, gave his report first. The crowd wanted to kill him. When he started speaking, there were jeers and catcalls. I was only able to control the meeting by promising everyone they would have their say, but I told them that they had to listen quietly to Joe.

I did let everyone have their say. At 3:00 a.m., there were still 100 people in the hall. The meeting broke up at 6:00 a.m. We deliberately did not take any action that night and postponed the vote for two weeks to give ourselves time to assimilate all the information. Besides, it was very difficult to listen to grown men cry at the thought of giving up the home that their grandparents had lived in and that they wanted their grandchildren to live in. We knew it would break up the neighborhood, the churches, friends, their whole lives. But we also knew how important the airport expansion was to the whole community.

I regret that those people were only paid what the market values of their homes were because when the land was re-zoned, it was worth a lot of money. I think they should have been compensated for the wrenching break up of their community, but I did not know how to make that happen.

I was the first woman chair of the Planning Commission, and I heard many comments from neighborhood groups that I was the first person who let them talk, the first person who really listened. I think because of my role, the neighborhood groups became stronger and participated more in the process. I was fair and objective and, long after I was out of that office, I got comments from developers and lawyers that they really missed the objective way I handled the meetings.

One of my big disappointments was Hurstbourne Lane. I was determined that it be designated a parkway and not become like Shelbyville Road. Sam Swope was one of the first developers to come out there. The Commission insisted that there be a 15-foot setback with a landscaped berm fronting the road. That became one of the binding elements, which would have set the standard for all of Hurstbourne Lane. Swope went to see Harvey Sloane who was county judge at the time, and he persuaded Harvey to amend the binding element to allow only a five-foot setback with no berm. So the rest of the road was developed pretty much the same way, even though it is designated a parkway and has different standards than ordinary roadways.

Because of my experience handling controversial issues on the Planning Commission, when I became a member of the University of Louisville's Board of Trustees, my first task was to chair a special committee on governance. It was a hotly-contested issue with the faculty, and no one on the board wanted to chair it. I really did not mind. In the end it took longer than the president wanted, but we came up with an agreeable solution for everyone.

When I became a trustee, I immediately noticed that there were no women vice presidents at UofL, and the only woman dean was the dean of nursing. I immediately started questioning the administration about this shortcoming and in response, President Donald Swain set up a committee to study the status of women at the university. An assistant to the provost chaired it, and I sat on the committee. The rest of the committee consisted of staff and faculty.

In six months time, the committee came up with a number of recommendations and President Swain put some of them into effect immediately. But then he announced his retirement, so the next president, John Shumaker, got credit for opening the doors to women. We now have women vice presidents at UofL and the university's provost is also a woman, but we are still lagging far behind in deanships.

I became the first woman chair of UofL's Board of Trustees, but I had a good deal of conflict with President Shumaker. I tried to curb his travel and his expenditures and he was not happy with that. So I stepped down as chair after a year and a half in that position. I did not ask the governor to renew my appointment. I feel good about my time on the board, however. I do feel I made a contribution in many ways.

I think that also describes my style of leadership. I believe that I am a public servant and all my actions are geared toward what is in the best interest of the public. I think that is particularly important in financial oversight. I also listen to what people have to say, and I always learn something from that as well. I am tenacious, but not obstinate.

Some of my mentors were Mary Helen Byck and Wilson Wyatt. Wilson was politically active as well as socially active. He really cared about the community and was a man whom I would always look to for advice. He would give it willingly, and he was accessible.

I remember vividly a story Wilson told me. Fifty years ago when any government entity wanted city water extended to their area, they had to be annexed by the city to get it. That was the way Louisville was growing. Mayor Charlie Farnsley was friends of the mayor of St. Matthews, which at that time was a very small city. St. Matthews wanted city water and the mayor of St. Matthews convinced Farnsley to let the city have water without annexation. Too bad. If that had not happened, Louisville would have eventually taken over all of Jefferson County. We would not have had to go through all those merger battles and we would not have the hundreds of small cities that we have now.

I think the expansion of the airport has contributed most to Louisville's growth. Bringing UPS here was very important. Equally important was the contribution that UofL made by creating schools and scholarships for UPS employees to keep UPS here. The program was unique and had not been done anywhere else. UoL provided classes late in the evening and early in the morning so employees could work during the night. It built dorms for those students and UPS paid tuition. The Jefferson Community College and the technical schools were invited to participate. The program was called Metropolitan College, and it has been a huge success.

Governor Patton's providing money to UofL under the so-called "Bucks for Brains" program has also contributed enormously to our growth in medical research and other areas. Louisville has an excellent medical community and that has contributed to our growth.

I do feel in small ways I have contributed to the city's development, first as consumer affairs director, then as a special assistant to Mitch McConnell, then certainly as chair of the Louisville and Jefferson County Planning Commission and as chair of UofL's Board of Trustees. I have also contributed in quiet ways by preventing some things that would be harmful to public areas. It is hard to say what my greatest accomplishments were, but I am pleased that many of the things I was part of are enduring.

My advice to young people aspiring to leadership would be to get on boards and be good contributing members. It's hard work, but it's the way to get to know the community. You will soon know enough people to be able to call whomever you need when you need help.

I think one of the biggest challenges facing our city is still making merger work for the whole area. I see all our small cities as a stumbling block. People in the county want all the services that the city used to provide, but they don't want to pay for it. I remember a real estate agent telling me when we were looking to buy a new home, "If you move to the county, your taxes are lower." It was a selling point. I think all that has to be equalized somehow. Also, a bigger challenge is to make downtown alive again. I think all the new housing going up downtown will be a boon, but we have to stop eating up our countryside for new development.

One of the most valuable lessons that I have learned and need to pass on to the next generation of leaders is that you cannot do anything alone. You always need help and you have to develop ways to embrace people so help will be given willingly.

BARRY BINGHAM JR.

Owner
Billy Goat Strut Publishing Co.

Former Editor and Publisher
The Courier-Journal and
The Louisville Times

Former Vice-Chairman
Standard Gravure Corporation
and WHAS, Inc.

BARRY BINGHAM JR. TOOK OVER Louisville's already-famous *Courier-Journal* and *Louisville Times* newspapers in 1971 and, as a hands-on editor and publisher, polished their luster even more, making them beacons of journalistic ethics.

Bingham has also been a devoted community servant and a strong patron of the arts in Louisville. He helped launch Actor's Theatre, has served on the board of the Fund for the Arts for more than 30 years, and has made large contributions of both time and money over the years to all of the city's arts programs.

Bingham has stepped back from some of his civic commitments in recent years, but he is still a strong presence – advising, sometimes scolding leaders in the arts and other areas when he sees things he thinks are not right or need improvement. One of his strongest desires now is to see the city of Louisville united, rather than divided along racial lines and economic levels.

Barry Bingham Jr. was born in Louisville, growing up with four siblings on his family's 50-acre estate in Glenview. His list of early mentors includes Curtis Madison, the Bingham family's chauffeur and handyman, and Lucy Cummings, who was nurse to him and his siblings, both deceased.

Barry Jr. began marching to a different drummer at an early age. He rowed crew at Harvard, taking on a grueling sport that remains obscure to most Kentuckians, but requires a good deal of physical effort and mental discipline. After graduating from college, he joined the U.S. Marine Corps and flirted briefly with buying a tea farm in Africa.

The family decided that he should lead the Binghams' broadcast stations – WHAS radio and television – so he went to work for both CBS and NBC as a documentary producer.

In 1963, he returned to Louisville, and was enjoying running the Binghams' broadcast companies when tragedy struck. His brother Worth was killed in a freak accident on Nantucket Island. Barry Jr. agreed to take over running the newspapers. "It would have been untrue to Worth to say the hell with it and go ahead and sell," he said later.

After he took the helm in 1971, the newspapers continued the family tradition of championing the urban poor, rural Kentucky, and reform of coal mining practices. Under Bingham's leadership as publisher and editor, the newspapers won three Pulitzer prizes. In 1976, the photo staff won for busing riot photos; in 1978, reporter Richard Whitt won for his story of the Beverly Hills Supper Club fire; and in 1980, reporters Joel Brinkley and Jay Mather won for international reporting in Cambodia.

By 1985, family and economic issues led to a decision to combine *The Courier-Journal* and *The Louisville Times* into one paper, and ultimately to the sale of the newspapers to Gannett Co., Inc. in 1986. Other Bingham radio and television properties were sold to other buyers that same year.

Bingham used part of his $76.5 million share of the proceeds to launch *FineLine*, a newsletter on journalism ethics. He had to pull the plug on the publication after two years, but the reputation he earned for running ethical news organizations continues to be one of the accomplishments of which he is most proud.

Bingham's commitment and contributions to his community continue. He has served on the boards of Actors Theatre of Louisville, the Greater Louisville Fund for the Arts, the Louisville Orchestra, the Kentucky Opera, the Kentucky Center for the Arts, the Governor's Scholars Program, Leadership Louisville, the University of Louisville Board of Overseers, Berea College and the Smithsonian Institution. He and his family continue to make generous donations to individual charities and arts organizations.

He is also an avid environmentalist, serving on the boards of the Kentucky Nature Conservancy and the Bernheim Forest Foundation. In 2000, he was one of three key contributors who helped Jefferson County buy a $1.6 million, 238-acre tract bordering the Floyds Fork of the Salt River, to save it from development. The next year, River Fields – a conservation and environmental watchdog group – gave Bingham and his wife, Edith, its Land Heroes Award for their involvement in conservation and preservation issues statewide.

The Binghams still live on the family estate in Glenview. They have four adult children.

Passing the Torch

LET ME START OFF by saying that if I sound vitriolic, and I probably will before I'm finished, I am really laying a lash on myself as well as the Establishment because, as publisher of *The Courier Journal* and *The Louisville Times*, I have been part of the Establishment, and I am part of the background of what I consider "The Louisville Problem." Our community is divided. It is not just divided between black and white; it is divided culturally, religiously, and certainly economically. This is what our community's leadership should be addressing. Louisville is divided in many ways, and to a great extent the leaders of those divisions don't communicate very successfully with each other.

I have tried to be an agent of change for at least the last 30 or 40 years of my life – in fact, all along. That's probably why I get into trouble so often.

One issue that was very close to me, and that I was very involved in, was the school busing crisis of 1975. The community rose up in arms and protested, but busing was federally imposed. We had school busing for many years, to the unhappiness of most of the people being bused both into town and out of town for racial balance. We now know that most of the members of the African-American community wanted their children to go to Central High School rather than to be bused out to Ballard High School or wherever, because they wanted their children to attend a neighborhood school.

We also know that while education attainment in the public schools seems to be on the increase, there is still a huge division between African-American and white students' academic accomplishment, especially male African-American and white students. There is even a division between African-American male and female students. This is an issue that has not been successfully addressed. If we are ever going to have one society, we have to provide everyone with at least a satisfactory education, no matter what their skin color, and no matter what their background.

Our community has other problems too, in addition to the education problem, like air pollution (mostly in western Louisville), sewage problems (much of it in southern Louisville), and water pollution.

So what are we doing now to solve these problems? We are now planning to build an East End bridge for billions of dollars, which will, of course, have nothing to do with solving any problems in the West End. It will actually drain jobs away from the West End.

For instance, we have obscene amounts of money coming from the federal government to fund local pet projects – both Democratic and Republican. I am not laying this on any one party. Everyone loves "pork."

For instance, we received $100,000 from the U.S. Department of Energy for rehabilitation of the old railroad bridge. I'm glad it's being done, but $100,000 is excessive from the Department of Energy, which has a Paducah nuclear plant to clean up, with billions of dollars of unfunded costs.

If this country were engaged in fewer wars and spent all its money on cleanup of nuclear sites left behind by the generating and weapons industries, we probably would do nothing else for the next 20 years. While we have money to develop a riverfront park in Louisville, we leave these other issues unaddressed or insufficiently addressed.

Our priorities, in my opinion, are out of line. Our present priorities make it possible for the Establishment to live the way the Establishment wants to live. When I need to get to Indiana, I don't mind going over the Clark Memorial Bridge.

Our priorities are to build one more golden subdivision and one more golden mall in eastern Louisville and to leave the problems of western and southern Louisville behind, maybe acknowledged but insufficiently funded.

We can all say we care about it, but not until we actually do something about it will we achieve one community. If Greater Louisville Inc. wants to lead, it is one of the organizations in our community that can do it. Rev. Louis Coleman and his people can also do their part, but I think it is an opportunity for Greater Louisville Inc.as well.

Let me just say once again that I am as much at fault as anyone else. I have been part of the hierarchy. I have now lost my journalism voice, but I still speak out occasionally and still get myself in trouble.

As long as we continue feathering our own nests, however, spending billions of federal dollars on "pork-pie projects," then I think we will continue to be a community in decline. Not until we make Louisville a community where Rev. Coleman can honestly go arm-in-arm with Greater Louisville Inc. to other communities and say this is what we've done – we've raised African-American and white education to top 16 in the country, not 38th or wherever we are now – will we be a city on the rise.

If the East End of the community were a little less golden and the western and southern parts of this community were more; if we shared the gold so that everyone has some, instead of some having platinum and others having lead; if we had an even distribution of worth around this community; then I think we would be in the heavenly state I think is possible in Louisville.

This is the Neville Miller/Wilson Wyatt/Charlie Farnsley legacy – the great mayors of this community who saw us as one great city, rather than as a prosperous East End and impoverished western and southern parts of the city.

Almost every city has a minority community. Almost every city has the same divisions – religious, cultural, racial – that we have. All cities also have educational attainment problems.

My advice is to find out which cities are handling their problems best and bring their ideas back here. If we could just be the collector of effective ideas, rather than thinking we have to originate them all.

This city could be a Mecca. We would have every hotel in this town booked every night of the year with people coming to Louisville to find out how we did it. We could have a great cultural community. We can't have everything, though. We can't have an NBA arena and team and everything else we want. We have to pick our shots. But before we do that, we have to make the community prosperous and happy and fairly administered. That means everyone getting the benefit of tax dollars, and those dollars not being spent to enhance the wealth and opportunity of the wealthy at the expense of the impoverished.

My leadership style is ineffective, I'm afraid. I have been saying these same things for years – maybe not quite as forcefully as I am saying them here. People are always polite to me. They nod and say, "Oh yes, we all want one community. We all want equality. We really want an East End bridge first, then we'll get around to all these other things."

Some would call me "phony" because I still live in the East End and I haven't bought a house down in Smoketown or western Louisville.

Well, I should be out in front. I should be down talking in churches in western Louisville every Sunday. I should be out every time Rev. Louis Coleman is on the street. I have been out with him a couple of times, but I haven't been out all that often. I participated in peace demonstrations to try to stop the war in Iraq before it started and after it started. My effectiveness, however, is about zero, or less than zero, because no one likes a preacher.

If I had moved to western Louisville when I first came to Louisville instead of moving to Glenview – if we had said, "We're going to live what we believe, we are going to put up with the schools down there and we're going to breathe the bad air and we're going to join Rev. Coleman and others and picket the Rubbertown plants" – then I think I would have been more effective as a leader. If I could start all over again, and if my wife and our children would be willing to do that (I actually think they might have been more willing than I would have been, because our children are remarkably understanding about things like that), I think we could have made that work.

When you get to the top or near the top of your company, everyone wants to bring you good news. I had a reputation for asking the people who worked for me to "bring me some bad news." George Gill, who was the president of the company at the time, would fish around and try to find somebody who had filed a sex discrimination suit against us or something. George would come in and, instead of talking about all the good things, we would talk about how we were going to work on this problem.

Martin Luther King, Jr. said, "Every time somebody says it's not time to solve that problem yet, it means it will never get solved." We have to turn our priorities around. We have to turn to the people who need us the most, the part of the community that needs us the most. And perhaps we need to scrutinize our accomplishments more modestly.

Every attempt to accomplish something is opposed – especially if it is going to change something. One of the few "accomplishments" that I was a party to was trying to bring an ethical standard to journalism – to Louisville especially, but elsewhere as well – and it has worked. I think the Louisville newspapers and, while we owned them, the broadcast companies in Louisville, had ethical standards that were considered admirable in the industry. If the industry had undertaken similar ethical standards, I don't know if we would be in the mess we are in today.

If I were going to give advice to young people in Louisville aspiring to become the next generation of leaders, I would tell them to form an organization that includes men and women, African-Americans, other minorities and low-income people; to make sure the organization is culturally diverse; then to go after the problems, go after the politicians, and go after the money. Politicians should stop wasting money where they know their votes are coming from. Many think that people in western Louisville and young people don't vote as much as adults in eastern Louisville do. Find those politicians and tell them, "You have to make this one community, or else we are going to vote you out of office."

To be a leader you have to be prepared to sacrifice and suffer – not only for yourself, but also for your family. Every sacrifice I undertake means a sacrifice for members of my family and the people who work with us and for us. When I suffer, they all suffer. You have to be prepared to sacrifice , but you can only go as far as you are humanly able to go.

My mentors are familiar names in Louisville. Let's start with my father, Barry Bingham, Sr.; former 12-term U.S. Congressman Ron Mazzoli; Edith Bingham, my wife; Jon Jory, the former managing director of Actors Theatre of Louisville; Wilson Wyatt, the deceased former mayor of the city of Louisville; Sally Brown, matriarch of the family that founded Brown-Forman and an avid environmentalist and conservationist; Sherry Jelsma, a strong advocate for the arts and education; Tori Murden, the first woman to row solo across the Atlantic Ocean; Neville Miller, a former mayor and an absolute genius who was mayor of Louisville during the 1937 flood, probably the greatest crisis this city has ever endured; and Charlie Farnsley, certainly a brilliant man in the history of this city and a mayor who has left us with many legacies – ideas like the Fund for the Arts and the Sinking Fund, and other innovations without which we would be virtually lost.

I'll add Rev. Louis Coleman to that list. The most important things Rev. Coleman has reinforced are that opportunities for fairness and equity are very important things in life, and that any society in which one part of the society prospers and major parts fail and suffer is not healthy and won't survive.

Of the people I have mentioned on this list, Rev. Louis Coleman is the one who has taught me these things most profoundly. My father certainly did; my wife, Edith Bingham, certainly did, and does; and all the rest have, too.

Neville Miller and Charlie Farnsley had this wisdom and these qualities imbued in their personality, and it is why they were so great. They were brilliant, but they also had a soul and a conscience. If we were all more like them, we could have a far greater city.

ULYSSES L. "JUNIOR" BRIDGEMAN

**Owner and President
Bridgeman Foods, Inc.**

**Chair
University of Louisville
Board of Trustees**

ULYSSES L. "JUNIOR" BRIDGEMAN led the University of Louisville Cardinals basketball team to the NCAA Final Four in 1975, then went on to play pro ball. While he was in his 12-year pro career with the Milwaukee Bucks and the Los Angeles Clippers and taking law courses, somebody talked him and a partner into buying a Wendy's Old-Fashioned Hamburger Restaurant franchise in Brooklyn and assured him the place would run itself. "Well, at the end of the first year," Bridgeman said later, "we lost about $300,000."

Bridgeman and his partner learned different lessons from that mistake, he will tell you. The partner went back to coaching. Bridgeman, on the other hand, took a Wendy's training course that started him off mopping floors, then he worked his way up through all the jobs in the restaurant.

Now he is owner and president of Bridgeman Foods, Inc., the 16th-largest restaurant franchise in America, according to the 2004 *Restaurant Finance Monitor*. He oversees the administration and operation of 153 Wendy's franchises in four states and employs over 5,320 people.

He has received business awards too numerous to mention. He was inducted into Junior Achievement's Business Hall of Fame in 2002. But despite his success and awards, you can still find him passing french fries to customers through the drive-through window at his Louisville restaurant locations.

Junior Bridgeman's basketball team at Washington High School in East Chicago, Indiana won the 1971 Indiana State Basketball Championship — the culmination of a youth spent concentrating on three things — school, church and sports.

He was a star basketball player at the University of Louisville, where he earned a psychology degree in 1975. From 1975 to 1987, he played professional basketball with the Milwaukee Bucks and the Los Angeles Clippers. During 11 of his 12 years in the National Basketball Association, he picked up leadership skills in the Players Association, serving as a player representative and liaison in negotiations with the teams' owners. He was also an officer in the NBA Players Association, serving as treasurer for three years and president for four.

During his professional basketball career, Bridgeman also worked as a sales and public relations representative for Howard Johnson. He took some law classes, but discovered that his schedule wouldn't allow him to get the courses he needed, so he quit studying law. He followed fellow players into the food franchise business instead, and that path ultimately led him to the successful career he enjoys today.

Along the way, Bridgeman got business tips from Wendy's founder Dave Thomas and from Wal-Mart founder Sam Walton, whom he met at a charity golf event in Arkansas. Walton put him in his red pickup and took him to Wal-Mart headquarters where, Bridgeman noted, Walton knew everybody's name.

Thomas could walk into a restaurant and tell, "within five seconds," Bridgeman says, what kind of shape the restaurant was in. "After Dave started doing the commercials," Bridgeman told *The Courier-Journal* in 2002, "it was like traveling with a rock star. It is just taking something from everyone along the way that makes you what you are," Bridgeman says.

Bridgeman and his wife, Doris, have three children. He gives back to his community by passing knowledge, and often monetary help, on to others. He currently chairs the University of Louisville's Board of Trustees and serves on the boards of the Louisville Free Public Library, the Louisville Convention and Visitors Bureau and Fifth Third Bank. He also co-chairs the capital campaign for the African-American Heritage Foundation.

Bridgeman chides Louisvillians to "get past" racial divisions, particularly in their churches, and to take advantage of what all groups have to offer. He also cautions the citizens of Louisville that they need to get over what he said is an attitude that other cities are "a little bit better, a little bit smarter."

He urges young leaders to hold onto their enthusiasm for change and the desire to make a difference, but to study why and how things got the way they are. "If our young people can get an understanding and knowledge of how the world, society, and the city got to this point, I think they can have a better idea of how to change things," he said.

BECOMING A LEADER in our community was not something I purposely decided to do, and it's still interesting to me when people refer to me as a leader. I think a leader has to be someone people will follow. To me, ministers and politicians lead people, because they have done things that have caused people to hold them up as examples – if that is the description for leadership.

I didn't want to be in politics or anything like that. Leadership just comes from being out in the community and becoming involved with the community. If you are in business and involved with providing jobs and livelihoods for people, and your business grows and you become successful, people naturally come to you, asking you to get involved with the community. If that is something you like to do and you feel, like I do, that it is necessary to give back, then you become a civic leader. For me it has been more of an evolution than a decision.

Leadership for me goes all the way back to my upbringing in the church. We were asked, as young people, to get up to give speeches at Easter and Christmas programs. Other kids were nervous, but I told myself that I was not going to be nervous, and I wasn't. That basic training set my ability to be a leader and a public speaker in later life in motion. Then I got experience exercising my leadership abilities in school – giving talks, speaking at my sixth grade elementary school, being an officer in my senior class of high school.

My parents played a role in all this too. They encouraged my school and church participation. Church was a great part of my life, and it provided me a lot of opportunities to build my confidence. I was never really comfortable getting up in front of people, but in my mind I knew I could do it. That confidence helped build a foundation in me that has stuck with me and been helpful to me all through my life.

My parents were my first mentors. They were the ones who set the first examples. I have been fortunate to learn something from a number of people along the way, however. We are all a culmination of all the people we have met and the experiences we have had in our lives. We are all a product of our encounters, whether good or bad.

I was fortunate enough to have an opportunity to learn from the richest man in the world, Sam Walton. But I was also fortunate enough to have an opportunity to learn from the janitor at our high school, and many others.

I met Sam Walton at a charity golf outing in Bentonville, Arkansas – the home of Wal-Mart. I was invited to his house to play tennis. We simply drove right up to his house – no guard, no gate – a regular ranch house. He did have a very impressive Japanese garden, but it was simple.

We jumped in his red pickup truck and rode up to the tennis court. The next day he invited us over to Wal-Mart. His office wasn't massive. He walked us around Wal-Mart and he knew everybody by their first name. It was impressive to see this humble man at work.

I became president of the NBA (National Basketball Association) Players Association after serving as a team rep, an officer. Because I had a law school background, I had an opportunity to be in the room through collective bargaining and negotiating with a number of very sharp people. I got to talk to players and, in many cases, discovered that basketball was not even their main business, it was their pastime. Some were producing movies – they were doing a wide variety of things. Business was exciting for them, and they were having a whole variety of experiences.

My opportunity with Wendy's came from Larry Fleisher, who was the attorney for the Players Association. He and John Havlicek, who had played for the Celtics, were Wendy's franchisees. I had a friend who was a backer in Chicago and he had some clients who were getting involved with Wendy's. He suggested that I get involved with them too so that when I retired, I would have other income. I made that initial investment and got involved with Wendy's. Now here I am, over 17 years later, with over 150 Wendy's franchises!

Early on, I read a quote: "When a job is all said and done a good leader will say, 'We did this ourselves, not just one person.'" That is what we try to do here because in our business, we rely on so many individuals.

When you become a leader in a business, it is important to establish the culture of your company, to determine what your values are, your do's and don't's, and what type of company you are going to be. Our culture is this: We allow people to do what they do best, yet be part of a team. This all goes back to my athletics experience, of course. Everybody on a team is not always the best shot, or the best passer or rebounder, but when you put all the players together on a team, they are collectively a pretty good group, and that is what we try to do here.

In any project, business executives are interested in seeing your goals – what you are trying to accomplish, and maybe the initial idea of how you think you are going to accomplish those goals. But employees are also hoping to be given an opportunity to add their ideas. If you can bring out people's creativity, energy and enthusiasm, and if somehow their ideas can get built into your overall goals, I think you have the basis for forming an energetic and exciting team.

I think you can often learn more from failure than from accomplishing things. You can learn more by going through adversity than by going down an easy path to success.

Let's go back to winning the Indiana state high school basketball championship. The reason this is significant for me is because to accomplish that great feat we first had to be a part of a group of individuals who grew up in the same city.

Passing the Torch

We all had to enjoy playing basketball, we had to be committed to the team and the team's goals and try to be the best we could be. In order to win, we had to put our egos and influences from family and friends in the background. The result of all that was the winning of the state championship.

The year before my junior year, we actually had more talent, but we lost. The lesson we learned was that everybody had to have a goal to win. The year we won, we cared about winning and picked up everyone along the way. We didn't let any outside influences, accolades or pressures affect the team.

If you can get a group of individuals to focus on what they are trying to do and to withstand all the outside influences, you are unlimited in what you and your team can accomplish.

The first Wendy's store that we opened was in Brooklyn. Looking back on it, the one mistake we made was listening to Wendy's, who tried to make us believe that all we had to do was get involved in their business as franchisees and we would be successful.

So when we opened that first Wendy's restaurant, we thought all we had to do was open the doors and we would be successful. Well, at the end of the first year, we lost about $300,000. We had no clue about what we were supposed to be doing. I went back to Wendy's and actually went through their training program. I learned every job. I started by mopping floors and worked my way up. Eventually my partner went back to coaching, but I stayed with it.

That experience taught me that if you are going to be successful, the head man has to understand and know as much as possible about all aspects of the business. You can't just rely on other people. Every day you learn something personally. There is always a surprise, and you learn from it, good or bad.

In athletics, you always remember the games you lost. We lost to UCLA in the Final Four by one point. It was our senior year, and we had been striving for a long period of time to get there. The irony for me was that two people I played with in high school had won the championship the year before, so it seemed like it was my turn. It was a severe disappointment when we lost.

I don't know if there is any real lesson you learn right away from a loss, but later on in life you look back, reflect, and you learn from your mistakes.

Probably the biggest lesson we all learn in life is realizing that we only have so many opportunities and chances in life. You have to take advantage of the opportunities that come your way in life. The worst thing you can do is go through life and look back and say, "I wish I had," rather than, "I'm glad I did."

Life is a culmination of experiences. When I was in the NBA, I filled the role as the sixth man for a number of years (the person who sits on the bench).

You have to have the attitude that a good follower should have, and that is to understand and adopt the goals of the team. If your strengths are X, Y and Z, but the team needs Y and Z to be successful, you have to take X and place it in the background of your mind, and just do Y and Z.

Good followers are the same way. They need to understand the team's goal and do what they do best to help the team reach that goal. When you reach it, that person has just as much joy and happiness by saying that they contributed to the success of the team as a follower, because they did what they did best.

If I had a chance to do things differently, I would eliminate all the mistakes I have made in my life. If you are honest with yourself, you will always "wish you had," about something, whether it's related to something personal or whether it's about getting involved with the community in some way. Perhaps you wish you had tried to make a change in your community. If anybody says they are happy with everything they have done in their lives and have no regrets, then in my opinion, they set their sights too low.

Young people have enthusiasm. They see the world differently, hopefully, and they see things as they think they should be. It's always a question with them why things aren't a certain way. I think all that is great. The one thing I would say to aspiring leaders in our community is, "Keep your enthusiasm for change. Keep your enthusiasm for wanting to make a difference, but go back and understand why things are the way they are at this point." If they get an understanding and knowledge of how the world, society and their city got to this point, then I think they can have a better idea of how to change things.

A number of factors have contributed to the growth and deveopment of Louisville over the last few decades. Employment is one of the first things you look at to measure a city's growth.

When I was in college, the manufacturing community basically left Louisville. I'm thinking of International Harvester and others that have left. The leadership that helped transform us from a manufacturing community to a service community took a huge step forward. That helped re-establish the Louisville community as a good place to live.

Housing development has been a big boon to the East End of town. Some people had the foresight to go back and look at the West End of town as well, and to re-design and rebuild deteriorating neighborhoods like Park DuValle. However, there are still whole sections of the city and any number of residents whom we can't just leave behind. You have to take your hat off to those forward-thinking people who plan a city's development.

For a long time, our educational system has been failing. So much goes into teaching a child that I don't know if you should ever say a child can "fail."

Perhaps it is better to say that they are just not as successful at learning as we or they would have wanted them to be. I recognize that, and want to do something about it. I am making a small contribution toward improving educational opportunities and learning success levels for young people in Louisville by being involved with the University of Louisville. I enjoyed working with UofL, then-Governor Paul Patton and then-president John Shumaker to help start the "Bucks for Brains" program. "Bucks for Brains" has not just made it financially attractive for our brightest students to stay in Louisville, but it has also recruited the kind of faculty, researchers and staff who are now letting UofL compete with other prestigious institutions on a national level.

A successful program like "Bucks for Brains" increases the self-esteem of the community and the self-esteem of all the people in the whole state. That is what I think has been the biggest problem Louisville and Kentucky have had. We have had this lingering attitude that everybody else – all these other cities – are just a little bit better, a little bit smarter, just a little bit more than we may be. That is the most detrimental mindset, and it's just not true.

"Bucks for Brains" was a risk. There was a lot a money raised, people weren't sure whether it was going to be successful or not. There are always naysayers. "Bucks for Brains" has been successful, and with the progress that has been made, we can't stop. From heart transplants to hand transplants, those all came about through the "Bucks for Brains" program. Even the person working on an assembly line feels good about what's going on in the community with successes like that. They feel a little bit better about where they live, and all that helps make the Louisville community a better place for everyone.

Opportunities for new leaders to take their chances, and to try to make Louisville what it can be, are going to be more difficult in the future because the competition is out there now. When I look at Nashville, Indianapolis, Cincinnati – they are a good three steps ahead of us right now.

The competition is fierce and the next generation hopefully can move forward. We have been hindered by the naysayers. There are so many people who want to see Louisville remain the type of city they always wanted it to be. As young and more talented people stay in town to make a career, and as they want to make changes, they will surpass other communities. But it is not going to be easy, and it is going to take a collective effort by a number of people in a number of different walks of life to make it happen.

I had a science teacher at UofL who made the statement that in order for mankind to exist and prosper in the future, there had to be a combining of all the races. He felt that in order for mankind to continue to be successful on this planet, we would have to take some good from every race, and eventually that human being would be the one who would survive and prosper.

Louisville has to get past its racial problems. Its majority has to understand that there are people who look and act different than they do. There has to be an effort to interact and to understand people from different walks of life.

A number of organizations have failed. The most segregated time in this society is 11:00 a.m. on Sunday. You would think with all the churches that would not be the case.

You go to the African-American or black churches, or to the East End where they are all white. You say to yourself, "If everybody believes that you have to go where 'everybody looks like me,' then all those things have to change."

It won't be with our generation, but I am seeing differences with the next generation. I just hope that the naysayers don't influence them too much. That will be a big challenge for the next generation. That is the only way this community is going to prosper.

CHRISTINA LEE "CHRISTY" BROWN

Owner
Louisville Stoneware

Co-Founder and Past President
Cathedral Heritage Foundation

CHRISTINA LEE "CHRISTY" BROWN bought Louisville Stoneware in 1997, and she has now transformed the landmark Louisville pottery company from a largely wholesale operation to an upscale retail business with two locations.

Before buying Louisville Stoneware, Brown helped found the Cathedral Heritage Foundation, a multi-faith organization that took on the daunting task of restoring Louisville's historic downtown Cathedral of the Assumption to make it both an architectural showcase and a vibrant spiritual center for the city. Brown served as the Foundation's president, chaired the fundraising campaign for the cathedral's restoration, and is widely credited with putting the cathedral and its multi-faith programs, including its annual Festival of Faiths, on the international map.

The Foundation's purpose is to develop spiritual, educational and cultural programs and experiences that inspire and foster individual growth; to increase understanding among people of diverse cultures; and to advance interfaith understanding.

Brown was a civic leader and community activist long before creating and leading the Cathedral Heritage Foundation. She served on the founding board of Actors Associates, which supports Actors Theatre, and on the boards of the Washington-based American Arts Alliance, the Greater Louisville Fund for the Arts and the Kentucky Opera. She also has served on the University of Louisville's Board of Overseers and on a variety of other boards, including River Fields, Louisville Collegiate School, Downtown Development Corporation, Historic Homes Association, Junior Art Gallery, Junior League of Louisville, the Kentucky Arts Council, Kentucky Educational Television and the Kentucky Progress smart growth commission.

Brown is a native of Maryland. She is an alumna of Stone Ridge Convent of the Sacred Heart in Washington, D.C. and has an associate degree in child study from Garland Junior College in Boston. She was teaching preschool at the National Child Research Center in Washington, D.C. in 1966 when she first met her husband, Owsley Brown II, then an army officer serving at the Pentagon.

The couple married in 1968, moved from Washington to Louisville, and immediately became active in community affairs. Christy Brown agreed to chair the third annual "Les Boutiques de Noel" in 1970, which was then Actors Theatre's major fundraiser.

Brown has chaired innumerable events and fundraisers for other organizations as well. She is a co-founder, for example, of "Collecting," an annual antique show that was a major source of funding for Louisville Collegiate School. She also co-founded a corporate sponsorship program called "Corporate Family Night" that has netted hundreds of thousands of new dollars for the Kentucky Opera.

Archbishop Thomas Kelly said it was Brown's leadership skills, vision and impressive fundraising capabilities that inspired him to ask her to serve as president of the Cathedral Heritage Foundation. Brown says she agreed to take on the presidency because the archbishop asked her, and because her own knowledge and instincts about preservation told her that the cathedral was very important to Louisville's history and culture. It wasn't an easy project to tackle, though. The building itself was in terrible shape when the restoration began. Many Catholics were ready to tear it down and sell the land to someone to build a high-rise building.

Brown's interest in Louisville Stoneware developed in a similar way. She talked with former owner John Robinson for ten years, asking him to sell the company to her if he ever decided to sell. "Louisville Stoneware has a huge history, and that's something worth preserving," she told *Kentucky Monthly* magazine last fall. "What I look forward to doing with Louisville Stoneware is to help us understand and market the value of this region's rich art and craft history."

Brown currently serves on the boards of the Cathedral Heritage Foundation and the Kentucky Opera, and is a trustee of the International Council of the World Conference for Religion and Peace.

The Browns have three children.

IN 1968, OWSLEY BROWN II and I married in my family's historic house in Frederick, Maryland. I then moved from Maryland, my family's home state for hundreds of years, to my new home state of Kentucky. It was my love for Owsley that brought me to Louisville, and it has been our 37 years of partnering and growing together as a family that has enabled us, I believe, to share ourselves more generously with our community.

Becoming a civic leader was not a specific goal of mine, but because of Kentuckians' remarkable openness and hospitality, I was immediately invited to become involved in a variety of different types of civic, political and cultural activities.

Owsley and I were both raised to believe that, as we have been given much, we have a responsibility to give much in return. We have had a life that has continuously afforded us truly immeasurable personal learning opportunities while serving others.

I gained a deep appreciation for the importance of knowing one's own ancestry and the history and heritage of an area from my parents, who had tremendous pride in their respective families' ancestry and in their beloved state of Maryland.

Owsley and I have always been very interested in genealogy, history, and land preservation. He is much more the true historian in an academic sense. I have an intuitive approach and am particularly interested in how our contemporary lives are connected to our heritage, knowing we are our history. We are all here to be stewards: of this great earth, of our heritages, of our spiritual, natural and economic resources, and of our many cultural traditions. Much of my work has been based on those fundamentals, whether it was in raising our three wonderful children or the preservation of an island, a building or a cultural event.

Reflecting on my 37 years in Louisville, it is true most of my community work has revolved around the importance of preservation in one way or another. The human spirit thrives through a deep connection with our heritage and the land. An understanding of the people who have gone before us enriches our lives in profound ways, connecting shared values from generation to generation.

I have learned, and hopefully always will be learning, from many wonderful Kentucky visionaries – leaders who unselfishly give of themselves, such as Senator Thruston B. Morton, Amelia Brown Frazier, Barry Bingham, Sr., and dear friend Moritz Bomhard, founder of the Kentucky Opera. As I turn each page of a book by my friend, Wendell Berry, the brilliant Kentucky author, cultural historian, philosopher and conservationist, I continue to be overwhelmingly inspired by his remarkable intellect and deep levels of holistic wisdom.

Of course, my parents and my grandparents were really my first mentors and role models, and stories about many of my ancestors, such as Thomas Sim Lee, the first Governor of Maryland, continue to inspire me.

Regarding my own leadership style, I begin every project by researching its history as well as by talking with the best experts in that particular field. Then I lead by consensus, by gathering lots of like-minded people together and creating large, fun and exciting visions – some of which have ended up having local and national significance.

An example of this is when Owsley and I invited international historic preservationist, Rev. Brown Morton, to study and evaluate the national architectural significance of Louisville's Cathedral of the Assumption. Brown, together with his co-worker, Peter Rathbun, made us aware that the 1852 Cathedral was one of America's most important pieces of early American Gothic religious architecture. As we were learning about our Cathedral's national significance from these national experts, many people in Louisville were advocating that it be destroyed and replaced with a high rise or a parking garage. Archbishop Thomas Kelly wisely and boldly knew that his dilapidated Cathedral should be revitalized and shared with the Archdiocese, the Cathedral parish, and Louisville's interfaith communities. He delegated the revitalization of the Cathedral parish to the brave visionary, Father Ronald J. Knott, who taught us the importance of "celebrating our commonalities and our differences" and to "trust in God, believe in yourself and dare to dream."

Even though I went to Catholic schools all my life, curiously, I really didn't have much of a theological education. I was frankly bored with most of my schooling, until I went to Garland Junior College in Boston to study child psychology. I then went on to teach pre-school at the National Child Research Center in Washington, D.C., where my studies at what I call "the University of the World" truly began.

When I first moved to Louisville, I audited a course at Bellarmine University on inter-religious thought, taught by Father Eugene Zoeller. Between that course, my reading of Rev. Clyde Crews' histories of Louisville's religions, reading Gandhi and re-reading some of Thomas Merton's writings, I realized that considering the state of the world, we really must continually find creative ways for inter-religious understanding and dialogue that celebrate our commonalities and our differences.

Thus, with the creation of the Cathedral Heritage Foundation and its theme of "Many Faiths, One Heart, Common Action" my family, many friends and I began an adventure into what is now known as one of our world's most important areas of need: interfaith understanding. The Cathedral Heritage Foundation, with its inter-religious programming and unique annual Festival of Faiths – an international model – serves as a forum to share the insights of great inter-religious thinkers.

I feel truly blessed to be able to contribute to a community so full of cultural diversity and uniqueness. Kentucky has always attracted a rich collection of people from all over the globe. Louisville and this region were settled by a diverse group of individuals seeking religious freedom and economic independence, which explains the richness of Louisville's interfaith history. Fifty percent of our population growth in this decade is coming from the arrival of worldwide immigrants.

There is tremendous value in having a strong regional identity. I envision our region becoming known as the cultural tourism center of America. With our region's rich cultural history, we must obtain the necessary confidence to achieve this important goal.

On the business side, clearly, it is my connection to the earth, my belief in preservation and my love of history that influenced me to purchase Louisville Stoneware, a historic landmark business that is an important part of our community's and our region's cultural heritage. The fact that the stoneware is made from clay that is 250 million years old and comes from the middle of our country literally makes that connection with the earth as each piece is used and enjoyed. Louisville Stoneware/Louisville Pottery can trace its roots to the 1800s, and it continues to be a family-owned company. Using the very ancient craft of pottery-making, we hand-make and hand-paint functional art. I'm very proud that we are able to continue that craft tradition, creating objects for people around the world to use, enjoy and pass on to their families and friends for generations and generations.

In looking back and thinking of what I would do differently in my life if I were given an opportunity, I wish I had understood more deeply as a younger adult the type of serious positive change each of us is truly capable of affecting. I wish I had figured out how to be more goal-oriented with much larger and more holistic visions. I also wish I had had the self-confidence early on to become more involved with public issues and political movements that truly reflected my deep-seated values.

The people who have contributed the most to Louisville throughout its history are the visionary and brave risk-takers who have founded major cultural and arts institutions, social service and educational institutions, and businesses which have stood the test of time and are still with us, growing, serving and inspiring us today. They are the passionate, hard-working individuals who lead by consensus, not bullying. They are leaders who understand the art of listening and lead by love, not fear. These leaders understand the importance of honesty and being impeccable with their words and deeds. They deeply understand that if you want happiness for a lifetime, you help someone else.

The tremendously important contributions of the young leaders of the '60s were made possible, in part, because of their deep understanding of the value that healthy art, civic and educational life brings to our city, state, and region. I feel honored to have been involved in some of these efforts which have greatly enhanced our community's pride and quality of life.

As a region we need to study much more seriously our history, our environment, our food supply needs, economics, educational, religious and our social service needs, while finding ways we can best build on our past to improve the future for all generations that will follow.

Our community and world are yearning for compassionate leaders who know that it is not the government or someone else's responsibility to fix problems. Each of us has tremendous gifts and talents to share, and it is our absolute duty to do so. We've been placed here to serve as the stewards and guardians of each other and of this great earth.

I urge aspiring young leaders to write their own script, paint their own canvas, and get to work. I urge them to never stop growing and developing their curiosity and their desire to be positive problem solvers. I urge them to always have fun while finding new ways to reinvent their leadership skills and their desire to leave this earth a better place.

OWSLEY BROWN II

Chairman
Brown-Forman Corporation

OWSLEY BROWN II BECAME CEO of his family's Brown-Forman Corporation in 1993, and added the title of board chairman two years later. Though he relinquished the title of CEO in August of 2005, he has dramatically expanded the company's international presence and orchestrated a total makeover of its marketing program, leading the company in bold new directions.

The strategy has worked. Brown-Forman brands – with Jack Daniel's whiskey, Southern Comfort liqueur, Finlandia Vodka, Korbel Champagne and Fetzer wines in the lead – have produced stellar financial returns and double-digit profit growth. The company also owns Hartmann and Wings luggage and other wines (Bolla, Bonterra, Sonoma-Cutrer) and spirits (Woodford-Reserve, Canadian Mist, Early Times).

Brown, whose breadth is of the renaissance sort, is well known in Louisville, for his donation of time, talent and treasure to a variety of civic organizations and endeavors. The concept of giving back is not lost on Owsley. Referring to his family he said to *Kentucky Monthly* last fall, "we are very fortunate people, so we need to be very responsible people."

Brown was born in 1942, into the fourth generation of a spirits dynasty founded in 1870 by George Garvin Brown. His father was W. L. Lyons Brown, who took the family firm to national prominence as the long-time leader of the company in the middle of the 20th century. He and his wife, Sara Shallenberger "Sally" Brown had four children, including Owsley.

Owsley went to high school in Virginia, graduated from Yale University with a bachelor's degree in history in 1964 and obtained a master's degree in business administration from Stanford University in 1966. He then served for two years in U.S. Army intelligence, and ultimately was stationed at the Pentagon. While living in Washington, he met a dynamic young teacher named Christina Lee. He married her, and moved to Louisville in 1968.

Christy and Owsley Brown immediately jumped into civic affairs, starting with Actors Theatre in 1969. Owsley Brown served as president of Actors during two major initiatives, when the Main Street theatre was built in the early '70s, and again, when it expanded in the early '90s.

Though he is an Episcopalian, he helped his wife lead community-wide efforts to restore the Catholic Cathedral of the Assumption in downtown Louisville, and to establish the inter-faith Cathedral Heritage Foundation.

The Browns — and Brown-Forman — have been generous patrons of arts organizations and arts-related events and exhibits over the years as well. They have given generous donations to, among others, the Kentucky Museum of Art and Craft, the Kentucky Author Forum, the Greater Louisville Fund for the Arts, the Kentucky Center for the Arts, Actors Theatre, the W. L. Lyons Brown Theatre, the J.B. Speed Art Museum, and the city's orchestra, opera and ballet. They have also stepped up to support pivotal city projects when asked. They were anchor sponsors, for example, of the National Trust for Historic Preservation's annual conference when Louisville hosted the prestigious event in 1983 and again in 2004.

Brown-Forman has donated to help build the Muhammad Ali Center and was a lead donor to the critical first phase of the city's waterfront development project, and continued that role in its second phase, which included construction of a 1,500-seat riverfront amphitheater that bears the company's name. Brown received the Waterfront Development Corporation's prestigious Silver Anchor Award as a result of his company's commitment to the project. "Waterfront Park is a magnificent place," he told *The Courier Journal*, "a beautiful refuge from the activity of city life and the jangled nerves of suburban traffic jams."

Like his wife, Christy, with whom he has three children, Brown says he gets as much as he gives through his civic activities. The couple are indefatigable hosts, constantly opening their home for philanthropic and civic receptions and dinners. "One of the things you quickly learn is that the people who are involved in these organizations, both the other volunteers and the staff, can be incredibly interesting. Working with people on a common goal to do things for the common good is an extremely rewarding thing."

I GREW UP IN LOUISVILLE AND SPENT my youth in Harrods Creek, which is where my family lived. But from the second grade through the eighth grade, we moved to Florida for five months a year. I would start school in Kentucky, then study with a tutoring service in Florida for five months, then finish again in Kentucky. I went to Ballard School, then Eastern, then Woodberry Forest in Virginia for high school.

I'm the fourth generation of Browns to live here. My great grandfather, like his father, grew up farming in Central Kentucky. After the Civil War, farming didn't look like it had a very bright future, so he moved to Louisville. He went to Male High School when they were still teaching Latin and Greek. After he graduated, he went into the pharmacy business and not long afterwards started Brown-Forman.

I went to college in New England (Yale) for four years, then studied in California (Stanford) for two years. After I finished school, I worked at the Pentagon for two years as a second lieutenant. It was an unusual place for a second lieutenant to be, but I was ordered to go there. I had to assemble masses of information and make it cohesive and correct very quickly. It was a forecast for the skills I would need later in life. Making the best judgment you can with information you have is something you have to do in the business world, the civic world, and even in family life.

I learned about the importance of leadership in the community and in the business world from my father's father, the first Owsley Brown, who was very active in Democratic politics in Kentucky. He was an attorney who practiced law briefly before he came to help his father at Brown-Forman and he never lost his interest in politics and government. On my mother's side of the family, there were several generations of people who served in government. My great grandfather was governor of Nebraska and served in Congress for 38 years, and his father served in the Illinois legislature. My maternal grandfather was a career army officer and his wife came from an Army family. So with all this, the importance of public service was instilled in me.

The member of our family who taught me the most about the art of giving was my aunt, Amelia Brown Frazier. She was the first member of our family who was a very generous giver. She would donate very thoughtfully and boldly. I tried to learn that lesson from her, though I had to apply it on a much smaller scale.

I first became involved in the community when I moved back to Louisville as a 26-year-old ex-lieutenant. I always felt a real obligation and desire to use my good fortune to help others. When people asked me to get involved in civic organizations, I would try to help. The same was true of my wife, Christy.

We found that there were very interesting people involved in these projects, some of the most interesting people we would run into in Louisville.

There were some very good things going on here in the late 1960s and early 1970s, though not nearly as many as there are today. Looking back, I hope that in some small measure, our efforts over a 35-year period have helped to produce this richness and abundance in civic organizations – strength in the arts, a major revival of historic preservation efforts, appreciation of open spaces, and so on. All these areas have been of particular interest to us and we have been involved with many of them, now, for a long time.

Historic preservation, conservation of green spaces and placemaking where art, architecture and landscape come together are important issues for me and my family. We have always had a very strong interest in trying to revitalize the downtown of Louisville in a meaningful way. The downtown is the soul of a metropolitan area, the centerpiece of a city, but it has not always been easy to keep it that way as people become increasingly suburban-oriented, no longer work downtown, or have little reason to come there. People tend to forget that the suburbs, if they are going to be great, are very dependent on a strong and vibrant core.

In 1968, Louisville looked not unlike photographs of Hamburg after World War II. It was being bombed, though not by terrorists. In a misguided attempt to do good, our city and national leaders were destroying part of our unique infrastructure. This was called Urban Renewal, an effort that was well-intended but, sadly, it eventually tore down the center of Louisville, hoping that better things would quickly spring back. They didn't, and Louisville's downtown is just today recovering from that self-destruction of the late '60s, early '70s.

I have great appreciation for history. The past informs the future and gives meaning and identity to a place. I've been able to avoid some mistakes and to do some good things in my life by reading of the experiences of how other people in societies and cities have led their lives well and poorly.

I am fortunate that I had an opportunity to visit Europe at an early age. It makes an impression to see that the buildings in Florence are different from the ones in Venice and those are different from the ones in Munich and those are different from the ones in Brussels. Buildings reflect and eventually influence the ethos of a particular place, embodying the social convictions and personal values of a people. So to tear down buildings that have given character to our city and to replace them with cookie cutter designs all coming out of one school of modernism doesn't seem to me to be a very wise course.

Historic preservation really involves two things: one, getting people to appreciate the value of their architectural heritage; and two, getting people to find uses for buildings so they can survive economically and at the same time preserve their attractiveness. It's important to combine your historical aesthetic interests with business interests, if possible. You have to find what businesses can work in these buildings. I've spent a lifetime doing that, particularly on Main Street. Brown-Forman also has done a great deal of historic preservation at our corporate campus on Dixie Highway, near Broadway; at the Woodford Reserve Distillery, a national landmark, in Kentucky's Bluegrass region; and at the Jack Daniel's Distillery and Homeplace in Tennessee.

The company has been blessed with owning some amazing buildings that have survived and continue to be used. It was my study for our Main Street area of how other cities were re-using old buildings that was the impetus for Brown-Forman's restoring our first building on our Dixie Highway campus — the Garneau Building, an old whiskey warehouse that we converted into offices around 1979. We later restored the much larger building behind it, a 1930s whiskey warehouse which is now offices. Our most recent work was on Brown-Forman's oldest office building on Howard Street, a building that we restored and reopened in 2004.

Putting buildings to new use in a viable way is the key. Actors Theatre is certainly one of Louisville's best examples of adaptive reuse. The lobby of ATL was once the old Bank of Louisville building. When the U.S. Department of the Interior was doing their first survey of the United States to pick the most important buildings and sites to be national historic landmarks, they only picked four in Kentucky, and this building was one of them. Hidden and probably doomed, it was a spectacular piece of architecture that virtually nobody in the city was familiar with. They were tearing down buildings on Main Street left and right. There was an Italianate warehouse building from the 1870s right next to it. A lot of civic-minded donors joined our adaptive re-use efforts in 1970 and helped us convert the old bank and warehouse building into a contemporary theater.

The next building Christy and I were involved in restoring was the first major office redevelopment project on Main Street at 600 West Main. Three couples, led by John Greenebaum, together undertook this project. It was the old Seelbach Hotel and quite a marvelous building. We were ultimately joined by another seven or eight couples who helped pay for the project with good help from cooperative bankers. We renovated what would be the equivalent of five large Main Street lots into what appears from the street to be two office buildings. Today the Louisville Bar Association is in the ground floor and other offices are upstairs.

More recently, Brown-Forman has renovated three buildings at Seventh and Main known as the 626 West Main Complex. We engaged Robert Stern, one of America's finest architects, to help us and it has turned out extremely well. We moved many of our Brown-Forman employees to this building and leased the upper floors to other firms.

Christy and I are proud that we have planted seeds that have brought a real renaissance to Main Street, enhancing a sense of place, engaging public participation and getting people to value the character of the area where our city began. It may have taken three decades but it was certainly worthwhile. Try to picture what Louisville would be like if Main Street was a bunch of a plain facade shiny glass boxes. I don't know how one could distinguish it from Wichita or Omaha.

It is important to protect and preserve this character. I have a great appreciation for Kentucky's rich history and wealth of historical sites. Many important things took place here, and our state played a prominent role nationally at various points in our nation's history. It was the breeding ground for people who populated much of the West, so it's a very interesting place to study. I was once head of the Filson Club, now the Filson Historical Society and I enjoyed that experience very much.

When we first came to Louisville, the Orchestra was the core of the arts community. We had a lively opera, but it was operating on a very low budget. We had a ballet, but it too had a very low budget. We had no theater; traveling companies would come through from New York. We had community support for a united arts fund which at that point was called The Louisville Fund (now the Fund for the Arts). But there was no paid full-time head of the Fund for the Arts in Louisville. Campaigns were run by a very smart guy named Addison McGhee. He would come in for three months to run campaigns out of rooms on the ground floor of the library on York Street. He would begin a campaign, finish it, put the files away for another year in the basement of the library, and go away. I think the Fund for the Arts raised about $275,000 back then. Inflation has been about tenfold over that period of time, so that is equivalent to $2.7 million now. Remarkably, today we are raising more than three times that amount for the Fund for the Arts.

There was virtually no corporate giving to the arts; they were almost entirely funded by individuals. There was little to no organized employee giving and no sponsorship of any art organization or art event by corporations or individuals. I credit Christy for having the energy and the vision to tackle this problem. In the very early '70s, she got several key Louisville leaders to back her in having a big day-and-a-half symposium on how to have a major boost for the arts and other cultural efforts here. We got speakers from all over the country to come in to talk about how businesses in other cities were giving to the arts because they had realized the arts help give a city shape and experience by fostering participation and community engagement.

This dialogue laid the groundwork for a deeper and broader realization of the importance that the arts could play in the life of our city. Shortly after that, I became the head of the Fund for the Arts. I hired the first full time executive director of the Fund, which of course meant we needed to figure out a way to get community support to pay that person. So the whole idea of how to support the arts moved from a seasonal thing to a permanent grassroots organization that could help Louisville more strategically in a variety of ways, including raising money.

Christy and I had a good friend from New York who used to come down to Louisville from time to time on business. He would usually stay with us and we would talk about these kinds of things. On one of these visits – around 1980 – he said, "Well, you know, we're doing a great thing at the New York Philharmonic. We have all these corporate sponsorships. Don't you have those here?" And we all said, "What are you talking about? Tell us more."

From this conversation we basically introduced that idea of corporate sponsorships to Louisville. It had taken seed in New York and probably a couple of other places, but nobody was doing it here. I'm proud to say Brown-Forman stepped up to become the first major corporate sponsor of any arts event I can think of, with the exception of production-stimulating grants made by *The Courier-Journal* in the 1970s.

We underwrote the production of *Carmen*, copying the idea straight from the New York Philharmonic. Brown-Forman employees got free tickets to the dress rehearsal and some of our employees were invited to be in the chorus. To get interest going, an opera singer came down and sang a couple of arias to the people in the bottling house. After the grand opening the company hosted a party across the street in what is now St. Francis School. This was the old YMCA Building, which had a great big public room. We invited civic leaders from all over the city to join us and the cast. The sponsorship idea caught on quickly, thereafter, and now corporate giving to and individual sponsorships of the arts are a very large percentage of funding for our arts organizations. It's gratifying to have helped develop some of these ideas in Louisville. The cultural institutions in Louisville are now much stronger and much deeper, but you can't just take them for granted. Success requires nurturing and care. This is work, but very rewarding work.

The arts have also enriched my life personally. I am a miserable, very occasional amateur painter, and that certainly helps me appreciate other painters who know what they're doing. I wish I could play an instrument or sing well, but I can't do either of those things. I do enjoy music enormously, and theater and I enjoy sculptures very much. These things enrich you greatly. I think the interaction with people who are also enjoying those things is rewarding as well. Sometimes some of the most interesting conversations you have stem from going to a gallery to look at something. The subject may not even be art, but the situation invites people to talk about more serious and more interesting things than the weather.

Brown-Forman recognizes its responsibility to be a leader and to be involved in the life of our community. Corporations like ours can help lead civic efforts so that, over time, the city ends up being a marvelous place for employees to live and to raise families. To do well in business today – certainly in our business – you need people working for you who have stimulated, creative and active minds, so giving them a city that allows them and their families to exercise their minds is a good thing. We have great schools and interesting things for children and families to do in our city. In general, Louisville is an extremely desirable place for people to live, a place with a creative and intellectual life.

Maybe it comes from my being a student of history or from my coming from a family that has a long connection with one particular company and place. We take the approach that we will help good things continue to flourish and to reform and improve things that aren't so wonderful. The actions that we take today absolutely have a positive collective effect on our future.

When I think of leaders I knew who have influenced our community the most, Barry Bingham Sr. always comes to mind. Mr. Bingham was an important mentor of mine. He was probably the single most active civic leader in Louisville when I was growing up. I was lucky enough to be a very close friend of one of his sons, so I knew him from my infancy. When Christy and I moved here, he and Mrs. Bingham were extremely supportive of us and helped us take on civic leadership. If we were having a little fundraiser for a project, they would be there with the first check. This gave us such encouragement.

I also learned something else from Mr. Bingham that had a big effect on me. He taught me the value of actually stepping up to the plate and taking the lead as a company in a big way for a few things. As he pointed out, none of us can do everything, but selective endorsements can be huge and stimulating examples.

At Brown-Forman, we often reflect on the value of leadership giving. It is usually accompanied by our being sure that whatever organization or effort we are supporting has very good direction and board participation. Sometimes we support one of our own officers, or someone whom we've watched civically for a long time who is very capable. When we know something is extremely well led, and it doesn't look likely that someone else can provide a leadership gift, we consider whether we should be the ones to do it; and often we have said yes.

I would advise young professionals who are aspiring to leadership and who want to get involved in the civic life of Louisville to just do it. Don't hesitate. People are always worried that it's going to take time away from their work or family, but I think people way under-estimate the value of what one gets back in return for that time given up. You get an enriching experience to bring home to talk about with your family and children, and you give them a model of how an adult citizen should lead life in contemporary society. You also provide an example to your business colleagues about how modern corporations and firms need to conduct themselves if they want to benefit from the society we're all a part of. You teach people that it is important for them to participate, too.

From a corporate point of view I've always found that the contacts, the experiences, the ideas one gets from non-profit involvement benefit your business in a significant way. You get a view quite unlike your daily work that makes you approach something in a new way, or you meet somebody interesting who gives you a completely different and diverse perspective. You almost never end up with the business having made any net sacrifice, as the business benefits because the individual brings back ideas, contacts, experiences and is simply a better employee or partner.

I describe my civic leadership style as "persuasive." When you are working with volunteers, coercion doesn't work. You have to make things appealing to people or they will simply find one of a hundred valid reasons not to show up for your next meeting. Everybody's busy. Doing things in a persuasive, collegial fashion works far better for civic endeavors made up of volunteers. This approach works very well with employees too. You can force certain people to sit there, but you can't force them to be open-minded and cooperative. It is much, much better and more long-lasting, if you can persuade and work with people and unleash their creativity and team spirit.

As a leader, one should also keep in mind that half the reason people keep coming back as volunteers is because of the other people they're working with, so you need to give people time to interact with each other. Have four serious meetings but at the end of the fifth, have the meeting at the end of the day and give people a cocktail, or some wine and cheese so they can talk to each other and have fun being with each other. I have found that you will make some of your best friends at those meetings, and they aren't necessarily the people you know from your other life experiences. You'll be very enriched by it.

Looking back, I think my leadership in getting Actor's Theatre built is one of my most significant civic accomplishments. I was president and either chief fundraiser or assistant chief fundraiser at two critical times, once in the early 1970s and again in the early 1990s. That I did it for the first time at the very early age of 28 or so means age should not be a deterrent to one's desire to try to take on leadership.

Young people should just step in and get involved. When I moved back to Louisville in 1968, you could have gotten the people who were active civically in one not-very-large room. They were fabulous people, but they were worn out. They were doing many of the same things over and over again for lots and lots of organizations. It was actually a good time, as these people didn't hesitate to let you lead. I've no reason to think that leadership, even by what would be considered very young adults, will be treated in any less friendly way now than it was in the early 1970s. So I would encourage people not to think "Oh, I'll do that when I'm older." Go do it now, have fun with it! You get a lot of good done and you'll enrich yourself at the same time.

When I reflect on the biggest challenges facing our city in the future, and the advice I might give to the next generation of leaders, first and most importantly, I would say that we have to keep concentrating on strengthening our downtown; and together, as a community, we have to find and develop those reasons for it to be of value. The difficulty of reconciling old traditional values and suburban demographics has never been more apparent than as we struggle to reinvigorate our core city and our arts organizations and simultaneously respond to a rapidly changing world that places huge new demands on people's time.

Secondly, we need to encourage our local companies and other institutions that are here to grow and build rather than to grow and sell. All too often people will build companies, then sell them; or they become leaders of an institution and get tired, and instead of turning it over to somebody else, they sell it. It's an extremely destructive process for communities when that happens. We can all think of circumstances where it's absolutely the best thing, but in most cases, in cities like ours, it's a pretty terrible thing when it happens.

We shouldn't spend our time trying to lure more warehouses to the fringe of Louisville. I'm not sure that really adds a lot to the viability of our metropolitan area for the long term, and I don't think it's the answer for the future. I think we need to concentrate on the things that will get people to re-focus on the center of our city, and encourage local companies to stay here and expand in our urban core. A flourishing central business district with businesses, thriving retail amenities and wonderful cultural institutions will define our entire region, and this is the key to our city's future.

Louisville is so centrally located with such a fine quality of life and there are many small and medium-size companies starting up now that I think have an incredible future here. I would also concentrate on attempting to find small to medium-size firms that can move here when they are displaced in their home cities. These will be the Brown-Formans of tomorrow. Those of us who are leading today must encourage these companies to build on Louisville's competitive position, and to succeed and expand right here in one of our country's most distinctive and livable cities.

Malcolm B. Chancey Jr.

**Retired Chairman and CEO
Banc One Kentucky Corporation
Bank One Kentucky, NA
Liberty National Bank
and Trust Company**

MALCOLM CHANCEY MADE HIS LIVING as an executive of Liberty National Bank and, later, of Banc One Kentucky Corporation, which acquired Liberty. But he may be remembered longer in Louisville for the many roles he played as what former Jefferson County Judge-Executive Dave Armstrong called "Citizen Chancey" – a community mover and shaker who has given his time, talent and energy to every major issue of significance taken on by civic leaders in the decades of the 1980s and 1990s.

Chancey has spearheaded a broad range of civic activities and has been a staunch supporter of public libraries and area schools and universities. He adopted public education as his "number one extracurricular concern" and played leadership roles in the selection of two county school superintendents and a University of Louisville president. He promoted business and community involvement in the Jefferson County Public Schools, chairing both the Louisville Education and Employment Partnership and the Jefferson County Public Education Foundation. He raised over $9 million for a New Kid in School initiative, which provided computers for Jefferson County Public Schools.

Chancey chaired the Louisville Area Chamber of Commerce in 1992 and has served on dozens of other community boards. He has raised millions of dollars for the arts, the Louisville Free Public Libraries, Metro United Way and innumerable civic and charitable organizations.

He's been a strong advocate for downtown development, and community leaders still seek his advice. "There has not been a project or an issue of significance that the individuals involved have not sought his advice, guidance and support," Louisville Mayor Jerry Abramson told *The Courier-Journal* when Chancey retired from Bank One.

He chaired the University of Louisville Foundation from 1998 to 2004, and chaired UofL's Quest for Excellence and its Bicentennial Campaign, which raised $350 million between 1994 and 1999. He helped recruit Howard Schnellenberger to coach football at UofL, then led a community campaign to build the university a new $56.7 million football stadium. His ability to attract private donations and to wield influence with both university and government leaders were considered crucial to the success of these fundraising projects.

"Malcolm is one of those guys who just doesn't concentrate on his own narrow area," former Liberty CEO Frank Hower told *Business First*. He said Chancey has a "wealth of talents," citing marketing, sales and his analytical nature – just the sort of abilities that come in handy when one is involved in civic activities as well.

In an interview in *Business First,* Chancey admitted that he loves marketing and sales. "I'm a fan of the power of persuasion," he said.

Chancey applied his considerable skills to the banking business, and served as chairman and CEO of Liberty National Bank, a position he retained after Liberty was acquired by Bank One. He also applied them to a long list of civic organizations as well, including: the University of Louisville's Board of Trustees, Board of Overseers, Athletic Association, and Foundation; the Bellarmine College Board of Trustees; the Louisville Area Chamber of Commerce; the Greater Louisville Economic Development Partnership; the Jefferson County Public Education Foundation; the Louisville Free Public Library Foundation; the Cathedral Heritage Foundation; the Workforce Development Council; the Louisville Education and Employment Partnership; the Prichard Committee for Academic Excellence; the Louisville Fund for the Arts; Metro United Way; and the Louisville Science Center.

Chancey has received innumerable awards and honors over the years. His decades of service to the University of Louisville inspired UofL to change the name of its University Club and Alumni Center to Chancey Center in 2004.

But he will tell you that the honor for which he is most proud occurred in 2002, when the Jefferson County Public School board named a new elementary school after him – Malcolm B. Chancey Jr. Elementary School on Murphy Lane.

Chancey and his wife Gail have four children and live part-time in Louisville and part-time in Naples, Florida.

THE "WHEN" OF MY BECOMING A LEADER in the community was about 1975. It was the year of forced busing, the merger of the city and county school systems, the forced integration through busing, and the chaos that came about for a few years because of that. I was chairman of the Public Education Committee of the Chamber of Commerce, as a representative of Liberty National Bank. I had always had an interest in education because I was the first in my family to graduate from college and I had stayed close to my high school teachers. As this crisis evolved, I went to the Chamber and said, "The Chamber really ought to get involved and try to massage and arbitrate and mediate this division we have in the community, because we're busing black kids to white areas and white kids to black areas and so on. So I chaired an effort to merge the administration of the two school systems, which included all the back office areas and student record-keeping and that kind of thing. Then we evolved into other areas that were programmatic.

From there I was on the search committee that hired Don Ingwerson (Superintendent of Jefferson County Public Schools) and Don and I worked very closely together for a number of years in public education. I was the original chair of the Public Education Foundation, which was an offshoot of the Chamber's Education Committee. We worked with the school system to raise money to do things for which there wasn't any public money. We tried a couple of times to get taxes passed to get more money for the local school system. We couldn't get it done, but we raised a lot of money over the years to fund computer labs for the students, and things like that.

So I got involved initially through public education. Roughly around that same time, I got deeply involved in higher education at the University of Louisville, and then got involved in all the other things that, as a banker, you typically get involved with like the Greater Louisville Fund for the Arts, Metro United Way, one civic effort after another. At one time I was on 19 civic boards. That is way too many. I wasn't as active in all of them as I would have liked to have been, but I helped where I could.

Now, it's not all unselfish. You have to remember that banks do well if the community does well, and if the community doesn't do well the banks don't do well. So there's some selfish motive in it. All banks participate in the growth and development of the community, so it's not like I was just doing it for Liberty Bank, but for the industry. There were other bankers out there doing it too, though, in different degrees perhaps than I was.

I always felt like I really could make a difference. The network that I built touched all facets of the community. It wasn't just other bankers, it wasn't just people in hospitals, it was everybody. It was black, white, poor, rich, East End, West End, South End, even across the river.

It's because of that network that I built that I got involved in all these other things. I remember one day somebody said, "If you can put all those computers in schools, and raise $9 million for computer labs for all the public schools, maybe you can help us with the Fund for the Arts campaign or maybe you can help us with the Bicentennial Celebration for UofL, because I had built up this tremendous fundraising network base. I could pick up the phone and call 15 or 20 people and build a committee to do something. Those are the reasons you get involved, and you feel good when it's done and things get accomplished.

I had several mentors. Frank Hower (former Liberty National Bank president and CEO) certainly was one. Another one who doesn't get discussed a lot is Don Ingwerson. Don was a great negotiator, a good personality for mediating and arbitrating. He was great with the public and the press, and I learned that from him. I got along very well with the press, and I think that people in the press were mentors of mine, because we were on the same side of most issues in education, for example, and in a lot of community projects. We were always looking for the best in people to do the right thing for the right cause. So the newspaper had an influence over what I did.

I think that most people would say that I'm a forceful, strong personality. I get that from my mother. My mother was really focused. Once she set her mind to do something, come hell or high water, it was going to get done, and I have some of that quality. Some may say that I have tunnel vision, but if I see a project that really needs to get done in a certain period of time, I devote almost all my energy to doing it. Like the computer labs in schools. For four or five years, all my energies went to raising the money to do that. The same with the UofL football stadium project and UofL's Bicentennial Campaign.

I'm not afraid to tackle tough issues; I've always been that way. It's easy to say, "Okay, I'll be chairman of the Metro United Way campaign this year because it's expected of me and I'm in line and I'm supposed to do it, so for a year I'll put all my effort into doing it." That's fine for that person to do that. But that's not my cup of tea. I don't do things simply because I am in line to do it. I want to do it because it really needs to be done.

For accomplishments, I go back to the public school system. My most significant accomplishment in all of my civic life was helping the Jefferson County school system become one of the better large school systems in the country. And I worked a lot of hard hours. I'm going to guess 20-plus years of my time went into helping the school system.

What I learned was that there's a tremendous divergence of people in terms of attitude, race, opinions, impressions, judgments. You have to deal with all of that. When you're dealing with something as public as a public school system, you're dealing with parents, you're dealing with students, you're dealing with teachers, you're dealing with principals, you're dealing with superintendents, you're dealing with the press, you're dealing with labor because they're all organized for the most part, so you have to deal with all of these people and bring them together however and wherever you can. I learned a lot in that process. Nothing is ever 100%, and nothing is ever black or white; there are shades of gray. If you can't get 100% but you can get 90%, settle for 90%. You just have to learn to compromise and negotiate. I learned all of those things from working with the public schools.

The one thing that disappointed me the most, and we did it twice, was not passing the library tax. Our public library here, for a city this size, does the best it can with the resources it has, but the resources aren't good enough. We're one of the very few public libraries in the state of Kentucky that is not its own taxing district. Most other libraries in the state of Kentucky are self-funded. Twice we had a proposed library tax on the ballot here, and twice I was deeply involved, and twice it went down to defeat. It was because selling taxes is hard. If we could have gotten that tax passed, we would have had a tremendous library system. Someday it's going to have to happen.

One of the things I learned was that you can't assume that everybody is as knowledgeable about certain things as you want them to be. I think the key to education and self-improvement is, pure and simple, reading. If you learn to read at an early age, and to read well, you can do darned near anything. For most people it starts with the library. When kids don't get the basics to start with, they have a handicap going in. It's hard to get that support. They will say, "We have the Internet and we have computers, we don't need books." That's ridiculous. You're still going to need the printed word. You still need to be able to pick it up and put it in your pocket and take it with you on the plane. How many people are going to sit down with a computer monitor and read a book? Or even a whole article? Darned few. What they'll do, the icon will say "print" and they'll print that article off and put that article in their pocket and read it when they get a chance to. If it's a book, obviously that's not going to happen. So the printed word is always going to be here and we need to make it available in more abundant numbers and categories than we currently do in this locality.

To me, the characteristics of a good follower are commitment and follow-through. If I'm working with a group, and certain people in that group have committed to perform certain tasks in order to get certain things accomplished to meet the end goal, I expect for them to do that. The way you ride herd on that is with constant communication. Constant telephoning, sending faxes and e-mails – there are a lot of ways to do it today that we didn't have 15 years ago, but that's what you have to do. Then those who simply say, "I'm going to work on this committee because it's a committee I ought to be on, but I'm not going to spend any time on it," I'm going to get rid of that person. If they're not going to put the time and effort in, I don't want them. I don't want somebody in that group who's not going to put out the effort.

I don't know that I'd do anything different if I had it to do over again, except I might have organized the library campaign differently. I would have put a lot more pressure on the politicians to get behind the tax effort. They were quiet. They weren't saying anything. I think they were afraid to spend political capital on something they weren't really sure would pass. That's the one hangup I have about people, particularly politicians, they are afraid to spend political capital because something might fail. They only want to spend political capital when it's a sure success. Well, hell, that's not strong leadership. Strong leadership to me is to take a project that is somewhat risky, use your political capital and get the damned thing passed. Now that's strong leadership. If you take a no-brainer and say, "I'll use my political capital to get that no-brainer done," that's not leadership. Not in my book, it's not.

My advice to young people who are aspiring to leadership is to join as many organizations as you can, then sift them down to three or four and concentrate your efforts there where you really think you can make a difference. Find the cause or the project where you think you can make a difference and maybe bring some unique talents to the project. Don't join just because somebody said you ought to be a member of that particular group. I'll give you a good example. Leadership Louisville has been around forever, it's a great organization, but I'd say that most of the people who've gone through the Leadership Louisville program, after they are through with it, disappear. They go through it because they want it on a résumé that they were part of that class. I have a strong opinion that if a company is willing to commit an individual's time, and if that individual is willing to commit their time to go through the class, then they ought to make a commitment at the end of that class for a project or two projects, or for a year or two years to do community service work. They should not disappear. Then those who decide that they really do like it will emerge as your next leadership group. Will it be all of them? No. But if you can only get five or ten percent of them, it would be wonderful. Most of the time, they simply disappear.

Without question, the one factor that has contributed most to the growth, development and improved quality of life in Louisville over the last 50 years is education. Our school system is better than it's ever been, even though it's a major metropolitan school system. The University of Louisville is leaps and bounds ahead of where it was when I was a student there. I graduated in 1954. I was a student there when it basically was a private college. I can remember my tuition rates were $18.75 per semester hour. The reason I remember that is because it was the cost of a Defense Savings Bond. That $18.75 would buy you a $25 bond, and that was a very high tuition cost back in those days. Tuition would be $350–$400 per semester, and back in the early 1950s that was a lot of money. One of the reasons that you have so many high achievers out of the University of Louisville, and you do have a lot of high achievers, is because they were people who lived here, grew up here, went to school here, and stayed here. You now see those people everywhere. They run projects and organizations everywhere. So I'd say it's education, without question.

Louisville's biggest challenge is to build on our strengths. I set up a task force with GLI's help to commission the Boyle Report, and we tried to do what Boyle said. He said in his report, which I agree with, that Louisville is trying to be everything to everybody. We can't do that. We have limited resources. So we said, "Okay, let's see what our strengths really are." And our strengths were the obvious — we are a major distribution center and we are strong in the health and medical fields because of our downtown medical center, the medical school and the research efforts that are going on there.

Louisville has a lot of potential, but I think that Louisville has to recognize that we are a city of potential with some limitations. There are people who will say that Louisville has great potential with unlimited opportunities, and that's not true. There are certain things that we just can't afford to do. We don't have an Eli Lilly Foundation here. We don't have any $40 billion foundation. We have the Brown Foundation, which is a couple of hundred million dollars — which is pretty nice, but it's not $40 billion. Eli Lilly drives and has made Indianapolis thrive. We don't have those kinds of resources.

The city of Louisville is also changing. We don't have the corporate entities headquartered here like we used to. It didn't start with the banks; it started years ago when Cochran Foil sold to Anaconda, Reynolds moved out, and somebody else merged with somebody or sold. A lot of family businesses sold. Those weren't really big, but they were headquarters companies that were generous to the community. They went away over the years. Then the bigger stuff started happening like the banks. When these things happen, decision-making generally moves out of the community.

Some decision-making is still here, but the major decision-making things we used to participate in and be involved in are all done somewhere else now, like Pittsburgh or New York or wherever. The headquarters operations in those other cities help some here, but to a much smaller degree. That's had an impact on how we do things here.

At one time, this city used to be run by five or six people, if you exclude the politicians. Then gradually, because of the power structure changing, with mergers and acquisitions and untimely deaths, that's changed now from a small leadership group to one that has to be much larger and that needs more consensus-building. That's not all bad. The good part of it is that you get more people on the same page. The bad part is it takes a long time to do it. That's where people like me might become impatient. I could work in that environment because I get along well with people and do a fair job of selling ideas. But it does lengthen the life span of decision-making. Many times we're on a short string and we want something done quickly. It's hard now to get things done quickly.

I do have some advice to share with young people aspiring to leadership. I still think, and have always felt this way – I guess this goes back to my family and my upbringing – number one, you must be honest. Somebody brings a project to you and says, "This is a great idea. This is something we ought to do," and you agree and say, "Yeah, I agree with you." But if it's not, say, "No. It's not going to fly." Just be honest. Be ethical, and operate with no conflicts.

If you are a civic leader and you're in the business world, there are too many opportunities to have conflicts of interest. You don't ever want to damage your credibility by having people accuse you of having a conflict of interest. There's still a lot of it out there. The surprising thing is that the people who offend in that area don't realize that other people see it, which makes them a lot less effective.

If somebody comes to me and says, "Look, this is a great project and we really need your help on it," and I look at it and say, "Yeah, it's a great project," and I get involved with it and I find out three months later that, if this thing flies, this guy is going to make a lot of money out of it, I get more than irritated. So my personal method of operation is always to do a lot of checking before I agree to do something, to make sure that I don't have people surrounding me who have conflicts. If I saw something happening where there were conflicts, I would be very quick to point it out.

So my advice to the next generation of leaders is just work hard, be honest, be free and open with your opinion, and don't be afraid to tackle the controversial issues.

DOUGLAS COBB

Chairman and CEO
Appriss Inc.

DOUG COBB WAS A BRIGHT YOUNG man from Louisville's Atherton High School who went away to college, found success in the information management field, then brought his entrepreneurial skills back to Louisville.

He "retired" at age 35, co-founded a venture capital firm, became volunteer chairman of the Louisville Area Chamber of Commerce, then was hired as the first president of Greater Louisville Inc., the Chamber's successor. Now he heads Appriss, Inc., the nation's largest privately-managed integrated criminal justice information network. Appriss provides innovative technological solutions that help hundreds of local, state and federal government agencies serve and protect their citizens. The company's services include V.I.N.E. (Victim Information and Notification Everyday) and Justice Xchange.

Cobb is also a champion of encouraging bright young people who grow up in Louisville to stay in their home town, and of luring them back if they have moved away. "I don't see how we can think of ourselves as a healthy, competitive city if our young people don't think there's enough opportunity to keep them here," Cobb told *Louisville Magazine*.

Cobb started college at Southwestern (now Rhodes College) in Memphis. He later graduated from Williams College in Massachusetts. While he was working on a master's degree in accounting at New York University, he came across an Apple II computer at the New York office of his future wife, Gena, and became fascinated with the technology.

He soon left his job with the Arthur Anderson accounting firm to work with computers, even though the company had just transferred him to Boston so he could be with Gena, as she pursued graduate study at Harvard.

Cobb got a job as a salesman for a computer store, began writing software support literature, and set up a consulting company in Cambridge, Massachusetts. As it happened, the Lotus Corporation, which developed the best-selling Lotus 1-2-3 spreadsheet program, had an office in his building. He learned everything there was to know about Lotus 1-2-3, then co-wrote a "how-to" book on the software program that sold 1.5 million copies.

A year later, in 1984, Cobb moved back to Louisville to start the Cobb Group with his wife, his brother Steve, and Tom Cottingham. Software developers shared information about new software programs with the Cobb Group, and the company started producing instruction manuals as new software was being released to the public.

The Cobb Group published both books and newsletters for software users and eventually grew to 150 employees. In 1992, Cobb and his partners sold the business. He worked for the new owners, Ziff Communications Inc., for two years, then retired. In 2004, *The Courier-Journal* counted 11 companies founded in Louisville by Cobb Group alumni, including Cobb.

In 1994, Cobb co-founded Chrysalis Ventures, a firm that lends start-up capital to entrepreneurs, with his friend David Jones Jr. After that, he served a term as chairman of the Louisville Area Chamber of Commerce, during which he helped merge the Chamber with the Greater Louisville Economic Development Partnership to form Greater Louisville Inc. (GLI). Cobb became GLI's first president and CEO.

He put his personal mark on the GLI business plan by making an improved entrepreneurial climate a central goal — reasoning that Louisville has a better record of growing its own Fortune 500 companies like Vencor, LG&E and Tricon (later YUM! Brands) than of attracting the headquarters of such firms.

"No one I have seen in 16 years in the state of Kentucky has taken on entrepreneurism quite as passionately as Doug," said Brad Richardson, former president of the Greater Louisville Economic Development Partnership.

In addition to his work with Appriss, Cobb serves on a number of boards, including Genscape, Inc, Summit Energy Corporation, International Voting Systems, and Golden State Overnight, Inc. He is also active in a variety of community activities, and serves as a volunteer on a number of local boards and committees. Until recently, he also served as chair of the Regional Leadership Coalition.

Cobb has received numerous awards and honors. He is a three-time Inc. 500 CEO and a two-time Kentucky/Southern Indiana Entrepreneur of the Year. He was inducted into the Junior Achievement Kentucky/Southern Indiana Business Hall of Fame and, in 2003, the Atherton High School Hall of Fame.

Cobb and his wife Gena have two sons and one daughter.

MY DAD, STEWART COBB, was clearly one of my earliest mentors, and the preacher at our church, Dr. Mobley at Highland Presbyterian. I went to Southwestern, now Rhodes College, in Memphis, because it was Dr. Mobley's alma mater and he suggested it to me. I admired both of them for being people of integrity, people who held it together, and I thought that was good.

There were others too. I had a teacher at Atherton, Mr. Worful, who was a great teacher and a believer. One day, somebody asked him a spiritual question and he just laid it out there on the table for us all. I wasn't a believer at the time, but I was really impressed with his conviction and his willingness to just lay it out there. That goes back 30 years, but at the time it was considered a "no no." You just didn't do stuff like that. I also had teachers in college I really respected.

I was never in student government, captain of a team or anything like that. I was in the Boy Scouts, but I can't really think of any leadership experiences I might have had from youth or childhood. When I was a senior in high school, the president of our class and a couple of other officers were really close friends of mine. I didn't have a title, but because they were friends of mine, I just started hanging around with them and doing a lot of things with them. I unofficially became part of that leadership group. I had no title, but did what needed to be done because they were my friends and I liked hanging out with them. It also kept me out of homeroom!

The first really significant leadership experience I had in my life was when I started the Cobb Group. That was in 1984 and I was 27 years old.

Gena Cobb and I had been working with a company in Indianapolis, Que Corporation, that published books about computer software. We had seen how that business worked, and we invented an idea for a newsletter concept for software. We didn't invent it, we actually borrowed it. We had seen it done once and thought we could do it again, so we decided it would be a great business. We tried to get Que to do it, but the guy who ran Que didn't want to do it, so we quit and came to Louisville to start that business.

I think we always had a sense that this was going to be a great industry – that people were going to have to learn how to use computers and software programs and that people were going to make money teaching them. We could see that, and we set several goals for our business.

We really had a high desire for a great culture when we started the business. Apple was beginning to emerge as a company and we were big believers in that West Coast style of management. We had a goal to be on the Inc. 500 list. We wanted to build a fast-growing company and we achieved that. We wanted to take the company public or sell it, so we started the company specifically with the idea of cashing it out sometime. We had some very clear ideas about what we wanted it to be and what we wanted to do.

Tom Cottingham worked with us at Que. We left in May to come to Louisville and he left in August to come join us. Tom co-founded the business with us. He was a guy we really liked a lot and we knew he was really talented.

I learned many things about how to manage a company by working at Que, then deciding to do the opposite thing. The guy who ran Que, God bless him, was a terrible manager. It's amazing the people he ran out of that company – me; Cottingham, who did the Cobb Group and Tech Republic; a guy who two years later invented the whole idea of the "For Dummies" book series, because he left and went to work for the competitor; Patty Stonesifer, who went to work at Microsoft then rose up through the ranks to run the Bill Gates Foundation. He ran off some of the best talent I've ever worked with. You learn a lot by seeing how people do things and by doing them a different way. The company ended up still being very successful despite all that.

I think there are different leadership styles for different situations. The way we try to run my current company – Appriss – may be somewhat different from the way I would have conducted myself when I was in the public eye at Greater Louisville Inc. We basically have three values we use to define our culture here.

First, we lead with trust and respect. A lot of what we are about is making sure our leaders are people who conduct themselves in a way that is worthy of being trusted and respected. They tell the truth, they do what they say they're going to do, they invest time in people. And those leaders return trust and respect to the people who work for them. They earn trust and respect from their people and show trust and respect by trusting their people to do what they say they're going to do, not micro-managing them, not being harsh with them. We don't scream at people here. We don't punish people for making honest mistakes. If you do something malicious or stupid, of course, that's a whole different thing.

Two, we strive for excellence. We have gotten to be as good as we can possibly be, and in our company that's a little strange because our main product really doesn't have any competitors. We don't have anything pushing us to be great. Our customers are the government, and they don't necessarily demand perfection from us. So it would be easy for us to be less than great if we wanted to be. We don't get pushed and we don't get pulled; we just motivate ourselves by the pride we feel from being great.

Three, we energize our teammates. We behave in a way that is energizing. We're polite, we're pleasant, we're honest and we're responsible, and if we all behave that way, we lift each other up and the result of that is a great work place.

These are just three simple principles, but if you think about it, those three principles really define the three relationships anybody has at work.

We have a relationship with our customers, and we define that as a goal of excellence. We have a relationship with our teammates, and with our leaders and followers, and those relationships are all based on trust and respect. If we could do these three things perfectly, we would really be great.

I talk about these things so much that our people get a little sick of it sometimes. If you're a worker here, you get reviewed on excellence, energy, and sub-characteristics under that, and if you're a leader you get reviewed on those two things plus trust and respect, so you can see how you're doing every year when you get your review. We have posters around the company that talk about it. I have one on my door. We talk about it a lot. I do the last interview with everybody we hire, and I give them a little sermon about this. I say, "If you don't want to do this, don't come to work here, because we don't want you if you're not going to buy into this. Here's the kool-aid, drink it." We are all about this. Its good kool-aid, but don't try to work here if you are bringing a cynical attitude.

Some guys have developed a concept here called "gift work." At the core of your employment relationship there is a contractual relationship. The contract says I will work for you and do these things and you will pay me this much and there are certain holidays and benefits and perks, and that's the contract. Too many places have a "union mentality" about work. Work is defined as this contract, and I'm not going to do one thing I'm not required to do, and you're not going to do one thing you're not required to do, so we have this contractual relationship. It's rigid and cold, inhuman, impersonal, and untrusting. Everyone's attitude is that if you're not going to give me any more than you have to, then I'm sure not going to give you any more than I have to either, because then you would be taking advantage of me.

"Gift work" goes beyond the contract. It's about what we each give each other that we don't have to give. We have a policy here that if you get married or have a baby, the company gives you $500. Five hundred dollars is "Congratulations, here's a little money for the kid's college fund." Or maybe you need a new dining room table or something. We don't ask, we just say, "Here's a little money." We don't have to do that, and we wouldn't be thought of any worse if we didn't do that, because it's so unusual. That's just something we do because we want to show people we really care about their personal lives.

Same thing on the worker's side. I really can't make people stay here until six o'clock at night, I can't make them make that last phone call. I can't make them get something done. What I have to do is create an environment where people believe we are going to give more than we have to give, then you look for people who see the world that way. There are some people who see the world as a contract, but those people are unsuccessful here. Our success depends on getting the right people on the bus, then managing them.

It's like building a championship basketball team. Rick Pitino, the University of Louisville's basketball coach, has had great teams the last couple of years. They have done a great job, but he would be the first to tell you, "I have to have better players before I can win the national championship." We have to have great players here too, or we can't be great. Good people bring out the best in other people.

When I was in a leadership position at Greater Louisville Inc., I didn't spend much time on the culture at GLI. I think the culture improved at GLI because we went from being ineffective to effective and people felt proud about that. We brought in some new people to change some things. But I didn't focus on the culture there because in that job, my focus was on the outside, not inside the organization. I delegated running the organization to Steve (Higdon) for the most part. My job was to cast a vision for what Louisville could be and to talk about that constantly. I gave one speech a thousand times in three years. There was often a request for money attached to my speech, but basically I gave one speech and the speech was "We can be better, and we need to be better."

For whatever reason, people responded to that and we started building an organization that I was lucky enough to be the father of. I'm so impressed with how well it's held together and how well it has continued to move forward. It hasn't lost focus and it hasn't lost talent, which often happens. The thing I'm really proud of is that that organization got built in a great way.

I was also proud that we attracted good talent to GLI. We made a few mistakes, of course, but you always do that. My experience has been that hiring is a little better than a 50-50 proposition. If you can do 70-30, you're doing pretty well. If you can do better than that you're really doing well.

When my son Wes was about eleven or twelve years old and I was working at GLI, I heard him say to one of his friends, "This is my dad, he can't keep a job." He saw that I had worked ten years here and three years there, five years here, ten years there. A lot of people stay in one place. I'm in career number five or six, and I'm 47. Hopefully there will be more.

I've done a lot of things, but I would say my greatest accomplishment so far, hands down, is that I've been married 25 years to the same person. I have a 19-year-old son who's great. I have two other kids. and I don't want to curse them by saying it yet, but I think they're going to be pretty good, too. All the other stuff really is secondary to that, in my opinion.

Most of the credit for our 25-year marriage goes to my wife. I did a lot of things along the way to try to screw it up, but we've hung in there and we've made it. When I meet people who have kids who are grown and are still together, I just think that's the greatest accomplishment in life.

Passing the Torch

In the temporal sense, the only thing you leave behind is the children that you've raised. They reach beyond you to their children and things pass along. You see dysfunctional families where the sins of the fathers are really visited on the children in the third and fourth generation. That's not a curse, it's just a fact, and when you see people who've done it well, that's really great.

From a professional point of view, I'm really proud of the Cobb Group and I am proud of GLI. We're not done with Appriss yet, but that seems to be going well and I'm very fortunate to have been involved with it. I just think it's fun to start things and make them work. I've been involved in a variety of things, but they have all had one thing in common: I've started them and helped make them work. It really gives me joy when I see a plan coming together. When it really starts to click, it's great. I felt that with GLI in late 1999 and at the end of 2000 when it became clear that we had raised the money and knew what we were doing.

I've had plenty of personal disappointments, which I won't talk about. Some businesses we've invested in should have worked and didn't. I've made some dumb decisions with investments that should have never been made. Those things are always clear in hindsight. You look at them and think, "How could I have been so stupid?"

I think the disappointments I would focus on would be personal things: Telling a lie when I didn't need to do it, violating my principles or being disingenuous with somebody. I've done that, and I hate it. I won't talk about specifics because they are personal, but those kinds of things have been personal disappointments for me.

I've always rebelled against the whole "followership" concept and, to some extent, against the whole "leadership" thing too. People do different things in different parts of their lives. Everybody who works for me is a leader in his or her own home. They're raising kids, they're involved in a hobby or something else that calls for them to lead.

My job here is to be the leader, but everyone here has a different job. One of the things we used to say at the Cobb Group is, "Leadership is a job, it's not a rank." We don't have lower-level people and higher-level people. The organization chart unfortunately always makes it look like that. We have people whose job is to write software, we have people whose job is to put sites online, we have people whose job is to talk to customers and to sell and maintain things. My job is to organize the work and lead. That's my job, and it's one of the jobs that's required to make this company work. But if it were up to me to do any of those other jobs, we would be in real trouble.

I'm thankful for the people who work with me. It really fires me up that we have people on our team who are so smart about things I know nothing about. I am proud to be associated with and surrounded by people who know how to do what they do as well as I know how to do what I do. People think this is Doug Cobb's company, but I don't really think about it that way. I think about Mike Davis being great at going out on the road and selling things, Brian Oldham being a genius about the organization of technology, and Jesse Steer, one of our software engineers, who is just a genius on Java programming. It takes us all.

They are all there to help build up the body. We used to say at the Cobb Group, if a job isn't important enough for us to respect the person who has it, let's eliminate the job. If it doesn't merit our respect, then obviously it's not something we need to be doing, so let's eliminate the job and just have jobs that we know are critical to what we are trying to get done. I learned so many things there. If I ever write a book on management, a lot of it will come from the Cobb Group. At the beginning, it was just the commitment Gena and Tom and I had to building this kind of place. We are all low BS, low protocol. We're not about the trappings of position and power and hierarchy. We looked for people there who wanted to work in a principle-driven environment. As we grew to a certain scale and began to get a reputation, we attracted more people.

As I look back on my life, would I do anything differently? In general, we've been fortunate. In venture capital, you expect some decisions to be bad; you just don't like it when it happens. If I had waited until 1998, when the Internet bubble hit, to sell the Cobb Group instead of selling it 1991, I could have probably sold it for a billion dollars, because who knows what a content company with an Internet play would have been worth. That was completely unknowable and unpredictable at the time, however, and something bad could have happened in the interim that would have messed it up.

I've really enjoyed all the different things I've done, and I'm very excited about seeing what comes next. I will at some point have this company fully baked, and it will be time to earn a return for our investors. I would like to do it one more time.

I would give young people today who are aspiring to be leaders the same advice we give our leaders here: conduct yourself in such a way that you earn the trust and respect of the people you work with. That involves competence, humility, authenticity, integrity. There are plenty of people who are successful as leaders and successful in business who absolutely fail in all those things. It's possible to become a leader and be effective, but to be dishonest and inauthentic. I think you can sleep a lot better at night if you know that you are who you pretend to be.

Passing the Torch

All the failures I mentioned earlier happened because I was inauthentic or did not demonstrate integrity. We are all people, we are all human, and we all make mistakes. You learn to seek forgiveness for those things and go on. You hope to have a high probability that you're going to do things right everyday.

I think for a long time in Louisville, the community had an attitude that we really didn't want things to change. We got exactly what we wanted. Things didn't change, and as cities around us were growing and prospering and changing and taking on new risks and new possibilities, we got left behind. Our population didn't grow. We just sat dead still. A few good companies formed, but not nearly as many as in other places. There are reasons for these things.

There's a joke about Kentucky that it is the state that sided with the Union in the Civil War, then with the losers immediately thereafter. We decided to become southern as soon as the war was over. We've got the rural/urban thing in Kentucky that has really hurt Louisville and sucks cash from us for other purposes in the state. It's a difficult thing to overcome.

I think at one time we had a leadership group that wanted to build a fence around Louisville and not let anything change. We exported a lot of our young talent and we started to shrink. Some things have begun to change that. The person I would point to who has really changed that has been Jerry Abramson. His ability to succeed himself as mayor and his charismatic leadership of our community has been a unifying and uplifting force for Louisville.

David Jones would be another person I would give a lot of credit to, a guy who was a Louisvillian, stayed committed to Louisville and has invested a lot in Louisville and provided a lot of leadership here. There are other business leaders who would qualify too, but Mr. Jones would clearly be the guy at the top.

I would like to think that over the last seven or eight years Greater Louisville Inc. has been a big factor, too. It's not so much the entity or the employees, although they are great. It's the unity that it has brought to our efforts. If you think about a lot of the things we fought for in the early days and are still fighting for, they are battles to maintain the integrity of one organization that holds this mission and drives it forward. I think we have been pretty successful. The thing that used to drive me crazy about the old Chamber is that the new chairman every year created a new agenda every year. I did it too — I am just as guilty. Leonard Hardin was about education. Malcolm Chancey was about workforce, transportation and community planning. Doug Cobb was about entrepreneurship. We always had some economic development going on, but there was no strategy, no long-term theme for the community.

The one big thing the business leaders in our community did right is the Ross Boyle Report. Ross wrote down the things we asked him to write down, but our overall goal was to come up with a long-term strategy for the community.

Once developed, the report would then drive things we thought were important: workforce development, for example, which really has become a critical attraction; entrepreneurship as a strategy. But even the things we were doing before as a community, like basic business attraction and business retention, we have been able to do much better because it's now efficient and effective and everybody knows what his or her role is. I don't know that Louisville had a strategy before that. I think the first thing in making anything happen is deciding what you want to do. If you don't know what you want to do, it's hard to get it done. So getting our community to decide what we wanted to do was a start.

There are some trends that have been going on in the last ten to 20 years that we better be aware of. The exodus of corporate headquarters from town is not going to stop, so strategies to deal with that are essential. We need to grow new companies, so our strategy for encouraging entrepreneurship is a long-term strategy. It may take 20 years for that to get to the point where we want it to be. We've made a difference, but we have a ways to go.

The workforce issue is still a critical issue too. The competitive struggle between cities today is primarily a struggle to attract and retain talented people. It's not about attracting jobs, it's about attracting people. There are cities that are dramatically advantaged in that game. Jacksonville, Florida, because it has a great climate which we can't compete against. Another would be Denver, Colorado or Colorado Springs. These are places that have strong built-in advantages. We probably have some too, but we should sell ourselves better than we do. People don't think of us that way, and it's hard to change their minds.

What we have to do is be sure we are doing everything we can to overcome the disadvantages we have and to stress the advantages we have. This is a great place to live and work. Go to Denver and sit in traffic two hours every day getting to and from work, then tell me how often you get to the mountains. Not often, because life is too complicated. Cities have to sell what they have. This is a great place to live and work. We have solid values, we embrace diversity, we have short commutes, cheap houses – it's a good place to live.

Building a community is like building a wall – you have to do it one brick at a time. There may be important bricks and less important ones, but you always want to be thinking, what brick am I putting in now, what is the next one going to be, and what's the one after that.

We've put some really important bricks in that wall in the last few years. Papa John's Cardinal Stadium; Louisville Slugger Field; eMain; the Kentucky Derby Museum; the Hillerich and Bradsby Museum; the Frazier Museum; the Muhammad Ali Center; the Extreme Sports Park; Fourth Street Live! All of these are bricks that have contributed to our community in a big way.

A downtown arena would be high on my list of next bricks we ought to lay, but it will be a pretty expensive one. It should be within our reach, though. We want to lay bricks as fast as we can lay them. We should never stop laying bricks.

So what else can we do? We were behind. I don't know if we've gotten ahead or just caught up. One thing we tend to do as a city is get happy with ourselves when we make some progress and we think, "That was great! Let's go have some lunch!" I am always thinking, "No, we need to work through lunch because we're behind."

The Glassworks Building and other downtown housing projects are exciting. There's a lot to do downtown now. There are a lot of cranes down there – there's a lot getting built. We have to remember that it's one brick at a time. Nothing in the Boyle Report is something we have to do. Let's just value the things we have now and add some things we don't have.

When I am asked to join an organization or to lead an effort I first decide whether it sounds interesting to me or not. If it's something that I like or respect, I'm inclined to do it, out of respect for the people who ask me. I'm trying to shed some things, however. I won't tell you which ones, but there are some things I've been involved with that just don't interest me anymore.

I just asked to be on the board and to become an elder at Southeast Christian Church, so that's a big new time commitment that's interesting to me. It's a little bit challenging because church boards are challenging organizations, but it's a unique opportunity, because nobody knows how to run a church that has 20,000 members. We are making it up as we go, and it's kind of fun. It's another case of create it, then make it work. It's fun to have a chance to participate.

Right now, it is my job to run Appriss, and when that's done, my assumption is I will probably start another company or become the CEO of one. Who knows? There might be something different around the next corner. The one thing that has been true about my career is that I've made several left turns, so I don't try to predict what might come next.

I was writing a memo to our board last night, and it occurred to me that the thing I really most like to do is to write. I used to do that years ago as a career. I don't think I am a fiction writer. I don't think I have that talent. I'm not sure if there's a way someone like me could make a living writing, but it would be very interesting to try.

I feel like Louisville, overall, is really doing well. That's not to say that we can't do a lot better, and I think we need to do a lot better, but when you compare where we are in 2004 to where we were in 1994, its incredible how much difference there is.

I think we need to continue to set ambitious goals for ourselves and to strive to hit them. Before we merged our governments, I used to say that the most important thing about merger had nothing to do with government or efficiency. Merger showed that we could do something hard like that — that we could actually make a big change like that. And we did it. I'm not sure that we have leveraged that as much as we could. It may be that we are still working on it and it will take a few more years to get it done. But I think the Abramson team has done a great job. I give them an A or maybe even an A+ for their efforts.

REVEREND LOUIS COLEMAN

Pastor
First Congregational Methodist Church

Director
Justice Resource Center

IN 1999, FORMER *Courier-Journal* Public Editor Linda Raymond discovered she had to write a column to try to answer a charge frequently made by *Courier* readers – "Do we cover Louis Coleman too much?"

"The quickest answer to the question," she wrote, "is that Coleman's crusade for social and economic justice is so omnipresent that it's hard to ignore."

That's by design. Coleman has spent long hours since 1975, in the name of his Justice Resource Center, complaining about alleged civil-rights violations in employment, education and housing, and defending people who are not in the mainstream, often using demonstrations, picket signs, prayer vigils and other confrontational means to make his points.

He has "considerable public relations skills," Raymond said in the newspaper's defense. Once he set up a card table and folding chairs and ate homemade sandwiches with other protesters on the sidewalk in front of the Pendennis Club, charging it with exclusionary membership practices.

Humana Founder David Jones Sr., a friend of Coleman's from YMCA basketball games in the 1970s, said it was "brilliant" – a stunt "the best PR people around" probably would not have come up with. Jones calls Coleman "the conscience of the community."

Coleman is a gadfly in the same way Socrates claimed to be – a person who sees people asleep to social ills and persists in trying to wake them up, but in ways that sometimes irritate them. A *Courier-Journal* article written in October of 2003 said that "while most acknowledge that Coleman is a polarizing figure, some area residents see Coleman as someone who helps give a voice to those without one." He said himself in that same article that he doesn't mind upsetting what he calls "the power structure, as long as the people in pain get some relief."

Louis Coleman was born in Louisville in 1943 and grew up in the Smoketown neighborhood, east of downtown. He had a passion for baseball as a boy, and often played it to the exclusion of other activities.

It seemed to pay off when, after his graduation from Central High School and Kentucky State University, he was signed by the Pittsburgh Pirates. He never moved up to the majors, though, so he returned to Louisville and got a master's degree in community development at the University of Louisville. He also obtained a master's degree from the Louisville Presbyterian Theological Seminary.

Coleman took jobs as director of housing and urban affairs for the Louisville Urban League and for the Presbyterian Community Center. He spent 18 years as pastor of Shelby Congregational Methodist Church in Shelbyville, before moving to his post as pastor of Louisville's First Congregational Methodist Church in West Louisville.

Coleman founded the Justice Resource Center in 1975, and the Louisville Black Chamber of Commerce in 1998. He has long been a familiar protest figure, gathering most often with a small band of people he calls "leftovers from the '60s," but sometimes with considerably larger groups.

He purchases guns to get them off Louisville streets. He has gathered with supporters in an anti-drug vigil for more than 800 consecutive nights. He traditionally serves Thanksgiving dinner to hundreds of residents in Louisville's Park Hill neighborhood each year.

His major victories include a $14 million payment from E.I. duPont de Nemours and Company, Inc. to black workers and their families for discriminatory practices stretching back decades, and a $3.9 million award for police department discrimination against black applicants.

Mayor Jerry Abramson who, as a highly visible public official, often finds himself a target of Coleman's barbs, acknowledged to *Business First* in 1996, "There needs to be someone like Louis Coleman who questions everything" in the community.

Coleman has been the target of a good deal of criticism and vitriol over the years, but he remains even-tempered through it all. He tells a story about an incident at a PGA tournament in Louisville that he feels explains the public's attitude toward him. "They were arresting us," he told *Louisville Magazine* last year. He said a young black female officer who was leading him to the paddy wagon said she had a message for him:

"My grandmother told me not to arrest you because you are a good man and that you stand for what is right. I told my grandmother that if I had to put the handcuffs on you, they wouldn't be tight."

I GOT INVOLVED IN THE LOUISVILLE COMMUNITY by default. So many of the organizations who had the name for challenging issues and problems in our community were not doing it as much as I felt they should. This was my personal perception, and I just felt more needed to be done. So in the little town of Shelbyville, Kentucky where I was pastor, I began to have a little office and began working on issues.

One of the first issues we addressed was an issue that dealt with state government's not observing Martin Luther King's birthday as they should. Other cities were celebrating it as a holiday and Kentucky workers were still at work on that day. I remember Governor John Y. Brown, Jr. saying that he thought Martin Luther King would want folks to work on this holiday. I wrote him a letter and said "You need to stop playing games with Dr. King's birthday, Governor. You don't play games with anybody else's birthday." I saw that folks were just going along with the program. So every year we started to protest in front of the State Capitol on January 15th. Sometimes I wouldn't have enough people to protest with; sometimes I would get some inebriated friend to walk with us in front of the Capitol. We started our protests the year Dr. King's birthday was instituted as a national holiday. We ended them 13 years later, when all state workers could go home and not work on this holiday.

About that same time we were dealing with school district issues too, and Jefferson County had a few we had to address. For example, the teachers were having an in-service day on Dr. King's birthday. Students could come to school if they wanted to. I said, "No, you celebrate the holiday as intended, like everybody else." Finally, that became a reality about four years ago when my classmate, State Representative Jesse Crenshaw out of Lexington, passed a bill in the General Assembly. He pushed that bill. We had filed complaints against the Kentucky State Board of Education for not being more forceful. We challenged the superintendent of Jefferson County's school district. When a school district in Kentucky decided they would celebrate the holiday in schools for students and teachers, we went to that city and gave that district an award. We spent a lot of time going to districts giving awards out. It was just a picture, with a plaque of Dr. King, saying thank you for celebrating Dr. King's birthday.

My calling to be a pastor came from wanting to do God's will. I saw man's will in many instances was not fair. It was not just. Every year the call continued to grow. Mine is actually a continual call.

My role models, my idols, have been people of the gospel, people like Paul, people like David. I love David because he was so human. But despite his humanity, God said, "Here is a man molded after my own heart."

My idols have included one sportsperson – Jackie Robinson – and later, Whitney Young Jr. and Martin Luther King Jr. As a boy, I just loved Jackie Robinson. I worked under Whitney Young Jr. at the Nashville Urban League. I was with the Louisville League at the time but felt a kinship to him.

A deceased friend of mine, Reverend Hosea Williams, was another idol. I went to some of the programs he did in Atlanta. His Feed the Hungry and Homeless Program in Atlanta inspired my Thanksgiving program here in Louisville. Every year, we feed close to 1,000 people Thanksgiving dinner – outside, in the housing projects.

I pastor at two churches – one in Shelbyville on Saturday, and one in Louisville on Sunday. Reverend Ralph Abernathy and Reverend Hosea Williams spoke on Martin Luther King Jr.'s birthday at our church. I brought King's men to the people in Louisville so they could communicate and feel some of the trials and tribulations these men went through. There was a lighter side to these men. Reverend Abernathy had a beautiful personality. I took him to meet my mother and father. They didn't talk about civil rights. He saw my mother had a lot of flowers in the house and he talked about flowers the whole time he was there.

You never knew what to expect out of Hosea Williams. We would ask him to come to the pulpit to preach, but sometimes he would use profanity to the point where you would say, "My goodness, you need those censored." He was a super human being.

I have learned from these people, particularly from their lighter side. I used to kid Abernathy about praying with his eyes open. There is a film from their march on Montgomery, when they were in Selma. Horses ran over the people and Abernathy was praying with his eyes open. I would tease him about that and he said "Coleman, if you saw what I saw, you would pray with your eyes open, too. They had horses and cattle prods coming at me. The good Lord could have taken me home right then. But I felt that I had accomplished most of the things the Lord wanted me to accomplish on this earth."

I've had fellowship and been involved with men and women like this and they have been people who have had a direct effect on my life.

Let me talk about Rosa Parks. I was trying to get her to come to Louisville. She is a strong Methodist and a member of a church in Detroit. I told her I was calling from First Congregational Methodist Church and she said "What is Congregational?" I said, "That means we broke off from the bishops and presiding elders." She said, "That's interesting. I like that." She said, "Reverend, if you can afford me, bring me in there, but you have to go through my agent." I said, "Ms. Parks, we have had most of your partners here in our humble abode. When we try to work with an agent it makes it very difficult." We had a good conversation, but we never brought her in to speak.

Passing the Torch

Most every January 15th, we have brought nationally-renowned people to Louisville to speak to the community. This year we are inviting the kids from the schools in the area to hear from people who marched with Dr. King.

Not a lot of people take time to take you under their wing. In the civil rights struggle, you had to get your baptism with on-the-job training. Continued protests and continued demonstrations are the learning tool for you.

This year I have been involved in protests in eight or nine cities in Kentucky, where I have met with people who do not really have a voice. I was in Mayfield, Kentucky last Sunday. The community was having problems with police abuse and with politicians not being honest with them, so we had a community meeting. Mayfield is going to establish a chapter of the Justice Resource Center. There is a bold minister in Mayfield who is a God-fearing man. Usually when the system sees you coming at them, even though you are with an agency, they single you out so they can personally attack you, to take attention off the issue. So I have learned from those kinds of struggles. You get singled out for attack.

Before I left Mayfield, I met with the mayor and presented him with a strategic plan. They need to name a street in that town after Dr. Martin Luther King Jr., and do the same thing in Richmond, Kentucky. Not only that, they need to hold police accountable.

That's what I do in every city. I give a strategic plan on the issues. Then I document it. Because what you find in many of these small cities like Mayfield is that people with power, like the mayor, have a very good hook-up with the media. These small town newspeople help maintain the status quo of that town.

Mayfield is a perfect example. The mayor said, "I don't want to meet with that group." I said, "I just want to meet with you and the police chief." He said, "That is fine, Reverend." When I got to the meeting he had a black person from the Human Rights Commission there, the NAACP person, and his attorney. So before the meeting I said, "Mayor, I am going to continue meeting with you, but you're not being honest. No disrespect, but if the problems haven't been resolved and these people around this table have been a part of this community all of these years, then why do you think it is going to be resolved now with them being here?" I make it plain that I do not involve some of these groups that blend in with the power structure. That's what makes our organization unique. We are unbound and unbought.

After I met with the mayor that morning, a Mayfield newspaper came out with an article that quoted the mayor. He said what a great meeting it was and that he, the mayor, had met with a person who is truthful and honest in this community. When I got home I wrote a letter to the mayor saying I felt the meeting was positive, but I gave him a list of the things that I felt needed to be addressed in his community.

The mayor never dealt with the things that needed to be addressed, so at the next community council meeting, my letter was read by a member of the community center. The *Paducah Sun*, which is right next to Mayfield, printed the letter as it was written.

Those are the kind of things we have to deal with in Kentucky. Some of these cities are just closed. They are going to continue to do politics the same way they have been doing it.

Louisville is so huge compared to these other communities I work with, but most of these communities are like Mayfield. They will pick out blacks who will go along with what they are doing. Usually they will hand-pick a person from an organization and include them and say "Now you are going to speak for the black community. You're going to speak for the Hispanic community," while the mass of the people are suffering. That is the reason we come to the community. We are the bad guys, though we don't think we are.

I like the mayor and the police chief here in Louisville, but politicians do not move fast enough to address community issues. Maybe it's the red tape they have to go through. The Metro Council isn't coming up with any answers either. I spoke to them the other night about naming a street after Dr. Martin Luther King, Jr. and they just sat there. Twenty-six people. Maybe that's the decorum they have – not to say anything. It's amazing. I think my tax dollars deserve better than somebody who will just sit there. It bothers me when you go to a meeting and you don't get a response.

If you have problems, get it done. I worked with Mayor Marshall Long in Shelbyville. He was a dream to work with. I went to him to say they needed some people of color and culture on his police department, and he got it done. It wasn't window dressing either. He actively recruited two people to be police officers. It happened, and they stayed on the police department.

There is a different mayor now in Shelbyville who is more in tune with the status quo. Right now there is one police officer of color in the police department. The chief was one, too. The officers would go around the chief and go to the new mayor, and the mayor let them get away with it. I don't blame the chief for saying he wasn't putting up with it. He left.

The mayors we work with are basically wanting to maintain the status quo. Marshall Long was one of the best I have worked with. Mayor Jenkins in Shively was head and shoulders better than any mayor before he resigned.

Governor Brereton Jones was a good governor. They thought he was going to run after Patton. He called me and said "Louis, I appreciate what you're doing in the state." I said, "What are you doing?" He said, "I am out in my barn.

I'm shoveling hay and manure. I'd rather shovel hay and manure than be in state government." He said he wasn't even thinking of coming back, but he offered to send me a contribution for some of the educational things I was doing with young people.

This morning I received the achievement scores from the Jefferson County Board of Education. What is going on in Jefferson County is disgraceful. The learning achievement level of African-Americans in this county is disgraceful. We sit around and talk about the issues, but we need to work with the system to try to come up with some alternative solutions. We discuss models. Greater Louisville Inc. is working on a reading program. I said, "Let's intensify and magnify that model, get it going and let it grow and grow."

I have the privilege of working with our kids in the school system everyday. I work at Iroquois Middle School and Westport Middle School, so I have first-hand knowledge about what many of these kids are lacking in the school system. Reading is one of the issues, and one of the skills they lack. We are working on a model right now for the school system so it can benefit young people in this community. That is one thing that we see as a problem.

I think people would describe my leadership style as an advocacy style, involving everyone in what we are doing. It's collaborative. I lead people in a coalition type of way. Before I take on an issue, we talk about it. Our board chairman, Maddie Jones, and I talk about issues with other board members, like Dr. Joseph McMillan and Reverend James Tennyson. We talk about issues before we address them. Then our next step is to get facts and sit down with the parties to educate them. If parties aren't concerned, aren't going to try to correct the situation, then we educate the community about what is going on. That's why I have these two meetings. They are friendly, objective meetings. We believe we are living in an age right now in which the media is making the news, not reporting the news. We refuse to deal with some media in this community, because we know they are newsmakers. WLKY is one, WHAS radio is another one that we have had issues with about how they create news.

I have my own talk show on WLOU radio on Saturday. I have some young people who talk on WLOU. They don't like to protest. They don't like to march. Their expertise is talking on the radio. We have a show on WLOU every Saturday morning to inform people about what's going on, and to listen to people discuss issues coming up in this community.

One of the things I've worked on that I am proudest of are the lawsuits we have finalized for citizens who have been oppressed. They have received compensation for past negatives that have been implemented against them.

Start with the E. I. Dupont lawsuit, which involved 157 men and women. We had to protest almost three years in front of E. I. Dupont. Dupont management said, "We're not going to settle this." We had to get out there and protest. That suit went on for 19 years, but it was a $4.3 million award.

Then there's Ford Motor Company. We won three cases against Ford. One of them was won without a lawsuit. The folks from Dearborn came down and said "Let's work together." That was about eight or nine years ago. We sat around the table and we worked on some issues. They moved the plant manager, who was a problem. They brought in a more reasonable person. They also made improvements in the Ford Motor Trucking Plant. Women were being put in some of the hardest positions in the plant by design – lifting heavy guns over their heads – to weed them out. The employees said this is wrong, and this is what we shared with the people in Dearborn. They began to address those issues. Ford still has issues, but we won two lawsuits against Ford. These were people in management who were engineers, who have graduated from Purdue University. They were at the top of the educational ladder. They filed lawsuits and we worked with them against Ford.

Then there was the Louisville black police officers' suit which took about 13 years to win. Ninety-three individuals who had applied to the Louisville Police Department won $3.4 million.

The most recent issue was the country club issue. We filed a complaint with the Kentucky Commission on Human Rights against Louisville Country Club, Idlewild Country Club and the Pendennis Club for their membership practices. They would tell us their policies say they do not discriminate, but they practiced it. We had to protest that. Our complaint was upheld by the Supreme Court of Kentucky about a month ago. It takes that long for justice to be actualized in the state of Kentucky.

In late 1989, the Justice Resource Center began to voice concerns about pollution in Rubbertown, and the pollution the Metropolitan Sewer District was placing in Louisville's West End. This year, the Louisville Metro Air Pollution Control Board has a Star plan with the intent to reduce toxic emissions in Rubbertown and throughout the city. It took 15 years to be actualized.

We have longevity in our protests. We are not going to be there for just a moment. People who are familiar with us know we are not going away.

The construction trades in this city and in the state of Kentucky are unbelievably bad to African-Americans. We have minority contractors, African-American contractors, women contractors – but this city and state are good at bringing in contractors from out of the state.

I go to Senate committee meetings in Frankfort. I go to Metro Council and share with them that it doesn't make good sense to constantly keep giving money to people out-of-state to do construction projects in the city when you can benefit people locally. It would raise our economy. To me that's common sense. They still haven't come up with a plan.

We had a protest on the building that Greater Louisville Inc. is in because the contractor had no minority subcontractors, no women subcontractors. They used a contractor that had an African-American name at the time. The company has improved. It has gotten better. But at the time, they were using another black company to say, "This is our minority participation."

My biggest disappointment is with our government. I wish government would be more for the people. It is sad to go to school with people and see how politics can change their mind set. I've grown up with quite a few of these African-American councilpersons, and I see how politics can cause them to lose their commitment to the community. I guess if I was there in a political office, I wouldn't be there long. I would bang out the gavel for the people. I could care less about making deals and getting re-elected.

The sad thing is to see things that you know are wrong, that should be addressed, and the powers that be know they are wrong and they should be addressed, but they leave them undone. That's the frustration. But because we work on many other issues, you keep your mental state focused. You keep hope alive. You go from issue to issue. If I get too frustrated, I go work on buying back guns or something else that I feel will better this community.

The people who work with me on these issues and I all walk side-by-side. These folks aren't followers. They would jump on an issue real quick. If we do a news conference, I don't always open the news conference. It might be Maddie Jones, it may be Dr. McMillan, or it may be George Edwards, my mentor at the Presbyterian Theological Seminary. I had to learn from watching others who have done news conferences and are in the forefront, to see how they dominate. All the attention is focused on them. I've learned if you are going to be halfway successful, people have to be used for the strength they bring to an issue. It also keeps criticism down, though we are open to constructive criticism. We are always looking for other ways to do things.

We were buying back guns and somebody wrote an article in *The Courier-Journal* saying, "We think it is a good idea that the Justice Resource Center is buying guns off the street, but some of these guns may have been involved in crimes in the community." I stopped immediately and tried to find a way to get these guns looked at by the officials.

But an official said to me, "Reverend, if you bring those guns in here, there is a state law that says they will have to sold back on the street." The state law was passed four years ago, when we were successful in our gun buy-back program. Somebody in the General Assembly from rural Kentucky wanted guns we bought back to be turned in to the state police department so they could be sold back to the public. I responded with an immediate, "NO!" The news media thought they had me. I responded, "I respect what this person wrote, but I will not have these guns put back in the community after I buy them. We will find a way to work this out."

I asked the police chief, "Why can't you bring your people here to the Justice Resource Center where we have the guns?" That's what he did. His people got around the table and inspected about 100 guns. After they inspected them and found none of them were involved in any crime, I was getting ready to destroy them, to take a hatchet to them. But instead we got in touch with a couple of artists who took the guns and made an art display out of them to send a message to this community that guns are a "NO."

You kind of grow as you continue to work on issues in the community. I get more satisfaction when I am pleasant and when I can be harmonious with people. I feel better, and it makes people around me feel better and more comfortable. I'm out of character when I have to bang my fist on the table. I'm out of character when I'm demanding.

I think if I had to do some things over again I would be more in tune with my own character. Many times I have had to over-compensate because of the laid-backness of Louisville. I've seen people go along to get along. You'll have two African-Americans on a jury of twelve and nine times out of ten they will not stand up and be that voice of dissent. They will go along with the rest of the jury. I've watched too many juries and it's a mindset in this community.

There are times when you have to be out of character to get your point across. I played organized baseball for 30 years, and I was on the Louisville Redbirds professional baseball team board for awhile. Baseball is a passion of mine. I'd rather go hit some baseballs than go to meetings. But when you get to be 61, you should have certain privileges. I just loved being on that Louisville Redbirds baseball committee and board. Then they built the new stadium and I saw it didn't impact local blacks or minorities, and I had to get out there and protest. We tried to work it out. We said, "This is not right." There wasn't any black contractor. It was business as usual.

What bothers me is these are the kind of issues that don't get better. I had to deal with David Karem on the Waterfront. I like David. He is my parents' lawyer. But we have to attack if it's not right. David is in the General Assembly.

When I am talking to people in Frankfort, David is an advocate there and a proponent of "let's get this thing right." Then when I look at what is going on in Louisville, it gives me some concern. When you have the facts, you have to stand up for what you believe is right. We have to over-compensate many times because of the laid-backness in the community.

On the 4th of July six years age, 12 of us got arrested at the PGA Golf Tournament. They were bringing in a few minorities from Chicago when the PGA could have easily encouraged minority participation here, and they didn't do it. The lady that was arresting me said, "My grandmother told me not to arrest you." I told her, "You do what you have to do." Out of that protest, the Urban League every year has benefited from the resources from the PGA — about $100,000, I believe, to do a youth golf program in the community.

The last Senior PGA golf tournament here spent $1,500 for minority participation by ordering some sandwiches from Jay's Cafeteria. I protested for five days at the tournament entrance. Not only did the Louisville Urban League benefit, Reverend Joe Lowery (Southern Christian Leadership Conference) and our agency worked together to get a person hired for the PGA now, whenever they go to other cities, to be a recruiter for women and minorities all across the country. I said to my friend Ernie, "I've got to educate the people, because you are misusing our community. You bring the PGA in here, the most prestigious golf tournament in the world, and then you don't benefit the community. That is asinine. What good does it do this community if you don't affect the community in an economic way?" We protested for five days against the Senior PGA tournament. We plan to meet with them again to discuss the Ryder's Cup.

The issues we are addressing will not be resolved overnight. You have to persevere. You have to stay on the case. You cannot be bought out. I hope the next generation in our community will not sell out. When you get frustrated, do something else. Get into some other venue, go to some other city. When I get frustrated in Louisville, there is no problem. I drive down to Paducah or Springfield to address some issues in those towns. There are enough issues around to last a lifetime.

I don't see Louisville getting better or the quality of life being raised, especially for the oppressed and the disenfranchised. I just see it getting worse. I see the hippy to bippy generation getting good jobs due to the many protests of the '60s, but many of them have forgotten to reach back.

Louisville is growing, and we are now dealing with a community that is besieged with drugs and crime.

But in our growing pains we need to address our issues. I just don't see the city addressing these issues. I was encouraged when I met with the Jefferson County Board of Education briefly this morning that Greater Louisville Inc. would be addressing this reading problem in Louisville. I believe reading is a core problem. Reading and poverty. Poverty is a serious problem in this community and the poor are all not black folk. I have seen some poor people in this community who would make your hair stand up. Some pockets of Louisville look like Eastern Kentucky. That really, really bothers me because many of them see no hope and see no light at the end of the tunnel.

I had to deal with this last killing that occurred in the Portland area last Sunday. I was coming back from Mayfield and before I went home, I went to that house, because one of our board members, Reverend Tennyson, who used to pastor Portland, called me. He said. "We need to get over to where this gentleman was killed." What is sad, besides someone dying, is to hear the family explain the situation. They said the woman should not have been there. They said she had more to do with the killing than the police officer did. Reverend Tennyson said the police chief said it was justifiable homicide. I said, "How can it be justifiable homicide when you haven't had time to investigate the situation?" I called Chief White up as soon as I got there. I said, "I am going to disagree with you. I'm going to write a letter to you and try to have a news conference to show that we support a longer and more detailed investigation."

Those people were poor and it didn't matter to that department. Poor black, poor white, poor Hispanics – when they get killed, it just doesn't seem to be a great issue of concern. That's when we took issue with the police chief, who is black. I can disagree with him and be agreeable with him, but the news media would not cover it. They will cover every black killing when we call a news conference, that never seems to fail. In fact they will call me, " Louis, are you going to do it?"

Yes, we are an African-American agency, I make no apology for that. But we will also stand up for a white person who was killed in this community if we feel an investigation was not done thoroughly. Nobody will report it though. I think they want to put agencies and individuals in a mold so the community will see them in a certain way. That's the only way I can figure it.

I think the city has to become more accountable to the people. I don't see the Metro Council men and women being accountable to the people. They are going to have to get into the trenches. They find an easy way out with the churches. They fix them with political money. The Board of Education is upset. The churches have tutoring programs and they are getting them from the politicians, but they are not bringing the students up to the standards.

What is the use in having a children's program if it doesn't bring the students' achievement levels up to the standards? When I looked at the standard achievement gap study done by the U.S. Department of Education, black kids are not even on the reading chart. Hispanic kids, bilingual kids, Asian kids are on the charts. African-American kids are not even on the chart.

I'm not being racist when I say African-American. When I go out with my Latino chapter in Owensboro, we're dealing with Latinos and I'm a Latino. They put me right in there because we think alike. When you hear me use that word African-American, or black, we have to make that distinction.

A church can't be confined to four walls. You have to go outside of the four walls. Believe it or not, most of the complaints I get are not from my church members. A member will come to me and say, "My pastor is not into that, Reverend. He doesn't believe in protesting, so we came to your agency, because you do that all year round." We don't mind taking those people in, but we need those same ministers to help us with our membership drive.

That's the only way to fund our program. When you get money from state government to do recruiting programs, you shouldn't bite the hand that feeds you in this state, but we did. We brought people to state government – African-American contractors and minority contractors, and they didn't hire them. We brought them to the door and they wouldn't let them drink. I criticized them. I found fault.

When we recruited 97 black police officers into the Louisville police department, they didn't hire those 97, so we filed a lawsuit. We didn't get contracts anymore from the city's finance department because we bit the hand that fed us – because our commitment to people was more important than our financial rewards.

I would advise the generation of leaders coming up behind us to listen. Listen and watch. If you listen long enough, the issue that you are dealing with will bring itself to the surface. I've gotten to the point in my ministry where I say very little at church meetings. I listen. I think people who work around me in our organization love to talk, and while they are talking, I'm listening. When you learn to listen and look, and you're dealing with people who want to be honest, you can work things out.

One frustrating thing I haven't yet mentioned is that there was a study done by the University of Louisville recently that found that 13 out of 27 of our judges were biased toward blacks when they did sentencing and bonding. I asked this committee, "What are you going to do about this?" Their response was "Nothing." Sitting next to me was Chief Justice Lambert.

I said, "Chief Justice, you see the issue here in Jefferson County. You have biased sentencing going on, according to the UofL survey." The commonwealth's attorney's office and some of the judges sitting around that table said, "Reverend Coleman, this report is not as accurate as it should be." They attacked the university professor who came up with the statistics. He had the facts, but the city will still look in a different direction. They feel more comfortable not admitting that they are wrong.

How can you grow as a great city if you don't admit that you have some problems? I admit I have some problems. That's how we grow. People do not admit their wrongdoing. Companies in Rubbertown do not admit that they are putting out toxic, health-harming chemicals. You can't get a corporate company manager to say our chemicals are harmful, even when the EPA says that they are carcinogenic. They are blaming the victim instead of dealing with the issue. This is very frustrating in this community, and it has to change if we want to grow.

Most of the young whites and blacks are saying until old Louisville becomes a younger Louisville in its decision-making process, this city will be bogged down. Young people in our community think things can happen overnight. When we ask for a commitment, the commitment is not always where it should be. You get a moment here and a moment there. Commitment means you have to hang in there whether the work is dirty or clean. Sometimes you don't get that from young people. There have been a lot of young fellows who say "Reverend, I want to do what you are doing." I say, "What is glamorous about this job? There's no pay, there are no benefits. Lots of people get mad at you, and it's not eight hours a day. It's a commitment, seven days a week."

Even though I am a pastor, I have learned to put God first, then my family, then the church, then this work. I spent more time on this work than I did on my family at one point, but I learned my lesson. I learned that my grandchildren are important. I had to remember that my mother and father were still living. It wasn't there at first. Civil rights took a priority. I had to learn. I had to learn that family has to be pushed right under God, and the church right behind that. The church can forsake you, but your family and God will still be there.

REVEREND KEVIN W. COSBY

Senior Pastor
St. Stephen Baptist Church

President
Simmons College of Kentucky

REV. KEVIN COSBY BECAME the pastor of St. Stephen Baptist Church in West Louisville in 1979. He was 21 years old at the time, and a student at Eastern Kentucky University. As the grandson of St. Stephen's beloved first pastor, Rev. B. J. Miller, he was invited to come home to take over the "little church on the corner" of Fifteenth and Kentucky Streets and he answered the call.

Over the 26 years he has been pastor, he has increased the church's membership from 300 to 9,000 members, and has overseen construction of a new 1,700-seat sanctuary in the church in Louisville and a 1,000-seat satellite church in Jeffersonville, Indiana. He has built a Family Life Center, a computer lab education center, a substance abuse recovery facility and a music conservatory.

Cosby and his father, Laken Cosby, who had a career in real estate and home construction, have built homes in the church's neighborhood for first-time home buyers. He has run gangs out of the area and attacked drugs, teenage pregnancy, violence and other problems challenging today's inner cities. His church has bought up liquor stores and nightclubs in the neighborhood and converted them into alcoholic rehab centers, homeless shelters, restaurants and other viable neighborhood businesses.

In 1998, Cosby converted the campus of the old Simmons University/ Louisville Municipal College at Seventh and Kentucky Streets in Louisville into St. Stephen's Lifestyle Enrichment Campus that gives youth, adults and the elderly a place to go for wholesome and supportive activities. To run all its ministries, the church employs more than 60 people from the low-income neighborhoods around the church.

He has hit a chord in West Louisville. He has built his congregation by preaching that people should move beyond a "victimization consciousness."

"I think the primary message I preach," he says, "is how Christ empowers us to be useful and productive, not weak and dependent."

Cosby now presides over Kentucky's largest African-American church and is a respected community leader, author and sought-after preacher and lecturer. He's also a strong proponent of education at all levels and, in April of 2005, he was offered an additional position – president of Simmons Bible College, now Simmons College of Kentucky. He plans to expand offerings and to attract secular as well as ministerial students to Simmons.

Kevin Cosby was born in West Louisville in 1958 and grew up at St. Stephen Church. His grandfather was St. Stephen's first pastor, his father was a deacon there, and his mother was music minister. He had to pass through the crucible of disparate, often conflicting cultures, however, before finding his own calling in the church of his youth.

His mother died when he was a teenager, and his father – who was a businessman and later a member of the Jefferson County Board of Education – moved him and his sister to a new home in eastern Jefferson County. The younger Cosbys entered Waggener High School and, as the only two black pupils in the school at that time, life sometimes proved challenging for them.

After ultimately graduating from Ballard High School, Cosby earned a history degree from Eastern Kentucky University. While in school, he served as an assistant to the pastor of the First Baptist Church of Richmond and as founding president of the Madison County National Association of Colored Persons. He also met his future wife, Barnetta, there. They married and now have two children.

Cosby sought an interim pastor's position at St. Stephen after that, and was soon asked to take the pulpit as senior pastor. He later earned a master's degree from the Southern Baptist Theological Seminary in Louisville, and a doctorate of ministry in African-American church studies from United Theological Seminary in Dayton, Ohio.

Although he assumed the reins of St. Stephen at the very young age of 21, Cosby has risen to become one of the most powerful and influential leaders in his community and in the Commonwealth of Kentucky.

He is pleased with his life overall, he says, and is delighted that he finally found his calling in the ministry.

"If I had ten lifetimes, I wouldn't want to do anything else but pastor," he said in a *Business First* profile in 2000. "I believe strongly in evangelism, seeing people connected to God. When we're connected to God on a vertical level, life falls into place on a horizontal level."

Passing the Torch

I WAS BROUGHT TO ST. STEPHEN CHURCH as a child. My maternal grandfather, Dr. Benjamin Miller, was the first senior pastor of the church, so my mother was reared in St. Stephen Church. My parents were both influential members of the congregation — my father was a deacon and my mother was music minister — so I was reared in St. Stephen Church as well.

I always dreamed of one day becoming a preacher, a minister. My grandfather was quite influential in my life. He was my childhood role model. He was a man of great pride and tremendous scholarship. Among other things, he was the first African-American to graduate from the Southern Baptist Theological Seminary in the 1950s.

Leadership has been a family tradition on both sides of my family. My grandfather came to Louisville at the age of 22, unable to read or write. He came from Peyton Town, Kentucky in Madison County to get an education, and he had to start in elementary school. I have a picture of him — at age 22, with other adults — in elementary school.

He had such a passion for education that he attended Simmons University, which was a major black university in Louisville and one of the premier universities in the South at that time. For 50 years, it pre-dated Kentucky State as the school of education for the state. It had a medical school, a law school and a seminary.

In the 1940s, during segregation, there was a law that prohibited African-Americans and whites from attending school together during the day. My grandfather could attend the seminary, but he had to sit in the hallway or take a class in the teacher's office. He could not sit with the regular students. But his passion for education did not let him get discouraged. He overcame all of those insults, got his education, and graduated with an A average. There now is a scholarship in his name and honor at Southern Baptist Theological Seminary.

When St. Stephen Church was formed, they were looking for a minister. The president of the school, Dr. C.H. Perry, sent my grandfather over and St. Stephen hired him to be the first pastor of this church.

An African-American who was the first to graduate from a prestigious institution like Southern Seminary was held in high esteem. My grandfather was held in high esteem, not only by St. Stephen's parishioners, but throughout the community. He was also a professor at Simmons Bible College.

I looked up to him, and I always wanted to be a minister. I played basketball for awhile at Ballard High School and remember one of the coaches saying, "If you can't put basketball above everything else, then you won't be successful in basketball." My passion was basketball. But in the back of my mind was the God question: "Should basketball come before faith?" I don't know if I resolved the question when I was playing JV basketball, but the fact that the issue came up in my mind is very important to me. The seed had been planted.

Reverend Kevin W. Cosby

For me, the call of God to be a servant was more important than basketball. I always wanted to be a minister, and believe it or not, I always dreamed of one day becoming a pastor of the church of my childhood. Most kids were playing cowboys and Indians, Batman and Robin. One of our favorite games was playing church. One of my sisters would serve as a deacon in our church, one of my sisters would serve as a choir member, and I was always the preacher. They would bring monopoly money and give it as tithes and offerings and I would baptize their dolls. I always wanted to be a minister, always.

The pivotal institution in the black community, historically and presently, is the church. The church is the mother of all of our institutions. It gives birth to so much in our community. Clergy persons are held in high esteem in the black community. As a minister, I have an opportunity not only to impact the spiritual lives and spiritual development of the people, but to have impact on economic development, politics. The church and its ministry covers the whole gamut of issues important in life.

John Maxwell is probably one of the greatest authorities on leadership. He defines leadership as influence. It's not position-holding, it's influencing people. I wanted St. Stephen Church to be a leader in the sense that I wanted our church to be influential and to make a difference in our community and in the lives of people. That is something we intentionally wanted to do.

All leadership is born out of crisis. Our leadership was born from the pressing needs in our community. There was a survey done on the most popular presidents in U.S. history and the most popular presidents were George Washington, Abraham Lincoln and Franklin D. Roosevelt. It is interesting that these were all men who gave leadership during times of crisis. George Washington, the American Revolution; Lincoln, the Civil War; and FDR, the Depression. The crises gave birth to leaders.

In our community, there are crises. The crisis of the breakdown of the family, the crisis of African-American males, the high rates of incarceration, the high crime rate in our community, the gap in educational performance between black kids and white kids. These are crises. Just like tea gets activated in hot water, leadership gets activated at a time of crisis. All leadership emerges as a result of a desire to affect the crises we are experiencing in the community.

The church is only the church when it exists for others. Whenever the church becomes a self-serving institution, it is no longer the church. We have been commissioned by Christ to be the salt of the earth and the light of the world, so we want to have an impact beyond our parishioners, on the local community. We have always been mission-minded.

I came to St. Stephen Church in 1979 at a time when the church was declining and the community was transitioning. Success meant leaving the California community. It was also a time when the church was dead broke because one of our members had embezzled some money from our church.

When I arrived here, the church itself was a solid, stable church, but it had declining membership. I think we had 400 on the roll, and we would see half of them at our services. Twenty-five years later, we are close to 9,000.

True leaders are people who are willing to face reality. You cannot fix what you do not face. True leaders always want to know the facts. As painful as the facts may be, as frightening as the facts may be, you need to know them. The congregation didn't know all the facts so I had to share them in a meeting one day. They rallied around the vision I cast.

Before I could develop the congregation though, I had to first develop myself. Leaders are always developing. Whenever you stop developing as a leader you stop leading. So I developed myself by going to Southern Baptist Theological Seminary. I enrolled in the Masters of Divinity Program and I worked hard and studied to become a more competent pastor.

Leadership, finances, I had to learn it all. I grew as a person. I exposed myself to out-of-the-box thinking. I was not restricted to the black Baptist tradition. I also wanted to learn from outstanding white pastors. I wanted to learn from Korean pastors. I wanted to learn from business leaders who were not pastors. I wanted to learn from philosophers. I was open to learn as much as I could. I developed, and people lit matches from the fire that I generated.

I did a lot of reading. I exposed myself to successful models. For example, I think the impetus behind our church is something that most black churches don't emphasize, and that is Sunday School. I went to Houston, Texas and saw a model of a church that was growing through Sunday School. I was taught how to do Christian Sunday School development in seminary, but it wasn't a priority because in the black church, the priority is worship. Preaching, singing, worship – we are a worship center. White southern Baptist churches tend to be Sunday School-centered and they grow their churches through small groups in Sunday School. I saw that model and I embraced it, and I adapted it to meet the black church experience. The church took off in 1986 as a result of that. It was the turning point of our church.

We broke the church down into small groups. Not only was there bible study, but there was fraternity and fellowship and mission projects and evangelism. People started inviting their friends to come to their Sunday School class to participate in church activities. The Sunday School grew as a result of it, and the church itself grew large very quickly.

We went to two services, and that still didn't accommodate all the people who attended. People would come and stand around the walls of the church because there was no room to sit down. It was phenomenal.

Today we have five weekend services. We have a 6:00 p.m. Saturday night service. We have an 8:00 a.m. service, a 9:40 a.m. service, and we have a service in Southern Indiana because we created a church in Southern Indiana three-and-a-half years ago. We have a 10:45 a.m. service there, then we have an 11:30 a.m. service here. We still try to have Sunday School, but it's very difficult to have a strong Sunday School when you have multiple services.

In the 1980s, St. Stephen became the first African-American church in the state to build a Family Life Center. Family Life Centers are now popping up all across the states in African-American churches. We were the first, and we were criticized initially. We said we wanted to have a seven-day-a-week ministry that would serve people holistically, like the Catholics do. So we built a Family Life Center and we opened it up to the community. We try to serve the community by offering recreation and family-oriented activities.

My role in the Family Life Center was to cast the vision, help people buy into the vision and to generate the revenue to finance the vision. I helped secure the land to build it as well, because when I came here the church was land-locked and broke.

My first mentor, as I said, was my grandfather, Dr. Benjamin Miller Sr. I just adored him and it was because of him that I wanted to be a minister. During my teenage years, I was mentored by my uncle, Rev. Charles Mims Jr. He was a student of my grandfather, an uncle by marriage, and pastor of Centennial Olivet Baptist Church, a prominent church here in Louisville. I lived with him in my senior year of high school. He taught me so much about ministry and how to present myself as a minister. He was quite influential.

Three other men influenced my life. One of them was Dr. Mack King Carter. He was a minister and a pastor in this community and he really helped me appreciate the black church experience. Rev. Michael Cunningham gave me a greater appreciation for bible preaching, and Rev. Andrew Carnegie Goodloe was a 90-year-old man who gave me practical experience in ministry.

I learned preaching methodology from a local pastor whom I still hold in high esteem and respect, Rev. A. Russell Awkard. He really influenced my preaching style, probably more than anyone. He is the pastor of New Zion Baptist Church here. I emulated his style, his energy, his charisma, his reckless abandon when it comes to preaching. I would listen to him preach and try to talk like him, walk like him. I incorporated so much of him into Kevin Cosby that my wife teases me.

She will say, "I can tell when you preach and when A. Russell Awkard kicks in," which is a compliment because of the respect I have for that man.

To prepare for preaching each week I study, study, study. I try to prepare my sermons months in advance because basically I have two responsibilities: I have to prepare fresh new sermons every weekend and we have a major mid-week service. One of our largest services meets on Wednesday night – 1700 people. So I have to get ready for that.

I try to use the Bible to preach on life-related topics. I don't think people are really concerned about who wrote the Book of Revelations or who wrote Genesis. People are more concerned about what the Bible has to say about relationships; what the Bible has to say about their private pain; what the Bible has to say about child-rearing; what the Bible has to say about financial freedom and how to get out of debt; what the Bible has to say about their anger, their fears, their grudges, their addictions, their self-defeating behavior.

Someone very wise once said that a preacher should have the newspaper in his left hand and the bible in his right-hand to make sure that the bible relates to current events. And that is what I tend to do with my preaching and teaching style. I take the Bible in one hand and the issues that people are dealing with in the other hand and create a nexus between the two.

I will address community-related issues during the course of my sermon on occasion, but our ministry and programs of the church also speak to the needs of the community.

I think my father was the driving force in my life who instilled in me the importance of education and hard work. My biological mother passed when I was 11 years old. My father's parents always stressed education. My father was the first in his family to graduate from high school and college on either side. He came from Alabama, and he was behind academically, but he had a passion for learning and getting an education. He graduated from high school and went on to get a bachelor's degree from the University of Louisville.

Both he and my biological mother expressed to our family the importance of education. My three sisters and I not only graduated from high school, but each of us graduated from college. One of my sisters went on to get a doctoral degree. Another sister is an attorney. Education was stressed in our home.

When my mother died, we moved from West Louisville to eastern Jefferson County and my sister and I went from the Jackson Five to the Osmond Brothers, from the Temptations to Three Dog Night. We had been in an isolated black community. My whole world was black. The only thing I knew about the white community was what I had seen on television, because all my friends were black, my total experience was black.

Reverend Kevin W. Cosby

The church I went to was black, my neighborhood was black, my school was all black. I had some white friends who lived in my neighborhood but for the most part, they were black also, culturally speaking. Everything I knew was black until my mother died, and we moved to eastern Jefferson County.

I went to Waggener Junior High School at age 11 or 12. My sister and I were the only blacks except for the janitors. We moved to Mallgate Apartments and were the only blacks in the apartment complex. It was culture shock.

It was a difficult, difficult transition. Getting to know other students' culture and getting them to know my culture was very difficult. I would not be who I am today, however, if I had not had that experience because it helped me at an early age think beyond the black community. It exposed me to so much that I never would have been exposed to in an exclusively segregated society.

There were other leadership people who were influential in my life. My father and my mother were the spiritual foundation in my life, but I also had a stepmother. My father remarried a woman, Connie Bussey, and I am blessed to have two mothers whom I adored – my biological mother and my intellectual and spiritual mother, Connie Bussey – because she stressed the importance of my becoming culturally diversified. As painful as it was, she expanded my world beyond the world that maybe my mother could not have exposed me to. Being exposed to a multi-cultural experience was very good for me. It expanded my vocabulary, it expanded my cultural horizons. It was difficult at times, though, because we are talking about the early '70s.

When my father moved us to the East End, we were the only blacks in the Mallgate apartment complex. Racism was overt. I remember once I was swimming at the Mallgate pool and a white guy who was drunk pushed me into 12 feet of water. He made me tread water, and every time I tried to swim back to the edge of the pool, he would put me back in the middle of the water and would not let me come to the edge of the pool until I said some self-deprecating things about myself. I was out there treading water and he said, "Call yourself a nigga, call yourself a nigga, call yourself a nigga." I wasn't going to do it and I was crying. I would swim to the other side of the pool and he would run over and wouldn't let me get to the edge of the pool. Finally I gave in and called myself that name and he finally left me alone. That hurt me so bad, because he lived in the same apartment complex. But what hurt me more was the lifeguard later came to me and said, "Kid, I'm sorry that happened to you." That let me know he knew what was taking place and didn't do anything.

It was a very, very, painful experience. In fact, it hurts even now when I re-live it. But there were others in the community – other whites – who treated me humanely, so that was not my only experience.

When I want to get bitter, I say, "Wait a minute. What about a white guy named Guy Tucker who was at Waggener? His father took me and two other kids to a University of Kentucky football game. He took me to the game, paid my ticket, took me over to his house and was so nice to me. I have looked in the phone book to try to find Guy Tucker because I want to say thank you.

There was also a guy named Gary Davis, who played on the basketball team with me at Waggener. His dad would pick me up and take me to the basketball game. Ron Spencer was a star basketball player at Waggener and was a brother to me. Jamie Carrico, other whites. A guy named Sydney Baxter was the principal at Waggener. He was a white man who took a special interest in me. An art teacher, I forgot her name, took a special interest in me. In fact, when I was at St. Matthews Baptist Church, the pastor told me about a woman at the church named Mrs. Baxter. I later found out it was her husband Sydney, who is deceased now, who befriended me back in the early '70s at Waggener and welcomed me. I thought, "My God, no wonder he did, he was an active Christian and I didn't know he was a member of this church."

The point I am making is that as painful as that experience was in the swimming pool, it was countered by so many whites of goodwill who went out of their way to let me know that I am okay. I try to dwell on that. There is a dog in all of us that wants to be bitter. There is another animal that takes the high road. Instead of being bitter, be better. Those two animals are both pulling us. I can be bitter about this, but I can be better when I think about those who have helped me. The animal that wins is whichever animal we feed.

I try to feed the memories of all the wonderful people who did so many wonderful things for me. How blessed I was to have these people in my life. How blessed I was to have a stepmother who stressed to me the multi-cultural experience and who did not let me give up.

I've told young people these stories to make points about not giving up, and to be careful about what side of your nature you feed.

I'm a risk-taking leader. A risk-taking leader is not afraid to be controversial if he has a conviction about something. We were pioneers in building the Family Life Center and now others are building Family Life Centers. We were pioneers in developing a church in the black community through Sunday School, and now others are using the Sunday School model. We pioneered the importance of appreciating and celebrating the African-American culture. We pioneered the work in Southern Indiana. We are the first black church to have two churches in different states. So I have always been a risk taker. I believed that it was the right thing to do and I have not been afraid to go against the grain, or conditional thinking, and to be the trendsetter. I think people would see my leadership as wise, creative, innovative and risk-taking.

I think I have the type of leadership that stresses the importance of excellence. If you are going to do a thing, do it with excellence. I believe in empowering people and entrusting other people. I don't like lax people.

I develop future leaders and leaders around me. In order to achieve success, it takes more than one person. There is no such thing as solo success. Leaders have to give birth to other leaders.

Every congregation has generals, lieutenants, sergeants. Generals are those who are self-motivated or gifted, who have committed themselves to you. Lieutenants are those who are gifted, who are visionary. They have not yet proven themselves, but have potential for leadership. Sergeants are those who are committed, dedicated, but are less gifted than a lieutenant or a general. Then you have a fourth group – privates. Privates are those who have a nine to five mentality. They do just enough to get by. You have AWOLs too – those are the people who do nothing. You have snipers, and those are the people who will hurt you if they have a chance. You can only build a strong organization with generals, lieutenants and sergeants. I try to surround myself with generals, lieutenants and sergeants and use them to develop the ministry of this church.

You also have VIP's – very important people; VTP's – very teachable people; and VDP's – very draining people. You build strong organizations with VIP's and VTP's. Many times, leaders make the mistake of wasting a lot of time on very draining people and they have no emotional resources for the VIP's and the VTP's. I try to focus on the VIP's and VTP's.

You learn how to deal with people through experience and study, but most importantly, through experience.

I can't express enough how important it is for leaders to know the facts, face the facts and be willing to make hard, tough decisions. That's leadership.

I think my most significant accomplishment has been the growth of St. Stephen Church. People were willing to become a part of this church that grew from a little facility into one of the largest black churches in the South.

I've had a few failures, however. I guess my biggest one occurred during a period in which I was too confrontational with some traditions in the black community. There was a great controversy in the '90s around school desegregation, and I took a position publicly that I should not have taken and I regret that now. Not because it was right or wrong. The media portrayed me as something I was not, and at that time, I was naive about the media. I learned the hard way that when you make a statement or talk to people in the media, it doesn't necessarily mean that what you say is going to be communicated correctly in a newspaper article or on television.

Louisville Magazine often features me or the church as one of the leaders in the community. But just for a brief period of time, I didn't understand how the media works and I regret that. I learned to be very careful about what I say and to whom, and to be careful that I don't allow others to control my image or to control how others perceive me.

There were also times when I should have been more decisive. I've kept people around whom I wanted to carry just because of friendship, or because I didn't feel good about letting them go, and I probably should have let them go much earlier.

There were times when I was thinking small when I should have been thinking much larger. When we were first building the Family Life Center, I said, "All we can build is a half gym." One of my staff members said, "Why are you thinking so small? Build a full court gym in the Center." We did.

I expect my followers to be committed to me as a person. I expect them to understand the important role I play, as senior pastor, in the development of the church and to have concern about me, my family, my wife and my kids. I expect them to be committed to the vision and to help enhance the vision so the vision can constantly be re-cast. That is what I expect from followers.

My followers and I are constantly in dialogue about what we should be doing. We try to improve upon our annual events, and they constantly help me cast the vision. They helped cast the vision for this Family Life Center, and they supported it and were advocates of the programs of the Family Life Center.

They helped me with the goal and the vision of Southern Indiana. We have a major campus now, and it is growing by leaps and bounds. We talk and share ideas, and they bring ideas to me as well.

If I could do anything differently, I would probably not have emotionally invested so much of my time with draining people. I also would not have taken things so personally when people didn't see the vision and wanted to leave. Everyone is not going to buy into a leader's vision. So when people don't see the vision and want to leave, instead of taking it personally or trying to convince them to stay, it is better to let them leave to make room for somebody who does buy into the vision. It's hard, because you personally invest in people, especially in this setting, much more than in a business setting.

I would advise young people aspiring to leadership to find out, and to be clear about, what it is they want to do and be. Then once they know what it is they want to be and what they want to do with their life, they should study and learn everything they can about it and surround themselves with people in that area who can help coach and mentor them.

I was blessed. At every point in my life, coaches were there. I needed them and they needed me. My uncle, for example, was an alcoholic who needed me because I was helping him. I helped him go to AA when I was 17 years old. I found someone at AA and introduced my uncle to AA to get him help.

Rev. Goodloe was a mentor when I was a student at Eastern Kentucky University. He was 90 years old and pastor for a Baptist church. He needed a young man and I needed an older mentor.

Michael Cunningham married my sister, and helped me appreciate Bible preaching. A. Russell Awkard, whom I patterned my preaching after, invited me to come on staff right before I became a pastor at St. Stephen Church, so I got to be around here and a relationship developed.

I loved Dr. Martin Luther King Jr. I read King. I read Malcolm X. I read Booker T. Washington, W.E.B. DuBois. I tried to synthesize, I guess the term is "collectivize," the tradition of King and the self-empowering traditions.

There are two traditions in the black community. One is the tradition of Martin Luther King Jr., W.E.B. DuBois, Frederick Douglass, and that is social justice, the change of society. The second is the tradition of self-help and personal empowerment — of Marcus Garvey, Malcolm X and Martin Delany. I try to live the two traditions of social injustice and personal empowerment together. You personally empower yourself by coming to know who you are and what gifts you possess that you have not maximized. Pastors who are excelling are those who are trying to take the best of the traditions and weave them together.

As a church member, I think the faith community in Louisville has done a tremendous job. It is shaping the character of the community. The foundation of personal success is character. By character I mean the heart and mind, knowing right from wrong, and having the will to choose the right over the wrong. Churches in the black community have set the tone.

I am part of the local ministry coalition and I have a great network. I am a member of the local Central District Baptist Association, and of a state body called the General Association of Kentucky Baptists. I am a member of these organizations and participate to try to help them reach their goals.

Finding viable jobs for people is one of our community's biggest challenges and it pains me to see so many people in our community hopeless and not knowing what to do. The unemployment rate in our community is so high. Part of the problem is that even when jobs come, you must have certain skills to obtain those jobs and you don't obtain the skill levels if you don't prioritize education and academics.

Character education is vital for our neighborhoods. It will teach the importance of studying, and will instill the kinds of values in people to give them employable skills.

Creation of jobs and creation of employable people is the greatest challenge our city faces, in my opinion, and it is going to take everybody working together to overcome those two problems. The business community, the faith community, and our educational systems have to work together to solve this problem. Educational systems can't do their jobs if the faith community doesn't do the job of teaching values. If you don't value education, you won't study your math. So the faith community can go a long way toward assisting youth.

We have a program in our church called "Dare to be Great." We get the kids at St. Stephen to embrace five core values:

"G" – Get connected to a faith-based institution where you can get good values. Come around the church. Kids who attend church do better than kids who do not attend church. Kids who come to church are less likely to get pregnant, less likely to have problems with judicial systems, less likely to drop out of school. It is an empirical fact, regardless of your faith base. Even if you are an atheist, you cannot negate the church as a positive influence on kids. That was the whole importance behind George Bush's faith-based initiative, which first started under Clinton. Bush has expanded it and emphasized it more, but Clinton first emphasized faith-based institutions, because the data showed that the way you could overcome predatory behavior is by getting kids into church. Studies showed that where there is a high concentration of liquor stores in a neighborhood in the black community, crime increases. The same studies have discovered that kids who attend church are less likely to have some of the problems associated with urban life. So "G" stands for "get connected to a faith-based institution."

"R" – Remain in school and get a good education.

"E" – Eliminate all behavior that gets you in trouble with the police.

"A" – Accept an honorable job to become acclimated to work culture.

"T" – Teenage pregnancy prohibits blacks from being able to accomplish many things.

Embracing those five core values is the track toward success. Our goal in our institution is to shut the highway from West Louisville to Eddyville, LaGrange and Pewee Valley. We want to create new highways from West Louisville to the University of Louisville, Western Kentucky University, Bellarmine University, Eastern Kentucky University. That is our goal – to build highways to those institutions that prepare kids for life.

All we have to do is look at what is on the highway from West Louisville to Eddyville or LaGrange, and you will find that on the highway are kids who are not in church; kids who get pregnant or are teenage parents; kids who have had trouble with school and who would not prioritize education.

We want to shut those highways down. Individual choice determines what people will become tomorrow.

I have learned a lot of lessons in my life that I would like to share with the next generation. First, that the key to success is discipline. Anyone who is successful as a leader or in any other endeavor in life is a person who has incorporated discipline. By discipline I mean delayed gratification; saying no when you want so desperately to say yes, or saying yes when you want so desperately to say no.

For example, I want so desperately to eat everything I see over the Christmas holiday, but my discipline says no. There are times when I don't want to get on that treadmill to stay in shape. My discipline says "Yes" to the treadmill when my body says, "You are tired." To succeed in life, you must have discipline.

Secondly, I would advise the next generation that there is another very important component to success and that is preparation. Success happens when preparation meets opportunity. If an opportunity is there, but you are not prepared to meet it, you will not be successful.

Sometimes opportunities are limited for some reason. For my father's generation, it was because of race. Fortunately, those opportunities that were restricted for my father are available for our generation. Sometimes you can't do anything to create an opportunity but you can do something to get ready for it, and to prepare yourself for it.

You also have choice about what you are going to do and who you are going to be. No one can make you do anything. I think instilling that message – that you do not have to be a victim – is important. What makes a person poor is not money, not address, not zip code. What makes a person poor is not having values and dreams. If you are living in a shotgun house in the California community but have aspirations and values, you won't be in that shotgun house all your life. You will move up.

True wealth is knowledge. True wealth is values. When you have those things, you are wealthy. If we give our young people their true wealth, they will be successful.

STEPHEN W. DAESCHNER

**Superintendent
Jefferson County Public Schools**

STEPHEN DAESCHNER IS A SELF-PROCLAIMED "DATA WONK" who gets high marks for dedication to children and belief in the possibilities of education. He wants children to learn, and he collects large amounts of information to determine whether they are learning. If the numbers are not there, he changes the way things are done to get them there. He has one goal: to help kids learn and achieve.

In his last job as superintendent of schools in Cedar Rapids, Iowa, and in his current position as superintendent of Jefferson County Public Schools, he had one sentence inscribed on the backs of the name plates of school board members: "How does this decision affect kids?"

Daeschner has been head of the Louisville system – the 28th-largest in the country, with 97,000 students – for 12 years. The average tenure for a superintendent in an urban school system is about three years. His tenure has not been without controversy, however. He had a difference of opinion, for example, with state education officials over installation in Jefferson County of a computer system compatible with the state's. Daeschner said the changeover would cost a lot of money and make the Jefferson County system less useful to Jefferson County. He is working hard to get it done.

He gets praise for early childhood education programs and all-day kindergarten, which he pushed through the year he arrived in 1993, and for boosting literacy and overall achievement among students. In its latest evaluation of Daeschner, the Jefferson County Board of Education praised his performance in increasing professional development for teachers, creating a literacy initiative that aims to get all students reading up to grade level in four years, and maintaining an effective level of student services in the face of difficult economic times.

Daeschner believes strongly that when high-achieving students mix with other students in a classroom, both groups perform better. He taught a ninth-grade biology class at Cedar Rapids that had been set up to include gifted and average students and some with learning disabilities. He told the brighter students that to earn A's, they'd have to make sure the slower learners earned B's. Except for one student, they did.

He argues vigorously against parents taking children out of public schools and putting them in private ones. "I can educate any child in this district as well as or better than any private or Catholic or any other school," he told *Louisville Magazine* in 1995. "I'm sending kids to Stanford, to Yale, to Harvard...with an incredible understanding of diversity."

Daeschner is credited with making Jefferson County Public Schools one of the most racially integrated school systems in the nation. He also created a "no expulsion" policy and has established a wide range of alternative schools to serve students with varying strengths and needs.

He is perhaps most passionate, however, about expanding early childhood education programs and increasing the public's understanding about the importance of a child's early years. "We cannot afford to lose the war," he said in a *Business First* article in 1993. "Our kids are our future."

Stephen Daeschner was born in Hiawatha, Kansas in 1942. He earned a bachelor's degree in physics and mathematics at Baker University in Baldwin, Kansas, and a master's degree in secondary education at Kansas State University, intent at that point on becoming a coach. But he taught four years in California and did research in Oregon and decided he would like to become a school administrator instead.

In 1972, after he earned a doctorate in Educational Administration from the University of Wisconsin, he served as principal of a school for the deaf in Washington D.C. He directed research, evaluation and planning at the St. Louis Public Schools for four years, then moved to an assistant deputy superintendent's job in Anchorage, Alaska. He was deputy superintendent in Anchorage and superintendent in Cedar Rapids before recruiters hired by the board of education lured him to Louisville.

Daeschner has been active in the Louisville community as well. He has served on boards and committees of Greater Louisville Inc., the Louisville Science Center, Junior Achievement, the Bell Awards, the Fund for the Arts, the Greater Louisville Economic Development Partnership, the Community Health Alliance, the Louisville Downtown Development Corporation, the Muhammad Ali Center and many others.

He and his wife, Stacy, have two children, and he has two adult children from a previous marriage. He also has two grandchildren.

I NEVER NOMINATED MYSELF to become a community leader in Louisville. I was recruited to come here, to become the superintendent of the Jefferson County Public Schools. I wasn't interested in the position at first. I was already a superintendent of schools in another community. The recruiter said, "Just go look." So I came and looked. My wife and I liked what we saw in the community, and we liked the interview process. We had a chance to meet with the Jefferson County judge-executive and the mayor at the time, and our discussions progressed. The community leaders, the board of education and I all agreed that it was a good fit at that time, so I agreed to come to Louisville.

We are all in the people business. The people we work with are why we come to work every day. When you add working with super-altruistic, motivated colleagues to that and the desire to do it is deep inside you, it all fits.

My job is all about influencing and working with kids. If I didn't believe that down to my soul, I would have problems. I spend hours investigating ideas, thoughts and methodologies that will help a child learn. I'm interested in both cognitive and affective learning. Our number one customers are our students. I am extremely happy with what our school district is doing to enhance kids' education.

I consider everyone I encounter to be a mentor. Usually when you think of mentors you think of someone who has coached you, but I think all people are mentors in the truest sense. Many people have driven me, but two people who have particularly been strong mentors to me come to mind.

I had an uncle who grew up on a farm who let me go to the field to plow. That's a very hard task at the age of 12. It's before you have a driver's license, before you can really reach the pedals. He put me on a tractor and said, "I want you to go plow the south 40 that's a mile away and I'll see you at noon." Well you wouldn't think he could do that, but he did. People like my uncle, who just allow you to do things, bring things out of you and help you grow.

I have worked with some superintendents who were excellent. One was John Peper, a former superintendent in Anchorage, Alaska, who hired me to be his deputy. John was the brightest educator I have ever encountered, even to this day. I would sit down and talk with him and he had insights.

I have also read some great books that have inspired me. Jim Collins' *Good to Great* is so right on, for example. The whole systems approach that W. Edwards Deming uses is true. It is not about the person, it is about the system. The system is always the problem. These people are mentors I have never met.

Peter Senge with *Fifth Discipline* is another author who is an influential mentor. These people are all influences. We are all influenced by what we hear, see, and feel.

Just yesterday, I was having a conversation with a principal and he said, "Boy, these people are very much in compliance, but they are not committed." Well that is a powerful statement – "in compliance but not committed." You have heard of form over substance? Well you don't forget a powerful thought like that. You ask "How can I use it?"

So if you ever ask me who I would go to for advice, I would say there is not any one person. I would borrow bits and pieces from a lot of different people, books and situations.

My leadership style is situational. I don't think there are any two situations that are alike. The people you work with probably determine your true leadership style. Some people I work with would describe me as "that damn tyrant," or they would say I am "too democratic" or "too autocratic" or they would say I "favor." That's the way it ought to be. Every situation is different. As a leader, you need to understand a situation and find the right people to assist you in that situation. Some you will find quiet, others more dictatorial; but it will depend on the situation. I think I would question people who think they have an actual leadership style. It's all situational.

I've been the superintendent of public schools here in Louisville for 12 years. The average stay of a superintendent is five years, probably two and a half years in urban districts. I've had some difficulties with the school board over the years, but I've had staying power.

It's important to try to understand what is motivating people and to try to understand them better by asking good questions. You need to question and listen before you get too deep into a situation because that will drive a situation as much as anything.

You also need to have a good grasp of a situation you are going into. I'm a data person, so I like to study a situation first, then to go in, pose questions, and listen.

I had situations like this already twice this morning. I had two principals in my office who I thought were better principals than their performance data showed. The data said they were not getting it, but I perceived that their knowledge base was a lot better. We had long conversations about that.

One reacted wonderfully. I said "This is the data, this is where I got it, this is what you can do, this is the way I perceive it. I haven't been in your school recently, so I don't know." She said, "You're right." Then I said, "Now what are you going to do? Do you need help?" She said, "Well yes I might." Then I said, "Here's where to go to get it."

The other principal wanted to make excuses through his kids. I said, "Well it's interesting that your population is no different than this other school's. How come their scores are higher? I can't get around it. The data shows you are not teaching content in science, in math, and in writing." He said, "Well I think we are doing it." Then I said, "Well you can't be and have these scores — it's inconsistent."

We have a system in place. What we do is look at data and determine how and how closely a school needs to be monitored. I take a team of six people in to the school for two days to look at everything going on. If it is more severe, then I send a team of individuals in to monitor the results of that school on a weekly or monthly basis. Everybody's now familiar with the system and the lingo. A dialogue, a monitoring, a weekly, no dialogue — that is our system.

As superintendent of schools, I serve more constituents than most — legislative mandates, parents, teachers, unions, my board and, of course, my students. For every group, there is a counter group or a pressure group in our district. Many of the attacks appear to be personal, but when you step back you realize that the attack was really about the system. The problems are usually not personal; they are about the system. Once I understand that, I can deal with an issue a lot better because I believe the system can improve.

Change is always hard, and we've had a lot of change at JCPS. Some has worked and some hasn't. I have worked in smaller districts where it has been much easier to get faster change. The larger the district, the slower the change, and I am not a patient individual. I have to work longer to achieve things here. It takes a great deal of patience and focus. I just have to talk the talk, walk the walk, and stay focused.

I think my greatest accomplishment as superintendent has been student achievement. We have been fortunate that we have been able to measure it. That makes all the difference in the world. It's a huge goal, but it's one of our main drives. We have had a lot of successes.

We have certainly had success with our early childhood endeavors. We have had the right curriculum, the right pedagogy, and the right testing system. What you test is what you will get. We may actually over-test in this district. It has been a long process and it's been hard. The teachers fight it a little bit. They say, "If I am testing, I am not teaching." My answer is, "If you're testing, you are teaching." You have to inspect what you respect.

Successes are also born from partnerships, in my opinion. Partnerships are about win-win. In my position, everything is about a partnership. We may be collaborating with the teacher's union, or we may be collaborating with the YMCA to create a success for every second grader who swims.

We may create a partnership with the mayor to do a particular program. We also partner with universities in many ways. We try to go into every partnership so it's a win-win for everyone.

Our bottom line is always student achievement. Everything else is ancillary. In 30 years, it could be that our most significant success story will be that we took 4,000 kids in one year and got them to be better readers. Before, they were below their reading level and now, they are reading at grade level or above.

It happens very consciously. We put the right leaders in place and find the right curriculum, the right pedagogy, the right in-service, the right assessment, and the right system that gets them quality educators. It combines to create the right outcome. We can examine it on another layer and discuss why that particular curriculum works and what we had to do to get there. We spent months adopting what we thought would be a better reading curriculum that was prescriptive, web-based, and goes deeper and deeper.

The vision for all of it comes from narrowing, focusing and thinking. Notice the words I use. Everybody in the district knows we are about seven systems: planning, leadership, assessment, curriculum and instruction, school culture, organization, and professional development. The vision or focus comes from many individuals' sitting around brainstorming about what we need to get there and what's the driving force, then doing it and sticking with it.

I have made some huge mistakes along the way. Seven years ago, I really believed that our curriculum was not prescriptive enough: teach this, within this time frame, like this. A group of naysayers said that was bull, "Teach me how to fish, then turn me loose and I'll fish."

What I was saying was "I am going to give you the fish." The naysayers said "No, just teach me how to do it, then let my creative nature take over." There was a huge number of naysayers seven or eight years ago who said "No, let's just teach people. We don't have to give them the curriculum, we don't have to give them the pedagogy, let's just teach them." I knew seven or eight years ago that I did not feel comfortable with that, and I did not touch it for three or four years because the number of naysayers was huge. Finally I said, "It's over, we are not getting the results we should, and we can get them faster." I ended up having to move some of the major naysayers because we had a huge philosophical difference.

We just said, "We are going to do this." Once we went there and told them why, the naysayers got on board and we became the masses. Now we are rocking and rolling. However, we made a mistake eight years ago when we felt intuitively that this was wrong. It was a mistake. I should have pushed it much harder than I did. If I had pushed it then, we would have educated kids faster; we would have been so much further down the road now.

I've changed. I'm getting older now. I'm a little bit less tolerant and I'm beginning to be angry at myself because I should have acted on that intuition. I should have found the right sort of people and made the changes instead of procrastinating and being where we are now.

I was willing to ride with them where they were, but the results weren't where they should have been, nor did they happen as fast as I wanted them to. That's when we began to change.

I have had disappointments every place I have been. Some of the biggest ones centered on my inability to put something into place that I thought would work for my kids and something on a larger scale overrode it.

Far removed from this district, for example, are the state and federal governments. The state's mandated enterprise system, for example, is a terrible disappointment to me and we are still paying for it. An enterprise system is how you connect with your student outcomes or your technology from a student and financial standpoint. Our district is so large, we have a customer-based financial system, and we built payroll on how we did things. We also built a student outcome system. This is how you know when your kids are in school, what your suspension rates are, and what your test scores are. An enterprise system is technology-based, interwoven, and web-based.

We had an outstanding system. It was a centralized system, which means we could push data down and pick data up. Nevertheless, the state board said they wanted a statewide system. I spent a long time trying to convince the state that it probably would not work here because we are too large. The system they wanted us to adopt had never been done in a district this size, and they wanted a distributive system, based in the schools. I fought it through my board, but the board finally looked at me and said, "You will implement the state board's new system." Every technology person I brought in said we couldn't get there. I brought national consultants in. I did not have the ability to move the state or to persuade those in political power to allow me to build interfaces with their system. Here I sit today with a system that can't provide some of the data I need.

We still have not met the state board's goals. It is a huge disappointment, considering all the labor and money that has been invested in it. I did not find the right way to leverage my position.

Most problems usually stem from bad communication or from bad leveraging. My failures can usually be blamed on my failing to leverage something correctly or my misinterpreting how to leverage or broker something and, therefore, not doing it the right way. In this situation, I did not do enough to communicate appropriately how hard the implementation of the state's plan was going to be, and we are paying the consequences today.

Individuals who work with you have to have trust and loyalty, but I don't think you gain their trust and loyalty through blind expectations. I think you have to lead people by trying to promote stewardship. Stewardship is a higher calling, for a different purpose than leadership. I like John Doe, not because he demands my loyalty or my trust, but because he earns my loyalty and trust; we have a common goal that is above both of us; and we respect each other. For example, we can both enjoy biking and competition, but we don't demand trust and loyalty from each other to achieve that goal.

The same thing occurs in the school district. Stewardship implies that we try to get individuals to follow the major focus and direction of the district, but it does not mean that I expect blind loyalty from people just because of my position. There are many individuals in this district who want to commit to Stephen Daeschner or to the superintendent out of blind loyalty, and that is wrong. It has to be for the commitment itself, which is a bigger reason. One must earn trust, not require it; and one must earn loyalty, not require it. This is what the concept of stewardship is all about.

Everyone at some point is a follower. At any given point on the leadership team, I have to follow as well. Why? Because I trust and have loyalty to an individual's position who is trying to make change. I think that's key.

Some individuals have great discussions on stewardship. I've had staff read books and we've had conversations about it, but I still have people who I am uncomfortable with who give me blind loyalty or blind trust because of my position or name. It makes no sense to me.

I want followers to believe in the overriding concepts we are trying to promote. By buying into the concepts, we can trust each other. There is a higher calling. We have loyalty to each other – not as individuals, but because we both believe in the concept or system.

As a leader, I have to communicate with my team by having passion for a concept, by having knowledge about the concept, and by rigor. Rigor is the ability to take knowledge to a higher level in multiple situations.

A good leader will try to bring a person aboard with rationale and passion, which carries emotion. Emotion is always more powerful than rationale.

A good leader has to use a combination of emotion, passion and communication skills against rational concepts to try to get people headed in one direction. You have to make sure you get everyone's thoughts and input.

There is one thing I would do differently now if I could do things over again. I am not happy with the pace at which I've learned. Why am I sitting here in front of you now, knowing so much more than I knew ten years ago? Why didn't I know the same things ten years ago?

Some would say knowledge comes with maturity or experience, but that is bull. There is no reason I couldn't have learned the same things ten years ago. I am dissatisfied with my own learning curve. I think it has made a huge difference. The way we communicate, the way we drive, the way we lead, the way we follow, the way our systems work – I am very angry I didn't have all that information ten years ago because it would have made a huge difference, in my opinion, in kids' learning.

Why didn't I know at 40 what I now know at 63? There is no reason for it. I know so much more now about motivating, systems, pedagogy, and assessment. Why did it take me so long to put these pieces together? It's a frustrating situation for me, in all walks of life – marriage, kids, play and work. It's about our own learning pace, and I am not happy with my own.

It's about knowledge, but it is also about experiences. I want to apply what I know, see, and have learned. I really wouldn't go back now and say I would have done this or that differently – what's done is done. It is just that I am not happy with it.

I could have been a better learner, and I could have spent more time and more effort accelerating my learning. We can immerse; we can expand, we can ask questions, we can accelerate our learning if we choose. One of the capabilities we have as human beings that sets us apart from animals or any other species is our rational learning process, and I am not happy I did not accelerate mine. Everyone has that choice. Some of us choose to read, some of us get engaged in technology. It's about time management and knowing the techniques of acceleration.

I would advise young people to prepare for the challenge of community leadership, because it is difficult work. We live in an interpersonal arena. Leaders have to learn how to be great listeners, in my opinion. The one piece of advice I would pass on is to be a listener first, and to learn appropriate questioning techniques. I think that's what makes leaders.

We think of leaders differently. We expect them to tell us about their great visions and to inspire us. Great leaders have to ask the right questions using good techniques, to listen intently, and to get others to buy their concepts.

Always watch ego. It's a dangerous thing. You have to know how to ask the right questions to get creative juices flowing. Not one of us is smarter than all of us. A good leader should question more and talk less and find creative ways to change systems and to get the people they work with to buy into them. There is nothing better than a passionate rational person who buys into some concept of something, then gets out of the way.

I have only been here for 12 years, but I think our community has had good leadership over the last 50 years. I have had an opportunity to deal with some of the people who probably had their most magnificent acceleration before my time – people like David Jones Sr., Malcolm Chancey, Bert Klein. Those individuals saw things and operated very differently from today's world. I hate to say it, but I don't think the way they got things done would work today. They certainly had huge influence, though. I think Jerry Abramson is an example of someone who's made a huge difference too. He is a charismatic leader and he has accomplished so many things as our city's leader.

Other people who have had great influence in our community include Ed Glasscock and Henry Heuser Sr. Today more things seem to get done as partnerships, many of which are created by groups like GLI.

As I look at our community, I am a little disappointed in some people I think could be great leaders but don't seem to be overtly helping the community. Some are people who carry huge prestige in the business community. Maybe it's just because I don't know them or have not seen any action, but I don't see them greatly engaged with the community, and that's wrong. What have they done for the welfare and quality of life in our community? They have the positions; you would hope they would exert more influence.

I think there are a lot of new people who have the desire to help the community and who may emerge. I'm looking for people who are willing to step up to try to find partnerships that can really advance this community.

I would advise the next generation of leaders that they better have a passion for the community. Their contributions will not be measured by how much money they make in their lives, but how much they do to better this community. They are going to have to worry about our environment, health, quality of life, amenities, and infrastructures. All of those things are important to people and are most important to our kids.

Kids are receiving less value today than in any point in the history of the United States. What does that mean? It means that you cannot value everything equally. There is an economy of value. But because our population is aging and becoming seniors, people are now worrying about themselves first, and I understand that concept.

The political structure has turned its attention to the needs of older individuals now, more than ever before – to Medicaid, Medicare, and other needs of senior citizens. I admire all that, but it takes value away, whether you like it or not, from our most important resource in my opinion, and that's our kids. If we do not have our kids' needs in mind then what do we have in mind?

There has never been less attention given to their needs. Less value translates to less money, less worry about whether kids are educated. Leave it all to somebody else. I worry about these things. I worry about them for my own kids and I worry about them for your kids. What are we leaving our kids? What kind of environment? How are we training them? Do all kids need to go to college? What is the legacy we're leaving them? Legacy means all the things that in my opinion make the quality of life good. It's not about the dollar sign.

I consider one of my most significant accomplishments to be creation of early childhood and preschool programs in our schools. It's just logic. The fastest growth in our brains occurs at three, four and five years old. Habits we shape then are habits we use today, whether we like it or not. It's so rational, but we are working against mama's power structures. There is always a power struggle.

I worry deeply about the "haves and have nots" in our community. Some people can afford to send their children to a private school instead of a public school. I know there is no difference in the quality of education, but we are creating a "have and have not" structure that hurts everyone. It hurts the ones who go there and it hurts the ones who don't. All of these things make me worry for our kids. We can't afford in this nation to have a "have and have not" structure in a democracy, or we will end up in a bad way. It is a huge issue.

We need to drive away from "me" concepts and drive toward "us" concepts. It's going to be hard because I see the "me" becoming even more pronounced than ever. People are changing jobs without loyalty to their employer's vision and they are wanting this and that for themselves. A lot of what motivates people is all about "me." I understand it, but if it all becomes about "me," then we will have many problems.

We are seeing the results here in Louisville. All the banks are being bought by national banks and companies are moving in and out. They don't have as much loyalty anymore, or a passion or commitment to the community. This is a philanthropic community. We do a wonderful job, but watch how even that can creatively become all about "me." I think we are losing a lot as a result of it.

Here is some advice I would like to give the next generation of leaders in our community: Have goals and set priorities. Focus, focus, focus.

Success is all about systems. You can't do everything, so don't spread yourself too thin. Commit to have passion. More than anything, as you become leaders, remember that it is not about you, the leader; it's about the people who work with you. Choose good people to work with you and get out of their way, then watch what can get done.

As Jim Collins says in his book, *Good to Great*, "Ask the right people to get on the bus and get the people you don't want off the bus."

Most important, build a good team.

GORDON B. DAVIDSON

**Senior Counsel
Wyatt, Tarrant & Combs, LLP**

GORDON DAVIDSON HAS BEEN A MOVER and shaker in Louisville for more than 30 years. His achievements include spearheading the construction of the Kentucky Center for the Arts, negotiating the merger of Kosair Children's Hospital with Norton Infirmary, and persuading Governor Wendell Ford to build the original Kentucky International Convention Center downtown. He also helped city leaders develop Fourth Street into a mall and Galleria, which were less spectacular successes at the time but paved the way for what is now Fourth Street Live!

One of the most famous pictures of Davidson is one taken in 1963. He is the lawyer in the photo, ducking for cover as a young Muhammad Ali – then Cassius Clay – tries to get at Sonny Liston before their first title fight. Davidson was the attorney for a group of men from Louisville and elsewhere who put up the money that launched the young fighter into his spectacular professional career.

At about that same time, he began having a hand in just about everything significant that happened in Louisville for several decades.

Gordon Davidson was born in Louisville in 1926, and he recalls it as a wonderfully vibrant place during his childhood and youth. He liked to take dates down to Fourth Street to movies and dances when that area of town was a lively scene.

He is a 1944 graduate, *cum laude*, of Louisville Male High School, and he has a 1949 B.A. from Centre College in Danville. He has law degrees from the University of Louisville and Yale Law School. He served as an assistant staff judge advocate in the U.S. Army during the Korean War and as a cadet-midshipman in the Atlantic and Mediterranean during World War II.

He spent the 1954-1955 term of the U.S. Supreme Court in Washington as a clerk to Justice Stanley Reed, a Kentuckian. He and other clerks did research on the difficult issues in the famous Brown vs. Board of Education school desegregation litigation.

Davidson flirted with big city law firms after law school and had offers from some, but he had married a Kentucky woman, Geraldine Burgess Geiger of Ashland, whom he met at Centre College, and they decided to return to their home state. He signed on with Wyatt, Grafton & Sloss in 1955 and became a partner in 1960, practicing civil law with emphasis in the areas of corporations, taxation, estate trusts and appellate work. He became managing partner of the firm in 1976.

After a merger in 1980, he found himself chairman and CEO of the new Wyatt, Tarrant & Combs firm and served in that capacity until 1995. He continues to work there as a senior counsel.

As a top attorney at a top law firm for over 50 years, Davidson has served on the boards of important companies like *The Courier-Journal* and *The Louisville Times* and BellSouth, and he has held leadership positions on the boards of a long list of civic, charitable and educational institutions: the Louisville Area Chamber of Commerce (now Greater Louisville Inc.), Louisville Central Area, the Greater Louisville Fund for the Arts, the Louisville Development Committee, the Kentucky Derby Festival, the Local Government Reorganization Commission, Centre College, the University of Louisville Board of Overseers, among others.

As president of the Louisville Theatrical Association, Davidson got involved in a long string of initiatives that culminated in his obtaining state approval and ultimately spearheading the construction of the Kentucky Center for the Arts. The effort started in 1967 when Davidson tried to persuade hotel mogul J. Graham Brown to build an arts center so he could regain control of his Brown Theatre property. Davidson eventually helped convince Kentucky Governor Julian Carroll to commit state money to build the Kentucky Center for the Arts in Louisville. He was appointed chairman of the Kentucky Cultural Complex Committee in 1977 to oversee the project. He served as the Center board's chairman or vice-chairman from 1979 to 1992, and has been a director emeritus since 1995.

Mayor Jerry Abramson saluted Davidson's leadership when he retired as chairman of the Kentucky Center in 1992: "Gordon is a visionary who, while leading the development and growth of the Kentucky Center for the Arts, never lost sight of the fact that it serves as a center for the arts for the Commonwealth of Kentucky as well as Louisville."

Davidson shares this advice with young people who would be leaders: "Set goals. Don't just set goals, but be active in pursuing them and be active after you have achieved them."

I THINK MY WANTING TO BECOME a community leader started in the seventh and eighth grade. I had a teacher, Mrs. Fontaine, who taught me at Melbourne Heights School, a county school with small classes, excellent teachers. Mrs. Fontaine was a lovely and inspiring person. She was interested in government and history and had a broad cross-section of interests. She knew what this country was all about and how it worked and what the government was all about and, as a result, we worked on a number of projects.

The class drew up a constitution for our little nation, the seventh and eighth grade, and I was on that committee. We followed our constitution, had an election and, for lack of a better candidate I guess, I was elected president of the class. Once or twice a week we would have a meeting of the legislative branch of our class. I just loved participating and I loved being president. I thought boy, this is great to be a leader of my class and to have my classmates recognize me as such and adhere to my demands. So that's really where it started. I knew then that I would rather be in front of the class than just a member of the class. I wanted to be a leader.

That feeling continued through school. I was interested in similar activities in junior high school, at Male High School, in college and in law school. So this urge or compulsion to be a player continued all through my schooling.

I was born and raised in Louisville and had a very active family – not a leadership family in the true sense of the word, but one that was interested in civic and church affairs. My focus was on Louisville from the start. As time went on, I realized there was a bigger world, but I still pretty much wanted to be a success in my own hometown.

I came back to Louisville after being a Supreme Court law clerk. I could have gotten any job in America and had offers from Los Angeles and New York, but my wife, whom I met at Centre College, is from Ashland, Kentucky. We decided that if we had anything to contribute, we wanted to contribute it back in Kentucky, particularly in Louisville. I always felt that unless you can make it in your own hometown, you can't make it. Perhaps I could have done a lot better financially in other towns, but I'm completely satisfied with our decision to come back to Louisville. My interest in Louisville and in the progress and success of Louisville never wavered. Even though we moved eight times in five years, Louisville and Kentucky were and still are our principal interests.

My greatest mentor was my mother, which is not an unusual answer for many people. She was more than just a mother, she was an inspiration. I was an only child. My mother and father were divorced, which was unusual in those days. It was a pleasant divorce, not a knock-down, drag-out sort of thing.

It was just one of those things where two people got married young and it didn't work out. I was four years old when they divorced, so we moved in with my grandparents, my mother's mother and father. My grandfather and an uncle lived there who was relatively young. I had plenty of male mentors at home but mother was, in her way (and I use the term in complimentary way) ambitious for me. I was all she had, so she tried to do the best with what she had to work with. She was always urging me to participate. If there were a poster contest or some sort of debate contest, she urged me to do it. It didn't take a lot of urging, but without her pushing me and nurturing me, I don't know what would have happened.

My grandfather was also very ambitious for me, in the good sense of the word. He felt he hadn't gone very far in school. He came from a large family of German immigrants and I guess was trying to get me to achieve what he hadn't been able to succeed in. One of his favorite sayings was "You have to learn how to speak. If you get a chance to speak publicly take it, because that's important." Things like that.

I had a number of inspiring teachers. I mentioned Mrs. Fontaine, who was a very important mentor and taught me about the world in general. There were several teachers at Male High School, in college and in law school who were mentors to me.

In later life, there were two standouts. One was Wilson Wyatt. One of the reasons I came back to Louisville was to join a firm that had similar political and civic interests to mine. Wilson, of course, having been the former mayor and an outstanding citizen, believed the same thing. His was the only law firm I applied to when I decided to come back to Louisville because I wanted a small firm and I wanted an activist firm. I was fortunate enough to make what I think was the right choice because Wilson was a great mentor to me in how to practice law, how to be a good citizen and how to take part in civic activities.

The other standout mentor, of course, was Justice Stanley Reid, for whom I clerked at the Supreme Court in 1954 and 1955. He was a Kentuckian, so we had that in common. I was the only Kentucky law clerk he had ever had up until that point, which was kind of interesting. He very much wanted me to come back to Kentucky, even though he knew there were other very attractive opportunities. He was very close to his law clerks. Justices just had two law clerks in those days, and his other one was from Massachusetts. We had lunch and dinner together and spent a lot of time with him on a personal basis. He, of course, had had a very distinguished career in public service before he was appointed to the Supreme Court.

So I had two standout mentors, Stanley Reed and Wilson Wyatt. It's good to have a number of mentors. What you gain from each one is hard to measure. I was very fortunate to be exposed to people like them.

Whatever sort of leadership style I have came naturally to me. I have always tried to build consensus. My style has never been dictatorial. That's true of when I was head of the law firm too. I always tried to listen to everyone, get their views, bring them together and serve as a mediator or a leader to try to reach a result.

I guess another thing I learned was when to zig and when to zag. I learned when to make a move or a proposal or an action and when to shut up and do nothing or delay things. I'm pretty pragmatic. If it can be done we ought to do it, but if it can't be done, let's not beat our heads against a stone wall. I hope I was never a zealot for a cause, but you'd have to ask others. I don't know how others would describe me.

I didn't take any courses or read any books about how to be a leader. I don't think you can make a leader out of everybody. I think a leader must have a desire to lead, make a commitment to do it and have sincerity about it. There are a lot of people who would like to be leaders but who could never be one. They just don't have the talent or the inclination or the personality. And there are a lot of people who could be leaders but are sitting on their rear ends not being leaders, which is sadder. I think a good leader has to have a sort of DNA, knowing what to do and having the talents needed to do it.

There are three things I have accomplished in my life that I think are significant. One was getting the Kentucky Center for the Arts built. I worked on that project for many years, on one committee or another, headed by different people at different times for different reasons. But it took well over ten years to finally find a governor, in Julian Carroll, who shared our vision here in Louisville and who was willing to support it both personally and monetarily. He appointed me as chairman of what was then called the Cultural Complex Committee, after some very interesting dinners and twisting of various people's arms. That was the beginning of what ultimately turned into the Kentucky Center.

We had a wonderful committee. I suggested the nominees and the governor appointed them. We hired the first director, Marlow Burt. We had to make peace with all of the user groups and others who didn't believe the money ought to be spent for it. They thought that we ought to rehab an old theater. It was not an easy chore, but it was so challenging it was fun. One thing led to another and we now have it today. After working on it for all those years, I have to say I feel good that I played a part in that effort.

Another accomplishment I am proud I played a role in is the merger of Norton Infirmary and Children's Hospital in the Medical Center. That was another difficult project because there were people who thought it was a terrible mistake. Despite what they thought, it was an absolute necessity.

Three people from Norton and three from Children's were appointed to serve on the committee to try to make the merger work. They were all outstanding people, heavy hitters. I was fortunate to serve on the committee with them. We worked hard and long and you can see what has happened today, as a result of that merger. It led to the Kosair affiliation. It led to a new hospital for children and to what Norton Healthcare is today, with five hospitals and thousands of employees. When we started, Children's was about bankrupt financially. Both Children's and Norton's were in old hospital buildings and they needed to be in a medical center. There were many reasons for them to want to get together but, interestingly enough, there was a lot of opposition to it within the families of those two hospitals.

Another accomplishment I am proud of happened when I was president of LCA. We twisted Governor Wendell Ford's arm to help get the original Convention Center built downtown – not the new addition to it, but the original building. Again, there was a lot of opposition to it and to the architecture, but we pulled it through and that's been another great success.

Now let's talk about some failures. I was involved in a number of civic activities, including LCA. I was also on the Chamber board, and we had Forward Louisville and all kinds of committees hoping to revitalize downtown. We hired some experts to come in and tell us what we needed. One thing we needed, we all decided, was a mall on Fourth Street. That was the "in" thing in those days. As strange as it may seem, we got all of the landowners on Fourth Street to agree to become a special taxing district to pay for it. The people who owned property on Fourth Street agreed to pay the taxes. We hired what we thought were the best designers in the world, and, for what it was, it was a very attractive place. Well, what happened to it?

First, the landowners, including the large department stores, committed verbally to pay the tax and to make changes. Stewart's Department Store agreed to open up the front of their building on Fourth Street, to create an indoor/outdoor winterized place that would make the stores and the building part of the mall. Well, that didn't happen. It was a bad economic time.

There was another big department store here – you might remember it, Kaufman-Strauss. Well, the day it was announced I was becoming president of LCA was the day they announced they were leaving Louisville. So that was kind of an unfortunate start.

Parking was another problem downtown. It was very difficult to get the kind of parking you could get in the suburban malls. Another challenge was attracting magnet stores. We tried very hard to get Saks Fifth Avenue, who was then owned by Brown & Williamson, later Batus.

We courted Saks, but they showed us statistics of what the disposable spendable income was in Louisville compared to other cities. We weren't in the ball park, so they went to Cincinnati.

We were unsuccessful luring others to the mall, we couldn't get the landowners and businesses to spend money to help the mall, we couldn't solve the parking problem even though we built parking garages, and we didn't have a magnet. We thought the mall was the answer to our problems revitalizing the downtown retail core and the office core and it ultimately didn't work.

So we shifted gears and moved toward what later became the Galleria. Again, several of us were on that committee. We selected Oxford Properties to build two new buildings, and again we thought we had the answer. But the same problems haunted us. We still didn't have a magnet and we didn't have the private sector saying okay, we'll commit to it. So needless to say, we were unsuccessful and we were disappointed.

Now that, of course, is what they're trying to do with Fourth Street Live!, but in a different way. They have a magnet and there is no other place like it. That's the theory and I hope it works.

The third disappointment for me was working on four campaigns for metro government in Louisville. The only one in my lifetime that I didn't work on was the one that passed. I don't know whether that tells you something about me, or something about the situation.

County Judge Mitch McConnell and Mayor Harvey Sloane were behind initial attempts to merge city and county government. The first time we were shot down by the volunteer firemen and sixth class cities. We tried it again and raised a lot of money and spent millions of dollars on the campaigns. We came close a couple of times, but we didn't make it.

I was also involved in a failed attempt to write a new constitution for Kentucky too. That was a long time ago, but the blue ribbon panel that got together to write a new constitution to modernize it came close, but failed. So, in my personal life, I've had a lot of good winners and I've had some losers.

In each of these endeavors, we had to learn how to make peace with user groups. For example, when we were trying to build the Kentucky Center, the user groups felt that by siphoning money into bricks and mortar, we would injure their ability to raise money for their own arts organizations. They of course felt that more money should be put into their organizations than into bricks and mortar. I approached it by meeting with every group involved one-on-one. We didn't have a mass meeting. We approached people individually and listened to why they felt this way, why they were reluctant.

We asked them what kind of commitments they wanted from us and the state if we did build it. I met with all of them and ultimately peace broke out because concessions were made, and because we involved them in decisions about the center. We also gave them a lower rate in rent. There were gives and takes, but I don't know you could say that all of them were enthusiastic.

The interesting part of it all is that all of their fears were 100% wrong. I didn't know it was going to turn out this way, but the Arts Center's opening and providing the forum for all these local groups, at least in the early stages, increased the amount of money they were all able to raise. It also increased their ticket sales, and there was an increase in enthusiasm of the audiences as well. I don't know where a lot of these performing groups would be without the Center. If they had continued to play in the Brown, which didn't have enough seats, we wouldn't have been able to get the big Broadway shows, because we would have had to charge $1,000 a ticket or something.

The Kentucky Center was a real shot in the arm to our arts community. The benefits that were reaped by the entire cultural arts community were tremendous. All of our arts are better now than they were, and it has a lot to do with the Center.

Plus, look at the wonderful things that have happened there for the people of Kentucky. We have bus tours that come up from Owensboro and Paducah to see shows at the Center. We have the Governor's School for the Arts which was spawned by the Center. The Center helps every other little arts facility in the state. It helped Lexington. It helped Owensboro. It's had an absolutely wonderful effect on the cultural life of our state and, of course, particularly on Louisville. It also has had a very positive effect on drawing business to Louisville and making Louisville a first-class city. It was a very important thing, but it took a lot of time and a lot of effort and a lot of hand-holding.

Barry Bingham Sr. was very much for it. His son. Barry Jr., who was then the publisher of the paper, was very much opposed to it, however, not on the principle of the arts, but on the principle that we were spending too much money on bricks and mortar. I can remember Mr. Bingham called me in Florida one day when I was on vacation and he said, "I want to give you a heads-up about tomorrow's *Courier*. Barry's written a very strong editorial opposing the Arts Center. I felt like saying, "Buddy, if you can't control him, who can?" Obviously, we had a lot of give and take.

We also had a problem initially with J. Graham Brown, who wanted his theater back and we had no place to go. We kept saying, "Mr. Brown, if you'll give us the money, we'll get out of your theater and build another forum, but we can't leave here without having a new venue to house all these arts groups." He said, "I'll take care of it. Just give me back the theater and I'll make a donation." I said, "Mr. Brown, I appreciate your offer, but I can't sell that."

I've got to be able to tell people 'Mr. Brown said he would give us poopteen million dollars.'" He said, "Oh you'll just have to trust that I'll do it." I couldn't sell it, and I didn't sell it. There were a lot of rocky roads along the way.

The Children's Hospital and Norton Infirmary merger was easier in a sense because we were dealing with smaller constituencies of people who supported and opposed it. Norton felt if they merged with Children's, Children's would bankrupt Norton. Children's felt that if they merged with Norton, the merger would eventually obliterate Children's. Neither of course happened, or were going to happen, but you had to satisfy each constituency. I think there were three directors of Norton who resigned over it and at least one from Children's who said "I'm not going to be a party to this. You're just killing Children's Hospital." Fortunately there were enough who stayed and we got through the merger. You just have to work with people and see what the problems are and face them head on. You can't go around controversy; you have to run right to the center of the line.

Wilson Wyatt was really the catalytic force who got Governor Ford to agree to build the Convention Center downtown. He had a close relationship with Ford and he's the one who was really able to persuade him to do it. I was president of the LCA and just went along for the ride. I told them we would do whatever was necessary to staff the thing and augment it and get it popularized. Ford was very much concerned that unless it was popular with the community, he didn't want to do it.

Interestingly enough, Governor Carroll said the same thing about the Kentucky Center. He said "I'll do this, but I want to be welcomed with open arms if I do it. I don't want to catch a lot of static about it." So we had to pave the road with rose blossoms to get the governors to do both projects. Their support was crucial. We couldn't have done either project without the state.

You ask what it takes to be a good follower. I don't want someone who is going to salute me every morning and say yes to whatever I say. I think what you want is someone who is committed to whatever cause you are asking them to participate in and, most importantly, who is willing to work. They can't just fill a seat or, as they say, an "empty suit." You want people who are as enthusiastic as you are and who perform. Both of those things are essential if you're going to have any successful organization. You have to have people who are committed to the cause and people who will then act upon their commitment and perform.

If I had a chance to do it all over again, I wouldn't do much differently.

I've had thoughts about what might have been if I hadn't come back to Louisville or if we hadn't done things in Louisville this way or that way. But as far as my personal life is concerned, there's nothing I would do differently.

I always wanted to be a lawyer, from the ninth grade until this very moment. I've been luckier and more fortunate than I ever imagined and I have exceeded my fondest expectations. I hope I'd be better than I was the last trip through, but I really don't want another trip. I am absolutely delighted with the trip I have had and I wouldn't risk it again. I don't think I would do as well the second time around.

I would advise young people aspiring to leadership to get into the action. Make a commitment. Go out on a limb. Make the effort. Get into the action, but be a good listener. Listen to your mentors and learn from them. You learn by your mistakes and you learn by your successes but most of all, you learn from other people. It's as simple as that. If you don't jump off the diving board, you'll never know if you can swim or not, so jump off the diving board and get in the water. Then listen and learn and work.

It would be hard to say who or what has contributed most to the growth, development and improved quality of life in Louisville over the last 50 years. But when I lived in Louisville as a young person, the city was controlled by two very strong political parties. The Democrats were a little stronger than the Republicans, but the Republicans had a very good organization in those days. Those parties, particularly the Democratic Party, provided the continuity, the succession, the power, because we didn't have a mayor who could succeed himself or herself. We had a four-year chief executive who took two years to find out where the conference room was and two years to do something, then the next person would come in and undo everything he had done.

Most of the cities that have succeeded over the last 50 years have had good mayors and Louisville, by and large, has always had good mayors. Most of them were selected by the parties, but they didn't have primaries in Louisville. The party picked who was going to be the candidate for mayor or county judge or board of alderman and so forth. They had primaries, but you were beating your head against a stone wall if you tried to run against the parties.

Atlanta had three successive two- or three-term mayors who could start on a master plan and keep it going for 20 or 25 years and continue to build on it. Indianapolis had a series of superb mayors. Senator Richard Lugar was mayor for one or two terms. When I was a kid, Indianapolis, Indiana was noplace. It was nothing. Now look at Indianapolis today. Why is Indianapolis the way it is today and we're not as far along as they are, at least by my standards? There are several reasons.

One, of course, is that Indianapolis is in the center of the state and everything funnels in to them. We're on the edge of the state. Another reason is that Indianapolis has metro government. Nashville has metro government. Jacksonville, Florida has metro government.

Now, finally, we have metro government. I think it is going to be a great move. It has to be. We have a mayor now who can succeed himself or herself, so we have some continuity. We're able to put programs into place, then follow through with them.

I think Mayor Abramson is a perfect example of what can be done. Look what he did with the airport. You talk about a tough sell! I talk about the ones I had that I thought were tough sells, but he had a really tough sell getting that done with federal, state, property owners and other interests. But that's what it takes, continuity of leadership.

Over the last 50 years, we had political parties that provided continuity to our programs and our developments. When the parties fell out of favor, the business community took over. The political parties, the mayors, the county judges were all good people, but they were directed in one way or another by the business community because the business community could not only provide money, they could provide continuity of leadership. Neither the mayor nor the county judge could do that.

During my golden years, the business community was 100% gung ho and they put their money where their mouth was, providing leadership. If there was a program coming up, you could make ten phone calls and find out whether you could do it or not. Probably the last call would be to the government. The first would be to the heads of the banks, *The Courier-Journal*, other major employers, and so forth. They were all willing, they were all dedicated, they all served on committees when asked and they provided what successes we had, with the help of government. You can't work without government, but the spark plug came from the business community.

I'll give you an example – Dan Ulmer and the Redbirds. He was second in command and later took over command of the old Citizens Fidelity Bank, now PNC. Mayor Stansbury was very much a baseball fan. Ulmer wanted to get the thing moving. The mayor was supportive of it. But neither could have done it without the other. The continuity had to come from the Ulmers of the world, however, because Stansbury was going to go out of office.

I remember the day that the first game was played. Harvey Sloane, who had just become mayor, threw out the first ball and Bill Stansbury was sitting in the stands. He got no recognition whatsoever. Without him, Ulmer couldn't have gotten the Redbirds. But without Ulmer, Stansbury couldn't have gotten the Redbirds either. Now that's the way it worked.

Frank Burke was the mayor during most of my activities. He was always supportive, always helpful, and of course he was innovative too. He would throw his weight behind what he thought was right and things he didn't like, but he was always supportive of what we needed. We bought the Brown Theatre when he was mayor and I was head of the Louisville Theatrical Association. Without him, we wouldn't have been able to save the Brown. But without the business community, he wouldn't have been able to save it either.

It was a hand-in-glove relationship between civic leadership and City Hall, and this was true with both Democrats and Republicans. Former Mayor William O. Cowger and former County Judge-Executive Marlow Cook were both supportive and active with the business community. They were both Chamber of Commerce types, and they frequently brought some good ideas from the government sector. So, whatever we have achieved in the last 50 years has been achieved by that partnership between civic leadership and government.

Unfortunately, that has changed. I don't know where we go from here, except that we have achieved metro government and we have a strong and good mayor, and if we continue along that road we'll be able to do what we did in the past. But the shifting of initiative has now gone from the business sector to the governing sector, because that's where the leadership has to come from.

The mayor is going to have to fill the vacuum. The focus of the leadership of moving this community forward has to shift now and be focused on City Hall, and the mayor needs to enlist other members of the community to help carry forward any ideas that come forward. Instead of all of us going to the mayor and telling him what we want to do, however, the mayor is going to have to assume a significant leadership role. Let's take this issue of whether we need a new arena or a professional basketball team, which is a hot topic now. That idea is going to flounder until the mayor, or the president of the University of Louisville, or the two of them get together and say this ought to be done.

When we did things, the business leadership in the community would go to the mayor and say, "We think it would be good to do this. Will you help us?" Without the mayor and county judge, we wouldn't have the Kentucky Center. The mayor got the land for us because it was city property. The county judge built a garage. We definitely needed them, but the idea didn't come from them. It came from somewhere else. And the same was true of other things we did. The idea would evolve from either the Chamber of Commerce or the business leadership groups, then we would go to the government leaders and say, "Can you help us with this?"

That was the system over the last 50 years. First, things were run and got done by the political parties and the business community, then by the business community and the incumbents, then we tried for metro government and worked to let mayors and governors succeed themselves. As far as our local government was concerned, we were riding in the 20th century in a horse and buggy. It's only been different in the last few years.

Metro government is the most important thing that's happened to this community in my lifetime, because it's not just a new building or a hospital, it is a mechanism to bring the community and the clout of the community together. It takes a strong, talented leader to harness that, however.

I'm sure Mayor Abramson has heard me speak on the subject, but it's amazing how age plays a part in your ability to be active in civic affairs. Before merger, the mayor and county judge didn't call on the old guys. For good reason. They shouldn't. It's a new generation, a new century. That's the way life is. I don't think George W. Bush is going to call Gerald Ford and ask him what he thinks he ought to do.

We now need to make a conscious effort to groom a new set of leaders in the community who are going to make things happen. That ties in to the point I was making about how much the business structure in Louisville has changed. I'm not being critical, but how many times in the last three or four years have the banks changed leadership? We can't have continuity. We can't have the same dedication from corporate leaders that we've had before.

I'm a permanent resident of Louisville, Kentucky. We now have a lot of very attractive, talented young people here, and a lot of people with money. But we don't have that synergistic force of the golden years, the ability to get something done. Maybe we do, but if we do, I don't see it. I'm not in it, so maybe I'm all wrong. I just know that if I called five or six people back in the 1970s or even the 1980s, I could tell you whether something was going to fly or not. I don't think I could do that now.

Let's take lawyers, for example. We have some very large law firms here, relative to our city's size. We have excellent leadership in those law firms, and they're important cogs in this wheel. But they don't control the money. They can't deliver the clout the corporate world used to be able to deliver.

We have always had some civic-minded, excellent doctors who have been leaders in the community and volunteered, but they can't deliver. They can deliver their good, hard work but they can't knock the ball over the fence.

In the old days, we had people who could hit a home run whenever they wanted to hit a home run and fortunately they did, and the progress we made over the last 30 years was a result of this business/government relationship. We still need the local, permanent, talented citizens to get active in civic affairs, to be devoted to the cause, to turn the screws on the government and the business community to ensure that things happen. There's more of a need for leadership now at all levels, but it's going to be much more difficult now.

Belknap Hardware and a lot of locally-owned businesses have been taken over. Devoe-Reynolds, Celanese, I can go down the list. Corhart Refractories is closed. It's going to be much more difficult, because a lot of these businesses are going out of business and are being bought by outsiders. And while they are going to have a budget and give to Louisville, the community and the Metro United Way, they're not going to build.

I'll give you an example of committed leadership here. I'm looking out the window at the Muhammad Ali Center going up. If Ina Brown Bond weren't the dynamo that she is, that sucker would still be a Kingfish. She is a dedicated, committed leader who went out and raised the money and who also has money and is able to do some things. There are a lot of other people who could do that, but they would have to have the commitment to do something like that.

That's an excellent example of how government can partner with an interested group and do something together. The Muhammad Ali Center could not have gotten the land and done a lot of things without government help. But on the other hand, the government could not build the Muhammad Ali Center. It has to be built with private money and it is being built with private money. Ina has raised millions. A lot of other people have been involved in the project and contributed, but Ina is the driving force.

There are other examples like that, of course. In the arts community, there are a lot of driving force leaders, and we need them more than ever. We need individuals to form a group so when we don't get the money from banks, we get it from people. You ride through Hurstbourne, you ride through Lake Forest, you ride through Sutherland. There's a lot of money here, but you don't see it coming out too much in big globs. Two young men I do not know, the Blues, are an example of entrepreneurs who are willing to put their money where their mouth is. Our community is going to need a lot of those types of people. Ina Brown Bond is an example. Owsley Frazier is another example.

I also think the University of Louisville and Bellarmine need to get more involved in leadership activity. I'm not talking about from a money standpoint. They have the standing in the community and the connections to know who the leaders are and to enlist them, and to serve as a catalytic force to help form new leadership groups we're going to need.

It's a new day. It's a new configuration. But we have so much more to work with now with metro government, and with the mayor and governor being able to succeed themselves, and strong senators and representatives on the national scene. A lot of good things are happening in Louisville that weren't happening when I was working on projects. I'm not pessimistic, but it's going to take a different configuration.

The most valuable lesson I have learned that I would like to share with the next generation of Louisville leaders is to have goals in your life. I'm talking about having goals in your personal life, as well as in your professional or business life. Have goals. I don't want to just be a regular lawyer, working for a firm. I want to be an outstanding lawyer and have my own clients, as well as firm clients. I'm using the only example that I know.

You know when I first came to the firm, I had to work for partners. I enjoyed it and continue to enjoy it, but I really wanted to build my own practice within the firm. I wanted to be more than just one of 150 lawyers. I wanted to be in the top three or four of those lawyers. That was a goal of mine, and I worked very hard to try to achieve the goal.

What is your real interest? Have a goal. I want to be on the board of the Louisville Orchestra. I want to be on the board of the Opera. I want to be on the board of Greater Louisville Inc., our Chamber of Commerce.

Have a goal and work toward that goal. Get to know the people who make the people. You are not going to get asked to do things sitting at home at night waiting for the phone to ring. You have to get out in the community, and you have to get to know people, and you have to serve your stewardship as a young minion, but make yourself known.

Show that you have the talent, the ability, the desire, and you will achieve your goals. And don't just set goals, be active in pursuing them and be active after you have achieved them. End of scripture.

OWSLEY BROWN FRAZIER

Chairman and Founder
Frazier Historical Arms Museum

Chairman
Bittner's LLC

Retired Vice Chairman
Brown-Forman Corporation

OWSLEY BROWN FRAZIER RETIRED from a 45-year career with his family's company – the Brown-Forman Corporation – in June 2000. For the last 17 years, he served as vice chairman and point man for the company's public and community affairs, communications, corporate and stockholder services and considerable philanthropy.

It was a perfect position for a man personally committed to making a difference in his community. In addition to the generous gifts he bestowed upon worthy programs and projects in Brown-Forman's name over the years, he personally raised over a half-billion dollars for a variety of community causes, a quarter-billion dollars of it for education alone.

Frazier still serves as chairman of Bittners LLC, a business founded in 1854 that specializes in interior design and custom-made furniture.

He has an impressive record of public service. He chaired the Greater Louisville Economic Development Partnership, the Downtown Development Corporation and the Business/Industry Political Action Committee in Washington, and served on the boards of Greater Louisville Inc., the Kentucky Economic Development Corporation, the Louisville Housing Development Corporation and a dozen other organizations. He also served on the boards of Jewish Hospital Healthcare Services and the Frazier Rehabilitation Institute and, in July 2001, he chaired a $75 million campaign – kicked off by a gift from his mother, Amelia Brown Frazier – to build the new state-of-the-art Frazier Rehabilitation Center.

He has raised money over the years to preserve historic buildings, to support arts programs and special community projects, and to build low-income housing for families. He spearheaded Brown-Forman's Adopt-a-Neighborhood program, for example, which resulted in an investment of over $6.5 million from various sources to construct and rehabilitate over 50 houses in the California neighborhood around the company's plant in downtown Louisville.

Frazier's real passion, however, has been education, and he has chaired multi-million dollar campaigns for the University of Louisville, Bellarmine University and Kentucky Country Day School. He restored historic homes for the presidents of both UofL and Bellarmine. He has served as a trustee and as chair of the Board of Overseers at UofL, is chair emeritus of the board at Bellarmine University and is chair emeritus of the board of Kentucky Country Day School as well.

After retiring from Brown-Forman, Frazier continued to give back to the community. He bought and restored an historic building on the corner of Ninth and Main Streets in Louisville's museum district and built a world-class museum – the $32 million Frazier Historical Arms Museum, which houses his priceless personal collection of arms. The Museum is also the home to the Royal Armouries USA, the fourth and only location outside of the United Kingdom. Other locations include the Tower of London, Leeds and Fort Nelson. In an unprecedented alliance that was approved by Parliament, the Armouries has artifacts from the 11th century forward, on rotating loan at the Museum.

Owsley Brown Frazier was born in Louisville in 1935, into the fourth generation of the family of Brown-Forman founder George Garvin Brown. He finished high school at Louisville Country Day, then attended Centre College in Danville, Kentucky. He earned undergraduate and law degrees at the University of Louisville, and was well on his way to a business master's degree there when duty called at the family company.

Frazier first went to work at Brown-Forman as a trainee in 1955, became assistant to the resident counsel in 1959, and company attorney in 1960. He was elected to the board of directors in 1964, and became vice chairman in 1983. When he retired, he was proud to tell *The Courier-Journal* that Brown-Forman, which had sales the year he joined the company of $65 million and a net profit of slightly under $4 million, had sales of well over $2 billion, yielding more than $200 million in profit. Frazier remains a member of the Brown-Forman board of directors, and continues to be active in the community.

Frazier has received a long list of awards over the years for his philanthropy and public service: honorary degrees from both UofL and Bellarmine and the prestigious Minerva Medal from UofL, the Louisville Urban League's Equality Award, the Lincoln Foundation's Spirit of Excellence Award, the Louisville Historical League's Founders Award, and Greater Louisville Inc.'s 2005 Silver Fleur-de-Lis Award, among others. He was named the *Voice Tribune*'s Man of the Year in 1999 and was inducted into Junior Achievement's Kentuckiana Business Hall of Fame in 2004.

He has two surviving daughters and eight grandchildren.

I AM NOT SURE THERE WAS JUST ONE SINGLE THING, event, or person that truly motivated me to become a leader. Of course my mother, Amelia Brown Frazier, was very civic-minded and growing up in her home we were taught to give back to the community. She taught us by example.

When I was a child my mother was in a car accident and needed serious rehabilitation. There wasn't a local facility with the treatment expertise she needed so she was forced to travel to New York. This was exhausting and aggravating. She believed there were others in Louisville who must have similar needs, so in 1951 she became a catalyst for the creation of The Rehabilitation Center, Inc. Watching her give back to the community made a lasting imprint. I try hard to emulate her kindness and generosity and, in a small way, sometimes measure up.

Actually both the Brown and Frazier families have a long history of educational, civic and charitable involvement so I guess I come by it naturally. I was taught it was my responsibility and privilege to give back to the community. Some of these notions were reinforced when I was at the University of Louisville attending law school. My initial plan was just to get through school and go to work at Brown-Forman. But by the end of my freshman year, I began to focus on learning and accomplishing as much as I could. I got involved with academics, student activities, became president of the Student Bar Association and Chief Justice of the Moot Court. I guess you could say that is when I decided that being involved was more exciting than sitting on the sidelines. Plus, Louisville is my home. I love this city. There isn't any better motivation than that.

Other than my family, I had many mentors. I learned a lot from Charlie Dobbins. He was president and later chair of old Liberty National Bank. Charlie and I became friends through the University of Louisville athletic council. I was part of the student body and he was the chairman. He taught me the banking business. He taught me how to turn over every rock, so to speak, and to be thorough, yet polite. I still practice that today.

I try to lead by example, and I am always moving toward a goal. You have to know where you are going to encourage others to follow. You also have to know your values and what role they play in your everyday life. Very, very few people are able to stay back in the trenches and tell people to go attack an army and be successful at it. It is the people who actually go out onto the battlefield and fight alongside the troops the entire time who are the true and respected leaders.

Over my many years, I have helped raise or have personally given probably a billion dollars or so, for education, health care, sports, and various other civic and charitable causes. I particularly love the University of

Louisville. I have tried to promote all aspects of the school, from academics to facilities and sports programs. I have watched UofL grow and excel with great pride. Whenever I give money, whether it is for education, healthcare, the environment or even political campaigns, I hope and believe it helps Louisville and in turn helps all of Kentucky and its citizens.

As I mentioned earlier, the Frazier Rehabilitation Center is particularly important to me as it was to my mother. Especially meaningful to me was helping raise money, about $87 million, to build and expand the Center. The Rehab Center has benefited people not only in our city, state and region, but all across the country. What I learned from that experience is if you have a passion for a cause, you will succeed.

Another thing I am proud of is the relationship I negotiated with Great Britain's Royal Armouries Museum. In essence, we have treasures from the Tower of London right here in Louisville at the Museum. It was not an easy task to come to an agreement. England's Parliament had to confirm the collaboration and a few members had some sticky questions. After many, many assurances from the folks from Parliament that we absolutely understood the significance of national treasures, we signed the agreement of collaboration in February 2003. Louisville is now the fourth home of the Royal Armouries and the only location outside of the United Kingdom. As an international museum, the Frazier shows businesses, those here and those considering Kentucky, that we are serious about education and global relationships. But the biggest thrill for me is that the museum provides people from all walks of life, in Louisville and America, an opportunity to see and experience international treasures.

At my age, 70, I look back on my life and wish I could do it all again. Of course, I would change a few of the mechanics, but none of the projects themselves. I have a passion for education and the city of Louisville. When the museum opportunity came along, I dived in head first. I was so excited about sharing my collection and other great pieces of history with the city, and the world for that matter, that I poured my heart, soul and finances into this project. If I were to do it again, I would give myself, the museum developers, staff and the community more time to plan and develop the project. The museum is a much bigger undertaking than I ever anticipated. But when I get letters and speak with people who rave about their wonderful museum experiences, see busloads of kids learning about history and enjoying the museum, it is all worth it.

Good followers are just good leaders in training. They are willing to listen, and then execute what they have been asked to do. It has been my experience that most great leaders can also be good followers. They can lead one group or direct a project and still be of benefit by following in other areas.

I would tell young people to get as much education as you possibly can. Gain knowledge from everyone you meet and every circumstance that comes your way. Look for a mentor. Learn to listen. Start building a career, not necessarily in a top leadership role, but in some lesser position. Work your way up. Learning the fundamentals of a business and building a solid foundation will make you a better and more respected leader.

I don't think you can narrow down any one person or specific thing that is responsible for Louisville's major growth. Sometimes you only need one or two visionaries to make a huge impact on a city and start the ball rolling. We have had some good economic development leaders who saw the need to upgrade our road systems, expand the airport and bring in companies such as UPS. Look at what UPS has meant to our community over the past ten years and imagine what the next ten can bring. Of course, we cannot discount the value of other established international companies that have their plants or corporate headquarters in Louisville, such as a Brown-Forman, Papa John's, Ford, Yum!, and General Electric. They give roots to our community that influence others to want to start their growth here.

I have been privileged several times over the last 20-25 years to have been put in leadership roles to make a few things happen. Knowing the mayor, county judges, governor and other influential leaders has helped. When these people know you and understand you only have the community's best interest at heart, you can sit down and talk with them to discuss the benefits that could be realized from certain projects. It doesn't always work out, but at least you are heard and it is considered.

The arts have certainly contributed to our quality of life. Louisville has one of the most sophisticated arts and theater programs in any city its size or a hell of a lot larger. When you get outside New York and Chicago, you are not going to find many folks that beat us out in terms of quality, quantity, expertise and skill.

As a city, we face some challenges. Many major corporate groups have split, no longer exist or have their corporate headquarters outside Louisville. You no longer have local newspaper ownership, a Barry Bingham Sr., to go to for financial and editorial support. *The Courier-Journal* is so important. I don't know of a group even today that is trying to put forth a major product that doesn't start with the editorial board of *The Courier-Journal*.

We have some great leaders in our community, like Owsley Brown of Brown-Forman, David Jones of Humana and John Schnatter of Papa John's who have given huge local support for many various projects, including the environment, arts and sports programs. Yet in the last few months, each of these men has stepped down as CEO from their respective companies. I have, however, met the new generation of leaders who have stepped into these positions and believe they all remain committed to this community. Plus, there are a number of new Louisville companies growing rapidly. With good leadership and a little more growth, maybe they will start replacing some of the companies who have closed or moved on.

To all future generations of leaders, I leave these words: Nothing comes easy and nothing comes without a great deal of hard work. Life is short and passes quickly. If you want to make an impact, a difference, a contribution, don't put it off to tomorrow — start today.

Get an education. Your education is exclusively yours. You are going to get out of it in exact proportion to what you put into it — little effort, little results; big effort, BIG results. I am referring to education in the broadest sense of the word, way beyond just pure academics. The whole learning process is something that is solely yours forever and cannot ever be taken away. Find something you love to do, something you are passionate about, and then do it.

GEORGE N. GILL

**Retired President and Publisher
Courier-Journal and
Louisville Times Company**

GEORGE GILL CAME TO LOUISVILLE in 1960 to take a job as a copy editor with *The Courier-Journal*. His ambition then was to lead the C-J news operation some day – a heady expectation for a young man with a couple of years of newspapering under his belt, at a time when *The Courier-Journal* was considered one of the best newspapers in the country.

But he reached the goal in six years, and became one of the country's youngest managing editors in 1966. After eight years, he took over the business side of *The Courier-Journal, The Louisville Times*, WHAS, Inc., Standard Gravure Corporation, and some other, smaller, Bingham subsidiaries. Then, when the Bingham family decided to sell its media empire, they asked Gill to handle the negotiations. He sold it all for more than anyone expected, then stayed on to run the newspaper company for the new owners – Gannett Co., Inc. – for seven more years.

While he was leading the papers, he took on the chairman's job at the Greater Louisville Economic Development Partnership and led a $10 million fundraising effort to find ways for Louisville to recover from a dramatic hemorrhage of manufacturing jobs in the 1970s and 1980s. The partnership later merged with the Louisville Area Chamber of Commerce, which Gill also chaired, to become Greater Louisville Inc.

George Gill was born in Indianapolis, where he was an Eagle Scout. He took a run at Indiana University after high school but, finding beer parties more interesting than studying, he took time out for a two-year hitch in the Navy. "Smartest thing I ever did," he said. After he completed his service, he returned to Bloomington, exchanged his C's for A's, ensconced himself for a period at the Ernie Pyle desk as editor-in-chief of the *Indiana Daily Student*, drove a taxi cab, met his wife Kay, then finished college.

He reported on the early space program for the *News Leader* in Richmond, Virginia for three years, then moved to *The Courier-Journal*. He became acting Sunday editor, then assistant city editor, then city editor. In 1966, he reached his goal and became managing editor. He always said his tenure in that job coincided with an era that was "awful" for the world but good for the news business, spanning the civil rights movement, Watergate, the Vietnam War, student riots, assassinations, and sweeping social changes.

But when he got a chance to jump to the business side of the newspaper in 1974, he left the news behind. He moved from general manager to vice president to president of *The Courier-Journal* before economic and family pressures led Barry Bingham Sr. to put the companies on the market in 1986. Barry Bingham Jr., who was then publisher and opposed to the sale, said Gill "handled a very difficult time very, very well." Others on all sides of the issues agreed.

The papers and other companies sold for $445.8 million, which Bingham Jr. said was $100 million more than anyone expected. At the recommendation of the Binghams, Gannett kept Gill on as president and publisher, then made him vice president of the company's metro newspaper division, with responsibility for newspapers in Louisville, Des Moines, and Nashville.

Gill became involved with a number of civic organizations as he moved up the ladder at the newspapers. He started as a member of the board of the Louisville Area Chamber of Commerce, then moved up to become its president, which led to his serving on the Louisville Development Committee and the Greater Louisville Economic Development Partnership. Along the way he served on a number of other boards: Liberty National Bancorp Inc., Alliant Health Systems, United Way of Kentucky, Louisville Free Public Library Foundation, and others.

He received an Outstanding Alumnus Award from his alma mater, Indiana University, in 1984, and received a Doctor of Humane Letters honorary degree from IU in 1994.

In his retirement, Gill likes to garden and travel but he still finds ways to give back to the community. He especially enjoys driving around in his pickup truck now, framing up houses for Habitat for Humanity.

Gill credits much of his success to advice he got from Abraham Lincoln by reading an inscription over a fireplace in the IU Memorial Union Building. He recommends the same advice to young leaders. "Study and get ready," Lincoln said, "and some day your chance will come."

MY FIRST LEADERSHIP ROLES in the community began as a result of my working at *The Courier-Journal*. As I got higher up in the Bingham organization, some roles just came with the territory.

WilsonWyatt asked me to be on the board of the Chamber of Commerce, for example. I was flattered and became a board member. I was on the board of Leadership Louisville the year it was established (1979). I progressed on and became president of the Chamber, then later led the UnitedWay campaign. If you were the head of or high up in a locally-owned company, it was kind of expected that you would do community service, which I thoroughly enjoyed.

As I was working my way up the ladder at the *Courier*, I saw some places where I thought I might be able to make a contribution, maybe even make a little difference. I looked forward to serving on these boards, and once I got on them, it was a lot of fun.

In the late '60s and on into the '70s and '80s, most of the banks and companies in town were locally-owned, and that made a huge difference. You used to be able to walk down Fourth Street and do business at lunchtime and see friends who were all CEOs. It's not that way any more. Most everything now is owned by out-of-town companies or has its headquarters out-of-town.

Gordon Davidson was one of my earliest mentors. We began to work together in the '60s when I was in the news department of the *Courier*. Gordon's law firm, thenWyatt Grafton and Sloss, was the company's firm and did a lot of libel work. So in the early days, Gordon was one of my idols and mentors; and in later days, we ended up selling the companies together.

WilsonWyatt was another mentor. I tangled with him as a reporter when he was running for governor back in the early '60s. He asked me one time what he had to do to get on page one when he was running for governor and I told him "Well, you might try shooting your wife." He didn't like that very much. He called my boss, Barry Bingham Sr., and I got in deep trouble over that. Later I did a roast of Wilson at the Rotary Club and told that story. His wife was in the audience and we had a big laugh over it. Wilson was also one of my advisors and a good friend.

My editor at the newspaper was another mentor – Norman Isaacs, who was managing editor of the old *Louisville Times*, then was executive editor of both papers later on. I was managing editor under him for a number of years. My wife used to joke with me, wondering who would die first of a heart attack, because he was a terrible task master. I both loved him and hated him, but I learned an awful lot from him, not only about journalism but about Louisville and how the city worked, because he was very active in the community as well.

I guess running through all three of these mentors of mine was a sense of ethics and a sense of doing the right thing. I also learned the art of patience from them, and maybe the art of negotiation and the art of listening. You had to really listen to these men, and you had to respond in a gentle way. One of the things I learned from Gordon early on was if you had an adversary in a situation, it was always better to have a smart one than a dumb one. There were a lot of smart people in town back then. I learned that lesson from Gordon.

Before I became president of the Bingham companies in 1981, I always thought that I had two heads. I had one head in the business and one head in the community, and I tried very hard never to mix those two together. The classic example of that was the airport expansion. I knew all about the airport expansion and had consulted with Jerry Abramson, who was mayor back then, and with attorneys and so forth, and I did not tell the news department. When the story finally broke, it was a big surprise to everybody, and a lot of people in the news department criticized me for not telling them what I knew. I explained to them that I have two heads, one is in the community and one is in the company, and I never tried to mix up the two. I think that was very important.

My leadership style was to listen and encourage dissent. You just need to do your homework and try to persuade people of your point of view. The most important thing is to do your homework. I always tried to go into every situation knowing as much or more about it than anybody else in the room. I didn't always succeed, but I tried to do homework in advance of anything I got into.

Others might describe my leadership style as authoritarian, but I don't think they would describe me as weak. Somebody has to make decisions, and I was never afraid to make a decision. I always knew, though, that I had to be accountable for my decisions, whether they were right or wrong. I guess there were those who thought that I was kind of a bulldozer. Maybe I was, but given what else I have said, I think I had some balance about it.

The first time I really stuck my neck out was when I was president of the Chamber. The city was kind of on the rocks because of the loss of manufacturing jobs and I was very concerned about that.

I commissioned what was called the Economic Inventory, which the Chamber paid for and the University of Louisville's Urban Studies Department conducted. My whole objective was to have a document that we could hold in our hands that told the truth about what the real economic situation was in the city. The results came back and, as we all suspected, the loss of manufacturing was tantamount to pending disaster down the road if we didn't do something to reach out and begin replacing those jobs.

As an example, at one time the General Electric Appliance Park had 20,000 employees, now it has 5,000. I think we had lost about 50,000 or 60,000 manufacturing jobs in the ten years before that, and this was done in the late '70s, early '80s. That led to the formation of something called Project 2000.

A group of guys ran companies that were all locally-owned. I remember we had an organizational breakfast out at Bauer's Restaurant on Brownsboro Road. Guys like Charlie McCarty, David Jones and Gordon Davidson attended, and the mayor and county judge. I kind of honchoed this thing. We got them all together, and I will never forget it. We sat down at the table. We needed some money. So I said, "Well, I'm in for $35,000," and someone else said "I'm in for $35,000," and suddenly we had a quarter of a million dollars raised right there at the table to develop some kind of economic development thrust in the community to address our economy. That led eventually to establishment of the Economic Development Partnership, which was chaired initially by David Grissom at Citizens Bank, then I succeeded him as chairman.

We were somewhat successful at raising money and attracting new jobs. We brought Zeon Chemicals to town, for instance. We put some money into Jeffboat across the river. Jeffboat was in desperate straits then, as it is now, but it's still here. The Economic Development Partnership was directed at bringing jobs from outside into the community.

One of the things we found out in trying to raise money was that the donors kept saying, "Don't give it to the Chamber of Commerce," because the Chamber in those days (which I headed, as its president) had sort of a "keep a steady hand and don't rock the boat" approach. It wasn't assertive and wasn't aggressive, and that was something that was very much needed. The Partnership eventually merged with the Chamber of Commerce, which later became Greater Louisville Inc. From the outside looking in, I think, GLI is a pretty spiffy organization now. It has gotten its act together.

I can remember going to UPS right after they were beginning to establish their airline and suggesting to them that they had a marvelous opportunity to offer logistical support to companies that had to transfer a lot of material overnight very quickly. Because UPS was located here, they could also attract warehousing and that sort of business because there would be discounts for shipping. In those days, the old brown truck guys were running the company and they said, "No way." You see what UPS is today, and the guy that runs GLI today, Steve Higdon, worked for UPS.

Another accomplishment I was pretty proud of was that I ran the Metro United Way fundraising campaign in 1983. We were the first campaign to reach $10 million, which sounds like peanuts today. It was a big deal back then.

We missed our goal by about $200,000, and I can remember being disappointed. But I can remember saying, "Hey, if you don't reach, you don't ever get there." We had hoped to raise $10.5 million and we only raised $10.3 million. So what? That's a pretty decent performance. That was another little axiom of mine: Never fear to set a "reach" goal and if you make it, great, and if you don't make it, great — at least you tried.

Back to the "two heads" thing, I remember the headline the year that I ran the Metro United Way campaign said "United Way Misses Goal." Well okay, that was their judgment. I didn't try to influence it. I just took it on the chin.

I guess my biggest disappointment over those many, many years was the failure to merge the governments. We failed twice. That was back in the Project 2000 days, and we held some seminars and public forums on merger. One of our members took it upon himself to go into the West End and told people, "You will vote for this merger," and of course it backfired. The lesson learned there is that to make democracy work, you have to have a good case and you have to persuade people. You can't hammer them and tell them to do something. Now of course the governments have merged, but it took 20 years. I think we could have progressed a lot faster if we had merged 20 years ago.

What's it take to be a good follower? If you say you're going to do something, do it. Don't commit to something, then slough it off and not do it. And don't be afraid to admit your mistakes. If you've made a mistake, say so. Nobody's going to hold that against you. Everybody makes mistakes, and I think we just have to admit them and go on, and learn from them.

I think a good leader or a good follower knows his or her own weaknesses. I always had a good rule of thumb to surround myself with people who were a lot smarter than I was. My role was to lead the band, to be the orchestra director. I knew what my weaknesses were, and they were many, so I tried to shore myself up with those who had great expertise in such things as finance, which is not my strong area.

If I had a chance to do everything all over again, I would be more patient. I'm healthy today at 70 years old, and it's a wonder. There are a lot of miles on those 70 years. A lot of angst and a lot of anguish, a lot of controversy and a lot of confrontation. I think I would try to be more patient.

I would advise young people aspiring to leadership to, first and foremost, learn as much as they can about the community. I used to have a rule when I ran the news department which illustrates that point.

We would get new employees in the news department and copy editors from all over the country, and one of the first things I always insisted a new person do when they came to work for the *Courier* news department was to go down and spend a day at the McAlpine Locks and Dam with the lockmaster. I wanted them to learn something about the river, because the river is very important to us and very dangerous to us if we don't know what we're doing. That paid off, I think, over the years, when flood times came. You hear news readers on television and radio today, mixing up the upper gauge and the lower gauge of the river, and they don't know what they're talking about.

So young people should learn about the community and learn about its people. Not only the leadership people, but the people down in the streets. Get out of the concrete bunker. So many folks who aspire to leadership want to do it in the boardrooms. There's a concrete bunker mentality that within these walls "what we know is what we know, and what we do is what is right."

I work with Habitat for Humanity. One of the marvelous things I have learned in retirement is a lot more about the people in our city, particularly in the western part of Louisville. I like to do rough and dirty work. I have a truck and a bunch of tools and, two days a week, I work for Habitat, mostly in the West End, in Smoketown and so forth, on a framing crew, forming concrete, pouring concrete, putting in floor decking, putting up siding, putting up walls. I don't have the patience to do fine cabinetry or fine finish work, but I love the rough and tumble stuff.

Merger has probably contributed more to our community's growth and development over the years than anything else I can think of. It is very important. I think the emergence of Greater Louisville Inc. is also very important, because I think now we have a place at the table for business and we have strong economic growth. I used to laugh about Cincinnati's, for instance, having 15 or 20 FORTUNE 500 company headquarters in town. The loyalty really is to the corporation, which may be in Delaware, or the company is owned by shareholders around the world. Combining a strong economic development effort with merged government is a real asset and can combat that. Of course, we are more like Cincinnati today, because everything is owned out-of-town. You're looking at a guy who led the sales team that sold newspapers and television stations and printing plants and subsidiaries for $445 million, all to out-of-towners.

The most important issue challenging our community today, I think, is trying to balance growth with tradition. I think we have to continue to grow in terms of infrastructure. I will never live long enough to drive across the new bridges, and we've been talking about new bridges for 25 or 30 years.

I applaud the preservation effort from a distance. But I think it can be an obstructionist at times. Those who would protect tradition at all costs, I think, are just as wrong as those who would protect growth at all costs.

My advice to the next generation? It sounds kind of corny. Study and get ready and some day your chance will come. This is what Leadership Louisville is all about – knowing the community, networking, knowing its people.

The most valuable lesson I have learned in my own life is how important it is to study and get ready. I started out majoring in beer parties at Indiana University and I piddled along as a C student. I fell in love, and my girlfriend threw me out, so I joined the Navy and went away to see the world. Smartest thing I ever did because when I came back, I finished college and met my wife. We have now been married 47 years.

When I was a college student at Indiana University in Bloomington, I saw a quotation above a fireplace at the Student Union Building that said, "I will study and get ready and some day my chance will come." People attribute that quotation to Abe Lincoln. I made straight As after I saw it, so I think that was a lesson to me even way back then. I want to share it now with Louisville's next generation of leaders whose chance will also come, if they study and get ready.

C. Edward Glasscock

Managing Partner
Frost Brown Todd LLC

ED GLASSCOCK PERSONIFIES leadership. Whether serving as managing partner of Frost Brown Todd, working with clients on significant business deals or chairing and advising regional and local civic endeavors, he is constantly moving things forward.

In his role as business adviser and legal counselor, he helps clients with corporate mergers and acquisitions and advises them on new business ventures. His peers use a lot of superlatives to describe how well he does it. In comments to the newspapers, they have said he brings intelligence, knowledge and humor to his job, that he is a conciliator and consensus builder, that he is "intelligent, kind, considerate, and loyal," that he is "dead honest" and a good catalyst for bringing investors together, and that he's a "lightning rod for entrepreneurial activity."

Add to those accolades an extraordinarily high energy level. Glasscock's friends say he never stops moving. Louisville Metro Mayor Jerry Abramson, no slouch himself, says he envies Glasscock's energy.

What you have, *The Courier-Journal* said in a 2001 article about how Glasscock almost salvaged a doomed effort to lure a professional basketball team to town, is "a towering figure in Louisville's business and legal world."

At Frost Brown Todd, he has managed the evolution of the law firm for almost three decades, and over that time has made a name for himself in the civic arena as a hardworking achiever and a skillful community catalyst.

During his tenure as managing partner, the firm has grown from 38 lawyers, with offices in Louisville, into the premier law firm between Chicago and Atlanta, with approximately 400 lawyers and offices in seven cities in Kentucky, Ohio, Tennessee and Indiana.

He was born in Leitchfield, Kentucky in 1943, and his father had prepared him for a career in the family's trucking, concrete supply and road construction businesses. He drove a truck at age 16, and supervised a large construction crew at 17.

He earned a civil engineering degree at UK, where he met his wife Mary F. who, he says, is the reason he has been able to accomplish what he has. He was working on an MBA, when a business law course stirred an interest in him in the legal profession. He changed direction at that time and graduated at the top of his law school class at UK's College of Law in 1969. While attending law school, he was selected as the recipient of the Outstanding Student Award, out of 14,000 students at the University of Kentucky. He left the family businesses in his brother Tom's hands and joined the Louisville law firm of Brown Ardery Todd & Dudley, which ultimately became Frost Brown Todd.

Most people would say that Glasscock has mastered the art of corporate law. With its dialogue, parlaying, negotiating and potential for building something, he found his cup of tea.

"Deal-making is where the action is. I like deal-making because I'm working with intelligent entrepreneurs willing to take risks," he told *Business First* in 1988. "I also like the give-and-take of negotiations, and the structuring of deals in terms of legal, business and tax issues."

In the 2005 issue of *Chambers USA: America's Leading Lawyers for Business*, Glasscock was described by the authors, after interviewing peers and clients, as follows: "Clients could barely find enough superlatives to describe 'the extraordinarily energetic, extremely thorough, highly imaginative and incredibly reliable' Ed Glasscock. His 'strategic thinking and effective marshalling of the wealth of resources at this firm' continue to earn him the accolade of 'probably being the number one corporate attorney in the state.'"

Glasscock's extraordinary civic spirit has been evident in the roles he has played in the community. He spearheaded the 2000 drive that raised $1.6 million to support merger of Louisville and Jefferson County governments. He has chaired Greater Louisville Inc. and its predecessor, the Louisville Area Chamber of Commerce. As a Chamber of Commerce leader, he pulled the Louisville business community together to present bills and business-friendly proposals to the Kentucky legislature. He helped launch the Chamber's Advanced Technology Council, as well as helping to establish the Louisville Venture Forum, Inc.

He has also received numerous honors and leadership awards, including Greater Louisville Inc.'s Gold Cup Award for Outstanding Community Leadership (2003); Louisvillian of the Year Award (2001); Member, Junior Achievement Business Hall of Fame (2002); Tom Simons Leadership Award, Leadership Louisville Foundation (2002); Member, Hall of Fame, University of Kentucky College of Law (2003); and UK Jefferson County Alumni Club All American Award (2001).

Passing the Torch

I HAVE ALWAYS BELIEVED that each of us has a duty to give back to the communities in which we live and work. There is plenty of work to be done outside of our chosen professions.

The best way to "do something" is to contribute time and talent to make our community even better. I am happy to have the opportunity to serve our city. Louisville has been good to me, my family and my law firm, Frost Brown Todd. It has been my pleasure to serve the many outstanding organizations in Louisville and throughout Kentucky. I hope, in my own small way, I have shown my appreciation by using my talents to do some good for our community.

In that spirit, I have been given the opportunity to chair the Board of Trustees of Bellarmine University, Greater Louisville, Inc., the Regional Leadership Coalition, Junior Achievement Free Enterprise Center Capital Campaign raising $5.5 million, the Kentucky Center for the Arts, the Greater Louisville Fund for the Arts and the Fund for the Arts Annual Campaign.

I have been fortunate to serve on the Metro United Way Cabinet and other boards in the community, such as the Leadership Louisville Foundation (Vice Chairman), Center for Women and Families, St. Xavier High School, the Louisville Free Public Library Foundation, the University of Louisville Board of Overseers, MetaCyte Business Lab, LLC, and Louisville Baseball Club, LLC ("Louisville Bats"), among others.

My attention has been focused on education, arts and entertainment and economic development, because each of those areas help to enhance the quality of life in our community and keep young people in Louisville. It is important to keep our young people here. The future of our city is in their hands.

I have had a chance to admire and be influenced by many wonderful leaders, family members and friends, like my uncle, C. D. Lucas, Jr.; my friends, Milo D. Bryant, James A. Patterson, Samuel R. Rechter, and James H. Thornton. But I would have to say my father, C. E. Glasscock, was my best mentor. He told me, "Whatever you do, do it with integrity, enthusiasm, and a positive mind set. Do not worry about who gets the credit for a task, but be concerned about getting the job done. Be passionate about every worthwhile endeavor and remember that failing is a part of growing." His words have been words to live by throughout my entire life. Those words have made me into the man I am today, and I am truly grateful.

There were other mentors as well, including all of the founding members of Brown Ardery Todd & Dudley, Brown Todd & Heyburn and Frost Brown Todd. They were all men and women of integrity and, like my father, stressed the importance of having integrity in all aspects of your life and consistently striving for excellence. Gordon Davidson, Bob Doll, Michael Fleishman, Fred

Goldberg and a number of other very talented lawyers in Louisville have also been very helpful to me throughout my career.

In my opinion, leadership is a concept not easily defined by words, although many have tried. I would describe my own leadership style as dynamic, and constantly evolving. Donald H. McGannon once said that "leadership is action, not position." And George Van Valkenburg said that "leadership is doing what is right when no one is watching." I would have to agree with both of them. That is the exciting thing about leadership – each new leader has an opportunity to redefine it. I hope others would describe my style as passionate, active and committed.

To be a good leader, you need to be a good listener. You need to respect others and their ability to contribute to a desired outcome. You also need to be willing to assume a role that is not necessarily a leadership role, depending upon the situation. You need to be a good follower when it is necessary for you to fill that role. It all depends on the team members and what type of leadership is needed to complete a particular project.

I have read numerous books about leadership. Some of my favorites include, *Good to Great*, by Jim Collins, a terrific book that provides excellent insight and information about why particular companies have become successful. I also like Jack Welch's book, *Jack – Straight from the Gut*, *Leadership*, by Rudolph W. Giuliani, and *Iacocca*, by Lee Iacocca. Each contains wonderful advice about effective leadership.

Another outstanding book on leadership is *The Cycle of Leadership*, by Noel M. Tichy. My friend, Coach Rick Pitino, has written a number of books on leadership which contain excellent advice and strategies about leadership for all ages.

Stay informed about theses authors and their companies to see how effective they are after their books are published. Some leaders remain true to their values, but others get caught up in their own recognition and veer off track – like Lee Iacocca. He lost his focus after his book was published, even considered running for president. It is important to stay true to your core values.

I believe in being prepared for everything I do. As co-chair of Frost Brown Todd's Mergers and Acquisitions Practice Section, I believe the more you know about the companies involved in a deal, their executives, and the industries in which they operate, the more effective representation you can provide. With preparation, you can help others stay focused on the ultimate outcome, whether that is accomplishing the merger of two companies or, in the community, achieving a goal that benefits the community as a whole.

Working on the strategy committee and serving as chairman of the finance committee of our community's campaign for merger – the Unity Campaign –

was one of my most significant accomplishments. We raised $1.6 million. Teamwork, commitment and hard work truly pay off when you put passion and focus into an important project.

The prospect of merger was tentative at best, since it had failed three times in the past. But this time, a number of key leaders came together in a true bipartisan effort to promote what was in the best interests of the community. Mayor Jerry Abramson, U.S. Senator Mitch McConnell, Congresswoman Anne Northup, former Mayor David Armstrong and former Jefferson County Judge-Executive Rebecca Jackson all worked together. That was true teamwork. We used the money we had raised as effectively as we could. We conducted extensive polling and, as a result, were able to better understand why people were opposed to merger, and we specifically addressed those key issues in advertisements and mailings. I was particularly proud of the way the young leaders got involved with the merger campaign.

You win some and you lose some, but life's biggest lessons come when we fail. My biggest disappointment is that we did not succeed in bringing the NBA to Louisville a few years ago; therefore, we could not build an arena in downtown Louisville. It is an effort that became somewhat controversial. I learned that in order to tackle other challenges in our community, we must first reverse the negative attitudes that greet almost every major proposal in Louisville. The negative attitudes were disappointing to me. In hindsight, we could have done a better job of polling and listening so that we could have educated the community about the significance of the arena. It wasn't just about the NBA; it was much bigger than that. It was about enhancing the quality of life in Louisville by building a state of the art multi-purpose arena here. The NBA was the centerpiece because we were using a tax increment financing plan to pay for the arena. The arena would have been used for University of Louisville sporting events, entertainment events, concerts, major tournaments and conventions.

We did not do a good job of getting that message across, and people focused too much on the NBA component. The effort also suffered because we did not have the broad-based support that we had with the merger effort. From an overall community perspective, the arena was important and something that our young people would have enjoyed. Its appeal would have extended far beyond Louisville. People from throughout the Commonwealth and the region would have looked forward to coming to Louisville to attend a wide variety of outstanding entertainment events. I am confident we will build an arena in the near future.

The foundation of many of Louisville's successes was *The Visioning Report* that was developed in 1997. It has contributed very significantly to our city's growth, development and quality of life. Approximately 100 business and community leaders came together to develop a vision for our community. The first thing decided was that we needed to merge our city and county governments so that we could speak with one voice. We also felt that we needed to have one economic development organization in our community, so we moved forward to merge the Chamber of Commerce, the Louisville and Jefferson County Economic Development Partnership and the Office of Economic Development.

In terms of economic development, we focused on logistics, distribution and transportation, and on biomedical and health care.

In the logistical, distribution and transportation area, UPS has been a significant economic development force in our community for many years, and its continued expansion has been very important to the entire Commonwealth of Kentucky. UPS is now the largest employer in Kentucky, employing approximately 20,000 people.

Jewish Hospital has been very successful with respect to innovation in health care. The first mechanical heart implant and the first successful hand transplant happened at Jewish Hospital. In addition, the University of Louisville has done an outstanding job utilizing the "Bucks for Brains" program to attract scientists and their teams to our community. A number of companies have been formed when the research has been commercialized. Jewish and UofL have formed the Cardiovascular Innovation Institute to commercialize cardiac devices. Norton Healthcare has also had its share of important medical innovations, including the outstanding medical innovations at Norton's Kosair Children's Hospital. The health care industry now employs approximately 72,000 people with an annual payroll of approximately $2.5 billion.

During the planning stages, we also decided that we needed to expand entrepreneurship and venture capital in our community. At the time, we had three venture capital firms. We now have approximately 20 venture capital firms in our community, with $365,000,000 in available capital. Entrepreneurship is flourishing throughout metro Louisville.

The merger of our city and county governments has also contributed significantly to the growth, development and improved quality of life in our community, especially in the downtown area. Our city has seen a surge in the development of downtown residential housing, commercial real estate, entertainment attractions, restaurants and biomedical services. Construction sites can be seen on many downtown streets. Louisville is definitely a city on the move.

In 2002, we pushed for merger during the Vote Yes for Unity Campaign. During that campaign, community leaders promised a vision of a merged government that would reflect our entire community. I think it has and will continue to do so.

Our city faces many challenges in the future. Among them are attracting regional and national corporate headquarters; continuing to focus on other economic development opportunities; and raising venture capital for emerging companies. We also need to continue our focus on educating our workforce and maintaining the excitement that has developed over the last few years.

With the recent boom in downtown residential development, more people are deciding to live downtown. The increase in attractions with Fourth Street Live!, the Frazier Historical Arms Museum, the Louisville Slugger Museum, Louisville Slugger Field, the expansion of the Kentucky Center for the Arts, expansion of Churchill Downs, and the construction of the highly anticipated Muhammad Ali Center have made Louisville a wonderful destination, not only during the first weekend in May, but year-round.

The next generation of leaders should continue to strive to make Louisville unique among other cities across the country. We should continue to build residential housing as well as more retail to make Louisville "the place to be" once again. I am hopeful that the next generation of leaders will focus on doing that by holding on to what sets us apart from other cities, keeping our southern hospitality charm, but with the benefits of a "big city."

We do not want Louisville to be like other cities. We have enough character, resources and talented people to make our city a model for others to follow. I have full confidence that the next generation of leaders will carry on the rich tradition of our city for many years to come.

Funding for Louisville Metro will also be a challenge in the future. There is significant revenue leakage from Louisville to the rest of the Commonwealth through state government. Louisville does not receive the full value of the tax dollars it sends to Frankfort. Louisville recognizes that it has a duty to share resources with other parts of the Commonwealth and is happy to provide some financial support, but not to the detriment of its own citizens.

We must receive a fair allocation of revenue from Frankfort. The scales are now tipped against us. Louisville as well as other major urban areas in Kentucky are economic engines. As such, their interests need to be financially supported. The more these engines can produce, the more tax dollars that will be available for the rest of the Commonwealth to share.

Kentucky's leadership needs to work together on this issue in a spirit of true bipartisanship — to focus on what is good for the Commonwealth as a whole. Progress can be made and Kentucky can continue to raise its national stature in a number of areas. We will all benefit from this effort.

A major challenge for Kentucky will be how to increase revenue. We need to give serious thought to this issue, be open-minded about the choices, then make the difficult decisions.

There is nothing I would do differently if I had the chance to do it all over again. Everything in my life, both successes and failures, has made me into the person I am today. Everyone wants to be successful, and I am no different, but with successes come failures. The key is not to let those failures keep you down. You learn from them, then you keep on moving. You should never let the fear of failure stop you from taking a risk.

The most useful advice I would give to young people aspiring to leadership is to be devoted to your family; be passionate about your occupation; serve your community and your religion; and continue to network and build relationships. Leaders will undoubtedly face opposition, and sometimes failure. Some of our community's most popular advancements were once the scorn of skeptics, (e.g. merger). But no matter what happens, never give up. Keep pushing for change.

Finally, I encourage young people to never stop learning. Perhaps the most valuable lesson I have learned in my life and career is that education and experience are essential to advancing your professional and personal lives. Ask yourself each day, "Did I learn something or do something today to help make a difference?"

George Bernard Shaw once said "My life belongs to the community and as long as I live, it is my privilege to do for it what I can. I want to be thoroughly used up when I die, for the harder I work, the more I live." I agree.

J. David Grissom

Chairman
Mayfair Capital, Inc.

Founder and Chairman
Glenview Trust Company

Chairman
Centre College Board of Trustees

DAVID GRISSOM HAS a long and distinguished history of service to Louisville's and Kentucky's economic and civic life. He has served as chairman of the 1979 Metro United Way Campaign, the Louisville Development Foundation, the Kentucky Council on Higher Education, the Louisville Area Chamber of Commerce, the Kentucky Center for the Arts, the Kentucky Economic Development Partnership and the Center City Commission, and he has had leadership roles in many more. He is currently serving or has served on the boards of 12 privately held companies and 13 publicly held companies.

Grissom's secret to success was starting young. He graduated from Centre College in 1960, and from the University of Louisville Law School in 1962. In part because he shared the Centre background with Gordon Davidson, a partner at Wyatt Grafton & Sloss, he launched his legal career with that firm. He later became a partner in the law firm of Greenebaum Grissom Doll Matthews and Boone.

Grissom met David Jones Sr. and Wendell Cherry there as well, and the three of them partnered to launch Extendicare, a nursing home company that, in turn, spawned Humana Inc. When Extendicare went public in 1968, the three young lawyers became millionaires. Grissom was 29. He served as a board member and as executive vice president of Humana Inc. from 1969 to 1973.

He also joined the board of Citizens Fidelity Bank & Trust Company in 1970, and Citizens chairman Maurice Johnson took a liking to him. Johnson offered him a job as vice chairman and chief operating officer of the bank. It reportedly ruffled a few feathers among Citizens executives who had more experience in banking, but it turned out that the canny Johnson apparently knew something they didn't.

Grissom, a businessman rather than a banker, ran the bank like a business and was very good at it. In 1977, at the age of 38, he became chairman and CEO of the bank and of Citizens Fidelity Corporation.

As a bank executive, he was committed to being active in community affairs as well, and once told *Louisville Magazine*, "A bank has two responsibilities – to enhance the value of its shareholders' investment and to improve the quality of life in the markets it serves."

David Grissom grew up in Louisville's Highlands neighborhood. He was more interested in track and football than studying hard back then. His father, a chemical company executive, turned him around, however, by pointing out that people who don't do well in school often don't make very much money. Grissom worked in the cafeteria and as a bus driver at Centre College, and worked for a construction company during law school, but he managed to graduate from both schools on schedule.

Gordon Davidson said he was phenomenal as a young lawyer, bringing in business much earlier in his career than most lawyers expect to. Besides Jones and Cherry, he met other interesting people while he was practicing law at the Greenebaum firm. One was John Y. Brown Jr., who had already made his mark with Kentucky Fried Chicken. Grissom helped Brown move the company's headquarters from Nashville to Louisville.

In 1969, Grissom told *The Courier-Journal* in a profile after he became chairman at Citizens that he and Brown – and Cherry and Jones and others – "got a wild hair" and bought the Kentucky Colonels professional basketball team. Grissom said it was an early attempt at a civic contribution. The team didn't last long, but its legend lives on.

PNC Financial Corp. acquired Citizens in 1987, and Grissom stayed on as PNC vice chairman. He retired from the bank two years later, however – at age 50 – and teamed up with Bill Lomicka, a former executive of Humana and secretary of Kentucky's Cabinet for Economic Development, to form Mayfair Capital, Inc., a private investment firm. Grissom serves as chair and Lomicka serves as president of Mayfair. They are equal partners and, most would agree, a formidable investment team.

Grissom also founded and continues to chair The Glenview Trust Company, and he remains devoted to his alma mater – Centre College in Danville – by serving as the chair of its Board of Trustees.

He and his wife, Marlene, are both active in civic affairs in Louisville. They are generous supporters of the arts and of community initiatives like the waterfront development project. Grissom also currently serves as chairman of the Executive Committee of Churchill Downs, Inc., and is a director of Providian Financial Corporation and YUM! Brands, Inc.

THE FIRST OPPORTUNITY I HAD to be a leader was when I was at Citizen's Fidelity Bank, working primarily with Maury Johnson. He was one of the most extraordinary leaders of our community at that time. Whether by example or by osmosis, I learned at his feet. Maury taught me how important it was to assume roles of leadership and to try to make the community in which you live and work a better place.

Maury was of course an important mentor to me, but I had three extraordinary mentors before him. Wilson Wyatt, former mayor of the City of Louisville, was my primary mentor and leader. Close behind Wilson was Gordon Davidson who, like me, graduated from Centre College and the University of Louisville Law School. Gordon was very involved in a variety of community affairs. Finally, there was David Jones Sr. I couldn't have had any better mentors teach me respectful leadership. For them, life wasn't just about making your career successful or making money. It was about making Louisville a better place from an educational standpoint, a civic standpoint, and from an artistic standpoint.

I've always tried to lead by example. I never ask people to do anything I haven't done already and that I don't already know the difficulty and challenges of. I never ask people to work any harder than I am willing to work either. I think the way you lead is to extend what your own personal resources permit. You try to make the leadership gift. If you're the chairman of the campaign, you try to make the largest donation. Nothing speaks more loudly than what you've stepped up and done. You can't ask other people to make a major gift if you haven't done so yourself.

I think others would say that I don't suffer fools gladly. I am very focused and concerned with the priorities of the day. I don't waste time with incidentals. I try to drive the truck to the finish line.

I've been privileged to be involved in a number of activities, but I would say that I am most proud of whatever role I've had in making Centre College an exceptional liberal arts college. I've served as chairman of Centre's Board of Trustees since 1987, and during that period of time it has become a much better place. I've learned that if a group of people put their shoulders behind a cause, they can make a difference.

I've had a few failures or disappointments. I served as chairman of an initial effort to bring metro government to our community. I knew that it was the right thing, but we came up short. Now that we have metro government,

I think the proof is in the pudding. It's a much better form of government. The community just wasn't quite ready for it before.

A follower, to use military vernacular, has to be a good soldier and take his cue from his leader. While he may disagree with the leader's strategy, he has to embrace it and do what he can to carry it out.

If I could live my life over again, I would attend college out-of-state. I feel my educational experience would have been significantly enriched.

Young people today have to be willing to pay their dues. They need to start out doing small things, the most menial tasks. You can't start at the top.

I think Mr. and Mrs. Barry Bingham Sr. made a huge difference in our community and contributed significantly to the growth, development and improved quality of life we enjoy today. You see their tracks everywhere, whether it be in the medical community, in the educational community, or addressing the social needs of this community. They were extremely generous, both with their resources and their time.

We also have a combination of arts in our community that is disproportionate to our population. We have a wonderful menu of cultural offerings that most cities would envy greatly. The arts have enriched the cultural fabric of our community significantly.

Lastly, with our new metro form of government, we've finally gotten it right! We have a form of government that seems to be working. The political leadership in this town is better than it ever was. When you have quality leadership at the top that is focused on the issues of the day, good things happen.

What are our community's biggest challenges? I think in the area of social needs in our community, we still have a lot to do to take care of the underprivileged. With the cutback in federal and state support, we just can't leave that segment of our community behind.

Secondly, we have to continue to strive to make our public school system even better.

I've learned some valuable lessons in my lifetime that I would like to share with the next generation of leaders in Louisville. But most importantly, I would advise them that tenacity is an important characteristic in getting anything done, whether it's in your personal career or in community leadership.

As Winston Churchill said, "Never, never, never give up."

MICHAEL N. HARRELD

**Regional President
PNC Bank
Greater Washington, D.C. Area**

**Former Regional President/ CEO
PNC Bank, Kentucky**

MIKE HARRELD SAYS HIS CAREER at Citizens Fidelity Bank & Trust Company, later PNC Bank, began as a fluke. He was in law school at the University of Louisville, bent on a career in politics, and he took a part-time job filling out inheritance tax returns in the Citizens trust department. He graduated from law school in 1969 and decided to stay at the bank until he could decide what he really wanted to do.

By that time he'd figured out it wasn't law, or politics. "I was way too impatient to be a politician," he told *Business First* in 1991.

Citizens Fidelity started adding to Harreld's responsibilities. In 1975 then-Citizens president David Grissom and then-chairman Maurice Johnson pried him out of the trust department. They told him they wanted him to try the marketing department, and to become its head. It seemed like a strange move to Harreld, from trust to marketing, but he gamely moved over. He found he learned a lot about the banking business and actually enjoyed promoting the bank's products.

Grissom was interested in making a banker out of him, however, not in letting him get comfortable. So he continued to move him into new positions from time to time, usually into some job he had never thought of doing. It made life a bit unpredictable, Harreld told *The Courier-Journal* in 1989, but it also offered him an "opportunity to never be bored."

Grissom later observed that Harreld seemed to have "the ability to keep a lot of balls in the air without becoming flustered."

One of the jobs Harreld moved through was correspondent banking, through which Citizens sold services to smaller banks across the state. What he learned there came in handy a short time later when banking rules changed and Citizens began looking for banks to buy out in the state.

While Grissom was seeing to Harreld's business training, Maurice Johnson was instilling in him the same passion for community service that he'd previously drilled into Grissom. Harreld was soon busy chairing the Kentucky Council on Higher Education, Greater Louisville Inc., Metro United Way, the UofL Board of Overseers, Leadership Louisville and the Housing Partnership Board. He became president of the Louisville Orchestra Board and the Kentucky Bankers Association, and a member of the boards of the J.B. Speed Art Museum, Norton Healthcare, Inc., the Muhammad Ali Center, the University of Louisville, Bellarmine College, Western Kentucky University and Murray State University.

All a step up for the young man who grew up in the Hikes Point area when it was still mostly rural, and who dug potatoes for money as a young man. Mike Harreld is a graduate of Seneca High School, where he mostly sat on the bench of the basketball team, but once had the honor of having his finger broken in a scrimmage by Westley Unseld, later a UofL and National Basketball Association legend. Harreld discovered in himself, though, a competitive streak and a reluctance to lose.

He dabbled in politics as a Republican precinct committeeman while he was still at home, an activity made all the more interesting by the fact that his father, who was in the stone quarry business, was the Democratic precinct committeeman and the precinct voting place was in the family garage. He attended Western Kentucky University for a time, but both his undergraduate and law degrees are from the University of Louisville.

Maurice Johnson's eye for talent, and Grissom's instincts about Mike Harreld's leadership capabilities, were confirmed when Harreld became president and CEO of PNC Louisville in 1989.

He served in that position, and was an active and respected community leader in Louisville, for 16 years. In spring 2005, he accepted one last career challenge to move to Washington, D.C. to become the regional president of PNC Bank in the Greater Washington, D.C. area.

Harreld amassed an impressive array of awards and honors for his community involvement during his years in Louisville. He received the Advertising Club of Louisville's Louisvillian of the Year Award; Distinguished Alumnus Awards from the University of Louisville Brandeis School of Law and its College of Arts and Sciences; Greater Louisville Inc.'s Gold Cup Award; and the Metropolitan Housing Coalition's Different Hero Award for his persistent commitment to affordable housing programs in Louisville.

Harreld has one daughter from a first marriage. His wife Susan has one son from her first marriage, and they have another son as well.

I DON'T THINK I EVER REALLY DECIDED TO become a leader in Louisville. When I went to work for Citizens Fidelity Bank, it was more or less expected that we would be engaged civically in the community. It was good for business, and it anchored deals.

Maurice Johnson was our Chairman and CEO. His legacy encompassed everything from Leadership Louisville to much of the rebuilding of downtown Louisville, so he expected all of his young officers to be engaged in the community and he nurtured, supported and assisted us.

That was my first nudge to get involved in the community. I had not been involved in anything up to that point except my political party. I had been active in local politics when I was in college and law school, but this was a new ingredient for me.

Maury and other mentors like Joe Rodes, David Grissom and Dan Ulmer were all civically involved. Your mentors, for the most part, dictate where you go and what you do. I became engaged, and stayed engaged throughout the 36 years at the bank.

I think it's too strong to say you emerge as a civic leader. You emerge as civically engaged. You tend to gravitate toward the things you like and things that are fulfilling to you, but activity, in my opinion, is almost just as valuable as leadership.

I'm concerned that business is more difficult today, and people don't have as much time to devote to civic capital. It shows in our community. It's not just a Louisville phenomenon, it's a national phenomenon, and it has put pressure on governmental leaders and organizations like Greater Louisville Inc. to try to do more with fewer people.

Early in my career, I gravitated toward working on things that were of particular interest to me. One of those was education. We were all involved in raising money for Metro United Way and the Fund for the Arts and we served on civic boards. But then County Judge-Executive Mitch McConnell, who was a friend of mine, called and asked me if I would be interested in an appointment to the board of Western Kentucky University. When Mitch called, I jumped on it.

I had gone to Western for two years, my freshmen and sophomore years, and I was interested in public education, particularly public higher education. Public schools provided me with an opportunity for an education. I couldn't afford to go to a private school. I'm a product of the public schools from kindergarten through law school. It was also natural for me to be involved in higher education, since the most important reason for moving forward in business was my educational attainment.

Michael N. Harreld

On Labor Day, 1978, I went on the board of Western Kentucky University and now, nearly 30 years later, I'm still involved in some capacity with higher education. I've served on five university boards (Murray, Western Kentucky, UofL, and Bellarmine College) and I also served on the Council for Higher Education. I've loved every minute of it. I think it was my way of paying back a state that had given me opportunity.

Most of the preconceived notions I had about deficits in public education turned out to be true. The state schools, from UofL to Murray to Western to Eastern to UK, were run as sort of feudal kingdoms, with the presidents serving as political lords. There was a lot of waste and duplication, although over a period of 30 years, that has been substantially reduced. It's a much more efficient system now, and I think the quality of the leadership is inordinately better than it was 30 years ago.

I think overall it is a good system and it has educated many Kentuckians. We've put a lot of money into higher education, but we've had two frustrations. First, while our state's educational attainment levels have risen why, two or three billion dollars later, aren't the numbers of baccalaureate and masters degrees higher? Secondly, whether our graduates are teachers or engineers or business majors, the state hasn't been able to create jobs to meet their needs, so we've exported thousands upon thousands of graduates to other places.

I've always been comfortable with change. Most people are fairly satisfied with incremental change. Incremental change is perfect if you are an "A" player to start; but if you're a "B" player, we need geometric change.

I was comfortable with replacing university presidents or making dramatic changes. Two governors picked up on that and asked me to accomplish particular things at particular schools, or at least to be open to helping them make changes. They surrounded me with other people and together we were able to make some substantial changes in university governance and university policies in the state.

Since I'm such a history buff, I have loved being part of this history. There is much to be learned from it. I think too often, though, people are mired in history to the point that they are unable to change. They lack vision and the will to move forward and inertia sets in. When that happens, we aren't learning from history; we're wallowing in it.

Change is not easy, especially in public institutions. You have to chip some china, and you have to be willing to do unpopular things if they are the right things to do.

Many universities never had presidents from outside the system or from outside Kentucky. At several colleges, we brought in the first non-resident presidents. They brought fresh ideas and new ways of thinking but disrupted the old ways, the cliques. That was particularly helpful at Western and Murray, which needed to be shaken up. They really turned out to be much better schools because of all the changes.

Once we made the first series of changes, the next were easier. But making the initial change was very controversial because every inefficiency had a constituency, and we were disrupting it. It was pretty acrimonious at times. People didn't think you had a right to make changes at "their school." It got pretty nasty, pretty volatile.

It was not only a great civics lesson but it was a wonderful learning experience in business leadership – how to deal with the press, how to deal with building consensus among different constituencies, and how to build coalitions. It also helped us understand the organizations' tolerance for change. It's the same in business as it is in education. You can only move things so fast.

Peter Drucker has said, "Everyone knows what to do, it's only a question of when to do it." So how fast you can move a culture, how fast you can ask people to change, knowing when it is appropriate to shed your history and when it is appropriate to relish it – my judgment about those things was substantially improved by my experience in higher education.

I went on the University of Louisville Board of Trustees after I served on the Council on Higher Education, so UofL was the last public university board on which I served. Don Swain was president and I served during the last six years of his tenure. I was on the search committee that brought John Shumaker to UofL to succeed Don as president. I left the board the day John Shumaker arrived. My term was over and, after serving for six years, I didn't want to be reappointed. I felt very good about the choice of John, so I left when Dr. Swain left.

Both of those presidents were terrific for their times. I think Don Swain really made extraordinary changes at the university and made John Shumaker's platform easier. John was able to exercise clout in the system and to bring UofL to the forefront because of a lot of things that Don had actually done.

Don increased the university's involvement in the business community by bringing in Bob Taylor to serve as dean of the College of Business and Public Administration and by creating substantial activity at the medical school. Don himself was an active participant in the business community and served on many boards. During his tenure, and I think in my lifetime, prior to John Shumaker, Don Swain provided the most significant leadership I ever saw at the University of Louisville.

Don came from the University of California. His agenda was to integrate the university with the private sector, and he used his board to help him. He was brought in to do some very specific things because the university had not been visible in the previous ten to twelve years. His agenda was to make the university more vibrant and more engaging, and he did that. To do it, however, he had to make changes at the university that would help bring about this new level of engagement with the community.

I saw him make some tough changes in the last year he was there. He said to those who were on the executive committee, "These are things that need to be done before I leave. I will do them, and when I leave I will be very unpopular within the university for doing them, but they need to be done." He made the changes with board support, and he was correct. He was criticized when he left, and was not given full credit for what he achieved.

The things he did removed the next president's obstacles from the table. It was a great profile in courage and leadership at the expense of his own popularity, but it was the right thing to do. All we had to do was support it, take a little bit of heat for some of it, but make sure he achieved it before he left. All of those lessons from watching good and bad university leadership over a period of 30 years were great chapters in my own history, observing what works and what doesn't in running, changing and motivating organizations.

The bank gave me "civic time" to work for the community, and I learned some of my greatest lessons about how to be a better leader in my own organization by working in the community. It was almost like on-the-job training, where you can try things, watch, listen, learn and bring ideas back. You get more adept at integrating things and knowing, once again, the strategy of timing.

I'm a student of history and an avid reader, not just of current events, but of business and political history as well. I think you can learn extraordinary things from smart people – what they did, what they said, what worked and didn't work, how they handled themselves in certain situations, personally and professionally. It's hard to be successful these days if you are unwilling to be a thoughtful student. You can learn from the people around you or from people who've been dead for 200 years.

There is so much to learn. I'm saddened by those people who really don't understand history, whether it's Louisville, Kentucky or world history.

You also learn by watching people who do things well, by watching good communicators and poor communicators, by watching domineering, arrogant people versus good listeners who inspire. You can learn what works and doesn't work and what feels comfortable with your own personality.

To be a good student, you have to be a good listener. Don Swain was a great listener. David Grissom, with whom I worked daily for so long, was and is a great listener.

Passing the Torch

Ballard Morton is a good listener, and a good person to reflect on things, too. He was a director of the bank for a long time, then taught at UofL, and I visited with him often. Joe Rodes was a good listener. I've been fortunate to have had a lot of people around me who listen well, and who come at things very differently. But they never dissuaded feedback. If I had been in an organization where the leadership had dissuaded feedback, I wouldn't have been able to do what I did, live and grow as I did, so I was very fortunate. I had good mentors and good people around me who were always there for me when I needed them.

Several things in my life have disappointed me, and I might do them differently if I could. First, I had a very difficult time affording my education. From my freshman year to my last year of law school – that seven-year period – I had to work so many hours, and it took such an emotional toll on me that I made a pact that my own children would never have to make those choices. I committed to myself that I would make sure there were enough resources for them to go to school without working and worrying like I did, and I've kept that commitment. I always had strong support and strong incentives from my parents, but worrying like that takes away from your educational experience. Shielding young people from worrying so they can optimize their education has been a big driving force in my life.

Many people have to work and go to school, and it's very difficult for them. A lot of people are critical of the University of Louisville because their graduation rates don't match with other schools, but I never criticize the university for that. I'm a veteran of having to work to pay my way through school, and I know it's even more difficult to do today. It's more expensive, and sometimes job access isn't as good as it was, because so many more people are looking for jobs.

Part of an urban university's role is to be there for their students whenever and however they can get their education. That may not be as I did, seven years straight. I think it is harsh for people to criticize UofL because its students may take five, six or seven years to get through school. That's how public education works.

The second thing I might do differently relates to my personal life. My professional career has been relatively straight-lined, but I've made some personal mistakes that I deeply, deeply regret. They were errors in judgment and things I needed to learn about myself. I will never overcome the disappointment and guilt I feel over that.

It's become "in vogue" in the last ten years to blame your environment or your upbringing for the mistakes you've made. I had the most wonderful parents in the world and grew up in a very stable, loving environment, so I can announce without any fear and with humility that all of the mistakes I've made have been mine and have had nothing to do with lack of nurture and encouragement. I've made them all myself.

Because of that, I do reflect a lot on what I've learned and what I did right and wrong. I've made terrible professional mistakes and personal mistakes. I've made some great personal decisions and some great professional decisions too, but you have to keep things in perspective and learn from all of it. You also can never give up. You just have to keep on going on.

I have worked in the same place (PNC Bank) for 36 years, so it would be hard for me not to feel what I call a fair sense of duty toward the bank and this community. I think I have a duty to be fair to my employer, to the people who are dependent on me and to this community which has given me so much. I believe I have an obligation to those things. That's a little bit out-of-fashion now.

A lot of people have said to me, "Wouldn't you have been better off to leave the community for some job or to do something else besides stay at the same institution for this number of years?" I don't know. It has worked well for me personally and professionally. I'm not unhappy over the fact that I've stayed the course. There have been good years and bad years in the institutions I've worked for, and there have been good years and bad years personally, but I think you can build a full life within the template you are given.

There is enough change in life, even in the same pasture, so you don't have to seek greener ones. You can adjust to the one you live in and try to make the best of it unless you run across something that is really intolerable professionally or personally.

The enemy of tenacity is impatience. Tenacious people have to modify their tenacity with patience and learn to make the system work for them. There have been 25 reasons why I could have left to do something else, but there were always 40 reasons to stay. I looked at opportunities elsewhere and I was approached with opportunities both inside and outside Louisville. I occasionally considered these opportunities and came very close a couple of times to leaving to work for another bank. I was approached with very attractive places to live, very attractive jobs, but the draw was the attractiveness of change, not being unhappy. It was a challenge, but I think I was smart enough to understand that challenge is fleeting. If I wasn't unhappy, why was I looking for more happiness? I never found enough reason to make a change. I like what I do. It may be old-fashioned to say it, but I like this community, I like this state, I like the institution I work for and I understand the assets and liabilities of all of these things.

I'm not blind. I'm not in some myopic nirvana. I understand what is good and bad about Louisville, the state of Kentucky, the bank I work for, the industry I'm in – I get all of that. But reflection, maturity and patience will dictate whether it is unrealistic to run to something that could be some sort of false promise.

It is very important for young people aspiring to leadership to have intellectual nimbleness. There is no substitute for a person who is very bright, but who will listen well and not be wedded to something anachronistically. Very often the competitiveness of younger people gets in the way of their objectivity.

One of the real enemies of success is unbridled competitiveness. It's the very thing that makes people successful and it's very often their greatest downfall, particular when they move up a corporate or professional ladder and have to work with a lot of people and form partnerships, work with teams, etc. Competitiveness can cause envy, so one of the great lessons everyone learns as they mature is how to be an effective partner in business and personally. They learn more tolerance for differences. People today are more talented, better educated and better prepared to be leaders than any generation I've ever seen. But their impatience and competitiveness sometimes gets in the way of their effectiveness.

I've always been impatient. What's important is what you do with it. There's nothing wrong with being aggressive, assertive, impatient, pushy, and probing. But there is a time to shut up and accept a 20% victory, or to fight the battle on another day. It doesn't have to be all or nothing.

That's a lesson I've learned from lots of personal experience. Compromise is not weakness, unless it's on a moral or ethical issue. If you have an important business or civic point you want to accomplish, remember that if you get 35% of it accomplished, that's still okay.

Leaders can't always be right. The days of dogmatic, arrogant CEOs are numbered because people won't tolerate it. They have too many other options professionally and they simply won't put up with it.

As we are migrating toward a different style of community leadership we are migrating toward a very different style of corporate leadership. We've seen a lot of CEOs fail over the last half a dozen years because of their inability to keep a team going, or their tolerance for ethical missteps.

You always have to be mindful of the arrogance of success. Corporate leaders think because they have been successful in business, their knowledge transcends all fields. They will be critical of non-profits they work with because they aren't doing things like a business, but the truth is half of all businesses aren't very efficient either. These corporate leaders are removed from the reality of things, and they for the most part don't make good civic leaders because they are too aloof.

Others have an attitude that "I can get by with it." We've seen some governors and professional leaders who thought they were smart enough not to get caught doing something unethical, either personally or professionally. Ethical missteps are brought about by the arrogance of success. A high net worth or a big title does not keep you from making mistakes. It actually makes you more vulnerable. There are a lot of people who believe they are entitled to do things their way, but it will always catch up with them.

Louisville has been blessed with good government. I'm a 60-year-old who has been moderately involved politically. We've never had bad local government. We have had some government leaders who were better than others, but we've really had no bad mayors or county judges in my lifetime. There has been little or no corruption. They have for the most part been people of great character devoted to this community who stayed devoted after they left office. Not many communities in this country that can say that.

I think we have always been blessed with at least "B" government and very often "A" government here. You can't say that about our state. Our state, I think, has had mediocre leadership throughout the 20th century. Both the legislative and executive branches have been particularly undistinguished. It is part of the reason Kentucky, for all of its attributes, is still constantly struggling like a salmon going upstream. We inherited a legacy of colorful but not very competent leaders at the state level for most of the 20th century.

I think if you go back to the post World War II era in Louisville, you had some people like Mayors Charlie Farnsley and Wilson Wyatt who stepped up and who were extraordinary in their vision. They were people of great character, and the people who followed them were thoughtful, good people.

County Judges Marlow Cook and Mitch McConnell, Mayors Frank Burke and Harvey Sloane — some of our political leaders were more successful than others, some were more visionary than others, and some were bolder than others, up through the Abramson era. They were all good people, however, and they always had this incredible legacy of people helping who previously served.

For the most part, the political parties in Jefferson County, both Republican and Democrat, moved pretty good leaders to the forefront, and *The Courier-Journal* and *Louisville Times* nudged them forward. There was an expectation that we would always have good government here, watched over by the press, all news media and by the legacies of former political leaders who were always there. At the state level, however, it's been wildly inconsistent in Frankfort.

You have had a lot of mediocre people in the General Assembly and in the governor's office.

I think one of the great liabilities of this state from the early 19th century on is the fact that there has always been a disconnect between urban and business interests in state government and, as I read history, that is not true of Indianapolis, Nashville, Atlanta, and Columbus. The great historical compromise, made by our forefathers, to locate Kentucky's state capital in Frankfort has significantly contributed to our state's being out-of-step, always a half-step behind what was going on in the rest of the neighboring states in the mid-south.

Over the last 50 years, Louisville's business environment has made an incredible transformation. It has gone from manufacturing to more breadth. It didn't happen as traumatically and quickly as Pittsburgh, but it happened steadily. We steadily lost our high-paying manufacturing wage base over the last 50 years, and we have adjusted to that enormously well. Adjusting to it enormously well is not the same thing as being a success, however.

Over the last half dozen years, we have paid more attention to how we improve ourselves, instead of just surviving. We have gone through terrific changes in our community business-wise, but have managed to get through them okay. We did not come out of it decimated like a Cleveland, with poverty and incredible problems. We've done pretty well. That doesn't mean we're a winner, it means we are a survivor.

Now we are trying to define what winning is. All the reports are coming out on how well we are doing, why we are making great progress, the number of people with high school diplomas, the number of people with baccalaureate degrees, etc. We've made great progress, so has the rest of the world. But we are playing catch up ball here in Louisville and we are still trying to decide if we want to be a big city or not.

That decision, by the way, is getting made by osmosis. Everyone is getting there on their own terms. If you asked people ten years ago if they would like to be an Atlanta, they would have said yes. They really don't talk about that as much anymore because of the enormous problems Atlanta has managing itself. We love being the 16th largest city in the country, but frankly we probably don't want the problems of the top ten cities, the true MSAs. Louisville is not a community for making an optimal living, but it is still a manageable community where you can make a reasonable living. We are just having a hard time deciding exactly what we want to be.

There are so many people who have moved here from outside Louisville in the last 20 years who have made us reflect on that, coming from places they don't want to go back to, that were bigger and seemingly more successful. We are a little bit schizophrenic about what we want to do. We have an infrastructure that for the most part works; we have a school system that for the most part works. Unlike most places in America, the public school system here is a decent option. That is an unbelievable strength.

We would like to see more growth in our per capita personal income and in white collar jobs. The truth is, I think what we really want is a place our children can stay. That's always at the bottom of the list, after you get through eight other things. People will say, "My child doesn't want to leave but can't find a job here," or "My child would like to come back if they could just find a job here." It gets to be very personal. Everybody has an opinion about what Louisville should be, but it is very often driven by family and what they personally want out of our community.

We're working very hard to create the kind of jobs that can help our children who obtain a good education to stay here. It's not easy and, in my judgment, we don't have a very good partner in Frankfort for a whole host of reasons. We are learning that there are more resources there to help us do things here, yet we are still trying to do it on our own. That's very hard to do. Once again, if the state capital was Louisville, instead of Frankfort, it wouldn't be as hard.

In 1996 and 1997, Louisville had a real eye-opener when the Boyle Report was released. We learned about all the things we still needed to do here despite our growth and development. We had seen a lot of physical improvements in our city and were living on the new high of UPS. We thought we had survived all the changes well and were doing better than we thought.

It was a bit of a bubble-burster when we learned that there was still much to do. The Boyle Report reinvigorated a new generation of people to become engaged in civic capital.

It's easy to be satisfied living in Louisville. It's a better place to live than it is to make a living, so if you can live here and have a decent job it's hard for you to get panicky about things. It's such a sociable place to live, and we have nice cultural attributes for a town our size – arts, athletics, etc. Reports like the Boyle Report jerk you up short to remind you that, as Robert Frost says, "We have miles to go before we sleep." They are a great reminder of where we are in the larger world. The negative is that they tend to separate us from the rest of the state, which causes Louisvillians to get angry or disappointed with what is happening in Kentucky. The business/political discourse in Louisville and Lexington is for the most part unrelated to the business/political discourse that goes on in Frankfort and, until that gets in sync, we are going to have difficulty.

Building two bridges was something that came out of the Boyle Report. The bridges are ten years overdue and it will probably be seven to ten more years before we see them built. They are long overdue, they're natural, and with all due respect to my friends at River Fields, I don't think they will be nearly as damaging as they think they are going to be to the quality of life in the community. They are mandatory for business distribution, they are mandatory for the circulation of people, and they are long overdue.

The light rail concept is appealing to me, but I'm no expert in it. I watch our commutes here increasing, along with the percentage of time people are devoting to getting to their jobs. Then there's Atlanta, where no one wants to live because commutes are so horrible. There has to be a middle ground.

I don't know whether light rail is a good answer to our commuting problems or not, but there have been a lot of studies. The issue has not seemed to ignite the public or our political leadership. There's been no call to action. I don't know if that's because they've been so focused on the bridges or not.

We need more money to spend on bridges and on roads in this community. We have so many side roads and back ways. My wife moved here via Los Angeles and has found it more complicated to get around here than she did there. We need to improve the infrastructure of our roads here to make things more efficient. It's long overdue, but it takes resources and money.

We have an airport second to none now. It took a lot of bold leadership by a lot of people to do that, but it's been the lifeblood of our business community for the last ten to fifteen years.

We also desperately need an arena downtown. Forget the NBA, forget basketball altogether in my judgment. We can fill it up with other things. One of the organizations most concerned about our earlier arena issue was the group that runs Rupp Arena. They were very concerned because all the concerts and other activities they do at Rupp Arena would start coming to the new arena if we built it, since there's not enough space at Freedom Hall.

I'm a big proponent of the arena for a lot of reasons. I thought if an NBA team could have come here that would have helped pay for it, but I wasn't interested in building the arena just for an NBA team. I'm still not. I think the University of Louisville would benefit from a new downtown arena. I think the community needs it for a whole host of reasons. It's ten years overdue.

I have watched Cincinnati tear down two stadiums since we've built any, and they've already built their second generation. Pittsburgh did the same thing. Indianapolis is getting ready to do the same thing. We just don't get it. People tend to see it as an investment only in the place. It is much more than that, but the investment in professional athletics or better venues for college basketball is well worth it. Entertainment is very often the flag under which communities fly now for visibility. No one was paying attention to Indianapolis until they had the Colts and the Pacers. That gave that town personality, as much as the Packers gave Green Bay a national personality.

I understand that Fourth Street Live! is very successful but, as in most things, we need to measure whether it's still successful 36 – 48 months from now. You can't re-create the past, and you can't make downtown Louisville the way it was when I was a child. You can still make it a vibrant place for entertainment and conventions, though. I think we've done some things pretty well, but we have, in my judgment, missed the boat on the arena.

I'm at the tail end of my professional career. I don't know what I'm going to do next, but I'm going to do something. I would be bored to death if I wasn't active. I have begun to think about what's next in my life. I've thought about a lot of things, but I haven't settled on anything that has given me as much satisfaction as what I've done. I'd like to move away from some of the time constraints and pressures of business, but I will have to do something that gives me a little constructive pressure. If not, my mind will get soft.

There are civic things I could do, but I can't make a living or a life doing that. I want another vocation. I have no desire to retire or to try to find part-time interests. I don't own a condo anywhere and I have no intention of finding a way to avoid work. I want something interesting to do in the next phase of my life, and I'm not going to stop until I find it.

(Editors' note: This interview was conducted in early 2005, before Harreld accepted a new position as regional president of PNC Bank, Greater Washington D.C. area.)

John A. "Jack" Hillerich III

Chairman
Hillerich & Bradsby Company

JACK HILLERICH III HAD LEADERSHIP thrust upon him in more ways than one. In 1969, when he was 29 years old and working his way into his family's world-famous baseball bat factory, his father, company president Jack Hillerich Jr., died suddenly. Hillerich III had to take over.

"I didn't know anything," he told *The Courier-Journal* in 2001. But when bankers urged him to sell the firm to one of several larger companies very interested in acquiring it, he decided the company's ownership belonged in Louisville — and with his family.

He had a pretty good handle on it by the early 1980s, when city and business leaders asked him to rise to another occasion. They said it was time to bring professional baseball back to Louisville and asked him to help. It seemed to him something a baseball bat maker should do. So he worked with a group of civic leaders to persuade A. Ray Smith to bring his Redbirds to town. He joined a group of local investors a few years later to buy the team from Smith so it would be able to stay in Louisville.

That pretty much launched him into a legacy of involvement in community affairs. He took a big step in 1996. His headquarters was in Louisville, but his bats were being manufactured in a large plant in Indiana — and had been for 20 years. Hillerich brought the bat factory back. He made the move in style, creating a museum with the factory on West Main Street in downtown Louisville, and propping a six-story bat against the building. The bat, made of steel that looks like wood from as close as across the street, has become one of the city of Louisville's most photographed attractions.

Inside the building, along with the much-visited museum, is a 15-ton baseball glove, expertly carved from a huge block of Kentucky limestone.

Passersby on the street can look in the factory's windows and watch craftsmen turn bats for the country's most luminous baseball players.

Now Hillerich is on the board of the Louisville Bats baseball team — formerly the Redbirds, then Riverbats — which is ensconced in the city's landmark Triple-A Louisville Slugger Field. He also serves on the board of advisors of Indiana University Southeast and the boards of the Louisville Downtown Development Corporation, Goodwill Industries of Kentucky, Demptos Glass and MPC Louisville Promotions.

Louisville Slugger bats were internationally famous long before Hillerich was born. His grandfather and namesake — John A. "Bud" Hillerich — made the first ones in the 1880s, when he was an apprentice in his father's Louisville woodturning company. The story is he was an amateur ball player and he skipped work one day to watch Pete "The Gladiator" Browning play for the Louisville Eclipse. Browning broke a bat, and Hillerich took him back to the shop and turned a new one for him. "The Gladiator" took a few trial swings between spins on the lathe. The bat worked well for Browning, and Hillerich & Bradsby bats have worked for baseball greats ever since.

Jack Hillerich graduated from Vanderbilt University in 1961. Eight years later, while he was working in the company division that secured its ash wood from forests in the East, his father died. The company's torch passed to him. He recalled in 1971 that he was able to quiet his bank's fears about his taking the helm with little experience by putting several prominent business leaders on its board.

In 1984, Hillerich became an advocate of W. Edwards Deming's Total Quality Management philosophy, which espouses that all workers are willing workers and should participate in managing their company. Hillerich put Deming principles into effect at Hillerich & Bradsby, and the company has subsequently won several awards for good labor relations.

Hillerich serves on the board of the Center of Quality of Management in Boston and is a trustee of the Deming Institute in Washington D.C. as well. He teaches entrepreneurial leadership classes at Purdue University and Indiana University Southeast.

In 2001, Hillerich stepped down as president and turned the company's reins over to John A. Hillerich IV. There is a John A. Hillerich V still growing up. Perhaps the company's torch will pass to him in the future.

COMMUNITY LEADERSHIP WAS SORT OF FORCED on me. Our Hillerich name is fairly well-known. People have come here looking for guidance on a lot of issues, like bringing a baseball team back to Louisville. Louisville Slugger certainly had to play a role in that, and we were anxious to do it.

I wanted to play a leadership role because I'm concerned about quality. I'm a manufacturing guy, and I'm always concerned with quality. I thought I could help our community by bringing a quality initiative to the community that would deliver a better product, better people, better management.

Moving our southern Indiana plant back to downtown Louisville was an opportunity that was forced upon us by pressing issues at that time. We were in Indiana in a 260,000-square-foot warehouse (from 1976-1996), and all of a sudden we were looking at a different way of manufacturing. We started making aluminum bats and we just had too much space.

We also asked ourselves the question, "Do we want to move back to an industrial site or do something for the community?" It just happened to work out. We had a great mayor (Jerry Abramson) who was as responsible as anybody for bringing us back to this location. It just all pulled together. All of the museum people in the community partnered with us and helped us. We had never had a museum before — a factory tour, but never a museum — and they all pitched in and taught us lessons that really helped. It was a community effort, as well as Hillerich & Bradsby's effort.

My mindset has always been to "do or die" for the company. The Hillerich family has never entertained the idea of selling the company. It's "We're going to make this thing work. We have to make it work. That's our only choice." I'm not going to sell it; my son's not going to sell it. It has to be successful for us and for the community and for the people here.

So when we looked at the options, we realized that we had to do this. It was the right thing. You do a lot of things that you can't put a number to, but you just know you've got to do them. This just happened to work great for us. We had to make some decisions, and so far it's been okay.

I learned a lot from the great people who made this company what it is. It's small, but it's so well-known, and the leadership, starting with my great-grandfather, built this company into what it is. It's hard to turn your back on that. There's so much pride in seeing what my predecessors did, and I can tally up what I've done. Hopefully someone else will come after me. I feel great pride in what we've all accomplished here and what we have built.

I've learned an awful lot about my grandfather, although he passed away when I was five or six years old. The stories about him were just outstanding.

My father was a great mentor to me, too, in the way that he ran things, and he was honest. People looked up to him. They would say to me, "You're Junie's son." He was known everywhere, not for making money or anything like that. He was just a guy who people wanted to be around. That really has guided me through my life, probably more than anything. I don't want to be famous or anything. I just want to be somebody that people like to be around, and I want to do good things. I got that from my father.

In 1984, I went to a Dr. W. Edwards Deming seminar in Minnesota, and it virtually changed my whole outlook on business. I learned things that had just never entered my mind before. Things like "all of your workers are willing workers." I had been brought up to believe that 20% of your workers are bad and you have to weed them out. Then he came in and said, "They're all willing workers."

His principles were a shock to me – things I'd never understood or even heard of before. Since that day, though, we have tried to follow his principles. I've done everything that I can to try to adopt his philosophy because it works. I'm a trustee of the Deming Institute and I'm trying to help them spread the word. If we could do that in a big way, we'd have a heck of a community. His thoughts and teachings describe basically how I try to operate this company. Looking at the history of this company, I would say that the style of the owners and leaders has been to let professional people come in here and run the company. I try not to run anything. I try to hire people who are experts, who have a burning desire to work in their area. I try to guide the ship instead of running the ship. I'm not a hands-on guy or one to tell you how to do things or insist that you do this or that. I just put people in place who want to run things.

We really need good people, and if you try to run their lives for them, they're going to leave, because there's no top for them. They are always looking at a Hillerich. They know where their own limit is, and you don't want people to look at their limit and say "I can't go any farther." You want people to enjoy their job, love what they're doing, and have a feeling of accomplishment. I've always felt that's the way to lead this company.

I hope the people on the floor of the plant would say that things are different now than they were a few years ago when we didn't have all this automation. I don't think that anybody would say that I'm an operations person, but I'm sort of there, getting in everyone's hair, asking stupid questions, making things work better.

Deming says that 95% of all problems in a company are caused by management, and management doesn't like to hear that. They like to think that there is something else wrong, but the problems are always in the system.

And who runs the system? The managers run the system. They have to look inward, which they don't like to do, and see what they need to do to make the system run better. It's not the people on the floor doing the job. It's the system.

I've tried to make that the biggest thing we do here. If you go to our biggest success story – our plant in California – management/union relations let the people run the show. They give them encouragement, they give them support, they're at their beck and call, but they never tell them what to do.

If you go in that plant, you'll see production that's just outstanding. You'll see clean like you've never seen clean. The floor is immaculate. At the end of the shift, there's not a piece of a bat anywhere. Not a single bat, anywhere. They're all put up somewhere. Management couldn't have done that. People had to get it in the system, be proud of what they're doing and take ownership of it. That's something we're trying to drive through the rest of the organization.

One of the things I'm most proud of is the fact that we took our company back to its roots. In the early 1980s, we were an also-ran in the aluminum bat business. A fellow came here from a major softball team and he wanted us to pay him $40,000 to sponsor his team. The most we had ever given a softball team was $100 or something like that. He dared us to come and watch a softball tournament so we did, down in the Smoky Mountains. Every time a super player would come up to bat, people in the crowd would say "He's using this bat" or "He's using that bat. Last week he was using another bat." Everybody knew what these guys were using and what they bought. Here we were trying to sell K-Mart and Wal-Mart a fence buster for $15. These guys were going to the plate with a $100 bat. We didn't even have a $100 bat. We sent the guy a check immediately, and sent them bats. They literally threw the bats in the dirt. I had to go pick them up. They told me, "This is no good. Let me get your competitor's bat and put your name on it." I said "No, we can't do that. We're just going to keep trying and keep trying."

And that got us out of the hole and put us on par with the best aluminum bat manufacturers. It really turned the company around to be more focused on the customer than we were. And who was the customer? The customer was the guy playing with the bat, not K-Mart and Wal-Mart.

No one believed me. I was pretty young, about 33 or 34, when this happened, and I was saying "Yes, sir" and "No, sir" to people because I didn't know a thing. And this was my first experience at going against the grain. I knew we had to get into major softball; it was something we had to do. Everybody said "No, we don't want to do that. That's crazy."

When it turned around and worked, then the whole company started listening to Jack. It was a major change in my life. Instead of asking people for help, I started making decisions.

I learned from that experience that I could make my own decisions and that people would respect them. One of the biggest lessons in leadership I have learned is that the mistakes I make are not the things that I do, they're the things that I don't do.

Throughout my life, I've abandoned a lot of little minor things because they didn't seem to work. We tried to design a couple of machines and had to give up on them. I'm not sure it is a failure, but I am missing a quality – being a good speaker, being able to communicate better. I'm not good at it and I know it. It bothers me that I just can't get past it. I feel I've done so much. I'd just love to be able to speak better. I'm terribly dyslexic. When I dial a phone, I have no idea who's going to be on the other end. But I've learned you just accept your mistakes when you put things where you can't find them, and you just go on.

That's what I've done with all my mistakes in life. I've just thrown them over my shoulders and moved forward. I've made so many of them, but I just don't dwell on them. It took me a long time to learn that. I would get mad about doing stupid things, but now I don't. I just say, "Hey, sorry buddy, wrong number." I know I'm going to be dyslexic all my life, and I just live with it.

Good followers listen to you and talk with you. I've seen a lot of people in business who just don't hear anything. They don't want to listen. They have their mind already made up about things. It's not that I want to tell them what to do, but I want to understand how they feel about an issue and be able to listen and comment, or to challenge them to understand where I'm coming from. All they want to do is talk. They have their mind completely made up, and it's their way or the highway.

I've seen that in our own employees from time to time, and usually they get the highway. If they won't listen to their fellow employees – not just me, but their peers – they're not going to make it. They have to be able to work with their peers.

The most important thing for leaders is not what they do, but what their people do. Leaders don't run machines anymore. They don't even know how they work. They just have to make sure that a machine or a process works. Their ability to interact with their employees is the most important thing.

Who runs Louisville? The mayor? I don't think so. The people in our community run Louisville. It's how we citizens all interact with each other that makes Louisville what it is.

That's what I look for in subordinates. What's their main job? It's to communicate and share knowledge, work together, and make things better.

Passing the Torch

The Deming seminar changed me so much. I wish I could eat it and sleep it, but I'm not that intense. I just gained so much from that experience, watching others get the idea and go "Aha!"

But I don't regret anything I have done here for this company. I don't think I have made mistakes and I can't think of a way I could improve upon things. The only thing I might do differently if I could do things over again is to intensify my efforts to get people on board, to understand each other and to work together. If I had known about Deming's principles earlier I would have focused on them more. If I have a weakness now, it's that I don't focus on them enough. I should do these things 24/7 but I can't do that. I wish I could, because there's so much gratification in seeing people learn and accept and enjoy what they're doing.

I would advise young people aspiring to leadership roles today to remember that there are all kinds of ways to skin a cat. The Deming approach is my way. The authoritarian way is another way. Some people just go in there and, by God, run the ship their way to try to make a jillion dollars or whatever. You can work that way if you want to. But my way of leading is working with people, and getting them to work with and for me, and with others.

You also have to pick the right place to work. You need to try to find a company or an atmosphere that will let you be yourself. If you come in to our company and try to be authoritarian, you're not going to make it. It doesn't work here, and I hope it never does. But this is just our way. There are plenty of authoritarian companies you can work for if you want to.

Don't work in an atmosphere that doesn't allow you to do what you want to do. We've had so many people come here and say "We love what you all do. How can I get my boss to do what you're doing?" You can't. It's not possible. That boss has to create his own atmosphere. I've heard people say, "I just don't think I can work under these conditions. We're not doing so well right now, and the board voted my boss a million dollar bonus, and we're laying off people." I can see the frustration in their faces. The important thing is to try to work in an atmosphere that you like, someplace where you can make a difference.

I think the corporate structure in Louisville has really changed since I first started getting involved in the community. We used to have a few major leaders, usually bankers or government types, and they pretty much ran the city.

When our home banks disappeared and other people came to town with new ideas and different ways of doing things, it really opened up this community. I can remember people saying, "We don't want more business coming here."

John A. "Jack" Hillerich III

"It will be a strain on our pay scale. We don't want the pay scale to go up."
I think changes in local ownership were in some ways not good, but they sure
brought in talent that we were suppressing.

What role did I play in all this? We've had many, many opportunities to
sell our company. We get approached all the time. But the fact that we've kept
our company in Louisville under family control is one of the most important
things I've done for this community. People appreciate the fact that our company
has stayed here. We've been a part of this city for a long time. We are one of the
icons in Louisville: Louisville Slugger, the Kentucky Derby, Brown-Forman —
people are proud of these things. We wouldn't be here or be a part of the
image of Louisville if we had sold the company.

Our talent pool here in Louisville has also been one of the keys to our
community's success. We've had some great benefactors in companies like
Humana who have stepped up to the plate, so to speak. There are cases where
the home-town leadership and new people, not the old guard, exploded our
community into what it can be. These people have taught me that even if you
don't get personal benefit out of some of the things the city accomplishes,
look what these things can do for the community. This big bat outside, for
example, cost a lot of money and we're not getting a dime for it. But what it
brings to our city is worth millions.

At one time, I didn't appreciate the need for a downtown. I believed I
could get everything I wanted in the suburbs. But then I started visiting other
cities — like Denver, for example. I saw how bright and cheerful and neat that
place is and I just loved it.

Building downtown is good for us, and I don't see that as much of a
challenge. The challenge for our community is addressing the problems we
have in some of our neighborhoods. We have to structure things better to address
the abject poverty and crime in those neighborhoods because people don't
have things to do and don't have jobs. This is not a racial issue. There are
neighborhoods all over our city that need attention. We need to go into these
neighborhoods and rebuild them instead of fleeing to the suburbs. That's our
challenge. There's beautiful property here in the city that's just not being
developed correctly. You can open the paper and see all the crime. It just puts
a dagger in your heart to see it.

I would put as much focus on those neighborhoods as I would building
downtown. We need to interact with the people in these neighborhoods too.

How can we make things happen? How can we work with them? And how can we work with the kids in these neighborhoods to get them to stay in school and to stay out of trouble?

Again, I would advise young people aspiring to become leaders in our city to read Dr. Deming's book. It's all there. There's so much advice in his book about how to live – business advice, ideas for incentive pay, questions about things like why we grade kids in school.

Why do we give you a "C" in the second grade, for example? You'll be a "C" the rest of your life. I've learned that we are all "A's" in some respect, at some point, and in some way. I've seen it here in our company a million times. A guy's a "D" in his job, and you want to fire him but you can't because he has 35 years here and his father had 42 years before him. Our challenge is to find his "A." It works every time.

You just have to get to know people. You put them in a different situation, talk to them. You don't, at the end of the year, sit them down and say, "You've done this bad and this bad and this bad so you are only going to get a raise of 2% versus 7%." You don't do that. You sit people down and talk to them and say "What do you like to do? Where are you going with this job? Do you like this job, or would you like to do something else here? Where do you aspire to go?" Believe me, this approach works every time.

I've tried to set up policies in our company that allow that to happen. We've abolished incentive pay. We've abolished annual reviews, per se. I've tried to set up policies that can make things happen. It's important to look at your company's policies to see if they are helping you or preventing you from doing the things you want to do. It's an ongoing process.

Deming says, "If you come to me in five years and say 'I've got it licked, I know what's going on,' then I know you don't know what you're talking about. If you come to me in five years and say you're 15% of the way there, I'll know that you know what you're talking about." We are never through – there is always plenty yet to do.

I've been teaching a class at IUS and Purdue on entrepreneurial leadership, and there is some good stuff in what I am teaching. I would advise anyone interested in business to try a couple of courses. You have to turn your light bulb on. It's all there to learn. It's available, and it's right. My courses are about Deming and other people like him. Deming is not the only guru; he's just the one I picked.

Some people call me a zealot. I can't help it. I've seen my ideas work. There are others out there too who can help you understand that interaction among the people in your organization is the key to making it work. A night course can open your eyes to a lot of things you've never been exposed to.

John A. "Jack" Hillerich III

We're still in the old machine age. We still dig a ditch with a shovel and if we fall over, we put another guy in there with a shovel. We teach people not to think — that only the owner of a business thinks, not us. We're still hanging on to some of these old ideas.

But business and everything else in life has just gotten faster and faster and faster. One man, one brain, can't make things happen now. We need a hundred brains to make things happen, and I don't think we're going fast enough in that direction.

ALICE K. HOUSTON

**Executive Vice President
Houston-Johnson Inc.**

**Former President and CEO
Automotive Carrier Services Co.**

LEGENDARY CENTRAL HIGH SCHOOL basketball coach William L. Kean, who died in 1958, would be proud if he could see his daughter Alice now. She is vice president of a large family-owned logistics firm, was president and CEO of the Automotive Carrier Services Company, where she doubled revenues, and she is on all kinds of community boards: Greater Louisville Inc., the African-American Venture Capital Fund, the Louisville Community Development Bank, Jewish Hospital Health Care Services, and the Muhammad Ali Center, among others. She is also co-chairing the University of Louisville's Community Partnership Advisory Board, exploring "town and gown" partnerships between UofL and local community service organizations.

Kean set an example for his daughter as an achiever, compiling an 856-83 win-loss record in 36 seasons at Central, which is still a Kentucky record in high school basketball. Alice's mother sent her to meet the University of Louisville's first group of black basketball players in 1962, and to invite them home for dinner. One of the players who came to dinner that night was Wade Houston, whom she married in 1969.

First, though, she got her high school diploma in 1964 and in 1968, she graduated *cum laude* from Baldwin College in Berea, Ohio. She received a Danforth Foundation Fellowship in Latin American History to attend graduate school at Vanderbilt University. After a year, however, she left to marry Wade Houston and go with him to France, where he had a job coaching and playing basketball.

Wade Houston soon returned to coach high school basketball in Louisville, and Alice Houston launched a long and successful career with UofL. She served as assistant, then associate director of financial aid, and she earned a master's degree in education in college student personnel services in the process.

While they worked at their respective jobs, Alice and Wade – and Charlie Johnson, Wade's college roommate – began casting about for business ventures. They settled on a grocery store at the corner of 38th Street and River Park Drive, in West Louisville. "We were going to be the Kroger of the West End," she told *The Courier-Journal* in 2000. They bought out a competitor who had been in the area eight years, but then "destroyed both businesses within a matter of 18 months."

Their next venture went better, though. The Houstons and Johnson formed a new company – the Johnson-Houston Corporation – which started transporting automotive parts to Ford Motor Company's Kentucky truck plant in 1985. In 1987, they established Houston-Johnson Inc., and began storing engines and transmissions for Ford's Louisville Assembly Plant.

Alice left her job at UofL in 1988 to concentrate on building the family's new business. By 2000, through a series of acquisitions and transactions, the Houstons and Johnson owned four companies which, when combined, had annual revenues of $120 million a year and made them the second-largest minority-owned company in the United States and the largest minority-owned transportation company in North America.

Alice ran one of the companies – Automotive Carrier Services. Under her leadership, ACS doubled its revenues and received a number of industry awards, including Daimler-Chrylser's prestigious Gold Pentastar Award.

The Houstons divested their interests from the larger business, but continue to run Houston-Johnson Inc. Alice also enjoys expanding her passion for technology, through investments with AKH Enterprises, Inc.

Alice Houston takes a good deal of pride in her family. She had the pleasure in 2003 of announcing that her son, Allan Houston – a standout player with the New York Knicks in the National Basketball Association – had established four academic scholarships to honor his father at the University of Tennessee. Wade Houston was head basketball coach at Tennessee when Allan Houston was in school there. Allan was a star for the Volunteers, and set the school's career basketball scoring record.

The Houstons also have two daughters. Lynn was a two-time Atlantic Coast Conference high jump champion for Georgia Tech, from which she graduated and is now employed. Natalie is a graduate of the University of Louisville's School of Medicine.

Alice Houston has been an active fundraiser for the United Negro College Fund, Big Brothers/Big Sisters of Kentuckiana, the Boys and Girls Clubs of America and the Presbyterian Community Center, among others. In 2002, Spalding University recognized her leadership in business and educational endeavors with an honorary doctor of humane letters degree.

Passing the Torch

I NEVER REALLY THOUGHT OF MYSELF as a leader, even in school. I was in organizations, and I was active and participatory, but I really wasn't a person who was the president or vice president or even an officer of any of those organizations.

After I went to the University of Louisville, I became active with the Urban League. I was in my early 20s. I quickly became engaged with Art Walters, the League's executive director, who was an icon in Louisville. Art was one of my early mentors. I saw him negotiate board rooms and address problems in Louisville in the late '60s and early '70s. He must have seen something in me because soon I became a part of the executive board of the Urban League. Then I was nominated to serve on the board of the national Urban League. Vernon Jordan was then the executive director. Later I was placed on its executive committee. So very quickly, I was in a very select group of people engaged in economic development, government and politics. I was so much in awe, but some of it rubbed off on me.

I've had so many mentors. I have to start with my parents. They definitely were my first mentors. My father was Central High School's head basketball coach. It's between him and Adolph Rupp who has won the most games. I grew up in athletics, but education was always terribly important in our household. You had to complete your education. My father died when I was only 11. My mother was a high school teacher – a single working mom. She worked hard before it was popular to be a single mom.

My teachers were my other early mentors. I grew up when Louisville was making a transition from a segregated to an integrated city. Our teachers taught us that the playing ground was not fair, that you had to play your card game with 26 cards instead of 52. They essentially prepared us for unfairness, and that it was not going to be an acceptable excuse that things were not fair. We were taught to rise above unfairness to compete in any arena.

From a local civic perspective, I have to mention David Jones Sr., who showed me early on, once I got into the business arena, that we all have a real responsibility to give back, to be involved, and to be engaged. As soon as we were able, my husband Wade and I and our partner Charlie Johnson began sponsoring a gala to support the United Negro College Fund.

We have now raised millions of dollars. David Jones Sr. contributed the first $100,000 ten years ago toward that event. Had he not done that, I am not sure our event would have been able to sustain itself in its embryonic stages of development.

When I serve in a leadership position, I like to get everyone involved, engaged and informed. I also want everyone working with me to believe in what we are doing. If you believe in and understand what you are trying to accomplish, you can be more supportive. I often tell our employees, "This is kind of like a democracy, but it is a vote of one. Anything can be debated. Don't let it be like the emperor's new clothes. Once we decide on something in this room, we're all on board to get it accomplished." I am honest to a fault. My door is always open, although sometimes that is not always a good thing.

Some of these traits come from growing an organization from the ground up, from starting at the dining room table and growing to a $400 million organization. Not all of these leadership characteristics are a good thing.

To summarize, I think I am an open leader. I lead by example. I don't require our employees to do things I am not willing to do myself. I teach them, mentor them, and let them make their own mistakes, as long as it is not going to kill them or us, personally or financially. My goal is to empower the people who work with us.

One of our employees describes our style this way. "You want us to draw an elephant. You will look over our shoulder as we are drawing. As long as it looks like an elephant, even though it's not the perfect elephant, it is okay with you. But when you see that we are deviating too much or the elephant is now looking like a horse, you say, 'Hey, you need to come over here!'"

I spent 17 years at the University of Louisville working with young people. Running a business is a lot like running the work-study program. You have to do a certain amount of stopping and listening and teaching.

Parenting is my biggest success. But from a business perspective, my decision to leave the University of Louisville's Financial Aid Office to branch out and devote myself full-time to our family business was one of the smartest and most important decisions of my life. We were able to grow our business. Our first year's revenue was $16,000. But when we left the businesses, we were a multi-million-dollar company.

I learned many of the skills we needed early in our business while I was working at the university. As our business grew, I also learned how important team effort is. The Johnson-Houston Group succeeded because the public and private sectors, financial institutions, and our entrepreneurial spirit all came together to make it happen.

Although bringing the business to Louisville and growing it was my biggest success, it was also my biggest failure. We were involved in the business for almost 13 years, from 1989-2001. I saw things in that process that did not evolve like I wanted them to evolve.

This area of the trucking business was not diversified in gender or race. There were four partners, three males and one female. Many of the things I tried to initiate and develop, I was not able to do. They are now being done. But at the time there was either opposition to who was saying it (the messenger) or to the message itself. I gave up after a year or two of frustration.

The corporate offices were eventually moved to Joplin, Missouri and to Kenosha, Wisconsin. I think now about what could have been or what Louisville could have sustained or developed, and I have to say, "Okay, was I just being stubborn?" No, we took the business to a certain point. Sometimes things have seasons. That was the kind of leadership needed then, and this is the kind of leadership needed now. I do consider that my lack of ability to "stick to it" was a negative consequence in the total scheme of what could have been. But it is what it is, and I am happy for all.

Good followers understand that their role is a critical and important one. Comparing it to athletics, since it has always been such an important part of our lives, you always have a leader, the star, the "go to" person. But Michael Jordan wouldn't be anywhere without his team. The New York Knicks couldn't do anything with just Patrick Ewing or my son Allan.

The word "follower" seems so negative. It implies a person who only does what he is told to do, who is clueless, mindless – so unlike a good follower. But followers are always in the room when we are having dialogue – challenging, questioning, and every bit a part of our decisions. Once we establish a direction, that person then assumes the role of follower. It is like the body – the head can't do anything without the neck and the rest of the body.

I select people a lot like me as followers. Not aggressive, but intelligent, outgoing people comfortable with themselves, who can make others comfortable around them.

We have certain values in our company. We value family, honesty and integrity. A good follower in our company is probably different from traditional followers because everyone has his or her role, and everyone is important. Everyone just can't be the leader.

I have enjoyed every phase of my life as it has evolved, so I am not sure I would do anything differently. The best part of my life, at least the most rewarding in terms of external affirmation, was my time spent at the University of Louisville. That is where I thought I made the biggest impact and had the greatest effect on other people's lives. It was something I could see, feel and touch. I could see someone coming in as a freshman, then see the finished product when they became a senior and graduated.

So, I often think if I could do it over again, knowing what I know now and having had the opportunity to savor and appreciate everything that I have experienced, I would go back to the university setting.

I often tell Wade that when we retire, what we really need to do is to go back to a college campus. I think now we have even so much more to offer on the right kind of campus. You can really mentor college students — not just share information about financial aid, but teach things about business and life, giving and responsibility. I think the college campus is the arena I would like to spend time in again. The university was the launching pad for me and still is.

It sounds so hokey, but it is just so important for people to be willing to get engaged and remain involved in their community. It is so easy, especially for young leaders, to get caught up in their own world. They need time for their families, starting their careers, the Internet — so many things that we were not even affected by ten or 20 years ago. If we don't watch it, we are going to look up one day and this thing we call the community, where we live, work and play, will not be here. Our community has to be more than a networking mechanism that allows us to transform our family or business. It has to be something that we care about and are actively engaged in.

My advice to young people who are going to become the leaders of tomorrow in our community would be to discuss issues with older people. We like to be asked and encouraged to give advice. There is nothing like getting involved. I think leaders have certain traits in common. They have to be able to operate with a certain level of anxiety at all times. I think people are more inclined to follow leaders with these traits.

I believe that integration has probably contributed more to the growth, development and quality of life in Louisville over the past 50 years than anything else. On the other hand, I believe that race relations remains one of our community's most serious challenges. It will continue to negatively impact the community's growth and development economically. We need to provide federal, state and local initiatives, especially in the downtown and western corridors, and include plans for job creation and economic incentives for new and existing businesses.

I grew up in a segregated Louisville where my boundaries were essentially Chickasaw Park on the west and Sixth Street on the east. Walnut Street (now Muhammad Ali Boulevard) was the economic and social center. My teachers were excellent and my world was secure, safe and shielded. I can't imagine developing in that arena long-term, however.

217

Passing the Torch

In the '60s I marched, participated in sit-ins and was part of the generation that changed Louisville and America forever. This community responded and has benefited greatly from that movement.

The University of Louisville, through its athletic programs and national championships, provided a unifying bond which bridged all races, colors, creeds and geographic areas of Jefferson County. The glorious '80s eased racial tensions and laid the foundation for the development of many minority businesses that are in existence today. Fortunately, Wade and I were a part of that wonderful era too.

I still believe that the education of our young people – having an educated workforce – is the biggest challenge our community is facing. I meet young people of all races every day who appear to have missed it. I don't know if there is a gap between this age and that age or if we have just not been as effective as we should have been.

An educated person, one who can function at a minimum-level skill set, is more self-assured, more confident and has less potential for drugs, sexual abuse or other kinds of coping behaviors. It is terribly important for us to create an educated populace that will be able to respond to the technological initiatives that our community has to support for our region and state. Sometimes I am very concerned about our community and our ability to respond to businesses that want to locate or relocate here.

Another thing I am really concerned about is our ability to retain our young people. I have three children. I am prejudiced of course, but they are extremely talented in different areas, and I can only get one of them to come back home or to stay home.

I certainly hope that initiatives like Fourth Street Live! succeed. Somehow though, it has to be more than an entertainment district. Our leaders need to engage young people and ask, "Why do you not want to stay here?" This has a spiraling effect on how our community is going to look, not in the next ten to 20 years, but even in the next two to four years. There is so much to value about Louisville.

We have a good mix of young people coming into leadership roles in our community. They now need to "take the torch," use those of us who have come before them and begin a dialogue. Maybe an extension of this book could be using the people featured in this book to mentor young professionals.

People commit their time to what they are passionate about. A person only has so much time to give. People are increasingly selective in how they spend their time.

This is an important lesson for leaders. When you get involved as a leader, you can find yourself stretched and overextended. Your voice can become so fragmented it is meaningless. You can become completely ineffective. You can't be everything to everybody.

We have to make choices, and I have had to do this as a seasoned leader as well. Somehow this has to be communicated to the next generation of leaders because the demands in their lives are even more fragmenting than ours have been. They need to become focused and have primary areas of emphasis. They have to define what components within this community they are going to focus on, whether it's education, economic development, the arts, etc.

We should also bestow the title of "leader" on more individuals in our community, in my opinion, instead of trying to get one person like me to do five things. Go out and find four other "me's." They won't be like me, but I wasn't "me" when I started out. Engage other individuals. People like to be asked to do things, but we continue to ask the same people to do everything. Nobody can assume all the demands that are made of them.

We need to broaden the base of leadership in our community. I have always been interested in how we choose our leaders. Whatever the criteria are, we need to broaden them. This book could feature 200 people telling their story.

We have so much to be proud of in this community. Our diversity is a major strength that needs to be embraced, cherished and developed for the good of the community.

ALLAN WADE HOUSTON

**President and CEO
Houston-Johnson Inc.**

WADE HOUSTON HAS HAD A CAREER of firsts. He was the first black to sign a basketball scholarship at the University of Louisville, first black to coach an integrated high school basketball team in Louisville and he became the first black to be a head coach at a Southeastern Conference university when he went to work for the University of Tennessee in 1989.

While he was working his way through that athletic career, he also was tending to the business of life after basketball. He formed a business partnership with Charlie Johnson, his college roommate, and his wife Alice Kean Houston. Their company, the Johnson-Houston Corporation, delivered automotive parts to Ford Motor Company's Kentucky truck plant, where Charlie worked. Before long, the friends expanded into the business of hauling trucks from factories to dealers and, through a series of acquisitions, became the second-largest minority-owned company in the United States and the largest minority-owned transporter of heavy machinery, aluminum, steel and military equipment in the country.

After forming JHT Holdings, Inc., which operated three trucking entities, the two Houstons and Johnson left the company to a fourth partner and put their energies into Houston-Johnson Inc. Houston-Johnson is a logistics provider and warehouse management company, with involvement in a broad range of activity related to just-in-time delivery.

Wade Houston was born in Alcoa, Tennessee, a small town not far from Knoxville. He came to Louisville after his high school graduation in 1962 to become the University of Louisville's first black basketball player. One of the people who tried to make him and other black players feel welcome when he arrived in Louisville was Alice Kean, daughter of the legendary Central High School basketball coach, William L. Kean. At her mother's urging, Alice invited them all to dinner at the Kean house. Sparks flew between Wade and Alice and they later married.

Houston became a starter on UofL's basketball team in two years, and lettered in three. He graduated in 1966 with a bachelor's degree and later earned a master's degree at UofL as well.

He was assistant coach, then head basketball coach at Ahrens High School in Louisville. He spent a year as a professional coach and player in Strasbourg, France. As head basketball coach at Louisville Male High School from 1973 to 1976, he had a 90-12 win-loss record. His team lost the state high school championship game in 1974, but won it in 1975.

He went to work for UofL in 1976, first as director of corporate relations, then as a member of head basketball coach Denny Crum's staff. UofL went to four NCAA final fours in his years there, and won the championship twice, in 1980 and 1986. Houston was named associate head coach at UofL in 1988. A year later, he became head basketball coach at the University of Tennessee and remained in that position until 1994.

Houston made his first foray into business during his Louisville coaching days, buying a convenience grocery in West Louisville with his wife and Johnson as partners. All three were busy with careers elsewhere and they hired others to run the business, an approach they decided later was a bad idea. They sold out after 18 months.

They went on, of course, to found the Johnson-Houston Corporation, then Houston-Johnson Inc., and became some of the most successful entrepreneurs in Louisville. While they were busy building their highly successful automotive warehousing, transportation and logistics businesses, however, all stayed busy with community commitments as well.

Wade Houston's civic activities have included service to the African-American Business Alliance, Old National Bank, Big Brothers/Big Sisters of Kentuckiana, the Kentucky Center for African-American Heritage, the Kentuckiana Minority Business Council, and the UofL Athletic Board.

The Tennessee Sportswriter's Association named Houston the University of Tennessee's top coach during his time there. He is a member of the Athletic Hall of Fame of the University of Louisville and the Kentucky and Male High School Alumni Halls of Fame. Spalding University also awarded him an honorary doctor of humane letters degree in 2002.

He and Alice have three children, a daughter Natalie, who is a graduate of UofL's medical school; a son Allan, who is a professional basketball player with the NBA's New York Knicks; and another daughter Lynn, who is a former Georgia Tech track star, and is now an employee there.

Allan, who played for his father and was all-time leading scorer at the University of Tennessee before joining the NBA, honored his father in 2003 by establishing four Wade Houston Scholarships at UT.

THERE WASN'T ANY PARTICULAR TIME when "bam, it hit me" that I wanted to become a leader in our community. It started back in the 1980s when I was coaching at the University of Louisville.

We were having some success, and I was getting some recognition for my recruiting, and I guess people started to realize I had some talent. They also saw that I was doing humanitarian things in the community. So they started calling me to ask me to join boards and to participate in the community. At that point, I suppose, I realized I was being looked upon as a leader and actually recognized myself in that category.

My father, Charlie Houston, from Alcoa, Tennessee, was my first mentor. He was like a lot of other African-American men back in the '40s and '50s. If you weren't a teacher, undertaker, doctor or professional person in your community during that time growing up in the South, you really had to manage how you were going to put bread on the table and support your family. He always managed to do what we called "hustle." He would hustle and find different ways to support us, to keep us going and to encourage us. He was never bitter and he never blamed anyone for what happened to him. He found ways to put food on the table, put clothes on our backs and encourage us to go to school and get our education.

My next mentor after my father was an assistant coach I played for at the University of Louisville, Coach John Dromo, who worked under Coach Peck Hickman. He was a guy the players could really go to for anything. I think all successful coaches have someone like that on their staffs. Coach Dromo would always have an answer. I was the first African-American student to sign a basketball scholarship at UofL. So I came in with lots of questions and things I wasn't sure of. He was the one I would always go to. I learned from him that you have to conduct yourself with class, you can't react to certain situations, and if someone calls you a name or is disrespectful, it takes a stronger person to stand up and accept things and be positive than someone who will start a fight or react. He told me I was a trailblazer and was setting a tone for the guys who would come after me. He told me that how I reacted would be noted and would become a blueprint for those who followed me.

Another mentor would be Ernie Green. Ernie played in the National Football League for the Cleveland Browns. He was the blocking back for Jim Brown. He frequently returned to UofL and spoke to athletes. He cautioned all of us that we really needed to find something besides athletics to fall back on when our collegiate or professional athletic career was over.

After Ernie's professional football career, he became a successful minority supplier for General Motors. I really wanted to do what Ernie had done and to be as successful as he was in business.

I would describe my leadership style as a coaching style. A leader is a coach, getting everyone to understand their roles, to want to overachieve, not caring who gets the credit as long as the team or company gets the victory. There is no "I" in the word "team," as the old saying goes. I think I've tried to pass that on to my managers, employees and the people I've coached. People who are able to get that across to their constituents are good leaders.

It is also the same style I have used with my family. Just as my father did, my wife Alice and I have led by example. To my children, I've tried to pass this on: "Get up every morning, go to work, stay till the job is done, even if you don't feel good or you'd rather be doing something else." Discipline is the key word. Discipline to get up and do what your job is and to do what you say you are going to do. Don't deviate from commitments you make. I think others would describe me the same way, as well as my family members.

I've had a lot of "firsts" in my life. I was the first African-American to coach at an integrated high school in Louisville, Kentucky; the first African-American to sign a basketball scholarship at UofL; and the first African-American head coach at a Southeastern Conference university. Those are accomplishments to me. What I learned about leadership from these experiences is to leave a legacy for those who come after you like, I mentioned, I learned from Coach Dromo.

I don't consider this a failure, but my biggest disappointment in life is that I didn't stay longer at the University of Tennessee at Knoxville as a head coach. But from that experience I learned that a lot of times the Lord has a different plan for you and you just have to rely on your faith, trust in the Lord and see where it takes you. It took us to an even higher level, as a company and as a family. Not long after we left Tennessee, we were running the largest minority-owned transportation company in the United States — the second-largest minority-owned company (next to Beatrice Foods) in the country. You have to learn how to turn adversity into a positive. You have to learn not to hold any bitterness. That is critical in this arena. And you have to learn not to take things personally. That's the way this business operates.

I always saw a bigger picture, even back when I was coaching under Coach Denny Crum. Occasionally his name would come up for other positions. Even if he left, I knew there was no guarantee that I'd be selected to replace him. While I was an assistant, I started looking at ways to feed my family. I started cultivating relationships with Ford Motor Company. I learned from these experiences that a vision is critical. There is an old saying in coaching, "As long as you are standing still, someone's going to be passing you." Continuous improvement and having a vision is very important.

A good follower has to be a good listener. Good listening is a lost art, in some circles. Everyone tries to impress by sharing knowledge. A critical component of business or other endeavors is to be able to listen and analyze what you hear, weed out the unimportant things and retain the things that are important. My father used to always tell me you could never learn with your mouth open. To learn, you have to be listening.

In managers, I am looking for team players – someone who will put the team first. Hire the best people and get out of their way. I want potential employees to have "people skills" – people who can get along with people; people who understand changes in the world market and a global economy; people who understand minorities in the workplace and are sensitive to single-person families. A lot of things are changing in the work force that we didn't have ten to 15 years ago.

If I could live my life all over again, I would probably still consider coaching. The chance to impact young people's lives is important. I've always been sincere in trying to help young people. I would still consider getting into the coaching field. I am a sports fanatic.

I can't think of anything I would want to do differently. I was a high school coach and loved coaching at that level. I had an opportunity to be an assistant coach at the college level at one of the top programs in the country. I went to Europe and played professionally and did some coaching there. I was a head coach at a major university.

I couldn't have started in business any sooner, but when Charlie Johnson left Ford and my wife Alice was able to leave the Financial Aid Office at UofL, we were ready. We had the pieces in place at the right time.

From a business perspective, I would probably not lean as much toward the service industry, but more toward the manufacturing arena. As African-Americans, we need to be in production. We need to be making things. A lot of income gets away from our community. To that end, I would lean towards manufacturing. But with so many manufacturing jobs going overseas, I am not sure where that would have led us.

Young people need to understand changes in the marketplace, diversity, make-up of families, why and how businesses have changed and how technology has changed. You learn this information from attending conferences and volunteering at agencies where you encounter people less fortunate.

When we start thinking about people or things that have contributed most significantly to our community's growth and development, three people come to mind: Mayors Dave Armstrong and Jerry Abramson, and Louis Coleman.

Former Mayor Dave Armstrong was a visionary with the African-American Heritage Museum. Mayor Jerry Abramson is a great ambassador on the local and national level. He has initiated a lot of things for our city. He is very visible.

I also have a lot of respect for Rev. Louis Coleman. He is in many cases the "conscience" of our city. Sometimes we go about our lives at such a hectic pace, we forget about our conscience and what we should be doing. We need to make sure we include all people in society – from the factory worker to the union worker, from the business owner to the people on the street. We need to discuss important local issues like those involving our city's police force.

I have always tried to give back to the city through fundraisers for Big Brothers/ Big Sisters, the Boys and Girls Clubs and the Fellowship of Christian Athletes. I have wanted to set an example for others to give back.

I am a proponent of minority businesses and I work with the Kentucky Minority Business Council. The KMBC gives minority businesses a chance to network with large corporations, present themselves and hopefully get a chance to do business. When you are inclusive, everyone has a fair opportunity. The chance to create wealth stands out when young people are looking to come back to work in our community. We need to retain our youth. Wealth is then passed on to charitable groups and improves our community.

Education is the biggest challenge facing our community today, in my opinion. Retaining jobs and companies and avoiding the loss of companies due to our tax structure are other issues facing our city. With our global economy, it is a new ballgame to recruit and retain companies. We have to be prepared to compete.

I would advise young people today who want to become the leaders of tomorrow in our community to get involved politically. They need to find out about our laws and what can most affect our city. They need to understand that they are going to have some bumps and obstacles to overcome in their own lives. There is no easy path to success. The road to success is filled with potholes and peer pressure. They need to surround themselves with the right kind of people, those who are going in the same direction as they are.

I have had many opportunities in my own life to be "first" – but it was education that gave me the preparation for many things to happen in my life. In every case where I was a "first," there were many reasons for me to say no or to stay where I was and be comfortable. I wanted to prove people wrong.

I've had a lot of blessings and I have a strong faith. But one important lesson I have learned is that it is important how you treat people. Always remember that no matter what is perceived as success for you, you are going to pass the same people on the way down that you did on the way up.

FRANK B. HOWER JR.

**Retired Chairman and CEO
Liberty National Bancorp, Inc.**

FRANK HOWER MADE QUITE A NAME for himself and will long be remembered as a respected banker and business leader in Louisville, Kentucky, but his favorite activity, anyone will tell you, is flying.

Hower was fascinated by the exploits of airplane pilots he heard about on the radio and saw in movies during World War II. He sold his bicycle and BB gun to take flying lessons when he was just a teenager, and got a license to solo in a plane on his 16th birthday. After he landed the plane, his mother had to drive him over to apply for his driver's license, which is something Hower still chuckles about today.

Later, after becoming a banker and community leader in Louisville, that early love of flying played a role in his being appointed the chairman of the Regional Airport Authority, where he played a key role in the $300 million expansion of Louisville International Airport. The expansion led to the establishment of the UPS air hub and package handling center in Louisville, which became Louisville's and Kentucky's largest employer.

By the time he was involved in that project, though, in the late 1980s and early 1990s, he had been in the top stratum of Louisville's civic leaders for many years.

Frank Hower grew up in Louisville, the son of an oral surgeon. He graduated from Louisville Male High School in 1946, and received a BA in 1950 from Centre College. Casting about for a career, he took a job totaling checks in Liberty National Bank's proof department.

The Korean War interrupted his career, and he ended up spending two years in the U.S. Marine Corps, six months of it in Korea during the war. He returned to the bank after his service, following his boss' advice that getting a Harvard MBA would be a waste of time. Hower also reasoned that working at the bank would give him a chance to learn firsthand about a number of different types of businesses.

His progression up the ladder at Liberty started early and was steady. In 1954, he became assistant manager of the credit department, and a year later assistant cashier. He became assistant vice president of the bank in 1957, vice president in 1958, secretary to the board in 1965, director in 1966, executive vice president in 1967, president in 1971, chairman and CEO of Liberty National Bank in 1973, and chairman and CEO of Liberty National Bancorp in 1980. He retired in 1990 – after 17 years as chairman and 40 years at the bank – at age 61.

He turned down offers to move to bigger banks and cities. "I love Louisville and Kentucky," he told *Business First* when they profiled him in 1985. "There are a lot more things in life than making the biggest salary."

During Hower's tenure, Liberty grew from a community bank with $430 million in assets to a $3.2 billion regional banking company. He also had a hand in every important community endeavor in Louisville.

He chaired the Louisville Area Chamber of Commerce, the Metro United Way Campaign, the Regional Airport Authority, the Board of Trustees at the University of Louisville and the Kentucky Independent College Foundation. He also chaired the board of NKC, Inc., and served on that board for over two decades.

Hower served on the boards of a number of other organizations as well – Centre College, Actors Theatre, the Kentucky Center for the Arts, the Filson Club, Alliant Health System, the American Life & Accident Company, Blue Cross Blue Shield and the Kentucky Historical Society, among others. He served on 16 corporate boards and 32 civic boards over the years, and still serves on five, including Churchill Downs, the James Graham Brown Foundation and the University of Louisville Foundation.

Through it all Hower has maintained a reputation for integrity and basic kindness. When he retired from Liberty, his friend and colleague David Grissom said of Hower, "He's one of the few people I've known that you'll never hear anybody say a bad word about."

Bill Joe Phelps, who was Hower's able sideman at the bank for more than 30 years, said when Hower retired that he was convinced he was doing it early to give an old friend, Phelps, a chance to be chairman and CEO before he retired, too.

Hower will tell you he has had a good life. "I guess the thing I'm most proud of," he told *The Courier-Journal* when he retired, "is running a good, clean, profitable, sound bank. Now that may sound kind of corny, but in this day and time, when we're reading about what's happening to a lot of financial institutions, I'm very proud of that record."

He and his wife, Sissy, have two sons.

Passing the Torch

I REALLY DON'T REMEMBER ANY particular point when I decided I wanted to become a leader. I knew that whatever field I entered, I wanted to be a success. I also knew, most importantly, that wherever I ended up working, I wanted to leave the place better than when I entered it.

I wanted to give something back. I began in the latter part of high school and into college to sense that I had a desire to lead. Actually, however, this realization peaked during my active duty in the Korean War. That experience made me realize that I didn't just want to be average, I wanted to be motivated.

I graduated from college right at the time the Korean War broke out, so I guess you might say I was destined to lead at that point in my life. At one point, I was responsible for 235 Marines.

When I began in banking, I sat in the proof department and totaled checks for awhile. That was not a very stimulating activity. It motivated me to do something better than that. When I returned from active duty, I looked around again. I enjoyed banking, and I saw so many old people in banking. So I thought as a young man, the odds were in my favor.

I looked at other jobs that were a lot better financially than I was offered, but I decided I'd rather do what I want to do and make less and be happy with it than make money without personal motivation. What I learned from that experience is that you need to make a career out of what you enjoy doing.

The bank encouraged us to lead and be involved with the community. There are not many industries that do that. Things have changed so much today, though, I really don't know if that is still the case. I was in the banking business during the "salad days." It was just fun, a people-oriented business, with a lot of wonderful customers and wonderful competitors, believe it or not.

I don't know that I had any one mentor. As we recall the 55th anniversary of the Chamber, I can remember when the first president of the Chamber was elected, Tom Ballantine. He was a person I had great admiration for. Later, I served on his board at the Louisville Title Insurance Company when he was president. It gave me a great thrill because he was someone I looked up to at that time. He was a real factor in the community.

I thought it would be wonderful to be someone who was involved. I ended up being the chairman of the board of the Chamber. I really enjoyed it – it was one of the most interesting things I ever did in Louisville.

There were a number of people who had an influence on me. A man by the name of Bill Dabney was one of them – president of DeVoe Reynolds Paint Company, quite a hero in World War I, distinguished service cross, Croix de Guerre, company commander in Teddy Roosevelt's outfit.

He started a little paint company in Louisville known as Jones Dabney, which later became a national corporation. He offered me my best job, but his son was one of my very best friends, and I was not sure that our friendship could survive that.

He told me one thing that was very interesting, though. He said, "You know, I am president of this company and you can look in the annual report and see that there are five people who make more than I do because they are valuable in the areas they are in. It doesn't bother me to pay them for what they are doing. I don't always have to be the number one guy." That was interesting to me and I thought that was a very valuable lesson to learn about leadership and management.

It was also memorable that he never forgot his friends. They were not top business people – just good, solid people – and he stuck with them.

My father was an oral surgeon – actually he was the first dentist to be a resident at the city hospital in Louisville, and the first dentist asked to speak to the Kentucky Medical Association. He was very involved in his own dental community.

During my young childhood, the war was going on and things were rather slow, so I went to almost every movie in town. Movies were a wonderful influence. The good guy always prevailed. The white hat won the battle. That whole atmosphere was very inspiring. There was an awful lot of integrity in that period of time. I'm not sure I see as much of that today.

One friend I looked up to was Thruston Morton, vice chairman of Liberty, a U.S. Senator, head of the GOP and one of the smartest men I have ever known in my life. When I had a problem that I couldn't solve, I could always sit down and talk to him. He had the ability to slice through any situation, suggesting a better way to go

I was the treasurer of his campaigns and met a lot of interesting people. In fact, I offered him a job. I thought, "Gee, I've just hired a U.S. Senator and I don't really have the authority to do so." He helped any major industry in Kentucky to succeed and worked on a lot of boards to make a difference. He helped me through my thought processes and had a great deal of integrity.

One thing I learned in the Marine Corps is that you don't succeed as a leader by commanding – you have to lead, you have to try to convince people that your direction is the right direction. I've always tried to pick good people and let them run with the ball. If they drop it, I'll make some changes. I never did try to take anybody's glory for their job successes.

I would describe my leadership style at Liberty National Bank as almost a partnership with my colleagues. Bill Joe Phelps and I worked closely together.

Bill, Malcolm Chancey and I also worked very well as a team. A team proposition was a wonderful experience.

I followed Wilson Wyatt as Chamber president. He ran against Thruston Morton for the U.S. Senate and was a Democrat. He was an absolutely fabulous guy, even more conservative than I was with Chamber decisions.

I find it hard to believe that people say such nice things about me. I have always tried to operate with integrity. In the banking business, you periodically have to turn people down on loans. In one case, I turned down a loan for a bigger gas station. Later the owner came back, opened up an account and told me I turned him down nicer than the others did. That certainly proves a point, that you should never write anybody off.

The thing I am most proud of is being chairman of Louisville's Regional Airport Authority when we expanded the airport. It was a tremendous team effort. UPS was the catalyst that really made it happen. John Y. Brown Jr. was governor, and Bruce Lunsford was Kentucky Commerce Secretary. We wooed UPS. We worked in many directions and figured it out. J.D. Nichols, for example, figured out how the runways could be fixed to accommodate UPS. We knew it would be difficult to sell to the Board of Aldermen and state.

The Courier-Journal kept the planning process quiet. If this had been planned in public, it never would have happened. George Gill, the publisher, took an awful lot of flack from his own reporters because he helped us keep it quiet. We were also lucky that U.S. Senator Wendell Ford was chairman of the Senate Aviation Committee. As governor, he had turned down the first attempt for a new Louisville airport in the '70s. It was a big disappointment. I think Wendell realized that was a mistake, so he really worked to help us get federal funds for this airport. Things just started working.

We met often, with a lot of committees instead of the full board, since working in that environment would have been more public. We lobbied aldermen, and I am still contributing to some of their campaigns.

We had a story so important to Louisville as far as payrolls and taxes were concerned, it was a growing industry. I got great satisfaction from being a small part of a major initiative that really pushed Louisville forward.

You know, Louisville was founded because of the Ohio River. Then we were a railroad hub, but we fell behind in aviation. We could have been Atlanta. Maybe we ought to be glad we are not Atlanta. We had to do a lot of catching up. It's amazing, you know, we were bigger than Atlanta before World War II.

We have to grow successfully — with quality growth — to give opportunities to our young people.

Frank B. Hower Jr.

I am not pessimistic about things like "brain drain." More and more people seem to like Louisville. It is a wonderful place to live and work – it really is.

One of the things I was most proud of is the fact that even though there were a lot of people unhappy about the airport expansion during that whole period, we never lost any accounts at the bank. And I was chairman of the Regional Airport Authority board at the time.

I really don't think I have had a failure – perhaps some minor disappointments, but no failures. Developing the Fourth Street Mall, for example, may not have been a successful venture at first, but it was a good idea at the time. We tried to do something different.

The Galleria on Fourth Street worked the same way. I learned that cities the size of Louisville have a very difficult time trying to reinvent themselves. You have to keep trying, however.

Today we continue to try to make Louisville a wonderful place. I think it's a jewel. Selfishly, I hope a whole lot of people don't find out about it. For the sake of the community, though, I want to see it succeed, with better schools and better health care, better places to live.

Louisville is blessed with a lot of real estate, and people want convenience. A lot of suburban conveniences drew people away from downtown. Corporate headquarters moved out to the suburbs, because they could provide parking for their employees. I don't think any city our size really succeeded while I was active in the community, except Indianapolis. They found a niche in athletics. I believe it will happen for Louisville.

Our niche has been cultural, more than anything else. We have supportive arts and wonderful schools, great private colleges and a style of living that is the envy of other cities. We also have a choice of neighborhoods and housing to live in. It's just remarkable.

Networking with other leaders, working with groups of people on successful projects – it pushes you in other directions. Banks used to push you in that direction, although I don't know if that is done as much today. For example, when I ran the United Way campaign, I wasn't asked to run it – I was told to run it. My chairman was asked and said, "Of course. Frank will do it."

In those days, all the banking leaders got together in a community way. We never tried to step on the other guy's foot, even if they were competitors. I was involved in the airport, the Galleria, and the attitude always was, "What can I do to help?" We accomplished a lot. There was a sense of collegialism that I am not sure exists today. We also got a lot done.

I remember one time, early in my banking career, I thought I had been passed over for a promotion. My boss said, "Well, Frank, you can't have all chiefs, there have to be some Indians." I said, "I don't want to be an Indian."

What I have learned is that if you want to go from being a follower to a leader, it takes a little extra effort. But it takes so little extra effort to get ahead of the crowd. There are a lot of wonderful people coming to work eigiht to five everyday. They are happy going home. Few stay late and come in early to do whatever it takes. If a person has get up and go, he has a wonderful chance to really use it in almost any organization. What followers have to learn is that you have to educate yourself in the business. You are in a constant training program in every phase of your career. Try to learn the next step up on the side.

In our days, if we did a good job, we didn't have to worry about anything. It is so different today. You have to keep educating yourself. In our industry, I was responsible for the bond portfolio. There was no textbook on that, so I just had to start talking to people and asking. "How do you do this and that?"

Push ahead and try to get information. It really takes so little effort. I was surprised there weren't more people interested in that.

My military background was very helpful. I often think it is a shame that more people can't have the experience – hopefully in peace time. I was in a group that was asking the Secretary of Defense, Casper Weinberger, some questions one day. "Why can't we have compulsory military for our young people?" He said, "We'd love to, but it would be very expensive social programming and we can't afford it."

I don't think I would do anything differently if I could do it all over again. I toyed with the idea of going to Harvard Business School after I got out of the military and Merle Robertson, the chairman of the bank said, "Frank, if you know what you want to do, don't waste time going to business school. Spend that time learning our business. If you don't know where you want to work – General Electric or Ford, for example – then go to business school.

Having two years in the military was a good experience. Young people need to kill a couple of years to gain that maturity. I think business school can do it, but it is not a panacea.

I am very pleased with my career. I was very lucky. I like people in banking. You get a chance to meet a lot of different people, and it's fun to meet people.

I would advise young people aspiring to leadership today that they need to work hard and dive into their business. They need to keep educating themselves too. We are going to be in training programs for the rest of our lives.

I think it is important to use interpersonal skills with your colleagues, too, both above and below you, if you want to be a leader. And you should enjoy what you do. You have to like what you are doing to be successful. If you are in it just for the money, you won't make it.

I think Louisville's getting the GE plant back in 1950 was one of the most significant things that happened to our city — 23,000 people at that time. Louisville is sometimes kind of a closed community, but GE employees ingratiated themselves to the community. Most who came here ended up staying here and retired. That spawned a lot of things. Those employees all had a sense of responsibility to the community.

Why did GE pick Louisville? Louisville had the Fund for the Arts and GE believed that made Louisville a great place for their employees to live. In the last ten years, the airport expansion played a major role too.

I think one of the biggest challenges our community is facing in the future is making sure that we develop a good, educated workforce. We have been a blue collar town for a long time and that's changing, but it is not easy.

We have a good public school system, and a good set of independent colleges in Louisville. We have good parochial and private high schools in Louisville and I think we are on the march. I think the University of Louisville is really doing some marvelous things too.

I don't want to be an Atlanta tomorrow. I'd like to work in that direction and be a better quality community without all the problems they have. You don't have to be the biggest to be the best.

Making your social friends your business friends is a terrible mistake. Sometimes it's okay, of course, but I see so many people disappointed when they leave a company. They lose their power, then they become of no use, then the friendship ends.

One of the most valuable lessons I have learned in my life that I want to pass on to the next generation of leaders in our community is that you have to have integrity. It makes me sick when I see what's happened in industry today.

Don't ever try to shade something. Be honest, forthright, upfront. Integrity is so important.

CHARLIE W. JOHNSON

**Former President and CEO
Active Transportation Company**

**Owner and CEO
C.W. Johnson Xpress, LLC**

CHARLIE JOHNSON HAD MIXED feelings about Louisville during his first lonely, hard days as a University of Louisville freshman football player from Columbus, Georgia. He had left behind four brothers, a sister, and his mother. His father, a Methodist minister, had died suddenly when Charlie was 13, but his parents had instilled in their children a strong Christian ethic which has grown stronger and stronger in Charlie's life. Charlie has a deep Christian conviction as evidenced by his devotion to his local church, his constant witness to his friends and co-workers, his extensive speaking engagements to various religious groups and, most of all, his love and compassion for people. The six-foot-three, 288-pound high-school graduate had turned down 83 college scholarship offers to accept an offer from the University of Louisville. Also this was his first time away from his hometown and his family.

But all of this was to change. In the early '70s, after four years at UofL and six years with the National Football League, Charlie decided to return to Kentucky and to make Louisville his home.

His first business venture was a neighborhood grocery project which he launched with his friend and former roommate, Wade Houston. This attempt failed and cost Wade and Charlie some $80,000. Johnson blames this failure on the fact that both men had full-time daytime jobs, and they had to rely too heavily on paid employees who were inexperienced and in many instances unreliable. However, Johnson vowed to keep trying. He said, "It's something you have to learn in sports — don't give up after the first setback!"

Johnson began his successful business career in the late '80s when he and Wade started a company to deliver parts to the Louisville Ford Motor Company truck plant. At that time, Charlie was employed as a supervisor at the Ford plant. His experience on his job helped prepare him when, in 1983, Ford Motor Company began looking for minority suppliers to transport parts into the plant and to deliver vehicles to dealers.

Thus was launched Johnson-Houston Transportation Company which later, after some mergers with other companies, became Active Transportation Company, with Charlie Johnson as CEO. The company soon won opportunities to do business with other vehicle manufacturers, as well as recognition in many business publications such as *Forbes*, *The Wall Street Journal*, *Minority Business USA*, and *Black Enterprise Magazine*.

In 1996, Charlie Johnson told *The Courier-Journal*, "If you truly believe you have been given an opportunity and you want to make a difference, you should give an opportunity to others." This attitude, no doubt, accounts for the fact that, by 1997, Active Transportation was spending over $25 million a year with other minority firms, Johnson said, "We have a commitment to the whole community, but our emphasis is on developing and having an image and visibility in the minority community."

Johnson's years in sports had also taught him how important it is in business to develop a team that sets goals, then to work hard together to achieve them. "Football teaches you that you are part of a group," he said, "and as long as that group functions as a team, everybody wins."

Johnson has served on a number of boards over the years, including those of PNC Bank, Benedict College, University of Louisville, Spalding University, Greater Louisville Inc., Louisville Private Industry Council, Lincoln Heritage Council of the Boy Scouts of America, Muhammad Ali Center, Greater Louisville Convention and Visitors Bureau, African-American Venture Capital Fund, Kentuckiana Minority Business Council, Louisville Urban League, Minority Business Roundtable, Joint Center for Political and Economic Studies, and Quinn Chapel AME Church.

Johnson has received numerous awards and accolades for his achievements and entrepreneurial spirit, including the Advertising Federation of Louisville's Louisvillian of the Year Award, Ford Motor Company's Entrepreneurial Role Model Award, the NAACP Minority Business Freedom Award, and the first Ronald H. Brown Leadership Award. In 1998, he was one of five honorees who received an Economic Development Leadership Award from then-Kentucky Governor Paul Patton. Johnson holds honorary doctorates from Benedict College and Wilberforce University.

Johnson and his wife, Bettie, are both active in the community and have given millions of dollars to churches and to many educational causes, including the United Negro College Fund and the University of Louisville, which named a new dorm "Bettie Johnson Hall" in honor of Mrs. Johnson.

I HAVE LEARNED HOW TO STAY in there and work with other people to make sure we all reach our goal. Most leaders have also been a role player; so it should not be hard for a leader to go back and forth — to step down into a role on a team and later to move back up into a leadership position. When you are a team leader, it is important that your followers are loyal. They have to believe in what you are presenting and they must subscribe to the team mission. Then, hard work and loyalty will usually produce favorable results.

I would advise young people who are aspiring to leadership that they should make good decisions about who their friends are and what places they frequent. Young people should avoid putting themselves in harm's way. They must be dedicated to whatever project they select to join and they must really work hard to make positive things happen.

In Louisville, we have several groups which have strong positive influence on our community. Foremost among these is Great Louisville Inc. (GLI), the former Louisville Chamber of Commerce. This group represents the business community and it has been a strategy-setter for this area over the years. Along with GLI, there are several major corporations such as Brown-Forman, Humana, Capital Holding and LG&E, to name a few, that have been good corporate citizens in participating in the growth of the Louisville metro area.

I worked with GLI even before it was a Louisville partnership. My company participated financially and we worked with the Chamber in activities to attract new businesses to the city, to develop studies of current problems, to encourage growth of educational projects, etc. In my opinion, it is crucial that we develop a strategic plan to grow our city. At one time, we were bigger than Nashville, Indianapolis and Cincinnati. We need a strategic plan to attract business, and such a plan usually is developed through an organization like GLI — that is our challenge. By using all the appropriate groups in the metro area, the necessary research can be done to come up with a plan to guide this community in future growth. GLI can and must accept this challenge.

Furthermore, a viable strategic plan will assist us in finding solutions to some of our pervasive community problems. We have a serious drug problem in the metro area and we must develop a better relationship between the community and the police department. We have to start looking at how we can target jobs. In the areas where we have the highest drug use, we also have the highest rate of unemployment. Churches have to get involved and not just West End churches either.

Our community needs to improve our educational system. We need to increase the money we give our schools so that we can pay our teachers more. Also, there are many other needs in the school system that we should address. However, it has been very difficult in the past to get the public to vote to increase taxes for the library, for schools, etc. A strategic plan would assist such efforts by making the needs and needed corrective actions clear.

First, you have to learn to be involved and accessible. Be accessible to work on a task force that the mayor might create for a certain cause. Be accessible to other civic activities. Help raise money for worthwhile causes in our city. Let the community know you are available when needed to support other leaders who are working on good causes.

Secondly, aspiring young leaders need to develop skill in problem solving. You must correctly define a problem and then work out a plan for solving the problem. Then you must determine how you assist in the solution.

I care about Louisville and where our city is going. This is my home; this is where I live. I don't live in Montana or Arizona, or New York. I live in Louisville, Kentucky. I want this to be a good community for everybody.

My advice to anybody is to work to make Louisville better for everybody and in doing so, you will make it better for yourself and you will feel good about living here.

I really did not consciously choose to be a community leader, but as our business grew, I became more and more interested in community issues. Soon I was projected into a leadership role as a result of my responding to the many civic and social needs of our city that were presented to me.

More and more often I began to be placed in situations with other civic leaders where decision-making was taking place and this broadened my view of the city and how the system works. Meanwhile our business was growing and this made it possible for me to participate financially in a wide range of community efforts.

Two people significantly influenced my business life and helped me in the development of my business perspective. They are Lenny Lyles and David Jones Sr.

I played professional football with Lenny and soon got to know him both as a football player and later as a successful entrepreneur. We worked out together and he was the epitome of hard work. He taught me if you want to achieve anything, you have to work hard and stay with it. Later, I went to him often for business advice which he gave freely. I did not fully understand how business worked – I knew how athletics worked but I did not know business. I learned from Lenny Lyles some of the things business can do for you and how you must hang in there to work things out.

When I was playing professional sports, had I possessed a working knowledge of the business world, I probably would have started sooner to participate since I did have income to invest. Business opportunities came along during my playing years but I did not fully understand how to make things happen and work for me.

I met David Jones early in my business career and he became a mentor and a good friend. He continues to be a valuable friend who is always available to share what knowledge he has to assist me in my professional growth. For example, I remember when I was considering taking my company public, he personally took me to Wall Street so I could tell my story. He has been and continues to be a real asset, not only to me, but also to our total community.

David told me never to depend on others to run your business because no one is motivated to make another person rich. You must always be hands-on and be there to make sure things are going the way you want them to go. I learned there is no easy way to make money — you must dedicate yourself to your business and stay the course.

One of the greatest accomplishments one can experience is to create a business plan and watch that plan develop into a viable business. Our business plan was my guide but I attribute my being able to stick to the plan until we could see it through to three things — first, my religious faith in God was and will always be the source of my strength. I depend on God for daily strength and guidance. Secondly, God has placed good people around me to support my efforts; and thirdly, my years as a professional athlete taught me how to be a good team player.

Within our company, I was the CEO, so I set a vision for everybody to aim for. Next, we defined our goals and how we intended to achieve them. We then stayed the course, persevered, and we won. In life you must set goals early on and work to achieve them. People who do not set goals and work to meet them are not going to be successful.

I would describe my leadership style as rather laid back. I am not a point person. I take everything seriously though and I carefully analyze each situation to understand the facts fully. My employees probably see me as demanding and something of a perfectionist. However, in our community I think people consider me a laid back person who does not have to be in charge or on top in order to be a good member of a group.

In my opinion, I also see myself as a good follower who can work hard in a group and assist in working through problems. Early on, I learned that once a game plan is in place, it is my duty whether I am a leader or a follower to do my part in working for the success of the plan. In life we are all role players or members of groups, and we have to know how to play our role as a part of a whole.

David A. Jones

**Co-Founder and
Chairman Emeritus
Humana Inc.**

**Chairman
Hospira Inc.**

KENTUCKY GOVERNOR BRERETON JONES ONCE referred to him as "the heaviest of hitters." Others have called him the "best friend a home town ever had." Mayor Jerry Abramson once described him this way: "He's a guy who's never forgotten his roots, someone who appreciates his home town maybe more than sometimes his home town has appreciated him. He's awesome. I wish I had 20 of him."

If people in Louisville, Kentucky were asked to name one man they think is the real "godfather of civic leadership" in their city, most would immediately say his name – David Jones.

As a businessman and as a community leader, Jones is a standout and an exemplary civil servant. He is chairman emeritus of a company, Humana Inc., that he founded with some partners and 1,000 borrowed dollars 44 years ago. Humana has now become a $14 billion health benefits company, and business analysts credit the company's growth and long-term success to its ability to reinvent itself. One nursing home in 1962 became the nation's largest nursing home company in 1969. One hospital in 1968 grew to become the nation's largest hospital company in 1978. A first insurance sale in 1983 led to the $14 billion company that Humana is today.

Despite the meteoric rise of his businesses and his own personal wealth, however, Jones has never forgotten that he came from humble beginnings and he, his companies and his family have been inordinately generous with their time, talent and treasure over the years. A list of just the major things they have done for their hometown would quickly swamp this page. The family won't talk about or quantify their giving, but Humana and Humana Foundation gifts alone, from 1975 – 2004, not counting personal and family gifts, are estimated at $160 million.

The Courier-Journal's Dianne Aprile hit some of the highlights of David Jones' community contributions in a 1997 profile. Jones, she said, has "built affordable housing in marginal neighborhoods, put computers in schools, supported an international play festival that put Louisville on the theatrical map, helped launch an African-American business venture fund, championed Kentucky education reform, spruced up parks, lured the Presbyterian Church USA headquarters to the riverfront, pumped a million dollars into Catholic schools and, for a brief time in the 1970s, helped to bring professional basketball to Louisville." Since then, among other things, Jones helped raise nearly $750,000 for local flood victims. He donated $400,000 to build a playground in Louisville's California neighborhood where he grew up, and an additional $175,000 for Cherokee Park improvements. He gave the University of Louisville $1 million to help establish the McConnell Center for Political Leadership, as well as funding for a significant humanities program. He has funded additional programs to try to attract the best and brightest students to Louisville and to keep them here after they graduate.

Jones chaired the fundraising efforts and personally provided major funding for the initial design and development of Louisville's award-winning Waterfront Park. He recently stepped up again to chair an ambitious new community-wide initiative called "City of Parks." Civic leaders hope to raise $20 million over the next 15 years to fund long-term development of open spaces and parkland in the Louisville area. Jones immediately pledged $5 million to the effort himself, and challenged others to follow his lead. He's already raised a total of $12 million.

Jones and former Humana partner Wendell Cherry, who died in 1991, played large roles in the construction of the Kentucky Center for the Arts, which was built across the street from their Michael Graves-designed Humana Building. In recent years, Jones' philanthropy has spread to places as far away as Romania, where the Humana Foundation has created a program to improve health care and health care education. The impact of this initiative, involving hundreds of Romanian and American volunteers, is so vast that a former Romanian minister of health refers to the last 15 years as "the David Jones era" in his country's history. And in 2003, Jones received the Order of Merit, the highest civilian honor bestowed by the Romanian government.

Speaking about the city of Louisville's future to a Venture Club audience in 2001, Jones said there is a lesson in his success and that of other Kentucky entrepreneurs. "Creating a culture that attracts and retains entrepreneurs — not just young professionals, or technology experts, or people of certified brilliance, but the rough-and-tumble, brash, glass-breaking folks who will tackle big tasks and occasionally succeed — is important," he said.

In 2005, Jones and his board passed the Humana chairman's torch to an entrepreneur trained personally by Jones — his son, David A. Jones Jr.

I MADE NO CONSCIOUS DECISION to become a leader in Louisville. As Humana grew, I was asked to participate in a variety of things in the city.

I was lucky enough to work for Wilson Wyatt and Robert Sloss at the Wyatt law firm when I first came back to Louisville. They were both extremely able professionals and they taught me to be fully prepared for any task.

I had another mentor away from Louisville – Peter Drucker, who is quite a management guru. Wendell Cherry and I ran into him by accident about 30 years ago, and he taught me something that was critically important: If you want to build a great enterprise or a significant enterprise, you have to create the conditions in which people can do their best work; and if you create that kind of an organization, wonderful things can happen.

The first thing that is important is not to throw roadblocks in people's way, and the second is to encourage them to be willing to take risks, to follow their passions. Obviously there has to be some direction – there has to be a goal. Setting the goal is necessary, but if you try to tell people how to do their work to achieve that goal, then you're going to restrict them greatly. So it's mainly a matter of letting them have the freedom to fall on their face every now and then, as long as they get up and try again.

I would say my leadership style is being a good delegator. I'm good at holding people accountable. I am also able to abandon initiatives, even if they were my idea, if it seems to be the right thing to do, and it often is. I'm very strong-willed and very competitive. That's how people see me, and I think they see me that way correctly. I have very high expectations for people with whom I work.

Founding and leading Humana, and creating 100,000 jobs as we built three great businesses here in Louisville, is by far my most significant business accomplishment. We built the largest nursing home company in the country, the largest hospital company in the country, and now we currently have a $14 billion health benefits business. The current revenues of those three businesses are well over $25 billion, and they were all built right here in Louisville. So in business terms, that would be my greatest success.

But a far greater success, from my standpoint, is my family. That has always been more important to me than anything else. I was very lucky to find Betty at a very early age, and we've been married now for 50 years. We have five great kids and nine, soon ten, wonderful grandchildren.

In raising a family, you learn a great deal of humility. I have learned so much from my family. Let me share an anecdote.

I was chairman of Humana for 44 years. We had times when the media would get after us for something or other, usually unfairly in my not unbiased view – and I would often write a letter to get it off my chest. But then I would take the letter home and Betty would edit it. She would strike all the adjectives, and then it was too boring to send. She was tremendously helpful to me. I've learned to curb my temper a bit.

But let me tell you a couple of really important things that I've learned from my life experience. Good character is the most important asset of any executive – of any person really. I've already mentioned this, but I'll mention it again: If you really want to build a significant enterprise, you have to be able and willing to work through other people. To work through other people successfully, you have to do what I said before, and that is to create the conditions where people can do their best work. If I want to hire someone, I like to be able to look that person in the eye and say, "You're a great student. If you were to come here, we probably won't pay you more than someone else for your equivalent experience, but this is a place where you will be allowed to do the best work of which you are capable."

Doing good work is one of the great things in life. When you've done a job and you know you've done a good job, there is a great deal of satisfaction. Wendell and I could never have built this business single-handedly. Neither one of us had an MBA, but what we've been willing to do is to work through other people. I love to see young people succeed and that, in turn, built all of our successful businesses right here in Louisville, Kentucky.

I've certainly had more than one failure, but I'll tell you about one. In 1969, we became the largest nursing home company in the country. Less than two years after we became a public company, 83 other companies also became public as nursing home companies and suddenly there was no need for additional new nursing homes. We had grown from eight to 50 nursing homes in a two-year period because we had capital for the first time, and we had skills we had developed through sweat equity – through doing things ourselves when we didn't have the money to hire others. We asked ourselves, "What can we do with these skills?" And we answered, "Zoning and borrowing money." Getting zoning was tough, because no one wanted a nursing home in the neighborhood, and financing the real estate side of it wasn't easy. So we said, "What's like that?" We said, "Mobile home parks." In a year's time, we built a dozen mobile home parks. We discovered, though, that the next thing you have to do is to sell the trailers to fill the parks. Suddenly, we were in a used car-like business, and it was a giant mess because we didn't know the first thing about it.

Having made the really bad decision to go into the business, we made a better decision which was to cut our losses and get out of it. We lost $5 million in 1970 in the mobile home park business, at a time when the company was very small and could hardly afford that kind of a loss. We learned a lot of things from that. The most important one is that just because you're good at one thing doesn't mean you're going to be good at something else. We also learned that to try to do two disparate activities at the same time is bad strategy. You spend all your time on the losing proposition, trying to make it work, when you should be spending your time on the successful proposition where you will get a lot further ahead. So that was a misstep that we made early in our careers. Thank goodness we made it early, because I think it probably kept us from making bigger mistakes later.

I think that good followers must have good character, be good listeners, be energetic, tenacious, intelligent, passionate, have a sense of humor, and be well-organized. Sounds like I'm after the perfect person, but those are the things I look for in executives and successful people and you often find them, especially if you give people the opportunity to take risks.

I really would do nothing differently in my life, if I could live it over again. Half the fun of life is not knowing what to expect.

I would advise young people aspiring to become leaders to learn to communicate clearly, both orally and in writing. Take advantage of your educational opportunities. The biggest shortfall I see in young people who have tremendous potential is their inability to express themselves clearly.

This isn't original with me, but I've said it for many years: "If you can't write your idea on the back of my business card, you don't have a clear idea." Being able to express your ideas clearly makes the difference between success and failure. So I try to encourage young people to get the best education they can, and really to concentrate on being able to get their ideas across. Ultimately, what you have to do is sell yourself, so that's my advice.

You use the same basic skills in whatever profession or task you may become involved in, and my advice to young people aspiring to be leaders in our community would be to gain the best skills you can. Gain skills as a lawyer or a doctor or a teacher or whatever it might be, then build on that. As you move into leadership, try to choose something where your knowledge and skills can be helpful. If you don't learn how to communicate clearly, though, you're really going to be crippled all your life, no matter what you do.

David A. Jones

I hope this doesn't sound vain, but I would nominate Humana as one, possibly "the" major engine of growth in our community over the past 50 years, especially in how it has raised the bar in civic participation, arts and education. Those are things that I think are really important. Others who made a major contribution in these areas in my lifetime have been Wilson Wyatt, Mary Bingham, Sally Brown, Ed Glasscock and, in recent years, Bob Doll. A current champion is Jim Gaunt over at Fifth Third Bank, who has taken a real leadership role. United Parcel Service – UPS – has been a major contributor. There are lots and lots of others. But when you look over a 50-year period that happens almost to coincide with the 44 years of Humana's existence and growth, I've been offered the opportunity to participate in a lot of things that have gone on in the community.

We've certainly stood up for a lot of things like improving education (Betty's and my passion), because that's what created opportunity for me as I was growing up in the West End in the Depression. We weren't poorer than anybody else – everybody was poor – but I've achieved what I have because I had a good mind and was able to obtain a good education. Maybe I would have gotten here without it, but I don't think so. So, it's been both an honor and a pleasure to be involved in most of the things that have gone on in Louisville during my time, and I hope to continue to participate in them. I always encourage other people to do that.

Education at all levels is still one of the greatest challenges facing our community. We simply must raise our level of expectation for educators and students alike. We must succeed in teaching all of our young people to read well, to write lucidly and to be numerically literate. If we fail, the city's future is bleak. If we succeed, Louisville will have a bright future.

I've been involved in KERA from 1990 through last December. I co-chaired the Partnership for Kentucky Education with Oz Nelson of UPS and John Hall of Ashland over that 13-year period. I am currently involved with "Every 1 Reads" locally and I see a lot of success.

Our schools are a lot better today than they were 15 years ago. The overall success masks the fact that there is a cohort of our students who are not improving, however. About 18-20% of our kids are not reading at grade level. They tend to be the victims of social pathologies of one kind or another. Having said that, they nonetheless need to be taught to read.

I'm reminded of a sign outside the post office in Middlebury, Vermont. My wife Betty is a trustee of Middlebury College, and I'm up there fairly often. The sign says "No parking" and beneath it there's a second sign that says, "Don't even think about parking." You know, "We're going to incinerate your car if you park here."

That's the kind of attitude we need to bring to kindergarten and first grade, and just not let up, because kids are curious and they will learn.

Some of our kids have terrible problems in the sense that they move so often. They come to school without ever having a book, although they have seen plenty of television. I don't have the science to know whether your brain develops well if it receives only visual stimuli, but whatever the problems are, we need to have an attitude that every child is going to learn to read.

My own experience has been that people typically rise to your level of expectation. If you keep it low enough, results will stay low. There are problems with public education. I've just seen one of them up close around Rowan Claypool's "Teach Kentucky" program. An inexperienced young man was placed in the Southern Leadership Academy — that's a euphemism for kids who are really troublesome. Instead of having young teachers with no experience trying to take on those problems, the most experienced and capable teachers should be doing that. But the way the rules are set up, experienced teachers can opt out of those jobs. I mean, who would want that kind of job? That's something that needs attention.

Related to that is the tremendous amount of money that we spend on busing – not just school busing, but TARC busing. The TARC ridership provides about 2% or less of the revenue of TARC, so it's a totally subsidized and vital public service. But those buses go empty most of the day, and at the same time we have all these school buses that are riding back and forth. It's all the community's money, and somebody with a logistics background ought to look at that and say how can we mesh these things together to improve productivity.

When I went to school, we used the city buses and were allowed to buy something called school checks that cost about half-price. It was a subsidized way to get kids to school. And if they can get there by public transportation, why should we have a separate and highly expensive system?

I'm just touching on a couple of the problems with public education and, if there were easy solutions, I'm sure they would have already been brought forward. But for our community, the one thing that we really need to do is insist on good education. I'm not just talking about in the public schools, but all the schools, including the universities. We need to do everything we can to help all of those institutions do their best work.

The man who really got KERA passed was a man who later on was vilified – Governor Wallace Wilkinson. Both he and his wife had grown up in a small town and were passionate about education. I did go over to Frankfort and lobby for KERA with some of my colleagues. I don't take any real credit for its passage, though, other than letting the governor know that the business community was strongly in favor of it.

The governor had the courage to raise taxes over a two-year budget period by about a billion dollars. He was goaded by the court ruling that the system was unconstitutional because the funding wasn't equivalent. But using that as the wedge, he was able to push KERA through a very reluctant legislature.

At the same time, the business roundtable sort of adopted KERA, and there were three companies – Humana, Ashland and UPS – that helped. The CEOs of all three companies had come from humble beginnings and gotten good educations and, as you can in this country, risen because of the skills that we've been fortunate enough to gain. We all agreed to spend ten years pushing KERA. We created an organization called the Partnership for Kentucky Education and it was open to anyone who wished to be a member. We recruited legislators, principals, administrators, union members, teachers, the teachers' union, parent-teacher associations and lay people. The only criteria for being a member of the committee was your agreement that if you wanted to change the legislation, you had to bring your idea before the committee, and we would then either support it or oppose it. It has worked really well for all these years. The teacher's unions often tried to remove the accountability sections of KERA. They didn't like those – they still don't like them. The teachers in schools where they have embraced KERA have seen phenomenal results, however.

I have learned some lessons in my life that I would like to share with the next generations of leaders in Louisville. One is that I would like all young people, or people of any age, to know that anything that can be accomplished anywhere in the world can be accomplished here in Louisville. I think we have proven that – not just Humana, but many others. I want young people who have integrity, energy, tenacity, intelligence and passion to feel free to dream and to act on their dreams here in Louisville. And if they fail the first time, or even multiple times, they are no worse off than the person who didn't try.

To me, there's just unbelievable opportunity in this country. Anything that is being done can be done a little better, so you never need to say that there is not anything left to be done. I'm optimistic by nature and, I think, by experience. I've seen a lot over a long period of time and I don't see anything that causes me not to be optimistic.

Now having said that, you know, our youngest son – Matt – is a Lieutenant Colonel in the Marine Corps. He has a purple heart and is often in harm's way. I feel deeply, from personal experience, for the families who have young people in harm's way. You can't be optimistic about everything, but I'm optimistic that the conflict in Iraq will end soon. I don't know if any Middle Eastern countries will ever become democratic, but I don't think it's a bad thing to have tried to introduce democracy, even if we fail.

The same philosophy that I feel about business, I feel about life.

DAVID K. KAREM

**President and Executive Director
Louisville Waterfront Development
Corporation**

**Retired Seven-Term State Senator
and Two-Term State Representative
Commonwealth of Kentucky**

OVER THE 29 YEARS HE SPENT in the Kentucky State Senate, David Karem built a reputation as a consensus builder. As a self-described "mostly liberal city slicker," he found enough in common with mostly conservative rural legislators to win leadership positions for 23 years. And he made his influence count, perhaps most noticeably in the key leadership roles he played in passage of the Kentucky Education Reform Act of 1990 and the 1997 Postsecondary Education Reform Act.

In Louisville, his hometown, he will also be remembered as the man who got rid of the junkyards and sand piles at the point on the shore of the Ohio River where southbound travelers enter the city, and replaced them with a welcoming splash of green lawn, soaring fountains and art.

Karem retired from the Kentucky State Senate in 2004, after spending a total of 33 years in the Kentucky Legislature. He spent four years in the state House of Representatives before being elected to the Senate in 1976. When he left, his status as the last survivor of the activist "Black Sheep Squadron" from the early 1980s was duly noted. Karem and other members of that group are credited with leading the legislature away from dominance by Kentucky governors to become an independent body and a force for change in the state.

Karem also was recognized for his sense of humor. *The Courier-Journal*'s Bob Garrett called him a "wiseacre." Once, when the secretary of agriculture was expressing concern about depressed prices in hogs, Karem told him, "If I was a feeder pig, I'd be depressed, too." His fellow legislators said he used his wit to defuse tension and smooth out wrinkles.

"Through the years," the senators said in a resolution when Karem retired, he has "demonstrated his diplomacy and amazing ability to keep people focused on a central issue and to help opposing groups resolve their points of disagreement in order to come to a final conclusion."

Karem stepped into his second claim-to-fame position, president and executive director of the Waterfront Development Corporation, through the door of service. He accepted a job on a committee appointed to find a way to implement ideas that Louisville Mayor Harvey Sloane and his successor, Jerry Abramson, came up with to try to clean up Louisville's riverfront — to make it a "welcome mat instead of a liability." As the committee cast about for a person to head its staff, it occurred to them that Karem, who had a longstanding love of the river, had contacts and commanded respect at all levels of government, would be perfect. So they hired him, and the wisdom of that choice is now evident from Chickasaw Park to beyond the Big Four Bridge. Louisville's award-winning waterfront development is a work in progress, with more yet to come.

David Karem came by his interest in the river honestly, by spending summers in a family cottage on Transylvania Beach, about ten miles upriver from the Louisville wharf. Both his mother and father were lawyers, but he didn't head that direction at first. He went to St. Agnes Elementary School and St. Xavier High School, and spent five years earning a degree in design at the University of Cincinnati.

He then shifted gears and returned to the University of Louisville to attend law school. He hadn't quite finished when he noticed no Democrat was running for the Kentucky House of Representatives from his Highlands district, so he threw his hat in the ring. That brought out other candidates, including Wilson Wyatt Jr., who beat him in the primary.

Karem won the seat two years later, however, and after two terms, sought and won the 35th legislative district Senate seat in 1976. His skill at bringing sides together emerged early.

"I believe there are two types of leaders," he told *Business First* in 1987. "The first kind is a single-purposed individual who, by his power or wealth or community position, can drag the community along. I'm thinking of a Wendell Cherry-type of person and what he did for the Kentucky Center for the Arts. I see myself as a person who is more inclined to bring groups of people together, a coalition builder." And that's what he has done, throughout his career, in every position he has held.

Karem was twice selected State Senator in the Public Interest by the Capitol press corps. He has given years of public service to his hometown as well, serving on the boards of the Louisville Science Center, Spalding University, UofL's Board of Overseers, Jewish Hospital, the Main Street Association and the Greater Louisville Fund for the Arts, among others.

Karem and his wife, Anne, live in the Cherokee Triangle neighborhood and have two sons.

I AM A LOUISVILLE NATIVE. My mom and her family go back six or seven generations in this country. My dad was born in Lebanon and came over as a very young man. I am a first generation American and a product of the parochial school system here in Louisville. I went to St. Agnes Elementary School, then graduated from St. Xavier High School.

I had an interest in design issues and got a job early on at Hubbuch in Kentucky, which is an interior design company. I went on to the University of Cincinnati College of Design, Architecture, Art and Planning, and I graduated from there in 1966. It was a five-year degree, and after the third or fourth year, I knew I really wasn't going to choose that as a full-blown profession. My dad and mother were both lawyers, and I have an older brother who is a lawyer, so I made a college shift. I started thinking about law school. I took the LSAT, and then went to the University of Louisville and got a law degree in 1969. I started practicing with my mother, father and brother shortly after I was sworn in. I practiced law a number of years, got into politics, and was elected in 1971 for the first time to the legislature. I served in the Kentucky House of Representatives for four years.

After four years in the House, I ran for a Kentucky Senate seat and remained in the Senate through 2004. I was in the legislature for a total of 33 years. I decided a couple of years ago that 33 years was enough, and that I would not seek re-election. I have always told everyone that I wanted to leave on my own terms, and I am pleased that I was not sent to the dugout by the voters. I got to leave on my own terms, which is important to me.

I had another kind of mid-career shift when the community was interested in revitalizing Louisville's waterfront. In 1986, I was approached by Mayor Jerry Abramson and Harvey Sloane, who was county judge at the time, about becoming the first chairman of the board of the Waterfront Development Corporation. As we began to think through how to organize it, it became clear that we needed someone full time — a president/executive director of the organization. In a series of meetings, we agreed that I would step down as chairman and become the full-time paid president/executive director of the organization. That was in 1987, and I have been in that position ever since. What was quite interesting about the whole situation was that I have a design degree from the University of Cincinnati, and I have a law degree, and I was involved in politics as a state representative and a state senator. If somebody had told me that the cosmic forces would come together, and that I was going to have all these skills that would make this transition possible, I would never have believed it. For me it was a neat mix. So the rest is history. The Waterfront Development Corporation is where I am now, career-wise.

It never entered my mind that I would become a leader in the community or that I would plot out a course to become a leader. I don't think there is anything wrong with doing that. I think there are people who want to become president of the United States. John Kerry, they say, knew when he was in the military that he wanted to run for president. I'm sure that President Bush never thought about that. It just never entered my mind that I would plot a course to become a community leader.

I just got into things. Young people ask me, "How can I get involved?" I always say, "There is a big void out there. You can either stare at the void, whine about it, or you can figure out how you can fill up the void." I think it's more like saying, "Why isn't somebody doing that?" Or, "Gee, it seems like there is another way to do it. I can do this."

I don't mean to sound smart, but the older you get, the more you look around and see other people doing things, and you say, "He or she is no different than I am. I can do that."

I never plotted a course. A lot of people get elected to the legislature who say, "Well, I'm in the House of Representatives, eventually I am going to become a member of the State Senate, then I want to run for lieutenant governor. Then I'd like to be a United States congressman." There are people who do that – it was just never my style. In fact, I served 33 years in the legislature, 23 of which were in some sort of leadership position – either as Democratic caucus chairman or Senate majority leader or Democratic floor leader – and I got into it all just by luck.

We were going through an upheaval in the legislature. There was a group of young renegades who wanted to take over. The group that was organizing it wanted to get someone from Jefferson County as one of the people in leadership. There was already someone from Jefferson County, from the other camp if you will. The guy who organized this is a wonderful guy – a friend of mine, John Berry from out in Henry County, who ended up becoming the Democratic floor leader. He said, "We have to have someone from Jefferson County, so it will be Karem." So I went on the ticket and I got elected.

A mentor is a person who is a counselor or an adviser or someone who assists you enormously. This may surprise you, but there is no question my greatest mentor is my wife, Anne Karem. I do not think in any way, shape or form that I would be successful if it wasn't for Anne. We've been married now for 38 years. I think she believed in me at times when I didn't believe in myself. Anne believed in me, forced me to have high expectations, and expected me to do the right thing. She expects me to be successful and work hard.

We actually met in college, on a fix-up date. My first date with Anne was funny. It was a football game. Our college fraternity, Pi Kappa Alpha, had a tradition. During one home game every year, we had a parade from the fraternity house to the stadium in pajamas. So we dressed up in pajamas on our first date to go to the football game. I think she thought I was really weird and off the wall – not because of the pajamas, but because I've never completely grown up, nor do I ever hope to grow up.

Women have played an enormous role in my life. My mom was a lawyer at a time when women did not go to law school. She went to law school in the '40s, after all five children were born. There were very few women going to law school back then, and the idea of going to law school when you had five children was unusual. My dad was a caregiver in a way that was untraditional at that time, because my mother went to law school at night.

I had two brothers and two sisters – the sisters were the oldest and the youngest in our family. My oldest sister is deeply spiritual person, with a compassionate nature. She's a wonderful person who has been a teacher and mentor in many ways. My youngest sister is a person with mental retardation. I always tell a story about her. She was born in 1945. In those days, people had the attitude that we should put her in a mental institution and leave her because she would never be able to take care of herself. The doctors all said this. They said she'd be a drain on the rest of the family. Of course, my parents never accepted that. Both of them refused to accept that, and if you met my sister today, you would never understand society's earlier attitude. She takes care of herself completely and does volunteer work. She actually comes down and volunteers at the Waterfront, and she does volunteer work at Little Sisters of the Poor. She's an inspiration, a teacher who sends to everybody around her very powerful lessons that anyone who has high expectations can do things. My sister is a mentor in a powerful way.

When the Kentucky Education Reform act was passed, I was one of the principal architects of it. Because the committee that I chaired really was the curriculum committee, it designed the framework. My own personal framework for this issue was that my parents had high expectations for my sister – we need to have high expectations for all our school children.

Another powerful mentor in my life is Marie Abrams. I have to say that because she would smack me up the side of the head if I didn't. Marie and I were a team in Frankfort that nobody ever completely understood. We worked together for over 20 years there. She was another woman who pushed me and had high expectations of me. So it's kind of interesting – starting with my wife, women have been a very powerful force in my life.

I'm a person who believes very strongly in empowering everybody I work with. I am not a person who needs to micromanage everything. I know many successful leaders who do that, but that isn't me. The Waterfront Development Corporation is a perfect example. If somebody works here in a staff position,

I want them to have a feeling of full ownership in the work they do, and I want them to feel like they are full a full partner in everything we do. I think that attitude instills in people a sense of pride and ownership. I think it's terribly important. I think if you micromanage, if you say, "Go and do this," they will do it, but they will never have a feeling of total pride and total ownership.

We have a lot of construction going on at Waterfront Park, and we have startled some contractors with our attitude about work at the park. We will have our initial meeting with a contractor, and I will sit down and say, "Obviously, we want you to stay on budget, stay on time, stay within your price, but we also want the people who work with you to feel some ownership in this project. I want the man or the woman working on a bulldozer out in this park to drive by later with their kids and say, "This is the park I worked on." I want the kids to day, "That's daddy's park." I think when they have that attitude, they are going to build it better. They are going to have a sense of pride and ownership. I think if we empower people, you're very likely to hear them talk about the Waterfront positively. Not just me, the spokesperson, but Ashley Cox, who handles the events, will be quoted in the paper, or Mike Kimmel, who is the deputy director, will be on the news talking about something at the Waterfront. Mike's picture was in the paper the other day talking about something. That's important. Marlene Grissom, who helps with fundraising here and does a lot of the art placement in the park, is quoted in the paper or on TV regularly about things. I think we do that across the board with people. My park manager is a guy named Gary Pepper, who is a young, dynamic guy. Gary is a knockout, he can sit there and talk to anybody. When reporters come up to him, he can sell Waterfront Park.

My style is to make sure everybody has information. Everyone comes to my staff meetings – all the outside and inside workers and event people. We are a pretty small staff, but I want everyone to know what's going on. I think that's the way you manage people. I want people to feel ownership. I think with ownership comes pride.

I think that there is no question that the most significant accomplishment in my career in the legislature was passage of the Kentucky Education Reform Act. It's another one of those situations I got thrust into to play a leadership role I was not expecting. I obviously represented Jefferson County, and the big issue going into education reform was whether we were going to lose money or not in Jefferson County – whether we were going to take money out of Jefferson County to award it to the state. There was a lot of pressure at the time, because I was in Senate leadership, to be sure Jefferson County didn't lose. You need to be on the finance committee, you need to make sure Jefferson

County doesn't lose money. I got a call from the floor leader's office that said, "Let's talk about assigning people to the three committees [that were going to do education reform]." The three committees were curriculum, finance and government. I told him, "I want to be on the finance committee – it's a very important issue to Jefferson County, I have seniority, and that's the committee I want to be on."

I hung up the phone, and 20 minutes later, Joe Wright, who was the majority floor leader at the time, called me up. After a 30-minute conversation, I understood that I didn't want to be on the finance committee; I wanted to be on the curriculum committee. Not only did I want to be on the curriculum committee, I wanted to chair it. I said to him after the lengthy conversation, "I'll do it with the caveat that what we come up with is legitimate." I expected to be supported whole-heartedly. He did so, and we came up with a good curriculum committee report and good legislation that grew out of it to be part of education reform. I think that to me is one of the real highlights.

A second thing that is important to me and was a great honor is that in 1992, I had an opportunity to chair the state's Bicentennial Commission. Out of that grew the *Kentucky Encyclopedia*, which was really sort of the signature piece that we did in the Bicentennial.

And then there's Waterfront Park. To have taken 100 acres of scrap yards and abandoned warehouses, asphalt terminals, concrete plants and industrial land and turned it into a public park has been extremely rewarding. We get a lot of good feedback on it from the community – the whole community feels a lot of ownership in that park.

It's amazing to hear people, "I'm from the East End – West End – South End, and we come to the park all the time." A million and a half people a year use the park in some way or another.

In the time I have been here, since 1986, there haven't been ten days when I said, "I just don't want to go to work — I just can't stand it another day." I haven't had those kinds of days. Every day has not been dancing on tip-toes, but I don't have very many bad days.

Seeing people from Glenview, Smoketown, Iroquois or wherever, using and loving the park makes me feel an enormous amount of pride. The James Graham Brown Foundation has been very generous to the park. Joe Rodes chairs the Foundation, and he always tells people that he takes his grandkids to the park and he just loves it. He had some out-of-town visitors a few months ago and he called up and wanted us to take them on a tour. Everybody takes pride in the fact that Waterfront Park has changed the face of this community – that's extraordinarily rewarding.

Anybody who talks about leadership and says that he or she has never had a failure is probably crazy. On the other hand, I have been very blessed in that I have not had to have anything called a tragic failure. One of the things that was a good lesson for me happened the first time I ran for public office. I ran for state representative and lost the first race I ran. I lost to Wilson Wyatt Jr., who is a very fine young man, about my same age at the time. He had a great family name from here, too. His dad was mayor and was an icon. My wanting to beat someone like that was an uphill task. I jumped in and ran, and everybody said, "Don't do it, get out." I filed before he did, and after he filed, lots of folks said, "You should wait your time."

That experience was a great lesson. "Wait for your time" is one of the worst pieces of advice anyone can give. Ignoring that advice was a good thing, because the lessons I learned, even in losing, were invaluable. I could have easily said, "I'm going to step back, sit this one out and wait my turn," but I didn't back out of the race. Wilson ran, and in fact, another individual, Dorothy Ezelle, whose husband Sam Ezelle was head of the state AFL-CIO, also ran. You normally don't get big media coverage in a state legislative race like that, but it piqued *The Courier Journal*'s interest that you had Wilson Wyatt Sr.'s son and Sam Ezelle's wife running in the same race. They did a lot of stories on it, one of which said, "By the way, there's a third candidate," – me. Wilson handily beat me, but I handily beat Dorothy. I carried six or seven precincts and surprised everybody – even myself. Two years later, Wilson chose not to run for re-election, and I used the experience and lessons learned in my first run to win the seat.

Had I not jumped in, had I taken the advice to "wait till the right time," there wouldn't have been the right time. It also taught me that nobody has an inherent right to an elective office – don't ever think you have some God-given right to a public office. While it was a disappointment, it was also a powerful learning experience.

Personally, looking back, I wish I'd studied harder in college, because I might have been better prepared for the legislature. It was always a disappointment that my father passed away while I was in my 20s, before I was in an elected position. I had an opportunity to show my mother, who died in her 90s, much of what I was able to accomplish. She lived through most of my political career and to see Waterfront Park, but dad never got to see any of that, and that was a disappointment for me. Dad died way too young. I always try to believe that there is something he instilled in me.

I don't have any problem being a follower. I think I'm a good follower, actually, because I use the same philosophy as a follower that I use as a leader. I'm a follower here at the Waterfront Development Corporation. If Margaret

Walker, my project manager, has a better idea, I'll follow that. If it's important that the governor or the mayor be seen as a spokesman on an issue or given credit, I have no problem with that. I think there's so much credit out there that it's completely unnecessary to worry about who gets the credit. Leading and following are coupled – I don't think you can be a good all-around leader unless you are also a good follower. You need to be open, to listen to others. I tell everyone in our staff meetings, there is no one perfect answer to everything. You're supposed to collectively come up with the best possible answer. I do ask that when we make a decision, people should move ahead on it – no back-biting or under-cutting a final decision. There are many things a team can do together. Generally, the more you empower people, the better answers you get from them.

I do have advice for young people aspiring to leadership in our community. I would tell them there are a number of things you need to do. First, understand there is no perfect path. You hear people say timing is everything. I believe you make your own timing. I remind people when we started the Waterfront Development Corporation, I went as chairman and met with a number of different people. I met with (former *Courier Journal* publisher) George Gill, and told him, "I'm interested in doing this on a full time basis." George looked at me and said, "If you decide to do this, you're the dumbest son-of-a-bitch I know. We've been working on [a waterfront redevelopment plan] for years."

About 15 years later, I was doing a presentation at the downtown Rotary Club and George introduced me. He was really funny – he said I'd been very successful at the Waterfront, and he confessed to the crowd that when I had come to see him in the early days, he had told me it would be a dumb idea. Then I stood up and said, "Since George doesn't work for the newspaper anymore, he doesn't need to tell the truth any more. He used to tell the truth all the time – truth is, he said if I took the job at the Waterfront Development Corporation, I would be the dumbest son-of-a-bitch he knew."

I went to talk to a number of other people who told me it was a good idea to take the job, but it just wasn't the right time. Then we moved on to fundraising for Waterfront Park, and everyone said the same thing: "Great idea, David, just not a good time." UofL was raising money. Jewish Hospital was doing a big fund drive. Spalding University was having a capital campaign. Metro United Way was trying something different. Fund for the Arts was launching its campaign. You get the drift. So I told people, "There is no right time. You have to make the right time." You have to say to people, "There is a void out there. Look out there and see there is a void. You can fill the void and participate, or you can just stare into space. If you're not going to come in and fill the void, you're in the wrong place."

If you sit around and think about everything that could inhibit accomplishing something, you will never accomplish anything. We jumped into developing the Waterfront with this wonderful abandon and naiveté. We just thought it was a good idea to do it, and it was time for the community to do it.

I tell people it's far better to ask for forgiveness than it is to ask for permission. Not in the law-breaking sense, of course. I think that projects or careers that are unsuccessful are ones where people sit around and plot in their own minds everything that can inhibit something, rather than thinking that there is something in the end to accomplish.

You sometimes see that in bureaucrats. We've gone into someone's office and said, "We're thinking about doing the following..." The immediate response is, "First you have to go through this regulatory process," or, "We've never done it that way." I think if you run into that, you have to have a blind naiveté — you just have to do things anyway. The Waterfront project and the Kentucky Education Reform Act would have never happened if people had sat down and started worrying about every potential negative thing out there. Kentucky Education Reform was replete with potential pitfalls, such as trying to raise hundreds of millions of new dollars for tax revenue. Trying to raise money for Waterfront Park or any large project is a show-stopper if you have that attitude. The lessons from all this are: Don't take no for an answer. Be naive. Ask for forgiveness, not permission. Barrel ahead. Empower everyone around you to feel like they are a part of things.

I went into this project knowing there was a budget and we had to keep it on budget. I immediately ran into people who worked with governmental units and thought change orders or add-ons were okay. Early on, a person who did work for the Waterfront had agreed on a price. When I got the bill, it was for half again as much. I said, "What is this about?" He said, "Well, I did more than I expected." I said, "Well, that's not my problem, it's your problem." This person, who is a good person, said, "Well, we've always been able to adjust these things." I said, "I'm not going to pay the bill." This went on for a couple of weeks, then the person called and said, "I'm going to come over." I said, "Come on over." We sat in this office and had a conversation, and this person said, "We've always done it this way." I said, "This is where it stops. Here's the solution. I'm going to have Phyllis Williams, my finance person, cut you a check for what we agreed on, and if you don't like it, then sue me." He left befuddled, cashed the check and never sued me. That was that.

I hope I have played some role in the development of our community over the years. From a selfish perspective, I believe Louisville's waterfront development has contributed significantly to our community's quality of life. Waterfront Park is an incentive and a driver for downtown housing. Some of the enormous amount of residential units and other development being built would not exist without Waterfront Park. The Medical Center has grown north toward the river because of it, and we certainly have more appealing things now as you get near the river. Employment in the Waterfront neighborhood has increased significantly. The park is enjoyed by everybody throughout the community, including southern Indiana. It clearly contributes to the quality of life.

I think it's important to say a couple of other things. The face of our community has changed enormously because of Jerry Abramson, and anyone who says otherwise is on another planet. Jerry is a constant cheerleader, a fabulous image for the community. I think he crosses the spectrum – Republican, Democrat and Independent people see him as "Superman for life." One of the things that helped Jerry greatly was a change in the Kentucky constitution. A constitutional amendment that I sponsored allowed the mayor to succeed himself. That was a very critical piece. We were able to amend the constitution to give Jerry the opportunity to run three successive times. Jerry's being at the helm for that period of time put us on the national radar screen.

You have to credit everybody involved in the movement to create metro government. That will end up as one of the most significant things our community has ever done. You have to credit people like County Judge-Executive Rebecca Jackson, Mayor Abramson, former Mayor Dave Armstrong, and U.S. Senator Mitch McConnell, who all spent political capital on this issue. I think metro's effects are already enormous. It's only two years old and I think we already think of ourselves as one community. Over the next three to five years, there are going to be some rough spots, absolutely. But it has broken a lot of barriers between neighborhoods and regions.

I think Louisville has come a long way in the last 50 years. A thing that really infuriates me is that I hear people say, "Back in 1952, Louisville and Atlanta were the same size. Look at how successful Atlanta is now." Atlanta doesn't appeal to me. It's too big, it's too spread out. I don't feel like there is a heart or soul to Atlanta. I think Louisville is a fabulous city, I love everything about Louisville. I don't want Louisville to be Atlanta. I want Louisville to grow in the way it is growing. I'm excited about downtown housing. The increase in dining opportunities over the last 25 years is unbelievable.

There is a wonderful ethnic diversity in this town now, too. Louisville is welcoming to everybody. The Presbyterian Church would not have located its world headquarters here unless they felt it was a welcoming community. The museum opportunities, the cultural opportunities, fine college sports – Louisville's got it over most cities. You can get around in Louisville. Our worse nightmare is a 15-minute traffic jam. You hear stories of people in other cities where it takes an hour and 30 minutes to go one way to work. Louisville is a good solid city. It's come a long way baby. I'm crazy about it. The Lebanese came here to this town and settled in the Haymarket areas, where there were also Jewish and Italian vendors. There is a lot of diversity. A lot of Hispanic culture, Irish, English, German, Asian, African. Louisville is a good city where you get a lot of balance.

Policing is clearly a problem, but not just in Louisville – it's a national problem. We are working, and I think with some success, to build trust between the police and the community. I think our community is well-policed. I have gotten to know many of the police officers through the Waterfront and they are all really fine, caring people.

I'm pleased about the partnership between the Jefferson County Public Schools and the Louisville Metro administration. It's incredibly important. We need to have the best-educated workforce possible. We need to prevent school dropouts. There should be high expectations for everyone in the Jefferson County School system. We can't say that any area of town can have second-class schools. It's just intolerable.

Louisville Metro is the biggest economic engine in the state. The engine must do as well as possible. Education, community tolerance, continuing our hospitable, welcoming attitude – these are the things that will make us continue to be successful.

I have traveled because of my positions in the legislature and at the Waterfront Development Corporation. I have been invited by numerous cities to do presentations about Waterfront Park. I've talked to people about education. Invariably, every community is unnecessarily down on itself. My pet peeve is that people dump on their own city. That drives me crazy. If you want to do something in this town, you have amazing opportunities.

People gravitate toward what they enjoy. We have significantly more recreational boaters in the Louisville area than Cincinnati has. Why? I don't know. People in this community like that. For our size, we support our arts at a greater level than most communities. College sports here are an insanity. There are fine college sports in this town. Yes, we don't have an NBA team, but we have UofL and UK, and a huge rivalry with IU. High school sports here are great. The largest high school football game in the country is the St. X/ Trinity rivalry. The community puts its arms around what it wants to.

When we started developing the waterfront, there were no housing units around this park – now, there are numerous residential units under construction.

Waterfront Park Place is a fabulous condo development. At the east end of the park, ICON Properties is getting ready to build a major residential development. I believe there are more good things to come.

When Waterfront Park started, there were only 400 employees in the immediate neighborhood, and now there are in excess of 5,300. If this community wants an NBA team, then there will be one. I don't think you can force it – you have to show it's an asset. We support Churchill Downs, and ticket prices for Churchill Downs on Derby Day are not inexpensive. The resources are there.

The medical center is a huge success story for Louisville. We are not some little bitty medical center. Our medical center has an international reputation – the Kleinert & Kutz Hand Care Center and the Rudd Heart & Lung Institute have put us on the map. I think we do what we need to do and we do it well. We need to appreciate what we have and cheerlead it. A prime example of this is Jerry Abramson – he's a cheerleader for education, Waterfront Park, the medical community. You can send him anywhere in the world and he will represent us well.

The river is a phenomenal force in the community. People are so drawn to it – it's almost subconscious. Mother nature gave us the most powerful river in the United States. It carries more tonnage than the Mississippi River, more than the Panama Canal. It's a powerful economic and recreational tool.

I have learned some lessons in my life that I would like to share with the next generation of leaders coming up in the community. First, I would say to people, "Please let us celebrate our diversity." That sounds like a cliché, but I mean it very seriously. I do worry that there is some resistance to celebrating our diversity. We are primarily a nation of immigrants – German, English, Italian, Greek, Lebanese, Indian, African, Asian, Russian, Mexican. We're all from someplace else. This is the strongest thing about America, and we need to celebrate it. Our system of common schools that are open to everybody is the backbone of the nation. We need to keep our schools and education affordable for everyone. We just can't have a successful nation if everybody doesn't have an opportunity. That's what makes this country amazing. We have to figure out a way to make health care accessible and real for all in this community.

We need people to come into the next generation with fresh views, and with the attitude that you can't take no for an answer. This all goes back to education.

It we listened to the naysayers, Waterfront Park wouldn't exist. We wouldn't have housing and all of the exciting development taking place in the downtown area.

There are two ways to do something. One, you can sit and look for every impediment. If you do that, you will never get there. Or, two, you can say, "That's where I want to go, so damn the torpedoes, I am going to get there."

George N. King Sr.

**Member and President
King Bridgeman Bosse
Constructors, LLC**

**Owner and President
King's Management Group, Inc.
and Time Engineering, Inc.**

GEORGE KING GREW UP in West Louisville. He didn't finish school, but he had a father and an uncle who instilled a sound work ethic in him at a very young age. He started out working as a waiter at the Pendennis Club and as a janitor at the old J.C. Penney store on Fourth Street. He made friends with people at the Pendennis Club who believed in him, respected his work ethic, and gave him a wealth of business advice and support that helped him launch himself into the business world as a successful entrepreneur.

The MacLean family – owners of the old Wood Mosaic Corporation – were some of King's most ardent supporters and they hired him. After 14 years at Wood Mosaic, King and the MacLeans figured out that if King formed his own janitorial company, he could clean the plant for less than the job was costing the company. Wood Mosaic set him up in business.

He knew a lot about directing a workforce to clean a building, but he had limited experience running a business. Joe Gauss from GE told him he needed guidance and a board of directors, so King looked around. His lawyer, his banker, his insurance man and his accountant all seemed to know what they were doing, so he put them all on his board.

In 1967, after they advised him for about three years, he had his first million-dollar revenue year. His company – Mr. Klean's Janitor and Maintenance Service – eventually grew to have more than 1,300 employees and was cleaning buildings in seven states. In 1982, King was named the Small Business Administration's Kentucky Small Businessman of the Year.

And a businessman he was. In the late 1970s, King was asked to join the board of directors of the Louisville Area Chamber of Commerce, now Greater Louisville Inc. His service there led to positions on the Jewish Hospital Foundation board, the Louisville-Jefferson County Economic Development Commission, the Lincoln Foundation board, the National

City Bank board and the boards of trustees of Murray State University and the University of Louisville, among others.

He started a Bluegrass Barbecue Cook-Out to raise money for the Lincoln Foundation, and was asked to judge a barbecue competition in Tennessee. He became intrigued, and talked his way onto one of the barbecue crews as a volunteer. By 1998, he was cooking 100 pounds of barbecued meat and fish a month for friends, and traveling to ten contests a year, all as a hobby.

King says now he regrets his failure to finish high school, but he doesn't think it has hampered him. Neither his father nor his uncle ever had a car. His uncle walked from his home on Dixie Highway to a job at the Brown Hotel for many years. His father worked for the L&N Railroad for 33 years, and missed work only once – when he was injured by a mugger.

When King was 14 years old, a barber named Fred Stoner took him under his wing and gave him a job. Stoner trained boxers on the side and King said Stoner made "a pretty good little boxer" out of him. But not as good as one of the other young men he worked with – Cassius Clay, later known as Muhammad Ali.

Mr. Klean's eventually created several subsidiaries, which distributed industrial chemicals and janitorial supplies, supplied construction material and equipment and did electrical contracting. King sold the company to Burns Enterprises Inc. in 1995. Burns changed the name to Mr. Klean's of Kentuckiana, Inc., and kept King on as president and CEO. King doesn't disclose revenues, but he describes Mr. Klean's as a multi-million dollar enterprise.

King also formed King's Management Group, Inc., a management consulting firm, in 1995. In 2000, he became president of King Bridgeman Bosse, a general contractor and construction manager of commercial and industrial property. The company participated in the project that turned the old Male High School into the Spectrum Building and is currently involved in a number of development projects, including the construction of the Muhammad Ali Center.

Despite how busy King stays running three successful businesses, he spends a great deal of time mentoring young men and women in Louisville who are aspiring to become successful business people. He suggests they get involved with people they recognize as leaders and do whatever they can to spend time with them and to learn from them, as he did. He also advises them that when they become leaders, they should try to include as many people as they can in whatever projects they are leading.

King and his wife Fannie have four children.

I DIDN'T DECIDE THAT I WANTED to become a leader. I was in an environment with a lot of leaders. I had opportunities to be on various boards and committees, and when you are affiliated with certain people in your community who are movers and shakers, eventually people feel that you are a mover and a shaker. But that's not really true. I'm not really a leader, but I do lead sometimes, because I've learned from leaders.

Being in the environment means that you are around these executives, these leaders. You are invited to join the Chamber board, the banks' boards, and the Rotary Club. You are in an environment of business people and leaders. Being in that environment led to opportunities for me.

My first mentor was my uncle. He was quite a man. I liked his demeanor, his style. He was a very quiet man, but anything that he agreed to do he stayed with it till the end. He didn't talk much about religion, believe it or not, but he went to church every day. He walked to work at the Brown Hotel, and he lived on Dixie Highway. Every day he would stop at St. Augustine Church at 13th and Broadway and say a prayer, then he would go on to work. That's just the way he was.

The next mentor I had was my father. He was also a person, like my uncle, who never had a car, lived in the same house all his life. My father worked for the L&N Railroad for 33 years. He never missed a day of work until somebody robbed him and injured him. He was off then for about three months. But other than that one three-month period, in 33 years he was never off work. I learned my work ethic from both my father and my uncle. I copied my style from them too, then I decided that I wanted to go to work.

I quit school, which was a dumb thing to do, and went to work at the Pendennis Club waiting tables. At the same time, I met my boxing trainer, Fred Stoner. Fred took me under his wing and taught me things.

From there I went to work at the Wood Mosaic Company. The MacLean family took a liking to me when I was working at the Pendennis Club, so they hired me. I worked with them at Wood Mosaic for 14 years. They were very successful men. They were born in the "silver spoon" era. I was always real honest with them. I would say things to them that my bosses at Wood Mosaic Company would tell me I couldn't say, because the MacLeans might not like it. But I still would just tell them the truth about things, and they began to like me. Then, after 14 years, they put me in business. They sponsored me. That's when I formed Mr. Klean's Janitor and Maintenance Service. I showed them how I could save them money, and I did.

When I started my own business, my own board of directors influenced me: Marshall Eldred, Jr., Thomas (Wick) Gaines, Bob Timmerman, Gerald Tyrrell, Bill Kline, Patrick Byrne and Bill O'Neil. The list of people who helped me just goes on and on. Another gentleman from GE, Joe Gauss, mentored me. My business was a mess, and he told me I needed guidance, and that I needed a board of directors. I was paying the bank interest on my money, paying a lawyer a fee for being my attorney. I was paying my insurance man a fee, and my CPA. So I decided to call all four of those people. I asked them to come together once a month at my expense to have breakfast and look over my company and give me advice. They helped me develop a business plan, and Joe Gauss at GE put me in touch with Bernie Block, also at GE. Bernie asked a group of Bellarmine College seniors to look over my books. All those guys came together and really got me rolling and helped me get my company going. Then, after about three years of working with them, we did our first million in sales. So, I've had a lot of mentors.

I'm an accessible leader. I feel I'm on the conservative side. I like working with others who need my help. As far as leadership is concerned, I try to talk people into business plans if they don't have them, then I tell them to work the plan. I try to teach people the conservative side of business. I'm more of a mentor than I am a leader. To me, I'm always learning from others. I like to learn what I can, then pass it on to others I feel can use that experience.

The fact that my community accepted me and took me in was a significant accomplishment for me. I've served on 20, maybe 30-plus boards and committees and organizations that have asked me to come and be with them and to work with them. To do those things, in most cases, was to help other people. That's meant a lot to me.

It was a big deal for me when I was voted the Small Businessman of the Year for the whole state of Kentucky in 1982. About that same time, our company went regional. We had been a local cleaning company that was doing well, but we needed to reach out and grow. We ended up in seven states with over 1,300 employees. Those are some accomplishments that I will never forget.

I was the only member of my race in an awful lot of the things I got exposure to. People like Woodford Porter asked me to serve on the Chamber board. He also made himself available to me, so that if I needed somebody to consult with, I could come to him. I was able to get there.

Our community was beginning to change. Our community leaders realized that other communities around us were moving forward and our community was beginning to lose some industry. We were beginning to go down slowly in tourism. Because of those circumstances, the community wanted to move forward. And that's when people like Barry Bingham Sr., Wilson Wyatt, Tom Simons (Capital Holding), Steve Miles (First National Bank), Charlie McCarty (BATUS), Charlie Herd (Chamber of Commerce) and others came together.

There were a few women, but not many, and certainly not many blacks. Woodford Porter was invited to a lot of those meetings, along with Art Walters. Both of those men saw something in me. What, I can't really say that I know, but in both cases, Art Walters and Woodford Porter would approach me. Another fellow who was well-respected in our community was a man named Joe Hammonds, who owned Joe's Palm Room. William (Bill) Summers III was another one. Those men at various times gave me words of encouragement. The Louisville community was moving forward and I was there. I had been given some notoriety about all the labor I had, and the company I started had grown to be a multi-million dollar company, and when those things got publicized, it made it a little easier to go with a winner rather than someone who hadn't quite gotten there yet. It looked better for the community, as people were coming into it, that they could see the "polka dot effect."

I learned so much from all these people: the way they plan, the way they communicate, the way that even when it got tough, they told it like it was, they told the truth. They were very dedicated to changing this community.

A lot of people would think that these people would come late and leave early but, believe it or not, even though they were executives, some of these people worked Saturdays and weekends. They burned some coal oil at night to keep things going. They were hard-working.

I don't beat myself up about it, but when I look back now, I wish I had gone to school. I don't suffer from it, but I would also have liked for one of my relatives, especially one of my three sons, to take over my cleaning service business. I have only one daughter. At that time, people weren't thinking about girls entering the business world. Of course we know what that was all about and how different it all is now. I would have liked to have kept my cleaning service because it was really doing well, and I would have liked for one of my sons to have come in, or all three of them, but they all have built pretty neat careers themselves now, and you really can't knock that.

I merged my business with Tommie Burns. I realized that in the type of business I was in, the minute it's in the paper that you've passed your competitors, there is something there to sell, because your competitors will go out and get your work and get your contracts. I wanted to sell my business while I was still healthy, and I would have an opportunity to maybe even try to do some other things. I learned through my board of directors how to dedicate myself to running that business, and when I had done that, the business became a lot more successful.

A good follower is one who can follow a good leader, and when that good follower makes an error and is told that he made one, he or she can take the criticism. They can still overcome the problems that they may have had, and go right on with following that leadership. I expect followers to tell the truth, to be frank, to speak up if they don't feel comfortable with something. Then we have to see if we can alter it for their comfort some way. If I get up in the rain and the snow and come down here to meet you, don't tell me that you couldn't make it because it was raining, or because of the snow. If you break your leg, you get a crutch. That's the way they taught me.

The only thing that I would probably change in my life if I could live it over again is that I would definitely have gone to school. As far as my business career and my relationships with other people are concerned, though, I don't think I would alter anything at all.

Believe it or not, the type of industrial cleaning business that I was doing was not the most sought-after business in the world, because it's not a glamorous type thing. But I enjoyed it, and I enjoyed working with people. I don't know of a person I worked with who I couldn't go back and have a conversation with, even some that I terminated, because they still thank me, even ten years later. I worried that I wouldn't be successful at times, then when I got to be successful, I stayed up because I didn't want to lose. If I was in the black, I wanted to stay in the black, and at times – maybe at a particular quarter in the year – my comptroller would come to me and say "We're not in the red, but we're certainly getting pink." I learned to really tune in and find ways to get the business back in the black.

So those kinds of things at times would bother me. When I was in these other cities, there were lawsuits because of unions and various things. I was in Boston, and I worked with people from the Dominican Republic. I didn't bring those people to this country. They were already here when I went to Boston. When they wanted to get out of the union and be on their own without organized labor, then the union sued me too because they thought I was a part of it. I had nothing to do with it. Those kinds of things bother you some, but we worked it out. Everybody shook hands. On my last day, there they were – all there – and they threw a little party for me. We got along fine.

Relationships in my life became the foundation for everything else I accomplished, and that's what I try to tell young people right now. I'm mentoring two young men, and I've told them that building relationships is what is going to get them success. Otherwise, it's really hard to get there. These guys are sharp young guys. They are beginning to build relationships. I think they would have done it anyway. They didn't do it just because I told them to, but the fact that I keep that before them reinforces it.

I would suggest to young people aspiring to leadership today that they get involved with people whom we all recognize as leaders and do what they can to spend some time with them. One way that I encourage young people to get involved is first to join Greater Louisville Inc., the Chamber. Then once they join the Chamber, we explore whether there is any committee they can work on. By working on these committees, they are going to get to see what leadership is all about. They are going to get to meet people and build relationships. Committees are the way that things get done. Things don't get done through boards. Committees bring all the success to the board, and they talk to the board about what they've done, but the work really gets done in committees. So let's join the Chamber and let's pay our dues, make sure we are always up front.

One of the things that helped me, that I teach young people today, is that they need to step up when they read in the paper that someone is going to have a fundraiser and each business is being asked to give a minimum of $10,000, like David Jones did when he was bringing the Presbyterians to Louisville and putting them in the old Belknap property. I couldn't give him $10,000, but I gave him $2,000 over three years, which gave him $6,000. So what I'm teaching these people is that if they can't give but $100, the person that is in the fundraising mode will accept that $100, even though they asked for more. They'll accept that, and then when they have the "thank you" dinner, you will be at the table. That's the way I did it.

Today, we're running a construction company, and it seems like the more we do for others the more that is done for us. I don't think I've ever had a year in 42 years or so that someone hasn't picked up the phone and called me and invited me to come somewhere or to give me something. The president of the University of Louisville, for example, will invite me to a tailgate party or to be his guest at a ballgame. Those kinds of opportunities put you in the environment of a lot of people with whom you have something in common, mostly business. Of course, I would give to these worthwhile community causes anyway, whether people gave me something in return or not.

I look at how many blessings I've had – an awful lot. People realize I haven't gone to school, and here I am – a small businessman, a minority and all, yet people take me right in. I feel I've been blessed.

I used to beat myself up because I didn't have an education, but at the age of 45 or 50, that was taken off of me because of the exposure I was getting. Once I realized I was making progress and accomplishing some things, and I realized also that others had made mistakes, then I stopped beating myself up.

George N. King Sr.

I overcame my insecurities, because all those people I thought were tall and handsome, regardless of whether they were black or white, I realized that they have messed up just as much as I have. Mentally, I took my saw and cut their legs off because they were no taller than I am anyway. At that point, I could like other people. I could respect them more, even really care more for them.

I work here everyday. I don't weigh myself versus them. I just go on. Even the racial things. As a black man, I mess up sometimes, but so do good white friends of mine. They get it wrong. So I go on, and can truly respect them and really care for them, because I'm an equal. We all do it right sometimes, and at times we all get it wrong. So I don't beat myself up anymore.

I think a large group of people have contributed to the growth, development and improved quality of life in Louisville over the last 50 years. The first person I remember who really made an impression on me was Steve Miles of First National Bank. Steve, Morton Boyd and Leonard Hardin of First National (now National City) Bank; David Grissom and Dan Ulmer of Citizens Fidelity (now PNC) Bank – these men were leading the charge from that era. Then you had Tom Simons, Wilson Wyatt, Barry Bingham Sr., Bert Klein, Sammy Klein, the Brown-Forman family, Brown & Williamson. These people came together and realized where the community was. Then the newer business people – David Jones, Wendell Cherry and John Y. Brown Jr. came in, and Capital Holding – they all got together and decided which way they would build this community. They formed committees, and that was a very exciting time. Tom Meeker had a lot to do with that also. Bernard Trager was right in there, along with Bob Allison and Nana Lampton. I was in there. I got exposed to all that. Woodford Porter got exposed to it. Art Walters got exposed to it. I served on boards, and I gave financially when I could afford it. I never remember ever refusing to give. If I was on a committee, I realized how important it was to be on time and, if I wasn't coming, to call and let the people know it.

Donald Swain, former president of the University of Louisville, did some unique things in this community that a lot of people probably don't even realize. When he took over 20-some years ago, he got the business community really involved with the University of Louisville and, since that time, UofL has really moved forward. Donald Swain was the guy who threw that pebble in the water that caused that ripple. Judge Bill McAnulty and Art Walters and a few others were on the Board of Overseers at UofL, and we saw growth in the community. I saw Tom Simons and the Bingham family come together, along with the Brown-Forman family, and when you look back, Al Schneider made a big investment in this community.

I would have liked for some other people of my race to have experienced some of the things I've experienced. A lot of blacks were not in business as I was and, if they were in business, they were in a business that was just in their neighborhoods, like a grocery or a barbershop or a service station. But as far as industry, there weren't many like me who were dealing with commerce. Art Walters and I were out going to industries to ask them to hire and promote African-Americans. I would like to have seen more blacks. Today I do see that blacks are on more boards than back then. Sometimes I was all alone.

One of the biggest challenges facing our city in the future is that we have to try to get our community to come together, all four corners of it. We need to let everybody be a part of the plan to keep this community going. We need an awful lot, especially my people, the black race. We need an awful lot of mentoring, and exposure is still short on this end. A lot of my people have not gotten the exposure that I've gotten. Of course, a lot of people from every race have not gotten it, but we are so far behind when it comes to certain things, because we haven't had those opportunities in the past. Some of us are slower about taking advantage of them now that they are here. I am trying to provide that exposure. I work at it all the time.

I would advise the next generation of leaders to include all people in whatever it is they are leading. Try to make sure that everybody is included, or at least a portion of everybody. In some things you're doing you can't use the whole army, but you can still include others on your committees and cut things up, and set goals for the community, and let everybody feel a part of the goal.

I thought of some things I would like to see leaders do in our community, because when you really look at it, the movers and shakers of the community can still go to just about any area of this community and form an organization and put us all to work and get us all going in the right direction. I think if you went to the churches and asked the ministers, "Let's do these things. Let's do this." I think it would be hard for them not to get it done for you. I just think that leaders need to think of ways to include others. I know people right now who haven't been past Sixth Street. They don't know what it means to go way down in the West End. That's not good for our community. I know people in the West End who don't know how to get past Preston Street. They don't know what's going on way up town. It works both ways.

There is one person I've been watching for awhile now, and I definitely think he's growing into the role of what I call real leadership and leading this community, and that's Ed Glasscock with Frost Brown Todd. I see Ed as an outstanding person – straightforward, honest. I see Doug Cobb, I see Greg Fischer, I see David Jones Jr. I see a guy who's not quite as young as those people, but I feel that Ben Richmond has gotten an opportunity to be in some of those leadership roles. Audwin Helton definitely has a role to play. Jim Beckett, who left Louisville to go with Brown & Williamson, was on his way. I feel that the Blue brothers are on their way. And last but not least, I don't know who would not enjoy working with Junior Bridgeman. He's just an outstanding person.

This may be a little naive on my part, but I've learned to be honest, even when the truth is going to get me in trouble. I've learned to be honest with people about any mistakes that I've made. I feel that if you are passing things on to other people, we all at times are a little bit shy about going upstairs to where the big guys are. I think you've got to make your plan, lay it out, look at it and, if you need their help, go and ask them for it.

I have some advice to share with Louisville's next generation of leaders. Go on and get involved, and ask people to help you. Offer to help them, too.

When I help others, it helps me too. I like to be around younger people to teach them, to share my experiences with them and to help them with theirs. I like to see them grow and make good decisions. When you scold them, you see that they come right back. That means a lot to me. It really gives me the freedom to be honest with them, because if I have to watch what I say to them, then I can't always say what I really want to. I like to say it the way I feel it, and if they accept it, and still come back the next day for more, I think we're getting closer. I think we're building something.

I'm kind of humble, in a way. When I'm by myself and I've done something real well, I can feel that bubble coming up and, if I don't watch it, I'll actually shed a tear or two. Success is funny. It has most of the time humbled me. In all the things I have ever done, I've never really thought as much about the dollar as I have about the success. Usually the financial end of it, if you're watching it closely and managing it right, takes care of itself, as I see it.

I want to thank everyone in Louisville for helping me be successful, and for giving me the opportunity that this community has given me, because a lot of the jobs and things I have gotten weren't a case of bidding, they were just negotiations. There's a difference when they call you in to negotiate. That means they want you. I want to thank my community for helping me succeed.

⚜

BAYLOR LANDRUM JR.

**Chairman Emeritus
Alexander & Alexander
of Kentucky
(now Aon Risk Services)**

INSURANCE EXECUTIVE Baylor Landrum Jr. graduated from the Wharton School of Finance at the University of Pennsylvania in 1940. He was involved in the original formation of the Louisville Area Chamber of Commerce in 1950. More than 50 years later, he still serves on the Board of Overseers of the University of Louisville, on the board of the Louisville Community Foundation and a host of other organizations, and is revered and respected as a devoted community servant.

"Landrum is a legend among community leaders for a life spent helping others," *Business First* said in 1997. Besides getting the Chamber going, his accomplishments include restructuring and rejuvenating the Community Foundation of Louisville after retiring from active management of the insurance business in 1982. As president from 1983 to 1993, and as chairman from 1992 to 1993, he grew the Community Foundation's assets from $1.1 million to almost $200 million. The fund collects charitable donations and distributes them to worthy causes and organizations in the community each year.

Landrum has made many contributions to his community over the years, and has served on a number of prestigious boards and committees. Among others, he chaired the Metro United Way Campaign, was president of the downtown Rotary Club, and served on the Louisville Development Committee and the board of directors of the Kentucky Derby Festival.

He has been a champion for improving education. In the late 1970s, for example, he served on the Chamber's joint Task Force on Public Education, which raised money to hire consultants to recommend how to make significant improvements to the public school system. In the 1990s, he was instrumental in organizing School Choice Scholarships, Inc., to help low-income families afford tuition for private schools.

Landrum served on the University of Louisville's Board of Trustees during that institution's transition from a municipal to a state institution.

He has also served as chair of both the UofL Foundation and the UofL Board of Overseers.

Throughout his career, Landrum has been active on many boards, among them Hospice of Louisville, the Louisville Presbyterian Seminary and the Cathedral Heritage Foundation.

His many awards include receiving the prestigious Gold Cup Award from the Louisville Area Chamber of Commerce in 1981, being named Man of the Year by the Advertising Club of Louisville in 1976, and induction into Junior Achievement's Kentuckiana Business Hall of Fame in 1993.

Baylor Landrum was born in Louisville but spent his early years in Lexington. After graduating from Wharton in 1940, he served as a special agent for the Federal Bureau of Investigation, then served three years as a pilot for the Army Air Corps during World War II.

He became a certified public accountant in 1946, and joined the Vaughan Insurance Agency a year later. It later became Vaughan & Landrum Insurance Agency. Landrum led its merger with six other local agencies in the 1970s to form Nahm, Turner, Vaughan & Landrum.

The firm became Kentuckiana's largest, most diversified insurance brokerage and self-insurance service organization, with Landrum as its CEO. He developed and introduced an employee stock ownership plan to create team spirit in the company and, within ten years, the number of employees increased from 12 to 120.

NTVL merged with Alexander & Alexander — the world's second-largest insurance brokerage firm — in 1981, and later with Aon Risk Services. Landrum retired as chairman emeritus in 1984.

He became a Louisville Jaycee early in his business career and was involved in that organization's participation in the formation of the Louisville Area Chamber of Commerce. He became one of two Jaycee members on the Chamber's first board. Later he served as vice president and president of the board.

In 1997, he created the "Landrum Prize for Leadership" at UofL, a $5,000 prize to be awarded annually to two aspiring MBA graduates in UofL's College of Business and Public Administration who make a commitment to help stimulate civic leadership over a three-year period.

"I believe that everyone needs to be involved in some worthwhile project to have a full life," he told *Business First* in 1997. "The young men of Athens, Greece, followed the creed, 'Leave the city a little better than you found it.'"

Landrum and his late wife Mary Wallis ("Wally") had three children. He later married Jean Elliott Merritt, who passed away in 2005.

I CAN'T EVER REMEMBER ASPIRING to be a leader. Perhaps in a large business or organization someone could hope to move up to the top, but I don't think you decide to become a community leader. I certainly didn't. I always found a lot of inner satisfaction from being active in those activities that would benefit the community. My spare time was mainly spent, other than with family and friends, of course, with community leaders. I enjoyed being part of a team, a group of people moving in the same way and whose direction I might be able to influence. I found satisfaction in being active. If you're active in volunteering, people say, "We've got a live one we can put to work," and away we go. So that's kind of how it happened.

I first got involved with the Junior Chamber of Commerce – the Jaycees – which is dormant now here in Louisville, but I think still active in other places. I moved here from Lexington, where I had grown up. From Lexington, I went off to college, to the Wharton School at the University of Pennsylvania. When I came back, I couldn't find a job in Lexington so I came to Louisville. The war intervened, then I came back to Louisville to my profession of CPA. I became involved in the insurance business a year or two after that.

In the insurance business especially, and in the CPA profession, it's important to have outside contacts. Being a comparative stranger to Louisville, it seemed to me not only important but pleasurable to be involved in the Jaycees. I held a lot of positions in that organization. In fact, I think I held almost all of the positions in the organization. That meant a lot to me, and got me started in the community. It helped me feel I was a part of Louisville to sell tickets at the State Fair, or to put strips of reflective tape on kids' bicycles, things the Jaycees were doing. That was my first introduction to community service. After that, I just gradually moved onto some boards and activities that were not very significant, honestly, in those early days.

My first mentor in Louisville, other than my parents, was Culver Vaughan who had the Vaughan Insurance Agency. He wanted to find someone to join his proprietorship because he was so busy. He needed help, and I convinced myself that I belonged. I wanted to try the selling game. So I joined him, thinking that perhaps my talents might lie in that direction. I didn't feel obligated to stay forever, but I thought I would give it a try for a year or two to see how it went. I never left the insurance business after that. I had 50 years in the property and casualty insurance business, helping businesses and non-profit organizations with their property and casualty insurance – not life insurance, not health insurance, but everything else that businesses and individuals needed.

The main thing I learned from Culver Vaughan was to look at every issue from the standpoint of how others would be affected by it. He never wrote a letter without perceiving in his mind how the recipient would react. I think it's a very important perspective to have in dealing with people. I learned that from him, and I have never forgotten it. I have preached it many times to people in our organizations.

After Mr. Vaughan, I can't say there was anybody else outstanding in my life until Wilson Wyatt and I became friends. We were personal friends, mainly civic friends, but we were not political friends. He was a Democrat and I have always been a Republican. I respected him tremendously, however, and we became friends in his later years. He was a tremendous mentor to me. I learned from him to be very careful about following an orderly process of decision-making and leading. One has to listen carefully. That means gathering the fundamental facts and the ideas of all people involved, as well as political aspects. After listening to all that, make a decision. Wilson also taught me how important it is to express yourself forcefully, in print and verbally, to get those decisions in front of other people, hoping that they will go along with your plans. That's a simple process, but Wilson practiced it to a degree of perfection.

Wilson Wyatt and I first met each other at the Chamber of Commerce. I always respected him tremendously, and I may as well tell you this brief story. Louisville's Community Foundation was a brain-dead organization in the early '80s. Mary Norton Shands invited 50 community people to lunch one day. She had as the guest speaker the head of the Community Foundation in Cleveland, which had been very successful – even to the extent of meeting the city payroll up there once, because they were broke. The concept grabbed me, "This thing makes sense. Why don't we have anything like this in Louisville?"

Well, that ultimately led to my being involved. The story I like to tell, because I think it makes a point about leadership, is the story about my consenting to be president of the organization. My first condition was a change in staff leadership.

The next thing I realized was that we needed a larger community board because we needed to get people to learn what a community foundation's goals and objectives should be. We did a lot of this work one-on-one, and we got together about 30-35 people to say, "I will be on the board of directors." The next thing we did was to get consensus on the search committee to select an executive director, which we did. Then I realized that my capabilities could be enhanced if I could persuade Wilson Wyatt to come aboard as chairman. So I went to Wilson and said, "Wilson, here is your board. You know most of these people. Here is your executive director. If you need to spend some time with him that's fine. I will stay aboard and do anything you want me to do. My time will be spent in a priority way on the Community Foundation, but we need you to be the chair."

I did need Wilson Wyatt to be chair, because he had such respect in the community. He had access to a lot of people. Let's face it; he was a treasure to the community, and was respected by everyone. He had grown up here. He had known important people in a social way forever and had their respect. He also had the respect of community leaders and both political parties. I went to him with as much selling technique as I could employ, with a board and executive director that he had confidence in, and with my willingness to stay as president. He said yes, and away we went. The whole thing took off from there.

Back in those days, it was probably a little bit harder to become a leader in the community than it is today, because the people who were part of the leadership of the community were old, respected families and took their part. For instance, the city board of education was a position that was elective, as it is now. The way the people of Louisville were assured of leadership and capabilities from that board was that a few people would get together and agree, "I believe it is his (or her) turn to be on that board of education." These two or three people would approach their candidate one day and say, "Joe, it's your turn. Your number's up and you are going to be on the board of education." That's the way leadership was parceled out.

You didn't move into those restricted circles very quickly. Today it's much more of an egalitarian system, and newcomers to town can have an impact. I think of one banker, Jim Gaunt, who until recently ran Fifth Third Bank. He came into Louisville as a complete stranger, into a bank that was at least fourth, and he has made a tremendous impact. That would have been far more difficult 50 or 60 years ago. I would encourage people not to hold back, to let their activities shine.

There were other people whom I have attempted to emulate. Mr. Henry Heuser Sr. was an example to me. A more retiring person than Wilson Wyatt, of course, but he still was a wonderful man, and a great influence on me.

I could name others. Mike Harreld, for example. When he is speaking to a group, it's amazing what he can accomplish. And Jerry Abramson. And Doug Cobb. There are many others. I hate to leave people out because there have been a lot of people whose talents I have tried to glean something from and utilize.

It's very important that we look for leaders like these to emulate. You must constantly search for the correct way to express yourself. You must realize the importance of clear writing, and use our wonderful English language to the fullest extent. You will never, ever succeed without that capability of communicating effectively. I just wish I could tell that message over and over again to young people aspiring to become leaders in the community, because they don't realize today how important it is to listen, to write, to speak.

You would be surprised how many of our employees I've taken aside over the years, quietly, one-on-one, and said, "Do you realize what you said in that meeting a minute ago?" The statement may have been: "I wish that you had given that to my sister and I," instead of "to my sister and me." There are many such common mistakes. When I have taken them aside, sometimes it has helped and sometimes it hasn't. But I keep trying.

As a leader, I always try to be available. That's pretty easy for a man in the insurance business to do, when I have excellent partners and a staff that I can rely on. I think I have the ability to listen. I think that is an essential quality, of course. I consider options carefully, then once we decide, we implement. I guess one of my strong points is once we decide to implement, then delay has to be stopped. You have to move ahead forcibly once a decision is made. It may require time to convince people to come aboard.

My son Baylor III died at age 52. I don't know where it came from, but he had a wonderful quality of bringing appropriate people together for maybe an hour, a day, three days, depending on how long it took. Before they left that meeting, they all agreed to go in one direction. I may be mistaken, but it was an unusual quality. He had a tremendous way of giving everybody an opportunity to speak, making sure not only that he heard them, but that others took the time to listen to what a person had to say as well. Then he would pull it all together and essentially require people to respect all the ideas that were on the table – or in Baylor's case, they were generally on the floor on white note cards. Then he would require everyone to work together to sort through all the ideas and, lo and behold, there would be an obvious path for the group to take, and everyone would decide to take it together. He called that method "facilitation". He also had another good trait – the ability to restrict input from people who were bores.

I don't know how other people would describe my leadership. I think in my firm they would describe it as compassionate. I have fired people, but it wasn't easy for me to do. I have also corrected people. Most of the time that's very difficult to do. You can correct people's deficiencies only to a limited extent. You must work on their strengths to have an effective organization. That is a truism most businessmen know, but it certainly is true.

I have tried to rate my accomplishments, not as how significant they were to me, but how significant they were to the community, now and in the future.

I think my number one contribution has been the rejuvenation and the growth of the Community Foundation, and having considerable input in the selection of the executive director, now called president, and the initial board members and committee members, (a lot of the latter are not board members). The chair of each committee was always a board member, but we had people from outside whose talents could bring a lot to the foundation's committees.

Baylor III and I also started a Rotary Leadership Fellows group. About 12 years ago, I decided – again, a truism – that nothing happens without leadership. I am not a rich man, but I did have some surplus. I wondered, where could I contribute some money, and some of my time, to improve the possibilities for effective leadership within the business and civic community? What can I do?

Well, I started dreaming about it and I started talking to people about it. I interviewed about 12 or 15 local community leaders one-on-one about what to do. I was not interested in high schoolers. I was not interested in people who had not had a chance to show, as Don Swain said, "propensity for leadership." So what we worked out was a prize of $5,000 to each of two upcoming MBA graduates at the University of Louisville. Why UofL? Why not include community-wide MBA programs? One reason was simply that we could get staff support if we restricted it to UofL, which had the largest program at the time. Their staff support was invaluable.

Baylor III was dedicated to this idea, and he would have carried it on in my later years, and after I had gone. He would have picked it up and run with it because he was dedicated to it also. Once he died, I realized that I was getting up in years and I could not run this program by myself. So Dennis Riggs, bless his heart, who runs the Community Foundation said, "You love your Rotary Club. You have been president, and you have respect there, why don't you turn it over to the Rotary Club?" He said, "You will have to keep funding it for awhile, but they will take it on, and they are a permanent organization that you would like to have take control of it." "Boy," I said, "that is brilliant." So about five years ago, we turned it over to the Rotary Club and it has now become a Rotary Leadership Fellows program.

We select two people for a three-year program. They are committed to staying in Louisville for that three years. They get $2,500 each at the start of the three years. They must stay in the program, attend Rotary meetings, and utilize a mentor, who changes periodically as their needs change. The mentors can come from Rotary, but not necessarily. Mentors can also come from the outside if the person wants. About half of the participants are men and half are women. Almost exactly 50%. They are all mature MBA candidates, not necessarily 22-year-olds. They are usually part-time students and full-time employees. The program has gone along fine. Rotary is thrilled with it. The third thing they must do is community service. They belong to committees in Rotary and they are all very busy young people. We appreciate the fact, as they climb in the organizations they work for, that their outside activities can be somewhat restricted. But they do belong to Rotary. They select a committee in Rotary to work on and they participate in mentoring, networking and service. They have to attend Rotary meetings once a month. We have about 450 to 475 members in Rotary and they all have to attend 60% of our weekly meetings.

The students do that, too, and at the end of the three years, if they have complied with these criteria, they get the next $2,500 each.

The Rotary Leadership Fellows program is operating today. I have been able to get outstanding people to be chairs of the committee and they have done a wonderful job with it. Ed Swartz was first, and Kathy Dawson and Maria Hampton have followed. It is a program that I predict ten years from now will be different than it is today, but I have set up a permanent endowment that will pay half of these expenses as needed. I don't have enough money to pay all of it out of my estate, but my estate will pay half of it, and the Rotary Club has agreed to consider carefully picking up the expenses of the other half after I'm gone. I am pleased with that.

I get to know the students who are selected for the scholarships. We interview them very carefully. We have made some mistakes. We discovered after six months or so that one man was just in it for what he could get out of it. We want people whose heart is in Louisville. So we told him, "You're out." That was the only occasion we did that.

Another thing that I have been proud of is our School Choice Scholarships, which I had a major hand in getting started. School Choice Scholarships is a program that we copied that is now in every major city. Private funds are raised, not through an endowment, but through annual giving. The program pays partial tuition for children from low- income families, who are on the federal lunch program, to attend a private school of their choice. Several people of means are interested in the concept and willing to supply most of the money. It's been a wonderful thing, and it has been going since 1995.

The program now pays the tuition of about 400 children per year. About a half million dollars of private money comes into School Choice Scholarship Inc., which is a 501(c)(3) organization. It is not a lobbying organization for vouchers or for charter schools or for tax credits. Our mission is to help poor kids. I think our mission should be expanded.

Kentucky does not have some type of charter schools or tax credits or tuition vouchers, or whatever they are, for poor kids to attend a school of their choice. It's a coming trend in this country. I believe in it very strongly, and yet in Kentucky – with KERA being significant in the eyes of the public, as it should be – it is difficult to get past the talking stage and to some action stage in Kentucky. I wish I could live long enough to see that change. I think it will change.

I guess the fourth thing that I am proud to have had a part in was the rejuvenation of the Board of Overseers of the University of Louisville. The trustees of UofL are the decision-makers. I was a member of the trustees of UofL at the time we moved into the state system. The trustees choose the president.

The overseers are a non-decision making body, a larger group of maybe 50 people now. At the time I was selected, there wasn't much happening. The president of UofL was half-way interested in it, and UofL wasn't supplying much staff. Every organization has to have staff to be really successful on a meaningful basis. Jim Hendershot, who was president of Reliance Universal at the time, and I decided we were going to rejuvenate the board, and we did. Don Swain was president. He saw the advantage and cooperated, and supplied excellent staff. Kathleen Smith has been with it ever since. She is a wonderful support person, along with others. That has done a lot to improve the university's way of communicating and getting feedback from people who love UofL, people who realize the vital importance of having a good university in any metropolitan area. We'll never ever have any metropolitan area of any significance without fine higher education. The overseers realize that, and they have meetings once every month or two months. The president always comes, gives a report "to the nation," so to speak, and counts on these people for counsel and advice and communication back and forth.

Those are four things that I had a major impact on. Other people have done so much more, but you asked me mine.

One of my biggest disappointments was that I chaired the Metro United Way Campaign one year, and we didn't make our goal. You can always find a lot of reasons for that, but the buck stops on the guy at the head.

I am also disappointed that the vouchers and school choice have not moved along as quickly as I had hoped they would in Kentucky.

Another disappointment was failing three times to merge our city and county. We came awfully close each time; the devotion of people and leaders trying to get it done was tremendous, but it just didn't pass. It finally happened, and it has been extraordinarily successful.

We are so fortunate in this town. Certainly politics gets bitter sometimes and gets exaggerated from the extremists on both sides but, generally speaking, in the Louisville political scene, politics has never been dirty, to my knowledge. I don't know of any big scandals. We have been lucky in that regard.

One of the things I look for in a follower is someone who can listen carefully, and be constructive. I don't want them to be a "yes" man, or a "yes" woman, but once a group reaches consensus about a fundamental path to follow, people should either follow the path or get out of the way. They may be right, but they should fight another day. I feel strongly that followers have to be part of a team or they have to get off the team.

Baylor Landrum Jr.

A good follower must have dedication to an agreed-upon plan. I grew up with the above organizations and became a part of them because I thought their mission was correct and I had a stake in solidifying that mission.

I'm not so sure I would change much if I were given an opportunity to do things all over again. Louisville is a wonderful, wonderful city. We're not as progressive as Atlanta, Nashville or even Indianapolis, but we live in a stable community, and we are generally unified on major issues. We also have the arts and sports and many other assets.

I am confident that I would have been more successful financially if I had spent the same amount of time in my business or profession as I did working on community projects. That wasn't my life, though. I wanted to be a part of the community's advancement. I enjoyed the stimulus of working with people I respected.

Education is so, so important. UofL and its scholarship programs are examples of that. Nothing happens without leadership, and that is why our Rotary Fellowship is so important to me.

I wish that I could live and be healthy for another 20 years because I'd like to see what happens with two things. One is how we fix our education system to make it more effective, especially for poor, economically-deprived people. The other is how the war in Iraq, and our push for freedom, plays out. The potential impact is vast.

Our country has not been asked to make any sacrifices to speak of, at least in a personal way to many of us. Our country can borrow a lot of money, of course, but our personal pocketbooks are not being tapped; nor is our time being tapped; nor is there a draft of people who are not willing. We have a coalition of the willing that wants to serve. I think it is a noble cause and I want to see this concept of freedom be extended to a part of the world that has never known much freedom. Our country's concept and operation of freedom has lasted longer than any other civilization in the history of the world. We have 200 years of freedom now, and no other country has even come close to that in any other area of the world. We need to be willing to make some sacrifices to try to extend this concept of freedom.

I hope in 20 years something can happen. I would love to be able to be here to see that. The other is our education system. It has to be remodeled in some way to make it more effective. Every 1 Reads is a program that is now starting that I am going to contribute to. It is an effort to help every child read at grade level or above in four years. I am not optimistic, I'll be honest with you. I think I'm realistic in that regard. But if we get 90% of it, we have done something. I hope we can be helpful in that regard.

Passing the Torch

I have worked with a lot of people in organizations, encouraging them to become involved, but over the years I have learned that there is something about a caring heart that can't be developed. I believe that it is very difficult, almost impossible, to get people to get involved in an effective way unless they really enjoy it and feel they must spend a part of their lives on behalf of others. I guess that is a discouraging note, but I try to be realistic about it. Once you find those people who have a caring heart and help them develop, that is about as rewarding as anything an older person can do. I encourage anybody who has some time to expend it on the right kind of folks who can become significant.

I don't think there is any one person over whom I have had a major influence. I still meet with people on a one-to-one basis and enjoy talking to them and helping them with their future. Some are executives of non-profit organizations, one calls on me regularly to counsel with him as to how his responsibilities are proceeding. Sometimes you don't know who you have influenced. But don't waste a lot of time on those who don't rise to the bait.

We haven't made tremendous progress in Louisville over the last 50 years, but it has been steady. There are advantages in not moving too quickly and taking on obligations that we can't afford. I look at Louisville's waterfront and how it has improved. It looks like a big lake out there. It doesn't look like a river. What a wonderful thing it has done for Louisville – and it was all done with private and public money.

The airport and its expansion have meant so much to our community. It is so convenient for Louisvillians to have an airport within twenty minutes of most people. We have facilities and businesses, UPS in particular, that have utilized that airport and made it even more meaningful for Louisville. This kind of physical development in our community has been productive.

The merger of the city and county has gone so smoothly, and I attribute that to the leadership of our mayor, Jerry Abramson, whose talents are tremendous and who has been a dedicated, able leader in getting this done. When I think of the prior conflicts that were there between city and county, as far as budgets and personnel were concerned, I am gratified to see that they have been reduced to almost nothing. We are making steady progress, without its being sensational.

Officials from the Brookings Institution, who came down here about four or five years ago, said the biggest need for Louisville is improving education. We need to tell people this over and over again. I do think in the economic development area that it is wonderful to have Greater Louisville Inc., the old Chamber of Commerce, working together with the new merged government, combining both public and private dollars for effective economic development.

I think our community's emphasis on conventions has been most successful. But we must concentrate on the agreed two-pronged aspects of medical research and biotechnology, and the distribution business. UPS is a vital force and our city is strategically located within the U.S.

Those who are aspiring to leadership should work toward agreement as to what our prime objectives are. That is always a challenge, because there are selfish interests, political interests, and social issues involved that tear people apart. We have to learn to respect the minority and to work effectively with them.

I'm not just talking about the ethnic minorities. Some people think government should be involved in social issues facing people. I don't. I think less of these social issues belong on ballots. They belong in the hearts of people.

One man I respected a lot was an ardent Christian and he said the most important things to him were faith, family and friends. I can't quite say that as forcefully as he did, because my emphasis is not only on my friends, my family and my faith, but also on trying to make Louisville a better place for all of us to live and take pride in. All of us need to magnify our "sense of community" and act accordingly.

We should all do whatever we can – for our faith, family, friends, and for the future.

LEONARD E. LYLES

**Owner and President
Lyles Enterprises Inc.**

LEONARD LYLES HAS WON ACCOLADES for speed and prowess in college and professional football, for pioneering diversity hiring as an executive with BATUS, Inc., and for launching thriving businesses in West Louisville at a time when other entrepreneurs were reluctant to try.

But *Louisville Sports Report* columnist Billy Reed said in a 2003 piece that Lyles doesn't get enough credit for just plain bravery for being the first black to win an athletic scholarship at the University of Louisville – in 1954, a time when race relations had a long way to go in Louisville. "Can anybody except Lenny ever truly comprehend the courage it took to become one of the first blacks willing to play for a university located below the Mason Dixon Line?" Reed asked.

Lyles told *The Courier-Journal* in 2000 that he wasn't so sure he wanted to be a hero at the time. But coaches and his friends ultimately talked him into taking the job of breaking the color barrier, and he soon was taking fellow players like Johnny Unitas to his place for his mother's home cooking. He was also setting records at UofL, including a rushing record that stood for years, and a scoring record – 300 points and 42 career touchdowns – that still stood in 2000.

In 1957, he was known as the "Fastest Man in Football." He led UofL to its first bowl game. Coaches say he probably would have set a world record in track and been an Olympic runner too if he hadn't been injured in that game.

He followed Johnny Unitas to the Baltimore Colts after he healed, was traded to the San Francisco 49ers in 1959, but returned to the Colts in 1961 to play eight final seasons. His pro football record was stellar as well.

Lyles was inducted into the UofL Athletic Hall of Fame. His #26 jersey was retired in 2000 and a $100,000 sculpture of him, created by nationally renowned Louisville sculptor Ed Hamilton, was unveiled at UofL's Cardinal Park. The sculpture was commissioned by Owsley Brown Frazier, who was a student at UofL when Lyles played for the Cardinals. "I've long been an admirer of Ed Hamilton's work," Frazier said at the unveiling. "I'm thrilled we are able to put together a trio of greats in Lenny Lyles, Ed Hamilton and Cardinal Park."

Lyles now tells young people they would do better preparing themselves to be president of the United States than professional football players. That way, he tells them, they will pick up more skills that will be helpful to them if the president thing doesn't work out.

Lyles started positioning himself to put credibility into that advice early in his 12-year pro football career. He took an off-season job in sales with Brown & Williamson Tobacco Corporation in Louisville. By 1982, he was director of minority affairs at B&W's parent BATUS. Three years later, he was vice president of minority affairs, plowing new ground in the hiring of women and minorities into the workforce.

Also that same year, 1985, he opened Lyles Mall at Broadway and 28th Street in West Louisville, following his development of other retail space at Lyles Plaza nearby in 1975. The developments provided groceries, banking and other amenities, including jobs, that residents of the area needed. He spearheaded these retail projects at a time when no one else was willing to take the risk.

"He faced so many stumbling blocks," Louisville Urban League President Ben Richmond said in 2000. "But he endured and persevered, and nowadays it's a lot easier to do development there because of the price Lenny Lyles paid."

Lyles decided early in his career that community involvement is "part of the charter" that goes with success. Improving the community's quality of life is good business, he told *Business First* in 1985.

Toward that end, he has served on a number of boards and committees, including the Louisville & Jefferson County Private Industry Council, the Mayor's Economic Development Advisory Committee, the University of Louisville Board of Overseers, the Kentucky Council of Higher Education, the Spirit of Louisville Foundation, the West Louisville Economic Development Task Force and the Bluegrass State Skills Corporation.

Lyles continues to serve as a mentor and adviser to young people, and to individuals and organizations interested in neighborhood revitalization and retail development projects.

He is married to former television personality, Faith Lyles.

Passing the Torch

I DON'T FEEL LIKE I'M A LEADER. I think a leader has to be chosen. I think followers are more important than leaders. People who follow you must want to follow you for a reason. All of us could be leaders to some degree.

I didn't intend to become a leader. I had great running speed in my youth, and it helped propel me into a position of celebrity as a football player. I am a different person today, however, because I believe in the Word and have incorporated it into my life. Some people may not recognize me any more.

I have had several mentors in my life, beginning with my mother, who was a good woman and taught me honesty and trust. Jim Martin taught me how to develop properties. My high school coach, Ben White, taught me about another kind of lifestyle (remember I grew up in the 1950s). Gene Lipscomb, Lenny Moore and Milt Davis, my Baltimore Colts' teammates were mentors to me, because we were a good team. Raymond Berry influenced me because he was a righteous man, and Ms. Emberger, a teacher at the University of Louisville, taught me how to speak, write and make presentations.

I had a tremendous job working for Brown & Williamson Tobacco Corporation. It gave me the opportunity to travel, exposure to other countries and the opportunity to work on big projects. That job was one key thing in my life that propelled me to think and act like an executive. It had a major influence on my life. I always tried to take the best of the best from people. My own phrase is, "I'm going to make it because of you, or in spite of you." I had to be a pioneer. I was the first black man to blaze trails. I feel that we all are human beings – that we must live together because we are linked through the Word.

I'm a good communicator, and I have zeal and passion. To be a good leader, you also need knowledge and the understanding of how to measure your progress and results. I'm honest and truthful, and I believe in consistency, discipline and completion. You also have to be part of team.

Others would say that I'm not selfish, that I'll help and participate if I can. They will also say that I'm a team player and fair. Some might even say that I'm aloof, that I won't attend meetings; however, if you want me to participate, you have to show me the end results. Don't waste my time.

My most significant accomplishment in life has been the recognition that through the Word, there's more to me than flesh. I think that when you see something greater than what you are, or think or feel, then you begin to humble yourself to want to use these principles. I know people will let you down, so I'm learning to forgive.

I have spiritual fruits in my life now that I can pass along to other people, so they can see in me the attitude of kindness, forgiveness, love and understanding while I am building relationships. Everyone should try to build relationships and connect, because each day is a day unto itself. You have to know the secular world and how it works, and if you require something greater, then you have to walk in that Light and be an example.

I believe I failed with my children. I could have done a much better job with my two sons. Both of them passed away – one died of a heart attack, and one shot himself. I also have a son at home with us who is bipolar. There's no question in my mind that I was a failure with my family. I have had to correct that over the years. Love is not just something that pleases me. People don't understand what love is. Today, I try to show my family that I love them by my works.

I've also failed in business, in that I've lost money. I had to fold the Ollie's Trolley restaurant I owned and pay off the debt. My partner left, and I was left "holding the bag." I had to overcome that one. Sometimes you look up, though, and there's somebody in another room that has it harder than you. You have to understand that, and take your own place on the team. You just have to have a commitment to others.

Good followers need to have confidence and forgiveness, because every leader has impediments. Commitment and sacrifice are required. Most of all, followers have to pray for their leader to lead them in the right direction. Leaders have to lead and provide for their followers. Leaders must be willing to self-sacrifice.

If I could live my life over again, I would hope that I could have understood the Word sooner. I'm still studying and learning. I will always look for the truth. I wish I would have been wiser, had better knowledge and, maybe, forgiveness. You have to have peace in your life, because you can't worry, especially about things you can't control.

I would advise young people aspiring to leadership that there are things you can do that go beyond just telling a person what's right and what's wrong. You have to meet people where they are. You have to help them spiritually in some way, and once they know you care and love them, then you can share your own life experience. Why not start thinking right now about your life – what you have, where you want to take it and what you have to do to contribute to what's around you? Make good choices. It's because of Grace that you can make choices, so make good ones.

Passing the Torch

A lot of people like me have contributed to the growth, development and improved quality of life in Louisville over the past 50 years. As I have said, I worked at Brown & Williamson Tobacco Corporation and BATUS for 27 years, and I had to show others how to include women, minorities, Asians, and all others in the workforce. We all hear about individuals who probably don't put themselves first, who have spent their money, time and effort to give of themselves. David Jones impresses me. Mayor Jerry Abramson seems to understand that the community is really one family. I don't want to do more naming, however, because as soon as you name one person, there is another one that has done something.

It depends on how you measure growth, but there is one thing that has made a big difference – merging our city into metro Louisville. We're trying to become one body. But we can't say we want to be one body when we treat some people in that body different from others. If you keep pulling the parts away and giving more to the "toes" than to the "fingers," then it's not going to be effective. I think we still have a way to go to get where we need to be.

I used to work hard in politics, but I got a little disenchanted with it. I just moved away from it, and got more involved in saving souls and spreading spiritual good news.

I'm not sure I can tell you what the biggest challenges are facing our city today. I think we all have an idea of what the perfect family is, and if we want to have the perfect family – meaning everybody in our community – then we have to design our relationships, design our buildings, and measure our progress against the objectives in such a way that it represents our family. If we can do this, then whoever is in a leadership role can base decisions on what is best for the whole community. I think the fruits of their labor will tell the truth.

Many people have been instrumental in my life, and I have learned from them. But the best advice I can share with the next generation of leaders in our community comes from the Word. If God is on my side, then I can conquer anything, and there's nothing that can hold me back. I now have inner peace.

Someone has to step up and lead, so I urge everyone to do it.

Make good choices, and make every day count.

ROMANO L. "RON" MAZZOLI

**Retired Twelve-Term Member
U.S. House of Representatives
Third Congressional District
of Kentucky**

RON MAZZOLI'S FIRST STEP into elective politics may be instructive to any would-be leader. A lawyer and an admirer of John F. Kennedy, he walked into Jefferson County Democratic Headquarters on Fourth Street one day in 1967 and asked, "How does somebody get into politics?" The woman at the desk — Kate Smith (Mazzoli remembers her name to this day) — showed him some precinct and district maps and noted there was a seat open in the Kentucky State Senate from his district. She told him that one way to start would be to work to get the party's backing to fill it.

He didn't get the party's backing, which might explain his independence within the party for years afterward, but he did win that primary, and the general election, and he served for two years in the Kentucky State Senate. He went on to win 24 more elections, counting primaries and general elections, and to serve 24 years (12 terms) in the U.S. House of Representatives. He defeated 33 political opponents along the way, but did lose one election, the Democratic primary for Louisville mayor in 1967, and he will tell you that defeat still smarts. He will quickly add that he learned more about politics and effective campaigning in this race than in all the races he won.

In Congress, Mazzoli chaired the Immigration, International Law and Refugees Subcommittee for 12 years. He also served on the House Small Business, Intelligence and District of Columbia Committees. He made a name for himself by co-authoring landmark immigration legislation (the 1986 Simpson-Mazzoli Bill), and by championing legislation in the areas of election finance reform, gun control and family leave.

Opponents often attacked him in primary and general elections for failing to bring home "pork," and he almost lost the primary in 1988 after he was abandoned by labor supporters for declining to vote their way on minimum wage and other labor-related legislation.

His fellow Democrats in Congress sometimes carped at him about his independent stances, and once even took away his chairmanship of the Judicial Subcommittee on Immigration for two years.

Mazzoli argued that his job was to vote for what was best for the country and his district. He wouldn't follow legislators who talked of trimming the deficit but still bragged about snaring "pork" projects for their home districts. He once said he would never have courthouses or highways named after him, like Congressman Gene Snyder, who represented the neighboring Fourth Congressional District. He said that wasn't what he was trying to accomplish in Congress. Ironically, however, his colleagues in the House congratulated him on his retirement in 1994 by naming the federal building in Louisville for him. The Romano L. Mazzoli Federal Building now stands directly across a parking lot from the Gene Snyder Federal Courthouse and Customhouse in downtown Louisville.

Ron Mazzoli grew up in Louisville and graduated from St. Xavier High School. He went on to graduate *magna cum laude* from Notre Dame University, and from the University of Louisville Brandeis School of Law. Between his two degrees, he sandwiched in two years of active duty in the U.S. Army, from 1954 to 1956. He worked in the L&N Railroad Company's law office when he first graduated from law school in 1960. In 1962, he opened an office of his own, from which he practiced law until 1970.

After returning from Washington, Mazzoli spent five years as Senior Distinguished Fellow in Law and Public Policy at the University of Louisville, joined the University of Louisville Board of Overseers and served on the boards of the Louisville Community Foundation, Louisville Area Chamber of Commerce, the Cathedral Heritage Foundation, Father Maloney's Boys' Haven and St. Xavier High School. He also lectured widely at the U.S. Naval Academy and other venues, and was a visiting fellow at the Institute of Politics in the John F. Kennedy School of Government at Harvard University.

Lecturing at Harvard in 2002 proved so rewarding that he quit his job at UofL and headed back to the Kennedy School as a student in 2003. He recently returned home to Louisville with a master's degree in public administration from Harvard under his belt.

Mazzoli says he plans now to organize his papers, which he has already donated to UofL, and to do "some writing and reflecting."

He and his wife, Helen, have a son and a daughter and two granddaughters.

I DIDN'T SET OUT TO BE A LEADER, it occurred accidentally as a result of my going into political life, public life, and the experience thereafter, which put me in contact with a lot of interesting people. Leadership wasn't anything I set my cap toward; it occurred as a byproduct of the life that I led.

Politics wasn't anything I thought about at Notre Dame, or at the University of Louisville Brandeis School of Law, or even in the years of my law practice. My wife Helen and I got married in 1959 and, in 1960, when John Kennedy was elected president, we were part of a group of young married people with children who would visit from time to time and discuss lots of things, including politics. It planted a seed that germinated many years later.

The next thing I can recall is walking into Democratic headquarters in 1967 and going up to a lady behind the counter named Kate Smith and asking her, "How does somebody get into politics?" She was patient with me, showed me maps of where I lived, and she explained that there happened to be a state Senate seat open in the district in which I lived. So Helen and I and my dad and some friends just put a little campaign together in our basement. It was as much an effort built on love and excitement as it was a crusade based on issues. We put this campaign together almost overnight and ended up winning the primary, although the Democratic Party had supported someone else. In those days, parties took an active role in primaries.

I ended up getting elected. Being in that setting, with a lot of very talented and accomplished people, and seeing how they got things done left me with certain elements that I incorporated into my leadership style. I was also intrigued by how they didn't get things done. I would see successes and failures, how people got votes they needed to get something passed. I was fascinated by watching that process – both in the Kentucky State Senate and, later, in the House of Representatives in Washington.

From the time I was a little boy, I was always observing people, asking people questions, wondering what they did for a living and why they did it, for how long, and asking if they enjoyed it.

My parents were my first mentors. They were very interesting people. My father was an immigrant to the U.S. He came here as a young boy of 11 in 1914 with nothing – no money, no language skill, no education. He got very little education here, because his uncles took him out of grade school and put him on a job. He was a wonderful man – very strong, very intelligent, read voraciously in his lifetime. He considered the public libraries to be his real college. He started a tile business out of our basement and garage. My mother helped run the office. They managed to make a living. I saw hard work, devotion, honesty, "the customer comes first." In a profound way, my mother and father were my mentors.

Once I got into political life, I had many more mentors – U.S. Congressman and Louisville Mayor Frank Burke, State Senator and Kentucky Adjutant General Richard Frymire, State Senator Gibson Downing, of Lexington; U.S. Senator and Governor Wendell Ford. These people all had common characteristics – they were ethical, honorable, effective legislators, intelligent people. I had other mentors in Congress in Washington – people like Tip O'Neill, John Anderson, Tom Foley, Jim Wright – all of them honorable, intelligent and effective legislators.

I did not have one patron who guided me along, but I had people around me whom I admired intensely. I should mention Congressmen William Natcher and Carl Perkins of Kentucky, two of the preeminent figures in Kentucky politics. They were indefatigable workers, well-respected within the Congress. They were not well-known outside the walls of Congress, but they didn't care to be. Their purpose was to serve the people of their districts and of the Commonwealth. I learned from them that being stagey, showy and flamboyant are not necessarily the characteristics of an effective public person. I learned that being a work horse, rather than a show horse, is sometimes the way to be.

I'm not sure I have a management style. If I had to characterize myself, I'd say I have led by example, derived from my mother and father, whom I saw get up at 5:00 a.m. every morning to work hard and sacrifice for their children. For me, it was hard work, trying to take advantage of whatever talents God gave me – being honest and forthright with people, being alert to the issues and prepared for the legislative matters that would come my direction, showing up early, getting the day's work done before I left the office. That was my style – being respectful of people, being interested in their well-being. In my office, I did anything the staff was doing – opening mail, getting there earlier than any of them. A few times, I had to dismiss someone. Those were difficult times for me. Personnel was always difficult for me. Fortunately, we recruited carefully.

In the House, I agreed to do the "scut work" of Congress – to sit in the chair and preside over the House during those interminable sessions late at night when almost no one was there (although TV cameras came in the '80s). I did that because I really wanted to see how the place worked, and I wanted to get to know the members. I knew the names of all 435 members of the House. If I walked behind them, I could recognize them by their gait. So when I was later a chair of a committee, as I was of the immigration sub-committee, I knew the members as people. It wasn't a matter of expediency; I really enjoyed them. When I needed votes on a bill, they knew I wasn't trying to con them – that I wasn't trying to advance myself at their expense, but was just trying to move a piece of legislation that I felt was worthy.

You have to be ambitious to run for office every two years and survive that bloodbath, but I wasn't ambitious to the point of scuttling someone else in order to advance myself. One of the reasons I don't work as a lobbyist now is that I want people in Washington to know that when I come back to visit (which I do fairly often) I have no ulterior motives.

My advice to young people thinking about or aspiring to leadership is don't get too mesmerized by leaders and by leadership – reading too much about it and thinking about it – because then it becomes a means on your part to gain something, rather than a means by which to get a job done.

All of the Speakers of the U.S. House of Representatives, from Speaker Albert up to Tom Foley, my last Speaker, would call on me to preside over the House when it considered some of the tough bills, just as Congressman Natcher had been called upon to preside over some very tough items. The Speaker wants to have someone in the chair who is responsible, understands the rules and who is respected by his or her peers. Part of keeping order in the House is the respect that the members hold for the Speaker Pro Tem. I never ever turned any of the Speakers down. When the members see you often in the chair, later when you're chairing a subcommittee or trying to move a bill, they are more likely to give you the time of day.

Leadership is patiently built over a number of years. It's an assemblage of personal characteristics – of your knowledge, your trustworthiness. All of that bubbles up to create a situation where people are chosen to be chairs or to be Speaker. A lot of it is, "Do I like this guy? Is she smart? Is he or she going to embarrass me out there by using a double negative?"

Legislatively, I am most proud of the immigration work I did for ten years, chairing the Subcommittee on Immigration and passing the 1986 Immigration Reform and Control Act which then, and even today, is known as the Simpson-Mazzoli Immigration Act. Senator Alan Simpson and I authored the bill that was originally introduced in 1981. The issue was considered peripheral to Kentucky, but I didn't think it was. I felt then, and feel today, especially given the 2004 elections in which immigration was an issue, that we were on to something important back in the '80s.

Clean air legislation came through for renewal in the late '80s or early '90s. I also presided over some defense bills. Once, late at night, early in my career in the House, there was a very senior member from California who was steamed up about something that occurred during the day, and he saw this as a chance to spring a trap for this new guy (me). He came back to the floor and teed off on the chair's ruling. I knew enough to realize that if I gave up or showed wimpiness or lack of resolve, I was dead meat, probably for the rest of my career. With the help of the parliamentarian, I was able to get through the parliamentary thicket that this guy wove. We later became great friends, in part because I handled the situation with aplomb and didn't get upset or slam the gavel. I look back at that as "my blooding." It taught me about how you stand your ground when you're right, even in the face of a very senior member who could hurt you later if he were of such a mind, because you're there representing the Speaker, the institution of the House and, by extension, the rest of the country.

Professionally, I'm most proud that my colleagues in the House, once I retired in 1995, felt it proper that the federal building here in Louisville where I had my office for 24 years be named for me. And they did it while I was alive – a real vote of confidence. I am also proud of the fact that I was invited to be a visiting professor at the University of Louisville Law School when I retired, which led to my becoming a Fellow in Law and Public Policy for the university. That in turn led to my fellowship at Harvard. The four months at Harvard in 2002 planted a seed in my head to become a student again at the age of 70, and to enroll in the master's degree program at the John F. Kennedy School of Government at Harvard.

Personally, the thing I am most proud of is the fact that strangers come up to me and say, "Congressman, I just want to thank you for what you did, for your years of service." A lot of politicians have burned bridges in their home towns, but at no point did I betray my constituents or do anything to embarrass them, to denigrate public office or to reflect badly on the community or the state.

Not winning the Democratic primary for mayor of Louisville in 1969 was one of my biggest disappointments. However, the only race I ever lost was the one I learned the most from. I learned more about my hometown than I ever had before, when I had to campaign in all the segments and areas of it. I had to be on my feet in forums and debates involving the other candidates, and had to react to the questions. It was a wonderful learning process. But that night I lost, almost exactly a year before I won the primary to go to Congress, was so demoralizing. My wife and I had poured everything into the campaign – all of our money, every ounce of our energy, our hopes and our beliefs in the future. Still, the mayor's race was probably as important for me as winning my first political race to get into the field, so when I did campaign for Congress, I was a better candidate.

I was really disappointed that succeeding administrations never funded the 1986 Immigration Act adequately, despite our entreaties that they do so.

The bill hasn't worked as well as Senator Simpson and I had hoped. The lesson learned is that the work isn't done even when the bill is signed. We moved on to other issues too quickly (work permits, for example). In Congress, you don't get pats on the back for oversight. You get them for passing new legislation. But if I had it to do over, Al Simpson and I would have spent the next two to four years overseeing the implementation of the 1986 Act.

My other disappointment is with my party – the Democratic Party. It hasn't seemed to learn that there are a lot of people in this country who aren't demented or religious nuts or conservative troglodytes who need to be reached out to. The Party is losing races it could win.

I've never been a great follower. If I had been back in 1967, I would have listened to the admonitions of the Democratic Party leaders who said, "Ron, why don't you wait for awhile and two years later we'll run you."

Followers have to be loyal, but they are not going to be loyal if they have no reason to be. The person they are following has to earn their loyalty. That's why leaders and followers are part and parcel of the same thing.

Blind followers are not good for the country, the community or for society. When it comes time to disobey an illegitimate order, a blind follower is not going to disobey it. When the leader is not on a good mission, you have to be able to tell that person what is needed. So followership, in a way, is leadership in a little different direction. I've looked at followers as leaders in waiting or in training.

If I were to live my life over, I actually don't think I would change much. Coming out of law school, I had three choices: being counsel to the L & N Railroad (which I did choose); being a teacher at the Chase Law School (now part of Northern Kentucky University); or being a clerk for a federal judge – Judge Henry Brooks. I have often wondered, "What if I had gone to the law school?" I think I would have been a very happy academician. Fittingly, when I retired from Congress, I taught at UofL and also at Harvard.

I would have loved to be a federal judge, but you have to be appointed, and I would never have passed muster to be appointed. The Democrats wouldn't allow it because of my pro-life stance, and the Republicans because they have their own people. I could have run for a state or local judgeship here in Kentucky, but I never wanted to be anywhere but the Congress – except for a federal judgeship.

If anything has been a detriment to me in politics and political life, it's my temperament. I think there are always two or three sides to an issue. I don't think I'm indecisive, but I'm just not of the belief that everything that is "liberal" is right or, like some of my friends, that everything "conservative" is right. For them, life has no gray. But for me, life has a lot of gray. There is black and white, but there is also gray. As a judge, that would have been my job, to try to untangle all the spaghetti and to try to figure out what's best for the litigants. So it might have fit my temperament almost better than politics.

I would advise young people aspiring to leadership not to dote or dwell too much on leadership, as this can lead to cynicism and becoming manipulative, being interested in people only because those people can advance your career.

To become a leader, do something you really want to do – something you're prepared to do and that you have talent to do – and do it to the fullest of your ability. Leadership roles will emerge from that. If you think on it too much, people will know you're sailing under false colors, because you're not really interested in them.

I think we've had inspired leadership in Louisville over the last 50 years. Just last night I saw that wonderful statue of Mayor Charlie Farnsley sitting there on that bench on Main Street. Wilson Wyatt and Frank Burke and Jerry Abramson and Dave Armstrong have all been wonderful mayors – farsighted.

What's made Louisville a great city, though, is its people. We have a cadre of very good people here. We're known as a hard-working community. There's a structure here, and it's reflected in our neighborhoods. Look how zealous we are about saying, "I'm from Schnitzelberg," or "I'm from St. Matthews," or "I'm from the Highlands." There is still a central core of what was here at one time – a small town with a lot of deep roots. Look at our location, on the Ohio River, at the crossroads of the highway system. We have air cargo service through UPS, so our location is attractive to business.

I am proud, as a former congressman, to have played some role in our city's development. Over 24 years, I helped bring a lot of federal money into the community for a number of projects – things like the McAlpine Dam; the conversion of the Naval Ordnance Station into a technology park; money for roads and highways.

I was in office at the time of all the mayors from Frank Burke to Dave Armstrong, working in partnership with them, and with governors like Wendell Ford and Julian Carroll and others to help advance the community. I wasn't the one that turned the key in many of these projects, but I was their partner.

I think the biggest challenge we have in our community, and always will have, is education. From the statistics I've read, Kentucky is abysmal. We're something like 45th among all states for the number of our people who have bachelor's degrees or higher. We are very much down in the last tier when it comes to elementary and secondary education. So if we have a challenge, it is education, education, education. We need to educate our workforce in addition to our young people and college students. I don't think we're prepared for the changes in technology. I don't think we today have the workforce for it.

We also need to re-educate people who are already beyond the normal education age, who will need to do the jobs coming down the line.

How we do that, I really don't know. We need money, but it will take more than money. We have made some interesting starts with KERA, but there is an awful lot still left to do. Unless we concentrate on education at every level, we aren't going to be able to continue the growth and advancement that we've seen in our community in the last ten years.

I have learned some valuable lessons in my lifetime that I would like to share with the next generation of leaders in Louisville:

First, don't be daunted too easily, because life inevitably will deal you some upper cuts. You have to be strong and resilient, because disappointments will come as they have come to me.

Second, remember that you learn from your failures as much as from your successes.

Third, remember the words in Simon and Garfunkel's song, "The Sounds of Silence" – "The words of prophets are written on subway walls and tenement halls." Listen to people – not just Ph.D.'s or people with a string of letters after their names, but to the "little" people as well. From them, you can get some of the best wisdom you will ever receive.

Fourth, remember, too, that you have to be willing to carry the garbage out – to do the scut work in life – in order to be invited to the big dance.

Fifth, remember that there will be ups and downs in the general glide path to the pinnacle of your profession.

Sixth, never forget that the things in life that really count, if you want to be a leader, are your faith, your family and your friends. Paradoxically, that's exactly what we sacrifice on our way up the saw-toothed ladder.

Last, and perhaps most importantly, never forget that life is not just for making a living; it's for making a difference.

MITCH McCONNELL

**United States Senator
Senate Majority Whip
108th Congress**

SINCE 1984, SENATOR MITCH McCONNELL has piled impressive win upon impressive win in statewide elections. He is the longest-serving Republican in Kentucky history, and after 21 years, he is one of the most powerful individuals in the U.S. Senate, as well as the country.

"Mitch McConnell bestrides Kentucky like a political colossus," *Courier-Journal* op-ed columnist John David Dyche wrote in 2002, after McConnell secured a fourth Senate term, unprecedented for a Kentucky Republican. In 2004, a Republican won Kentucky's Fourth District congressional seat, the sixth to win a spot in Kentucky's congressional delegation since McConnell's election to the Senate. That same year one seat slipped back into the Democrats' column when the McConnell-backed Congressman Ernie Fletcher left the House to make a successful run for governor. Fletcher became the first Republican to win the governorship of Kentucky in decades. Over the past few years, Republicans have also engineered a takeover of the Kentucky Senate for the first time in generations. This Republican success has taken place in a state where registered voters are predominantly Democratic.

All of the campaigns that have brought about that Republican ascendancy have had Mitch McConnell's handprints all over them, his supporters and detractors will agree. His ability to raise campaign funds is legendary. He has used that prowess to help other Republicans in the Senate, as well as fellow Kentuckians, and he personally has risen steadily in national stature.

When George W. Bush was first elected president in 2000, McConnell chaired his inauguration. In 2002, he won the office of Majority Whip, making him the second-ranking member of his party in the U.S. Senate. It is now his job to count and ensure enough votes for the Republican leadership.

He may be best known in the Senate for his unyielding stance against so-called election campaign finance reform, which he says is a threat to the First Amendment rights of candidates and voters.

Mitch McConnell was born in 1942 in Alabama and grew up in south Louisville. He graduated from Manual High School in 1960 and received a bachelor's degree from the University of Louisville in 1964. He has a 1967 law degree from the University of Kentucky. Students of leadership will find it interesting that he served as president of the student bodies of each of these institutions.

He practiced law briefly, but politics was his calling. He served as an intern in the office of legendary Kentucky Senator John Sherman Cooper, who he says taught him how to be a senator once the job was won. He refers to Cooper as his hero, though they came from different sides of Republican philosophy. McConnell won his 2002 election with 65 percent of the vote, the only Republican ever to beat a winning-percentage record set by Cooper.

McConnell also worked in the U.S. Senate before he was elected to it, as a chief legislative assistant to Kentucky Republican Senator Marlow Cook. He later served as deputy assistant U.S. attorney general as well.

McConnell's political career actually started in Louisville, though, not Washington. He served two terms as Jefferson County judge-executive, from 1978 to 1985, before being elected to the U.S. Senate.

McConnell currently serves as a senior member of the Senate's powerful Appropriations Committee; as chairman of the State, Foreign Operations and Related Programs Appropriations Subcommittee; and as a senior member of the Rules and Administration Committee and the Agriculture Committee.

McConnell has a reputation for bringing a lot of federal money home to Kentucky, but he also has raised a good bit of private money for Kentucky institutions as well – most notably its universities. Since 1998, he has secured more than $100 million in federal funding for University of Louisville priorities alone. He is particularly proud of the $4 million he raised privately to establish the non-partisan McConnell Center for Political Leadership at UofL, which trains students to become leaders in law, politics, business, health care, the arts and community service.

One of his former staff members, Janet Mullins, explained in a 1995 *Louisville Magazine* article how McConnell has achieved so much in his lifetime: "He is nothing if not well prepared and methodical," she said. "When he decides what he wants, he makes a plan, and he realizes that every step is a step along the way to making it happen."

McConnell is married to Elaine Chao, who is U.S. Secretary of Labor, making her the first Kentuckian in half a century to be in a president's cabinet. He has three grown daughters from a previous marriage.

I THINK IT DAWNED ON ME IN HIGH SCHOOL that I liked the idea of trying to lead. I ran for president of the student council at Manual High School. It was a hotly contested race and I won, so that gave me the opportunity at a relatively early age to have a leadership experience.

I had a similar experience at the University of Louisville where I was president of the Arts & Sciences Student Council, and at the University of Kentucky College of Law where I was president of the Student Bar Association. So by the time I had gotten through having those leadership experiences, which in my case involved elections, I had decided that I wanted to pursue politics.

Previously, I had been interested in sports, and I think there are some clear similarities between sports and politics. You have two sides, you have competition, and when it's over somebody wins and somebody loses. Like a lot of young boys, my first competitive experience was in sports, and when I realized I had limited ability from a sports point of view – that I wasn't going to be a major-league baseball player – I shifted from sports to a more political environment, a place where you had wins and losses. In that case, when you won, you then had the responsibility for those who had chosen to give you the opportunity to lead. So all of that was happening during my formative years in high school and college.

As with many children, in my early days, my dad was my mentor. Then when I got to UofL in the '60s, I was beginning to see examples of people I admired, like Bill Cowger, who was elected mayor of Louisville, and Marlow Cook, who was elected county judge-executive. Then I had an internship at the end of my college years in U.S. Senator John Sherman Cooper's office. I was getting to know a little bit about some of the major political players in my political party during those days, and I watched them and observed them and tried to learn from their example.

I think one of the best lessons I learned in those early days was from Senator Cooper. It was during the great civil rights debate of 1964. There were a lot of people in the country, particularly in the southern part of the country, and even a number of people here in Kentucky, who were not very enthusiastic about that legislation. We received a lot of correspondence in Senator Cooper's office from those who were opposed to its passage. Senator Cooper, however, was one of those leading the charge for it. It was an opportunity to ask him about leadership in a situation where it appears as if the people who have chosen you may have a different view from what you think is the right thing to do.

He reminded me of the Jeffersonian model of representative democracy. The Jeffersonian model is essentially that once you're chosen, you're supposed to exercise your best judgment. If you chose to run again at the end of the term, and if people didn't like the way you exercised your judgment, they'd replace you with someone else. In other words, you were not sent to Washington simply to try to reflect the popular mood at a given moment. The voters expected you to have some independent judgment and, even though they occasionally might not agree with you, they might still support you. So that was an early lesson.

I think President Reagan was a really good example of the Jeffersonian model. Surveys indicated that many of the positions he took were never the majority view of the American people, yet he won one election by carrying 44 out of 50 states, and his second election by carrying 49 out of 50 states — overwhelming electoral successes at a time in which a huge percentage of the things he stood for were quite controversial. Why did people vote for him? They voted for him because they thought he was a person of conviction. They had confidence that he was doing what he thought was right, and they were willing to cut him slack even when they disagreed with him.

A good leader is not somebody who simply wets his finger and puts it in the air to see which way the wind is blowing on any given issue, but rather somebody who exercises his or her best judgment. Those are some of the leadership traits that I've observed over the years that I admire and seek to emulate.

It's hard for me to describe my own leadership style. I've been involved in public service for over a quarter of a century and have been in my share of battles. I think what I've learned is that most of these battles are not fatal, so the best thing to do is to exercise your best judgment. If it's really, really important, then you need to decide whether or not you're willing to sacrifice your career for the position.

On a couple of occasions, I've taken positions that I thought might well prematurely terminate my career. I like political figures who are driven by conviction rather than simply convenience. If you just operate on convenience all the time, trying to find out what the least-common denominator is at every given moment, then all you are is a reflection of the electorate on any given day. If, on the other hand, you use independent judgment, you sleep better at night and you're probably going to succeed politically anyway.

I have been blessed in my life, but being chosen Senate Majority Whip, which makes me the second-highest ranking Republican in the U.S. Senate, is the most significant position I've achieved to date.

In a place like the United States Senate, which is a melting pot of people from 50 different states, if you're going to be in leadership you need to be a good listener. Imagine this – you're in a club with 99 other people, all of them class-president types, and each of them would like to be in charge of the other 99. How do you go about earning a leadership position?

I think it's elementary that the only chance you have to become a leader among leaders is to be a good listener, because all of these people are bright and capable or they wouldn't have reached this level of American politics. Each of them has a significant contribution to make in some way to the country. So I think respecting their points of view, being a good listener and, where possible, promoting their interest is the key to being a leader among leaders. That's the kind of thing I have to do every day in my current position as Majority Whip.

I think I've been very fortunate, in the sense that I've had setbacks from time to time, but nothing that I found disabling that made me want to go in a different direction. I do think that every failure is an opportunity.

I have learned that the sun comes up tomorrow, and life goes on, and other opportunities are around the corner. I think one of the most important lessons, no matter what field or walk of life you are in, is that not many setbacks are fatal, unless you choose to think of what just happened to you, what success you just didn't have, as somehow the end. If you get up the next day and chart a new course and don't give up, the chances are overwhelming that no matter what field you are in, you're going to be a success.

I think for any organization to be effective, the majority of the people involved in it have to be team players. At some point, a decision has to be made to go in a certain direction. If the overwhelming majority of members of the team are not willing to be team players once a final decision is made, that organization is going to fail. So a leader's job is to try to develop a consensus for a course of action among enough people, so that once that decision is finally made, you have enough people together to move forward. This means that there have to be enough team players for the team to succeed.

No matter what organization you are a part of – whether it is the U.S. Senate, or the state legislature, or the Metro United Way, or a big corporation – 90 to 95 percent of people are probably going to be constructive players. Then you have five percent or so in every organization who see things a different way. Leaders end up spending well over half their time with the five percent, not with the 95 percent. So one of the big challenges is not having the 95 percent begin to feel like they've been taken for granted.

It's easy for a team player to think, "Here I am, always after a good argument, willing to follow the team, and yet you're spending all of your time with this person over here who's almost never with us." This makes the leadership challenge enormously time-consuming for a good leader.

I don't care what the organization is, it's not a nine-to-five job being a good leader. And you have to spend an awful lot of personal time respecting the views of a whole lot of people, consulting with them and courting them, frankly, to keep the organization together.

I hate to say this, but if I could live my life over again, I would not do anything differently. I have enjoyed my life. I feel very fortunate to have been able to have the kind of career I had hoped and dreamed I could have as a young man, and – it sounds funny to say it – I wouldn't do anything differently. I have loved my life and feel fortunate for the opportunity to do what I wanted to do.

I have a unique opportunity to give advice to people who are aspiring to leadership positions, too. I founded a program at the University of Louisville called the McConnell Center for Political Leadership. In spite of the title, it's not just about political leadership.

We have had kids pursue business majors, pre-med, pre-law and any number of other areas of focus. The idea is to get the best and brightest kids in the state to participate in the program. They get a free ride – tuition, room and board. We expose them to leaders, most of them political, but some of them business.

For example, Secretary of State Condoleezza Rice was at the Center recently, and Senator Joe Lieberman was there also. What we are doing is taking high school youngsters who have already demonstrated leadership capabilities and enhancing those leadership skills through this program, so that when they go into whatever field they choose to pursue – and it's a whole lot of different fields, not just government or politics – they will be the best leaders they can be for the community.

Leaders are needed in every field, not just politics. So I have an opportunity to interact first-hand with these youngsters from all over the state, with lots of different interests. The one thing they all have in common is that they have demonstrated leadership skills and are going to go out – hopefully, they will stay in Kentucky – and apply those enhanced leadership skills here in the state. The program is designed to help address some of the brain-drain problem, because a lot of our kids go to college outside the state and never come back.

Several things have contributed to the growth and development of Louisville over the last 50 years, in my opinion. Having a good and getting-better university is a very vital part of any community of any size. Here we have a good private school in Bellarmine, and an improving public university in the University of Louisville.

So much of the future is tied to knowledge, and the University of Louisville is doing a better and better job of attracting federal dollars for research and other things that give us the jobs of the future, rather than the jobs of the past.

I think governmentally, going to metropolitan government was also a big step in the right direction for the city of Louisville.

I was county judge-executive back in the early '80s when we tried to merge city and county government two years in a row and came up short. Fortunately, we were able to get it over the hump in 2000. I participated in that – I wasn't the main reason it passed, but I did support it. I think that it was good for the community as far as the government portion of it was concerned. I think we're still struggling in the private sector with what we're going to be.

There are some advantages that Louisville has that will always be helpful to us like location, which is the principal reason UPS is here, which in turn is the principal reason we have lots of warehousing and distribution and storage facilities here. That's good, it's all good. It's not enough, however, and I think we also need to put more emphasis on higher education. We're getting better, but we have a long way to go.

I'm trying to participate as a senior member of the Senate Appropriations Committee. I've had a chance to earmark more than $100 million in federal funds for the University of Louisville. UofL hopes to attract specialists for medical research, and we hope that's going to produce biotech spin-offs that will be beneficial for the whole community. Having a well-educated population and research-oriented expenditures, I really do think, are the most important things we can do for the future.

What I try to do, even though state government is the principal funder of universities, is to earmark federal funds. For example, in 2005 I earmarked nearly $30 million in funds for the University of Louisville alone. This is not competed-for money, this is money actually written into bills. A lot of this money that I've been bringing in is for these centers of excellence that have already gotten the state to match private dollars, and now federal dollars on top of it. We're trying to catch up – to push ahead to make this university and this community better than it has been in the past. So that's how I'm trying to target areas, through my job, that will make a difference to our community.

One of the great business leaders in the Louisville community is David Jones. David taught me something back when I was county judge-executive that stuck with me forever. He said, "The most important word in the English language is focus." Which is another way of saying, "If you've got a good game plan, stick to it."

I think we need to focus like a laser on the issues facing our community. Not flip-flop around, not change every year and go in a different direction. We know that great universities breed knowledge-based industries, which bring in the most successful people, which create the greatest growth. The communities that succeed will be those that have the focus to stick to it and keep pushing it in the right direction, rather than trying to change strategies every two or three years and look for some magic. Focus, that's what I think is the most important thing.

The most important advice I can give young people who are aspiring to leadership positions in the future is don't ever quit. The only way you will fail is if you give up. For some people, success comes a little quicker than for others, either because they are a little smarter or because they are a little luckier occasionally, but if you have the view that failure is not an option, simply not an option, and you refuse to be defeated by setbacks, you will be a success. It's an absolute certainty, because in this country, there are no artificial barriers to success.

JOSEPH J. "JAY" MCGOWAN

President
Bellarmine University

LOUISVILLE'S BELLARMINE UNIVERSITY is literally a different place than it was when Jay McGowan took over as its third president in 1990. For one thing, it was then called Bellarmine College. For another, it now has 14 more buildings and 15 more acres, 135 in total. Ninety percent of the faculty is new since then. The number of students has increased to around 2,500, with the number who live on campus increasing by 51 percent, and the percentage of full-time students also growing. As a result of these changes and McGowan's personal leadership, tuition and fee revenue has grown 172 percent over those years, from less than $12 million a year to more than $32 million. Stepped-up fundraising efforts have also generated over $50 million in new revenue for Bellarmine over the last seven years.

U.S. News and World Report has recognized Bellarmine as one of the outstanding liberal arts comprehensive universities in the South for 11 years in a row. The operating budget is up more than 180 percent, from $10.9 million to $33.1 million in 2003. Its endowment, annuities and trust values have increased from $7.2 million to $22 million. Plant assets are now worth $57.4 million, up from $20.3 million. Three new schools have been created – The Annsley Frazier Thornton School of Education; the School of Continuing & Professional Studies, and the Donna & Allan Lansing School of Nursing & Health Sciences.

McGowan came to Bellarmine from Fordham University, a Jesuit school in New York City. After 20 years of increasingly responsible administrative positions at Fordham, he decided to leave there, largely because Fordham's presidents have traditionally been clergymen. When he arrived at Bellarmine, he began to change things and began an aggressive fundraising and building program that continues today.

Jay McGowan was born in Shreveport, Louisiana and grew up in Scranton, Pennsylvania, and in the Philadelphia area, where he attended a Jesuit college preparatory school. He has B.A. and M.A. degrees from the University of Notre Dame, and a doctorate in higher education from Columbia University. He started thinking seriously of becoming a college president in 1985, five years before he came to Bellarmine, during study at the Institute for Educational Management at Harvard University.

Bellarmine's hilly campus off Newburg Road reminds him of an Italian hill town, he will tell you, specifically Montepulciano, a village in Tuscany where St. Robert Bellarmine, the Jesuit for whom the school is named, was born in 1542. He says Bellarmine's three hills, open spaces, great light, and beautiful buildings are consistent with the architecture and the rolling, terraced terrain of that beautiful Tuscan village.

McGowan stays busy as president of Bellarmine, and also is active in a number of professional organizations as well. He serves on the boards of the National Association of Independent Colleges and Universities, the American Council on Education, the Association of Independent Kentucky Colleges and Universities and Kentuckiana Metroversity.

His community service activities include serving on the boards of Greater Louisville Inc., the J.B. Speed Art Museum, the Young Professionals Association of Louisville and the Greater Louisville Health Enterprises Network. He served as chair of the NCCJ 2001 Humanitarian Awards Dinner and chaired the 1994 Metro United Way Campaign as well.

In his spare time, McGowan loves to read voraciously and to play golf with humility. He has also been known to sing an Elvis Presley ballad or two from time to time, but says that "for these sightings to be truly valuable, they must also be quite rare!"

McGowan has definite ideas about leadership and draws a clear distinction between leading and managing. "In the final analysis, management is about your skills while real leadership is about your vision, substance, values, character, and soul."

McGowan and his wife, Maureen, the Chief Financial Officer of Louisville Collegiate School, have two sons.

I DIDN'T DECIDE TO BECOME A LEADER in the Louisville community; the Bellarmine Board of Trustees decided to make me one.

What I did decide after nine years as a vice-president of Fordham University in New York, was that I was ready to become a university president. I made that known to the president I was serving and other colleagues, and soon the search firm Bellarmine was using contacted me. It was a college I did not know a great deal about, but it was in a town I did know a great deal about because of my wife's mother's family – the Barrys. And I did know there was a Catholic college in Louisville with a world-class Thomas Merton collection. I interviewed with Bellarmine and found I was competing in the final round against two others who were already presidents of colleges. Fortunately, I was selected, so I never decided to become a leader in Louisville, but decided to become president of a college that was and is a leader in our region.

My greatest mentor was Fr. Ted Hesburgh, who served as the president of the University of Notre Dame for 35 years. His attention to person, vision, passion, as well as his common sense, courage and openness influenced me. He had such great staying power at Notre Dame, and a "stick-to-it-tiveness." He knew his priorities and he stayed with them.

Another man who was a great mentor to me was Michael Walsh, S. J., president of Boston College and subsequently Fordham University. I knew him at a time when there was a great tumult and unrest on college campuses, violence and takeovers of buildings. I was impressed with how many questions he asked in making a decision and how well he listened to a wide variety of perspectives, including those of his youngest staff members. Effective leadership it seems takes place when high advocacy follows high inquiry in decision making.

A third major influence on me was John F. Kennedy. As an undergraduate at the University of Notre Dame, I took great pride in having an Irish-American Catholic elected president of the United States. His political style, grace and intellect, wit and humor served as an inspirational model for me.

The leadership instrument called the Predictive Index (PI) fairly characterizes my leadership style. I am goal-oriented to a fare-thee-well, but am imaginative, flexible, and resilient about how to achieve my goals.

The more I learn about leadership, the more I am fascinated about how your leadership improves as you grow and mature as a human being. Who you are as a person is inextricably interwoven into who you are as a leader.

For instance, early in my career as a leader, I was so concerned with achieving the desired results, the goals, that too often I paid too little attention to matters of process. So sure was I that I understood the problem and understood the solution, that I would not be as careful as I might to seek the input, perspective, and advice of those I was trying to lead, and then would be surprised and frustrated by their lack of understanding of the problem and their subsequent lack of appreciation for the solution I had developed. I also observed that my "lone ranger" decisions did not have the life span that I desired.

As I have grown as a person, my love and respect for my fellow human beings and colleagues has deepened beyond measure. I have come to see the great richness and wisdom in perspectives beyond my own. And as a consequence, my leadership now is much longer-lived and more fully-owned by those I am leading and by those I am serving in my leadership.

Because of my belief in the cybernetic relationship of leadership and personal growth, of leadership accountability and responsibility with personal accountability and responsibility, I often am critical about leadership programs that focus too much on skills, strategies, and surface matters and too little on the philosophical, personal, psychological, and spiritual dimensions of leadership, the deeper dimensions of leadership.

As far as my achievements at Bellarmine are concerned, I feel very good about building a first rate library, like building a world-class kitchen for a world-class restaurant.

A great university, of course, begins not with its president but with its board of trustees and its alumni and alumnae. Our board has national membership because of the national placement of our 14,000 alumni, and to my observation is the strongest not-for-profit board in this region. Both our board and our alumni provide great financial support for the University and great moral support for me.

Since 1990, our faculty has increased from 65 full-time to 165 distinguished full-time members. Their academic credentials and the quality of their teaching and research are highly competitive nationally. While we will remain a teaching university at our core, you will see in coming years an increasing emphasis on graduate programs and on research at Bellarmine so we can help solve more problems and create more opportunities for our region.

The national as well as regional character of our student body of 2,500 continues to build. Of our 1,900 undergraduates, 1,600 are full-time; this year 720 will live on campus and 40% will come from out of state and from 15 nations. I am very proud of the fact that about two-thirds of our undergraduates graduate in four years. Our student athletes graduate in four years at an even higher rate and there are not too many universities these days that can make that claim. Our financial aid packaging is strong so that the average debt of our graduates is low.

Our Rubel School of Business recently achieved accreditation by the Association for the Advancement of Collegiate Schools of Business (AACSB), an international recognition of quality achieved by only 15% of business schools in the world. This academic year, we graduated our first cohort of students in Bellarmine's first doctoral program, the Doctor of Physical Therapy (DPT).

Something that reflects a priority of mine has been the dramatic growth in study abroad participation and in welcoming exchange students from other countries. Over 30% of our most recent graduating class studied abroad during their junior year, one of the very highest percentages in this regard in the nation. These are specific achievements that have been encouraging and very pleasing to me.

But in the larger scale of things, I am pleased with the fact that in some sense I have been a helpful advisor for Bellarmine. The Bellarmine I met when I arrived was like a really bright, good looking individual with enormous energy and talent, but with too little awareness of its own identity, tremendous strengths, opportunities, and future.

Through encouragement, affirmation and counsel in my presidency, I believe that I have helped this bright and beautiful institution get a much better sense of itself, a better informed sense of its identity, a greater self awareness and confidence. I feel as though I have helped unleash the great energy and competitiveness of the place, to help it become more focused and deliberate, to help it get a better understanding of who and what it is, where it wants to go, and how it wants to get there. There is a greater sense of efficacy, coherence, and intentionality to the place now.

So it is not that I have brought a lot to Bellarmine, but rather that I have helped the place discover and better appreciate the greatness that it has within it, and have helped encourage our nationally distinguished learning community to build confidently on its strengths and to create new ones. As a consequence of all of our work together, Bellarmine University is the leading independent, Catholic, liberal arts based, comprehensive university in the Commonwealth and the region. I am very proud of Bellarmine and our talented people for that reason.

My biggest failure is that I always wanted to be a rock star but not a single agent has ever called. Seriously, when I think of something I have not done well, I recall a couple unfortunate hires, in which instances I thought people were right for the job and they were not. When you are the president, you are hiring at the senior level and so there are real consequences if you do not hire well. In the two cases I have in mind, there turned out to be a lack of institutional, cultural, and personal fit and so these individuals were just not the right people, either for our institution or for me. It is humbling when that situation occurs because the people with whom I work are very important to me, professionally and personally and I depend on them and learn from them a great deal.

If I could do things over again, I would try to figure out a way to learn all that I have learned – earlier. For the life of me, I have no idea how I would have done that, but it certainly would have been easier. As a younger person, I would have listened to more people, more often, more carefully – a skill that I fully embraced by the middle of my career. And I also would have been more aware at an earlier point of the importance of integrating my person into my leadership.

I would strongly advise young people today who seriously aspire to leadership to first and foremost get a first-rate liberal arts education. During your undergraduate days, it is more important than anything for you to fully engage with and inform yourself about the great and ultimate questions in life and about the great answers to them developed across the history, experience, and collective wisdom of mankind. Only with a liberal arts education does an individual get a deep sense of who they are, what the world is all about, what is good, what is bad, how to think clearly and communicate effectively – all essentials for successful leadership. I am highly skeptical of someone who alleges to be a true leader of people who does not have a first rate liberal arts education.

I also would advise future leaders to always take care of themselves as persons, and to take care of their physical and emotional health. Leadership and achievement are seductive and distracting in a narcissistic way and can create a lot of self-delusion. Because work and achievement are seductive, they can consume your time, your relationships and your soul.

We have to take our jobs very seriously and do them well, but if we sacrifice ourselves, our health, and our personal relationships in the process, it contributes to less effective leadership and to an unhappy leader. Always be attentive to the center of your person. There has to be balance and integration in your life. You must always work to be master of your own ship. If you are so inclined and I recommend that you be so, nurturing a strong religious faith and a guiding spirituality will contribute greatly to your being centered. Then you can lead – from your center – and your leadership will be more effective and you as a person will be more satisfied.

For me, part of the fun of being at Bellarmine at this wonderful point in its young history and development is the sense that as we make our place and experience better and better for the students who are here, we also are helping to improve the region, the nation, and the world. One of the things I like most about my job is the opportunity it presents to have impact on our great part of the world. If I do my job right by improving the education of the students who are smart and capable enough to come to Bellarmine, then they will move on to improve the region, the nation, and the world.

Louisville is at a very exciting time in its history. Finally we have an enlightened, merged government. Having Jerry Abramson as our mayor is a gift from the gods – having that kind of experience and world class talent and vision. The Metro Council is great. I am excited about Greater Louisville Inc. and its superb work. I recently served on GLI's Executive Committee. It is a highly intelligent, thoughtful, and well informed operation. I was part of the development of the current structure as a follow up to the Boyle Report and the work of the Economic Development Task Force. In this time of technology and the global free market capitalism it encourages, I believe that Louisville can be anything it wants to be, and that Louisvillians can be anybody they want to be. We just have to be really smart, imaginative, persistent, and strong willed about it. But as the 16th largest city in the nation now, we have the potential to be a real player on the national and international stage.

Some of the things that challenge Louisville include some problems set up by regional levels of education and by parochialism or short term, narrow vision. Some people still think that what is around Louisville is all there is and needs to be in the world. I think one of the great ways one can really serve Louisville is to encourage local students and citizens to travel more, nationally and internationally – to help themselves better appreciate not only how spectacular Louisville is, but why it is spectacular. With some people I have met in the area, I occasionally sense a smugness, complacency and satisfaction with the status quo that is a function of not having gotten out of Dodge City enough, seeing what the rest of the world is like, or understanding or appreciating Louisville's strong competitive potential. The good news is that I am meeting more and more people in recent years, however, who are traveling more, and more and more people moving here and living here who have international perspective and experience. As that happens here, everyone benefits.

What has contributed to our community's growth and progress to date are a number of very intelligent and courageous key decisions on the part of the local government, economic leadership and the people. Louisville is an immensely welcoming, encouraging, and hopeful place now. We are making a lot of the right moves in the right ways.

Higher education, for example, with the support of government and economic leadership, is becoming a stronger and more visible player in forming the future of the region and that is a good thing.

Our community has to build strategically, persistently, and imaginatively upon what we have going here. We have to figure out rather quickly how to get a lot more educated people in our region. We have to continue to get more serious about the essential role of higher education. We have to become so good in the private and public higher education sectors that we attract the best and brightest from other places. We also have to become a more diverse and diversity-tolerant place. We live in a multi-national, multi-ethnic, multi-cultural world on all levels now, so let us embrace that reality in the great Louisville spirit of hospitality. Issues of race and multicultural awareness are related areas in which we need to make progress. We need to be more international, more welcoming of difference, and more diverse on all sorts of levels.

Sometimes in regional cultures like ours there can be a low tolerance for risk and too much affection for safety and predictability. We need to risk and experiment more and to fear failure less. One of the things we do so well here in Louisville is to create and maintain a culture of great pleasantness and comfort. Alone and in excess, however, these otherwise highly desirable qualities can qualify our spirit and competitive desire. Pleasure and comfort need to be balanced, therefore, by a real drive for competitive excellence. I would like to see Louisville and Kentucky as a culture become more confident in ourselves and in our ability to compete. We need always to seek greatness and excellence, and to skillfully integrate those things into the tremendous human quality of life in our city and region.

Louisville, Kentucky, is a spectacular place to live, learn, work, and play. It is my great privilege and blessing to have this terrific opportunity to lead and to develop Bellarmine University as the premier, private comprehensive university in the Commonwealth of Kentucky and as one of the best in the nation. It is my strong belief that as we continue to grow and improve the colleges and universities in our region to be competitively excellent in the national and international academic arenas, and to produce in the process many more talented college graduates, Louisville will become one of the truly great cities in the world – even greater than we already are!

A. Stevens Miles Jr.

Retired President
National City Bank

Chairman
First Kentucky National Corporation

LOOK FOR STEVE MILES in the newspaper these days and you'll find him in the sports pages. He owns a couple of thoroughbred horses, graded stakes winners Western Breeze and Lead Story.

For more than two decades, however, he was a bank executive in Louisville, and a civic activist whose name, along with others like Wilson Wyatt, Gordon Davidson, Maurice Johnson and Frank Hower, was on the list of every major community group or project.

Miles served as president of Louisville Central Area Inc. and chaired the Louisville Waterfront Development Corporation, Project 2000, the Old Kentucky Home Council of the Boy Scouts of America, the Louisville Science Center's Foundation Board, and the Kentucky Convention Center Planning Commission. He served on the boards of both the Louisville and Kentucky Chambers of Commerce and the Kentucky Center for the Performing Arts. In addition, he was a trustee of the J. Graham Brown Foundation, the Governor's Scholars Program, Louisville Collegiate School, the University of Kentucky and Washington and Lee University.

When he was coming up through the ranks at First National Bank, he will tell you, that's just the way it was done – people reached for leadership in civic affairs while they gained it in business.

In the mid-1980s, he was involved with Project 2000, casting ahead to see where Louisville should be in days to come. In the 1970s, he led Louisville Central Area, Inc., looking at where the hub of Louisville should be. Miles predicted accurately that it would be along the Fourth Street corridor from Broadway to the Ohio River — even though there wasn't much on the river end in those days.

As head of both LCA and WDC, Miles worked with civic leaders to develop Louisville's waterfront, as well as the river end of Fourth Street, including the Belvedere and Kentucky Center for the Arts. His leadership helped sow seeds that would one day transform sand piles and salvage lots into an award-winning Waterfront Park and Louisville Slugger Stadium.

He also worked with Maurice Johnson, Gordon Davidson and other civic leaders in the 1970s to find a developer for a downtown shopping mall along Fourth Street. The group eventually hired Oxford Properties, Inc., which developed the Louisville Galleria on Fourth Street, between Liberty and Muhammad Ali Boulevard – the precursor to Fourth Street Live!

Steve Miles was born in Louisville in 1929. He graduated from the old Kentucky Military Institute in 1947, then from Washington and Lee University, with a bachelor's degree in economics, in 1951. After he was drafted into the army, he went to officer's candidate school for a commission and served until the end of the Korean War in 1953.

He returned to Louisville without a clear idea of what he would like to do for a living, so he took the advice of a friend who worked at First National Bank. The friend suggested he give working at the bank a try, reasoning that the experience would be good for anything else he might want to do. He applied for a job at First National and was hired in 1954.

It wasn't long before Miles recognized that he'd found his career. He became bank president in 1972, and two years later moved up to president and CEO of First Kentucky National Corporation, a holding company formed for the bank. In 1988, his company merged with National City Corporation of Cleveland, and he became president and a director of National City Bank.

He retired at age 60, at the end of 1989, but only after he oversaw a successful merger. "I leave First Kentucky knowing the company that has meant so much to me is in good hands," he told *The Courier-Journal*.

When he retired, Miles announced he would not pursue other business ventures but would remain active in civic affairs – keeping chairmanships of the Louisville Waterfront Development Corporation and the Louisville Science Center's Foundation Board. He also continued to serve as vice chairman of the Kentucky Derby Museum.

Miles was married to the late Ann Berry Houston Miles, with whom he had two children. He currently is married to Dorothy Deane Miles. They spend quite a bit of time in Florida these days, but it is sometimes possible to catch Miles on the backside of the track at Churchill Downs early in the morning when a meet is on, watching his horses run.

ONE WHO BECOMES A LEADER obviously must be willing to assume responsibility, but I don't think a leader necessarily goes in and says, "I am going to take over this place and run it."

When you go to work for a bank, it's a very public institution. I think by virtue of its role in the community, the leaders in a bank and the people who work in a bank do become involved in community affairs, so it's just a natural phenomenon. I look back at J. McFerran Barr, John Barr's father, who was president when I came to work at the First National Bank in Louisville. Mr. Barr was involved in so many civic activities, as were Henry Offutt, Hugh Schwab and others. Many were involved in community activities, so it was natural for someone like me, who was coming along and gradually playing a leadership role in various aspects of the bank, to become involved in community things.

Those people were, in fact, my mentors. They were the ones who set the stage and encouraged me and others to play roles in civic activities. As I said, in a bank you probably find more of that than other institutions that aren't quite as public as banks are. There is definitely tradition, and it's good business, too, you might say, because you do get a high profile and that, in turn, translates into a benefit to the community and a benefit to the bank.

As a leader, I always thought it was important to set clear goals — to make sure that people understood what was expected of them, and to keep reinforcing those same goals. You don't just say, "These are our goals, we'll put them in the drawer and that's that." You have to keep reinforcing them, so there is no misunderstanding about what the goals are and what is expected of people.

As far as my personal leadership style is concerned, I tried to be demanding, obviously, and held people accountable for the decisions that they made in an effort to achieve whatever goals we set out. But I also wanted to be understanding with them, and I felt that I was. Above all, I think that you just have to be really honest and fair with people. To be a leader, that is so essential. You must be fair with people and honest with them in your evaluation. I guess that would be how I would like to see myself thought of. Jim Denniger, however, who was our personnel manager, used to call me the Velvet Hammer. He said I did things in a smooth way, but everybody always got my message. I took that as a compliment.

My greatest accomplishment in business was ascending to the leadership role of CEO of the bank holding company, a role I played for 15 years, and seeing the bank succeed in so many ways. Obviously you always have setbacks along the way, from time to time, but essentially we certainly succeeded in what we aspired to do and it gave me a great feeling of accomplishment.

I would also say the same thing would hold true at Washington and Lee University, where I was elected to the board and then served as rector for seven years. Here again, in that role, I felt that we made some great accomplishments. Washington and Lee certainly holds an esteemed position among liberal arts colleges across the country. So I would say, in short, that those are two things I feel were significant accomplishments in my life. Obviously there are many other things that I was proud of and that meant a lot to me, but those were the main accomplishments.

I had a couple of personal failures or disappointments. First, we tried very hard to get the banking laws changed in Kentucky so that banks could merge and we could form a stronger banking system in the state. I can't tell you how many times I met with the Senate Banking Committee in Frankfort, and others as well, to try to get this point across, but those men saw it as a big city grab. They felt that big city banks were trying to swallow up all the minor, smaller banks out in the state and they felt that they were protecting the smaller banks. I always said to them, "Well, why don't you go ask the smaller banks, because a number of them are coming to us and saying we'd love for you to buy us. No big bank is going to buy a small one unless that small one is willing to sell, so I don't think you have a good argument there."

The reason I felt this way, and my counterparts at Citizen's Fidelity and other banks throughout the state felt this way, is because we could see what was happening to banking in other states, notably states like North Carolina, Georgia and Ohio. Those states had very favorable banking laws which enabled banks to consolidate, and you can see the results today.

Charlotte, North Carolina is one of the biggest banking centers in the world, and it is because they had a jump on everybody else. Ultimately, our state law did change so that we could make those acquisitions, but it was so late in the game that we didn't have time to catch up. We put together a wonderful network of community banks that is thriving today, but by the time we got to the position we did, everybody was far down the road. That was a disappointment, and I guess I would have to call it a failure, and if you ask me what I learned from that experience, I learned that politicians are hard to convince, but I think also from an experience like that, you learn that you really need to persevere. We did persevere, but it was too late. We didn't persevere soon enough. Anyway, that was one thing I consider a failure.

Another thing that comes to my mind was how disappointed I was that we were ineffective in getting the city of Louisville and Jefferson County governments to merge. Ultimately we came around, and I am so delighted that we did. I give our mayor, Jerry Abramson credit for that leadership.

I know from personal experience that there were so many different factions involved. We had fifth- and sixth-class cities throughout the county that didn't want to give up their little fiefdoms and didn't feel they had anything to gain from it. We had others in various sections of the community who for one reason or another felt that they would be disenfranchised, but ultimately all those things were resolved. I haven't been on the scene downtown, but I have a feeling that everything is functioning very well and, again, I would say that Jerry Abramson's leadership has had a lot to do with that. I always felt so frustrated that those of us who worked so hard to get that done were unable to do it. But maybe, just maybe, the groundwork that we laid ultimately paid off.

We started working on that in the early '50s. Thruston Morton and Wilson Wyatt — the leading Republican and the leading Democrat in the state — joined hands, saying "Let's get this job done," and even they couldn't do it. Maybe I am being a bit unfair with myself when I say these are my personal failures, because if they couldn't do it, how could I expect to? I just felt it was disappointing. Now that we've done it, however, maybe we can catch up. I think we will.

A good follower has to, first of all, clearly understand who he or she is following and what he or she is supposed to do. It's largely the responsibility of a leader to define the goals and whatever job it is that he expects to be done. But on the other hand, I think it is the responsibility of followers to make sure that they clearly understand what is expected of them. Otherwise they are not going to be very effective followers.

No one can go through a business career as long as mine and not make some decisions that you subsequently wish you hadn't made. Maybe some of those decisions were wrong, but I can't think of any that really stand out. None of them was an "earth-shattering" deal that I stay awake at night thinking about. I am certainly not saying that I didn't make mistakes, but as I look back on my life, I dodged a lot of bullets. Overall, there is little I'd do over again.

If I were going to advise young people today who are aspiring to become leaders in our community, I would say that to be a leader you have to generate followers. You can't do anything alone. I think people who are aspiring to leadership really need to know what is expected of them and accomplish those goals. If they have leadership qualities, eventually they will find themselves with opportunities to be in leadership positions.

Believe it or not, some people just don't want to assume leadership roles. They are uncomfortable in leadership positions. They have to find that out about themselves early in the game, because there is nothing worse than finding yourself in a leadership role, then finding that you are not suited for it, don't like it or don't really enjoy that sort of position.

I think that my advice to aspiring leaders would be to do a little self-examination before you take on leadership roles. Don't try to do things alone. Get yourself into a position where you can really test not only your leadership skills, but your affinity for leadership. Are you really destined for a leadership role? Should you be in that position? Unfortunately sometimes we get people in a leadership position and we find out too late that they shouldn't have been in those positions, whether it's in politics or in business.

I could point to several people who I think have made great contributions to Louisville. Leading that list would be David Jones, whom I admire greatly. He has been tremendously successful with Humana and has been a very generous person. He has made enormous gifts of talent and fortune to the city of Louisville. So, if I had to name one person, I think it would be David. He has always been there and has been involved in so many different roles over the years. It may not have been 50 years, but many years. He would lead my list.

There have been plenty of others who have been wonderful leaders – Barry Bingham and *The Courier-Journal*, for example. The senior Barry Bingham was quite a leader in Louisville, so you certainly would have to point to him. I already mentioned Jerry Abramson. I think Jerry has been a wonderful mayor, and now we have metro government. Those are three people who I think have made great contributions, but there are many others who would be close behind.

You really can't say that merger has contributed to Louisville's growth over the past 50 years because it's such a recent phenomenon, but I do think that Louisville has been fortunate over the years to have people who are willing to work together – people who lead companies, yet they are willing to work together on community projects. I have worked personally and closely with so many people like that.

For many years in the mid-'80s, we worked on Project 2000. The purpose of Project 2000 was to focus on where Louisville should be in 2000, and how we should get there. It really was an extraordinarily interesting enterprise. I think it had a lot of positive results as well. We had the heads of four major banks working on it – Maury Johnson, David Grissom, Frank Hower, Bert Klein and me, along with Lee Brown of Brown-Forman, Tom Simons of Capital Holding Company and Charles McCarty of BATUS. We just dropped all of our competitive instincts and put on our community hats and made some decisions that benefited the community in the long run. Many of them were subtle, and we didn't see any evidence of them right away, but I think in retrospect, you can look back and say, "Well gee, those things that we talked about were really good."

For example, take Louisville Central Area. I was very much involved and was president of Louisville Central Area in the '70s. You know, we were taught back then that the center of the city of Louisville was Fourth and Broadway — until we had the Victor Gruen study done. We said, what direction should this city grow? He said, "All river cities should grow toward the river." His initial plan was that Fourth Street would be a spinal column which would be anchored on both ends. One anchor would be Fourth and Broadway, with the Brown Hotel and the Commonwealth Life and Capital Holding building at that end, then the waterfront would be at the other end.

At that time, there wasn't much at the waterfront. Gruen's study sowed the seeds for the development of the waterfront. He said that ultimately the waterfront end of this spinal column called Fourth Street would end up being the dominant end and, sure enough, if you look around today, it is.

We built the First National (now National City) Tower where it is because we felt that was the direction in which the city would grow. Capital Holding (now Aegon) then built a tower downtown, and Citizen's Fidelity (now PNC) Bank built a tower downtown. I was on the board of the Kentucky Center for the Arts when it was built on Main Street, and the Humana Building, of course, was a major addition. Al Schneider was very helpful in putting up hotels and a parking garage. It all just started falling together. But the momentum for all of it began when we finally stepped back and said "In which direction is this city going to grow, and where is the center of it going to be?"

At that time, we also thought about whether certain things naturally should go together. The commercial aspects of downtown were gravitating toward the suburbs, which is now where retail is strongest. But we all thought that the center of banking should be downtown; the center of federal, state, county and city governments should be in the center of the city. We said, "one of a kind things" should be downtown — things like the Kentucky Center for the Arts. You wouldn't want that out in the suburbs. You really want that downtown. Now we have a baseball field downtown, as well. So the seeds that were sown at that time, when we started thinking that way, have now really manifested themselves through this evolutionary period of 20 years or so.

We had subsequent studies done, but it was Victor Gruen who really got us thinking initially about all of this. We had sort of taken things for granted. Our mentality had been, "This is here, so it's always going to be here."

First National had to acquire its property through Urban Renewal, which had the power to condemn property. They didn't have any money to finance us, so we had to put the money up. There were hold-outs, so it was not easy to acquire all those parcels of property. Citizens Fidelity did the same thing, and they had a couple of holdouts that cost them dearly, but those things happen.

A. Stevens Miles Jr.

I think Louisville is in an interesting position right now. It now has many of the elements of a thriving, larger city. We are now a merged community – the 16th-largest city in the country – so we are a big city. But at the same time, we don't have a lot of the things that big cities have. All you have to do is look around you. Look what's going on in Indianapolis and Nashville, like football teams and those types of things. Nashville is lucky because they really capitalized on calling themselves Music City U.S.A. That has really elevated them and given them a high profile in the country.

I think Louisville is still a little bit of an enigma. We have the Kentucky Derby every year and other interesting things, and people say, "Oh, yeah. That's right. That's in Louisville." But we still don't have that one thing that identifies us. We are sort of a "branch office" city, with some exceptions.

Of course Brown-Forman is still here, and some of the big companies, but we've lost a lot of them. All of the banks were independent, but for reasons I already talked about, they are not now. The banks are branches, essentially. You can cite some exceptions to that, but I think that Louisville still needs to deal with its identity and find an identity for itself that will project. I think that's a challenge for our city going forward.

Louisville is a wonderful city. Please don't take the comments that I am making as derogatory at all, because there is no better and nicer place to live. You have heard the stories of the General Electric employees, when big executives came in saying they were going to move them someplace else, saying, "We're not going." It is just an absolutely warm place to live. But our city is now at that awkward age between teenage and adulthood. I just hope things are going on in Louisville now like Project 2000. I hope people who are now in the roles that I and others were in 20 years ago are still getting together and talking about where the city is going from here, because nothing is static. Everything is dynamic. Everything is going to be moving in one direction or the other and, to an extent, we can influence that movement in a positive direction. The only way that can be done, however, is through "think tanks" and people getting together. We have a terrific opportunity in Louisville now with metro government and so much progress. It's an opportune time to get together to think about where we can take this place from here on.

I have already talked about some lessons I have learned that I would like to share with the next generation of leaders in Louisville. I think that by working together, a community can accomplish an awful lot – if you get the right people together, focusing on the problems. Some way or another, the issues and the problems have to be identified. They are pretty easy to identify, you know. "Where are we going from here" is a good place to start.

That is certainly a lesson I learned — the value of being able to arrive at a consensus once everyone understands what the problem is and what the issues are, then having people in roles where they can help direct the effort.

I think the next generation of leaders in Louisville need to get their heads together. I mentioned how Nashville has capitalized on the name Music City U.S.A. You know it was just fortuitous that they had the Grand Ole Opry there and that they could capitalize on it. Look what they've done with it. Everybody knows Nashville is Music City U.S.A., and there are other places like Nashville that really have identity.

Lexington, I think, has done a good job creating its identity as the center of thoroughbred horseracing in the world. I think that's very exciting for them.

I think Louisville has some terrific opportunities as well, but somehow we have to weave our threads together into a cloth that all comes together and fits logically together and gives us something to sell.

Louisville is a great place to live. It's not like we are trying to sell something that is not attractive, but we need new blood. Cities always need new blood.

We can all think of new people and new companies that have come into Louisville and contributed so much. We need local folks too, of course, but it's always good to get new life into our city. Tom Simons was a perfect example. Tom came to Louisville with Capital Holding and he was a dynamo. Some of the GE folks who came along were really a big help too.

These are my words of wisdom for Louisville's next generation of leaders.

Elaine M. "Cissy" Musselman

**Vice Chair
Risk Management Services
Corporation of Louisville**

**Chair
Greater Louisville Convention
and Visitors Bureau**

**Founder
Women 4 Women, Inc.**

CISSY MUSSELMAN IS the first woman to chair a Metro United Way Campaign, the first woman to chair the Louisville Area Chamber of Commerce, and the first woman to chair the Greater Louisville Convention and Visitors Bureau. She is a pioneering woman who has dedicated her own life to breaking the glass ceiling and improving the lives of scores of women in Louisville for decades to come.

In 1993, she founded Women 4 Women, Inc., which raises money to improve the lives of women and girls in Jefferson County. The organization has already raised and distributed over $1 million to worthy programs over the past 12 years and is well on its way to establishing a $10 million endowment, in partnership with the Louisville Community Foundation.

In 1973, Musselman entered what was largely a man's world of commercial insurance, joining Louisville's Harris & Company insurance firm. Within ten years she had risen to the presidency of the firm. Subsequently, she became senior vice president of Alexander & Alexander of Kentucky, Inc. — the second-largest insurance broker in the world — and helped form a succession of new insurance companies with billings in the millions of dollars. In 1992, she became the first insurance broker in the United States to be computer-linked to the floor of Lloyd's of London.

Musselman says she learned to work hard doing chores around her family's home in the Highlands as a child, winning swimming races at Big Spring Country Club and volunteering for the Red Cross when she was a teenager. She grew up with four brothers and an older sister, and she said it was often her lot to wash windows. No slacking was permitted in those tight little corners.

Her hard work ethic is accentuated by a "personal warmth" blended with "a strong sense of determination" — traits attributed to her by Charles Lee Thiemann, president of the Federal Home Loan Bank of Cincinnati when Musselman left his board in 1982. In a letter thanking her for her service, Thiemann added that she possesses "charm, good humor, and keen intelligence, integrity, determination and grace" — a litany of qualities, which begin to explain how Musselman has been able to accomplish all the things she has in her life.

Cissy Musselman grew up in a strong Catholic family and was very involved in athletics, both at Sacred Heart Academy and in pickup games around her neighborhood. She was competitive, and counts winning a Duncan yo-yo championship in 1956 as one of her early victories.

She attended the University of Louisville after high school, but got sidetracked and delayed completion of her bachelor's degree in political science there until 1986. She worked in Louisville for three years as assistant director of a Red Cross youth program, then moved to Washington in 1968 to work as a lobbyist for Bristol-Myers Company. While in Washington, she was elected to the national board of governors of the American Red Cross.

In her Louisville career, Musselman has served on the boards of LG&E, First National Bank and Anthem Blue Cross Blue Shield of Kentucky. Her civic contributions have included service on the boards of the Louisville Community Foundation, the University of Louisville Board of Trustees and the Louisville Regional Airport Authority. She was a charter member of both Leadership Louisville and the Bingham Fellows, and was a founding member of The Committee of 200, a national association of successful entrepreneurial women.

Musselman is deeply committed to improving the lives of women and girls in her hometown. Her annual Women 4 Women golf tournament and festival has won national acclaim and has donated more than $1 million to women's causes since she founded it in 1993.

She chaired Benchmark 2000, a project that studied and documented the status of women and girls in Jefferson County at the turn of the century. The study's recommendations were published in a guidebook that was adopted by Louisville Metro government in 2002 as its blueprint for designing and delivering future programs for women.

She has received innumerable awards and honors over the years for her dedication to community service, especially for her years of work on behalf of women and women's issues. Musselman was awarded the prestigious Thomas C. Simons Award by Leadership Louisville at their fifth annual Leadership Conference in 2000.

I CANNOT REMEMBER MAKING A CONSCIOUS decision to become a leader in our community if, in fact, I have become one. I would suppose my first specific and significant leadership opportunity came in 1976 when I was asked to chair the Metro United Way campaign. That was an experience that made a difference in my life and what followed for me in community leadership. Let me talk about that by first surrounding it with some context.

In my formative years and early adulthood, a number of people influenced me in a variety of ways. Two who are somewhat obscure are my grandmother, Vera Bailey Underwood, and an Ursuline, Sister Brendan, who taught me at Sacred Heart. Two others were Frank Hower and Eric Tachau. While each of these people mentored me in different ways and at different times, the consistent thread that ran through their advice was to seize the life that came before me, to see all its moments as opportunities, to be fearless in all things and ever more fearless every passing day. It was the same advice, whether it was coming from my grandmother when I was young, from Sister Brendan when I was 17 or 18, or from Frank Hower, who was head of the Red Cross chapter when I was president of my high school Red Cross chapter and he heard me speak. He singled me out and said there was much more I needed to do.

I met Eric Tachau when he was 50 and I was being taught by his wife Mary K., who chaired the history department at the University of Louisville. Eric was in the insurance business and we ended up in the same agency – C.D. Harris and Sons. He became a great mentor to me, not just in insurance, but also in life. He was fearless in every passing day. When he turned 50, he decided to go back to law school, and I always thought that was amazing.

These are people who just got inside me. They were not just mentors, they were my guardian angels, and I am grateful every day that has passed that these people each took the time to give me advice.

So, I had been shaped by those people and their attitudes when the United Way came calling.

In 1975, Louisville and Jefferson County was going through a pretty emotional time. Forced busing of our schoolchildren was brought on by a decision mandated by the federal courts, and the implementation of that decision was very difficult for many people to accept. The labor community boycotted Metro United Way's 1975 campaign because there were those who felt the United Way had in some way joined the conspiracy that brought on busing, and that they had perhaps even bought some of the buses with United Way money.

The next year, 1976, I was asked to become the chair of the Metro United Way campaign. This was important because there were two pieces to it. One piece was that the United Way had to succeed. We couldn't have two years in a row of a failure. Secondly, this was a time that the women's movement was surfacing and, as the first woman chair of the United Way campaign, I was well aware that I would either advance the cause of women or, God help me, set it back. I was untested, unseasoned and had something of the look of a sacrificial lamb. Both Frank Hower and Eric Tachau said the same thing to me: "Cissy, you can't say no. You have no choice. You have to accept and you have to succeed." So I did. And it changed my life. I went straight into the heart of the problem. I met the union leaders – men like Marion Winstead and Ron Harsh and Steve Barger – in their offices and at their organizing halls. I learned my way around Okolona and Fairdale and Valley Station. I got comfortable drinking beer from a bottle at Kelly's Bar on Dixie Highway. And, over time, the union guys found their way back downtown to the offices of the United Way.

All the problems didn't fade away. Hostility and suspicion lingered for many years. Marion and Ron and Steve and many, many others decided that they wouldn't let the deserving beneficiaries of the programs of the United Way become casualties in a war not of their choosing. They carried the United Way that year – and me – to success. It would be easy to exaggerate my contribution in all this, to cast myself in a thirty year retrospective as Louisville's answer to Joan of Arc. Marion and Ron and Steve might even let me get away with it, too. But the truth is a better story. The truth is that the leadership skill that I think I learned was refusing to take no for an answer and to just keep talking. Communication became the most important element of that experience. I was the only thing I could be – a young woman who acted like I liked those guys – because I really did. And they knew it.

I think people tend to recognize in me that I am the ultimate "multi-tasker" and networker and I will use every resource available. My style has more to do with my upbringing in a large family – six children. Everybody had a job, and everybody was required to complete it. If you completed it early, you helped whoever wasn't ready yet. We were shown you could work together well. I try to do things in what I would call a consensus style. Whether it is work in my professional life or work in the volunteer world, I try to have fun. I have a permanent dread of excessive seriousness, especially among those who are volunteering their time. I think I should take my work seriously but not myself. I think I am supposed to have fun with my work, and I think everyone else is too. I hope people say they have fun when they work on projects with me.

I haven't had many disappointments in my life. One is that I never told my parents how grateful I am for all they did for me. I told them I loved them, of course. But I never, somehow, found the time to sit down at their feet and say, "I'm not sure how good I am or whether I've become anything or anyone special, but I know I would have been a huge doofus, maybe even a failure, if it weren't for what you've given me. I am grateful that you had me and that you made me be all that I could be. I just want to say thanks. A lot."

Most definitions and descriptions of leaders and followers I have seen and heard are wildly off the mark. There's not much difference between the two in the first place. Perhaps a willingness to make a decision is essential to leaders. I've always had that willingness, but successful organizations are those that have, at all the spots on the chart, people who will follow through. That's the difference. People who will do what they say they will do. The corollary of that is equally important. If a person won't follow through for whatever reason, there is no bigger favor they can do for the leader than to say so. The joy in working with groups is when you ask somebody to do something and you totally trust that it will be done – that's magic. I love working in that situation. Whether I am the follower or whether I am the leader, everybody knows his or her job. It's like the perfect team, the dream team.

Sometimes I reflect that I may have been born with an excess of versatility. And I wonder if I might not have accomplished more by bringing a narrower focus to my life and my work. And the answer, of course, is maybe so and maybe not. These reminiscences arrive when, for example, I ask myself why it took 13 years for Women 4 Women to establish its Foundation. I think, after all, that it may ultimately become the most important accomplishment of my entire life. If I had not served on those many boards, commissions or projects, and had used that energy instead to move the needle on creating the Foundation we might have gotten there a lot sooner. But then, is that really fair? I would have to look at "What was I working on?" "Who did I affect and help?" I am a great believer in God's plan, and She has a lot better view of this than I do.

I would advise young people who are aspiring to leadership to avoid thinking in terms of wins and losses. The problem with wins and losses is that it's a zero sum game. One goes up and another goes down. Half the participants feel like a failure, even if they may not have failed. All of our work is a journey, just as life is a journey. You keep on going. If you stumble, you get up. Don't start measuring yourself in failures. If you screw up, admit it and start over again. Nobody bats a thousand. And when you turn away from zero sum, from who won and who lost, you find out everybody is a potential friend. There is a much more level playing field. When you are with people, socializing, schmoozing, and other forms of mutually supportive activities, friendship becomes possible. Other people are not your enemy. I like playing sports as much as anybody does. I understand keeping score. I am in sales and I understand measuring accomplishment in that way. Too often I see people who beat on themselves, though. If we just turn that around a little, I think you can get maybe a million times more things done with others than you can alone. Maybe a billion. So forget winning and losing is my advice – until you're on the golf tee.

What I would nominate for what has brought about the most positive change in our community over the last 50 years would be the recognition and acceptance of our diversity. Fifty years ago, the power structure of this community was exclusively white, male and primarily Protestant. Today, while the representation of women in the councils of power is still less than they deserve, women clearly are a lot more visible than they were back then.

Today, at the tables where our decisions are made, men and women of all colors, all nationalities and all faiths are seated in greater proportions than ever before. It is still below the level of their entitlement, so I don't want to say we have quite achieved it, but we have embraced diversity over the last 50 years. It has made us stronger as a community. It has made our decisions and our policies more credible and acceptable. While we are not there yet on this one, and I suspect that we never fully will be, the force has been released and the results have shown it to be a benign force. I believe strongly it will move forward.

My role? I think I helped in that process. I was the first woman to lead a Metro United Way campaign. I was the first woman to head the Chamber of Commerce, in 1982. I am the first woman to chair the Greater Louisville Convention and Visitors Commission, elected in 2004. I guess I helped more than a little. I haven't stopped helping women, and I never will.

The challenges facing those who will lead this community in the decades to come are different from my era in a significant way, a way that made it easier for us and will make it harder, or at least more complicated, for the next generation. It is this.

In the latter half of the previous century, Louisville's corporate leadership was made up of a few homegrown, wonderful people like the Binghams who owned the paper; David Jones and Wendell Cherry, who owned Humana; John Y. Brown Jr., who became a millionaire with fast food; and the banks, which at that time were all local banks. All of that is no more. I wouldn't go so far as to say this community that I love is a corporate outpost, but the reality is that most of our civic leaders owe their loyalty, first and foremost, to someone far, far away. This imposes a greater burden on those who will organize our effective coalitions in the future. It will require more patience and a strong recognition of the complexity of the agendas of each of the participants seated around the tables.

More than anything else, we need to enjoy life. I think we get pretty intense about our world. I really appreciate joy in my life. My strongest advice is to find that joy and share it. Our family grew up with the mantra of "Work hard, play hard, and share everything."

I have learned a lot of lessons in my life and career that have been valuable to me, and I'm happy and flattered to be asked to share them. For whatever it's worth, and in no significant order, here goes:

First, show up. Fill that everlasting minute with what Kipling called 60 seconds worth of distance run. You're going to get plenty of rest when you're dead, so don't overdo it while you're alive.

Second, communicate with an understanding that it is a two-way street. Shut up and listen carefully and then, when your turn comes, open up and speak your mind and your heart. Respect the absolute right of others to hold and express positions that you disagree with. You don't know everything and you're not always right and if you don't know how to engage in a free and open dialogue, not very many good things are going to happen while you're around.

Don't whine, don't complain, and don't quit. Sniveling is strictly forbidden and nobody wants to hear how hard you think things are. It's like Churchill said, "When you're going through hell, just keep on going." When you stumble, and you will, get up, tell yourself and anyone who's nearby that it was entirely your fault, and then get back in the game. As long as you have breath you have untapped potential.

You're not as important as you think. And neither is anybody else. But, even so, each and every one of us is very important.

Finally, if you're not happy, go away and figure out why you're not and then come back with your chin up and a smile on your face. Because this strange and bewildering experience called life is way too good to miss.

GERALD A. NEAL

State Senator
Commonwealth of Kentucky

Attorney
Gerald A. Neal & Associates
LLC

GERALD A. NEAL, A 1972 GRADUATE of the University of Louisville Brandeis School of Law and a resident of the Chickasaw neighborhood in West Louisville, began serving as senator of the 33rd District of the Kentucky General Assembly in 1989. The 33rd District is composed of Shively, several West Louisville neighborhoods, Clifton, the primary business district, metro government buildings and the major health facilities. It is racially and economically mixed. Although he was focused on representing the interests of a diverse district, Neal soon recognized that as the only African-American state senator, he would have to pay close attention to issues that impacted the African-American community. "Very few others were carrying the waters on this," he told *The Courier Journal* in 1992. But, of course, there was plenty of overlap between issues of interest to blacks and those of the general population.

Senator Neal went to Frankfort with education as a high priority because he felt that this was one area where work on behalf of one group would clearly help others. In 1991, he formed the Kentucky Education Reform African-American and All Children Caucus, a coalition of parents, educators, administrators and others, to boost the chances of implementing the Kentucky Education Reform Act in a way that would make sure all children would get the help they needed. Although he had a particular focus on ensuring that KERA maximized its potential for African-American children, he noted that children in Appalachian areas and in such predominantly white, low-income neighborhoods as Louisville's Portland neighborhood, tended to fall below average levels of achievement as well, and would benefit from KERA.

By 1992, Neal was having noticeable success with the agenda thrust upon him. Along with championing and supporting other educational measures, he secured $800,000 to recruit minority teachers for elementary and secondary schools. The Minority Recruitment and Retention Program he created is now a permanent fixture in the Kentucky Department of Education.

Neal also shepherded through a measure to put teeth in efforts to increase the number of minority students and faculty members at state universities, and tacked an amendment onto another education bill aimed at making sure minorities are represented on Kentucky Education Reform Act-required school councils. Most legislators didn't oppose his efforts, they just did not see the need until Neal pushed for and demonstrated the need and the benefit.

In the 2005 interim, Neal serves as a member of the Senate's Education Committee and serves on the Post-Secondary Subcommittee. He also serves on the Judiciary Committee and its Justice and Judiciary Subcommittee. As well, he is a newly-appointed member of the Banking and Insurance Committee and formerly chaired the Health and Welfare Committee. He has significant knowledge and expertise in revenue and budget issues as a former long-term member of the Senate Appropriations and Revenue Committee.

Gerald Neal was born in 1945, in Louisville, Kentucky. He is a graduate of Kentucky State University, where he majored in history and political science. He then attended law school at UofL. He has engaged in graduate studies in political science at the University of Michigan.

He worked as assistant director of public health and safety for the City of Louisville, as a hearing officer for the Kentucky Workers' Compensation Board and as a juvenile probation officer. He also served five terms as chairman of the Louisville-Jefferson County Metropolitan Sewer District.

He was admitted to the practice of law in 1973 and is a member of the law firm of Gerald A. Neal & Associates, Attorneys At Law, LLC. He was former vice president and regional director of the National Bar Association, and served as president of the local chapter. He has created several crime and drug prevention projects, and has served on many boards and commissions including the NAACP, Urban League, Community Action Agency and Louisville and Jefferson County Crime Commission. He is a member of the Sigma Pi Phi fraternity, Psi Boule chapter.

Neal has a good deal of international experience and service as well. He served as a United Nations observer/monitor for the historic 1994 elections in South Africa and has worked on several projects to support South African democracy. He has worked with Africare, a non-profit African aid organization, to enhance linkages between African and African-American communities. He has participated in several African/African-American Summits in Ghana, Senegal and Zimbabwe and has received many awards and honors over the years, including several life-time achievement awards. He was inducted into the Kentucky Civil Rights Hall of Fame in 2001.

Gerald Neal and his wife, Kathy Cooksie Neal, have two children, Brandon and Kristin.

Passing the Torch

I DON'T THINK I EVER CONSCIOUSLY DECIDED to become a leader. I think it was more a matter of wanting to contribute to the community and to achieve. I was brought up that way. My parents instilled in their children the love of God, the value of education, contributing to the community, helping others, standing up for our beliefs and never giving up. This, coupled with developing my own skills and applying them to opportunities that presented themselves, placed me from time to time in leadership positions. I got a lot of satisfaction out of engaging people and doing positive things. I think one thing led to another.

You know when you are active in something, and if you are consistent and persistent, then eventually you get recognized. People call on you more and more, and sometimes they ask you to do things you didn't anticipate. I think just being out there a long time, wanting to contribute and getting better at it, put me in a position to do things that you might call leadership. If you add to that planning, preparation and determination, growth and development is inevitable.

It helps to draw from those whose past has been productive. You can put them under the general category of mentors. That included anybody I observed. The most important mentors I had were my father and mother, Sterling and Mildred Neal. They brought all of their children, including me, up in such a way that we developed a commitment to community service and involvement in the civil rights movement and other types of justice-oriented movements. They shaped the way we carried out our everyday business. They also got us involved and interested in politics and other issues that they thought were beneficial to people. They taught by example. My father was very much involved at a high level. He, along with my mother, laid the foundation. I think they really sort of set the tone and, somewhat, the stage for how I functioned as a young man, and who I am today.

My father also encouraged me to talk to older, experienced, knowledgeable and productive people. People like Lyman Johnson, Joe Hammonds, William Summers III, Woodford Porter, Georgia Powers and others whom I came in contact with early on. I can remember those I just named, and others, always setting the example and always being available to me. I learned a great deal from them.

One thing I learned was the concept of fairness – that if I became engaged in something, I should always use the standard of whether or not it was fair. I learned the concept of justice – that whenever there was no justice, I should support the fight for justice. Every man, woman, and child deserves respect and justice.

My father used a perspective that he borrowed from a poem. He said that you should be able to walk with kings but not lose the common touch. He spoke of that a lot. You know sometimes you can lose perspective, or the people around you lose perspective, but the fact of the matter is that you want to be able to relate to all levels, because all people really fundamentally want and need the same things and deserve respect and justice.

Like most active people, I have had many accomplishments, some with significant ramifications, and others more modest in effect. It's hard to say what is my greatest success, but there are many satisfying accomplishments. I had a lot of satisfaction working with the National Bar Association, which is a national legal organization that is dedicated to issues of fairness and justice. I served as vice-president, parliamentarian, regional director and president of the Kentucky chapter of the National Bar Association. It actually expanded my horizons professionally, but also gave me an opportunity to exercise the principles I have embraced throughout my life.

My involvement in law has been my primary instrument in helping others, contributing and participating in a key arm of our democratic republic, and making a living. It is part and parcel of what I do in and outside of my office.

In the Senate, my most satisfying accomplishments have been, I think, in education. I was very proud to vote for and support the Kentucky Education Reform Act. I came along in the legislature just at that time. I was eventually appointed to the Senate Education Committee and I saw deficiencies in the Act — things that many thought would just rectify themselves, but didn't. So I got involved in sponsoring bills that ensured minority representation on school-based decision-making councils, because this is where a lot of decisions about school policies would be made. I've been involved in requiring schools to dis-aggregate their data as it relates to student achievement. I sponsored a bill that required that we be able to see where student achievement deficiencies were. If you don't understand or can't identify them, you can't correct them effectively.

I sponsored Senate Bill 168, which we called the Achievement Gap Bill, which required that schools make an assessment of student achievement deficiencies with respect to achievement gaps between various groups based on race, gender, disability or class. If it was found, schools were required to develop plans to significantly reduce the achievement gap. I consider that significant in the area of education, but more encompassing and otherwise consistent with federal No Child Left Behind legislation. I passed legislation to address minority teacher recruitment and minority representation on superintendent screening committees. I sponsored and co-sponsored many bills and initiatives, and supported other efforts behind the scenes and on the front lines.

In the area of the judiciary, my most satisfying work was my role in supporting and advancing juvenile laws, primarily through my sponsorship of a bill which updated juvenile law. In addition, I was encouraged by my participation on the Kentucky Justice Council where we dealt with juvenile and other justice issues.

For years I have fought to eliminate consideration of the death penalty for juveniles under the age of 18, although this was blocked in the Senate. The U.S. Supreme Court recently finally ruled the practice unconstitutional.

I successfully sponsored the Racial Justice Act, which allowed statistical data in a criminal trial, reviewed to determine whether race was used as a factor in subjecting a person to the implementation of the death penalty. If that was found, then the death penalty could not be imposed. I also successfully sponsored legislation banning racial profiling in the state of Kentucky. Legislation supporting and protecting our seniors has always been a part of my focus.

It has been and is a welcomed challenge to address the issues of our Commonwealth, Louisville, and my district, whether it is through the various committees I have served on, constituent service, working behind the scenes, on the floor of the Senate, by speaking to issues, or by vote.

On the issue of leadership, you must look at its components. Followership and leadership are two sides of the same coin. One doesn't exist without the other. Someone has to provide leadership. If you are part of a body that is trying to achieve an objective and you are not the leader, then you have to learn how to follow. They are different roles, but a good leader understands and appreciates the role of a follower. Without followers, you can't lead. It is clear that to be a good leader, you must also know how to be a good follower.

I try to lead by articulating the needs, outlining the mission, then hopefully selecting the people with the right skills, motivation and commitment. I try to focus, sustain and organize efforts and to lead by example, whenever useful. My leadership style is inclusive but focused. It is always helpful to identify people with similar views and ideas who can work with you. It's easier to stay focused on your objective; however, it is important to listen carefully to those who may not agree on various sub-parts of your strategy.

It's important for people to try to decide what they think is important and valuable in life, then they should try to develop skills in those areas. They need to be persistent. They must also, I think, be flexible in their thinking. You can get very rigid and caught up in your own press sometimes, and you never want to do that. It is like wearing blinders.

You also have to learn the technical aspects of leadership, however. Leadership is not just getting out there and saying, "You all come." You need to develop a lot of skills if you're going to be an effective leader. I don't think it's a matter of my suggesting what someone might do differently than what I have done. I think it is a learning process. But I think being prepared and involved, and being willing to learn as you go, is a critical part of it. If you have a good plan and you have selected good people to execute that plan, you are more likely to succeed.

If I were going to advise young people aspiring to leadership in our community, I would tell them to get involved in areas that they enjoy, and to support things that the community needs. I would inspire them to join with other people in trying to correct things that need correcting. I would tell them that the key to it is involvement, focus, consistency, passion and planning.

You have to be persistent and consistent when you make commitments. You have to keep those commitments if you possibly can to maintain credibility. And you have to involve yourself and use your skills. If you do that, people will recognize it. So if you develop consistency and persistence, and if you develop skills, stay focused, and strive to keep your word as you go forward, you will find that you will begin to rise in terms of recognition and perhaps even leadership. At least you will definitely develop better skills and satisfaction.

I think our community's quality of life has improved a great deal over the last 50 years. However, I think there is an aspect of our community that is still teetering on the edge, that has not benefited largely from what's happening.

If you look at Louisville as a corporate entity, I think you would have to say that it has advanced. Right now I'd say that it's just become a real city, and is trying to shrug its "town" image. It is actually cosmopolitan in some aspects. It hasn't broken totally away from some parts of its historical past, which gives it a little character. It has the location along the waterways that it is building upon. It has diverse industry, and some pretty strong players, if you are talking about entities like UPS, Churchill Downs, Brown-Forman, Ford, General Electric and others in the community. Many have kept a commitment to downtown and understand that the general health of the community is predicated upon the success of our downtown.

Louisville has some steadfast players. It also has some prospective things on the drawing board that it's fighting for, that I think are going to take it even further. Waterfront Park is a tremendous development. I know there are plans to expand it, too, in terms of park area. It's tied into other types of business and corporate facilities.

You can look at our health facilities downtown, whether it's Jewish Hospital, Norton's or Kosair. We have some of the top health facilities in the country. So I think there are a lot of things going for Louisville right now. At the same time, I think Louisville struggles, as many urban and rural areas do.

We must lift up every part of this community, and improve everyone's quality of life and access to resources if we are going to continue to move forward.

Our community's greatest challenge is including everyone in the advancements that Louisville is making. Not everyone is benefiting from this. We have an economic floor that is much too low and it translates into many problems within our community. I think that Louisville as it is now — with a merged government — was predicated upon a concept called unity which implies bringing the community together — everyone participating and enjoying in the benefits of that community. I don't think everyone benefits adequately yet.

I think people are out there now, dealing with this challenge. There are many grassroots initiatives, corporate initiatives, and governmental initiatives. We have corporate sponsors of cultural and educational initiatives. We have grassroots operations addressing issues regarding the environment. We actually now have the government of Louisville on the same page with an advocacy group supporting an environmental package to push for clean air for the future. These are all positive developments.

I think we are bringing these forces together. People are now putting on their agendas things that are across town on someone else's agenda, and they are recognizing the common benefits. This leads to ultimate solutions to many of our problems, and we're not just talking about operating in our narrow interests. We're beginning to see that addressing the community's interests from one end to the other is going to accrue to everyone's collective benefit. We need to think locally, and act globally. Think neighborhood, and act community.

J.D. NICHOLS

**Chairman
NTS Corporation,
its subsidiaries and affiliates**

THE NAME J.D. NICHOLS will go down in Louisville and Kentucky history for at least three things. He developed the Plainview subdivision off Hurstbourne Lane and set the residential and commercial tone for Louisville's eastward expansion. He was one of the catalysts behind the expansion of Louisville International Airport and played a key role in saving the UPS hub for Louisville – twice. And as chairman of the Kentucky Council on School Performance Standards, he played a role in guiding the 1990 Kentucky Education Reform Act (KERA) along a constructive and ultimately successful course.

Only the first task was undertaken in pursuit of his main occupation. His company, NTS Corporation, is a multi-million-dollar development operation which has developed over seven million square feet of commercial and residential properties and 8,000 acres of land in 11 major markets throughout the midwest and southeast United States. Plainview essentially got it started.

But Nichols sees a strong connection between his development business and the other two accomplishments. Education, he told *Business First* in 1991 when the standards council was setting its agenda, "is an economic development issue." And a critical one for companies such as his, he said. Employment depends on education, and economic growth depends on new employment.

Nichols has served on the Prichard Committee for Academic Excellence, the Partnership for Kentucky Schools and chaired the Council for Education Technology. He urges education leaders to market education like he markets homes and commercial buildings. "Explain the cost-benefit ratio of education," he said. "Make the public realize that education is a benefit and not just a cost."

His attitude was similar when he worked on the airport expansion project, which ultimately led UPS to grow its operations in Louisville into the city's and Kentucky's largest employer.

A pilot himself, Nichols became alarmed in 1987 when a consultant told the airport authority its plan for paralleled runways wouldn't fly. Without paralleled runways, Nichols said, UPS would leave and Louisville would die. It would "blow every chance that we ever had to be anybody," and that would also, of course, be bad for the building industry.

So Nichols thought up some ideas of his own on how the project could be done, hired some engineers to check them out and called a meeting of city leaders to put them on the table. Ultimately, his plan wasn't chosen, but another plan was developed, and then-County Judge Harvey Sloane gave Nichols the credit. "He got us off the dime," Sloane said.

Later, when the airport had been updated and UPS still was worried about finding enough employees, Nichols spurred the creation of the Metropolitan Scholars Program, a partnership with UofL, that paid for college or post-high school technical training for students in the Metropolitan College Program who also worked part-time for UPS.

J.D. Nichols was born in Erie, Pennsylvania in 1942, and came to Louisville in 1954 when his father transferred here with General Electric. He is a graduate of Fern Creek High School and the University of Louisville's Brandeis School of Law. He also studied business at the University of Kentucky.

He left a management trainee program at GE to join some friends who were building houses in the early 1960s and formed NTS with two partners in 1968. Plainview was their first development and it was Louisville's first totally planned community. Other projects followed, including Lake Forest, Owl Creek, Oxmoor Woods and Sutherland. Nichols is a long-time member of the Home Builders Association of Louisville and was named their "Builder of the Year" in 1984.

He currently is chairman of the Louisville Regional Airport Authority and a director of Greater Louisville Inc. He has served on the Governor's Council on Economic Development and on the boards of a number of community organizations as well: the University of Louisville's Board of Trustees, Board of Overseers and Foundation; Actors Theatre of Louisville; the Kentucky Opera; the Louisville Zoo; Kosair Children's Hospital; and the Home of the Innocents. He is also a lifetime member of Bellarmine University's President's Society.

Nichols and his wife, Barbara, have three daughters.

I NEVER DECIDED TO BECOME a leader in the community; however, I have had leadership roles in some important community projects that some people might think are significant accomplishments for our city – the airport expansion would be one of those projects.

I've never really considered the development projects I have worked on all my life as a big deal. I am a lawyer by education. I never took the bar exam and never intended to practice law; I went to law school to learn the analytical thought process. In fact, I owned a business while attending law school – a pizza restaurant.

I worked in an Italian restaurant from the age of 13 through high school and that was my early grounding in business. My father transferred to Louisville with General Electric (GE) when I was young. I thought I might work my way through the ranks at GE too when I was young, but I really only worked there because of my dad and stayed only 11 weeks.

While there I was in this fabulous GE marketing training program, which turned out to be a fiasco. The supervisors learned that I was building homes and running my restaurant business on the side, and told me I would have to give it up. I was making considerably more money outside GE than I was inside GE, so obviously I chose the restaurant and building business.

Because my dad did not have a college degree, it was always a big issue with him. He wanted me to attend college and then go to work at GE, because he thought that if he had been able to earn a degree, he would have been able to rise higher in the ranks there. He did fairly well despite that, but I went to GE to appease him.

When I was just a kid in high school, I learned a lot from the man I worked for in the restaurant business, although I learned more of what not to do than what to do. For example, if he met with a lawyer he would try to tell the lawyer how to practice law. He was just one of those people who didn't take advice very well and didn't consult with other people. I learned a lot from his mistakes.

It was an interesting thing. I actually ran and managed a restaurant when I was 15 years old – not by design, but the man I worked for had two restaurants and the manager at the one where I worked had quit. He couldn't find a replacement, so for about six months I literally ran the restaurant. I worked 80 hours a week and went to school at the same time. I worked seven days a week through my senior year, until my girlfriend started wanting a little more of my time.

I never really had any mentors after that. I had business partners and friends, but no mentors. My father was not really a mentor. The truth is, I probably ran the family after I was 25 or 30 years old.

J.D. Nichols

I started off as a homebuilder with no others employees, just me. I was the bookkeeper, the sales manager and everything else. My undergraduate education really helped, since I had majored in business, thankfully.

I don't actively run my real estate development business and haven't for 20 years. I have always had somebody in the position of chief operating officer, and currently my partner, Brian Lavin, fills that role, as well as my former role as chief executive officer. I am more the financial guy and am pretty strong in that area, but I know that I'm not a very good manager, so I've surrounded myself with good people to manage our business.

The reason I know that I'm not a very good manager is because I know the process you have to go through. You meet at the first of the month to set goals and objectives, and then you meet at the end of the month to measure how well you have met those goals and objectives. By the end of the month I would have forgotten our goals and objectives. I have always had somebody work with me who is a professional manager and has been trained in this process.

About 30 or 35 years ago we would recruit IBM or Xerox people for these management positions, because they were well-trained marketers and managers. We built the Xerox office building that was located down the street from our offices, so we knew all the Xerox guys and recruited as many of them as we could.

The most significant accomplishment I've been involved with in the community was the expansion of Louisville's airport to keep United Parcel Service (UPS) from leaving Louisville in the late 1980s. The second most significant was the retention of the UPS hub when it threatened to move elsewhere in 1998.

I, like many others, thought that expanding the airport was an economic necessity for every business in our community. UPS and their air hub were going to drive our economy. Obviously, I knew what Federal Express had done for Memphis and I knew that UPS would do the same thing for Louisville.

The airport expansion took a lot of effort, time, and money. NTS actually paid for the initial engineering. At the time, (Jefferson County judge-executive) Harvey Sloane was very helpful. He was more instrumental in that process than a lot of people gave him credit for. Harvey wanted to appoint me to the Board of the Regional Airport Authority and I said, "No, you can't do that," because I wouldn't be able to do the things that I was doing behind the scenes if I was a member of the Board. It's not that anybody was trying to be secretive about things, but there just wasn't enough time to go through a ten-year process to determine what our community wanted. Somebody had to drive the boat!

I was also very involved in KERA (Kentucky Educational Reform Act).

Governor Wallace Wilkinson had sent me his education proposal and asked me to comment on it. Like a fool, I wrote him a ten-page letter full of comments. I didn't hear back from him – I don't remember the exact time span – until probably a year later. I was on my boat in the Virgin Islands and the captain came down and said, "You've got a call from the governor." I said, "Which governor?" It was Wallace! We had a long-range communications system on the boat and they tracked me down. During the conversation he asked me if I would chair his KERA initiative – the Kentucky Education Reform Act – and I said, "Wallace, I don't really know." Well, long story short, he twisted my arm a bit, so when I returned to Louisville we met, and I told him under what conditions I would accept the position. Actually, I met with his secretary of education and he said, "Well, this is what we are going to do." So I went to Wallace and said, "Wallace, if I'm going to chair this, I'm not going to be just the front guy," and he said, "I understand." Well anyway, I ended up doing that for about three years and it was almost a full-time job.

When you said "doctor in the room" to the group I chaired, everybody got to stand up except me. I learned a lot about education chairing that group and, actually, my own law school education really helped me. I coined a phrase, "application of knowledge as opposed to the accumulation of knowledge." In undergraduate school we memorized and regurgitated information. During my college days, I could go to class only half the time during the semester, stay up all night during final week memorizing all of the material, and made A's and B's. I never had to work very hard and still achieved a 3.4 or 3.5 GPA in undergraduate school.

Law school was different. You learn something and you have to apply it, as opposed to just memorizing and regurgitating it. It was an interesting change in learning. I got the first D of my life in law school.

KERA was all about measuring learning results. I will take responsibility for that. When we started pushing KERA educators were saying, "Huh? We don't know about this," but they finally came around and supported it.

In my opinion, what gets measured gets done. When I was in school we learned that adding two and two made four and we would ask, "Why do I have to know that?" The teachers would say, "Because I said so." What we tried to do with KERA was to explain to the child the benefit of learning whatever he or she was being taught.

Someone said, "But how are you going to show the benefit of learning percentages and things like that?" This probably isn't the best example, but let's say that Suzy and Johnny are walking down the street and there are two ice cream stores. The store on the right side says that ice cream cones are 50% off and the store on the left side has no discount. The child who knows what 50% off means knows that he can get two ice cream cones for the price of one.

This is teaching them the benefits of learning at a level they can relate to, instead of just saying it's something they have to know.

I haven't really had a major failure, but I've had a few disappointments. In hindsight, anyone can go back and say, "If I had known then what I know today." I have made some mistakes that have caused me to lose money on some business deals, but that's just part of life. Some of them were significant financially, but as long as you win more than you lose it all works out.

Like many others, we had a tough time for a period in the '70s during the oil embargo. That was 30 years ago, so I would have been in my early 30s. I had been in business a few years by then and honestly don't have any idea how we made it through those tough times. We had a chief financial officer who would say we made payroll every week, and at times, I don't know how we did it. After that period was over I said that I never wanted to be in debt again. It didn't work out quite that way, but we substantially reduced our debt to equity ratio.

I don't think I've surrounded myself with followers. The people who work with me, for the most part, are not followers. I like everybody I work with to voice his or her opinions. We don't like people who are just "yes people."

The only thing that I would probably do differently if I could live my business life over again, is I would not build any golf courses. We built only two, but that was enough. I think the problem was that we just didn't understand the golf course business; we understood the land development business. We stayed away from golf courses for a long time and still did very well. I don't know who decided to develop the golf courses or how it all came to pass, but I'll take the blame. While the golf courses and country clubs we built are beautiful additions to the communities we built them in, they were not successful financially.

What actually happened is we took over a failing development in Orlando, Florida that had a golf course. When we bought the development we valued the course as a negative $1 million. We didn't think it was worth anything and looked at it as a million-dollar liability. Consequently we subtracted $1 million dollars from the purchase price of the development.

We ran the golf course, fixed it up, and probably spent $1 million dollars or so on it. Then some Japanese investors came along and bought the course from us. We ended up making $4 or $5 million dollars from it, so we decided that developing golf courses might not be so bad after all. We built the next two courses at the same time; one in Louisville at Lake Forest and the other in Washington, DC., but we lost the $5 million that we had previously made and probably $25 million more on the new courses.

If I were going to give advice to young people today who are aspiring to a leadership position, I would tell them to develop a lot of contacts and get people to respect their opinions. The ability to get people to answer your phone call is extremely important.

You want people to listen to you. I will refer back to the airport expansion as an example. If I had not been able to get David Jones, Jerry Abramson, and others on the phone because I already knew them personally, then I wouldn't have been able to get the group together that saved the airport expansion project.

We had a meeting at NTS' corporate offices and we assembled everybody, including the top UPS people who flew in from Boston. I had already met one-on-one with all of the participants from Louisville and the meeting went very well. In the end, we made it happen.

David Jones was very helpful with the process. Previously, when he was putting the Presbyterian headquarters deal together, he called me and wanted to know if NTS could do something to help, so we offered discounts on lots and houses for all of the Presbyterian employees, and also raised some money for the project. The airport expansion was my project and when I called David to ask for his assistance, he more than reciprocated because of our help with his project.

Most of NTS' local development has been in eastern Jefferson County. Plainview was our first large land development. With my partners at the time, Dick Thurman and David Carney, we developed LaFontenay Apartments, which was really the first very large, "hot" apartment complex in Louisville. (All of the divorcees moved there after they got divorced.)

The Tways, who owned the Plainview Dairy Farm, knew Buzz Bush and Sam Miller, and contacted them regarding their interest in purchasing the farm. Buzz and Sam dabbled with real estate, but really didn't have land development experience. Having heard of our development experience with LaFontenay they approached us. That's how we got involved.

I think the Tway farm had around 700 acres – we're going back 35 years or so. That was really our first big entry into land development, but it's not nearly the size of Lake Forest, of course. We started Lake Forest in 1982 and there will be 2,000 homes in the development when we're finished with it. It's not very far from being finished – probably a year or year and a half.

Unfortunately, you can't develop these large properties in today's times with economics the way they are. The cost of land has gotten so high you just can't afford it. The only possible way you can do it today is if it's a project like Norton Commons, where the landowner is sort of a partner in it. At this stage in my life, however, I'm not sure I want that kind of challenge. I'm 80 percent retired, more or less, but I'm always going to stay involved. As long as I have my faculties, I will never completely retire.

I think the biggest challenge facing our city in the future is going to be attracting high-paying jobs. Louisville is a nice place to live. I think the retention of talent is an issue we can all relate to, but without opportunity we are not going to retain the really bright young adults.

I'm proud of the program we created for United Parcel Service (UPS) to help them recruit the workers they needed for their hub here – the Metropolitan Scholars Program. It was a group effort. We initially began the process by trying to establish how to make a full-time job out of part-time jobs, so that UPS could say, "Okay, if you work at UPS from 1:00 a.m. to 5:00 a.m. and you work at McDonalds from X to X, it ends up a full-time job." I didn't think that made a lot of sense.

I knew that UPS' preference was to use students to fill those part-time night jobs, so what made a lot more sense to me was to create a program that would enable you to take kids who might not otherwise have an opportunity to attend college and provide them with that opportunity. At one point in time 80 to 90 percent of the people filling the night shift sorting jobs at UPS were students, and 10 to 20 percent were from the general population. In recent years this had reversed – they were losing their ability to attract students. What we needed to do was create a program that offered potential students a package deal including school tuition, housing, and a part-time job to cover their other expenses.

Prior to the Metropolitan Scholars Program, I had heard that one of the problems discouraging the University of Louisville (UofL) students from working at UPS at night was the class times. Take an algebra class, as an example. The only time they offered the class was at 8:00 a.m. in the morning. So now you have a student who has been working all night and has to take an early morning algebra class, because it is the only time it's offered. Algebra is a brain-mangling course anyway with no flexibility, so I talked to Governor Paul Patton about it. Paul was a friend, and I shared our ideas with him and the possibility of organizing a meeting with UofL President John Shumaker, as well as the head of Jefferson Community College and the vocational schools. Paul understood the importance of solving UPS' problem and had the meeting called quickly. I had reviewed everything with Paul and what we were trying to do with the University to make it more flexible. I give John Shumaker a lot of credit – he jumped on it. During the meeting he said, "Yes, we'll do this." So the program evolved to allow the students who would go to work for UPS to get their college tuition and housing paid for, in exchange for sticking with their night jobs. They also received a nice paycheck to cover their other expenses. The theory was that UPS could get all the help they wanted. All you had to do was make the recruiting circle bigger, because it was an opportunity for young adults to get an education that they otherwise wouldn't have.

It worked. It reversed the problem. UPS had an 85 percent turnover rate on that night shift before the creation of the Metropolitan Scholars Program — now they have 85 percent retention and only 15 percent turnover.

UPS' biggest concern was that in five or ten years there weren't going to be enough people to supply the workforce they needed. The Metropolitan Scholars Program solved that problem. The program was good for the students, good for UPS, good for UofL, and good for Kentucky. Steve Higdon, who is now president of Greater Louisville Inc., should also get a lot of credit for his efforts regarding this program.

Transportation is going to be a big issue in our city's future. We (the Louisville Regional Airport Authority) have tried very hard to get more flights out of Louisville and worked forever to get a hub here, but now the hub concept is not working for the airlines and existing hubs are being closed or reduced in size, so there is little likelihood that Louisville will ever become a hub.

A lot of people don't know this, but Delta Airlines' choice for their hub was Louisville, not Cincinnati. I was told by Delta's president at the time, that unfortunately our leadership basically said to them, "We don't want you." Delta had a number of reasons for preferring Louisville. They wanted to be out of the northern flow that was flying from Chicago to New York, and they also wanted to be out of the lake effect of snow and ice, a problem that you incur in Cincinnati. Our weather is much better, but Delta's president told me that when they came to Louisville, the leadership at our airport said, "We don't want your stinking airplanes here." People would probably deny that today, but that was back in the late '70s or early '80s.

We're still going to have some hubs - we have to. Otherwise, there will be numerous places we can't get to. Southwest Airlines is wonderful and they do a great job, but you can't get to South America; you can't get to the Caribbean; you can't get to Europe, and you can't get to Asia or the Middle East on Southwest Airlines.

Additional advice I would give young people who are aspiring to leadership positions in the community is to get enough respect from other people who live here, and to try to get something accomplished that causes people to recognize them. The most important thing that anybody can do is to develop the ability to get somebody to listen to what they have to say. I really don't know how to tell you to do this. In my case I was very fortunate early in life, having built a fairly large and successful business, which had a way of getting everybody to say, "Hey I'll talk to him." If somebody doesn't have early financial success, however, I think they can still be capable of getting people to listen, but they have to do it politically or through community involvement. I don't know if that's the way it should be, but it's reality.

Jim Thornton of Thornton Oil Corporation had 150 gas stations at one time and he would look for certain numbers. He knew at each type of station what the labor cost per gallon of gas sold should be; this one at 1.3 cents a gallon - that one at 1.6 cents a gallon, etc., and if it was out of that range then he knew something was wrong. These were just rules of thumb and I think they apply to any business. I'm sure David Jones has some brackets he watches and he knows things ought to be this way or that way. I don't know the business, so I don't know what those parameters should be.

Anyone I've ever known who has been successful in business, however, especially in an entrepreneurial business, has to have a feel. If you have to call the accounting department to ask them to tell you where you stand, then you have a serious problem. I fight that problem here today. I ask people questions and they say that I have to talk to the accounting department. It is my opinion that you have to have a gut feeling or basic understanding of where you are at all times to be successful in business.

Most of my decisions were made by a combination of gut feelings along with a lot of study and knowledge of the market. When we bought the first section of Lake Forest out on Shelbyville Road, Dan Ulmer was chairman of Citizens Fidelity Bank. He said, "You're nuts! You're absolutely crazy!" He thought the site was so far out in the country that it would never be successful. He probably wouldn't remember that he ever made that statement, but that was in '80 or '81 and I'll never forget it. We knew the market and had analyzed the project in depth. Drive out to Lake Forest today and tell me if we were right or wrong.

ANNE M. NORTHUP

**Member
U.S. House of Representatives
Third Congressional District
of Kentucky**

ANNE MEAGHER NORTHUP FIRST BECAME widely known in the Louisville area in 1986 as the older sister of Olympic gold medal swimmer Mary T. Meagher and a candidate for a seat in the Kentucky House of Representatives. She won her first election and quickly made a name for herself as a gutsy Republican state rep who took on tobacco in a tobacco state because she wanted to reduce its use by young people and generate revenue by taxing it more heavily.

In 1996, two years after a Republican revolution captured the U.S House of Representatives in Washington, Northup decided to try to unseat freshman Democratic Congressman Mike Ward. She quickly raised more money than any other GOP House challenger in the country and, buoyed by a reputation from the state legislature as an intense and thorough worker, came from a June standing of 33 points down in the polls to beat Ward in the general election in November.

She was welcomed with open arms by the Republican House majority and was immediately placed on the prestigious Appropriations Committee. She made the most of it, applying to the job what supporters and even some critics described as a blend of intelligence, toughness, political savvy, hard work and, in general, support for Republican positions.

She became known as a polished, articulate congresswoman, who has been able to raise increasing amounts of money to win re-election to her congressional seat four consecutive times.

She has also been able to raise big bucks in Congress for her hometown. As a member of the powerful Appropriations Committee in the House, for example, she was recently able to insert $96.3 million in the fiscal year 2004-05 federal budget for local projects – including $68.5 million for continuing the replacement of the McAlpine Lock, $4.5 million to build the spiraling mound at Waterfront Park that will help connect the

Big Four Bridge with Indiana, $4.6 million to upgrade Louisville's Olmsted parks and parkways, $7 million to improve drainage and sewers throughout Jefferson County, hundreds of thousands of dollars for local churches for outreach, tutoring and after-school programs, and $2 million for the Ohio River bridges project, *The Courier-Journal* reported in December of 2004.

Mayor Jerry Abramson called the funding a "home run" for Louisville. She has also helped the city secure $20 million in Hope VI funding to pay for redeveloping the Clarksdale housing complex, $98 million for airport volunteer relocation, and $750,000 to equip police cars with mobile data terminals.

The Courier-Journal, a newspaper that does not often endorse Republicans, did endorse Northup for re-election in 2004, largely because of her ability to bring so much federal funding back to her hometown.

Anne Northup was born in Louisville in 1948 and grew up in St. Matthews, one of 11 children – 10 girls and one boy. She graduated from Sacred Heart Academy, and met her husband – Robert "Woody" Northup, who owns an electronics company – while she was a student at St. Mary's College in Notre Dame, Indiana. She graduated with a BA in economics and business in 1970.

Northup taught math at Atherton High School briefly after her marriage and worked a short time for Ford Motor Company before withdrawing from the work force to raise their six children.

She re-entered the work force as an aide to a Republican state legislator a year before running for her own seat. Besides fighting tobacco, she focused on helping business, creating jobs and improving education. She succeeded in eliminating state tax deductions for private clubs that discriminate on racial or other grounds and in getting girls' fast-pitch softball into the state's high schools.

In Washington, Northup now sits on three Appropriations subcommittees – Labor, Health and Human Services, Education; Transportation, Treasury, and Housing and Urban Development; Military Quality of Life and Veterans Affairs.

She is the founder and co-chair of the House Reading Caucus, a bipartisan caucus that raises awareness about the number of children who are failing to learn to read.

She is also a member of the Congressional Caucus on Adoption and is a proponent of legislation that promotes adoption.

I AM NOT SURE I EVER MADE A CONSCIOUS DECISION to become a community leader. I just wanted to participate in my church, my neighborhood, and my children's schools. I always got involved and often I would find myself chair of a committee or PTA president.

I have had an interest in public policy all my life. I have asked, "What does the community look like and need – the immediate community and the community at-large – the city, state, country? What are our challenges and our opportunities?"

As my children got a little older, I decided I wanted to get involved in public policy. Originally, I wanted to do research – analyze a situation, write it up, and work for someone else who would take action on it. But when the opportunity to run for office came, I took it.

The people who inspired me most were my dad and Ronald Reagan. My dad was a mentor. He was always involved in the community. He believed you could make a difference. He was very optimistic and encouraged all of us to take risks, to try. Ronald Reagan was more of an example and an inspiration. He always tried to reduce division and bring people together, but he stuck with his principles. With public policy, you cannot just add together everybody's different positions, average them out, and implement the result. Ronald Reagan understood that. He led from a principled position. He had a very clear idea of what was good for this country. But he also engaged people who did not necessarily share his political views to try to explain to them why a particular policy would make a positive difference in their lives.

It is hard to imagine how others would describe my leadership style, but I would say it consists of four principles: work hard; learn a lot; listen to advice; and seize the moment. In big things and even in smaller things, there is a moment when everything turns on what a leader does. If you haven't prepared yourself by practicing these principles, it passes – for better or worse.

For example, consider the legislative battle surrounding the so-called Patient's Bill of Rights. Going down that path would have driven the cost of insurance up very high. While there have been some problems with health-care insurance, the cost of insurance was an even bigger problem. So I opposed the Patient's Bill of Rights legislation. It was a hard stand to take originally; so few people were willing to do that. Yet today, nobody even talks about passing a Patient's Bill of Rights, because most people understand that it would be the worst way to try to solve the problem.

The ergonomics issue came along in exactly the same way. In this case, the government wrote regulations to force companies doing business in this country to absorb extraordinary costs for injuries they did not cause. These costs would only make it harder to keep as many jobs in this country as possible, which is the much bigger issue. While passing the regulations might have given everyone a sense of accomplishing something, it would have damaged the job outlook in the long term. Standing against the ergonomics bill was unpopular in the beginning; but by discussing it in depth, working with people, and building a coalition, those of us who opposed it prevailed.

It is very important to get to know a lot about an issue and to understand it fully. You obviously cannot do that with every issue, but when there is a situation that needs a good knowledgeable leader, the leader must seize the moment. In this way, I was able to play a small role and make a difference in some big issues, such as the Ohio River bridges project and the Kentucky Education Reform Act (KERA).

In considering the most significant local issues with which I have been involved since coming to Washington, two come to mind. First, inviting faith-based organizations to become part of the solution in delivering social services. When I was first elected to Congress, there were parallel but separate delivery systems for social services – the government on the one hand and faith-based organizations on the other. Joining these two service delivery systems together, inviting the faith-based organizations to become part of the solution that government previously had tried to monopolize, has begun to change our community for the better.

The other significant issue that is impacting the Louisville community is the Ohio River bridges project. I watched this project for years. When I was first elected to the Kentucky General Assembly in 1987, the bridges project was part of the six-year road plan. Then, despite widespread support, it was taken out of the six-year road plan due to the work of a small group who opposed the project. Someone needed to step forward and emphasize why the community needed this project. It needed defining – its scope, various stages, and its impact. It needed a leader who stays focused, wades into the details and complications, and makes the effort to move it forward. Otherwise, people would never get their arms around the issue.

I learned something important from both of these experiences. One is best summed up by the old saying, "How do you eat an elephant? One bite at a time." When our community confronts a major challenge, you have to chip away at it. Work at it, be sure to stay a part of it, but remember it will often take time and patience. Inevitably, there will be setbacks, conflicts, tradeoffs to build consensus, and delays that will disappoint you.

We are not going to get two new Ohio River bridges overnight. It would be a failure of leadership, however, if we in Louisville lost our focus on this project – at least until we start pouring concrete – because these bridges could still slip away from us. We have to seize this moment. That is so important.

So the first idea I would like to share with the next generation of leaders in our community is: stay involved, work hard every day on big challenges, and never relax. You have to know a lot about these issues to have an impact. You cannot just persuade Congress to appropriate money – in fact, that may be the easiest part. The hardest part is to work through the challenges, to overcome the inevitable setbacks. This takes hard work; it is not magic.

You will run into disappointments. For example, in working with faith-based organizations, there have been times when it just hasn't been possible to get a project to work, or to get it to work quickly enough, despite everyone's good intentions. At other times, programs have not materialized effectively, even though Congress and others provided the funding.

There is no question that my biggest disappointment in Washington has been the degree of partisanship. It may be different today, but when I was in the state legislature in Frankfort, the type of partisanship I now see in Washington, D.C. simply did not exist.

For a very long time, it was clear that every single day, a significant number of people on the other side of the aisle in Washington, D.C., were watching every word I said with one goal: How do we defeat her? They did not want to be friends. They did not want to be partners. They just wanted to win the seat back, so they campaigned against me.

Opponents have unfairly accused me of everything from putting arsenic in water to sending good jobs to China. Politics is a very rough business. But you cannot let partisanship obstruct what you are trying to accomplish and the good things you are trying to make happen in your community. You have to be tough. You have to be very tough.

The first step in becoming a good leader is to be a good follower. Good followers carry out their responsibilities, and they do it well. They do it better than anybody thinks possible. Good followers not only follow through on everything they are asked to do, but they carry it to the next step. They gain wisdom by being part of the team, then use that wisdom to develop insights that help the whole team accomplish more. They understand that the whole is made up of all the parts, and that the completeness of each one of those parts results in a better whole. Also, when a person takes the next step – providing new insights and doing more than he or she was asked to do – that person helps the whole. That is what good followers do.

So leadership starts early, with small things. You do not simply start being a leader by becoming the mayor, or a member of Congress. Sometimes people look for the "grand" and miss the "not-so-grand," or the detail that is key to a problem's solution.

Anne M. Northup

One way to enter the "circle" of leadership is to help somebody, whether at your workplace or in the classroom. Some people want to run the world, but they do not want to clean the chalkboards after school, or help clean up after the prom. There are many ways to pitch in.

People's leadership potential becomes more apparent by the quality of the job they do and by their ability to organize a task and move it forward. It is not hard to find a seat at the table unless you are trying to start at the top. But whatever your current niche, whether as a follower or a leader, it is very important that you do the best you can.

Young people aspiring to leadership — whether they want to be a leader or a participant — can start participating now, wherever they are. Younger children — say sixth-graders — can start being a leader on Mother's Day. Plan the dinner, and see if you and others in the home can bake the cake, make a card or plant some flowers. Do something that you organize, because it will make Mother's Day entirely different.

If you are a student, the same thing applies in your classroom. If there is a field trip, someone will have to plan it, collect the money and help make it happen. Someone must take the leadership role and ask, "Do you think we should make a card for the bus driver? Do we want to take pictures along the way and make a scrapbook?" Then recruit someone to take the pictures and someone to mount them.

You can practice leadership at any point. Without it, life goes on, but does not have the fullness that leadership can bring to it. Generally, the people who are the most effective leaders have served in other capacities first. I was a mom first, for example, before I was a PTA president. I learned about education, health care and so many things because I was involved in them everyday. At the time, I did not think of that as training, but today I look back on it and recognize that those roles brought me knowledge and wisdom.

When I became a state legislator, I gained new insight about everything from road construction to health care policy to education policy — the federal component, the state component, the needs of the rural communities versus the urban communities, and the relationships that make legislative bodies work better. The General Assembly was a good place to learn about these issues and to participate in legislative dynamics — experiences that have been invaluable during my time in Congress.

Some people think, "I want to know how to run for Congress," or "I want to be the mayor or the governor." What we need in those offices are the best people, people who understand all perspectives. The place to start is not at the top, however. You have to start by getting academic and real-world knowledge, and you have to learn to work with people who may think differently than you do.

The most significant contribution impact on our community's development during the last 50 years was United Parcel Service's decision to locate its hub in Louisville. That brought a tremendous amount of investment into our community and a new foundation of good state-of-the-art jobs. I did not play a role in that, but I work hard to help UPS stay on top.

Trade is growing. It is important that UPS remain a part of that wave of growth into the future. So I try to help ensure that the airport grows and that the federal government designates it an international port of entry with customs inspectors. I am very involved with that issue today. UPS is an enormous economic engine for this community in ways that many may not even realize. Not everybody's paycheck comes from UPS, but many workers – our neighbors – have good jobs because of UPS.

Our community's biggest challenge is how to foster future economic growth and development. Communities that are on the leading edge of a new technology often gain a significant long-term economic advantage as that technology expands and matures. Look at Silicon Valley and the computer software industry, for example. Because much of the early work took place there, it became a sort of industry hub.

Such leading-edge communities import money, investment and jobs, rather than exporting them. They develop a synergy that brings additional growth and investment. Our area must be the producer of something important, not just a consumer of what other communities produce.

We need to find a cutting-edge technology today and put the Louisville area in the forefront of its development. Right now, for example, there is an explosion of investment in the health-care industry – everything from biochemical companies to pharmaceutical firms. We must find ways to make Louisville the location of choice for high-tech health-care companies and put the infrastructure in place to make that happen. We have to be proactive; otherwise, we will always be playing catch-up in the competition for jobs.

Seize the moment. Opportunities come along and you cannot just tread water. If you do not seize the opportunity, it will pass you by. In order to do that, you have to take risks. That is true regardless of leadership position.

Leadership challenges often take you into unfamiliar territory. In those cases, your job as a leader is to blaze a new trail, based on the knowledge you have gained from others. For example, when I decided to run for state representative, I started knocking on doors, introducing myself. When people asked me, "Is that how you run for the legislature?" I replied, "Well, that is what I am going to do." There was not really a textbook to check. I had my own plan, based on years of involvement.

It is the same way with issues. For example, while in the Kentucky General Assembly, I became involved with the tobacco issue. I approached it from the standpoint of public health. I asked, "Why does Kentucky have the highest death rate? Why do we have the highest health-care costs? Why do we have the most smokers?" The answer to all three questions was our close affinity with, and appreciation for, tobacco's economic benefits. I started looking at those benefits and asked, "Will they last forever?" And the answer was "No." The tobacco companies were leaving Kentucky behind.

This was important to our state, so I learned as much as I could about the issue. Some people look for power by elbowing others out of the way or by just demanding it. My approach is to take an issue that I really care about and learn as much about it as anybody else. That gives you the confidence to speak up at meetings. When you thoroughly understand an issue, you can better define the solution.

But you cannot be an authority on everything. In fact, it is hard to give up and say you are not going to know as much as others do about a certain issue because you are going to concentrate on other areas. You have to choose your battles.

Right now, there is another significant issue for which I would like to help develop a solution – that is making Social Security sustainable so it will be there for our children. I will spend more time researching this issue, talking to people who are already involved, and then I will go from there. You have to assess what the emerging issues are at given periods. That means doing the research.

You should never think that an issue is going to be "served up" to you. Occasionally someone may invite you to be the "go to" person on an issue. But most often, leadership is not handed to you, and that is especially true for women in public office. I was part of many women's organizations. Often, these organizations selected female leaders by consensus, rather than through the hard knocks of a campaign. However, it does not happen that way in politics. If you are waiting for someone to invite you to run for state representative, forget it. There are ten men out there who want to be state representative. You have to step up on your own and say, "I am going to run for office." Even if someone asks you to run for office, you must rise to the challenge, devise a campaign strategy, and execute it. You must seize the moment, take the initiative and the risk, then define a route to your goal.

Being bold does not mean you plunge ahead on a pre-determined path and never make assessments or corrections. Sometimes you pursue a path only to reach a point where the best choice is no longer viable and you need new solutions or directions. As a leader, you must decide what that new direction should be.

Passing the Torch

I have learned a number of lessons in leadership:

First, surround yourself with people whom you trust and who are good advisers. My husband is one. He is very insightful, he is well read, and he knows the issues and cares about them. Select good people to work for you. Terry Carmack and Sherri Craig are very sound advisors. So are my campaign chairman and campaign manager. But you have to do more. You must actually take their advice. Sometimes, when you are in the middle of a battle, it is hard to step back and get the big picture. If you have trustworthy people around you who ask, "Why don't you take another look at that?" you are much more able to do so. You still decide the final route, but with good advice that you trust, you can avoid cliffs and blind alleys.

Second, you must develop balance in your life. You always have to work for that. You cannot lose sight of what is going on in your personal life. If your professional life is disorganized, it will affect your personal life. If things are not in order at home, that disorder spills over into your career.

I love being the mother of six kids. It is an adventure and the most important part of me. But there are challenges. My children are great kids, and they are hilarious. I had to make sure I met their needs just as I had to respond to the demands of being a state representative. When one of my children had a science project, I had to make time to sit down with my child and say, "Here is the plan for the science fair. What do we need? We will go to the library, we have to plant the seeds, and we will do the posters." Knowing I had done what I should for the children meant I could concentrate on being a good state representative while I was in Frankfort.

There is a lot more freedom for women today, but we should never think we are so super that we can do everything our mothers did and still have a career.

My dad, who recently passed away, always saw life as an adventure. Even in tough times, his attitude was to roll up your sleeves and work through it. He always looked at things with a sense of humor and optimism. If you want to be a leader, even in your own campaigns for public office, you have to maintain your optimism, confidence, and sense of humor. Do not think that what you do in legislative leadership is the sole description of who you are. It may not even be the most important description of you.

I always remind myself at the end of a campaign that no matter what happens, I am still going to be a mom. I am still going to be the daughter of two parents I love and haven't seen often enough. I am still going to be Woody's wife, and he is still going to love me. That gives me a perspective that makes everything else seem less desperate. It does not mean that there is not a night in every campaign when I lie awake, worried about the campaign. But remembering those other important parts of my life makes getting through the campaign a lot easier.

David C. Novak

**Chairman, CEO and President
Yum! Brands, Inc.**

THERE'S A GUY IN EVERY OFFICE who entertains his co-workers with fun things like rubber chickens or cheese hats or chattering teeth. At Yum! Brands, Inc., a world-wide $9 billion company with 34,000 restaurants now in over 100 countries and territories, that guy is David C. Novak, chairman, president and CEO.

He started his light-hearted fun when he was president of KFC (hence, the chickens) and also president of Pizza Hut (ergo, the cheese head hats). Novak would go around and hand them out to employees who had done well, wanting both to recognize their efforts and to create an impression that they worked for a company where people are appreciated and like to have fun. After he started doing it, sales went up.

Then Pepsico Inc. spun off KFC and Pizza Hut with Taco Bell to form Tricon Global Restaurants. Novak was made vice-chairman, president, and designated successor to then-chairman Andrall Pearson. Novak had marketing and corporate management strengths. Or, as *The Courier-Journal* said at the time, "acute marketing skills, a persuasive personality and – perhaps most important – a genius for recruiting people."

He needed a new gag for the blended company, so he came up with the chattering teeth, mounted on little feet, to back up a company slogan: "Walk the talk."

Novak had joined the Pepsico system in 1986 as a senior vice president of marketing at Pizza Hut, where he helped develop a new pizza delivery service and a successful promotional campaign. Sales doubled and profits tripled. Novak moved up.

He will tell you he operates the way he does because that's who he really is – a fun-loving, optimistic person who believes in people and wants to motivate and reward them.

"He is intense, yet he brings a spirit of joy that is contagious to everybody else," Bob Russell, Novak's pastor at Southeast Christian Church, said of him. It makes Novak a good builder of consensus.

He takes his upbeat demeanor on the road, popping up a couple of days a week at his brands' restaurants, asking customers how they like the sauce and asking employees what's working and what isn't.

Novak moved up to the chairman's job at Tricon in 2001. A little more than a year later, after adding Long John Silvers and A&W All-American Food Restaurants to its stable, the company changed its name to Yum! Brands. The new name was to acknowledge an expanding portfolio, Novak said, and to reflect a "unique fun and recognition culture" the company spreads around its entire system. Besides, he said, it encourages employees to strive to make people think, "Yum!" when they think of the company's products.

David Novak had affability and charisma thrust upon him, in a sense, as a child. His father was the leader of a government surveying crew that moved around the country in a caravan of trailers, changing towns every three months or so. He lived in 23 states before the family settled down in a suburb of Kansas City when he was in the seventh grade. Until then, he had to learn to make friends fast, and to be able to blend them with the friends he already had among the families that traveled with the group.

Once Novak settled down, he edited his high school newspaper, and became interested in journalism. He went to the University of Missouri, a premier journalism school, and two things happened to him there. He discovered advertising and developed a passion for it, and he met his future wife, Wendy, who happened to be from Louisville.

Novak worked in advertising for ten years, honing his branding and marketing skills, before he joined PepsiCo.

The couple, who have one daughter, moved to Louisville in 1994, and Novak has now lived there longer than he has ever lived anywhere before. He has said he plans to retire there.

He is a director of J.P. Morgan Chase & Company, the Yum! Brand Foundation and The Business Council. He also devotes his time to a variety of service programs and organizations in Louisville, among them the Dare to Care Food Bank, Metro United Way and Southeast Christian Church.

To be a leader, he told *Business First* in 1996, it's important to "act like a leader. Leaders don't wait for somebody to recognize how great they are. They go out and lead every day."

I DON'T KNOW THAT YOU DECIDE when you are going to become a leader. I think that sometimes you are in positions where you are a leader and you just assume that responsibility.

I think that when you get in a leadership position, you have a natural orientation to lead. I don't think I have ever consciously thought about becoming a leader in the community, and I don't know that I am one, but if people think that I am, that's nice to know.

My dad was a government surveyor, so I lived in 23 states by the time I was in seventh grade. We moved every three months. It was a great experience, because it taught me to go into new situations and make friends. My mom used to say to me, "Better go in and make some friends and take the initiative, because we are leaving soon." Because of that, I think I was able to develop an ability to get to know people, maybe a little bit easier than other people.

My mom registered me in every school. I would usually be there for three months, then move to the next school and register again and go to school there. I lived in really small towns, everything from Dodge City, Kansas to Detroit Lakes, Minnesota – basically up and down the United States, from Texas to Minnesota, never on the East Coast or the West Coast. This will be our 11th year in Louisville, which is the longest I have ever lived anywhere.

I first worked at Pizza Hut in Wichita, then became president of Pizza Hut, which was headquartered in Dallas. I became president of KFC in 1994. I lived in Louisville when I was president of Pizza Hut and KFC. That was difficult. I was the line president for two Pepsico divisions at the same time, so I spent most of my time on planes. I never knew which community I was in.

Becoming president of KFC obviously put me in a natural leadership position in Louisville. When we had the opportunity to be spun off from Pepsico to form a public company in 1997, we made the decision to make our corporate headquarters in Louisville. I think that elevated both KFC's and Yum! Brands' overall importance in the Louisville community.

Everybody I worked for in my career ended up being president of a company, so I've been blessed with many great coaches, all of whom were enormously successful in their careers and grew after they coached me. I worked with Steve Reinemund when he was president of Pizza Hut and now he is chairman & CEO of Pepsico. I worked for Roger Enrico when he was chairman of Pepsico, and now he is chairman of Dreamworks Animation SKG, Inc. Craig Weatherup was president of Pepsi Bottling Group and became CEO of the Pepsi Bottling Group when it was spun off from Pepsico. Everybody I worked for ended up running a major company, so I've been blessed with great mentors.

David C. Novak

I think the most rewarding relationship I have had in my career is with Andy Pearson, who was the former president of Pepsico. He then became a professor at Harvard Business School and worked in a leveraged buy-out company. He was the original chairman of Tricon when we were spun off, and he served in that role for the first three years. He is now 80 years old, and one of my best friends in life. His whole goal was to help me become the best possible CEO. He is an avid learner, and he really took the time to coach me on everything he knew about business, leadership and life. He is a great guy and has shown me a lot of things. I never thought my best friend would be 80 years old. Since I'm 53, that is a pretty big age gap, but I think he is actually younger than I am.

Andy has taught me how to stay young by being an avid learner. He wakes up every day with tremendous energy and attacks life. I think one way you can stay young and keep your vitality is to have a tremendous learning mentality. I've always had a learning mentality. That's why I think we get along. What's interesting about us is that we can finish each other's sentences. He may have had different experiences than I have, but we were so simpatico. That is why we were such great partners. We believed in the same things, and when you are starting out a new company, you want to have courage of conviction. You want to have a belief in what a company ought to be like. He was terrific because he was my biggest cheerleader and we both agreed and believed in the same thing. I think we kind of fed off each other.

I think first and foremost my leadership style is authentic. I am authentically who I am. I'm David Novak and I believe that I need to be true to who I am. I don't want to be anybody else. I admire a lot of other people, but I am myself and people see me for who I am. I don't put on any airs or try to pretend to be somebody that I'm not. I am who I am. I have an intense belief in people and the capability of people to do great things when they are put in a work environment that lets them know genuinely that they are appreciated and valued. I call it "people capability first", and it's helped me be a good team builder.

I think you go through your life, you mature, you evolve and you realize what really makes things work. When I became president of KFC, I can remember getting on a company plane to come here for the first meeting and thinking, "Gosh, I've always wanted to be president. Now I'm president. What kind of president am I going to be?" I thought about that and I said, "You know, I've just got to stay being who I am. Who I am has helped me get where I am so far. I don't know what kind of president I'll be, but I guess I'm going to be a president called David Novak. And I'm going to be David Novak."

David Novak has a lot of fun. I have always had a lot of fun in my career. I have always built great teams and I have always had a lot of enthusiasm.

I have always believed that you shouldn't look up, you shouldn't look down, you should always look straight ahead when dealing with people. I've always been very competitive and results-oriented. That's who I am. I am emotionally involved with people, too. I'm not distant. A lot of people think that CEOs have to have that emotional distance. I think that is a crock. That distance keeps you from high performance. People follow people who are in the boat with them, so I try to be in the boat.

I am known for my passion, enthusiasm, fun-loving spirit. But I am also known for being tough, demanding, high-performance driven, and competitive. I think I am a combination of those two things.

I think the most significant accomplishment that I've had is taking Yum! Brands and building a unifying culture around the world that's based on a formula for success that says if you put the "people capability first," and you satisfy customers, you make more money. This is all based on the notion that the culture you create really is the foundation, the bedrock for driving high performance and results.

When we started our company, we were in 100 different companies, three different brands, and three different locations. It would have been very easy for us to go off and have each of these brands do their own thing. But what we did is say, "Hey listen, we are going to build this business all around characteristics and values that drive great performance in our restaurants, and that one culture, that one set of values, is going to be universal all around the world."

We decided to have a huge belief in people; we decided to be totally focused on excellence. We decided to have lots of recognition, all kinds of recognition, high-energy recognition – both spontaneous and informal – and we decided to take this all around the world.

I used to give out these floppy chickens and cheese heads at KFC and Pizza Hut. People used to say, "Well you can't recognize people in Asia like that, because it's a much more formal culture." But Peter Hearl, one of our top international executives, now president of Pizza Hut, said, "That's not true, David. It will work in Asia, it will work everywhere." So we took that culture around the world, and now we're doing Yum! cheers in China and we're giving all kinds of recognition in China, Thailand and Malaysia.

People love to be valued everywhere. I think that we've created a high performance, people-first culture around the world that is getting the best results in the industry. I remember when we first started the company, I wrote down the idea that my personal mission was to build a reward and recognition culture that would drive the highest performance in our industry, and I think we are on our way to doing that.

We talked about these same things with our franchisees. We wanted to be equity-blind. We didn't care who owned the restaurant. We want all of our restaurants to be run on the basis of one thing, and that is satisfying customers. Customers don't care if it is a franchise restaurant or a company-owned restaurant. They just want to have a satisfying experience when they come there.

I have had a few failures or, shall I say, disappointments. One was an idea that would have been great but didn't do as well because of poor execution.

When I was with Pepsi, I came up with the idea of doing a clear cola — Crystal Pepsi. When we first went into test market, Crystal Pepsi was the lead story on the CBS news. "Pepsi is taking the color out of Pepsi. It's clear Pepsi." This was back in 1990. We did this back then because the alternative beverages were really taking off — teas, waters, drinks without caffeine. Pepsi the brand was kind of languishing, and it seemed like everything clear was really doing well. So I said, if that is the case, "Why don't we do a clear Pepsi?"

So we went out and showed it to customers, and consumers loved the idea, the formula was good, and we had a great thing. We launched it in test markets with tremendous results. But then, when we went national with it, there were two things that we hadn't uncovered. One, it didn't taste like Pepsi. It was a cola taste, but it wasn't identical to the Pepsi taste which I rationalized as being okay because we wanted to bring in an incremental user base. We wanted to have a different taste profile, but we were still going to leverage off the Pepsi name. The Pepsi franchisees kept saying to me, "Well, David, it doesn't taste like Pepsi." But I just kept pushing ahead on it. Then, when we launched it, we had problems in the plant making the product. There were some manufacturing issues. The taste wasn't as crisp as it needed to be and we had product quality problems.

So first of all, it didn't taste like Pepsi, but we called it Pepsi, which our franchisees rightfully pointed out to me. I had a rationale. I kept saying, "It's not supposed to taste like Pepsi." But they would say, "But it doesn't taste like Pepsi." And I would say, "But it's not supposed to." And they would say, "But it doesn't taste like Pepsi."

I pushed it through, then we had quality problems. As a result, the product did not do that well. It was the only product in the history of the Pepsi-Cola Company that was ever introduced at a premium price. The franchisees introduced it at a premium price because they said they knew it was not going to be around that long. And they were right. It was a disappointment to me, because the consumer loved the idea. It was an idea that was 15 years ahead of its time.

We actually made plan that year and it helped us make plan. But I looked at it as a disappointment. I thought if we had executed it well, it would have been a homerun. I probably should have been clearer with the packaging, saying it was a lighter cola taste – something that said it wasn't exactly like Pepsi. I could have done a better job there.

The learning I got there was first, I should have listened to the bottlers. I was so passionate about my idea that I didn't listen as well as I could have. Secondly, I learned that execution is everything. You can have a good idea, but if you don't execute it properly, it doesn't make any sense. That was just one of those big ideas that you know could have been huge if it had been executed properly. Now we are seeing it come back full circle, with all the flavors and other things we are seeing in the carbonated soft drink world right now.

A good follower does what we call "team together, team apart." Basically, when you are on a team, the leader needs to create an environment where everyone has an opportunity to influence and input. If you are working with me, I value your opinion, and I ask you to give me your opinion. Nine times out of ten, when you have ten smart people sitting around the room and they are looking at the same facts, they come up with the same conclusions and you have alignment. You say, "Yeah, let's go, this what we are going to do." In that case, it is very easy to follow, because you agree. So a good follower should provide good input into a solution, then follow-up through powerful execution.

Sometimes, though, when you have a discussion, everyone doesn't agree. They don't agree with the direction the leader takes after getting input. In that case, a good follower has to execute what I call "team together, team apart." That person had a chance to influence, but didn't get his or her way. The decision has been made, however. Good followers – even if they don't agree – have to execute that decision to the best of their ability. And until there is new data saying the team should go in a different direction, they should go out and execute with positive energy. That is what a good follower does.

What a good leader does is make sure that the followers or team members at least get a chance to have input, because there is one rule: "No involvement, no commitment." If you are not involved in a decision or you don't have the chance to weigh in as a team member, how committed are you going to be?

I think a leader has to create an environment where people can provide their input. But followers, once they have given input, must execute what the ultimate decision is.

Leaders have to create an environment where there is productive conflict. A leader has to ask people, "What do you think?" or "Where are you on this?" If you are a leader, you know where people are, and you know what their opinions are. You know that somebody might not think that you ought to take pricing and another person might think that you should take pricing. A lot of times people will come in and tell you, "I believe in this" or "I believe in that," then they will get in a room and they won't say anything in front of their peers. What I do in those situations is say, "What do you think, John?" "What do you think, Sally?" I know what Sally and John think, but I make them say it. Then I say, "Well, that is not what you told me," or, "I know you, Frank, you have a different point of view."

A leader also has to say, "Hey, am I missing something here?" I celebrate all the people who help keep me and others from making bad decisions. Those are the heroes and heroines in our organization. I always say, "Gee, I would have gone down this path if it hadn't been for John. I was going down this path and Sally told me I should go this way and boy, she was right. Thank God I didn't do that." You try to create that kind of safe haven, that it's okay to speak up and have opinions. In fact, you love it when people keep you from making mistakes. In fact, you love to talk about all the mistakes you would have made if it weren't for the people you were working with. Then people want to help you out and feel free to speak their minds.

You cannot have a creative or innovative organization if people are afraid to fail, so you have to create an environment where people are willing to try new things. Now that doesn't mean you should go out and try stupid things. But if there is good logic flow for why you are trying something, and it could change the game in terms of how you do business, or change the sales curve, or increase profits, but it just doesn't work out, what's wrong with that? How are you going to get better if you don't create an environment where people can do those things? Now if everything you try fails, and you have a track record of executing a bunch of dumb ideas that never work, then you are going to get fired around here. We have a high performance culture. But you are not going to get fired for trying to do the right thing, or trying to do a big thing, or a new thing that could be successful.

I would do nothing major different if I had a chance to live my life over again. I think life is a continual learning process. I've had my ups and downs, and I've tried to do the best I can in every situation. But I don't really look back. Of course, there are a lot of things that I might have done differently or mistakes that I made in the past that I wish I wouldn't have made. But I think that is all a part of living. I think that the mistakes you make make you a better person. Hopefully, you try to learn from them.

Fortunately, the big decisions I have made in my life have all been great decisions. I married the right woman. I worked for the right people. My spiritual life is great. Everything else is kind of trivial.

Passing the Torch

If I were going to give advice to young people aspiring to leadership, I would tell them, first of all, that they must realize that they have to work hard. I think people underestimate that fact. People who work harder than other people usually achieve more than other people. There are a lot of smart people in the world, so one way to differentiate yourself is just through harder work.

The second thing I would advise is something I believe very much, and that's that people get absolutely motivated by people who are passionate about what they do. If you have a passion, it creates a positive energy that is contagious and that makes other people want to go with you, and makes them want to follow you. You know that old saying "Do what you love and you'll be successful?" It's true. I always say to people, "What do you like that you are not good at?" I don't like anything that I'm not good at. I think it is important to get in a field that you know you are going to be good at because you like it.

I think the third thing I would advise is that you absolutely have to be an avid learner. There are three things that I would say to people: 1) Be passionate about what you do; 2) Work harder than the next person; and 3) Continually learn. When somebody comes in to interview with me who I know is passionate, who is going to be a hard worker and who has a learning mentality, they're a homerun. They will absolutely be a fantastic talent. I can tell when I interview them.

I think that Louisville has had a leadership that has wanted Louisville to stay small and has been very successful at it. I think that Louisville is one of the best small cities in the world. That's what we are, and I think that's what we are always going to be. I like living here. There is no traffic. We have great arts, a nice little Bats baseball stadium, great college basketball. Louisville is a fun, nice place. We should try to be true to ourselves and to keep the things that make Louisville really great, great. The worst thing that could happen now is to get caught in the middle – to have all the hassles of a big city without any of the benefits. This is a big challenge for Louisville. I think we need to continue to attract smaller businesses, which I think we are doing, and try to grow in that vein.

I think the most valuable lesson I have learned as a leader is that you should attack life. Don't wait for tomorrow to do what you can do today. Life is really way too short, and it can change in an instant. You never want to look back. Don't live a life that makes you look back. Always live for today and move forward.

I think the biggest sadness I see is when you see highly talented people looking back. The city shouldn't look back – it should always look forward. People shouldn't look back either – they should look forward. Take action today. Attack life. Live life. I know that when I die, nobody is going to say that I didn't live life.

I think Louisville is a great community. When I talk about the growth of Louisville, it is a fact that Louisville has been outgrown by surrounding cities in a significant fashion. That's okay, because Louisville is what it is, which is a great small city. Louisville has a lot of good things. A lot of people move here and love living here. They never want to live anywhere else. It's beautiful here. It is a great place to raise a family. It has good schools, a good arts community, great college sports, and it's growing. It also has world class golf due to the vision of Dwight Gahm who built Valhalla ahead of the curve.

There are very good people here, good leaders. I don't have anything but praise for Louisville for what it is. When people start talking about Louisville growing, I think that Louisville is going to have to grow in a way that leverages off of what it is — which is a great small city. A great small city has a great quality of life about it that you can't get in a big city. It doesn't have the hassles of a big city.

JAMES A. PATTERSON SR.

Owner and President
Pattco, LLC

Founder
Long John Silvers and
Rally's Hamburgers

Co-Founder
Chi-Chi's Mexican Restaurants

A STRONG COMPONENT of Jim Patterson's formula for success has been to look for people with a "proprietary mentality" to work with him. Rick Sherman, who worked with Patterson at Rally's, told *Kentucky Commerce* magazine in 1989 that Patterson didn't ask people to work for him. He asked them to have a vested interest in whichever of his businesses they were in, so they would really be working for themselves.

Patterson made many millions of dollars following that strategy. In 1989, he thought of 24 people who had made more than $1 million as a result of working with him. He said more recently that seeing his friends become millionaires is what has given him the most pleasure in his career.

And an interesting career it has been. Patterson grew up in a poor neighborhood in South Louisville, and worked to support himself after the age of 12. He was encouraged by a nun at his parochial school and by various employers, and he became the only member of his family to finish high school, working his way through all four years of school. He played football and baseball and saw the world outside his neighborhood by traveling with his teams. He liked what he saw, and he became determined to make something of himself.

Baseball earned him a scholarship to the University of Louisville and that, supplemented by R.O.T.C. and various jobs, got him through college with a marketing degree in 1955. In his senior year, he began selling insurance and discovered he had a knack for selling.

He honed his management skills as a captain in the Air Force and saved his money. Back in civilian life in 1959, he decided to invest his savings — $10,500 — in a Jerry's Restaurant franchise. He learned the business as he went along. He persevered, the restaurant caught on, and within eight years he had three of them.

He began to expand into real estate, and he got a big dose of confidence when he discovered that he could hold his own with classmates in a one-week course at Harvard for CEOs of small companies. That got him thinking. Kentucky Fried Chicken was riding high. As a Catholic, Patterson had eaten fish every Friday of his life. Maybe a carryout fish place would go.

Thus, Long John Silver's was born. Patterson took his idea to the chairman of Jerrico and they started a new company, with Patterson as president and 40 percent owner. By 1975, Long John Silver's was providing most of Jerrico's profits and the company wanted Patterson's 40 percent. He sold it to them for $20 million.

Patterson then founded an oil and gas company, and later sold it at a profit. At the same time, he and friends established Western Restaurants, a holding company that now owns 49 Wendy's Restaurants. With other friends, he founded Chi-Chi's, which was sold in 1988.

He founded AmeriCall Services and First Phone, which merged later into WorldCom. He started Rally's, then sold his share in 1990. He was involved in developing Resource America, selling medical software systems, and he sold that in 1999. His Pattco, LLC is an investment company with several interests, and he continues to invest privately in a number of other companies.

Patterson has served on the boards of the J.B. Speed Art Museum, the Kentucky Derby Museum and the Greater Louisville Fund for the Arts. But his strong belief in the importance of education has motivated him to give generous gifts to educational programs and institutions.

He founded a program called School Choice Scholarships, which helps lower-income families pay tuition for elementary-age children to attend private schools — children from backgrounds like Patterson's.

He's been a major contributor to Bellarmine University and to the University of Louisville, his alma mater. He recently made the lead gift to help UofL build a new 2,500-seat baseball stadium. The facility, which opened in spring 2005, is appropriately named Jim Patterson Stadium.

Patterson's career was officially certified a rags-to-riches story in 2002, when he was one of ten people in the country to receive Horatio Alger awards, recognizing a rise to success from humble beginnings. Recipients are asked to give advice to Horatio Alger Scholars.

Patterson's advice was simple: "Get an education and become involved in something you can be passionate about. Be persistent. Deal with people with integrity and forthrightness. Don't sell yourself short. Keep your antennae up for opportunities and then have the courage to take the lead."

I NEVER DECIDED I WOULD BECOME a leader. Sometimes, as things progress, people begin to ask more of you and if you're responsive, then someone someday might say that you're a leader.

My motivation in life was to become somebody. I never wanted to be a "wannabe." I was always economically driven to better myself from my South End neighborhood of poverty. Having become relatively successful and recognized for my accomplishments, I've now become – by default – a civic leader.

I had a number of mentors, but I particularly loved Wilson Wyatt. He took to me in his later years and lived some of my success. He used to tell me how he admired the things I did. Maury Johnson was not as close with me, but they were both very powerful in the city of Louisville. They opened so many doors and were regarded so well. It was easy to be inspired by them.

Sister Josita, who was my teacher for third, fourth, and fifth grade was also a mentor. In some respects, she was maybe even my first crush. She took a special interest in me during an era in my home life that was unsettled. My greatest pleasures were being an altar boy and singing in the choir. I was a teacher's pet. I loved her then, and I love her now. She gave me confidence, and she made me feel like I was somebody. I felt serenity with her when my life at home was in an uproar.

I don't really think I am much of a leader, but people with whom I associate all know that I am a regular person, unpretentious. At my core, I am humble. It's important to be honest and forthright when you're dealing with people, not a games-player. I try to lead by example.

In my business life, my greatest pride is the recognition that so many people are wealthy today as a result of their being involved with me and the successes we've had. Everybody has to have a goal and must be rewarded when that goal is met. When people know what you expect of them and they meet that expectation, that's a lesson taught by experience.

My biggest failure was being fired from Long John Silver's in 1975, a company I founded. When I was called in and told I was no longer president of the company, it was like someone jerking my baby out of my hands. I was disappointed. In retrospect, it was a wonderful thing that happened to me, although I couldn't recognize it at the time. Six months later, I received a lot of money from that situation, and I restarted my life.

I don't think there are good followers. A "good follower" has the connotation of being weak and hanging on. We don't have followers in our business. We try to create an environment with an entrepreneurial feeling, so that people who work with us have a feeling of ownership.

James A. Patterson Sr.

If I could live my life over, I might do a few things differently. I have missed several opportunities that I would have taken advantage of. We were always so conservative about the AmeriCall Company, for example. AmeriCall was a long-distance reseller, and we didn't do the things we should have done. We sold the company for several tens of millions of dollars in profit, but we should have sold it for several hundreds of millions of dollars in profit. It was there for the taking, but we didn't take advantage of it. The same with cellular. We just weren't smart enough to recognize it. I wish I had been smarter and braver and willing to leverage myself. That's the kind of thing I reflect on now that I would do differently.

I don't think David Jones set out to be a community leader. He set out to build a business and created a powerful position for himself as a result of that. My advice to the next generation of leaders in our community is that if you want to be a success in business, you first have to have a dream. Then you have to focus, be opportunistic, and be willing to pay the price.

I don't think I really played a role in the growth and development of our community over the last 50 years, but the people who did, in my opinion, are people like Wilson Wyatt and Maury Johnson. David Jones and Wendell Cherry have been most remarkable in the past 30 years. I speak of them as a team. It was so inspiring to see them build Humana and make something of themselves. They became leaders as a result of their success.

I'm not much on giving advice, but Louisville has seen failure before. In 1970, we wanted to expand Long John Silver's and I had the challenge of looking at three cities that geographically made sense. They were in a horse race, neck and neck. We came to Louisville because it was my home and my bias. But I looked up 20 years later and the other two cities were 20 lengths ahead of us. They left us so far behind, we were a speck in the background. The other cities had a stimulating political leadership that was both progressive and aggressive. They became merged city governments. They didn't have the divided city like we have had up until recently. We haven't had the stimulation, the leadership, and the aggressive growth these other cities have had.

I've learned some valuable lessons in my lifetime that I would like to share with the next generation of leaders in Louisville. It all begins with integrity. Integrity is kind of like virginity. You can't get it back once you lose it. Be honest with yourself, with the people you associate with. You have to be trustworthy. It's the primary ingredient for anybody who aspires to be successful. Success just takes application and dedication.

WOODFORD R. PORTER SR.

Chairman Emeritus
A.D. Porter & Sons Funeral Home

WOODFORD PORTER SR. SERVED on the University of Louisville Board of Trustees for 24 years before stepping down in 1991, and by all accounts set a tone for dignity and reason throughout his tenure.

"Woody Porter is a senior statesman," then-UofL President Donald Swain said when Porter retired. "There is nobody with a greater sense of history than Woody or a greater range of experience. He's one of the trustees who everyone turns to for leadership in a crunch."

Porter was the first African-American to serve on the board, and the first to serve as its chairman. He was chairman four times, and held that position when he retired.

In a way, he blazed that trail for himself, by getting elected to the old Louisville Board of Education in 1958. He was the first African-American to do that too, and the first to serve as that board's chairman, which he did three times. When he was named Louisvillian of the Year by the Advertising Club of Louisville in 1992, Citizens Fidelity (now PNC) Bank President Mike Harreld joked that he had outlived three school superintendents and three university presidents.

Porter told *Business First* in 1985 that he was proudest of being elected to the school board because it showed the white-dominated school system that blacks would fight for equal treatment. He said he ran because his wife, Harriet, and other licensed teachers were being denied teaching jobs because of their race.

Porter was a civil rights activist who took an "evolution rather than revolution" approach. "I believe in sweet reason," he told *The Courier-Journal* in 1991. "That's always been my theory, to whittle off a little at a time until I get what I want."

Which is not to say that he ignored the civil rights movement.

In the '50s, he marched with Lyman Johnson and others in the rain outside Memorial Auditorium to protest segregated seating during a performance by an all-black cast. He stood outside a Blue Boar cafeteria and saw a policeman poke a nightstick into the stomach of his demonstrating daughter, Marie. He knew Blue Boar owner Gene Johnson, who was also a member of the school board, and they talked. "I just told him we were standing up for what was right, and I told him I didn't think he'd lose any business" if he desegregated his restaurants, Porter said. He said Johnson opened his doors that day, and other restaurants then followed.

Woodford Porter was born in 1918. He was the son of A.D. Porter, who had started a funeral home business in Louisville in 1907 and who had run for mayor on the Lincoln Independent Party ticket in the early 1920s. When he graduated from Central High School, Porter wanted to be a lawyer. He was within 28 hours of graduating at Indiana University when his father became ill and he had to come home to run the business. He intended to return to college later, but never did. His business prospered though, and he became a mentor to other black businessmen.

Over the years, he earned many awards and served on many boards, including Mid-America Bancorp, owner of the Bank of Louisville. Occasionally he was urged to use his prestige for projects he didn't think seemed like they had his name on them. His friend, Philip Ardery, asked him to try to join the then all-white Pendennis Club, for example, and black leaders rooted him on. He declined. "I can't see spending that kind of money to be uncomfortable," he said. "I don't have anything to prove."

Former UofL trustee Norbert Blume said Porter has an even dignity. "I don't care how rough things get or how exciting, Woody always has his feet on the ground. Everybody respects Woody Porter. He gets along with everybody."

In 2004, Porter's wife, Harriett, lost a battle with breast cancer she had been fighting since her 30s. To honor her, and to help others facing cancer, Porter and his family decided to donate $250,000 to the UofL Brown Cancer Center's "Finding Answers to Cancer" campaign. Porter said he hoped his family's gift would help educate people about cancer, especially those in the African-American community. "We will be praying and supporting them in every way possible," he said.

It was A.D. Porter's dream that the funeral home business he founded in 1907 "be perpetuated from one generation to the next," Porter once told *The Courier-Journal*. In 2002, Woodford Porter Sr. sold his interest in his family's business to his four children and a longtime employee to keep his father's dream alive for at least one more generation.

I DIDN'T MAKE A DECISION TO BECOME a leader in our community, it just evolved. My early training from my father had a lot to do with what I've done. His philosophy was "You don't take everything out of a community and not put something back." We weren't wealthy, so he taught us that if you didn't have money to put into things, you put service. That's how I got involved in the community. The leadership came. I guess I had time, or I made time. I was sincere about what I wanted to do.

My community involvement goes back to the period immediately following World War II. Being second class had a lot to do with it. Trying to overcome that situation and change it had more to do with my getting involved than anything else.

When I got out of the Navy with a medical discharge, I was told to come here to Louisville to get a job in a defense plant or they were going to draft me into the Army. I sort of chuckled, because if they didn't want me in the Navy, I thought it was probably unlikely they'd want me in the Army. I went out to Naval Ordnance. The only job I could get was cleaning out torpedo tubes or sweeping the floor. I chose the torpedo tubes – it paid more – but it galled me that I couldn't get a job doing some of the things the Navy had taught me to do. The only thing that prevented it was being black.

I joined the NAACP and became very active in that. I worked with a woman named Elvira Williams. We led a membership drive and did very well. We ended up with over 5,000 paid memberships. I don't think they've had that many since. This sort of projected me out into the community a little bit.

Lyman Johnson and I became very friendly. We were pretty close, actually, but you have to take into consideration that most of the things I got involved in in the community were new things. I had a lot of on-the-job training.

One of the things I remember doing with Lyman was walking a picket line in front of Memorial Auditorium one night when it was pouring down rain and the all-black show *Carmen Jones* was playing. Whites, of course, walked by us like we didn't exist, but what galled us most was some blacks did the same thing. That convinced us we had to dig deeper. It got me involved in trying to change attitudes.

My church was always kind of a militant church – not violent, but it preached the philosophy that you're as good as you want to be and you can go as far as you want.

I got involved with the Chestnut Street YMCA. Like most people, the board members were busy, and one night we were looking for a representative to sit on the metropolitan YMCA board. Everybody else had a reason why they couldn't go, so I said, "I'll take a chance."

So I went and met some of the white leadership on that board and became friendly with some of them. There was a fellow named Homer Parker – without Homer, I would never have gotten my funeral home built. Nobody else would finance me. I told him I'd been to all the other banks and finance companies. They would say they would loan money to remodel an old building, but not to build a new one. "Woody," he said, "we'll finance it for you."

In the mid-1950s, the community began to get a little more cohesive and the Chestnut Street Y was like a Mecca. Everybody met there, all the groups. It was conveniently located to the black community at that point in time. A group of us got together to see who we could get to run for the school board. We had tried several times before with people we knew were competent, but they could never win. That night everybody said, "I don't want to do it" – just like at the Y – so I said, "Okay, I'll try." Using all my contacts, I got elected.

There were three positions up for election, but we figured if people voted for me and two others I wouldn't win, because I wasn't going to get any votes in the white community. So we did "single shot voting." People in the black precincts were told "Only vote for one, and that's Woodford Porter." That's how I got elected. After four years, the "slate" as they called it asked me not to run by myself, to run with the slate. In that particular election, I got as many white votes as black votes.

My primary mentor was my father – not that my mother wasn't a mentor, but my dad taught me a lot about people. We had a little stone bench that sat on the side of the building where the funeral home was, and he used to take me and my brother, put one on each side of him, and talk to us about people and how to get along. "Don't pick on people," he would say. "You've got to give some back." That sort of thing. He was born right after the end of slavery. He had been a hard-working man. He learned primarily from his own reading and from the college of hard knocks.

He ran for mayor of this city back in 1921. That influenced us too. As kids, we had a rough time because black folk weren't used to any blacks being Democrats. You were supposed to be Republicans because Abraham Lincoln freed us. That's what he set out to do anyway. My dad believed in principle. What he felt was right was right, and he was willing to sacrifice for it.

My father always told us, "Be honest and fair." "Pay your debts." Oh, he was a stickler for that, even in business. He would say, "The first thing you do is pay your help, then your suppliers, then you pay all the other debts, and if there is anything left, you take a nickel of every dollar for yourself." Back in the '30s, when everybody else was going bankrupt – and he was like everybody, he owed money, too – he refused to go bankrupt. He went to his creditors and they agreed to settle on some sort of percentage.

All my teachers, in a sense, were mentors. That was the one big advantage in the segregated school system. Not that I wanted it, I thought it was horrible, but the teachers cared. They were interested in your learning and your behavior. I actually had a lot of guidance outside the house. My teachers were pretty strict people. We didn't have any national Negro history month then, but they taught us the Negro national anthem and they taught us about Booker T. Washington, and about W.E.B. Dubois – in addition to the regular history – because those things were not in the books.

I was very fortunate in my marriage. My wife Harriett was influential. She probably controlled my temperament to a great degree, as I could get a little fiery sometimes.

But as a leader, I always tried to use persuasion, reasoning. One thing that stood me in very good stead is that when I was in high school, I was on the debating team – the only medal I ever got. You learned how to examine both sides of any question or proposition. I was always able to get people to look at both sides of an issue and reason. That was the greatest thing I ever used with people – sweet reason.

During the demonstrations to try to end segregation in Louisville, Gene Johnson, who owned the Blue Boar restaurants, and I were on the school board together. Gene called me and said, "Woody, you want to talk to me?" And I said, "Gene, you know I can't come up there to your place." And he said, "No, and if I come to your place the reporters will follow me." So I said, "Why don't we meet out at Sixth and Hill, at the old school board building." We met out there, had lunch, and started talking. We were there two hours or so. I convinced Gene and finally said, "Gene, go open your restaurant up to black people. You're not going to lose any money." And he did it. He went back that very afternoon and told them to open the door, and because he was head of the restaurant association, that broke the whole thing open.

I have had heated arguments with some people, but I learned on the school board that if you must have a fight, have it behind closed doors. I had a few of those. And when you come out, be friendly and gracious, especially if you won. I only made one real enemy, and he's gone on to glory.

Other people might describe my leadership style as "Move along, get along" or "sweet persuasion." A few would say, "He's a pretty good trader."

I chaired UofL's Board of Trustees when the city got to the point where it couldn't support the university. It was sell out – go belly-up – or go under the state. Jim (James G.) Miller was president of UofL at that time.

We went to Frankfort to make the appeal to the Council on Postsecondary Education for the state to take over the university. I made the appeal for the trustees and Jim made it for the faculty and staff. UK, bless their hearts, wanted UofL to come in as an Eastern or a Western Kentucky University – a regional university – but we came away as "the major urban university." Jim and I figured out that with that designation, we could do anything we wanted to do. So that's how UofL went into the state system.

If I were going to try to list my biggest, or most significant accomplishments, they would be these:

First, I feel a part of what UofL has become.

Second, I've opened a lot of doors and opportunities for African-American kids. I've always told people I'm not asking for anything but for you to give me an opportunity. Just don't say I can't come through the door. Give me a chance. If I go through and fail, I had my chance. But don't look at me and say "You're black, you can't come in."

Third, I am proud that we established the Porter Scholars at the University of Louisville. I meet with the Society of Porter Scholars once or twice a year. It's always 75 or 80 kids. It does my heart good. All the presidents have been very supportive and receptive to the program.

When I look back over my whole life, however, I perhaps feel I have not contributed enough to make the African-American community more cohesive and more concerned about leadership – about getting the qualifications and the will needed to lead, and having the real intention to become a leader. Maybe I should have gotten a little bloodied up and gotten involved in that a little more, but you just have so much time.

Getting elected to the school board the first time demonstrated one thing – that I could attract votes. Then I got away from the political side. Not that I didn't do some political things.

Joe Hammonds was a very tough, very smart politician. He was a Democrat, and he worked hard for the Democratic Party. Joe and I were very good friends. We could, I think, have caused a greater cohesiveness among African-Americans. Now you might say that's "bossism," and I guess it is in a sense, but a benevolent boss is better than a bunch of people running around with no objectives and no leadership. Right now our leadership is so fragmented.

Good followers must do three things: 1) be committed; 2) have access to leadership; and 3) be willing to share thoughts – both pro and con. Leadership must be receptive to its followers as well.

A lot of people want to give Rev. Louis Coleman a hard time, but he's part of the pot that must be there. He and others like him are the catalysts who help make things work. They are actually contributing a whole lot to our community.

For example, at UofL, back when everybody was talking about dis-investing in South Africa because of apartheid, the UofL Foundation had a lot of money in companies that did business in South Africa. Rev. Coleman and others made a demand that the university dis-invest. They came to the university and they marched around the rotunda and sang freedom songs. I was chairman of UofL's Board of Trustees. Rev. Coleman called and said, "I want to talk to the board." I said, "It's the day of the board meeting, Reverend, we have an agenda. But I'll tell you what. I'll give you the name of a trustee, and you can ask him if he'll make a motion that you be allowed to address the trustees."

Well, he followed my advice and he talked to the board (and made most of the board members angry, actually – I knew that was going to happen), but it gave me an opportunity to say to the chairman of the UofL Foundation, "I'd like to have a seat on the Foundation board." He said, "Sure, Woody." I took a seat on that board in September, and we dis-invested. But without Buster (Rev. Louis Coleman) marching and speaking to the trustees, that would not have happened. I'm not going to lie to you, I've enjoyed being under-estimated by people a lot.

I'd like to be 16 and do everything all over again. I don't know that I would change anything, though. If you could restructure things that way, you might change so many things. Back in the same situations, though, I'd probably do the same things, because I'm much the same person. I haven't changed much. I'm just older, maybe a little wiser.

When I think about what I could have done? Maybe I chose the path I did because I was chicken. The other path would have been harder. Putting myself through law school? My daddy didn't have any money, and didn't leave any.

I would tell young people aspiring to leadership in our community, you've got to be a fairly decent follower. Be willing to share thoughts and solutions. Be willing to help other people go up the ladder. You have to be willing to give of your time, too. I had no time for golf, but the world changes and a lot of decisions are being made now on the golf course. So if I was coming along now, I might try to learn to play golf.

There has been a great change of attitude, over the past few decades, about what I call "leadership," but I don't want to name specific people who have been responsible for the growth and development of our community.

Some of the changes have come out of a "conversion" philosophically, but I think most of it has come as a result of "conversion" commercially – the realization of the old adage that "no chain is stronger than its weakest link." Why have a big community, but have a part of the chain so weak that it can't really contribute anything to the strength of the chain? If you strengthen that link, you make the whole chain stronger, which is philosophically what I think a lot of the younger leadership thinks (Caucasian, primarily). While not totally inclusive of black leadership, there has been a great shift. Now even those people who have primary control stop and think and reflect, "What effect is this going to have?," when heretofore they didn't give a damn.

The role I have played in that shift was really to try to make it palatable for all. It took a long time for certain people in this community to really listen to me.

One of the biggest challenges facing our community will be getting the people of Kentucky to accept Jefferson County. The state has so much power. We need to find a way to get more power here locally, but it's probably going to take a change in the state constitution to make that happen.

I worry about this Metro Council now – how divisive its party politics is. It's going to hurt. Our mayor, Jerry Abramson, has been a pretty good leader, but Jerry can't live forever. I wish I had some solutions. I'm about at the stage where all I can do is pray.

I have learned some lessons in my own life that I would like to share with the next generation of leaders coming up in Louisville:

First, know what leadership requires and be willing to give it – time, finances, and any other things necessary to make a project succeed. You need dedication, in one word, that embraces all those things.

Second, consider everything before you embark on a project or a leadership role. If, by accident, a leadership role falls upon you – even if you weren't seeking it – if you are willing, take it. If you are not willing, be honest and say you're not interested in it, and let the community find other people.

You hear people say, "Why don't they do this?" But who is this "they" people are talking about? "They" is us.

JAMES R. RAMSEY

President
University of Louisville

JIM RAMSEY CONSIDERS HIMSELF a teacher, first and foremost. But the current president of the University of Louisville also has a good deal of experience in state government and in academic administration.

In 2002, when both UofL president John Shumaker and his interim successor, provost Carol Garrison, decided to leave UofL, Ramsey was serving as the Commonwealth of Kentucky's budget director, as a chief policy advisor to the governor, and as a professor of economics at UofL. He had served as the state's budget director one other time, and also as the state's chief economist. He had directed both the Office of Financial Management and Economic Analysis and the Office of Investment and Debt Management in Frankfort.

He had also served in administrative jobs at Loyola University in New Orleans, at Western Kentucky University and at the University of North Carolina, and he had taught at Middle Tennessee State University, Loyola, the University of Kentucky, UNC and WKU, as well as at UofL.

In tough economic times, and with all of the state schools facing budget difficulties, Ramsey seemed to the UofL Board of Trustees to be a good choice to serve as interim president while they conducted a national search for a new president. He declined at first to be a candidate himself.

During the course of that interim period though, friends of his — including UofL trustees, students, faculty, staff, alumni and state political leaders — urged him to consider taking the job permanently, Ramsey later told *The Courier-Journal*.

Ramsey knew that one of the most formidable tasks the next president would face would be moving forward with UofL's Challenge for Excellence, launched by Shumaker in 1998 in response to the state legislature's passage of a higher education reform package.

The initiative set benchmark goals for academics and fundraising and created the blueprint for UofL to become a nationally recognized metropolitan research institution, as the legislation mandated.

Ramsey, as it turned out – in his state position – had been largely responsible for drafting the legislative bill that set forth the requirements. He said he felt some obligation to see it carried out. "There was a little bit of a sense that this was the right thing for me to do," he told *Business First* in 2003. "This is a job, and it's my job."

So he agreed to be a candidate and was quickly chosen. He said he realized the Challenge for Excellence wouldn't be his only challenge, and he set additional goals for his presidency: improving graduation rates, addressing diversity concerns, and building on partnerships with Louisville Metro, state government, community organizations and other universities.

Jim Ramsey was born in Louisville in 1948 and grew up in Fern Creek. Both his parents were teachers and his father, John Ramsey, was later an associate superintendent of the Jefferson County Public Schools. His wife, Jane Ramsey, also became a teacher.

He has a 1970 bachelor's degree in business administration from WKU, and master's and doctoral degrees in economics from UK. He stayed on at UK for awhile as a research associate in the Center for Public Affairs, then spent two years at Middle Tennessee. He spent three years as a teacher and administrator at Loyola, then 11 years as an adjunct or visiting professor at UK while he held several state jobs. He worked at WKU for six years, then at UNC for one year, but he rejoined Kentucky state government in 1999.

Ramsey's contract to serve as president of UofL is for ten years, a term he doesn't think he will actually serve out. His hope, he says, is to end his career as a full-time professor.

"Education is my first love," he told *Business First*. "I always say the only thing I'm good at is teaching. I enjoy teaching more than anything."

In addition to serving as UofL's 17th president, he serves on several corporate boards in Louisville, as well as the boards of Greater Louisville Inc., the Greater Louisville Sports Commission, the Muhammad Ali Institute, the Frazier Historical Arms Museum, the J.B. Speed Art Museum, the University Medical Center and the Boy Scouts of Kentuckiana.

The National Governor's Association presented its Outstanding Public Service Award to Ramsey in 2001. He was named Kentucky Economist of the Year in 1999 and was inducted into UK's Gatton College of Business and Economics Hall of Fame in 2004.

Jim and Jane Ramsey live in Oldham County and have two daughters.

I FIRST BECAME A LEADER IN THE LOUISVILLE COMMUNITY when I was appointed president of the University of Louisville. John Shumaker had left the University of Louisville to become the president of the University of Tennessee. Carol Garrison, who was UofL's provost at the time, was appointed acting president. She was then offered the opportunity to become president of the University of Alabama at Birmingham, however, so UofL started looking for someone to step in to serve as acting president while the university searched for a new president.

I remember it like it was yesterday. I was doing some training for a group in Kingsport, Tennessee and I got a phone call from UofL officials saying, "Would you help us stay on course?" "We've lost John and we've lost Carol, all in about a three-month period of time. We need someone to come and fill in while we go through the search for a new president."

Because I had been heavily involved in the design and passage of the Postsecondary Improvement Education Act, because I had helped Governor Paul Patton with his focus on higher education, and because I had seen the University of Louisville fully embrace higher education reform, I felt it was important for me to come to Louisville to accept this role on an acting basis. So I guess if there was a moment in time when I made the decision to come to Louisville to serve in a leadership role, it was at that time. I felt it was important to keep the university moving forward and to recognize the contributions it had made to higher ed reform. So that was the point in time when I said, "This is something I need to do."

I talked to Governor Paul Patton and he said, "I don't want you to do that. I'm afraid you'll never come back." It was always my intent to come back and finish out the last year of Governor Patton's administration. But after four or five months, as the Board of Trustees went through its search process, they came back to me and said, "We like what you've been able to do in the first four or five months. We've interviewed some candidates, but we'd like for you to stay in the position on a permanent basis."

It was an easy decision for me to do that. I had had an opportunity to meet many of the faculty and staff, and I realized what a great place UofL is, and the city of Louisville is. Otherwise, I probably would have continued to stay in Frankfort. I had actually thought that at the end of the Patton administration, I would probably try to stay in higher education administration anyway, at the state level.

Originally, I taught school. I then became associate dean at Loyola University in New Orleans. When John Y. Brown Jr. was elected governor of Kentucky, some people in his administration knew me and asked me if I would come back home. So I have come back home a couple of times actually.

Governor Brown was bringing in some really smart, talented business people and to be part of that seemed like it was going to be fun. He was clearly going to be a change agent, and the area in which he wanted me to work was the financial management area. He wanted to change some things from the way that they had been done in the past. He wanted to make things less political, and to give them more of a public policy focus.

It sounded exciting, but it was also a chance for us to come back home. Jane and I are both from Louisville and our families still lived here, so this offered us an opportunity to come back home and to be involved in a very meaningful effort to make a difference in Kentucky. Even then, one of my requirements in coming back home was to have an adjunct position at the University of Kentucky. Later, when we left North Carolina to return home, one of my conditions on returning was to have a faculty position. At that time, it worked out for me to be in a position at the University of Louisville. UofL stepped forward and said, "We would like for you to be on our faculty." So we came back from North Carolina, and I became a member of the faculty here. I also served as budget director for the Governor's Office of Policy and Management.

Probably the person who has had the most profound influence on my life was a person whom I didn't really know for an extremely long period of time, and that was Michael Hooker – the Chancellor at the University of North Carolina. I knew of Michael before going to North Carolina. Michael was viewed as one of the new generation of higher education leaders in the United States. He was a leader in higher education who "got it" – understood the role of higher education in quality of life and economic development issues. Michael understood the transformation that was taking place in the economy, from a manufacturing to a knowledge-based economy.

I first met Michael when he came and spoke to the Council on Postsecondary Education's Trustees' Conference, immediately after the higher ed reform bill was passed. Michael knocked everybody's socks off with his presentation. His whole appearance, his whole presentation – there was a wow factor. Like everybody else, I went up at the end and said hello. But then later, when Michael was looking for a chief financial officer for UNC to help him get done what he needed to, he talked to people and they gave him my name. I really didn't know him. I only knew who he was. I had read some of his writings and some of his speeches as part of higher ed reform. When I got a phone call from him, I thought, "Lord, how did this happen?"

We were living in Bowling Green at the time. Michael called me one Saturday morning out of the blue. He was at the Gator Bowl, and North Carolina was playing that afternoon. He asked me if I would come and be part of his team at the University of North Carolina. I could not immediatly sign on since we were within weeks of heading into a legislative session. After the legislative session, however, I interviewed at North Carolina.

When I went to interview and we sat down to breakfast, Michael said, "You're the person I need. You need to go through all the interviews today, do the very best you can, don't blow it. But I need you to come here and help me make this everything that it can be." I started there that June.

Michael taught me a great deal. He taught me to think big. The University of North Carolina is a great school. It has great history, great tradition. I hadn't even been there a few days when Michael said to me, as we were driving across campus, "Jim, our goal is to make this the number one public university in the country." I was flabbergasted when he then said, "I can't do it without you, Jim. That's why I brought you here."

For some reason, Michael had a profound belief in me. I became a key part of his team. Then, within six months, he was diagnosed with cancer. And within nine months, he died. He was 53.

A lot of the progressive things that happened at the University of North Carolina took place before Michael got there. North Carolina had a lot of great higher education leaders. Michael was from Grundy, Virginia – just across the mountain from Pikeville, Kentucky. He was the son of a coal miner.

Michael was the first generation in his family to go to college, and he went to North Carolina. He went on to get his graduate degree at Johns Hopkins, then worked at some different universities before he came back home to UNC. Michael had a very clear vision that the University of North Carolina's job was to improve the quality of life and economic opportunity for the people of North Carolina. Of course, that's what we were trying to do with higher ed reform in Kentucky as well.

North Carolina was ahead of Kentucky. I could see where the things that we believed in Kentucky, and that we worked so hard for in the higher ed reform effort, were really making a difference in North Carolina.

My experience with Michael solidified in me the belief that what we had done with higher ed reform was the right thing to do, and that higher education really could make a difference in terms of economic opportunity and quality of life in our city and our state.

The second person who had great influence on me over a long period of time was Jack Segell, a local business person in Louisville. I met Jack when I first went to work for the Brown Administration in 1981. We stayed in touch until Jack's death in 2003. Jack was one of those people who was always there to offer advice, to offer counsel, to meet with you, to help in any way. Jack was probably 25 years my senior, but we maintained a relationship for 22 years, until his death. The amazing thing was that when I went to the memorial service for Jack, I saw a room full of people and I thought, "How did all these people know Jack?" It turns out Jack was a mentor to all of them as well. Later people told me, "Jack used to send me newspaper articles on certain topics." "Jack used to call me." "Jack and I used to have breakfast." He was a career counselor to so many people.

So those two people were the two people who have been strong mentors to me – one was a 22-year relationship, and the other was a very short but powerful relationship. Michael's impact and death is what drives me day-in-and-day-out, however. He helped me believe in myself.

I believe very much in teams. I like to use the analogy of a basketball team. We all have strengths and we all have weaknesses. Our basketball coach, Rick Pitino, needs a good power forward, a good shooting guard, somebody to come off the bench. I know I have limitations and I know I have weaknesses, so I like to work with a management team – people with different skills, different perspectives. I like the interaction from the team. I like the support from a team. So as a leader, I try to create a team atmosphere and encourage working as a team.

Others might describe me as haphazard. I'm a professor at heart, and I'm kind of absent-minded. I think sometimes that the professor in me results in people not always knowing exactly what I'm thinking, so I think people would probably say "He's probably a little disjointed or haphazard."

I don't think that I've really ever accomplished anything on my own. I think people working together accomplish things. But I do take a lot of pride in a few things. I was the point person on the revenue package that supported KERA – the Kentucky Education Reform Act. I think KERA has been a great thing for this state. When Governor Wallace Wilkinson made the decision that he was going to increase taxes – and that was a hard decision to make – he looked to me to put the tax package together. And we had a good tax package.

Governor Wilkinson had said that he was not going to increase taxes when he was campaigning. But the 1990 legislative session started, and we were under Supreme Court order to do something about our education system. A lot of legislative work and executive branch work had taken place regarding governance and curriculum and financing – all things that were part of KERA. The question was how we were going to pay for it. I think most political leaders in the state, and probably most of the press in the state, thought that Governor Wilkinson would not show leadership and put forth a tax increase and package. A small group of us had been working on one. We weren't trying to grab headlines or anything like that, but we had a tax package that was going to be part of the budget that we knew would pay for the KERA reform.

We called all the legislative leaders into the governor's office. Governor Wilkinson turned the meeting over to me and said, "Jim is going to explain the package." At that time, we had some real stalwarts in the General Assembly – people like Senator Mike Moloney from Lexington, Representative Joe Clarke from Danville, and others. And they came out of the room and said, "This is a good package." So being a small player in KERA, and being a small player in higher ed reform – those are things in which I take pride.

What I learned from these experiences is, again, the importance of team. When we were working on higher ed reform, we would sit in the governor's conference room. We would work late and order pizza. The governor would always come down and say, "Anybody ready for pizza?" It was a team, and we all kind of brought different things to the table and worked together. Those two efforts probably really reinforced in me something that I believed in – that working together, you can get more accomplished. Team members build off each other's strengths and weaknesses and can bring different talents and expertise to a project.

My biggest disappointment may be that I only stayed in North Carolina for a little over a year. It was a great place. I would have liked to have stayed longer and worked with Michael longer. My greatest disappointment was not having that opportunity. God does work in very strange ways, though, because we were sent there. And I couldn't have done this job without that experience – working with Michael, and being at a great research university.

We're trying to build the University of Louisville into a premier metropolitan research university, and I was at one of the greatest research universities in the country. I worked for a great leader and I learned a lot. I couldn't do this job without having had that experience.

When Michael died, we didn't know what the future would be at North Carolina. We were also being recruited to come back home. Michael's death made it easier for us to come back home, so we did. Within a year, Jane's mother died of Lou Gehrig's disease; and within two years, my mother passed away. So everything worked out the way it was supposed to work out by our coming home again. In a sense, living at UNC-CH for a short time was a disappointment, but it was meant to be.

In terms of failures, I don't know. Things that I think some people would interpret as failures, I really don't interpret that way.

When I was at Western Kentucky University and Tom Meredith left, I think everybody just assumed I would be the next president. Being president was not something that I had aspired to — it wasn't one of my lifetime goals — but I was a candidate for the job. Jane was much more disappointed than I was that I didn't get that. I was more philosophical that it wasn't meant to be.

I've had failures, but I've tried not to dwell on them. I don't know that I would single out any one failure as having had a profound impact on me or my life. You have a lot of experiences in life — some positive and some negative — and you try to learn from those experiences and move forward.

One thing I have learned from my experiences is patience. Sometimes we don't always understand why things happen, and we don't understand why they happen the way they do. Secondly, I have learned that we learn from all of our experiences. Thirdly, I have learned that we draw strength from our experiences. A lot of things happen to us in life that we don't like, but we don't have any control over them. We just have to learn from them and do the very best we can.

Good followers need to work hard to understand the mission and vision of the organization they are working for, and to understand where their leader is going. I think that's very important. A good follower also needs to be honest and straightforward and offer input and suggestions. He or she must realize that the ultimate responsibility to make the decision of "here's where we are going" lies with someone else.

A good leader has to take the time, however, to say, "Here's where we are going," and "Here's how I think we should move forward, strategically and tactically." I expect people who work with me to give me honest input and to make suggestions about that mission and vision. These are the major things I look for in people. I also expect people who work with me to work as hard as I do, but that is probably an unrealistic expectation.

I wouldn't change anything or do anything differently if I could live my life over again. I've made a lot of mistakes in my life, but I've tried to learn from them and I have no regrets. I am very fortunate. No one is more fortunate than I am. Cher has this song, "If I could turn back time." You can't. I don't know what tomorrow holds. I could be hit by a car this afternoon. So I just try to stay focused and to do the very best I can do.

I would advise a young person aspiring to leadership to take advantage of every opportunity you get. Sometimes we don't realize all of the opportunities that are presented to us. We don't realize that sometimes in life we are faced with things that look like challenges but they are really unique opportunities.

While you are young, in particular, you should try to meet as many people as you can and experience as many different experiences as you can.

Jane and I were born in Louisville. We are white Anglo-Saxon Protestants. So for us to have experiences at Loyola University in New Orleans, with its Spanish, French and Catholic influences, helped us grow and better understand people. That was a good experience for us.

People should take advantage of as many opportunities as they can to meet different people, and to enjoy different work experiences and diverse cultural settings. I would strongly encourage that. It gets harder when you start raising a family. Take advantage of all of those opportunities, because they are all learning experiences. Someday you'll look back at age 36, or 46, or 56 and draw on those experiences and things that you learned a long time ago.

I think the second thing I would advise young people is don't look back. Learn from your past, but set new goals for yourself. Think about what you can add to the world and what difference you can make. You have to be realistic, but it's important to keep moving forward and to stay focused.

If you look back 50 years in our community, to 1954, I was six years old. Louisville was a very different community. General Electric had just come here. It was still very much a manufacturing town, with International Harvester, the tobacco companies and so forth. Then you look at our city in 2004, and we're a very different community – economically, socially and culturally.

I think one of the most important projects in our community took place after the recession of the 1980s, when the community came together and said, "How can we really diversify our economy?" There was a community effort called the Boyle Report that said, "Here's how we can move from a manufacturing economy to a more diverse economy."

So our community made efforts to redefine itself. We will hopefully look back in the future and say that merging our governments was one of the most important events that happened in our community, because it helped bring our diverse community together.

In terms of people who have made a significant contribution to our community over the years, I think Wilson Wyatt clearly had vision and leadership and was a major influence, especially at the University of Louisville.

Finally today, we are beginning to appreciate and achieve the vision that Wilson Wyatt and other community leaders had back then for the regional cancer center and other major projects. Wilson Wyatt believed in the community and believed in the people of the community. I think sometimes we as Kentuckians probably don't do enough of that. We've sometimes been told that we are under-educated and that we like basketball because we're good at basketball, and that we are not good and can't compete at other things. I think Wilson Wyatt really set a positive tone for the community.

In terms of educational leadership – and this is probably more statewide – I feel David Jones, Oz Nelson and John Hall have had great vision and leadership and influence. They all believed that education was key, and KERA wouldn't have happened without their leadership.

I think even more modern day, we are going to lose a real giant in Hank Wagner. Hank's had a vision over the last 20 years of the importance of the medical community. Hank has for a long time understood the role of the University of Louisville in health care and in the medical community, and he has been a real visionary in that sense.

Any role I might have played in these things I played in the background, working from a public policy perspective. I always thought, up until this position, that my role was to do the policy analysis so that the political leadership could make the policy decisions with the best information they had.

From a state public policy perspective, I always recognized the importance of Louisville. There were a lot of projects here that I had the opportunity to be involved with. I take great pride in the first project I worked on with Governor Brown – the financing of the Kentucky Center for the Arts. I had an opportunity to meet a wonderful gentleman named Chip Grafton. Chip passed away shortly after we finished the financing of the Center of the Arts. His daughter, Sue Grafton, who is one of our graduates at UofL, is a famous novelist, of course.

I had the opportunity from a public policy perspective to work very closely with Louisville's governmental and business community. I worked on a lot of projects that were not successful, including a couple of attempts to build a new arena and to attract an NBA team. But my role was always more wearing my economist hat or making sure that the people who were making policy decisions had the best information they could have to make those decisions.

Coming back to higher education reform and "Bucks for Brains," I vividly remember being in the conference room of Jewish Healthcare with Ron Greenberg when the idea was conceived. Ron was on the Council on Postsecondary Education. At that time, I was a liaison with the Council. Leonard Hardin had asked me to be a special advisor to him as chairman of the Council. I was working with the council members and working with the institutions, and Ron Greenberg said to me, "We have this idea we've been thinking about at Jewish Healthcare. We could create a pool of state funds and be able to bring in research teams, the best talent in the world." He would always talk about research teams from Duke and, of course, that was painful to somebody from North Carolina. I understood the idea, so I give myself credit for that. I went back and talked to Governor Patton about it and his first reaction was, "I don't know if that makes sense." But to the Governor's credit, he thought about it, then he came back to me and said, "We need to follow through with Jewish Healthcare, because that idea has a lot of merit."

So we worked with the Jewish Healthcare people to flush out the idea. We then started talking to a lot of other people. One person we talked to was Lee Todd. Lee wasn't president of the University of Kentucky yet, but we had known each other for ten plus years. Lee had been a successful faculty member at UK – a successful researcher, businessman, and entrepreneur. We talked to a lot of people and out of that came "Bucks for Brains." We put together all of the financial analysis. We talked to bond rating companies in New York and sold them on the idea of bonding because originally we didn't have the cash. It turned out later we had the cash and didn't have to borrow for "Bucks One." We helped sell the concept to the General Assembly, we helped sell it to the bond rating companies – again, I saw that my job was to do all the things necessary to make the policy work.

I think our community has several challenges to overcome in the future. One is to develop the next generation of leaders. We have had some wonderful leaders in Louisville – from the David Joneses to the individuals from Brown-Forman, to some of the great leaders in our law firms, our financial leaders and leaders in our banking community. Who are the next generation of leaders?

I think the challenge to us is that the corporate world has changed. If you look at Louisville now, a lot of our banks are owned outside of Kentucky. A lot of our companies, like Commonwealth Life Insurance – a great Kentucky company – have external ownership now. Louisville Gas and Electric has external ownership. Many of today's corporate leaders are really working for someone in another community, so the focus of the leaders here in Louisville is the quarterly report and financial statement.

Where are the people going to come from who are going to step forward and worry about the arts, worry about education, and worry about the relationships between whites and blacks in our community? I think how we develop that next generation and who that next generation of leaders will be in Louisville is very important.

The second challenge our community is going to face is that we have made progress diversifying our economy, but we still have a long way to go.

My oldest daughter, who is 21, graduated from college last year. What's going to happen when she goes out to the job market? Will there be good-paying jobs in our community so that she doesn't have to go to Atlanta, doesn't have to go to California, or somewhere else? Diversifying our economy and providing good paying jobs to keep our young people here is still a very major challenge.

One of the goals of the governor's KEES scholarship program was to keep the best students in Kentucky, because the research shows if you go outside the state to go to college, the likelihood of your coming back is a lot less. We are trying to keep our better students here, but are we making sure that once they have graduated, they have job opportunities?

I think the third challenge that we as a community are facing is making sure that the whole community grows together – not just the East End, but the South End and West End and downtown as well. One of our community's great strengths is that we are a diverse city, in terms of race, religion, ethnic backgrounds and so forth. But that's also a challenge, and we have to stay together as a community.

I would see those three things as issues that we as a community need to be thinking about and working on everyday.

I would like to tell young people who are aspiring to leadership in our community that they can make a difference – a huge difference – in this community. The effort is worth it.

Sometimes I think as individuals we feel like there are things that are beyond our control, and they actually are. But I've been amazed here at the University of Louisville. I look around our organization and see the work that we are doing in our heart program, and the work that were are doing in our cancer program, in our college of education, in our business school, in our engineering school. We're a big organization, but we are making a difference in the quality of life of the people who live in Louisville and Kentucky.

I would advise the young people of this community to be engaged, work hard, do what you can to make a difference. I think one of the things that has been a plus for us as we have tried to recruit some of the top people in this country to UofL is that we've actually had people in our cancer program who have had job offers at Harvard, Yale and other major universities. They have come to UofL because they feel like here they can make a difference and be a part of a real change.

That's advice that I would offer to the next generation of leaders. In this community, you really do have the opportunity to step forward and guide how we as a community are going to grow and prosper in the future.

I have learned some valuable lessons in my life and career that I would like to pass on to the next generation. First and foremost, stick to your values. We are all driven by certain core values. They will differ from person to person. Your values will be a little bit different from mine. But stick to your values. Always come back to your value set as you are thinking about things and are trying to make decisions. That was a lesson I guess I learned 10 or 15 years ago. I went through one experience in my life and was questioning my own values and my own worth. As I moved forward, it was important for to me to come back to ask myself, "What are the values that are important to me?"

Secondly, I would say that I have learned to do the very best I can, to work as hard as I can, and to be persistent. Sometimes at the end of the day you go home, and you're pretty frustrated, and you yell at the dog and tell your wife "It's just not worth it and I can't take it any more." But stay focused, day-in-and-day-out, and work hard. Do the best you can, and at some point you'll look back and say "Wow, we were really able to do that."

Thirdly, don't be afraid to fail. I think that sometimes we don't do things because we are afraid we might fail. There was an old adage in state government that there were two kinds of people – those who were afraid to do anything because they were afraid to make a mistake and get yelled at, and those who were going to move straight on ahead, and if they went too far they were going to beg forgiveness, but they weren't going to be content to just sit there and not do anything. They were going to take the initiative and, if they made a mistake or went beyond their bounds of authority, they would just beg forgiveness and move forward.

I think that sometimes we are afraid to fail. As I look at this job, I don't think I have the skill set for it. I don't think I am any more suited for this job than the man in the moon. I think I've been asked to do the job, however, so I'm going to do the very best I can. I'm going to try to stick to my values. I'm going to work hard. I'm going to be persistent and focused and do the very best I can. That would be the advice I would give to anyone.

I may fail. People say, "Have you ever done fundraising?" No, I really haven't done fundraising. I may fall flat on my face doing fundraising.

But tomorrow we are announcing a $15 million gift – the largest gift ever given to the University of Louisville. You just can't be afraid and say, "Well, I can't do it." You've got to be like the little train chugging up the hill and just keep telling yourself, "I think I can, I think I can."

SAMUEL ROBINSON

**President Emeritus
Lincoln Foundation**

SAM ROBINSON CAME TO LOUISVILLE in 1960 to work for the Lincoln Institute, a school created by Berea College in 1912 in Shelby County to educate black Kentuckians. His boss was Whitney Young Sr., a Lincoln Institute graduate who had risen to become its first black president and served for almost 40 years.

Robinson jumped into civic activities shortly after he arrived, starting with the West End Community Improvement Association, which tried to stem white flight as blacks moved into West Louisville neighborhoods. One leadership position led to another, as his reputation for hard work and his enthusiasm for community projects became known.

He served on the boards of Bellarmine University and PNC Bank, the Board of Visitors of the Indiana University School of Education, and the National Board of the Presbyterian Health, Education and Welfare Association. He also serves on the board of the Muhammed Ali Center and the African-American Heritage Center, and he is a co-founder of the Louisville Chapter of One Hundred Black Men, and of the Kentucky Minority AIDS Council.

Robinson was very active in the civil rights movement in the 1960s and '70s, and when the Jefferson County Schools were ordered desegregated, he was co-chairman of the council that helped map out the plan.

Through such activities, he met a lot of people, and he parlayed his contacts into a career as a noted fundraiser. In 1994, for example, the James Graham Brown Foundation offered his Lincoln Foundation a challenge grant of $500,000 for its Whitney M. Young Scholars Program.

The grant called for Robinson's group to raise $500,000 in matching money in a little over a year. Robinson did it in less than six months.

He considers the scholars program, which picks up students in the seventh grade and guides them through high school with promise of a college scholarship if they maintain grades, to be his signature achievement.

Eleanor Stokes, sister of the late Rev. Vernon Robertson — with whom Robinson worked on Montessori schools for many years — told *The Courier-Journal* in 2001 that the two men were very much alike. "They both knew a lot of people in the community and they had the kind of personality that draws people to them," she said.

Sam Robinson was one of nine children, born in 1935 in Memphis, Tennessee. He graduated from Tennessee State University in 1956, with a bachelor's degree in biology. He served two years in the Army, before moving to Louisville. He started out teaching biology and math at the Lincoln Institute, then ultimately became dean of education and administrative assistant to the president.

The state took over funding of the Institute in the 1940s and, in 1967, changed the school's mission from educating black students to teaching gifted, but disadvantaged students. Robinson became principal. The state closed the school in 1970, with only one class of graduates, but Robinson likes to note that all 42 of them had four-year scholarships to colleges, including Harvard and Yale.

Robinson was principal at Louisville's Shawnee High School for a few years, then went to Indiana University to earn a doctorate in education.

When he returned to Louisville in 1974, he became executive director of the Lincoln Foundation, then became its president in 1991. The Foundation was established in 1910 to start and support the Institute, and it later supported minority scholarships in general.

Robinson retired as president in 2000, though he continued to work with Montessori schools. He also took a job as executive-in-residence at Bellarmine University, to help with recruitment of minority students.

He has received over 100 honors throughout his career, including induction into the National African-American Hall of Fame.

In 1997, *Louisville Magazine* named him one of Louisville's 50 most influential citizens.

In 2001, then-Louisville Mayor David Armstrong presented Robinson with the city's second Dream Award, which recognizes someone who reflects the principles of Dr. Martin Luther King Jr.

Robinson is married to the former Hugh Ella Walker, a retired Jefferson County Public School teacher. They have two adult daughters.

I THINK I DECIDED TO BECOME A LEADER during early childhood. In first or second grade, I decided that I always wanted to be the one in charge. I wanted to be the one to make the highest grade. I wanted to be the one who could receive some adulation from my classmates because they felt I had some things on the ball. That's when I decided I wanted to be a leader.

I decided I wanted to translate that from personal into community leadership during my middle and high school years, because I was very active in my church growing up, and I was involved in projects in the community, helping out with senior citizens projects, school projects.

When I first came here, I did not know anyone. My wife and I came here because I was offered a job opportunity. When I came here, I saw that there was a void in terms of youth leadership. There were quite a number of individuals who were older, middle-aged, in leadership roles. I had been very active in college. I was a campus leader, involved with student government, fraternities and other organizations. So when I came here, I began to look for opportunities where I could become involved and be a leader.

One of the first opportunities came about in the community I lived in – West Louisville, around 47th and Riverview. There was a group of individuals who wanted to begin a community club. They asked me if I would serve as president, and that was the beginning of my leadership here. I became the president of the Riverview Community Center and Club. We were involved in road improvements, lights for the community, community betterment. That had not been evident in that community before we began that organization.

I came here to work at Lincoln Institute, for Dr. Whitney M. Young Sr., who was the president of the institution. He offered me opportunities to assume leadership roles at the institution, with the assistance of Dr. Eleanor Love, who also worked at the Institute. I worked very closely with Dr. Love and her father. He gave me so many opportunities to represent the institution, and to become involved in professional development with teachers. In the meantime, I was still active in the community.

I came here in the early '60s, during the Civil Rights era. I became very involved with the West End Community Improvement Association, which was a group at the time working to advise and encourage white people to stay in the West End so that we would have an integrated, and more diverse, neighborhood in the community. I spent many Saturdays going from door-to-door, asking white families to seriously consider remaining in the community. That gave me an opportunity to become a leader in West Louisville.

Dr. Whitney M. Young, Sr. and Dr. Eleanor Love had a considerable impact on my life. I consider Dr. Whitney M. Young Sr. my mentor, and Dr. Love a colleague-mentor.

What I learned from Dr. Young was that you have to work hard. If you are interested in working in a typical nine-to-five or eight-to-five job, then that is not a good place for a leader. You have to extend yourself. You also have to be sincere about what you're doing, and you must set an example. That was one of the main things I learned from Dr. Young. If you expect others to be productive, you have to be a productive individual yourself, in terms of the amount of time you are willing to spend to do the job correctly, and so forth.

The other thing I learned from Dr. Young is that we have to prepare ourselves for leadership. Dr. Young strongly encouraged me to continue working toward a doctorate, because he felt like that would open up opportunities for leadership roles for me, as well as show my colleagues that I didn't mind taking the necessary steps to prepare for a leadership role.

My Christian upbringing has also always played a role in what I believed. I believe in God, and appreciate the many opportunities the church offers for leadership growth. I've often said that if I wanted to start a revolution, the first place I'd go is to the church, because the church is constantly looking for people willing to assume leadership roles. To me, one of the ideal places to get leadership training is in the church. I've always been active in my church and served in leadership roles. I served in leadership roles in my fraternity also. Once people realize you're serving in a leadership capacity in one organization, they look for you to serve in leadership roles in other organizations.

The challenge is not to spread yourself too thin – especially when you have family. That's one thing that I learned from Lyman Johnson, who also mentored me. He said, "Sam, once people know that you'll do, they'll wear you out." So you just have to work at it, establish priorities. You have to look at impact. What type of impact is this having on the community or individuals? What difference is it making?

Those are the criteria to use in making decisions about leadership involvement. Some people like seeing their names on stationery, or they like to see how many committees they can serve on. Once you're in a leadership role, people will say, "Oh we would very much like to have you, but you don't have to do anything. We just want to use your name. When people see your name, then they will be responsive." I do not adhere to that. Unless I am intricately involved in the operations, then I will not serve as a board member or in a leadership role.

I would describe my leadership style as participatory. I try to get others to share my vision, then I spread the work out, letting everyone find their niche within the organization, and giving them wings to do their job.

Others would see me a little authoritarian. I would call on experiences I've had, and maybe a person could benefit from that, but my leadership would be democratic.

While I was at the Lincoln Foundation, I was very involved in the founding of the Whitney M. Young Scholars Program. That would be one of the crowning successes of my career. I was able to convince the Foundation board that starting a program at the seventh grade level and continuing to assist students, and to assure them that if they maintain standards they will realize a college education, was significant.

But I accomplished some other things too. I was able to raise $1 million dollars in six months for an endowment fund for the Scholars Program. I thought that was significant, because it was highly unusual to achieve in such a short period of time.

I tried to be selective about organizations I would get involved with. I would look at the leadership an organization already had. As a board member, I would tap resources that would benefit the Foundation. Many of the gifts and funds I received came from my informal associations with individuals whom I had met by serving on boards like the Louisville Orchestra, the Kentucky Center for the Arts, the Kentucky State School Board, Bellarmine University. I would get to know people and arrange to tell my story and make it beneficial to the Foundation. If you're going to be a community leader and you want people to help you, you have to get to know them on a one-to-one basis.

Another crowning achievement for me was being involved in the Black Achievers Program. I was in charge of scholarship assistance for over ten years. We were able to identify millions of dollars in scholarship assistance for students who otherwise would not realize a college education. Black Achievers continues to be strong, as well as the Whitney Young Scholars Program.

I think one of my disappointments in life, however, has been that I don't think I've been as successful in improving academic standards for minority students as I could have been. The achievement gap has not decreased and, in some cases, has perhaps even increased, like in Black Achievers. Although we have these wonderful programs, it still seems like we have not made significant improvement in addressing the achievement gap.

In my leadership role in these broad-based organizations, we should have been able to collaborate with the school system, and with city-county government, to come up with some type of broad-based program that would have meaningful impact and that would be sustaining in terms of reaching economically disadvantaged youngsters. Many of the youngsters we help through Black Achievers would have done well in spite of us. Black Achievers didn't really reach the young people we had in mind when it was first founded.

We wanted to go after the extremely disadvantaged youngsters in the housing projects. When you took an inventory of participants, you'd find that there were very few youngsters from those types of environments who were actively involved in the program.

If I could start over and do things differently, I think I would start a stronger mentoring program among African-American professionals and get more of our professional organizations like the Links, Boule, fraternities, etc. to do something similar to what we're trying to do with the reading initiative in Jefferson County schools. We need a broad base of tutors to get involved in helping these youngsters, and we never have been able to do that. We just haven't been very successful. A lot of that has to do with individuals not being willing to do it. We have more and more retired teachers, but many of them are just not interested in tutoring.

Good followers have to have certain criteria. They have to be able to listen attentively, have a certain discipline about them, have an unconditional allegiance to the leader and be able to serve in the absence of their leader.

These qualities are not readily found in young people. I think what we're dealing with is young people want to be leaders. Not many want to be followers. They want to start off at the top – not realizing that they have to spend some time in the trenches and be willing to bleed a little to get to the level where you're in a leadership role.

Learning to become a leader gives you a chance to reflect. It gives you time to meditate and observe. If you start out as the leader of something, you haven't had a chance to observe your terrain. We know from a military standpoint that you don't start off heading or leading a group of men. You have to serve in the trenches; then you're ready to give advice and counsel to individuals who are following you.

I've had the privilege of working with academically talented, economically disadvantaged youngsters. If I were going to do something different, I think I might work more diligently with academically-challenged youngsters, instead of many of the youngsters I'm helping, to try to bring them up to a level of proficiency. I don't think I have been challenged, in terms of impact, by what I have been able to do through the Whitney Young Scholars Program. If I had a group of youngsters who were academically challenged, and I brought them up to a level of proficiency where they could function within a classroom and be able to graduate with B's and C's and go on to be productive members of society, that would have been more fulfilling. I could have done that. It would have taken more resources, more time, more talent, more hours of the day but I think I would have been more fulfilled.

I feel fulfilled by the accomplishments of the youngsters, but if I could say these were mainly kids operating below grade level, and now they're operating at grade level and they've gone on, it might have been more rewarding for me. Not that all of them would have gone on to college, but into postsecondary and technical schools.

The advice I would give to young people aspiring to become leaders is first, be observant of the activities going on within your environment. Be aware of what's going on. What are the issues and concerns and so forth?

Secondly, early in your career and early in your life, identify a mentor – somebody in whom you feel you have faith and with whom you can share your dreams and conflicts.

Thirdly, I would advise aspiring leaders that sometimes you have to toot your own horn. Sometimes you have to go out and let others know what you're doing. Just sitting back, thinking that someone is aware of everything – don't take that for granted. You need to do that.

And lastly, identify groups and agencies where there is a void in the leadership structure that will offer you an opportunity to exercise leadership. Go into an organization trying to find a niche. A good example would be the NAACP. That's how I became involved with the ACT-SO program – identifying youth with talent. So develop a niche for yourself, and work within that niche.

To be very honest, the best way to find a good mentor is to ask someone. I've had many young people come to me. Set up a structure that if one says no, then you try to find someone else who will say yes. Seek out opportunities where you can interact with that person. They don't necessarily have to be in your own field. It often depends on the type of leadership you're looking for. In general, all you're looking for is somebody who has exercised leadership in any given area. The attributes for success are the same for any area in terms of developing trust, a sense of people believing in you and what you can do.

If I had to identify an individual who has contributed significantly to our community over the last 50 years and who has made a big difference in our quality of life it would be Lyman Johnson, because of what he was able to accomplish as an educator, civil rights leader, and social activist. He helped our community develop a conscience, equalizing salaries for teachers, being able to confront people when need be and, at the same time, having courage. He forgot about his own welfare.

I always thought he probably could have risen higher in the educational hierarchy, but he had a firm belief in what we have been able to accomplish over a period of time.

Samuel Robinson

I think that in spite of the issues and concerns and problems we have in Louisville, there is a great amount of goodwill between African-Americans and whites who believe in diversity and achievement. I think this is a wonderful community. We have a great school system. All of that working together has made a difference. My role has always been as a facilitator. I advocated peaceful desegregation during my time as a principal of a high school. I served on the school board and was involved in education. I always felt that through education, I played some important role.

I think closing the divide – educationally, economically, and socially – is one of the greatest challenges currently facing our community – working for one community, so we have equity as well as equality. Those are our challenges. When we look at our school system, our work force, our social services, and our communities, we must bring them closer. I think we're on the move, but until we're able to get that really going, we'll have some problems. It comes from working together. We must work with people we may not ordinarily work with, develop a respect for people who have opposing views, and see if we can find a commonality in terms of things we can work on together. I think what we need to do is really work on developing a cadre of leadership among young people just out of college, avoiding the brain drain of leadership from Louisville. We hope that young people will come back here and find productive employment, then become involved in addressing these issues and concerns.

One of the main lessons I have learned in my lifetime that I want to share with the next generation of leaders in Louisville is to trust God and his redeeming grace. The second is the Golden Rule: Do unto others, as you'd want them to do unto you. The third lesson would be that hard work will not kill you. Anything that's worth cherishing and valuing requires some blood, sweat, and tears. We have to believe in our young people – believe that they can make the difference. We should not discourage them. We should give them advice and counsel on a regular basis.

Another piece of advice I would like to share with our young people is that they should work to increase diversity in their lives – social, economic, educational. They should get to know people who are different than they are. You learn a lot from that, and you develop a sense of community with people of other races, creeds, and ethnic groups.

Lastly, our young people should always think that they can make a difference. Some children don't believe they matter. They're growing up in homes where parents feel the same way. When we were coming up – a family of nine children – we were always told that we could make a difference, and although we were very poor, there was a certain amount of family heritage. We were proud of our family. I worry that hopelessness is rampant. I just wonder, in the next ten or 15 years if we are going to feel as if we have had any impact.

Mason C. Rudd

**Retired Chairman and CEO
Rudd Equipment Company**

**Retired Chairman
Board of Health
Louisville Metro**

MASON RUDD WORKED HARD for four decades to make money selling heavy construction and mining equipment. Since retiring from Rudd Equipment Company in 1993, he has worked hard to give his money away in places where he thinks it will make a difference.

His name is on the 14-story, $45 million Rudd Heart and Lung Center at Jewish Hospital, on a $500,000 endowment to fund research programs for the University ofLouisville School of Medicine's Department of Surgery, on the Bass-RuddTennis Complex at UofL, and on the RuddYoung Artists Program for groups that show up periodically at the Kentucky Opera for 15 weeks of additional training between conservatory study and full-fledged professional careers.

Rudd's fingerprints are on the Children's Lead Poisoning and Haz/ Mat programs, and the AIDS Task Force established by the Louisville Metro Board of Health, which he served on and chaired for 33 years. They are also on the high-tech equipment at the Louisville Free Public Library now, which permits electronic access to volumes from any of the library's branches, even from home – free. Rudd served as chairman of the Library Foundation for 16 years and gave a considerable chunk of his own money to that project. He continues to serve as a member of the Library Foundation board.

Rudd's stamp is on health clinics in less-affluent areas of the county, and on an expanded sewer system that has eliminated many smaller, less effective treatment plants around Jefferson County. When he retired from the Louisville Metro Board of Health last year, former mayor and county judge-executive David Armstrong said he had been "the most influential leader of any of our community boards and commissions."

Mason Rudd was born and educated in Minnesota as a petroleum engineer. He had a brief career with Shell Oil that was interrupted by his service as an artillery officer in North Africa, Italy and France during World War II. He had success as a sales engineer with a distributor of heavy construction equipment in Iowa. He decided to move to Louisville in 1952, because he thought it might be a place where he would be able to do well in a business of his own in that field.

His competition was Whayne Supply Company and Brandeis Machinery and Supply Corporation, two giants in the industry. Their size, he told *Business First* in 1995, made him think "there might be room for somebody else." An associate at that time said Rudd owed his success to an uncanny ability to match just the right person to just the right job.

When Rudd finally retired from Rudd Equipment Company in 1993, his company was operating in six states and had annual revenues of $150 million. He won't discuss his wealth or reveal how much of it he has given away over the years, but he told *The Courier-Journal* when the Rudd Heart and Lung Center was about to be dedicated, "I'll tell you how I feel about money. When I leave this planet, I don't mind if it's all gone."

Mayor Jerry Abramson has called Mason Rudd "one of the great leaders of this community." Besides chairing the Board of Health for 33 years, Rudd has served as chairman of the boards of Jewish Hospital, the University Medical Center, the Kentucky Certificate of Need and Licensure Board, the Library Foundation, and getCare, a network of health institutions that help people without insurance get health care. He has also served on the boards of Channel 15, Metro United Way, the Louisville Area Chamber of Commerce, the Kentucky State Racing Commission and the J.B. Speed Art Museum, among many others.

His generosity and dedication to community service have earned him many honors: a National Conference of Christians and Jews Charles I. Weisberg Humanitarian Award, a Governor's Distinguished Service Medallion, the City of Louisville's Fleur-de-Lis Award, the Advertising Club's Louisvillian of the Year Award, Junior Achievement's Laureate Award, along with honorary doctor of laws degrees from both UofL and Spalding University. The Kentucky Medical Association named him Layman of the Year in 1995.

At the 1995 ceremony dedicating the Rudd Heart and Lung Center at Jewish Hospital, Rudd quoted pessimistic statistics on the state's health status despite his decades of hard work to improve them. He was just frustrated, his daughter, attorney Elizabeth Rudd Bennett, said, because "he hasn't saved the world."

Rudd and his late wife, the former Mary Davidson, had two children. He is married to Peggy Welsh Rudd.

Passing the Torch

I CAME HERE TO LOUISVILLE IN LATE 1952 or early 1953. I came from Davenport, Iowa, where I was a sales engineer for a construction equipment company. I came here because I thought there was an opportunity. I've now lived in Louisville for 54 years.

I don't know if I ever made an actual decision to become a leader, but I probably was a leader for the first time in my adult life during World War II. I was a battery commander in an artillery unit. I was only 21 years old at that time, but I found that I was a good leader, and a successful leader.

Everyone has mentors. I met a number of mine in the military. They were career officers, older than me. I also had another outstanding mentor. After the war, my first job was in Iowa, and the man who owned the particular company I worked for was full of advice. He had started his company as a balloonist during World War I. I listened to him. He was an outstanding man. He had very high moral and ethical standards, and he was a high-quality business man. I learned a great deal from him. You learn all your life. If you close your mind to learning, you can forget about it. You will be in bad shape and you'll have problems. I'm still learning.

I became chair of a health-related board called "getCare" that provided health services to adults who are uninsured and don't qualify for any programs. I chaired the Louisville Free Public Library Foundation for 12 years, but I recently retired. I'm still chair of the Board of Health, although the newspaper said I retired. I promised Peggy that I was going to retire. I told the mayor that my plan is to resign when the Metro Council adopts some kind of plan on a smoking ban. I'm optimistic we will.

I love the Library Foundation. I also took on the Marine Hospital Foundation recently, at the request of the mayor. We plan to re-construct the Marine Hospital behind Family Health Care, on the same piece of property. Congress created it, and eight other Marine Hospitals around the country, in 1837. They targeted workers and passengers on river vessels. The one in Louisville is the only one left standing in the country. Some years ago I said to myself, we're going to have to save this building, and we are moving toward that.

You can't lead by demanding things from people. You have to make people understand what the problem is and what the plans are. You must be able to relate to people. I think that's the best way to lead. That's certainly how I lead. I think other people would describe my leadership style in that same way.

On a personal note, I was married to Mary who has passed away. I'm the father of a family that I'm extremely proud of and I am now also a grandfather. That's my major accomplishment. I've done lots of other things though. I've helped build a building – the Rudd Heart and Lung Center at Jewish Hospital. I've helped the Louisville Ballet and the Louisville Opera. I'm particularly proud of my work at Jewish Hospital. I started in the late '60s. I was chair of the hospital's board, and we bridged the gap with the older leaders of the hospital. That allowed me to connect younger people coming on the board and the older members. I was the first so-called "young" chair. I'm very proud of that and proud of other accomplishments.

I've been chair of the Board of Health for over 30 years, serving as we moved into the modern age of public health. We have done many specific things that have brought it to this point.

Another committee I worked on early was the Kentucky Council on Higher Education. Governor Louie Nunn asked me to serve. I really enjoyed working on this, and we had some genuine accomplishments.

I also chaired the state Certificate of Need and Licensure Board for four years. It was one of the most difficult jobs I've ever had. Because of what it's role is, members can sometimes become pretty unpopular.

Yes, I've made some contributions. Some good things are still going on, too, and I'm proud to be a part of them.

My son Mike is CEO of our company. The company has continued to grow successfully under his leadership. He must be doing the right things. I've always said that your success and failure depends on the kind of people you surround yourself with. You must select them carefully.

My daughter is an attorney specializing in environmental law. She became an attorney after her kids left for college.

I have been disappointed about our not passing the smoking ban bill yet. There should absolutely be no smoking in public places. I've talked to many people, and there is no question about right or wrong on this issue. I am very disappointed by our Metro Council. Some of its members are friends for whom I have a great amount of respect. We're going to get the smoking ban policy in place. This is a pure health issue, nothing more. I'm not giving up.

There have been times when I've been asked to lead this or that. Working on a project that someone else is leading is fine, as long as it is something I want to see accomplished.

I was a petroleum engineer. I worked for Shell Oil Company. I loved working in the oil fields. I have often wondered if I should have stayed. I enjoyed that kind of work, and the people involved in it. It was exciting.

World War II changed all that.

I might have been 21 when I joined the Army, maybe 22. I was just a baby. War makes you grow up fast. I feel so badly about the kids being killed in Iraq. I don't mean to get political, but they are 18, 19, 20, 21 years old. We are there with no way to get out soon. I feel so badly for them and have some idea what they are going through. I know what it's like being shot at. They have little idea of why they are there. They only think in terms of when they are going to eat, where they are going to sleep.

Here's my advice to young people today who are aspiring to leadership. Select something you have an interest in and get involved. The first time I was involved in helping was in about 1962 or 1963. I was an engineer and a business man and I had a very dear friend on Norton Hospital's Mental Health Board. He told me, "I think you'd probably enjoy it." I didn't know anything about it, but I did get involved with Norton. It was my first job in health care and I did fine. There was a need I felt I could fulfill.

There is a terrible need for health care in the world today. Did you know that approximately 25 percent of the kids in this world right now are hungry? I must try to help improve these things. We think we are a wonderful country and we are. The greatest in the history of mankind. But we have a big problem with homeless and hungry kids and other people. You can fight it and fight it. I hope to see it improve.

When I moved here to Louisville, it was a different community. It has grown up as I have grown up. I'll give you an example. I was at a reception and a couple of women included me in a conversation. One said she used to be able to stand on Fourth and Broadway and know everybody, and now she said she knows very few people. I said "Why do you have to know everyone who walks by?" I thought she was going to hit me.

That's the way things were at that time. We have a high level of culture here. There are only a few months out of the year when our weather is bad. Louisville is a pleasant place to be, and to have a corporate headquarters. It's very relaxed, just a nice place.

We also have a good education system – both public and private. Louisville is just a nice place to work and live. People talk to me about moving here, and how nice it is. We have also become a more diverse community. Places like GE have brought workers here from all over the country. I think that has changed our culture. If the culture used to be like the two little women I talked about, it's not that way anymore at all. We have a very large Vietnamese community here now, for example, and other significant groups like that.

Finding people to continue to lead this community is going to be one of our community's greatest challenges in the future. It's difficult finding younger people who will be willing to step up. I have spoken to several myself. I ask them to come join this or that. These are people from age 30 on. Many of them are running their businesses and just don't want to be involved. We need to find a way to make them feel they are a genuine part of this community.

Many things need to be accomplished here in Louisville, but there are always some people who want things to stay the way they are and who resist change. They don't want to see or do anything, but that doesn't make them bad. Everyone can find some niche, some way to make a contribution to our community to make it better.

We must tell our young people to look around, and to think about what they are saying and doing. They need to think in terms of how they can help make things better. Then we need to ask them questions and listen to their answers. Too many people don't listen. Lots of people like the sound of their own voices, but we need to be listening to others. We can accomplish that easily.

REVEREND BOB RUSSELL

Senior Pastor
Southeast Christian Church

BOB RUSSELL'S LAST CHURCH building was huge. It seated 2,500 people. But his congregation grew so large that he used to have to hold Easter Sunday services at Freedom Hall. So he and his congregation built a new church which seats 9,100, and that's only in the main sanctuary. You can see it from Interstate 64 in Louisville's East End, looming out on its 100 acres off Blankenbaker Parkway. But now the church has 18,500 attendees and they have to hold four services on the weekend to get all of the people in the doors. It is one of the ten largest churches in the country. It's still growing.

The size of the church has been the subject of some humor around town, but its ministry has drawn open admiration, even from people who aren't members. An interesting number of the community's biggest movers and shakers are members. Fundraising for the new $78 million church perhaps shows something about the members' support for Russell and the financial clout of the congregation. Church members donated $40 million and sold their old church for $7.3 million. It was easy for them to borrow the rest.

Southeast Christian is not a fire and brimstone kind of church. When Russell speaks, *Business First* noted in a 1992 profile, "his words fall gently on the ears."

The Courier-Journal's C. Ray Hall had a similar impression. "His soul-searching and soul-winning are done softly, in a low-key, low pressure way, suffused with humor, self-deprecation and an utter lack of presumption," Hall wrote. One of the ideas he preaches, Russell told Hall, is that the country has lost a "sense of moral values that have been handed down by God."

It isn't just those thousands of people in the sanctuary who hear Russell either. His sermons are broadcast on more than 35 radio stations, including Louisville's WHAS, and some as far away as South America and Europe. *Louisville Magazine* reported in 1998 that an arm of the church run by Russell's wife, Judy, was selling 6,000 tapes of his sermons each month.

Still, some of the church's growing appeal is attributed to its support programs, through which it creates a sort of Christian haven to address the stresses of everyday life on its members. It has more than 18 support groups, for troubles from alcoholism to divorce, and dozens of classes of many kinds.

Bob Russell was 22 when he came to Louisville in 1966, from a small Pennsylvania town by way of the Cincinnati Bible Seminary. Southeast Christian had recently been spun off from another church, and it had about 120 members — big for Russell, whose home church had 89. The congregation started off in rented space in a school, then bought a brick house and met in the basement. It tore the house down and built its first church on the lot, off Hikes Lane, the year Russell arrived.

In 1976, church leaders struggled with the question of whether to keep growing or to spin off some members. They decided there were plenty of small churches, and maybe they should see what a large one could do. Members backed that decision years later by pledging $1 million in one day to build the 2,500-seat church a few blocks down Hikes Lane. By 1987, when they moved into the new church, the congregation had grown to 3,000 members. By 1990, that figure doubled. In the ten years that followed, the Southeast faithful grew by an average of 900 per year, served by more than 30 ministers and a number of elders.

The congregation moved again — to the big church off Blankenbaker Parkway — in 1998. The building, its congregation, and its ministries continue to grow, still guided and inspired by the same charismatic pastor who was called to Southeast Christian almost 40 years ago.

Russell is a popular speaker and has written over a dozen books. One book, *When God Builds a Church*, subtitled "The Remarkable Story of Southeast Christian Church," gives guidance to churches on how to grow. Russell lists ten principles churches should follow, including evangelism, worship, a commitment to the Bible and honest, moral leadership. Russell claims that his principles are applicable to churches of any size and culture.

Russell and his wife, Judy, have two adult sons, both of whom are active at Southeast Christian Church. He told *The Courier-Journal* in 1996 that his plans called for 10 to 12 more years of preaching, then moving to a smaller ministry of some kind. But not in Louisville, he claims. "It's tough to retire from a church and stay in the community," he said.

Passing the Torch

I DON'T KNOW IF ANYBODY SETS OUT to be a leader. I guess there may be young people who say, "I want to be a leader," or "I want to be president of the United States," but I think most people don't. I didn't have those kinds of aspirations for my life when I first started out.

The first time I even thought about being a leader of any kind was when I was asked to be the quarterback on my high school football team. I was thrust into a position that required making some decisions and taking charge, and it surprised me that people responded to my leadership. Because it was forced upon me, I was able to grow into that position.

When I first started out in the ministry, I came from a very small church — only 125 people. My vision for the church was that we might grow someday to 300 or 400 people, but that's as far as my vision went. I felt I had to be a leader in the local church, because I had been called into ministry and I wanted to make my life count. I think my primary leadership has been to the fellowship and flock that God has entrusted to me. But as the church started to grow, I began to be asked to do some things out in the community. I was asked to come to the local school and be involved in the PTA. I was asked to speak at the PTA banquet, at a football banquet, at a commencement and at a baccalaureate. Sometimes people from the community would ask me for counsel about issues that would come up. It wasn't my saying, "I want to be involved in the community." "I want to be a big time leader in this church." The leadership came as a result, just like that quarterback illustration. Someone said, "You're the quarterback, now you have to lead." It was thrust on me. The more I did it, the more confident I became, and the more I could see that God was using me in a positive way. I can't point to one thing, however, and say "Okay I have to lead now," and it happened. It was a gradual process, over a period of time.

I was 16 when I became a quarterback — in my sophomore year of high school. I was a third string quarterback. The second string quarterback got hurt for the season and, three games into the season, the first string quarterback got hurt and he was out for the season, and all of a sudden I was a 16-year-old quarterback on a team made up largely of underclassmen. We got beat badly. The same guys stayed together and, in my senior year, we were an undefeated team. It was one of those experiences that you are thrust into, and you learn through hard knocks and gain confidence over a period of time.

When I first came to the church here, I was 22. I went through four years of Bible College and one year of a located ministry. I came here and was really still very green, but I started the ministry of this church and there are some parallels to that quarterback story.

My father was a blue collar worker who worked in a factory. He was my first mentor, because he had such a servant compassionate heart. He was a part of what Tom Brokaw called the "greatest generation." He had a sense of duty. He worked 35 years at a factory job. Never missed a day, though he hated his job. Although he was a one-talent man, he was an elder in the church, because he was asked to do things.

I have great admiration for my father because he was the 17th of 18 children. His mother died when he was three, and his father was an alcoholic, and he got tossed around a lot. When he married my mom, he became a Christian, and he had such a heart for people – a real love for people. He loved me and I learned compassion from him. I have one brother who is also in the ministry. I have four sisters. One is single, and she does a lot of teaching and speaking. Two of my other sisters are married to preachers. One is married to an elder. She's a black sheep – just kidding! So my dad was my first mentor.

When I came to Louisville, I met a man named Olin Hay. Olin was the minister of the South Louisville Christian Church over on Southern Parkway. He was the patriarch of all the Christian churches in Louisville, and he was a mentor to me. One thing I learned from him was authenticity. There was no pretense about him. If you talked to him, you knew he was not putting on any airs. People loved him because he was real. If he was mad, he let it show; if he was happy, he would let you know he was happy; if he was nervous, you would see that he was nervous. There was no phoniness in him.

Another man who was a mentor to me was a man named Bill Gaslin. He was the preacher at the Shively Christian Church. Bill and I have been friends for probably 40 years. He was the dean of White Mills Camp, by Elizabethtown. I would see him lead teenagers, and he had a balance of firmness and flexibility. He knew when to tighten, and he knew when to let it go. He was a good leader.

Here's an example. I was under a dean of camp who had a list of rules for dress code, and part of the list was that girls' shorts couldn't be more than two inches above the knee. It was a topic of discussion with the boys. When Bill Gaslin was the dean of that camp he said, "Guys and women, I expect you to dress modestly. I think you know what modest is. If you are not modest, I'm going to come and tell you and then that's going to embarrass you, so don't make me come and tell you." I think he approached one girl and that was it, end of discussion. They had such respect for Bill. He wasn't afraid to confront people if he had to confront them, and that made him a good leader. The key was balancing firmness and flexibility, and observing and being around a leader like that was really healthy for me.

Another mentor of mine was a preacher in our brotherhood named Ben Merold. Ben is probably 80 years old. The one lesson I learned from Ben is to have a spirit of joy in everything that you do.

You know your attitude is so important in leadership. The Carnegie Institute did a survey years ago and interviewed 10,000 people who were successful in business and they determined that success was 15% technology and 85% personality. In almost every field, so much of what we do relates to people, and getting along with people. Ben Merold has the ability to be a leader, to be under stressful situations and still be joyful. That is a gift.

I went to his church convention out in California. The first service was so overflowing that it went long, and they were forced to have a second service. There were people standing out in the hallway waiting for the second service to begin. It started 15 to 20 minutes late. I'm a stickler for time. If I say we're going to start at 9:00 a.m., we're going to start at 9:00 a.m. I thought, if I were Ben Merold I would be so uptight I'd probably get up and say, "I know you're all in a hurry and we're starting late, so we are going to cut out a couple of songs and I'm going to abbreviate my sermon so you can get out of here." Ben got up at the service and said, "I know we're starting late, but there were so many people at the first service and we had such a great service that I don't want to short-change any of you. You're not going to do anything more important this week than to be here to worship God. We normally introduce all of our visitors and we're going to do that again. We're just going to take our time. We're going to have a great time here. Let's just settle down and worship God and we're not going to short-change you." Everybody settled down, and he led that whole congregation and those visitors into a different attitude and a different spirit because of his attitude and his spirit. I observed him a lot in that kind of situation, and I saw that joyful spirit in spite of stress is a key for leaders.

You have to walk through life being observant of those softer skills. You need to observe people who are effective and whom you admire, and contrast them with how you would react at the moment and say, "I think I can learn from this person." You can sit down and read books and go through leadership training, but to deal with people in individual situations has to be "caught more than taught."

There is no question, my leadership style is high trust. I believe that 90% of good leadership is gathering the right people around you, giving them an idea of what their job description is supposed to be, then giving them a lot of freedom to accomplish it. Occasionally there needs to be accountability, and occasionally there needs to be adjustment – sometimes even correction – but most of the time you just need to give them encouragement.

If you get the right people around you and you empower them and encourage them, its incredible what they'll do, if they feel like they own the program and they are responsible for it.

I guess the best example that I could give to you would be Greg Allen, who is a great worship leader. After he was hired, he learned by heart some things that I wanted, then I gave him the whole first hour. There are many times that I'll walk into worship service and I don't know what's going on. I know that I'm going to get up and preach after a half hour, but he chooses the music; he chooses the person who is reading the scriptures; he chooses who is going to pray; and if he needs me, he will say something to me. I've empowered him to do that. He's not doing that first half-hour to get my approval. He wants to use his creativity and have his fingerprints on it. He wants to please God with what he is doing, and he is going to do a whole lot better than if I am micromanaging him. To be a high trust leader, you have to get the right people around you. If you get the wrong person, then you've got trouble.

I think if you were to talk to our staff, they would say "I think Bob Russell is easy to work for, because he believes in me." If one of them wants more oversight, they might say I am "disengaged" sometimes, but I think if I were in a position of leadership in this church, I would want that sense of support and empowerment, rather than someone lording it over me.

I think different people would describe me in different ways. Occasionally, I hear people say that Southeast Christian Church is a cult, that I'm a cult leader. It never bothers me, because it is so far from the truth that it is funny. I'm probably up-front less than and furthest from a preacher controlling a church than anyone I know. People see the rapid growth of our church and they see a high degree of dedication on the part of the members, then they see a television evangelist and other ministers, and they want to paint everybody with the same brush. They can't explain what has happened, so they say it must be a cult. There are some people who have an image of me as an authoritarian leader, but people who know me know that is not the case at all.

I think our biggest accomplishments at Southeast Christian Church would be moral leadership and the long-term strengthening of the moral fiber of our community. Hopefully, the majority of our 18,500 members are more honest in their daily transactions. I hope they are faithful to their families and loving and compassionate. I hope they are better workers. I hope they are more compassionate to the needy. I hope they are better citizens of the state because they are members of Southeast Christian Church. I hope that we have made a contribution morally to this community by strengthening the moral fiber of the people who come here.

With respect to accomplishments, I guess probably our first re-location project was the most significant and gratifying thing to me — even more than our relocation here. When we moved from our first little building to a building that seated 2,500 people, that seemed so impossible. It was so far beyond what I dreamed or imagined our church could be. At that time, it was $7 million dollars and we had a little over 1,000 people. That was beyond what I dreamed could happen.

When we first started talking about $7 million and the building committee came back to me, I said, "Look, I would like for us to build a building that seats 1,500 people because if we get bigger than that, like our Wednesday night service, we are going to rattle around in there. If we have 1,500, we can have two services and we can have 3,000 people, and that will be big enough. They said, "Bob, your gift is preaching. You are not big enough of a visionary. We're going to build the building, you preach."

The committee came back with this plan for a building that seated 2,500 people and boy, it made my heart skip. But I was forced to expand my vision and realized that I don't think big enough. God is able to do more than I ask or imagine. When we marched from the old building to the new building, it was probably nine-tenths completed before I walked in one day and said, "We are going to do this. This is going to happen." That was nearly 20 years ago, but it lifted my vision for what God could accomplish, through us.

So when we filled that building up and they said, "Let's relocate," it made my heart skip, but I believed it could happen if it was God's will. When we came out here and got a church building that seats over 9,000 people and cost $70,000,000, that is what people see. But in my mind, the big event happened 15 years before that, when I saw us try something so big that if God isn't in it, you are going to fail. Then you see that it succeeds, and you say, "Our vision of what God can do is too small." The lesson I learned from that first relocation project is that people will respond to a challenge if they really believe in something, and you have to dream bigger dreams as a leader.

One of the things that people don't see about this church is that I have been reinforced by quality elders, and by lay leaders and staff who are honest with me and I listen. I'm not an autocratic leader and I'm accountable to elders. I have had ideas and dreams and they have told me no, so I accept it as no.

I heard somebody say once, "If you are one step ahead of your people, then you are a leader. But if you are ten steps ahead of them, you are a target." If your vision gets so far out there that you are dragging people, they will find some way to disassociate themselves from you. Those who are following your leadership have to feel that you are right there in touch with them.

Sometimes the elders here at our church keep me from being one step behind because, quite honestly, they are often more visionary then I am.

But there has to be this sense of teamwork and consensus building on the part of the core of your leadership team. You all have to be on the same page, and that has been one of the great strengths of this church – that we have had this core of leadership.

Good leaders attract other leaders, I have found. I have observed that people who are "A" leaders – top of the line leaders – will gather around them other "A" leaders. People who are "B" leaders will gather around them "C" leaders. I don't know why that is, other than that people who don't have a lot of leadership experience or gifts are sometimes threatened by people who are more gifted then they are, or who are even just as qualified as they are. They gather people who will be "yes people" around them.

I have people on my staff who are more gifted than I am in some areas. We have a team-preaching concept here. There are two other guys here who do preaching, and they are extremely gifted speakers. People come up to me and say, "My children love to hear Kyle Idleman," or "My teenagers love to hear Dave Stone speak." If I'm threatened by that, then I am not going to gather those kinds of people around me.

If my vision is what is best for this church, and if I keep the big picture in front of me, then we are going to gather the best people around us to do the work that needs to be done here.

Jim Collins' book, *From Good to Great*, is the best book on leadership I've ever read. He talks about how a leader has to be a servant leader. It's not that he doesn't have to have ambition, but the ambition is for the organization, not for himself. If the ambition is for the organization, then the organization can advance. That means that the leader sometimes is not in the spotlight. If people sense that their leader is willing to make a sacrifice, then they will go to the wall for that leader.

The example that Collins uses in his book is: "More like Abraham Lincoln, less like General Patton. More like Sam Walton, less like Lee Iacocca." Lee Iacocca is a dynamic leader who is doing his own ads, writing his own book, promoting himself. That kind of leader can take you so far. The servant leader that I think we ought to be as Christians is called a "Level 5" leader: Somebody who is willing to sacrifice himself for the sake of the cause.

One of my biggest disappointments is that I wish we could be more effective in helping Louisville's inner city problems. As we became a larger church with resources, we tried several different approaches at helping take the gospel to the inner city – helping to alleviate racial problems with the black community – and we struck out. We tried starting a church downtown. We tried a basketball program in the West End, and each time, we didn't feel good about what we did. Eventually we said, "Maybe instead of us trying to do it ourselves, we should try to partner with people who are already down there doing it well."

So that is what we have done in recent years. We've partnered with Bates Memorial Baptist Church and their minister, Dr. Bruce Williams. We decided that we weren't just going to put money down, but that our people would go down and work with their people and have some interaction. A. Russell Awkard and his church are also a partner. We have developed relationships, and have been more effective, but it sure took us a long time to get there. I'm still disappointed that we haven't been a bigger help to the inner city of Louisville.

We have so much information about good leadership, but not very much about good followership. Everybody is a follower in some sphere. Almost everyone is a leader in some sphere too, whether it's your family, a small group, or the PTA. We all have to be followers. A real test of the character of a person is: Can you be an effective leader in one sphere of your life, then turn around and be a supportive follower in the other sphere?

Some of the people whom I love the most in this church are people who are high-profile leaders in their position in this community – the president of a university, or the CEO of Yum!, or a basketball coach – and they come in here and sometimes are my most supportive followers. They are not asked to follow blindly, but they know what it is to lead and how hard it is to lead and be led well. I can be a good follower if I'm being led well. It's when I get in a meeting and somebody is running it poorly that I start getting really restless. A real test of your character is: Can you be a follower when the leader is not so hot? That is why I appreciate so many people in this church who are good leaders, but who are also good followers, who say "I've got enough on my plate right now. I don't need to be critical, and I believe what's going on, and I endorse it 100%."

It's wonderful to see that. If I go on a golf trip with eight men, it is nice to feel that I do not have to lead all day long. I love for somebody to say, "Here is where you are staying, and here is your tee-off time, and here is who is driving." I love it when I'm not leading, if the leader is doing it well. It takes the pressure off. People who are good leaders are willing to be good followers because they realize that that's an important role too.

Young people aspiring to leadership need to learn to be accountable. Everybody is accountable to somebody. If I can't be accountable to the elders and the overseers of this church, then I can't be an effective leader. There's an interesting story in the Bible about the centurion who came to Jesus and said, "My servant is sick. I need you to heal my servant, but don't come to my house. I don't want to trouble you that much. I am a man under authority and I know what it's like to be told to go here and there. You are a man of authority, Jesus. Just speak the word and he will be made well." And Jesus said, "I've not seen such great faith in all of Israel," and the centurion's servant was healed.

The interesting thing was when the centurion said "I am a man under authority." The test of whether you can lead is how you respond to the person right above you. I can show you a gentleman on our staff who is a great leader from his position down, but he is not a great leader from his position up. He can handle the people under him, but he chafes a little being accountable to other people over him. Every leader has to go two ways. The president of the United States has to answer to the American people and Congress. If the people or Congress do not think he is answering them, then he is not being an effective leader. Leadership goes both ways.

I've already mentioned that I wish we had a stronger presence in the inner city of Louisville. Locally, what I would like to do differently for this church is raise the bar for being a member of Southeast Christian Church. I would say, if you are going to be a member of this church, you have to be involved in a small group. Since this church has gotten larger, it is easier for people to be anonymous and slip through the cracks. We are battling that all the time. So we are struggling to get everyone plugged into a small group. If everyone is in a small circle, then the big circle is wonderful. If the big circle is the only thing that they are involved in, they can get lost.

I went to the elders recently and said, "If people are going to become a member of this church, they will have to do three things, and one will be that they cannot be a member until we get them "plugged in" to a small group somewhere. The elders did not think it was quite fair, because we had not required that of previous new members, so they said no. That is where I have to be accountable to the elders. If I were starting a church again, knowing that it would get large like this, the first thing I would say is, "We are going to keep everybody in some kind of small circle, where people know your name, and you know their name, and you have this little church within the big church.

If I were going to give advice to the next generation of leaders coming up in this community, I would tell them these things:

First, be a person of integrity. More than anything else, your character matters in the long run. You can be a short-term leader by bluffing people, but if you are going to lead people over the long haul, they have to know that you are for real. Believe me, they will observe and watch you, and if they sense that you are being phony, they will back off.

The second thing I would tell young aspiring leaders is to focus on the area of your giftedness. Whenever you start leading, Boyle's law is: If uncontrolled, work will flow to the competent person, until he submerges. The reward for doing a job well is more work. People say "Thanks, you did a great job, now here's more work." Pretty soon, you'll find yourself overloaded.

The areas where you are gifted get pushed aside because you can get by without as much concentration. You start spending most of your time in areas where you are not gifted, and you do not have a passion for them and, all of a sudden, you get burned out and you're not happy doing what you're doing. I have done a lot of things wrong, but I did one thing right from the very beginning – and the Lord helped me. I always understood that, while I don't have a lot of gifts, one of my gifts is to stand in front of people and to teach and preach the Bible. So that is my focus. Everything else has to come and go. If it takes me 20 hours to write a sermon, I've got 20 hours of time blocked out first thing. That's my priority. I did this when I was 22 and, now that I'm 61, I do the same thing. I've stayed focused in the area of my giftedness. Not that I haven't done some other things, but that has always been my primary area of emphasis. I would say to a young person: Know what you are gifted to do, and what you have a passion for, and you never have to work another day of your life. You enjoy doing it so much that the other stuff just flows out of that. If you don't know where you are gifted, take one of those gift courses and they will tell you, "Here's where you are gifted."

One question I find myself asking young people in ministry or leadership is, "What do you do that makes time go the fastest for you? When does that clock start whirling for you?" Bill Hybels, a preacher at the Willow Creek Community Church in Chicago, is the strongest leadership personality I've ever met in my life. I asked him "When does time go the fastest for you?" He said "When I'm leading a meeting." For me, it is studying to teach or preach. Four hours goes by so fast that I know that is my passion, and I will never get tired of doing that. If you have to spend 75-80 % of your time doing things that you do not have a gift or passion for, it is going to show.

If you are the leader in a growing organization, you have to trim back the areas that are not your giftedness. Delegate those out, get someone else to do them. One of my struggles in ministry has been to stay in ministry because everything else is pulling. I could meet with people and counsel them all day long everyday, answer letters or phone calls – these are all legitimate things for me to be doing. But you know what? Some things are going to have to suffer because the first 20-25 hours of my week are already scheduled to stay in the area of what I think I'm gifted in and called to do.

Politically, I think Rebecca Jackson, Anne Northup, Mitch McConnell, and Jerry Abramson are the people who have contributed most to the growth and development and success of our community over the last 50 years. Educationally, I think it's Richard Van Hoose. I have been here for 40 years. Business-wise, I think Al Schneider contributed more than anyone.

Another person who has contributed a lot to our community in a very real way is Denny Crum. Other people are probably going to be more sophisticated and mention someone in the arts, or those who have made a big donation, but I think Denny Crum has made a real contribution to this community.

The people that I am mentioning are people of honesty and integrity, people who have made a long-term commitment to doing what is right. Let me come at this from a spiritual side. The way I see it, the community is like a tree. The moral values of the community are the roots of the tree that you do not see.

There are also leaders who most people don't see who have contributed a lot. I mentioned Olin Hay. When he was at South Louisville, he helped, sacrificed, and started the Shively Christian Church. He then sacrificed of his people and started the Okolona Christian Church, then the Lyndon Christian Church. He told me that he asked his people who of them was going to go to Southeast Christian Church the next Sunday to help start the new church and his heart sank. He said 50 of his best leaders stood up, among them his brother and sister and brother-in-law, his organist and a couple of elders. But he said that was the right thing for them to do. Southeast Christian Church helped start the Northeast Christian Church. The tentacles of Olin Hay's spiritual leadership back in the '50s and '60s, along with the spiritual and moral impact that he has had on our city, is significant. You mention Olin Hay and everybody is going to say, "I know who Al Schneider is, but who in the world is Olin Hay?" The Bible says that in heaven the last are going to be first and the first will be last. I think people like Wayne Dehoney from Walnut Street Baptist Church, Kevin Cosby at St. Stephen's Baptist Church, and Al Mohler at Southern Baptist Seminary are having a tremendous impact on the moral fiber of this community as well, and are keeping the roots strong.

God has enabled me to play a role, and to make a spiritual contribution, I believe, by being a part of this church. I probably have not played as big a role in the secular world, other than helping to spiritually reinforce people who have been involved in the secular part. If some of the people who go to church here come to me for counsel or they ask for my prayers or my influence in their life, then maybe I've played a role. If I've had a significant role in the community, it would be as an encourager and a counselor to those who are involved in education and in business and political leadership in the Louisville community.

Our community has some big challenges ahead of it and I'm going to tell it like I see it. Our biggest challenges are moral challenges. You name the challenges that we face — whether it's crime or race problems or prejudice or corruption in business or pornography or the breakdown of the family or the distrust a segment of our community has with the police.

Almost all of those problems, if not every one of them, has as its base the moral fiber of the community. Again, you're getting at the root of the tree, and if the root of the tree is rotting away, then it doesn't matter how good it looks on top of the ground. That tree is going to topple over.

John Adams, our country's second president, said, "Our constitution was made for a moral and a religious people. It is wholly inadequate for any other." Democracy is going to be a failure, as we see in Iraq and other places, if there is not a moral fiber at the core, a consensus of what is moral. An old-time example is if you put five people on an island and three are men and two are women and the three men vote to rape the women, then that is democracy at its worst. If you do not have a moral core, democracy will collapse.

So our community's biggest challenge is to return to moral values. The strange thing is we need spiritual institutions like the church saying that there is a right and a wrong, training people; training fathers to train their children; training corporate heads to be generous and fair to their employees; training employees to give an honest day's work; training business people to be honest in their dealings; training politicians to be honest, and policemen to be fair with people, and people to respect the police. Those are the core values that are all through the Bible. The church and spiritual institutions are trying to train people that way, while at the same time, a certain segment of society is saying, "We don't need the church anymore. We do not want to hear about the commandments anymore. We want to withdraw from God and altogether from our culture. Education used to teach those values in school. They've withdrawn them all together, so there's chaos in school. There's a vacuum of moral teaching, so I think the biggest challenge we have now is to determine what is right and wrong and to get back to moral training, so we won't have so many people in prison and we won't have all these people on drugs and crime. We need moral training so we can have integrity in business, and so we won't have so many people on welfare who are milking the system. All those things are moral issues.

Now I am going to go a step further. When you have the major media opposed to the teaching of moral values and not understanding that there are absolutes, and that the absence of those absolutes is causing moral decay, there is a constant sense of conflict in the city, and a disunity that has created an obstacle to overcoming all those problems.

An example of how much of a vacuum there is: We had this seminar recently called "Lead Like Jesus" and 4,500 area business leaders came to the conference. These are people hungry for leadership skills, but they are hungry also for moral values. You would not have that kind of turnout if people weren't saying, "We need the help."

I have learned a lot of lessons in my life that I would like to share with the next generation of leaders in our community: First of all, I love Louisville and I love living here. It is a great place to live. I didn't grow up here, but I fell in love with Louisville when I came to town at age 22. I love the climate here. I love the change of seasons. I grew up in the North, where I was familiar with 130+ inches of snow a year, and now one snowfall a year is enough for me. Louisville has warmth here, a little touch of southern hospitality. We have an accessible airport only 15 minutes away. I wouldn't want to live in a large city. We have a lot of advantages here, and it's a beautiful place to live, and we ought to love our community rather than always putting it down. I would like for it to be a better place in the future.

One of the lessons I've learned is that who you are is a whole lot more important in leadership than what you say. That's pretty much a cliché, but William Barkley once said, "A man's message will always be heard in context with his character." How people perceive you makes a big difference in whether they are going to listen to you or not. Billy Graham can get up, and whatever he says is wonderful because he is Billy Graham.

Dr. David Jeremiah, who has a radio ministry almost nationwide, two years ago battled cancer and overcame it and is doing well. While he was going through cancer, he got a number of letters from people who listen to his radio program. They said, "We've always enjoyed your ministry, but we have to tell you now that you're going through cancer there's a new depth to your preaching. We can sense the spirit of God is working with you through your difficulty." But the interesting thing was that they were playing old radio tapes. It demonstrates to me that the perception of the people listening to the leader is almost as important as reality itself. The leader has to be on guard as to what his character is, and how people perceive him.

I guess the one thing I haven't yet talked about that is really important to me is commitment to excellence. I think whatever we do, when we want people to follow us, they have to believe that there's something special about what we're doing. They want to know that there is something distinctive about it; that we're not doing it half-heartedly.

Marvin Rickard wrote a book that impacted me early on called *Let It Grow*. One of his principles was that quality produces quantity. If you do something right, and you do it well, people are attracted to excellence. You're better off doing one or two things with excellence than you are doing four or five things with mediocrity. Keep the main thing the main thing. That's something you have to battle all the time.

Passing the Torch

I heard someone say that everyone's ego has to battle either pride or fear. Either you become really proud of what's been accomplished, or you become fearful that you're going to fail and look bad.

My challenge to future leaders in this community would be: Do not be prideful and arrogant and think that you are above people. More importantly, be courageous enough to think big thoughts and that things can be done. There are some exciting things that can happen in this community if we have people of resource and influence who will step out and courageously take the lead.

Now it is frightening to be a leader. People take shots at you. People criticize you. But if big things are going to happen and important steps are going to be taken in this community in the future, there are going to have to be some young people who say, "I believe God's tapping me on the shoulder, and I believe I'm being called to lead, even if nobody's following, because it's the right thing to do." I just challenge future leaders to have the courage to think big things.

One verse out of scripture that means a lot to me is Ephesians 3:20 -21: "God is able to do immeasurably more than all we ask or imagine." That happens if there are leaders who are willing to step up to the plate and be courageous.

T. William "Bill" Samuels Jr.

President
Maker's Mark Distillery Company

BILL SAMUELS JR. CAN TRACE his ancestry back 1,000 years, and the family tree includes some people who made whiskey in Scotland. The ones with closest ties, though, go back to 1844 near Bardstown, Kentucky, where T. W. Samuels built the family's first commercial bourbon distillery.

T. W. was sheriff of Nelson County and a cousin of Dr. Reuben Samuels, who was the stepfather of Frank and Jesse James. T. W. arranged the surrender of the remnants of Quantrill's Raiders, including the James boys, at the end of the Civil War.

The James story might sound like a digression, but it's just the kind of thing Samuels Jr. likes to talk about in ads for his family's current bourbon, Maker's Mark. Those ads and a smooth finish have made Maker's Mark perhaps the best-known bourbon in the country. Samuels Jr., who has degrees in engineering and law and had a short career as a rocket scientist, found his niche when he started writing those ads. Maker's Mark had kind of simmered along since his father – Bill Samuels Sr. – developed it in 1953, abandoning the old family formula for T. W. Samuels bourbon.

The senior Samuels was kind of a tinkerer who didn't like whiskeys then being made, so he decided to develop a more polished brand. Having sold the family distillery years before, he bought the smallest distillery in Kentucky – a venerable, abandoned facility near Loretto, and started producing his new recipe. He didn't have much of an advertising budget, and the brand was known mostly around Kentucky and in places where Kentuckians go, like Washington.

Samuels Jr. finished up his law degree at Vanderbilt and returned home in 1967. He expected to work for his father a year or so, because there was no assurance Maker's Mark would survive as a brand. He told *The Courier-Journal* in 1998 that his father agreed to pay him half of what he'd been offered as a lawyer, and was specific about his part in the business:

"We do three things here," the elder Samuels said. "We make whiskey, we count money, and we sell whiskey. I'm in charge of the first two."

Samuels Jr. didn't know it going in, but he soon learned that marketing and advertising were things he liked to do. Working with the Doe-Anderson Advertising Agency, he began coming up with offbeat, easy-going ads that began to work. He still writes many of them himself. Then, in 1980, *The Wall Street Journal* published a front-page piece about this quaint little distillery down in Kentucky that made pretty good whiskey, and things took off.

The younger Bill Samuels was born in 1940 and grew up in a Bardstown steeped in his bourbon-making ancestry. His neighbor and godfather was Jim Beam. He met his wife, Nancy, in Bardstown. She was the daughter of a family friend, and he first laid eyes on her when she was 20 minutes old.

His father invented the whiskey when Samuels was still a boy, using soft wheat in the mash with the corn, instead of rye. Margie Samuels, wife of the elder and mother of the younger Bill Samuels, designed the bottle and named the product after markings on a collection of handcrafted pewter in the Samuels family.

Samuels Jr. graduated from Bardstown High School in 1958, and studied engineering at Case Western Reserve University when the U.S. space program was trying to catch up with the USSR's Sputnik. That's where the rocket science came in. He had worked on solid fuels, but liquid prevailed. He then headed for law school. While he studied law, he often had lunch with his father's friend, Jack Daniel's chairman Hap Matlow, and learned whiskey along with law.

Today, as one of the ten operating distilleries in Kentucky, Maker's Mark is one of the smallest, producing only a fraction of the millions of bottles of whiskey produced in Kentucky each year. The distillery has the industry's smallest batch size (200 bushels of grain) in its idyllic setting in Loretto, Kentucky — the typical distillery capacity in the late 1800s. It may be the smallest distillery in the state, but the whiskey that is made there — with its distinctive red wax top — is enjoyed and appreciated all over the world.

Though the company was sold in 1981, Samuels Jr. continues as president. He is also active on a number of boards in the community. He is a past board chairman of both the U.S. and Kentucky Chambers of Commerce, the University of Louisville Board of Trustees, and the Kentucky Distillers Association, among others.

He and Nancy have three children and live in Oldham County, Kentucky.

TO TELL YOU THE TRUTH, A LOT OF MY INVOLVEMENT in the community has been at the back end of the line with a shovel, and I've enjoyed that ever as much as I have at the front end, chairing organizations.

Things are situational. Maybe that's part of my approach to leadership – not to think of it as leadership, but to think of it as responsibility. Everybody like me who is really driven to accomplish things has a selfish motive behind what they are doing. That's just honesty.

My dad's family has been in Kentucky forever. We were really one of the founding families of Kentucky. We've never really gone anywhere. I'm the first member of my family since 1780 not to live in Nelson County. I broke with family tradition in a very small way, but I've gone back and looked at what the family has been up to over the years and, since I'm the family lawyer, I had some sense of where to go in the courthouse to find a lot of the records. I found that not only was my family engaged in making whiskey, they were engaged in founding Kentucky's first independent school district, which was in Bardstown. I found that Dad and his father served on the board of the Bardstown Independent School District for 70 straight years, and that they were elected and served most of those years as chair.

My grandfather was the mayor of Bardstown. My great-granddaddy was the Sheriff of Nelson County. So, in a sense, leadership is what was expected of us. It's what I saw growing up, sitting around the dinner table. We talked about public school matters. Part of it is the way I was raised. Neither Mom nor Dad said, "When you come to work for the company, we have expectations, blah,blah,blah." If anything, Dad thought I was maybe a little too involved, at times, with community leadership and giving. The other motivation – and I think this will touch a string with a lot of people, I may just be one of the first to admit it publicly – is that many of us don't sit still very well.

Many of us did not like the time we spent in school, and some of us didn't do very well in school. Yet most of us realize that to be successful, life is a lifetime of learning. We had to develop strategies to keep our brains fresh, to keep being challenged by ideas. Since I didn't want to go back to school to get a business degree, which is what I should have done, probably, I found it very stimulating to get involved in community matters.

That really led to my not having the need to run everything. I enjoyed just being exposed to the energy of a community. That's been the way I have tried to keep my brain sharp and my ideas fresh, rather than having to sit through seminars or going back to school, which I wouldn't do very well. I think there are a whole lot of others out there who are like me too.

T. William "Bill" Samuels Jr.

My family is very closely connected with our brand, Maker's Mark. And when our brand looked as if it was going to become a national icon, all of a sudden I looked smarter. Whether that's true or not – I suspect it's not – that really had more to do with my being seen as a leader than anything else.

Tom Meeker says it better than anybody because he has another one of those great platforms from which to look brilliant. When you retire, you instantly look un-brilliant. Tom has been very helpful in reminding me that it's more about the success of the brand than it is about any particular brilliance I've shown in the community. Now there are some exceptions to that, and David Jones would certainly be one of them, but there are some of us who are coasting along or are being recognized far beyond our own real abilities.

I think there's some instant credibility in just being who I am because of the brand, and that's a huge advantage. Coming into the company was a huge disadvantage, though, because everybody figured I wouldn't be here if my old man didn't own the company. And there's some truth to that.

I think people trust that I put the community first when I go to work on something. That's more what they think than, "Oh, this guy's a great leader." I don't think I fool too many people there, but I do think that, over time, folks have come to know that when I get asked to do something, any interest or agenda I might have gets subordinated way to the back of the line. I will always put other people and the community first.

I think I may have the most famous mentors who ever lived, a lot of them from early life. Jim Beam was the first older person I was mesmerized by. He was my godfather. He was our next-door neighbor in Bardstown for a short period of time before he died. I think about him everyday. He knew how to make business fun, and I'm absolutely convinced that there's a little bit of Jim Beam in all our communications and all the silliness that I propagate upon this company. I do think about that now. I think, "If the Colonel was sitting here with me, who would he want to screw with?" It would be somebody.

When I was young, everybody thought I should have been out doing stuff but I much preferred to sit with the Colonel and listen to some of his nonsense. He liked stories, but mainly he liked to mess with people – my father and my grandfather and others.

He made fun of himself, too. He was a legend. He really caused me early in my career to understand that we needed to take the business of what we do in Loretto very seriously, while that did not mandate that we take ourselves too seriously. I think the Colonel had a big influence on that.

The other big influence in my life, and I was his first employee, was Harland Sanders. He never paid me, but I was his first chauffeur.

That was right when he was first starting out with Kentucky Fried Chicken. I had just gotten my driver's license in the early summer of 1956. He was a good friend of Dad's. He was running around trying to sell his pressure cooker idea with herbs and spices because he didn't have any restaurants then, and I used to drive him around. There was a lot to learn from him, because he was the greatest public relations guy of all time. I mean, think about a guy at 65, who sold his restaurant in Corbin and retired. He received one social security check. Claudia threw him out of the house because he was trying to run the house like he ran the business and, 15 years later, he was the most famous human in the world. It's absolutely remarkable.

We spent all our time together – just the two of us – in the car. That was his office back then. He stayed at the house, so we'd get him all day, then I'd get to sit in the car and listen to him and Dad talk at night. It was absolutely priceless. It was all about promotion. I could see that he was able to use his charms strategically. I guess the word that comes to mind is "manipulate." I could see that he was different at it than other naturally charming people. I also saw the other side of him, when he would slip into the kitchen on his second or third visit and they weren't doing the chicken like he wanted it done. The roof was likely to blow off the place.

It was really interesting, watching Colonel Sanders get the word out. He was a gentleman and a very jovial person. While he was very serious when it came to the business in the kitchen, he never ever got too serious about the money. By that I mean he didn't have any paper, because it was all a nickel, a chicken, a handshake, and then whatever the folks said. That's what they paid him.

The one thing he was really serious about was his craft. And that's a pretty big lesson for somebody who is going to spend his life in the craft business.

Hap Motlow, who ran Jack Daniels for his family, was another mentor to me. I had three years of him every Friday while I was in law school in Vanderbilt. He was remarkable. The common threads were to have good values, focus on the craft, and never disappoint. Each of those people were just maniacs about not disappointing customers.

They went about it in different ways, though. Most of them were pretty fun-loving. The Colonel was probably less fun-loving than the others, believe it or not. They were big influences, though, and I reflect back on them a lot today.

I am absolutely sure I am not a good manager, and it didn't make any difference because I was in a position to be able to define my job. I was able to define it up against my strengths, rather than spending all my time doing what the nuns wanted me to do, which was to sit down, be quiet and conform.

A lot of my understanding about my strengths came early on from the results of personality tests. Understanding what they meant allowed me to understand me, and my father to understand himself, and how we could best develop roles in the company that were not hierarchical, but were more about "Okay, you're going to do this well, and I'm going to do this well." This is not how companies are usually organized.

Clearly, he was better at controlling and I was better at creating. So that's pretty much the way we organized the business. Creative people, as you know, generally don't have a lot of empathy, so they don't hear people very well. That's a bad thing when you're trying to manage something.

My role has always been to provide the creative leadership in this business. That's a good thing, because that's what I do naturally. It also requires somebody to look after the people, though, so we have organized the business so that we have other people — like our distillery manager — who have great empathy. He could have been and should have been a sales manager. Hiring him in that position was deliberate because I needed it, the organization needed it — we have complementing personalities. We have a finance director here — same skills.

Normally, neither one of those people in an organization can talk, okay? It was deliberate. We had to find people who could compensate for my management deficiency. Early on, it became clear that if we were going to create something out of nothing, creative leadership was more important than management. You can manage yourself around a small circle all your life. We had to get out of that circle, and that's probably been my role.

My father was better at managing, better at controlling, better at crafting, better at all the stuff we do. Once we did the personality test, it was simple. I did outside, he did inside.

Then we had some stuff in-between, like who is going to define the vision for the business. That was convoluted, but we worked our way through it by saying, "Well, I'm probably better at it, but you own the company, so maybe I ought to listen to you."

I also got some help from Doe-Anderson Advertising Agency here in town, and I got help from the Oliver Group, which is also here. Those would be my two mentors — the people who helped us get through this thing of utilizing the right talent, using the talent the right way, and building an organization that I think is second to none now. It doesn't make any difference that I can't manage. We joke about it in here all the time, so it's not a big deal.

There are a lot of books out there that talk about instead of trying to build up people's weaknesses, companies should define people's strengths, focus on their strengths, and neutralize their weaknesses.

Probably the biggest and most satisfying success I have had – from an outcome standpoint – is creating an American icon brand. Not many of those have been created in Kentucky. Colonel Sanders and I may be two of the few. But I think the real satisfaction came from my stumbling upon the Oliver Group early on. They were able to put my limited strengths and considerable weaknesses in order, hire around that, and build an organization where everybody contributes in significant ways today.

I became the president of Maker's Mark pretty early. Dad never trusted me with the checkbook, but he finally got comfortable enough with the idea that I was the one who needed to be leading the parade. I had demonstrated that I was going to check with him before I went and did a lot of stupid stuff. Early on, I joined YPO (the Young Presidents Organization), right after it was founded, and I became the education chairman. The first resource I offered the company was this predictive index, this personality testing, and how to use it as a management tool. It was like a major light bulb going off.

The most obvious failure we have had is taking so long to get where we have gotten. It took way longer than it should have. Part of that was because I'm a little hard-headed. The other part is because I didn't have any idea what I was doing. Mainly, though, it was because I was hard-headed.

I was ineffective, because I was the one who was supposed to be in charge of the outside of the business. I was supposed to get the bus going.

I would tell someone coming up behind me, taking my position, to read. Some of the stuff that is available now to read wasn't available then, especially a lot of the conventional wisdom like "find a niche and fill it." If Dad and I had gone down that business school route, we wouldn't have ever gotten started. If we had gone down the conventional, classical marketing route, we probably wouldn't have ever found it. But today there's a lot of good stuff coming out of the business schools on the "psychology of buzz" – on what they call "permission marketing." We were one of the really early practitioners of those theories, just in a not-very-disciplined way. Mentally, we had our head wrapped around the concept, but didn't know how to execute it.

I have a hard time reading because I'm dyslexic. It's terrible. I have to read in small spurts and have to do it in the morning. I still say, given a choice, you need to expand readiness and expand your scope, but I say participation in the community is number one.

Looking back, I do have a strong bias. If I had to get an MBA, attend a lot of seminars, read a lot of books, instead of just jumping in there and doing this job, I couldn't have done it. Dad and I learned from doing things, and being exposed to people in totally different industries with totally different ways of approaching problem-solving. That has been a godsend for me.

T. William "Bill" Samuels Jr.

My community involvement included industry involvement. I was on the job on day one and Dad said, "You're taking over our company representation in the Kentucky Distillers Association and in the distilled spirits industry."

I was like 30 years younger than anybody else and, of course, obviously knew a lot less than everybody else. We had the smallest company, so we were the least significant. But that was the beginning, and I ended up being really involved in the leadership of both of them.

From then on, my list of community involvements got really long. Most of it was in education – the DePaul School, the Ursuline Learning Center for handicapped children. When somebody hollered for help, I'd always jump. I prefer to work with the non-hierarchical organizations, where everybody just pitches in, figures out where they can be helpful, then works as a team.

Leadership is situational, and I don't know anybody – other than a born-again couch potato – who isn't capable and couldn't get seriously motivated in the right situation to lead. We really try to do that around here. We deliberately hire strong-willed people and try to give them responsibilities where they're in charge. Then the rest of us – me included – are at their disposal to serve.

I spend a lot of time around here doing what I'm told. Ginger is in charge of Kentucky, for example, and she does events and tells me what me to do. "Go here, wear this, do that." She takes the leadership role because it would be stupid for anyone else to do it. It would be stupid if the rest of us tried to pretend, just because we have position or power, that we could second-guess her. I'm a little nervous about calling people leaders and followers because I think it's really situational. I can name many more times when I'm following than when I'm leading.

I'd much rather lead. But there have been some times recently when I've been horribly uncomfortable because I really wasn't equipped to make a difference. When I was asked to chair the Workforce Investment Board, for example. It was going through a rebirth and we were having some leadership issues and it was scary at first. Now that I've been doing it for three or four years, though, we have it all together. We have some great internal leadership.

Every time I have been successful as a board chair, it's because the chief executive officer of the organization has been sterling. And every time I've been a dunce, it's because that person hasn't been sterling.

If I could have an opportunity to do things differently, I would spend more time with my wife and four children. I was – and still am – fortunate to have a wife who is an unbelievable mother. Now she has taken over the grandchildren.

Our family is basically in the entertainment business. We have been able to drag our family into entertainment situations, just like my father did me, where I received a lot of subliminal mentoring.

Our youngest son, Rob, is in Florida working for the company, which sells Maker's Mark all over. We do the operations and marketing part. He is in Florida looking after the package stores. He's 30 years old and he does quite well. His wife would like for them to come back to Kentucky. She is a Kentuckian, as he is, and they just had a baby.

If I were going to share advice with young people who are aspiring to leadership today, I would say that the first thing you have to do is earn it. You shouldn't be thinking about leadership, you should just think about getting into the trenches. See if you're capable of subrogating your own interests for the interests of the organization, and see if that really causes you to get excited. Because if it doesn't, you're not going to become a leader, you are just going to get in somebody's way.

What I see is that the more competitive things get – and we have no control over that – we're either going to suck it up and be competitive and succeed, or we're going to go away to France. And I think a lot of young people, at least the ones I've run into like the YPAL group, are very serious about their careers at an early age. That causes many of them to stretch themselves pretty thin, and it's awfully hard to dig into an organization. I have not met one that wouldn't like to.

Many of them just don't have the time to do it. Many of them do, though, and I think we have some terrific involved young people. The quality of the young people who are willing to bring their talent, energy, and passion to the community is much better now than it was in the mid-'60s, when I got out of college. I think YPAL may be one of the most important organizations in town. I am involved with that organization in every way I can be involved.

Things happened long ago in our community that set our future. Then everybody changed on the scene and all of a sudden we wonder, "How did we get here?" Who in the community consistently makes a difference at the top end of the funnel? David Jones comes to mind first, foremost, and almost only. It's not a slam on anybody else, but I've never seen anybody as gifted, and I'm not talking about his money. I'm talking about his incredible interest in and care for the community, along with his rare ability to see around corners and his incisive way of articulating gibberish into focus. I think that his ideas are so much better than anybody else's. I've just never seen anybody like him, and he's the nicest guy in the world.

If I were to pick a moment that changed the culture of our community, it would be the founding of Metropolitan College, which was driven by good political leadership — Mayor Jerry Abramson, UPS, Governor Paul Patton, President John Shumaker, at the University of Louisville, and Dan Ash of Metroversity. What I'm talking about is not so much about Metroversity, but about the concept of breaking down silos and working in a collaborative way to get an outcome, as opposed to everybody's building their own silos, which is the Louisville way, the Kentucky way.

I went on UofL's Board of Trustees shortly after Metroversity was created. I was absolutely fascinated by how it happened so quickly and the impact that it has had. Not only did it bring all the capital with UPS, it's been an incredible way to help Kentucky urbanize our population. Now we have a way for young people from the distant rural parts of our state to come to Louisville, get a job, and get an education.

Now they have choices. One of those choices might be to go home and do what Paul Patton did for his community, but it sure beats sitting at home on the step because the county judge doesn't want to lose a voter. The impact of Metropolitan College is a major cultural shift in how Kentucky thinks about the future.

Our community's biggest challenge is that we have to educate our people or we will not get to compete in the new economy. It is really simple. We are not just talking about scientists, we're talking about educational attainment for all our citizens. If everybody could bump up one level — if the dropouts could get a GED, if the high school graduates could get a two-year associates of arts degree, if more people could get bachelor's degrees, if we could keep the "Bucks for Brains" program and bring in and actually grow more Ph.Ds, this is what economic development is all about.

Unfortunately, not valuing education is one of the legacies of Kentucky. That has not been nearly as big a problem in Louisville as it has in other parts of the state, but we don't win any awards here either. When you look at how educated our population is compared to the 11 or 12 cities we consider competition, we're right near the bottom. The good news is that most of the problem is in people 50 years and up.

So we've done a much better job with people 30 years old and under. I think the community is focused on it. I think our mayor — even though he has no formal responsibility for education — uses the bully pulpit at all opportunities. We have terrific educational leadership here in Louisville. Everyone gets along and they all work together, and that's new.

As I get older, I do sometimes think about the one thing in my life that was really valuable. I also ask myself, "If it had been missing, would things have been a disaster?" I think that, without question, it's integrity. Talking about it sounds kind of self-serving. My parents never talked about it, they just lived it. But you have only one chance in life to lose your reputation and, if you lose it, you never get it back. So I would tell every young person not to get into financial trouble, just to do good. Build your reputation and protect it. It's the most valuable thing you have.

I don't like to throw stones, but some of our business leaders — not necessarily in Louisville — but some around the country whom we admired are now in jail. They not only haven't had integrity, they're just nuts. My grandfather went to jail once for moonshining, but that's what he was supposed to do.

Everything depends on the situation. I've developed reasonably good instincts. I know how to get informal input from a lot of people and to synthesize it. I even do disaster checks, as I've gotten older and have realized that I'm not as smart as I think I am. I see a lot of people, particularly uncreative people, use strategic planning as a crutch and as a waste of time. I mean there's nothing wrong with it — it's just not going to make a great plan. We do a lot of operational planning, but you still like to maintain the freedom to smell the roses.

Sometimes you just have to go with your gut instinct. That's easier for some people than others. I think it's probably related to one's personality. People who are risk adverse are going to have a lot of trouble seeing forward. People who are extroverted are more interested in pleasing others and are interactive, and that sometimes gets in the way of seeing through the fog. So there are certain personalities that are a little more objective and a little less baggage on risk avoidance.

Before my father died, he reminded me that the most likely reason that Maker's Mark has worked and been so successful is that God decided it's our turn to get lucky. He told me to try not to forget that. Well he was right, and that concept is reinforced by Tom Meeker, who keeps reminding me that he and I are just standing on top of a giant pedestal, and if we really get to thinking that we're as smart as we think we are, we better step off the pedestal.

JOHN H. SCHNATTER

Founder and Chairman
Papa John's International Inc.

AT JEFFERSONVILLE HIGH SCHOOL in southern Indiana, John Schnatter used to play water polo to build upper body strength and make himself a better shortstop. In college at Ball State University, he worked at several pizza parlors, learning about crusts and sauces while meeting the requirements for a business degree in three years. "The will to prepare," he told *Business First* in 1995, "is more important than the will to win."

Or, to put that another way, "Better Ingredients - Better Pizza." That slogan has taken Schnatter from baking pizzas in a bar's broom closet to the helm of a 2,700-restaurant chain that is now in 49 states and 11 international markets including the UK, where Papa John's owns 140 restaurants operating under the name of "Perfect Pizza."

Actually, completing college in four years was the slow way for Schnatter. He felt he was ready to go with his plans for a pizza business after his second year at Ball State, and he thought seriously about quitting school and starting a pizza place in Bloomington.

But Schnatter supplements the lessons life gives him with a lot of reading about inspiration and success, and he had read somewhere that character is the ability to keep marching after the initial thrill wears off.

He didn't believe in quitting anyway. He was born in Jeffersonville, Indiana in 1961, son and grandson of lawyers named Bob Schnatter and Louis Ackerson, the latter called "Papaw." Schnatter gives both of them credit for guiding him to success in business. Besides having a career as a prosecutor and judge, his father had a passion for running businesses. He experimented with 20 or so, none of which succeeded, but he never quit trying. "Not quitting builds character," Schnatter says.

His father and grandfather taught him two other important lessons he's never forgotten: the importance of having a strong work ethic, and of focusing your efforts on what you do best if you hope to succeed in life.

At age 11, Schnatter had enough of a work ethic to earn $300 for a motorcycle he wanted. In high school, he had a Camaro that he washed three times a week, while earning A's in his classes and working at Rocky's Sub Pub. After college, he cut a deal with his father for space to make pizza in a bar the elder Schnatter owned that was $64,000 in debt. All John Schnatter had to do was run the bar.

He turned the place around in three months and created space for a pizza oven in a former broom closet. The patrons gobbled up the pizzas, and Schnatter discovered he loved running a business.

So in 1985, he took over a building next door and launched Papa John's. He got the name from a dorm mate at Ball State who was studying marketing, though his special relationship with his grandfather may explain some of its appeal to him.

By 1987, he had acquired three more restaurants and a wife and business partner, Annette. He built more restaurants and struggled a bit with suppliers and expenses. But he said that in 1989, when *Louisville Magazine* declared his pizza the best in town, he knew he had something special. Today, for a record six years in a row, Papa John's Pizza is rated #1 in customer satisfaction among all national fast food establishments, according to research conducted by the University of Michigan's National Quality Research Center.

By 1995, ten years after he started, Schnatter had 701 restaurants in 20 states and was looking at $445 million in sales. A year later, when pizza sales approached $1 billion, he told *The Courier-Journal* that he always had a feeling his business would do really well, though perhaps not as well as it was doing. "I didn't think it would be worth a billion, but I thought maybe one day it would be worth $100 million dollars," he said.

Schnatter was quick to start giving back to his community. In 1996, he gave $5 million — $4 million of it his and $1 million of the company's — to the University of Louisville to help them build a new $63 million, 42,000-seat football stadium. To show its gratitude, the university named the facility Papa John's Stadium. He also helped the University of Kentucky build an on-campus soccer/softball complex, as well as a UK basketball museum.

Both Schnatter and his wife, Annette, are active in community activities. They made a substantial donation to help the Louisville Zoo build the region's only natural gorilla habitat. Schnatter has also served on a number of boards in the community, among them the Muhammad Ali Center and National City Bank, and he currently serves on the Advisory Board of the Cerebral Palsy K.I.D.S. Center. Papa John's sponsors many charitable events in the community, including an annual golf outing benefiting cerebral palsy.

The Schnatters live in Anchorage, Kentucky and have three children.

THE BIGGEST TURNING POINT in Papa John's history was when we won *Louisville Magazine*'s "Best Pizza in Louisville Award" in 1989. People in the Louisville community told us they thought Papa John's was the best. It was, and still is, a huge deal for us. After winning that award, I remember telling my brother, Chuck, "We finally did it." I think it was at this time that I realized that Papa John's and I owe a lot to this community. Louisville supported us and helped us in tough times. I owe it to this community to give back and provide support, as the folks in this town once did for Papa John's.

My biggest mentors were my grandfather, Louis Ackerson, whom we called "Papaw," and my dad, Bob Schnatter, whom we called "Champer." Papaw instilled in my brother, my sister and me the belief that we could accomplish anything we set out to do. He taught us that hard work pays off. He was very positive, a "can do" man. My dad was always trying new things and encouraged risk-taking. Over the course of many years, he embarked upon approximately 20 different business ventures, all of which failed. But Dad maintained an upbeat attitude and kept trying. He had a "never give up" approach to life. Dad and Papaw instilled in me the importance of integrity, mutual respect and hard work. Their influence on me tremendously enhanced my intuitive grasp on how a business should be run.

To be a good leader, I think you have to let your team do the things that they are the best at doing. You can't be afraid to bring in truly smart, energetic individuals who are good at things you're not. The price of leadership is responsibility, and a big part of that responsibility is addressing personal and professional weaknesses — looking in the mirror and not out the window. If you've imparted your core values on the right people around you, you can trust them to make the right moves and provide you with the strength you need to succeed as a team.

I'm not sure how others would describe my leadership style, but I would hope they would describe me as a fair, honest, energetic and straightforward leader. While I have very high expectations for myself and for those around me, I also believe some of our best learning comes from making mistakes. You get your learning from your burning.

If you hire bad, you have to manage tough. If you hire good, you don't manage, you lead. If you hire great, you don't lead, you follow and let those around you take you up the ladder to success.

I'm proud of the company we have built at Papa John's. Growing from a converted broom closet in the back of my dad's tavern in Jeffersonville, Indiana to nearly 3,000 restaurants has been extremely rewarding.

My biggest lesson learned from building Papa John's is that no matter how big you get, it always comes back to how the customer is treated at each restaurant, with each order. In our business, we are only as good as the last pizza we served, so the most important person at Papa John's is not me or the officers who run the company. The most important person at Papa John's is the front-line team member, making it happen one 10" pizza at a time.

Along the way, I also learned the importance of keeping things simple. Simplicity is the ultimate form of sophistication.

As Papa John's grew, it became physically impossible for me to visit every restaurant frequently enough to gauge the product quality and level of customer service being delivered at our restaurants. I think we all underestimated our ability to measure the customer experience throughout our system as the number of restaurants increased. Once we discovered this, and devised a mechanism to monitor the customer experience, I realized how important it is and that what gets measured, gets done.

The people who are successful at Papa John's generally have one trait in common – what they think, what they value, what they say and how they act is who they are. They have integrity.

We've been blessed with a lot of success at Papa John's, and we have to constantly remind ourselves that integrity – playing it straight with our customers and among ourselves – is critical to our continued prosperity.

I also believe a good follower isn't afraid to challenge and debate with their leader. I tell my leadership team, "If you don't challenge my judgment, you weaken me." I like constructive discontent or "collaborative confrontation" in my team. Then once a decision is made, we march together.

If I knew back in the beginning what I know now, I don't think we would have done what we did because we never should have been able to do what we've done.

I would advise young people aspiring to leadership in our community to focus on one thing and try to do it better than anyone else. The main thing is to keep the main thing the main thing. But young people should know that nothing comes easy. You have to learn how to handle and beat adversity. A big shot is just a little shot who kept on shooting.

Look at Michael Jordan or Abraham Lincoln – they never won anything in their early years. Michael Jordan sat the bench in high school. Abe Lincoln lost every election he was in, except the one for president. But the difference between winners and losers is, the great ones never give up. They just keep firing at it. As the great hockey player Wayne Gretzky used to say, "You miss 100 percent of the shots you don't take." In the game of life, you have to keep shooting.

Innovations in the medical field in Louisville have been tremendous: heart and lung transplants and the development of the artificial heart; the amazing advances by Doctors Kleinert and Kutz and their team in hand and related surgeries; advances in cancer research; the outstanding trauma work at University Hospital. Who would have thought 50 years ago that a hand transplant would have been possible or that a person could survive with an artificial heart? The amount of medical innovation in Louisville is amazing, and we must continue to nurture this.

The University of Louisville continues to be a bedrock of our community. From its Medical School, to the Brandeis School of Law, to Speed Engineering, to the Business School, UofL continues to be innovative and to train future leaders. We have to continue to support the University of Louisville, including in its quest to become a national leader in research.

Many leaders have helped shape Louisville over the last century and are too numerous to name. But I have been impressed with the work and good deeds done by Wendell Cherry and David Jones, Owsley Brown Frazier and James Graham Brown, among others.

I have also been impressed with the foresight of our city leaders to invest in our parks system. We are benefiting today from the wisdom and vision of our town fathers who hired the Olmsted brothers 100 years ago to design our parks system and boulevards. I appreciate and admire that.

The greatest thing about Louisville is its people. Louisvillians are genuinely nice people. They care, they are generous, and they are always willing to lend a hand.

Our community has some big challenges ahead, however. We have to continue to invest in our infrastructure. We have to continue to invest in education. We have to nurture creative and entrepreneurial thinking. We have to build the bridges, continue to recapture our waterfront, and continue to invest in our parks and our neighborhoods. We need to do things right, build things out of stone, and dream big. We also need to remember that UofL is an enormous asset and the bedrock for our community's future.

I have learned some lessons in my life I would like to share with the next generation of leaders in Louisville:

First: The real reward in life and business is the satisfaction that comes with knowing that you've done your best and contributed to something greater than yourself;

Second: Work hard, add value and have fun;

Third: Appreciate the opportunity you have been given to make a difference and to create something enduring;

Last, and most importantly: Remember to give thanks to the people around you who make it all worthwhile, and respect and give thanks for the ultimate gift that we have all been given – the gift of life.

DEBBIE SCOPPECHIO

**Chairman and CEO
Creative Alliance Inc.**

ANYBODY WHO KNOWS "Hurricane" Debbie Scoppechio would have a hard time believing she ever had a shyness problem, but her mother says she did. She was so shy, she was standoffish with her own grandmother, Scoppechio's mother told *Business First* in 1991. They had to send her to dancing school to try to snap her out of it. People who know her will have no trouble believing the next part: Nine years later she tap-danced with her class on the "Ed Sullivan Show."

Now Scoppechio is a real show woman. She moves around her chandeliered and balconied advertising agency with energy that has been compared to whirling dervishes and Tasmanian devils, calling out to her "creative people," her trademark rich, throaty laugh bouncing around the cornices. "If she says she's going to fire you about once a week, it's a sign that she loves you," a former colleague told *The Courier-Journal*'s Linda Stahl in 1994. She is the one who goes out into the world gathering up business for her growing firm, leaving the creative work to others.

After laying groundwork working for other advertising firms for 12 years in Buffalo, New York and for three years in Louisville, Scoppechio launched her own firm – Creative Alliance – in 1987, with two partners. They got started working for clients who liked their work at other agencies. Then Scoppechio went after other business like the whirlwind of nature people later compared her to.

It became clear she was serious in 1989 when she bagged the $6 million inaugural advertising account from the Kentucky Lottery Company, after competing against larger, more established agencies. That account later went in-house, and later to another firm; in 2001, Creative Alliance was once again named agency-of-record for the Kentucky Lottery.

By 1990, Creative Alliance was the largest advertising agency in Kentucky, with 140 employees in Louisville, Nashville, Chicago and

Pittsburgh, and with more than $109 million in capitalized billings. Her who's who list of clients now includes Yum! Brands Corporation, KFC Corporation, A&W, Long John Silver's, Brown-Forman Corporation, LG&E Energy, Kentucky Lottery Corporation, KFC CaribLA, Pepsi, Ken Towery, Aptis Medical, Louisville Convention and Visitors Bureau, Mikasa and others.

Debbie Scoppechio was born in Nutley, New Jersey, and grew up in Wappingers Falls, New York, not far from Poughkeepsie. Her father was a building contractor who thought she was a princess and didn't need to go to college, but her mother made sure she did. She studied psychology and sociology, then got a job as a social worker.

She soon decided she could do more for the disadvantaged by making money and donating it back to community causes. She met an advertising executive at a party, got a job, and found out she was good enough at it to become vice president of Faller, Klenk and Quinlan in Buffalo. After 12 years there, she left Buffalo in the midst of a divorce and, ultimately, landed in Louisville, Kentucky, a city she says she loves. There is no question that the city loves her.

Scoppechio is one of only two women who have been inducted into the Junior Achievement Business Hall of Fame, and she was named Entrepreneur of the Year in 1999 by the Kentucky Small Business Development Center. Presentation Academy presented her with a Tower Award for Women Leaders in 1999, and *Working Woman* magazine presented her with its National Entrepreneurial Excellence Award the same year. She received the Heart of the Community Award from Women 4 Women, Inc. in 2002. Both Scoppechio and her business have earned a long string of additional awards and recognitions over the years for their creative talents and for their considerable community service.

Creative Alliance has done *pro bono* work for a number of civic and charitable causes in the community, including the Louisville Orchestra, Operation Open Arms, Women 4 Women, the Festival of Trees and Lights, Junior Achievement, Collegiate School, the Dream Factory, the Kentucky Center for the Arts, Metro United Way, and Street Ball Showdown.

While serving on the board of Greater Louisville Inc., Scoppechio and her agency designed a *pro bono* poster for a GLI membership campaign, showing Louisville banker Malcolm Chancey soaring across his desk to slam dunk a basketball.

Scoppechio is married to Rick Duffy, who is her partner in business, as well as in life.

IN 1987, I DECIDED TO BE an entrepreneur, so I started Creative Alliance. I guess about three or four years into it, I decided it was time to give back to the community. That's when I joined a number of different boards, and I started enjoying it immediately.

I soon saw that it was time for the leadership in our community to change. There had been a lot of great leadership in the past, but I thought it was very important, back in the early '90s, to bring some young, as well as female, leadership to the table. I felt we were bringing new blood into the community, because many of the leaders then were from major corporations and that has now changed. The way I see it, if the major corporations don't lead, then the smaller businesses need to pick up the slack.

Being in a leadership position doesn't necessarily help you get business, but you work to help other people make business thrive in the community.

Certainly from a charitable standpoint, I think that Louisville itself is a leader in the country. That's another reason why I wanted to become a leader here, and to do what I could for other parts of the community.

I felt when I started the ad agency that, from a business perspective, Louisville was ready for change. I certainly felt that there could be more aggressiveness in the advertising community, and that we could make Louisville more of an advertising community, so we could compete with ad agencies in other surrounding cities. I think that's what got us started, and I decided then to lead our creative team to do "whatever it takes" to make a difference.

When we turned ten years old and had recently moved into this building, we remembered that we had had a big party when we were one year old, we had had a really big party when we were five years old, and we wanted to have a super big party when we turned ten years old. We got the mayor to give us permission to close down Jefferson Street. We had a huge tent, great food, beverages, and entertainment for approximately 1500-2000 guests.

The party was really not just for our clients, but a way to say "Here we are, thanks for all your help" to our clients, our people, our vendors and the people we do business with. We had a great time. The governor, the lieutenant governor, the mayor and the county judge all attended. We have some great memories from that party.

When I was "up and coming" and working for other people, there weren't leaders, there were bosses. I worked for lots of bosses. Now there aren't any bosses, there are only leaders.

I guess I knew I was a leader at Creative Alliance when *Ad Week* wrote something about our people drinking "Kool-Aid", implying that anything I asked them to do, they would do it. They made it sound like that was a negative, but actually I thought, "That's pretty good!" I never asked our team to do anything I wouldn't do, so we all had a big laugh over that. Then we had a little Kool-Aid party!

Those who know me may find it hard to believe that when I was about four years old, I would never go anywhere without my mother. I was a little shrinking violet, very shy. So she sent me to dancing school, then that was sort of "all she wrote." I'd say yes to everything. I was always a leader in school. I'd be in three different groups of friends, instead of just one. I was usually the one who led us into trouble, but I guess that's a leadership skill too. I was a cheerleader in high school and college, which is also "leading," so in those strange little ways, I became a leader.

I have also tried to be a leader with my clients. I have been in account services forever. Back in Buffalo, whether I was as an account executive or an account supervisor, I felt like I was leading clients as opposed to just doing what they told us to do. I hopefully played a little bit of a leadership role at the agency there.

My big mentor in advertising leadership is a gentleman named Bob Faller, who was president of Faller, Klenk and Quinlan back in Buffalo. He gave me my first job in advertising a couple of years after college. He was truly my mentor. He taught me that you never say no, and that there is always a way to get something done. "There is always a solution," he would say. "We can always figure it out." His attitude has led me through my entire life. No challenge or problem or issue has ever arisen that I haven't been able to figure out how to solve.

One year, I thought one of my clients was sending out an announcement for this event we were having in Chicago, and I got there and said, "What was your response?" They had never sent the announcement out. So three of their sales reps and I, in the Conrad Hilton Hotel, went door-to-door, to how many thousand hotel rooms, slipping these invitations (which I quickly printed) under the doors so people would attend instead of writing the whole thing off. Things like that are what he taught me. He was so service-oriented and so creative and I am proud to still call him a friend.

My father was also an entrepreneur. My parents were mentors who inspired me. That goes without saying. My other mentors are people like David Jones. I don't often seek his advice, but I certainly want to follow in his footsteps and have a great relationship with him. I think he is a fabulous mentor.

Ed Glasscock is our lawyer, so he is a great business mentor. But he is also a great civic mentor and has valuable advice on everything. He is someone I would call at two o'clock in the morning if I needed something. He is so civic-minded, and he is so "number one" right now.

David Novak is a mentor too. He is the best leader I know, but he's viewed as much more of a business leader. People don't know him as well for civic leadership, which he does, both personally and through the YUM! Brands' foundations. He is certainly a mentor in many ways, even though he is also a client.

This may sound odd, but Rick Duffy — my husband — is also an important mentor to me from a business standpoint. I'm probably his mentor from a civic standpoint, but he's my mentor from a business standpoint.

Leadership Louisville and the people whom I have met and worked with there are also mentors — both when I was in my class, and since then. I look at many of them as mentor types, whether it's formal or not.

I would describe my leadership style as "inspirational." I think the word is on the street about my leadership style here at Creative Alliance. Civically, my leadership style is "involved," in that I try to get to meetings and to stay involved with any boards and civic activities that I'm on. I try not to chair anything because for me, and the business situation that I'm in, if I commit to chairing something, I know I will fail and that's not failing me, it's failing the organization.

When people ask me for help, I try to make sure they get the best thing for them, not for me. I resigned most of the boards I was serving on after 9/11 because I couldn't commit my time. I had to commit my time here, and I try not to over-commit. I just don't want to be involved in something that I'm really not going to be able to be completely involved in.

One other word describes my leadership style, I think, and covers both my business and civic leadership, and that word is "motivational." I feel like a lot of organizations want to meet with me to try to get something done. I hope that I can motivate them and give them some great ideas so they can go do things. I can't do those things for all of them, but they can. I try to offer them creative thinking. I think I do that civically, whether I am on a board or doing *pro bono* work.

Creative Alliance is certainly innovative and motivating to people. I work very hard to keep everybody up and motivated no matter what's going on, which is not an easy task, but I think that's a very important part of being a leader. You have to be honest if there are issues, but to keep everybody excited about what they are doing — and that goes for civically, too — isn't always easy.

I believe if you are going to do something, you should get excited and do it well. Any civic cause I get involved in, I try to do things differently. Whatever they did last year, if I'm going to work on it, I want it to be different. So many people who get involved are corporate, and we're not. If they want our involvement, they should want something that isn't so corporate.

All the bankers (past and present) in our community — the Malcolm Chanceys, the Jim Gaunts, the Leonard Hardins, the Mike Harrelds, etc., are all fabulous leaders. They are a little more conservative than the up-and-coming leaders in our community, but they also have clout from their financial positions. It will be interesting to see if that changes now that more and more banks are owned by out-of-town entities.

One leader in our community is now gone — Susan Ivey, former president and CEO of Brown & Williamson. You couldn't find two totally different styles, hers and mine, but she did so much for the community while B&W was here.

Jay McGowan is brilliant and has an unbelievable personality, and he is a great leader in our community.

Look at Greater Louisville Inc's. Steve Higdon, and Doug Cobb, CEO prior to him. They have totally different leadership styles than I have, but both have done a lot. The only thing that matters is what you bring to the table. There are a lot of different styles of leadership in our town. We just need more people with styles that are not so conservative — people who have a little bit more "out there" thinking, for example.

I think our community should have more leaders coming out of the marketing and advertising community — and I don't just mean out of ad agencies. TV stations should have leaders. Steve Langford at WAVE-TV is a fabulous leader and he has done a whole lot civically.

A lot of businesses a couple of years ago just went inward to stay alive and to do their own thing, so I think the timing is excellent to be talking about leadership.

The way I see it, you have two kinds of leaders — one who has financial clout and one who doesn't have financial clout but may have other clout. I don't think we have enough "financial clout" leaders out there, so what are we going to do about that?

The ones who have had the financial clout in the past — Owsley Brown and Owsley Brown Frazier, for example, two more mentors of mine — they have done unbelievable things for the civic community. Who is coming next?

I've done a lot of things in my life, but my greatest accomplishment has to be Creative Alliance. I have loved every minute of it. The first couple of years we were in business, I can't believe anybody even worked here, though. I was a nightmare! As you grow, you turn into a better leader. Creative Alliance — under my leadership — is certainly night and day compared to 18 years ago. I am still as driven, but I try to make sure I drive through my leadership team now. I think I have a whole lot more patience, because I know I am leading a team that I know I want to keep together. I think I have learned a lot about patience and judgment. I think I lead more effectively now, and without fear. I don't worry so much about things, because I know there is always tomorrow.

I do think I learned a lot here, though, in the first two to four years. People who worked for me then probably wish they worked for me now instead, because back then, there were bosses. You did things because your boss said to do it, as opposed to "Wow, is this a great idea? Let's figure it out together."

I was so driven that everything went to the goal line. If we had to be here all night, we were. Now, if we have to be here all night, not only will I be here, but we will bring two people in from the outside to help, so we won't have be here all night. The whole agency, I think, is driven. But my personality, I think, has leveled out to the point that I am more of a leader. I also have a great leadership team, and I think that's part of it. Early on, we didn't have one. We had two or three creative guys, and me.

When I first started out, I didn't have fear based on "What if this doesn't work" because I would just go, "I sell, I love to sell ideas." I was more in fear of disappointing a client, of not making the right presentation. I wasn't afraid of losing business, but I had fear about keeping our clients happy because we really built our reputation by delivering what they needed from Creative Alliance. Between that fear, and the fact that all I did was work, I guess I figured I'd never have a life again.

I am very client-driven, which doesn't mean I'm a "yes person." If I tell clients "no," they understand there is a good reason behind it. I just think that not every agency remembers that we all wouldn't be here if it weren't for our clients. That was my catalyst for establishing and growing this agency. I felt our clients deserved better work, better treatment, better thinking than they were getting.

To be perfectly honest, I don't think I've had any "failures" because in my opinion, you learn from everything. I know I sound like Mary Poppins, but if I really had to identify failures, I would have to say that I have learned from every one of them.

My biggest failure happened when we pitched a piece of business years ago that we didn't get. We didn't get it because we weren't Creative Alliance. It was someone who liked doing business with men, so I sort of took a back seat. We went in to make the presentation and we really weren't us, so we didn't deserve to get it. We disappointed ourselves, and that was a lesson learned. Everybody doesn't want us. We're not right for everybody and vice versa.

I did get to know that client. I worked on getting the business for the next two years. I worked on a board with him, then we got the business two years later. The lesson again is to learn from it. Never give up. That's part of me now

– if at first you don't succeed, try, try again. So we eventually did get this business but the failure was that we didn't recognize that we had to be us. We are who we are. Like it or not, I am the leader. We can't change that overnight. That was a very important lesson.

I've also learned that it is a failure to be on a board and not give anything. That's a great failure. The lesson I learned from that failure was, "Don't over-commit." I can't do anybody outside civically any good if I don't take care of Creative Alliance. I over-committed and I feel like I failed some people. One failure that I have is saying "yes" when I shouldn't, then I let people down. That also goes for new business. Sometimes I take a piece of new business that I shouldn't. God forbid that I should say no, but again that hurts the team I'm leading if it's not the right piece of business.

Probably the biggest failure I've had since I've been in business is making a mistake in hiring. A bad hire is the worst failure you can make – for the person and for the agency. If a person is a rotten egg or is not a part of the culture and you keep him or her on forever, everybody gets upset with you if you don't make a change. You're either in the culture here or they will drive you out. Everybody blames me that they are working to take up this person's slack, then you try to make a half fix and that never works. I have learned it's best to just cut it off if it doesn't work. My biggest challenge is people, however, because it's terrible to make a mistake about a person when he or she has a family depending on them. I hate that part of my job.

The best employees are the ones who are proactive with good ideas, who don't wait for me to ask for things. I want my employees to give me their ideas, their proactive thinking on things. When we're in a meeting and we've all heard everybody's opinions and we make a decision, that's it – they understand that we have to move forward. Everyone doesn't want to be a leader, and everybody shouldn't have to be a leader. There are people who want to do what they do forever. I wish people would recognize that, because I love that. There is nothing wrong with you if you want to just be a good employee. Many of our employees here are going to be great leaders.

We have some wonderful talent that just needs to mature to become part of the leadership team. We have a pretty strong leadership team, too. Very interestingly, it is not so much the older ones, but the younger ones. I'm sending one of them now to one of the Leadership Louisville programs. They are very excited and want to get involved in the community.

I want to help anyone who wants to be a leader. Managing them is another story. Some are just on an automatic rise to the top.

How many of our people can we give up to the community, and for how long? That's a big question. The important thing is that more people are doing it for the future of our company as well. Letting them step into leadership roles in the community is an important part of our growth.

I certainly would be a challenging follower. I think I would be a good follower of a civic or political leader, but not a professional one. I really think it would be difficult for me to be a follower in my profession at this point.

If I had the time, I would love to be involved nationally and locally for women. I don't think we are diverse enough and I'd love to help do more. I'm sure before I lie down and die, I will do more for women. I should put my money where my mouth is when I talk about women and diversity. I've certainly given speeches, but that is very different from helping mentor young women.

If I could do things over again, I would probably want to erase all my hiring mistakes. Actually, I don't know that I would do anything differently. That goes back to my believing that I had to go through what I went through to get here. I probably would have done some pitches differently. I probably would be more of a leader and more proactive in the kinds of business we grow. Once we took off, if we got a call, we would make a pitch. We would not go outside and look for a new piece of business, so shame on us. I think if I went around again, that is something I would make more time for.

Civically, I think I could have offered more to certain boards, but there are boards I should have said no to, for their sake and mine. I wish I had done more for women's organizations, but I'll just make the commitment to do that in the future.

From a business standpoint, I don't know whether I would have set the company up any differently. But even though I have headaches every day, I love every day that I walk in here. From a civic standpoint, I regret over-promising.

I felt great about the time I spent on Greater Louisville Inc.'s board, because that's when we brought the Economic Development Partnership and the Chamber of Commerce together and I was one of the leaders in that. I felt it was the best and smartest thing we could have done.

Creative Alliance also did *pro bono* work on Louisville's merger campaign. We worked very closely with the mayor and were proud to be involved with that project. Furthermore, most of my financial commitments have been for children's causes, and I have always felt good about that.

If I were going to advise young people aspiring to become leaders in the community, I would recommend – if they have time to commit to something

— that they commit to one business board that will help business in the community. If business doesn't grow in the community, none of us can help anybody. They should get involved on one board or in one cause they believe in, whether it's kids, pets, animals — whatever. You should never just do a cause-related board because if we don't kick ourselves in the butt to grow business in this community, we won't have any money to give to causes.

I would ask aspiring young leaders, "Do you understand what a leader is?" Then if they answer that question correctly, my advice would be, "You need to be ready to work as hard as the people you are leading. Don't ask someone to do something you wouldn't do yourself. Know where you are trying to lead people. If you think you are a leader, what is your vision?"

I would also advise people aspiring to leadership in business to remember that their first line of attack needs to be their business. I would tell them that they have to have a lot of energy. Whether it's effervescent energy or not, they are going to have to have a lot of energy and patience to be a leader. They also have to be willing to be a mentor to others. They have to be willing to help others grow and be willing to listen to their followers. And they have to remember that there is a big difference between being a leader and being a manager.

David Jones, Owsley Brown, Christy Brown, Owsley Frazier, David Novak, Jerry Abramson, David Armstrong, Ed Glasscock, every CEO of the banks here — they have all been phenomenal leaders in our community. They have all played a part in our community's growth and development over the years.

Jerry Abramson and David Armstrong have improved the quality of life in our community as mayor. David Jones, the two Owsleys and others have helped finance it. I should mention the contributions of Malcolm Chancey and Leonard Hardin too, because no one can doubt what they have done for the community. I haven't been here the full 50 years, so my viewpoint is very different. David Novak located YUM! here.

I was proud to have served on the board of both the Chamber and the Partnership, and enjoyed working closely with Doug Cobb to create what we called the super board. Doug led it and did a phenomenal job. He's another one who has done a lot to improve the quality of business life in our community.

The biggest challenges I think our community is facing are how we are going to get big businesses to locate here to replace the big businesses we have lost, and how we are going to get a number of mid-size businesses to come here. When our governments merged, we asked our mayor, Jerry Abramson, to pull it all together and, in doing that, we gave one man about ten full-time jobs. We have to help him develop a vision for the future, and it has to be a vision we all agree on. Certainly the state thinks one way. Louisville may think a different way. I would like to play a role in helping us form that vision.

I think we need to be a little less conservative with that vision, but we need to be honest with ourselves about what we can attain. Are we going to move American Express here? I don't think so. But we do need to get beyond just telling people that our wonderful lifestyle is the reason to move here. That's certainly one reason why people move here, but we also have to have other things.

One of our challenges is, how do we get new business to move here, but take care of the businesses we have here now? The businesses that move here get all the extra things, like tax incentives. What about all the people who are already here? I'm not saying we are forgetting them, but we may not be doing as much for them as we should.

I think the sooner the next generation of leaders steps up and gets involved and understands what's going on the better, which is why I like what Leadership Louisville is doing. But I think our community is facing another challenge. We can have some great leaders, but if they don't have corporate money backing them, that scares me. For a long time, our city has received a lot of money from major corporations and, when those people retire, will the money still come from those companies or not?

It's important for our leaders to have brains and brawn, but they are also going to need to figure out what our vision is going to be, how we are going to achieve it, and how we are going to have enough corporate support to finance our dreams. Companies like Creative Alliance aren't going to be able to do that. They can be a part of it, but we are certainly not a Brown & Williamson.

Another challenge our city is facing is that there is a lot of high-paid talent out there in our community. People would kill to have it, but can't afford it; yet they can't find talent they can afford. I think there is a mismatch in this community between openings and talent. Maybe I should go back on the GLI board and make that an initiative. When companies like Brown & Williamson have people who earned a lot of money out looking for jobs, and when the people I need are account people, there is a mismatch in our community between openings and talent.

In some ways I feel a huge responsibility, because I've had such a successful business here. I attribute Creative Alliance's success to the community in many ways, and I feel like I owe everybody in the city. If you asked ten different people about the future of our community, I think they would agree that there are a lot of good things happening here, but where's the vision? Some of our young people are looking for change, so perhaps it should not be too conservative a vision, but it has to be a reachable vision, and Louisville needs to take ownership of the vision. The city needs to develop the vision and go forward with it, and it has to be something that young leaders and old leaders can all agree with.

Debbie Scoppechio

One thing I left out that's very important for a leader is that you have to share your vision. Sometimes I am great at that, and sometimes I'm not, and this could be said about many leaders in our community. Leaders have to share their vision. I can be the best at it and the worst at it. To me, if you don't have a business vision for this community, you are not going to have civic leadership. Louisville is the most giving community on earth, but we have to have a vision to keep growing so we can keep giving.

The next generation of leaders should always remember why they want to be leaders and a part of the community, and that's to pay it back. People should have some civic-mindedness if they want to be a leader. I do think it often helps to become a good business leader before you become a good civic leader.

I have learned some lessons in my own life that I would like to share with the next generation of leaders:

1) Be yourself;
2) You can never work too hard or too smart;
3) Remember those who brought you here and take care of them;
4) Be ethical, because it's a huge part of your credibility;
5) Make sure you have a vision, and that you can communicate your vision to the people who work with you;
6) Have patience, and never give up;
7) Be sure you have the talent it takes to be a leader;
8) Have empathy and understanding for everyone you work with;
9) Don't get frustrated;
10) Be positive;
11) Listen, learn, and get ready to step up; and
12) Never say no!

I think it is going to be very interesting over the next five years in Louisville as we create a vision for our community and continue to grow.

I thoroughly enjoy life. I wake up every day loving what I do. People ask me when am I going to slow down, but I don't want to slow down because I love what I do. I like myself so much better today than 15 years ago. If I died this evening I would die very happy. I do wish I had more time off, though. My entire life is business. A lot of my friends are business friends. The best thing that ever happened to me was meeting and marrying Rick, because I would have no life if he weren't there to make me have one.

WILLIAM M. STREET

**Retired President
Brown-Forman Corporation**

FROM THE TIME GEORGE GARVIN BROWN founded Brown-Forman in 1870 until 1966, members of his family never turned the reins of the company over to anyone outside the family.

In 1966, they decided to make an exception with Dan Street, who hailed from Cadiz, Kentucky, and who had come to work for them some years earlier as the company's lawyer. Three years before Street became CEO, the company had hired his son, William Street, fresh out of Princeton University and Harvard Business School, into a sales position.

The younger Street has said he thought with all that education, somebody should make him a CEO somewhere. But he said when he got into sales, starting off marketing Brown-Forman's beverages in south Florida, he soon discovered that he had a lot to learn.

One of the things he learned, he said years later, was that nobody can do everything. The thing for a person to do, he decided, is to pick out what you can do, then to focus on it until you've accomplished or mastered it.

Over the years, he decided that's not a bad idea for a community either. So he applauds the decision of Louisville leaders in recent years to focus their corporate recruitment efforts in the areas of health care and distribution.

Bill Street grew up in Louisville and graduated from Louisville Country Day School in 1956. He began his career at Brown-Forman that same year, as a summer intern.

After his return from Harvard, he progressed through sales, promotion, marketing, and general management responsibilities.

He became a member of Brown-Forman's board in 1971 and a vice president of the company in 1977. He was appointed president of domestic beverage operations in 1986.

In 1994, Brown-Forman created a global beverage organization responsible for its domestic and international wines and spirits businesses – Brown-Forman Beverages Worldwide – and made Street the president and CEO. It is the company's largest subsidiary.

He did very well there. "Bill's Leadership of BFBW. . .has been truly exemplary, as our financial and brand building results indicate," Owsley Brown II, Brown-Forman's chairman and CEO, said in 2000. "In addition," Brown said, "he is a superb counselor, not only to me, but to many in our company."

Brown was announcing Street's election to the presidency of the corporation, a position that did not change his job as president and CEO of the subsidiary, but amounted to acknowledgement of his value to the company. Brown said it gave "fuller recognition to the pivotal leadership role he plays in the company's continuing growth and prosperity."

Street stepped down as president in 2003, at the mandatory retirement age of 65, but he has remained on the corporation's board.

He subsequently served a year as chairman of the Greater Louisville Inc. board, and he has also chaired the boards of the Louisville YMCA, Louisville Collegiate School, the Leadership Louisville Foundation, the Kentucky Horse Racing Authority, the Governor's Scholars program and Metro United Way's "Success by 6" initiative.

Besides the Brown-Forman board, he serves on the board of Papa John's International.

Leadership Louisville gave Street the Thomas C. Simons Distinguished Leadership Award in 1998, and Metro United Way honored him with the Allen Society Community Service Award in 2000.

In 2003, he received both the YMCA's Spirit of Louisville Award and Louisville Collegiate School's Collegiate Service Award. In 2004, Street received the Gold Cup Award from Greater Louisville Inc., the organization's most prestigious award, bestowed to honor a lifetime of leadership and community service.

Street is married to the former Lindy Barber. He has one daughter and four stepchildren.

Passing the Torch

I'M NOT SURE I EVER MADE a definitive decision to become a leader in the Louisville community. My parents taught me by example that you need to give back so you can share your luck with others. I think that was what motivated me to decide that I wanted to become a leader. I wanted to pick some spots in the community where I thought I could be of help, then go to work in those areas.
Mother was involved in different education activities. My father was a lawyer first, then was at Brown-Forman from 1947 until he retired. My father did several things in the community, but I would say he probably focused more on his work at Brown-Forman than he did on anything else at that point in time. Both of my parents, when asked, always agreed to do something to help.

I got involved in the community almost entirely by working on organizational boards. Two are for-profit and the rest are not-for-profit boards.
The first was an organization called Bridgehaven. I had not been back in Louisville for too long a period of time when I was asked if I wanted to serve on that board. I thought about it and went and talked with the executive director, a fellow by the name of Roy Joseph. I listened and talked to him about what he was trying to accomplish and was very pleased with what I learned from him. I thought he was a good leader and, as it turned out, he was. I thought I could contribute something, so I made the time to go on that board. I was on the Bridgehaven board for a period of time, then became the chair. When I finished my term, I left the board and actually didn't do anything else at that point. Because of my workload at Brown-Forman, I ended up focusing almost all my time and effort there.

The next step I made was to go on the YMCA board, which was probably in the early '80s. I am still a director emeritus for that organization. After that, I found time to serve on more boards. I served as a director on some and actually became the chairman of a few to provide leadership to those boards and those efforts. I think my primary contributions to the community came through my board service. I selected organizations that I thought could have or already were having a positive impact on Louisville.
I happen to believe that committees are where the work of most boards gets accomplished. When I've been the chair of boards, I've always tried to select the chairmen of the committees with a lot of thought. Some of the boards I serve on frankly are so large that the meetings are agenda-led and not given to very fruitful discussions. The real discussion and thinking happens in committees.

My parents were my first mentors. I know now that my values and things I think are important in life came from them. I certainly learned hard work and integrity from them. I'm not sure how you say this, but my parents taught me that if you believe in something, you should go ahead and make it happen, even if it looks like the world is against you. So I guess they taught me determination. Some people would refer to it as stubbornness, from time to time, when they refer to me, but I prefer to think of it as determination.

My first boss at Brown-Forman was the sales manager for Florida. He and his assistant were both mentors to me. I had just gotten out of business school, had done some summer work and worked in Chicago between college and business school, but I really hadn't started a career so to speak. I came out of business school prepared to be a CEO, and I'd say in about a week's time I realized I'd better be a sales representative rather than a CEO and get on with that part of my career. They were very good about helping me with it and teaching me. They taught me the sales part of the business and they taught me the value of relationships.

When I was in Florida, working in Brown-Forman's south Florida territory, I learned which retailers I thought were good business people who could teach me something. I also hoped I could teach them something in time. But in finding those people, and working with them over time, I realized that it was not only helpful to my personal growth, it was also helpful to the business growth of my company. I have always tried to do relationship building throughout my business career. That meant finding people whom I thought understood what was going on, and learning from them.

There are other mentors in the community whom I respect and have learned from. I'd have to say the current mayor, Jerry Abramson, would be one. Mike Harreld would be another. Ed Glasscock would be another one who comes to mind. In a different sort of way, I would say the Brown family because I certainly have learned a lot from them. Watching the values of that family was important to me. I understood integrity with the Browns, and a sense of setting goals and making them happen.

My leadership style is definitely one of consensus building, not dictatorial, up to the point where my patience runs out, then I shift. I go from trying to build consensus to telling people, "It's time to reach a decision, so let's get on with it. We've talked about it enough, we understand it's tough to make the decision, but let's do it and get on with it."

So I'd have to say my style is to build consensus up to a point, then to use determination to make a decision and get on with implementing it.

I would hope others would see my leadership style the same way I do. My guess is if you were to ask an outsider who's been around me enough, they would probably weigh in more on the consensus building than the determination. I think it depends. If you were within Brown-Forman, you would probably see it pretty much the same way I see it, but if you were outsiders in the Louisville community, you might not quite see it the same way.

I have to say that my commitment to this community has gone down two paths. One is Brown-Forman. I've always felt that by making Brown-Forman as successful as possible, I was helping the community. The other path leads to the organizations on which I've served.

I'd have to say probably the one event that I remember most was at Brown-Forman. That was when the Joseph Garneau Company, of which I was a member, had a bad year. The senior management of Brown-Forman was pretty unhappy, so the decision was made that there would be a time period during which our division had to prove itself or they would disband it and fold the brands into other sales divisions. That was the charge that was given to me, and I was promoted to be the head of the Garneau Company.

I looked at the people and decided which of those people I thought could really provide the necessary leadership if I did my job and encouraged them to do theirs. I actually took a small group on a retreat and we literally wrote down the pluses and the minuses of our situation and listed what we would have to do to get ourselves more into the plus column. We wrote down some goals for ourselves for the next six months, then 12 months, and came back and started working on it. I'd say within 12 months, we had the senior management at Brown-Forman very supportive of what we were doing. Any way you measure it, whether it's how the people felt about working for the division or whether you reviewed the financial measures of the division, there was enormous improvement. I've always felt that was probably where my leadership did more than at any other time.

From that experience, I learned how to be willing to make tough decisions, because we let a few people go. That was always the hardest thing I ever had to do at Brown-Forman was to say goodbye to someone. But it was necessary. We changed the priorities of the division, which meant telling certain people that we were no longer putting quite as much emphasis on their brands and getting the consensus of the executive committee of Brown-Forman to agree with that strategy by explaining why to them. So, we had to make tough decisions. I had to make tough decisions. You figure out what the issues are as best you can, then make decisions and go and implement them.

Disappointment is probably a better word than failure, but when I retired from Brown-Forman I believe we had failed to acquire certain brands that would add to the company's strength. There were always good reasons why we didn't do it, but it's unfortunate we didn't. We did acquire some brands which I think will be very beneficial to the company over time. However, there were some big brands and some big opportunities that came along where we never quite had the resources or partnerships to bring them to bear. That is probably my biggest disappointment of my career.

I learned that there are disappointments, that things don't always fall your way, and you have to pick yourself up and say, "Okay, here's where we are, now what do we do with it?" "Here are the blocks we have to play with, how are we going to do the very best we can?" We had to get everybody past the disappointment and focus on what it would take to continue our success.

I don't know if I've ever quite gotten it in my head that some people are followers and some people are leaders, but I know that happens with organizational structure. I wouldn't call people followers, I would describe them as people with whom I have enjoyed working. I liked people who were focused, who would say what was on their mind. If they didn't like what you were saying, they would not only say so, but tell you why. They were willing to listen so you could have a real debate going back and forth. I don't know if that's being followers or leaders, but those are the kinds of people with whom I like to work.

There are a lot of shared values among the people at Brown-Forman. One of the things I've always said about them is that I don't think I've ever met anyone there with whom I wouldn't enjoy sharing a dinner. That was one of the nice things about the company. I didn't have anything to do with the hiring of 98 percent of those people, but there was a common feeling of what the company was all about.

I am sure if I gave enough thought to it there are some things I would do differently now if I could go back. There are probably some things in my personal life I would do differently, but as far as my career at Brown-Forman or any community role, I feel pretty good about where I have been involved and the organizations I've helped move forward.

I have some advice I would like to share with the next generation of leaders coming up in our city. I certainly think you have to work hard. I also think you earn leadership; I don't think it is bestowed upon you. For others to appreciate you and to willingly work with you, you have to work hard.

The word "focus" is important to me. I would advise aspiring leaders to focus on a few things and not get distracted. It's amazing how easy it is for people to get distracted. You can only get so much accomplished. I don't care how good you are, how smart you are, or how strong you are. There are only

24 hours in a day, seven days in a week. So I think focus is a critical word, and I would tell young people: "Pick the things that are important to you and focus on them and stay focused. You'll be distracted enough as it is, but try to get away from those distractions and stay with those things that matter." That's probably what I would tell young people and that's probably what I would tell the community too – "Stay focused. Don't get distracted, because it's so easy to do."

I would put the Brown family on that list of people who have contributed significantly to our community over the past 60 years. If you would allow me to go back 50 years, I would put Mayor Charlie Farnsley on that list. I would put Jerry Abramson on that list. There are a whole bunch of cheerleaders I remember, whom I would put on that list. Mr. and Mrs. Byck would be among them. The bank leadership around this community was very important to Louisville.

I think some of our civic leaders provided a great deal of leadership. The political leadership of this community for a period of time was not particularly outstanding. I think the civic leaders really stepped up to the plate and provided the real leadership. I would say David Jones and his partner, Wendell Cherry, provided that leadership.

My greatest focus was of course Brown-Forman, and I think I contributed to Brown-Forman's financial and personnel growth over the last 30 years. I was able to provide good thinking to help those organizations in which I participated continue their vitality. Certainly I was not the only person, but I believe those organizations had good people who found ways to get people to work together to make very positive things happen.

I think staying focused is one of the biggest challenges facing our community at this time. We have certain assets that we can build on over the next ten years. Louisville is a great logistics center, primarily because of UPS. There are ways to continue to build on that strength. There's a very strong health network system here in Louisville, and we are building on that asset. There's a willingness to support what I'll call entrepreneurial ventures, and Louisville is feeding them and supporting them.

One of the things our community needs – I don't think there is any doubt about this – is to find ways to get more venture capital in this community so we can feed these entrepreneurial engines. That's something we lack, and it's an issue that needs work. The mayor announced an initiative on this need not too long ago. It's being worked on – we just need to accelerate it.

I was so focused at Brown-Forman that I didn't pay a lot of attention to the growing entrepreneurism in our city. I certainly think there are a lot of young people who are ten or 20 years younger than I who seem hell-bent on developing their own businesses and being successful at it. I get the feeling there are more of them today than there were when I was that age.

There were a few who were doing it back in the 1960s and 1970s. I think it is different now, though. There's a good cadre of young people who want to do things, build things, and they are working very hard at doing it.

I think our support systems are stronger now. The University of Louisville is a stronger school. I give a lot of credit to the former dean of the business school, Bob Taylor, for stressing entrepreneurship and turning that into a strong asset for the university. There is just a lot more awareness of and support for entrepreneurship at this time than in the past.

I would definitely advise the next generation of leaders in our community that whatever they are doing, stay focused on it and be determined that it is going to be successful. Work like hell at it. I think that applies whether you are in a commercial venture, a research venture, an educational venture or whatever it might be.

I think education is another challenge for our community. I think there is a lot of good work going on around education. I'm very impressed with the current improvements in the school system. We can't let that dissipate. I'm a big believer in education. It's an avenue that gives everybody a chance to excel if they want to take advantage of it. I think our superintendent of schools, Steve Daeschner, is doing a first rate job at the JCPS. There is a lot that has been accomplished, but there is still a lot yet to be done.

I have learned some valuable lessons in my lifetime that I would like to share with young people today who are aspiring to take over the leadership positions in our community:

First – Think before you act.

Second – Stay focused.

Third – Put all your energy into your efforts; don't hold back.

Fourth – Believe in what you are doing and be committed to it.

I've been comfortable in high profile positions. I've never thought of my position in the community as particularly high profile, but someone told me, "Well, that's easy for you to say, but if you're on the outside looking in, you look pretty high profile to me." I've never considered my position high profile, but it was just something I wanted to do and enjoyed doing.

I think what I've been able to contribute, as much as anything, to these boards is to get people to think in terms of what they want an organization to be, as opposed to where an organization currently is. I have helped them determine what steps have to be taken to accomplish things. They call it strategic planning today but, in truth, people have been doing that for years.

I found what was lacking in a lot of not-for-profit organizations was focus, sometimes because of financial situations. Most of them focused more on today than tomorrow. I think I've been able to get boards to think forward, how to think and plan but, even more importantly, how to implement a strategic plan so that it becomes a part of the board's everyday work. It's important that you be able to look back after five years and say, "'Hey, look what we've done." I think I've been able to bring that perspective to most of the boards.

I always interviewed executive directors before I joined a board to make sure I had a good one, because executive directors make all the difference in the world to boards. I had great executive directors on all of the boards I was on, so that made it fun. There were always good people with whom to work.

I would advise tomorrow's leaders to find their own boards, because I am certain they too will find personal satisfaction from discovering their own unique ways to share their talents and to give back to our community.

A.R. "Al" Sullivan

President and CEO
The Sullivan University System

AL SULLIVAN IS IN THE CAREER education business. His company operates three schools on seven campuses in three cities, all training people for specific jobs where employers are known to need people. Norton Healthcare and Jewish Hospital, for example, have agreements with Sullivan through which they provide tuition for staff members to take training in specific medical fields.

Sullivan students take management support courses to be able to work in offices. They graduate and start careers as junior accountants, secretaries, industrial draftsmen, practical nurses and computer programmers, among other vocations. From its inception in 1962, the school has promised opportunities for students to learn how to support themselves, quickly and without extra courses they don't expect to use directly on a job.

In recent years though, the scope of Sullivan has expanded to include fully-accredited bachelor's degree programs which include English and other broadening courses in the curriculum, and an MBA.

The business school offers a "career-in-a-year," one-year program, a two-year junior college level program, and a four-year bachelor's program, all available in such traditional concentrations as accounting, management, finance and marketing. The graduate school of business offers a master's degree in business administration in such concentrations as management information systems, leadership, and management skills.

"Sullivan is focused on high-need vocations that pay well," Sullivan told *The Lane Report* in 2002. "Centre College would say it's a 'world-class liberal arts institution.' At Sullivan, we say we're a 'world-class career institution.'"

With over 7,300 students and faculty and staff of over 950 between seven campuses of three separate schools, The Sullivan University System is now Kentucky's largest independent college system. One of its institutions, Sullivan University, with an enrollment of nearly 5,000 students, is larger than the combined enrollment of the next two largest independent colleges in Kentucky

Its components are Sullivan University, which offers career-focused degrees at the undergraduate and graduate levels and offers a variety of programs in business, culinary arts, hospitality management, legal studies and early childcare management; Spencerian College, an associate degree school that concentrates on high-need allied health programs, including a school of nursing, plus specialized technology disciplines; and Louisville Technical Institute, which offers degrees in interior design, network engineering, robotics, computer security and a marine mechanics technician program. The System has seven campuses across Kentucky.

Al Sullivan grew up in Louisville and is a graduate of Male High School and the University of Kentucky. He holds a doctor of business administration degree from Johnson & Wales University in Rhode Island.

After his initial graduation from UK in 1960, he briefly considered a career as an Air Force pilot, but bad eyes sent him back home. He entered the education field as an instructor and admissions officer at Spencerian College, where his father, A.O. Sullivan, had devoted his education career.

His father sold his interest in Spencerian, a privately-held institution, and in 1962 the Sullivans together invested a total of $15,000 to start Sullivan Business College, then a one-year career school named in honor of A.O Sullivan. On the first day of classes, in June 1962, the College opened with five faculty members and seven students. By that fall, Sullivan – now named Sullivan University – had 150 students. Today it is regionally accredited by the Commission on Colleges of the Southern Association of Colleges and Schools at the graduate level.

As the System grew, the Sullivans never added another dollar of outside investment beyond the first $15,000, and they yearly reinvested after-tax proceeds back into the System's growth.

Al Sullivan built Sullivan through hard work and reinvestment. In 1972, he re-acquired both Spencerian College and the Louisville Technical Institute, which together now comprise the Sullivan University System.

As the colleges have grown, Sullivan has become more and more involved in civic affairs in Louisville, serving on the boards of Greater Louisville Inc. and the Kentuckiana Workforce Investment. He has also served on many national boards, including the prestigious American Council on Education in Washington, and as president of the Career College Association, which has over 1,200 college members across the country.

Sullivan has two children, both of whom have built careers within the Sullivan University System.

AS A LEADER, I am very hands on – that's just me. I like to manage processes. I like to see something done very well, not just good. Getting the best requires that you know what's going on, so I probably know more of what's happening than most presidents of large systems. I don't want any surprises, so that makes me very detail-oriented. I'm still hands-on, even after 40 years.

I haven't the faintest clue about how others might describe my leadership style. They might describe me as a tough, demanding manager who expects excellence (not just good) from those who work for me. I pride myself on challenging my staff to be better and not just good. Our students tell me that we provide an environment that gives them more than they were expecting when they enrolled in one of our schools, and I like to hear those comments.

From a business standpoint, I think Sullivan University's move to become the first privately-held collegiate institution in the South to earn regional accreditation from the Southern Association in the late 1970s was our most significant accomplishment and one that propelled Sullivan to where it is today as Kentucky's largest independent college. Some in the Association didn't want a privately-held, family-owned education institution accredited even when we met and exceeded their standards. That prejudice was hard to accept, and we didn't.

My biggest disappointment is not professional, it's personal. I am sorry that my father did not live to see Sullivan become a four-year college and now a university. He would have reveled in that accomplishment as an educator who devoted his entire career to education.

I have not had many regrets. Like most entrepreneurs, you just work hard and tough it out. We put our own money at risk, and work hard at getting results. I am proud to say that our last audit shows zero debt. Many educators somehow feel someone else should fund their success, but the taxpayers and donors are expecting more now than in the past from them, so now performance and results are being expected. I agree with that trend.

Integrity and loyalty, I believe, are certainly important qualities a good staff must possess. I am proud to have many colleagues around me who have shared my vision for the system for 20 or more years. They are the key ingredients of my success.

The most valuable lessons I have learned in my own life and career in building this organization I know will survive my tenure are:

1) Honesty counts;
2) Be a person who does what you say you are going to do;
3) Be fair with people;
4) Show up and work hard every day. Hard work is 80% of success;
5) Be involved with actions, not just words; and
6) Don't be a person who joins important organizations just to have your name on a list. Be involved and contribute!

Donald C. Swain

**President Emeritus
University of Louisville**

DON SWAIN WAS HIRED IN 1981 to do no less than transform the University of Louisville, and when he retired after 13 years as president, city leaders seemed in general agreement that he had accomplished it.

He was credited with "changing the face and the image" of UofL in the community, *The Courier-Journal* said. For one thing, he had overseen $151 million in construction that included a new campus library, classrooms, and a student center, that now is named for him. More important, community leaders said, he had changed the way the university relates to Louisville and Kentucky and increased its prestige in the process.

"He has clearly brought the university and the community closer together," UofL trustee Steve Bing said when Swain retired.

David Karem, then majority leader of the Kentucky Senate, said Swain had taken UofL from its image as a "fine municipal university" to that of an "important regional and even national-image university."

Swain accomplished such objectives as persuading Humana Inc. to take over the University of Louisville Hospital, and to run it while sharing profits and treating indigent patients. He raised more than $100 million toward UofL's endowment, pushing it to $145 million, one of the largest for any public university in the country.

During his tenure, the number of Ph.D.s graduating each year rose from 20 to 50. Swain also raised the school's admission standards, added new academic programs and increased the amount of money the school spends on research. He also increased academic standards for athletes.

Swain took pride in his record. By the time his tenure was up, he said, "I believe UofL was widely perceived as one of the community's and the state's major assets and as a source of willing expertise which could be brought to bear" on state and local problems.

His approach to the job included a good deal of participation in community affairs. He served as board member and chairman of both the Louisville Area Chamber of Commerce and the Greater Louisville Economic Development Partnership, unusual for a college president, and was heavily involved in the process by which the two organizations merged to become Greater Louisville Inc.

He championed adopting a regional attitude that Louisville is the hub of a large economic development zone, some of which is in Kentucky and some in Indiana. He also worked hard to "raise Louisville's collective self-esteem," so that leaders and citizens would understand that Louisville could become competitive with other metropolitan areas.

Don Swain was born in Des Moines, Iowa and received an undergraduate degree from the University of Dubuque. After a stint in the Navy, he headed for the University of California at Berkeley and didn't look east again until he came to Louisville.

After earning master's and Ph.D. degrees in history, he taught in that field, specializing in the history of the American environmental movement, an area in which he published two books and numerous articles. He was on the faculty of the University of California, Davis from 1963 until 1981, and received its Distinguished Teaching Award in 1972.

Swain was also an administrator in California's vaunted university system. His years at UC included six years as academic vice president of the nine-campus institution. He always loved teaching, however, and he was a professor of history, as well as president, while he was at UofL.

In Louisville, he served on many ad hoc committees and advisory boards put together by the mayor, county judge, governor, legislative or business groups to attack particular problems or to look forward creatively. He was a long-standing member of the board of the Speed Museum, chairman of the Lincoln Foundation and a frequent participant in Leadership Louisville programs.

Swain was named Louisvillian of the Year in 1995. Before he retired, he received the Wilson Wyatt Award for distinguished contributions to UofL, and both UofL and Bellarmine College awarded him honorary degrees to salute his achievements in education and community leadership.

At the national level, he served on the executive committee of the National Association of State Universities and Land Grant Colleges, and on the board of the American Council on Education.

Swain and his wife, Lavinia, who have two children, headed for a house on the river in Oldham County when he retired as president of UofL, instead of going back to California. They now live in the Highlands. "Louisville is the most hospitable city we've ever lived in," he told *Business First* in 1984.

I WAS APPOINTED PRESIDENT of the University of Louisville in 1981. At that time, community leaders felt UofL was not connected enough with civic, business and cultural activities in Louisville. I guess I was viewed as "new blood" – someone who could infuse some vitality, and boost the university's presence locally and throughout the state. Almost by definition, the UofL president, because of the university's central role in the community, should be involved in most of the important community initiatives.

At the request of the UofL Board of Trustees, I set out to build the closest possible ties between UofL and the Louisville metropolitan area and to correct the view that the university was lacking in responsiveness. By the end of my term in office, I believe UofL was widely perceived as one of the community's and state's major assets, and a source of willing expertise which could be brought to bear on Louisville's and Kentucky's educational and economic development problems.

That was probably my main leadership accomplishment. But I also played a leadership role in private fundraising – one that had an impact on the wider Louisville community as well as the university. UofL's endowment stood at about $20 million when I got to Louisville. It was approaching $150 million when I retired, more than any other public university in the Commonwealth of Kentucky. Building on this success, UofL's total endowments grew rapidly after that. The university's breakthrough in attracting large private gifts not only provided vital resources for its academic programs, but also demonstrated to Louisville's charitable organizations that they should be more ambitious in their own fundraising – that they, too, could raise large amounts of money from generous people in Louisville and Kentucky. Private fundraising at UofL and in Louisville has not been the same since.

I worked consistently to persuade people in the community to "think big" and to avoid an often self-denigrating style which assumed Louisville could not compete successfully because of the perception that the state was too poor and backward. Perhaps because I was an outsider who chose to come here from California, I was mystified by the prevailing negative attitude about the city's competitiveness held by some native Louisvillians. Louisville is a wonderful place to live because it has many of the attributes of an urban area, yet it has the friendliness and warmth of a small town. But the downside is that insular, small-town thinking often held this community back.

In my role as president of the university and later as chairman of the Louisville Area Chamber of Commerce, the forerunner of Greater Louisville Inc., I supported the concept of Louisville as the hub of a large economic development zone, some of which was in Kentucky and some in Indiana.

We worked to bring together the Chamber's economic development program with local government efforts, as well as to coordinate with southern Indiana. Along with others, I helped contribute to an all-out effort to raise Louisville's collective self-esteem. People came to believe that Louisville could be very competitive with other metropolitan areas, like Indianapolis, Nashville, and Memphis, and that Kentucky could successfully compete with neighboring states in attracting and retaining good jobs. One of the keys to success in economic development was mounting a long-term effort to improve public education in the commonwealth. That effort was an important focus during my tenure as president of the university.

A civic culture committed to partnerships and cooperation has, I believe, contributed to Louisville's success over the past 20 years. I certainly tried to make UofL a partner with the community and participated in that cooperative spirit as chairman of the Chamber.

My academic area is twentieth century American history, in particular the modern environmental movement. That academic background informed my approach to problem-solving and my leadership style, to a degree.

Using the historical method requires one to go back to the historical record to pursue the factual evidence and to place issues in context. Human behavior is not linear, and we humans tend to loop back and repeat familiar patterns of behavior. Understanding that fact, I think, helped me handle some tough decisions for the university.

I learned about leadership from two of my early mentors, A. Hunter Dupree, my major professor at the University of California, Berkeley, and James Meyer, Chancellor of the University of California, Davis, where I taught in the history department and began in administration. They taught me about getting people to work together and managing in the academic environment.

When I came to Louisville, Woodford Porter and David Jones Sr. were particularly valuable friends and mentors. Woody was an outstanding chairman of UofL's Board of Trustees, and David was chairman of the search committee that brought me here. They both introduced me to a broad cross-section of people and were great sources of advice and counsel. It was Steve Bing, a vice president at UofL, who introduced me to Frankfort and the sport of Kentucky politics.

For the most part, I think my leadership style meshed well with others in the community, and I was able to accomplish most of my goals at the university and in the community. I have always seen myself as very straightforward.

Occasionally my directness didn't fit with the Louisville style of indirect communication. I had to learn to adapt to that part of the culture here. But I think most people found me approachable and unpretentious. I am fairly forceful in making decisions. I'm also comfortable with change, and take pride in being responsive and flexible. Strong personal values are very important to me, especially honesty and integrity.

Change can be uncomfortable, and I'm sure there were people at UofL who saw me as too forceful. I should, perhaps, have been a bit more patient about some of the changes we had to make at the university. If I had it to do over again, I probably would push more slowly, especially in the last couple of years of my tenure. One example is the changes we made in the Redbook, the university's policy manual. There was a lot of resistance to those changes by some faculty members, and I regret the acrimony my efforts sparked.

However, the trustees and I knew the revisions needed to be made. Overall, I believe the changes enabled UofL to develop into the metropolitan research university it is today and will become in the future. I also recall some difficulty, now and then, reining in UofL's Athletic Department. During my tenure we established the Athletic Association to help manage athletics, and I instructed the Athletic Department to become self-sustaining. I believe then, and still do, that general funds should not be used to support athletics. There were many tough decisions, but I have very fond memories of my days at UofL.

Lavinia and I love this community. That's why we chose to stay here after retirement. Louisville has an inherent civility about it, and there is certainly a noticeable impulse for its leaders to try to work cooperatively. It is a warm-hearted place to live and has real potential for solid growth and economic development, while maintaining its warmth and character.

I believe Louisville will be an even better place to live as it continues to become more open to diversity, which includes women, minorities and others outside the traditional norms.

My closing advice to aspiring leaders is simple. Be prepared to work your hardest. Don't be easily discouraged. Learn to tolerate ambiguity; the world is shades of gray, not black and white. Think big. Take risks. And never lose sight of the fundamental place of a good education. A well-rounded education gives one perspective and places issues in context. And of course, something I learned long ago is to have really grounded, knowledgeable people around to advise you. That's why I always listen to my wife Lavinia!

BERNARD M. TRAGER

Founder and Chairman
Republic Bancorp, Inc.

BERNARD TRAGER ENTERED the finance business in 1952, as an outside collector for the Modern Loan Company. In 1955, Trager co-founded the Consumer Finance Company and upon its sale in 1957 co-founded Union Trust, an industrial loan corporation. Twenty years later in 1977, Union Trust – which by then had seven subsidiaries in Kentucky, Indiana and Ohio – was acquired by Commercial Credit of Baltimore, Maryland. Trager stayed on as president, CEO, and chairman of Union Trust, and became an executive consultant for Commercial Credit.

In that same year, Trager and his wife Jean bought a very small 80-year-old bank in Shelbyville, Kentucky. It was the first in a line of community banks that would become Republic Bancorp, Inc. Following a highly successful initial public offering in 1998, Louisville based Republic Bancorp has grown to be the largest Kentucky owned financial institution in the area with over $2.7 billion in assets and 33 banking centers in Kentucky and southern Indiana. In addition to traditional bank subsidiaries, Republic Bank & Trust Company of Kentucky and Indiana has become active in several national financial service businesses under Trager family ownership, including Tax Refund Solutions, a nationwide tax refund loan and check provider.

Bernard Trager was born in Louisville in 1928. Except for two years of service in the U.S. Air Force during the Korean War, he has lived in Louisville his entire life.

He's an adopted alumnus of the University of Louisville (UofL), and a member and former chairman of UofL's Board of Overseers.

In 1987, he was one of the leaders of a group called Business Advocates, formed by small business leaders who felt ignored by the larger Chamber. By 1992, with most of the group's members also a part of the Louisville Chamber, they decided to merge into the larger group.

Other community activities have included terms on the boards of the Greater Louisville Fund for the Arts, the Cathedral Heritage Foundation, Greater Louisville Inc., Boy Scouts of America, the Louisville Community Foundation, the Louisville-Jefferson County Redevelopment Authority and the Health Enterprise Network.

He is a member of the Louisville Male High School and Junior Achievement Business Halls of Fame. Louisville's Entrepreneur Society has named him Professional Entrepreneur of the Year, and he is an honorary member of the Golden Key National Honor Society.

Trager and his wife, Jean, their two children – Steve and his wife Amy and Shelley Trager Kusman, and their five grandchildren (Michael, Andrew and Brett Kusman, and Kevin and Emily Trager) – have donated generously to community causes in their names. In 1999, for example, they gave generous gifts to UofL to build the Trager field hockey stadium at Cardinal Park. Since then, the family has also given sizable donations to Jewish Hospital to build the Trager Pavilion of upscale patient suites at the Rudd Heart & Lung Center, a Trager Pavilion in the new Frazier Rehabilitation Center that is currently under construction, Baptist Hospital East for the Trager Pediatric Emergency Care Center, and to UofL Athletics to build Trager Center, an indoor football practice facility.

Trager and his wife received the 2003 Caritas Foundation Community Leaders of the Year Award, and were honored in 2004 by UofL with its Hickman-Camp Award, recognizing their strong support for UofL's Athletic Department and programs, and as the recipients of the 2004 Philanthropy of the Year Award.

Trager has played many roles in the community over the years. "I believe my greatest role is being a daily cheerleader, if you will, of the city," he said. "Hopefully, I have influenced many great causes through either direct involvement or by influencing someone to become involved in the city's development."

Trager regards his ability to provide career opportunities that encourage the best and brightest to stay in Louisville as his greatest success. His advice to young people who would like to be leaders is simple: "Respect others, listen, obtain a good education, maintain integrity, and carry a loyal work ethic that balances with a good family life."

I CAME FROM A FAMILY THAT HAD a Jewish word in its culture – "tzedakah" – which means sharing your blessings with others. I remember, as a very young man – even as a preteen – being at my grandmother's house where there was what we called a tzedakah box, a small blue and white metal box used to save money for charities. I can recall that bread was seven cents a loaf. My grandmother would give me a dime to get it. There were always pennies that were left. I got a penny and she got a penny and she put a penny in the tzedakah box. Were there a lot of pennies in there? I don't know, but it was all shared. If you walked into my house today and you looked on my wife's desk you would see a tzedakah box. It constantly reminds me and everyone in our family of the importance of sharing our blessings.

My family comes from the inner city, and we started out with the most modest of means. My father died when I was 16. My mother, a remarkable woman and role model, got a job in a dress shop and I got a job after school at a department store.

We never had much, but we always shared whatever blessings we had, even if we just gave a $5 contribution to the Boy Scouts or a $5 contribution to the Community Chest 50 years ago. The tzedakah box was always around, and our family always shared what we had. My wife and family feel very strongly about sharing, and if you went into my children's homes, you would see the same thing – a reminder tzedakah box.

I had no intention of starting a bank in 1952. It wasn't even a dream or a vision, because that was beyond any vision I could possibly have had at that time.

I was in a National Guard unit that was activated in 1950 during the Korean War and I was mustered out in 1952 on a Friday. Over the weekend I saw Judge Samuel Steinfeld, and he said, "What are you going to do?" I said, "Well, first of all, I have to get a job." "What kind of job," he asked, and I said, "It doesn't matter at this point. I'll take any job." He said, "Well, I have an interest in a small loan company, and you might want to go in and talk to them. They are always looking for collectors because they have a hard time finding them."

So I did, and I started to work that Monday. I think I earned $167 a month. That's how I got into not the banking business, but the lending business, because that's what it was – a small loan company. At that time you could lend up to $300. The company where I worked was called Modern Loan Company at 1021 West Broadway, right across from the train station. I worked myself up from an outside collector in two to three years, until I was manager of a three-person office.

Then one of the shareholders, S. Harry Linker, indicated to me that he might want to start another loan company of his own. I am not talking about something that was big and glorious, he put up the money and I got a share of the equity. That was the deal. I also got $400 a month, which was to me just fabulous. That began a great relationship with Harry Linker, from 1955 to 1977 when he died. So that's how I started Consumer Finance Company.

I have never been the brightest but I am hard-working. I have always been a guy who works 60 hours a week, at least. That's what I've always done. I come from a family of working people – not people who own anything, just people who work hard for others. That was the culture I was living in at that time. I was thrilled to get a job and happy to hold on to it.

At that point in my life –1953 or 1954 – I don't recall anyone befriending me to the point of helping me move up a ladder, because in my view there was no ladder. My goal was to move up from outside collector to assistant manager to manager and that was the extent of my vision. When we started this new small loan company – Consumer Finance, which was about the size of a desk, it was on Fifth Street behind what was then the Greyhound Bus Station. My goal or vision at that time was that we were going to have a one-office company.

I got married in 1955, and I'll be married for fifty years this year. Someone asked me once what was the best investment I ever made, and I said, "Marrying my wife." That's the easiest question anyone has ever asked.

I was working 60 or 70 hours, seven days a week, but that's the way it was. I think if you talk to anyone in my peer group, whether it is David Jones, who I think is a role model for everybody, or any of the people whom I know on the national scene, they are all hard-working. I don't know anyone who runs any business successfully off the coast of Florida or on the mountain tops of Colorado. They may go there after they make it. But I think the ingredient of a "just hard work" culture is critical, and I always have. Fortunately I come from a family of "work hard people," and I have a family of "work hard people."

As time moved forward, we financed the finance company with the earnings. I grew the company to the point that we had an opportunity to sell it. We sold it in 1957, and out of the sale I made a king's ransom of $50,000. I had never seen $50,000 in any one spot in my life. I didn't even know people who had $50,000. So we took that and we started an industrial loan company in 1957. And again, the vision was just to run a good company and make a profit.

When we got into the industrial loan business in 1957, which was called Union Trust, we needed additional financing. The people who befriended me were some of the bankers of that day: John Barr, president of First National Bank; Frank Hower, president of Liberty National Bank; Sam Klein, president of the Bank of Louisville, and Maury Johnson, chairman and president of

Citizen's Fidelity Bank. From that point on, those four gentleman, plus one – David Grissom, who at that time left Humana and went over to Citizen's Fidelity – were very generous with their time and commitment also.

I used to see John Barr after he retired and after I became a banker and I would say to John, "You know, I wouldn't have lent me money as a banker at that time. And if I did, the regulators would have criticized me." He would always say, "Well, what makes you think they did not criticize me at that time." So those four or five people were very supportive of me.

From 1957-1977, as president and CEO of Union Trust, I was able to grow it to a point where we then had offices in Kentucky, Indiana, and Ohio. It was a bustling company. The gentleman who had originally put up the money for the loan company in 1952 died in 1977, and his family inherited his shares. So we had an opportunity to sell Union Trust, and I sold it to Commercial Credit Company of Baltimore, Maryland.

When I sold Union Trust in 1977, I had an obligation to stay with Commercial Credit for three years. I reported to the chairman of Commercial Credit and became involved in a number of their subsidiaries. They expanded my role considerably and I did a lot of traveling. They were a great company. Not only did they treat me well, but they also treated the people associated with Union Trust who became Commercial Credit employees well too. That was partly because of the contract I negotiated, which said that the date of employment for the Union Trust people was the date of their first being employed with Union Trust. What that did was put our employees in line for pensions and retirement plans.

I got my money, and the other family members and shareholders all got their money, everyone was pleased. But I made absolutely certain, and held the deal up for a month or so, that the employees were protected. I am proud of that, because that is not usually what happens. Usually the principals get the money and run. What I tried to do – and did – with the blessings of Commercial Credit, is to get them to extend themselves into protecting the people who had been so loyal to us. That was a moment that I am very proud of.

The other day, someone told me that one of the ladies who started with me many years ago and who has since retired, thanks to that retirement program, has a daughter who is now working for us. So I called the daughter and said, "Welcome aboard! How's your mom? Where is she?" The daughter gave me her number and I called her. We had lunch, and this lady who had started working for me when she was 19 years old is now 69. She worked for me for over 25 years. She was with me at Consumer's Finance, Union Trust, and then transitioned into Commercial Credit and stayed with them until her retirement program kicked in. She said, "I don't think people really know what you did for us." We cried and hugged.

When I look back, I realize that it took from 1957 to 1977 for me to acquire enough capital to go into the banking business. I took my profit from the Union Trust sale in 1977 and I put it all back on the table again.

I am glad I did that, because I had savings and a good job with Commercial Credit that I could have retired, at age 49, and said, "Well, I put in my time." But I didn't, because I used that money to start what subsequently became what you see today, Republic Bank & Trust Company. It took me 20 years to get there, but we were the first new bank in Jefferson County in about 40 years.

Aside from the money in assets, we have given over 600 people an opportunity, with their stock options, to acquire assets and to have a place where they can have a career. I am proud of the people who come up to me and say their stock is worth a million dollars. I feel good about that.

I always knew and still think that you have to work hard. I don't think there is a substitute for it – I really don't. You have to be consistent. It's like riding a bike up a hill. You create something and try to keep its momentum going, and if you think there is a breeze that's going to come along to give you momentum, it won't. Even the smartest, the best and the brightest make wrong turns sometimes. I think through our diligence, and by having good people, we have been able to get out of some situations that consume other banks. You have to be careful that you don't get so big that you can't be light on your feet. You have to be able to change products or to change style, but you should always give good service.

A lot of people lose their culture. What we have tried to do is to keep management as close to the client as possible. We spend a lot of time out in the branches with "boots on the ground."

If you don't stay close to your customers or your clients, then all of a sudden you come up with this big dreamy idea and, by the time it gets from you down to the regionals, to the managers, then to the customers, it's not what the customers want.

We compete with the best and brightest by providing local decision makers and service, service, service. During the refinance period we have seen over the last two years, a lot of banks and mortgage companies found themselves inundated with applications. We added associates and extended our days. Rather than telling people we could not close a loan for four to six weeks, we were closing them in 15-21 days. Our people worked longer hours, put in double shifts and, "made hay while the sun was shining." And as a result, we have become the largest mortgage lender in the region for the last 4 years. A lot of times I think people in the banking industry think everything is only rate-driven. But a good deal of it is service-driven also. You can't charge an outrageous rate and give great service, but I think to deliver the product in a reasonable period of time is important.

Everybody who affects the bottom line in our bank is on an incentive plan. We have substantial bonuses based on a number of factors, including revenues and introductions to other people, etc. We are great believers of being involved in the community. We think that you ought to belong and have community responsibility.

I am a great believer in faith. Whether it's your faith or my faith does not really matter to me. I am a great believer in family too. I think everyone should work at having a good family life and, of course, you ought to do anything you can to influence your own and your family's good health too — whether it is exercise, or diet, or whatever. Because if God does not bless you and your family with good health, you have a problem.

I spend a lot of time with my grandsons — Michael, Andrew, and Brett Kusman and Kevin Trager — and granddaughter, Emily Trager. We are blessed and I really like to see that we share what we have with various and sundry people of all kinds. Sharing what we have is a culture in our family.

Some people are willing to share, some are not. I am working on a couple of fund drives now. David Jones and Owsley Brown Frazier are people who really stand tall. They are role models. They will take your call. A lot of people don't return calls today. We have a culture at Republic Bank that you must return calls, even if you have to take them home and call from home.

I think Louisville is a great city for growing a family. Anything you may want, if it is not here, it is within an hour or two. Our public (thanks to Steve Daeschner) and private school systems are good and the parochial school system is extraordinary. It doesn't cost $100,000 a year to belong to a good golf course. If you want to go to the theatre, the ballet, the orchestra, children's theatre, it's all here. There is also plenty of opportunity for people to get involved in the community. You can come to town and, in a very short time, become involved.

Louisville is alive. We are lucky to have Jerry Abramson as our mayor, because he has a lot of energy and is forward-thinking. We have good congressional leaders, and U.S. Senator Mitch McConnell is a fan, a booster, and a cheerleader for Kentucky and for the University of Louisville (UofL). Congresswoman Anne Northup also does a fabulous job.

One concern I have is that I think there are fewer and fewer opportunities for people at a certain level of income in our community. Many companies that have been acquired now outsource much of what they do. Take a lockbox manager, for example. We're the only bank of any size that does lock box processing locally, so we have a lock box manager in Louisville. Every other bank in Louisville now does it centrally in their home offices in Cincinnati, Columbus, Minneapolis, and so on. There is also a lot of other processing that the major banks don't do here now but do elsewhere. So if that's your skill and talent, you have limited opportunities here.

Another example is Brown & Williamson. There were numerous individuals there that were earning $100,000, $125,000, or $175,000-a-year as marketing, technology or other types of professionals. Brown & Williamson no longer has a market presence here, but their former employees would like to stay here, so where do they go? They can go to Humana, Yum!, health care companies, or Brown-Forman, perhaps, but where else can they go?

We just don't have opportunities for these type of people to stay here. That's Louisville's weakness – trying to retain people who spent 20 years with a company here and who would like to stay. They are a part of the fabric of our community, but there are no positions for them.

Republic Bank has provided an opportunity for over 600 people in Louisville. That's my legacy. We will certainly continue to share our blessings.

My son Steve is now chairman and chief executive officer of Republic Bank, and president and CEO of Republic Bancorp. Steve is a graduate of the University of Texas and has a law degree from the University of Louisville. After two years in the law firm of Wyatt, Tarrant & Combs, he joined Republic in 1987. In 1994, Steve provided the leadership resulting in the complex merger and reorganization of the Republic group into its current unitary corporate banking structure and was named vice chairman of the bank's holding company, Republic Bancorp.

In 1998 Steve was further appointed to the position of president and chief executive officer of Republic Bancorp (total assets at that time, $1.2 billion) and provided the leadership for Republic Bancorp's public offering.

Steve studies a lot, reads a lot, and rubs elbows with the best and the brightest, and that's being more of a student *and* a good businessman.

Steve is also a great believer in "sharing". The only difference is Steve tells me to do it now, not when I am no longer around. "Share your blessings now," he says.

At one time, up until 30 years ago, a person allied himself with a company and stayed there his entire life. Whether it was a steel mill or a bank or federated dry goods, a person worked there for 30 or 40 years, then their kids went to work there. Now it's not that way anymore because people are on the move. You have to come up with human resource plans that will retain people.

Until about 20 or 30 years ago, banking was a simple business. Rates were regulated and not competitive, how banks operated was regulated. There was no "marketing". The lines were defined regarding what banks could or could not do.

With de-regulation and technology, it became a very competitive business. So unless you are willing to make the financial commitment to technology and to people now, then of course you can't be in this business. You have to be a student of all those things. You have to understand the technology and what it does for you, and have a much greater understanding of people.

I took one of my grandsons to a ball game the other day. He said about a particular person, "He certainly is a mean guy." I said, "Maybe he has something bothering him," to which my grandson said, "But you are always nice."

What better compliment could I get from one of my grandsons than to say I am always nice? I don't know why people don't get it. I see people at the airport and some of them talk to other people like they are a bunch of dogs.

Remember I come from a family of people who waited on other people, served other people, sold to other people. It would be like someone being mean to my mother when she was trying to sell them a dress. I don't know why people don't get it. Just be nice.

At age 77, I feel great. I feel like coming to work, and I like our associates. Where else would I go? We go to Florida for two weeks, and I go nuts. I play golf every day, with my wife, then we say, "Let's go home." Someone said you have a home in Florida to which I say "Oh no. I have an apartment in Florida, but home is in Louisville."

I am a blessed man. It's that simple. I am a second-generation American. My dad was a naturalized citizen. This life of mine is not a dream, but a fantasy.

Title this interview "Only in America," because I often say that my story could only happen here in the greatest country in the world.

Daniel C. Ulmer Jr.

Retired Chairman and CEO
Citizens Fidelity Corporation

Chairman and Co-Owner
Louisville Bats Baseball Franchise

AFTER A 40-YEAR CAREER in banking, Dan Ulmer would like to be remembered as a good banker. He was, and is, and he also has been a prodigious civic leader. But like it or not, he'll go down in history as the man who brought professional baseball back to Louisville.

Ulmer and his son, Gary, had a notion in June 1981 that professional baseball would be good for Louisville's self-image and community spirit. The senior Ulmer approached Barry Bingham Sr. of *The Courier-Journal*, and Robinson Brown Jr. of the Brown-Forman Corporation, with a plan to make that happen. He got encouragement from both of them and began talking up the idea of finding a Triple-A club to bring to town. People wished him luck.

But by using his trademark tenacity and energy, Ulmer got his team — the Louisville Redbirds — in time for the 1982 season. In 1983, the team drew a Triple-A record-shattering one million fans to Cardinal Stadium in the Kentucky Fair and Exposition Center. Ulmer was called upon again in 1986, when Redbirds owner A. Ray Smith wanted to sell the team.

Ulmer put together a slate of buyers, including himself, and chaired the ownership group. The franchise — now called the Louisville Bats — plays home games at Louisville Slugger Field, a jewel of a baseball park the city helped build for them near Waterfront Park. The team is doing well and is likely to be around a long time.

Dan Ulmer was born in Louisville in 1932 and grew up in Crescent Hill. He has memories of getting friends together to ride a streetcar to Parkway Field near UofL to watch doubleheaders on Sundays.

He is a graduate of the old Flaget High School, the University of Louisville, Rutgers University School of Banking and a Stanford University executive program.

Ulmer joined Citizens Fidelity Bank in 1957, after a stint in the Navy, and he worked his way up through the bank. He became president of Citizens in 1976 and chairman in 1988. He retired in 1993, passing the presidential torch to his successor, Mike Harreld.

As he rose through the ranks at the bank, he felt his platform for accomplishing things in the civic arena improving also and he waded right in. He has held leadership positions with a long list of organizations over the years. They include boards of the University of Louisville and University of Kentucky, the Regional Airport Authority, the Kentucky State Fair Board, Actors Theatre of Louisville, the Greater Louisville Fund for the Arts, the Louisville Orchestra, Metro Parks, the Louisville Area Chamber of Commerce, and Metro United Way, among others.

He earned the reputation he wanted as a good banker, "a can do person," in the words of David Grissom, his former boss, "who focuses on the job at hand, and rallies people around him to get it done."

On civic boards, *Louisville Magazine* said in 1987, he had a "courteous but piercing manner of dealing with those who point to problems alone instead of looking for solutions." Ulmer worries now that he may have been too brusque with people on occasion, but the magazine writer said his style worked, and he was very successful.

He was known, the piece said, as an "undaunted salesperson, a relentless fundraiser with good contacts throughout the community, a tough negotiator, a visionary but pragmatic civic booster" and "someone who could twist arms and somehow make the twistee like it."

Although he believed strongly in the importance of being involved in key projects in the community while he was working at Citizens Fidelity Bank, Ulmer was selective in his choices and would caution future leaders not to over-extend themselves. "What I like to do is get involved in one or two really important community projects that benefit the whole community," he said just before he retired. "I don't want to be on 17 boards just for the sake of being on them. I just want a couple a year…and those will be the most important community jobs I have, at least for the next year or two."

The National Conference of Christians and Jews chose him as their Man of the Year in 1982, and the Better Business Bureau and Advertising Club of Louisville did the same in 1983. *The Voice Tribune* newspaper named him Man of the Year in 1993, and he was the recipient of a Catholic School Alumni Award in 2004.

Ulmer and his wife, Helen, have three grown children.

LEADERSHIP IS A PROCESS that evolves in each of us. There is no point in time when you say, "I think I'll be a leader." You just observe others, their management style and their leadership characteristics, and at some point you start thinking, "Maybe I can do something that will make a difference."

A certain amount of leadership in a community like ours is a function of your job. A high-profile position, usually with some considerable responsibility, develops leadership skills. From there, volunteerism opportunities come quickly. Each individual handles these opportunities in his or her own way.

I can't cite any one individual who was my mentor. I had many bosses and I paid a lot of attention to all of them. It was a habit that began in the Navy and I continued to use in my business career. The idea was to eliminate the flaws you saw in your superiors and to emulate all of the good things. We all have faults and good qualities and you do well by going through the process of eliminating the bad and copying the good.

I would like to think my leadership style is energetic, aggressive, candid and fair. Those would be the four things that I tried to develop as a style. My guess is almost anyone I've ever worked with would say, "Well, that all might be true, but he could certainly have used more diplomacy and tact, with maybe a little less aggressiveness." With the benefit of hindsight, I would agree. There were many times when I was just so interested in getting something done or moving a project to a certain point that I could have been more diplomatic in my relationships. Being involved in so many organizations and projects and fund drives probably resulted in a management style of being too direct on occasion.

There isn't any question that there were many opportunities and situations where I could have been a better listener and a more effective leader.

I take some degree of pride in believing that I was a good banker, my chosen field. Whatever business success I had became the foundation on which other community activities could be attempted.

Failures were many, but the most public one involved the Louisville Falls Fountain. The Falls Fountain was a project that Barry Bingham and I dreamed about and planned. With help from some very hard-working people at Louisville Central Area, we thought that we could create a significant signature for the community, along the lines of important fountains in other parts of the world. We visualized that this could be a water Fleur-de-Lis, a wonderful visual symbol that everyone would see when they entered the city from the north.

The project took two long years. Our committee thought that it would be wonderful and we were pleased when it was finally done after a great amount of time and work and money. Unfortunately, I learned that we didn't know nearly enough about engineering, the vagaries of the river currents and related issues. We trusted the engineers and it turned out that there were bigger mechanical problems than any of us imagined. There were political issues about who was going to pay for the power and the maintenance and the project bogged down.

It was never as spectacular as we envisioned. A four-hundred feet water display in the middle of the river just didn't have the same desired impact as four-hundred feet on shore. While it was a lot of hoopla and fun and satisfying at the moment, over a period of years the fountain project fell apart because of lack of money and engineering and finally was removed. I'm glad we tried it, and I was happy that Mr. Bingham saw it operate before he passed away, but it was a grand idea that failed.

Hard work and loyalty are the keys to being a good follower although you don't have to blindly follow a leader. I think good followers take part in the process and try to bring suggestions and ideas to the table. Good leaders usually come from good followers.

All of us can look back over a career and say there were many things we would have done differently. I'm just not too interested in going back and picking things apart. Rather I followed the creed that, "I'd rather be criticized for a decision made than one not made." You are going to make some wrong choices but you are also going to make many right ones. I'm a believer in being direct and getting to the root of the issue and moving on, and really not looking back too much. It's not productive to agonize over past decisions.

I would tell young people aspiring to leadership positions that one should become successful in your chosen field first. You will learn management skills in that process and, at that point, you transfer those skills for use in other ways in the community. I think in working on community events and trying to be a leader in the community, you should pick things in which you have a real personal interest.

I couldn't have done the baseball project, for example, without a real passion for baseball and knowing something about it. The special ingredient is having a passion and an interest in the subject. I don't think anyone can enjoy working the Metro United Way drive or the Fund for the Arts drive unless they are really interested in the arts or the community needs of these agencies.

Passing the Torch

My advice to anybody in the process of becoming a leader is not to take on things just to be taking them on or to get your name on a letterhead. Work on the things where you really can make a difference.

Fifty years ago, I was a Naval Officer in the Far East, and the first ten years back in town, I was just another young guy trying to make a living and raise a family. I didn't have any developed ideas about the community. I observed the old guard – how things were done during those years – but beginning in the 1970s it was clearer to see the potential growth of our community. The '70s were the time all the bank buildings were started, the Galleria was built, the Hyatt came to town, the Seelbach and the Brown were renovated and the downtown area became alive. If you looked at the skyline in 1980, it was tremendously different than that in 1970, so those ten years or so were the boom years in terms of development of downtown.

The Hurstbourne corridor and the suburbs started to blossom. Many other projects began during this time. The '80s were interesting because the community finally gained some swagger; and some of that came from the University of Louisville winning two national championships. Baseball returned successfully which gave the community more confidence.

In that decade, Waterfront Park was started, the Louisville Zoo blossomed, the airport expansion was started, UPS came to town. The '90s became an embellishment of the '80s. The medical community became a huge industry, one of the biggest growth industries in Louisville, and the one employing the most people in the downtown area. That's not to forget the contributions of Ford and other important company expansions. The Humana growth has been a great contribution.

The expansion of the Kentucky Fair & Exposition Center and the downtown convention center, both of which happened in the '80s and continues to this day, were very important to the growing convention business. Louisville Slugger was encouraged to come back to Louisville, and the Art Center and the Louisville Science Center stimulated Main Street. In addition to the physical component of development, metro government – after failing twice – finally was passed. All of those things were very important growth items.

No one thing is responsible for this positive activity in our community, but certainly strong leadership was the most important component of it. In the 1970s, I remember my chairman, Al Brinkley saying "We are going to build a new bank building and it's going to be 30 stories high" and so downtown development began.

Daniel C. Ulmer Jr.

There are those who criticize the community for not being as fast-growing as Indianapolis or Nashville or some other city. I don't pay much attention to that talk. I think this is a great community — it could have developed faster and accomplished more, of course. Maybe it would have helped to have had a different structure of government 20 or 30 years ago, but that again is hindsight. I believe you build on current situations and and not worry about how things were done 30 years ago.

We have plenty of objectives to achieve. Completing the waterfront; making sure metro government works well; trying to attract new businesses; continuing to work on the convention business which is so important to us and to any city of this size; getting those bridges built; making sure UPS and the airport and our distribution systems remain top grade. Vision has to come from private/ public partnerships which means the elected leaders have to have vision and some courage about how to enhance this relationship. The private/public partnership has worked really well in numerous ways.

The advice I would give to the next generation of leaders is to not neglect your family while you are working long hours. You will find out quickly that family is the most important support group you have. The second thing is to become successful in your chosen field. I think if you don't do that, you will never have a base from which to build success in other activities. Business success opens other doors which in turn allows one to take on civic responsibility. The final advice is that when it becomes time to leave the stage, do it gracefully and in a well-planned way. Stay active, if possible, in community affairs but accept a lower profile role.

Most of us have learned to be generous. It's obviously easier to be generous when you have substantial resources, but the truth of the matter is that the $100 you give to some agency or project when you are young is equally important and as significant as the $1,000 you can give when you are older. The spirit of generosity needs to be developed for most of us over a period of time and the feeling of "giving back" is most satisfying.

When my career began, Louisville was a pretty cloistered community. There were fewer entrepreneurs and decisions were made about the city by a mere handful of men. They were well-intentioned people, but there was little diversity of thought or active participation. Fortunately that situation has changed with the growth of entrepreneurial efforts which has produced more visionaries. Many more people are involved in the decision-making process in the community. All of this means the leadership of the community has moved from a handful of people to a much broader group. That's good news and I hope the trend continues.

Henry C. "Hank" Wagner

**Retired President and CEO
Jewish Hospital
Healthcare Services**

HANK WAGNER TOOK A JOB as executive vice president of Jewish Hospital of Louisville in 1973. In September 2004, after three decades of transplants — hand, heart, heart-lung, kidney, pancreas, liver and other organs; after a replacement heart implant; after expanding the Jewish Hospital campus to include a 15-story heart and lung center and other new buildings; after participating in the formation of the Louisville Medical Center Development Corporation, the construction of new medical research facilities on the University of Louisville's Health Sciences Campus and the creation of a successful "Bucks for Brains" talent recruitment effort at UofL, Hank Wagner announced he would retire in June 2005.

He spent 25 of his 32 years at Jewish Hospital as president and CEO — first of the hospital itself, then of Jewish Hospital HealthCare Services, as the hospital company spread and became the parent organization of a regional health care network that now has more than 50 locations in Kentucky and southern Indiana.

In announcing his retirement, the Jewish Hospital board of directors gave Wagner credit for a long list of accomplishments, including steady growth of the Jewish Hospital Foundation, which the board said "has enabled Jewish Hospital to conduct pioneering medical research that has benefited mankind and brought worldwide recognition to the Louisville Medical Center."

Board Chairman Julian Shapero said Wagner would be hard to replace. Even competitors sang his praises. "Hank's leadership always caused those in the hospital business to look at Jewish to see what Jewish was doing, because they raised the bar," Larry McDonald told *The Courier-Journal*. McDonald is on the board of trustees at Norton Healthcare, and was a long-time executive of Humana Inc. when it operated hospitals.

Hank Wagner was born in West Virginia in 1942. He received a master's degree in hospital administration from Duke University in 1966 and served two years in the army at Ireland Army Hospital in Fort Knox. He spent five years as associate director of the University Hospitals of Cleveland before coming to Louisville.

Wagner became involved in community affairs almost upon arrival in Louisville and, when he added them up after his retirement announcement last year, he came up with 20 organizations or fundraising events he has chaired since he's been in Louisville. He has also served on the boards of at least 20 other organizations, including Greater Louisville Inc., the Greater Louisville Economic Development Partnership, the Downtown Development Corporation, the Kentucky Chamber of Commerce, UofL, Spalding University, the J.B. Speed Art Museum and many more.

Though he served in many "conventional" civic assignments – chairing the Metro United Way and Greater Louisville Fund for the Arts campaigns, for example – he thinks he has carved his personal niche in more health-related activities.

He was involved, for example, in efforts to gather Jewish, UofL, and Norton Healthcare hospitals around one table to create a single Louisville Medical Center focused on getting the most out of Louisville's overall medical offerings. He organized and was the founding chair of Louisville's Health Enterprise Network, a network of health-related business leaders working for economic development in the health care area.

The idea for creation of the state-backed Research Challenge Trust Fund – also known as "Bucks for Brains" – which seeks to recruit top health researchers to UofL and the University of Kentucky, came from Jewish Hospital. Wagner helped shepherd it through the state legislature. He also worked with the Louisville Medical Center hospitals in the 1990s to work out an agreement for joint management of University Hospital.

Over the years, Wagner has been recognized for his leadership and stellar service to his community with such awards as the Leadership Louisville Thomas C. Simons Distinguished Leadership Award, the Louisville Urban League's Equality Award, Greater Louisville Inc.'s Silver Fleur-de-Lis Award and the Kentucky Hospital Association's Award of Excellence. He was inducted into the Junior Achievement Hall of Fame, was named *The Voice Tribune*'s Man of the Year in 2004, and received the YMCA's Spirit of Louisville Award in 2004 as well.

Wagner has three adult children from a previous marriage. He and his wife, the former Donna Kane, intend to stay in Louisville after his retirement and to remain active in civic affairs.

WHEN I WAS APPOINTED CEO of Jewish in the early '80s, I was invited to attend special meetings around town. I graduated from Leadership Louisville, struck up a friendship with Maurice Johnson, who was CEO of PNC at that time, and I struck up a friendship with Mason Rudd, Ben Richmond, Tom Simons, Malcolm Chancey, Bob Allison, Mike Harreld, and Bill McAnulty.

Malcolm asked me to sit on a stadium committee with him and, for a couple of years, we worked on the notion, "Could Louisville help build a new football stadium for the University of Louisville?" The idea eventually developed into Papa John's Cardinal Stadium.

Mike Harreld, Sam Robinson, and Ben Richmond asked me to chair the Black Achievers annual fundraising dinner. We decided to do something special by bringing in a celebrity-type guest speaker. In those days, the big thing was Alex Haley and the TV series "Roots." Lo and behold, Alex Haley passed away on us one week before the dinner, but we got lucky. Ben Vereen, who also starred in the series, filled in.

Tom Simons asked me to chair the Metro United Way campaign. Mason Rudd asked me to chair the task force on AIDS that was being put together by the Louisville-Jefferson County Health Department. Bill McAnulty put me on the Jefferson Club board. Bob Allison, with whom I was working on Jewish Hospital's advertising and marketing, encouraged me to grow the heart service at Jewish.

With those special types of opportunities coming my way, I began to think that I could make a difference. It was an incredible high to be in the company of that generation of leaders. I started feeling like I could add value. I think the notion and thought process of Leadership Louisville caused me to take pride in my hometown and to get interested in wanting to make a difference in Louisville. That helped me get off to a good start.

In addition to the people I have already mentioned, the people chairing the board at Jewish Hospital were good mentors. Shelly Weber, Marsha Schuster, Stan Bayersdorfer, Marty Margulis and Sonny Altman were all board chairs at Jewish for whom I worked. Members of my medical staff and medical staff presidents included Joe Kutz, Laman Gray, Norton Waterman, and Harold Kleinert. I would put all of those people in the category of being mentors to me.

I developed a level of confidence through their encouragement and support. I learned to take some risks. In my mind, it was an awesome responsibility to take on the chair of the Metro United Way campaign. The notion, back in those days of trying to raise $13-14 million seemed impossible.

I remember that we built the first outpatient care center on the Jewish Hospital campus in the early '80s, and I got a lot of criticism from members of the medical staff who called it a "white elephant."

In those days, we really did not know where outpatient care might go. We had a notion that it might grow, but we did not have a notion that it was going to grow as dramatically and as fast as it did.

I remember building the 15-story Rudd Heart and Lung Center – truly the first heart hospital of its time. A lot of people labeled that "Hank's folly."

I leaned on my mentors. I think that it was their wonderful way of giving me confidence, sticking with me, helping defend some of the things that we did, working with my medical staff to perform Kentucky's first liver transplant. Those were really major steps to take. They really put Jewish Hospital at the center of attention, but caused us to take some measure of risk. The mentors I had around me really helped me stay the course.

I think that I'm a consensus-builder. A hospital is a unique kind of business. Running a hospital is a lot like piloting an aircraft carrier. You have to think about trying to turn it miles and miles before you make that turn. It has a million moving parts. You can't run the business I try to run without building consensus throughout the entire organization.

I think I would also describe my leadership style as one of trying to be absolutely fair. Most everything I do affects someone on the one hand in a positive way, and someone on the other hand in a negative way. To do what I do day-in-and-day-out, long-term, I have to be absolutely fair or the whole business would come crashing down around my shoulders.

I think that I work in a high-energy kind of way. I have a willingness to work harder than most people around me. I pay a lot of attention to details. A lot is written about the whole notion of not drowning yourself in details, and I understand that. On the other hand, in the health care business, where the public wants a zero-defect outcome in the services we provide, you find out that you have to pay attention to the details.

I don't know how others would describe my leadership. You always hope that others would perceive you as you perceive yourself. A lot of people around me are afraid of me, I'm told. I just can't see that. I describe myself as a big teddy bear.

After being at Jewish Hospital for 32 years, I think I am most proud of building the Heart and Lung Institute. I think that was one of my biggest challenges.

Another challenge I've recently had is organizing and being the founding board chair for the Louisville Health Enterprise Network. We now have assembled some 400 health care businesses in town and are working off of a $300,000-a-year budget. That whole project got launched with the help of a lot of people.

Building Jewish Hospital's Medical Center East was no walk in the park.

We worked our way through all of the certificate of need authorizations. We got to a point where we felt all approvals had been obtained and had some $25 million of steel in the ground. We then were abruptly sued by the competition in an attempt to block the project. That evolved into a lot of heated words, as well as continued court appearances, and eventually we hammered out the authority we needed to complete the project. At the end of the day, the project ended up costing $2 million unnecessarily and ended up being delayed some 18 months. All of that happened four or five years ago. I find that with the passage of time, it all seems less and less important today. The project has turned out to be a wonderful service to the community. We thought that it would take us four years to break even and, as luck would have it, we broke even in 11 months.

I would put working with the hospital and our medical staff to perform the world's first implantable heart on our significant accomplishment list as well, along with negotiating a management governance arrangement for University Hospital with the University of Louisville's School of Medicine in the mid-'90s. Those are the things that come to my mind.

What I learned from doing all of these things is the sum of what it takes to get things done. You learn to be a little more patient. You appreciate and understand how many other people are critical and important to your success. You appreciate that a journey starts with one step at a time. I suppose, on balance, you look back and recognize that you've had a wonderful time doing all of these things. Your life becomes the sum of what your business life has been about.

I've given a lot of thought to this next point. My biggest failure has been on the personal side of my life – two failed marriages, four homes bought and sold for losses, four country clubs joined, then resigned. I have lived through those experiences and, as I look back, it seems as if I've wasted a lot of dollars. I also think I could have raised my kids better.

One thing I decided early on in my career at Jewish was to spend my time focusing on the Louisville community. You can only do so much, though. You can only spend so much time away from your main responsibility, which is your job. I got to a point where I was being pulled to get involved in some national-level organizations on the one hand, and I had volunteered to take on certain jobs in Louisville on the other hand. Chairing the Metro United Way Campaign in the late '80s, then chairing the Fund for the Arts Campaign right behind it were monster kinds of civic volunteer assignments. I found that I could not just get on a plane to go to Chicago to spend two days doing this or that. Because of all that, I did not pursue national opportunities that were there. That's a disappointment, looking back.

Henry C. "Hank" Wagner

The Jewish Hospital organization spent a lot of time during the mid-'90s negotiating a merger with the Norton organization. Back in those days, it was called NKC. After two years of money, time and energy being spent on that agenda, which was a failed agenda, I look back and regard that as a disappointment.

We bought a hospital in Lexington in the late '90s. We thought that we could take Jewish Hospital state-wide. I soon learned that it was pretty difficult to have one foot in Louisville and another foot in Lexington. So we eventually sold that hospital and decided to concentrate our agenda in Louisville. Those are random thoughts about disappointments, but that's what comes to my mind.

I get a lot of credit for leadership, but I think I have also been a good follower. I would be the first to tell you that you don't advance to the position of board chair without first being a board member. I counted up, not too long ago, that I had chaired 20 organizations or fundraising events in the community, and I have been a member of the board of 20 other organizations. So I feel I have done a lot of following.

I think a good follower must be willing to be a good foot soldier. Every organization has to have a number of people willing to help that organization meet its goals. What do I expect from followers today? I expect help. A guy chairing a board cannot do it all by himself. I expect loyalty to the organization. I expect everyone to put forth his or her best efforts. I also expect everybody to speak up and participate.

If I could live my life over again, I wouldn't be in health care management. I would be a banker. I can't think of any banker I know who hasn't enjoyed the opportunity to merge, consolidate and grow his bank.

Over the past 30-40 years, we've all lived through the greatest growth period in history, so I think that banking would have been a fun career if I hadn't been in health care management. I had this notion that focusing on health care was so much more important than focusing on some other walk of life. I thought that I would look back over the past 40 years and say, "What I've done has really been important and perhaps more important than two dozen other activities that one can get involved in."

I've learned that everybody is doing something important for the community they live in and for their fellow man, no matter what they are doing. There are so many ways to achieve that objective. Health care does not have the corner on making a high and valued contribution, as I perhaps thought 40 years ago. I have a world of respect for what everyone is doing. I can see something good in what everyone is doing, regardless of their walk of life.

My advice to young people aspiring to leadership positions in Louisville would be to chair the Metro United Way campaign. Anyone can do it – I'm a living example of that. I've given this some thought.

There is not another civic assignment that will get you into every CEO's office in town, and getting into every CEO's office, meeting as many CEOs as one can, I think is the single most important ingredient in aspiring to leadership. Every CEO is involved in some way in a leadership assignment. By meeting them, you get to know what their passion is. You get to know the assignment that they have chosen to take on. You develop an opportunity to re-visit. You have built in an opportunity to have your phone call answered. I can't think of another assignment that works so well – especially in the Louisville community – because every CEO embraces the work of Metro United Way and supports the work of the Metro United Way. Chairing that campaign is a good, fun assignment that is open to anybody. You just start as a foot soldier. You log your time. You take on small assignments, demonstrate performance, and eventually – as Tom Simons did for me – somebody turns to you and says, "It's your turn." I think it's a wonderful way to get off to a good leadership start.

I also think that aspiring leaders need to create a niche for themselves. They need to differentiate themselves from others. I would think that you would say that Malcolm Chancey's niche is UofL. I would think that you would say that Tom Simons' niche would be building the Aegon Tower. Hank Wagner's niche has been the development of the Louisville Medical Center. Most everything I do civically is done to help promote the notion that the Louisville Medical Center is the best health care address in the state. That's worked for me.

I would also recommend that young people aspiring to leadership in our community support campaigns for mayor. It has been a wonderful way for doors to open in my circumstance. I've had a chance to work on every mayor's campaign for the last 30 years, and it has always opened doors. It was always a wonderful source of continued support. Whoever is the mayor has the focus of trying to make this community work. If you are close to that mayor, and if you are close to that mayor's agenda, then you're close to the epicenter of what this community is all about.

The last recommendation I have is to get involved. Don't wait to be asked. Go knock on Metro United Way's door today and say that you're ready to sign on.

When you think about what has contributed most to the growth, development and improved quality of life in Louisville over the last 50 years, five things come to my mind. Because of my bias, Louisville's growth as a health care center – the Louisville Medical Center – would be first on my list.

Jewish Hospital especially, and the neighboring hospitals to some extent, have pioneered over 100 medical firsts for the state of Kentucky. Jewish performed Kentucky's first kidney transplant in '64. Jewish performed Kentucky's first open heart surgery in '67. Jewish pioneered the first cardiac cath lab, the first balloon angioplasty procedure, the first heart transplant, the first liver transplant, the first lung transplant, and the first work using implantable heart devices. Our physicians re-attached the first hand to an injured patient. They re-attached the first arm that had been severed in a coal mining accident. Eventually, we pioneered the world's first hand transplant. So health care has really helped Louisville grow to what it has become today. The Medical Center employs upwards of 15% of all the people who work downtown.

The University of Louisville is also on my list. It is a metropolitan-style university that gets very much involved in the leadership and economic development of our community. I would have to give UofL high marks for what they have done with athletics in recent years. I would have to give UofL's School of Medicine high marks for the pioneering research it has accomplished. The "Bucks for Brains" program was the brainchild of Jewish Hospital and was eventually assembled by many people in state government. It's done more to fuel the growth of medical research than any other single event in the last 50 years.

Downtown development is the next thought that I have. I really feel good about the growth that I see in downtown development.

Next, the expansion of the airport was huge. I really feel good about the way our airport has grown, and what it will mean to our community in years to come.

What will mean more than anything, however, is the accomplishment of merged government. In years to come, that will probably go down as a landmark point in time, when Louisville changed from being a very small town to a community that is now the 16th largest city in America and, therefore, has much more potential.

Jewish Hospital and I have been very much involved in the health care agenda. I helped develop the "Bucks for Brains" agenda. I helped develop the Louisville Medical Center Development Corporation, which I think will have an enormous impact in years to come.

In terms of downtown development, I have played a role on the Downtown Development Corporation over the years, though I can't take much credit for what has been done. Most of the growth of downtown has been fueled by our past mayors and county judges.

I have had zero role in the expansion of our airport and our merged government, but I am a cheerleader for both.

Our community has some big challenges in the years to come. I've only recently come to understand just how engrained the attitude of Kentuckians is about Louisville and the rest of the state. I never fully understood and appreciated the harm that tends to do and why it's perpetuated. I can remember being in conversations 30 years ago where people were saying, "Let's change it." "What do we have to do to change it?" I think that there are three things that paralyze our ability to change that attitude.

One is the fact that our state university in Lexington tends to steal attention away from Louisville. I don't think that it is done consciously, but I just think it happens. Being president of the University of Kentucky seems to be more important than being governor, or being mayor of Louisville, or being president of the state's largest bank. That's just a built-in problem.

The second problem is that Kentucky has 120 counties. We piecemeal the state into such tiny governmental entities that there are 120 little fiefdoms. There are 120 legislative representatives. It is almost impossible to develop a focus, consensus or common vision among them, given the complexities of geographies, distance, economics, culture and history. That is disappointing.

Lastly, Louisville has allowed itself to be taxed by state government in a way in which more dollars migrate outside of Louisville to Frankfort than are returned. Louisville has no way to grow without getting state government's participation and support, and that sets up a set of political dynamics that I think has a stranglehold on the Louisville community.

I have no idea how we are going to deal with those problems, but I would hope that the next generation of leaders at least attempts to define our problems so we know what we are trying to solve. Looking back over the past 30-plus years, that's what comes to my mind.

I would put in the category of valuable lessons learned the notion that an aspiring leader ought to start with the conventional civic assignments. You have to start somewhere. You have to somehow get a toehold and start to build your credibility and credentials for providing leadership.

The conventional assignments are Metro United Way, Fund for the Arts, and Greater Louisville Inc. Until you get those behind you, you will not have met the people you need to meet to create other achievements, and you won't have earned your way into whatever our leadership groups are. So, start with the conventional civic assignments.

Once you've done that, it becomes critically important that you then leverage what it has taken you several years to achieve.

Henry C. "Hank" Wagner

You now need to harvest what you have learned. That's the most wonderful thing about what any of us can do. We are now in positions to make some difference in what I would call our own special projects.

My special projects have been the Louisville Medical Center, the pioneering of new medicine, the development of medical research agendas, the creation of the "Bucks for Brains" program, putting together the Greater Louisville Health Enterprise Network, and putting together the Louisville Medical Center Development Corporation.

I believe that what I did as a civic volunteer in the '80s allowed me to do those special things that I found that I wanted to do in the '90s.

I just hope the next generation of leaders in our city will follow our lead, adopt their own special projects, and do whatever they can to make sure our community continues to grow and prosper.

Arthur M. "Art" Walters

President Emeritus
Louisville Urban League

ART WALTERS IS SOMEWHAT of a living legend in Louisville. His leadership in the Louisville Urban League from 1963 to 1987 is far from forgotten now, but last year the Urban League presented the first annual Arthur M. Walters Champion of Diversity Award, so people will continue to be reminded of the extraordinary service he has given to the Urban League in his lifetime, and of his devotion to increasing diversity in his hometown.

It's a well-named award. Walters was executive director of the Urban League from 1970 until his retirement in 1987, and was chief architect of its prestigious job training program. He was also a central force in securing civil rights for African-Americans in Louisville. Among other things, he was the first African-American member of the Louisville Rotary Club.

Walters' work for equality began long before he came to the Urban League. He served for 20 years in the United States Army where he earned several service medals and three decorations: the Soldier's Medal for Heroism, the Bronze Star Medal for Bravery, and the Army Commendation Medal for Meritorious Service. At a time when the Army was still segregated, he was chosen to lead integrated troops, helping to lay the foundation for President Truman's 1948 order integrating the U.S. armed forces.

Art Walters was born in 1919 and grew up in Magnolia, Kentucky, south of Hodgenville. He remembers walking with siblings four miles to a segregated school in Buffalo, Kentucky, and being called names by white students passing in a bus.

In 1942, he was drafted out of Kentucky State University, then an all-black school, and ended up building bridges and rail yards in France, near Omaha Beach, as an Army engineer in 1944. He lived and worked in five countries and eight U.S. stations during his Army career. He retired as a lieutenant colonel in 1962, after 20 years of service in the military.

Walters had bought property in Louisville during the war, so he returned to Louisville when he retired from the Army.

In 1962, then-Mayor William O. Cowger asked Walters and his wife to test Louisville's new public accommodations ordinance by visiting restaurants to see if they would be served, as the law required. Sixty per cent of the restaurants turned them away, Walters told *Louisville Magazine* in 1987. He was determined, he said, to "address inequalities in my own hometown," but could see he had his work cut out for him.

He joined the Louisville Urban League in 1963, as industrial relations secretary and director of education and youth incentives. He quickly wrote the first application in Kentucky for federal on-the-job-training funds and obtained $210,000 from the Manpower Development and Training Act.

The lesson was not wasted on Walters. He kept applying. As Congresses came and went and the Manpower Act became the Comprehensive Employment and Training Act, then the Job Training and Partnership Act, Walters stayed in step with the program.

As director of the Urban League, he continued a diversification of the board of directors that had begun earlier and broadened the League's relationship with the community. He led League involvement in implementing the Civil Rights Act of 1964.

Besides his workforce development efforts, Walters expanded programs in housing counseling, computer training and youth education. He developed programs in affirmative action monitoring and black adoption, and expanded an Equal Opportunity Day dinner to include annual printed reports to the community and scholarship assistance to eligible high school students.

He launched a $1.2 million capital campaign as well. And along the way, he integrated the board of the Kentucky High School Athletic Association and chaired Louisville's first Citizens' Administrative Advisory Committee. Committee action resulted in an increase in recruitment of black officers on the city police force to one-third of the force.

Walters has degrees from the University of Louisville and Colorado College and an honorary degree in humane letters from Bellarmine University.

He was formerly married to the late Noralee Bryant, with whom he had three children, all college graduates. His current wife, Mary Anne, has two children, and together they have seven grandchildren.

Walters has received numerous awards and recognitions for his many contributions to his community. In 1984, he received the Chestnut Street YMCA's annual award as Black Achiever of the Year. He was among the first 22 people inducted into the newly-created Kentucky Civil Rights Hall of Fame in 2000. And in 2004, he got a start on his career as a living legend when the Urban League presented the first annual Arthur M. Walters Champion of Diversity Award.

I FRANKLY NEVER DECIDED to become a leader. I did decide that I wanted to make a difference in the issues that impacted my life and the lives of people I cared about. I guess from that came the title "leader." But I was not seeking leadership. I just recognized that I had to take some action to address the problems I was concerned about.

My parents were my first mentors. My father and mother were not highly educated. They grew up on a farm in Larue County, but they taught me and my older sister and my younger brother (I'm in the middle), that we were not better than anyone and no one was better than we were. "God did not make any junk." That was their word. They taught us, "You are somebody, so act like it. Put some effort forth to make something of yourself. Do not do it selfishly, but so that whatever you do will accrue to the benefit of other people."

I had two more contemporary mentors in the military, which was my first career. I was drafted out of Kentucky State the end of my junior year. I finished all but one semester. I was on the dean's list the whole time. I'm glad of that, as a little country bumpkin. I had all women teachers in elementary school. Nothing wrong with that. I learned tremendous facts from wonderful teachers when that door closed in the one-room school in Buffalo, Kentucky, a mile from where I lived. My brother, sister and I walked four miles one way to school every day. There were no buses. Buses were running, but they were for white children. They would peep their heads out, roll down windows, call us "smokescreens" and whatever. I decided at that time that one of the things I wanted to do was to give children of color some exposure to individuals like themselves, particularly black boys. I was one, and it seemed to me that the fright of persons not of color – Caucasians – was more pronounced in women than it was in men. I've tried to find rationale for each position I hold about life, and I believe that that position was a no-no. The taboo of the intermingling across races, particularly black men with white women, was the fear of white men that their women would be treated as our women were, as slaves. Hence, we have multi-colors, like you and me.

The military was part of my orientation on how to become a leader as a black male. Some of my contemporary models were people like Lyman Johnson, who was a very close friend of mine and whom I admired greatly. He was in my fraternity at Kentucky State. I served as president of that fraternity while I was there. Dr. Maurice Rabb was a physician at Kentucky State. Dr. J.B. Bell, who was also at Kentucky State as the college physician, was one of our family's doctors once I moved out of the country into Louisville. He was my wife's parents' doctor, too.

I saw in those men that they were each the type of person I aspired to be. Lyman Johnson was an educator, an individual who was interested in his knowledge being the foundation for someone else's grasping for knowledge. He also had a big role at Quinn Chapel during the civil rights struggles, helping plan and implement programs. His basic philosophy was that if you don't plan it well, it will not turn out well. Poor planning makes poor performance.

Dr. J.B. Bell taught me that people mattered. I would be sitting out in the waiting room, talking to my wife or my in-laws, and I would know that Dr. Bell was back there asking people, "How is your family?" He was really interested in who you were and what you were when you came to see him, beyond your medical problem. I picked that up from him – that if you're only interested in yourself, it doesn't count for much. It's not what God wants. It's not what needs to be done in the community. You need to be concerned about other people and take whatever time is necessary to make them feel and act important.

My leadership style is "Organize it, deputize it, and supervise it." That's a military lesson I learned. I don't ever recall standing up and accepting any kind of accolade – and there have been about 120 of them. I have awards and plaques and certificates to prove it, without saying, "This is a very special moment. Someone has recognized me and given me credit for doing some things, but I want you to know that I did not do it alone."

What I'm most proud of is that I corralled around me in both careers – the military and the Urban League – people who knew how to do things that supplemented and augmented my areas of weakness. Now that may be a strange statement. Some people I hear saying, "I won't do that because they'll take over." I never found that to be true. Out of 42 staff members, which was the highest number I had in 24 years at the Urban League, only four reported to me. "Organize it. Deputize it. Supervise it." All the tasks at the Urban League were deputized to someone else. I oriented them, I trained them, then I turned the selection of their staff members over to them. The final stamp of approval was mine, but they selected their own team members and that's very important. It empowers them, and it gives them people who can relate to their style, which may be different from Art Walters' style. The credit goes to the selection process, and to the deputizing process, and the faith we put in persons who will do what gives them a sense of ownership in the process. When you have that, you have a winning combination for success.

I'm not puffed up. The Good Book speaks against that. I really try not ever to take credit without giving credit, but I believe that other people – corporate America, national Urban League, federal government, state government, local government – saw me as effective in my role.

Seven months into my role at the Urban League, I wrote the first proposal for a federally funded on-the-job training program for a non-profit organization. It was funded for about $220,000. The plan was innovative, because the grant reimbursed employers for the participants' wages during six months of training, allowing them to hone their skills to a satisfactory level, as determined by the person in the company who trained them. If the individuals demonstrated that they could do the job, reimbursements stopped, and the company agreed to hire the trainees full-time.

We started with four companies who made that commitment and we ended up with 44 companies, including FORTUNE 500 companies. The first checkout person at a Kroger store was trained through the Urban League's on-the-job training program. Seagram's had the first management trainee and George King is one of them.

I used to walk down Fourth Street and see all the beautiful showpieces in the windows and the mannequins never looked like me. I happened to be lucky enough to have a friend on the board of the Urban League. I talked to him about this mannequin situation and he put the first black mannequins on Fourth Street. I think that changed the feelings of young blacks. It said "I'm important enough to be on this main shopping street."

Believing strongly in education and youth incentives, we created the first organized effort to lift up kids who were dropouts, and to turn around its negative impact on their lives, at what is now the Plymouth Renewal Center. The program was headed by Morris Jeff, who served as its director. It was a settlement house. I used volunteers from the Urban League Guild Auxiliary — named after another mentor of mine, Mae Street Kidd. She organized the first volunteer group. It was made up primarily of women, but there were some men in it too. We paid transportation if they needed it. They were role models and assisted our children to make them the best that they could be. We had 165 youth, three nights a week, on the second and third floor up there. Morris Jeff was fully supportive of it. Bettie Taylor, who was the assistant principal at Central High School at that time, was very much in support of it. The Urban League Guild was in support of it, and the Future Teachers program from Central High School was a part of it. That was the group. Three nights a week, they tutored in reading, math and science.

The other two nights in Fifth Street Baptist Church's basement, a white union business agent taught us about asbestos and insulation. He got fined $250 for conduct not in the best interest of organized labor, and the conduct was that he was teaching us this field on his own, no pay. When it came time to build the Galleria, I sat with the blessing of Oxmoor Properties, the builder;

organized labor; and a committee called CUB (Committee of United Blacks). The pastor who just retired in the past couple of years from Zion Baptist Church headed that group.

As a result of that experience, we got organized labor to accept individuals almost like on-the-job training, but it had to be approved by organized labor at the state level. They took it as part of the Louisville Plan, a volunteer effort. I finally got money for that program the year after the on-the-job training program. It was the second labor education advancement program, and it was adopted by the National Urban League as a model. I remember them saying, "Art, when you propose this, ask for some money." This was in 1963 and 1964, and we had been used to getting $10,000. From that time on, we were funded on a year-to-year basis.

I retired in 1987. Each year, we had to undergo three levels of audit because federal money was involved: federal, state, and an independent audit required by the National Urban League. Not one time was there a penny not accounted for, and I am very proud of that. Our audits were satisfactory. We met our programmatic goals, and we pleased our funding source. We also later received private sector money as well. These are the things I am now most proud of. These were results that were measurable.

The dropout program we started resulted in a two-and-a-half-day statewide conference. We looked at "What's the cause? What's the remedy?"

Another program I am proud of was a dropout program we did in cooperation with the public school system. We became a resource to them. We brought volunteers in. We asked questions to try to make the public school system more accountable. "Why is the dropout gap more significant among people of color than among non-blacks?" "What is the fallacy behind this idea that black children can't learn as well as white children?" "Who is responsible for teaching?" Teachers are. "Who pays the teachers?" Parents, through their taxes. This was not threatening; it was partnering to get results. We haven't eliminated that problem. It was one of my last initiatives. It was called the Louisville Education Initiative. It made big headlines in the paper and has been adapted all over the Urban League. It's now called the Education and Youth Incentive Program. I want to see some accountability and some partnering to make a difference in the lives of our children.

What worries me is that I know a lot of teachers and I respect them highly. Our children have need of what the Good Book warns us about — building on sand, then the storm comes and blows the house down. Why? Because the foundation is bad. The same is true of children. If we put them out there in this world ill-equipped to deal educationally or interpretively with what's going on out there, they're going to fail. And so many of these teachers whom I believe in and respect so highly – many are my friends – are now saying that they can't wait until they retire. Who is going to fill this void? That's so sad. They are the ones who are equipped to do it. They have demonstrated accomplishments and have gotten results. And now, they are going to leave. Who is going to fill the void?

The first problem is teachers' pay. If we are going to try to build a foundation for this house that's going to withstand the rains and the winds, teachers ought to be the highest paid technicians on the job. That worries me. I used to be invited to go into classrooms to talk to individuals. I'll tell you who's still active in that is Buster (Rev. Louis) Coleman. He used to have me come on a regular basis and talk to students about the correlation between what they were having an opportunity to learn in the classroom and success. I would talk to them about how they would have success if they mastered their schoolwork, or failure if they tried to go out into the work world without mastering their schoolwork. I would tell them that it doesn't mean that they have to stay in their major, if you will. Seventy percent of individuals who major in a field do not end up working in it, the last time I checked. It would be better if they were prepared to build a solid foundation, without putting too much emphasis on what their major is.

The impact these training programs had on people's lives helped them build a solid foundation, and I am proud of these programs. They were a significant accomplishment. If you come up with a plan that is oriented toward problem-solving and you do what the Good Book says, the race to success will be won, not by the swift or the strong, but by those who endure, those who hang in there, those who have tenacity.

In Aesop's Fables' story of the hare and the tortoise, the tortoise won the race. He was not fast, but he hung in there and kept plodding along, and he stuck with it. Falling down is not a positive thing, but if we lay there, it definitely becomes a negative. If we get up, it gives us another opportunity to try again.

My biggest disappointment was in my military career. We served under the label of making the world safe for democracy. I served almost 100% of my 20 years in organizations in which I did not experience democracy myself. I went in as a recruit, and served the last four years and retired as a lieutenant colonel. That was unheard of in those days. I commanded white troops and battalions and companies.

Captain Harold D. Cannon was my commander in Europe. I was in Europe twice, landed 16 days after D-Day. I was in charge of all the vehicle equipment in the regiment, and I remember sitting in the seat of the jeep with water up around here. All jeeps were waterproof around the carburetor, with a snorkel like a submarine. We rode around in the water and dropped a landing thing that rolled off into the water and onto the banks. Military police were on the other side to lead each company to its pre-determined bivouac overnight.

My company commander, Captain Cannon, presented me with my first lieutenant bars. When I went to the command post the next morning, he said "I am a southerner, proud of it, grew up in Biloxi, Mississippi, and I have been told, taught and believed up until now that the black people were not capable of being commissioned officers in the United States Army. You have changed my feelings about that." "Oh, thank you, sir," I said. I thought it was a lot of talk.

Military regulations say that if a commander is going to be officially absent from his company, battalion or regiment, the next senior officer automatically assumes command, unless the commander leaving appoints a person other than the senior. After Captain Cannon said that to me, every time he left for more than a week, he published a company order: "I hereby appoint Arthur M. Walters Commander of C Company of the 354 Engineer's Battalion until my return." That lifted me more than anything else — right in a sea of segregation, separate but equal and all that old stuff.

Every commander used to give an overall efficiency rating to all the people below him. He would say, "This is an outstanding colored officer." Colored was the giveaway. I wasn't to be compared to anyone who's not colored. Within my little segregated rank, I was outstanding. They finally assigned the process of evaluating and computing the Overall Efficiency Index to the Department of War, now the Department of Defense, and they were prohibited from using race on the OEI. That resulted in my being promoted after I came out of World War II and Korea, above some of my contemporaries who were West Pointers.

My primary Military Occupation Specialty finally ended up being operations officer. In a military outfit, from the battalion up, there's an S-1, administration and personnel; an S-2, reconnaissance and intelligence; and an S-3, plans and operations. As S-3 of the 354 Engineer's Battalion, it was my job to decide a number of things: What is the situation? What do we need to do to prepare? How can we get the company to various locations? What tasks have to be developed? Who will do it? How do you allocate the equipment to the companies? That was my job.

I had a plane and a helicopter — both with two seats. We would go down and take notes and come back and have the company commanders assemble and give them their locations on a map. I used to teach map reading, and I enjoyed it. I already knew something about how you take a compass and map. That experience drew the attention of individuals other than Captain Cannon.

I have always been fortunate to have assistants whose competence allowed me not to be tied down to minutiae and detail. I could dictate a five-paragraph field order enroute to the next command post and when I got there it would be typed up and reproduced. I was the only one who had an air-conditioned van, cool in the summer and warm in the winter.

My biggest disappointment, as I sit here now, in 2004, is that so much of the negative, discriminatory acts that I have described are still going on. It's just more sophisticated. The individuals, in many instances, who are demonstrating don't understand what they're fighting against. It's all right to talk about things and demonstrate, but you have to come up with some action plans eventually that will move toward resolution of the problem. We had that during the civil rights struggle, but I don't see it happening anymore. There's no plan; they just get on television.

My other disappointment is that if you look at an organization table of a battalion, there's a CEO and what is the rank? Look at the battalion leaders. What are their ranks? Without exception, from my experience, the junior ranking officer was always a second lieutenant, and black. I was proud that a southerner helped me move around that bottleneck, but the disappointment is that I haven't seen that much change. It's still happening all around us.

Good followers are individuals who have the courage of their convictions, who will contribute to conversations involving the tasks they have been assigned – or that have been "deputized" to them – but who understand at the same time that the final decision rests with the individual who cannot delegate ultimate responsibility. The leader, or top individual, is responsible for the success and failure of everything that goes on. The only way you can achieve that is to "organize it, deputize it, and supervise it." The person whom you deputize must understand that you can delegate tasks to them, but they must do them to the best of their ability because they are representing not just you, but the person from whom the delegation came.

Good followers can internalize that and put their opinions in during the process. I ask them to tell me if there is a better way. Maybe things will change. But if they never do that, I expect them to do it the way we agreed initially. That's being a good follower. I want them to come back to report to me when their task is finished and let me go out and look at it. They need to report to me on an ongoing basis about how things are progressing, so I can be assured of telling my superiors that "the job's going well in C Company."

I am proud of what I have done in my life and I am proud of how I accomplished it. In two careers spanning 46 years, and in ten more as a retiree and in advisory roles, I think perhaps if there's anything I've learned it is that you cannot talk to funding sources anymore about pie in the sky. I have also learned that it is important to make sure that the people for whom services are being provided have a voice in whatever it is being done to alleviate whatever the problem is. People need to have a sense of ownership in projects. For so long, experts have tried to say, "I know what your hurt is." No, they don't.

Kim Burse, who ran Louisville's Community Development Bank , asked me, "Art, I want you to serve one year on the board of the bank." "Why me?" I said. "I don't even live in the area." She said, "But you worked in it for 20 years, so you know the community." I said to Kim, "Where are the individuals you are providing this service to? Who's hearing their voice at the board level?"

When I joined, there wasn't a single member of the board from the five target areas served by the Community Development Bank. There wasn't a single advisory committee member from the five target areas. There are now. I would emphasize very much, if I were doing it over again, that we need to bring these people in on the front end. We need to show that we have the courage of our convictions.

I told Kim, "I'd like to see a needs assessment done professionally of the five target areas, and don't sit here as professional board members and draw this up and approve it when it hasn't been tried on for size with the people you serve." When we tried it out on the people we served, we got burned. We thought we were doing such an outstanding job. Of all the individuals who moved out of Park DuValle, only 10% of the people dislocated had the opportunity to come back in under the guidelines that were developed without their input. It wasn't people living there in squalor, in barracks-looking buildings with nothing but dope fiends, in prison-type housing. I can speak to it because I had relatives living there. If I had one thing to do over, I wouldn't agree to serve on a board unless they were going to put somebody on it who represented the voice of the people we were trying to help. I would expect them to have recurring meetings, and to relate to what they're doing there.

I certainly think all of our elected officials – the mayor and the aldermen – now metro council – have had a significant impact on our community's growth over the last 50 years. I was on an exploratory board, looking at options, and I came down on the side of merged government and that's what came about. I got criticized for supporting the idea of metro government, but when you get representatives from various areas equal in standing as you to make policy, and those individuals look beyond their own sphere of influence, it's a plus.

I'm a strong supporter that people without means to get to a job ought to have some subsidy initially from the city. That program is now operational at Louisville's Nia Center. You look in the back and there are always TARC buses parked there. For the first 30 days, TARC will transport any individual who comes out of the learning center to their jobs – free of charge. I thought the city ought to subsidize that type of operation.

The biggest challenge facing our city, in my opinion, is to turn loose yesterday and embrace tomorrow. We are a slow-change community, kind of hick-townish. The biggest challenge is learning how to coalesce, how to plan together, and how to have the people we're trying to help and serve involved in the process. I hope delegations will continue to go annually to other cities to see how they are doing things. I think Mayor Abramson started this type of program.

I've learned a lot of lessons in my life that I would like to share with the next generation of leaders coming up. I've learned that truly, the best things in life are not free. The second thing I've learned is to seek to partner and coalesce with individuals who know how to take what is and make it better. And finally, I have learned to believe what the Good Book says: Seek first the kingdom of God, and his righteousness and all these other things will be added.

You've got to get some spirit. He sent His son to validate us again in relationship with a supreme being. Without Him, I am nothing. So I don't get puffed up about all these awards I have received.

I don't know why I'm blessed to have beautiful friends, a locker full of plaques. I'm sure God has something that he wants me to do. I'm really not sure what that is. But I do try to do a good turn, literally, every day. If it's nothing more than making you smile or saying to a child who looks downtrodden, "Is there anything I can do to help cheer you up?" "You look beautiful today." "You're going to do well in school." If nothing else, we just need to smile more.

STEPHEN A. WILLIAMS

President and CEO
Norton Healthcare

STEVE WILLIAMS ROSE FROM BEING a Livingston County, Kentucky farm boy in 1965 to president and CEO of Kentucky's largest hospital and health care system in 1993 without ever filling out a job application. Unless one's behavior might be considered an application of sorts.

Williams behaved like a leader early on. In high school, he was president of the student body in both his junior and senior years, and also president of many clubs and organizations. Because he was interested in health care, his family doctor got him a job as an orderly at the Livingston County Hospital in Salem, Kentucky while he was still in high school.

He liked that job, and he did it well enough to be moved up to a job in the operating room at Western Baptist Hospital while he was in college. By that time it was pretty clear to him that he was more interested in administration than in medicine.

He was given a job that summer as an administrative assistant, writing job descriptions for every job in the hospital for an upcoming accreditation evaluation. He said later it was a good way to learn how a hospital operates.

After graduation from Murray State University in 1972 with a bachelor of science degree in administrative management, he decided to stay on at Murray for an MBA, with hospital management as a career goal. He had about four months in when he got a call from the chief of staff back at Livingston County. The doctor said they needed a hospital administrator and it would be a good way for Williams to see if he liked the work.

Williams found himself running a 26-bed hospital — Kentucky's smallest at the time — where only one person on the staff was younger than he, and the chief of staff was the doctor who had delivered him 22 years earlier. He then heard about a program at the University of Minnesota where one could obtain credentials of advanced studies in health care administration through independent study – something he could do while doing his job at the hospital. One thing he needed, though, was an alumnus of the program who would meet with him once a month to guide his study. It happened that both Wade Mountz and Jim Petersdorf, president and executive vice president at Norton in those days, were alumni. Williams asked if one would be his preceptor, and Petersdorf agreed. They met once a month for three and a half years, until Williams graduated from the program.

Somewhere in there, Petersdorf saw something he liked in Williams, and in 1977 he offered him a job – a very good job, as assistant to the executive vice president. He worked as administrator of Norton-managed hospitals in a couple of smaller towns, and in 1985 he was named vice president. He became executive vice president and chief operating officer in 1988, and president and CEO in 1993.

Williams is recognized nationally as an authority on health care quality management. He has authored articles and has made dozens of presentations on the subject around the country. As a result, Norton Healthcare is considered a pioneer in developing Total Quality Management processes for the health care industry. The company receives national recognition for being on the cutting-edge in the field, and was recognized in 1988 as the first company in the nation to receive Healthcare Forum's "Commitment to Quality Award."

Along the way, Williams has discovered that leaders of causes in the community are interested in his services, too. He has chaired the boards of the Kentucky Hospital Association and Kentuckiana Works, a workforce development program.

He chaired Metro United Way's 1999 corporate campaign and has been active with its "Success by 6" initiative. He has served as co-chair of Greater Louisville Inc., and has served on the boards of Leadership Louisville, the Greater Louisville Fund for the Arts, the Greater Louisville Health Enterprises Network, the Boy Scouts of America, Bank One Kentucky, Fifth Third Bank Kentucky, the University Medical Center, University Healthcare Corporation and many other organizations.

The Kentucky Hospital Association gave Williams its Award of Excellence in 1994. Murray State University recognized him as a distinguished alumnus in 2000. The University of Minnesota also recognized him as a distinguished alumnus and gave him its first Jerome T. Bieter Award for Outstanding Leadership in 2004. He has received a number of additional awards over the years from organizations like ElderServe and Volunteers of America.

He and his wife Kathy live in Goshen, Kentucky and have two sons.

LEADERSHIP IN THE COMMUNITY and, in fact, leadership with Norton Healthcare, was just a natural evolution of my own personal journey regarding leadership. That journey really began in high school with my probably overloading myself. If you look in my high school yearbook, you'll find too much of me: president of the student council two years, president of several different clubs, on and on. From a very early age, I found myself naturally pursuing leadership positions, or being asked to.

Let me back up. In growing up on a farm, I obviously had lots of experience with raising livestock and I loved it. But I was attracted to health care for some reason instead of veterinary medicine. I had a real curiosity about it, and I had a good relationship with our family physicians. So I was considering whether I wanted to study medicine. Through our family physician, I was offered a job at our local hospital as an orderly when I was 15. I loved the work, the environment, being part of the health care team. As I got into college, I didn't get into leadership roles like I had done in high school, because I was working part time as an operating room tech. I took a few pre-med type courses, but I realized I really did not have an interest in the science. I took a few business courses and loved them, but I also loved the work I was doing at the hospital. I became intrigued with the business side of health care. By my junior year of college, I was working at a larger area hospital in the operating room, and had made friends with the new personnel director at the hospital. He gave me a job for the summer — writing job descriptions in preparation for an accreditation inspection. Over the summer, I wrote job descriptions for every job in that hospital. It was really a great experience, because it allowed me to have a full understanding of everything that happens in health care.

I think it was really that summer, in 1972, when I became interested in health care administration. Following my graduation from Murray, I decided to go into a master's degree program for health care administration. I was too late that year, however, to get into any of the MHA grad programs. So I started on an MBA at Murray with a notion of going into a health care administration program the following year. About four months into the semester, I received a call from the physician who delivered me 22 years earlier, back at my home county's hospital, where I had been an orderly a few years before. The doctor was leading a search committee for an administrator for the hospital. He had heard I was interested in hospital management. He said, "Steve, why don't you come back home, give it a try and see if this is really what you want to do?" So in November of 1972, I found myself, at age 22, running a 26-bed hospital, Kentucky's smallest at the time. I was thrust into a leadership position that was so far over my head that I didn't know what I didn't know. I had only one employee younger than me.

My getting involved in the community just evolved. Once I came to Norton and took on increased leadership roles inside the organization, it was just a natural to be called upon to be more active in the community. I have found that to be very gratifying. It was never really a conscious decision that I was going to go out and do X, Y and Z in the community. My leadership roles in the community evolved, just as they have in my professional career.

The only job I ever asked for was that orderly position when I was 15, and that was done very informally through a family physician. I have never filled out an application. I have never applied for a job in my life. I don't say that in a boastful way. It has simply been a journey where I have had opportunities come about, professionally and in volunteer work, where I would be asked if I were interested in doing this or that. It has been invigorating and gratifying to take on those kinds of roles, whether they have been an internal role in an organization or a leadership role in the community.

I consider my father to be my greatest mentor. He is a man of rock-solid values, strong work ethic, a steady voice of reason, and he has an understanding and appreciation of what's really important in life. I have always considered him my role model. At age 87, he is still teaching me important lessons of life.

Professionally, I really owe my entire career to the previous presidents of Norton: Wade Mountz, Jim Petersdorf, and Rod Wolford. When I came to Norton in 1977, Wade was president and Jim was executive vice president, then president after Wade retired. When I was running that little 26-bed hospital in western Kentucky, I decided that I did want to stay in health care administration. But I realized that if I was going make it a career, I needed more education and more experience in a larger institution.

So I began to do some homework. I found the University of Minnesota had a program in health care administration that allowed a practicing hospital administrator to do part of an MHA degree through independent studies. That same personnel director who I had written job descriptions for several years earlier had also decided to seek a graduate degree. So the two of us together applied to the University of Minnesota program and were accepted.

I had heard of Jim Petersdorf and Wade Mountz through the Kentucky Hospital Association circles, but of course I didn't personally know them. As it turned out, both of them were alumni of the U of M program. To get into the independent studies program, one had to have a U of M alumnus preceptor meet with you monthly to help you work through the program. Wade Mountz had just finished his term as chairman of the board of the American Hospital Association and Jim Petersdorf was a well-known, very reputable health care leader in his own right.

So I came to Louisville, fairly boldly, and introduced myself. I told them, in the context of being a young whippersnapper, that they certainly had no obligation toward me but I said, "You are alums. I want to get into this program and I need a preceptor. Would either of you be willing to do that?" They agreed.

Jim became my preceptor and I met with him monthly for three-and-a-half years. I worked my way through the master's program, spending part of my summers in Minnesota. By that time I was married, and we had our first child. In 1977, I was finishing up that program when Jim called me and asked me to come to Louisville a day early so he could talk to me about something. Of course, that was a job offer.

I should add that our newborn son had a birth injury to a right arm, and we had been researching nationwide where we should take him for the best care. The answers we had received were to take him to Louisville to the Kleinert & Kutz hand surgeons.

Within weeks, Jim offered me a job in Louisville. Kathy and I had known each other since elementary school and had dated since high school. We both were rural Kentucky kids, scared to death of moving to the city. But we felt without question that this was what we should be doing.

So we moved to Louisville with a six-month-old in late 1977, and Jim immediately became just an incredible mentor. I had made a deal with him that I would not immediately have operational responsibilities. I wanted to see the entire organization and learn the big picture. So I worked as a staff person for Jim, in his role as executive vice president. Frankly, it was a job he carved out and made for me. I was so young that even though I had been a hospital administrator five years, many people assumed I was in an administrative fellowship or residency at the time. Anyway, that began my tenure at Norton and an incredible mentoring relationship with Jim and Wade.

Finally, I should add, that following Wade's retirement and Jim's untimely death shortly thereafter, Rod Wolford was named president and CEO of Norton and, shortly thereafter – in 1988 – he named me chief operating officer. In that role, of course, I learned much from Rod, and it positioned me to be named president and CEO upon his departure in 1993.

As I age, I realize more and more valuable lessons I have learned over the years. But as I reflect on those early and most formative years with Wade and Jim, if I had to name one key leadership characteristic that was born out of my relationship with them as mentors, it unquestionably would be the development of values. They both taught me the absolute necessity of not only having strong personal values and integrity, but of leading an organization in such a way that you represent those values and present the organization as a values-driven one. Said a different way, if the CEO isn't visibly demonstrating strong values, then how can one expect an institution to have that kind of culture?

Now I am quick to acknowledge that I fall short of living up to that standard all too often, but it is a sense of purpose and the importance of values I am referring to. I'm sure that people within our organization get tired of hearing me talk about the importance of values; but I think it is the CEO's responsibility to lead the culture, and to do so in a very personal, sincere way.

Unquestionably, both Jim and Wade are revered to this day in our organization and in the community. And when you ask people what makes them so revered, it doesn't take long to get to the values of honesty, integrity and trust – intangibles which provided the foundation for them to do what they did for our organization and for the community.

In reflecting on my shorter time working for Rod, I certainly refined my business acumen. We completed a merger during that time, and I was given the opportunity to operationalize that merger. It was a lot of "trial by fire" over a couple of years, but it was a great experience and I learned a lot.

My leadership style has evolved over the years, and particularly as the organization has grown. Coming from those small, rural hospital roots, I have always had a fairly "hands-on" style: wanting to know details, some more than I really needed, but understanding what was really going on behind the scenes in order to best try to provide leadership and direction. As we have grown, it has not been possible or appropriate for me to know what all is going on in operations, but I have tried my best to hire really good people.

The author Jim Collins talks about the necessity of a CEO's "getting the right people on the bus." I think that it is extraordinarily important for a CEO to hire the right people with the right core competencies, the right values, and with compatible styles.

I believe very strongly that effective leadership is very much tied not only to values, but also to the issue of personal relationships. There must be a sense of trust, openness, and honesty within a leadership team if that team is going to reach its full potential. That said, I prefer a fairly "consensus-driven" decision-making process. I like to have "group think." I like to hear point-counterpoint, pros and cons and so forth when we are making a big decision. Of course, sometimes consensus isn't possible or timely, so I need to make a decision, having taken into consideration all the inputs. Regardless of how the decision is made, once it's done, the clear expectation is for everyone to sign on and understand that we then move in unison toward execution of the decision.

Over the years, the way people have described my style – whether as a compliment or critically – has been pretty consistent with the way I see myself.

But that isn't a surprise. I think I am fairly easy to read in the context of where I am going and the matter of my style.

From the standpoint of a specific project or initiative, certainly the acquisition of the former for-profit hospitals here in town and our doubling in size overnight in 1998 was probably the most significant professional initiative that I have undertaken. It was a bold move on the part of our board. Some have described it as courageous leadership. Others described it as near-insane. Nevertheless, I think anyone would say it was bold and high-risk. We felt it was the right thing to do for the community and that it was achievable, although we recognized it was going to take a lot of leadership and commitment to make it work.

We developed a strategy to integrate those facilities into a coordinated network of hospitals. Success required a lot of things – everything from developing the infrastructure to blending employee and physician cultures. I realized we needed a lot more breadth and depth on the management bench. So I have hired a lot of talent from throughout the nation over the last seven years. In fact, about 30 out of the top 35 people in the organization have come in the last six years. That gives you a feel for the scope of that one strategic acquisition decision. I think it was clearly the biggest initiative we have undertaken and it has resulted in a lot of hard work on a lot of people's part. But I think we have proven it was not only achievable but it was the right thing to do for the organization and for the community.

You can't do everything at once, in terms of blending organizations. Even if we had had enough money to do everything at once, it wouldn't be possible. Some things had to be done sequentially. You must have a very clear vision for what you want for an organization as you go forward. Clarifying mission and vision and values are all prerequisites to developing a good strategic plan. With that done, then you can focus on developing the tactical plan, the plan of execution. That includes determining the kind of talent you need to implement those strategies. Of course, all those things become a lot easier if you have a very clear understanding of what you are, how you want to behave, and exactly what you want to achieve.

I've had failures, of course. But rather than enumerating transactions or initiatives that failed, I would answer more from the standpoint of leadership with people.

Unfortunately, most seasoned leaders have, at various points in their careers, had to tell an employee they are not the right person at the right time, that they are not a good fit, or that they just can't meet the job requirements. For whatever reason, you have had to separate a person from the organization.

I have always felt strongly about the responsibility of a good leader to make leaders of others, to hire good people, to let them develop. Undoubtedly that comes from my own background. Here is a farm kid who didn't know anything about running hospitals. I was given incredible opportunities, even pushed by great mentors to develop and grow professionally. They always kept me out there with a 10 to 20 percent uncomfortable factor, giving me a challenge and an opportunity to grow, but within an acceptable margin of risk. I have tried to return the favor by hiring good people with a lot of potential, then challenging them to reach that potential. But it doesn't always work.

Even in hiring veteran managers and leaders, sometimes it just doesn't work out for one or both parties. What I have felt the worst about in my career, relative to failures, has been having to separate someone from the organization. In the end it was often a situation where it should have happened earlier rather than later, but I am one who usually tries hard to figure out a way to make it work. On occasion, however, that's just not possible. Either the agenda has changed, the person has changed, or for some reason, it's just not an acceptable match and you have to face that reality. It is always tough, though. Anytime I have to separate someone from the organization, I consider it a failure of mine, as well as his or hers.

It's a matter of continuous personal development and learning for a leader. You have to become more judicious about the initial matching of person to job. I think one of the failings of leadership, at least in our field of health care management, has been that we have not been nearly sophisticated enough to understand all of the things that go into making a good match between an organization and a person. But I believe we are getting a lot better at that. There are tools out there now like the predictive index that can be used in the process, and there is more acceptance of both parties "kicking the tires" through more extensive and better-focused interviewing. I think we need to put more energy into making sure upfront that it is the right match.

I think a good follower is one who makes sure he or she clearly understands the mission, vision, values, and strategies of the organization and exactly where he or she fits into the execution of that strategy — what part he or she can play or is expected to play. In other words, a good follower should understand the roadmap. Secondly, I think a great follower is one who provides value to that institutional journey, in the context of not just waiting to be called on but to step up and ask questions, provide constructive input, and volunteer for opportunities to contribute.

I believe the best kind of followers are in some ways leaders themselves in the context of their level of engagement. That's particularly so the higher up they are in the organization.

You might be following someone to whom you report, but you are also leading others who report to you or who are observing you. Most everyone within an organization is some kind of leader because people around them are watching, observing, seeing how that person interacts with the organization. They can be positively or negatively affected by how they see others behaving.

Obviously, anyone has things they would have done differently if given an opportunity, or if that were possible. But in terms of major career decisions, I would say I have been extraordinarily blessed to have had the opportunities I have had. I've been blessed to stay within the same organization for 28 years and to have had opportunities to grow personally and, hopefully, to contribute to the organization. I really don't think I would do things differently in major career decisions, however, even if I could do things all over again.

In terms of a specific issue or action, I certainly know from the standpoint of my own personal growth, and my experiences in followership and leadership, I would certainly do a lot better job of listening. As I have grown older, I have realized that one of the strongest attributes of good leaders is that they are really good listeners. I have increased my appreciation of that in terms of just listening, observing, and learning from others. Whether it is a positive or a negative experience, being a good listener can play an extraordinary role in one's personal growth and development.

I have also learned to be a much more productive questioner. I think that many times a leader doesn't get the right answer because he or she doesn't ask the right question. I think the art of leadership is also a lifetime journey, where you never quit developing and you never quit learning. I've heard so many folks who are near the end of their professional journey say "Oh, if I only knew then what I know now in terms of just listening and learning, I could have made so many contributions so much earlier. I thought I knew all the answers, and I didn't even know all of the questions."

I would advise young people aspiring to become leaders in our community to find a good mentor. I lucked into that. I was very blessed, but I was also aware that many didn't have that good fortune. Finding a good organization and mentor who has the right values, who provides an environment in which you want to learn and grow is a real blessing.

I think a lot of people fall into a circumstance that may not be consistent with what they want or where they see themselves going. I think one has to be much more intentional. In our field, there are so many opportunities for young professionals where they can contribute and grow. I think it matters less what the specific job is, in terms of entry-level these days in health care management.

For the people within our organization whom we have identified as up-and-comers — the people who have great potential and want to grow — it really hasn't mattered what particular position they are in. It is more about how they are contributing, demonstrating their interest, their core competencies, their compatible values and style, their potential to be good managers and leaders.

There are obviously lots of names that come to mind of people who have contributed to the growth and development of our community over the last 25 years, which is my frame of reference. I think we have been very fortunate to have a number of leaders in government or civic work — folks like Wilson Wyatt, Jerry Abramson, David Jones, Malcolm Chancey, Mike Harreld — I could go on and on. The list of people who have made extraordinary contributions to the community is fairly long.

There are many factors which have contributed to making Louisville a great place to live, to work, to raise families, in my opinion. There was no big bang or big event, but an evolution — a blending of factors such as improvements in our education opportunities, a good health care system, the arts, and those things that really contribute to what most people see as very important in terms of quality of life and work.

Many people would probably assume that I would talk about health care if asked to name the biggest challenges facing our community in the future. Obviously, health care is an important part of any community. But my priority focus would be education. I think Louisville has made positive strides in the area of education over the last number of years, but I think we have so much more to do. I believe if we are really going to be a successful community, regardless of what indicator you use to measure success, so much goes back to the quality of our education system — elementary through post-secondary opportunities. The quality of our workforce is only as good as the quality of our education system. While we have certainly made progress over the years, we have so much catch-up to do, compared to so many of Kentucky's neighboring states. I think if we are going to reach our potential as a community, education really has to become a huge priority for our community.

Secondly, now that we have merged our government, we have to think and act as a broader, greater Louisville. I think we have done a pretty good job over the last year or two. We have taken the first steps. But we have so much more opportunity to look at ourselves as a greater Louisville community and to take on issues and opportunities that are less parochial in terms of neighborhoods.

People often ask me the legacy question – what I think is the biggest contribution that I might have made to the organization. That is a fairly easy question for me actually. I need to be very careful how I say this lest I sound immodest, because it is in the area of values.

Back in the mid-'80s, when I was far from being the CEO, I authored a statement of values that is on the wall in our offices, on most printed material, part of our culture, and which, hopefully, is a guiding standard to which we aspire as organizational leaders. It was a recommendation adopted not only by our president and executive vice president, but by our board of trustees. That statement of values has remained applicable over the years and, hopefully, will continue to remain well past my watch. If it continues to have an impact on the organization the way it is intended, then unquestionably it will be a much more important contribution than any specific initiative I have led, or anything else which I have done as CEO or COO.

My admonition to young inspiring leaders is to do your homework, but also don't be afraid to take risks. Step out and reach for opportunities. Occasionally, we may be fortunate enough to have something handed to us just by pure randomness, but that very seldom happens in leadership. You have to engage in opportunities and be noticed as someone who can make a contribution, and do so consistent with the way the organization wants you to behave. If you are making contributions and are doing it in a way in which your behavior is considered to be positive, then you are going to be noticed and you are going to be given opportunities to lead. You will open doors for yourself. But it does take intention, willingness to take risks, and it doesn't always pay immediate dividends. If you do your homework well, however – if you engage, and if you do it with a positive style, it will pay off and you will have many opportunities.